Major Problems
in American Women's History

MAJOR PROBLEMS IN AMERICAN HISTORY SERIES

GENERAL EDITOR
THOMAS G. PATERSON

Major Problems
in American Women's History

DOCUMENTS AND ESSAYS

SECOND EDITION

EDITED BY

MARY BETH NORTON
CORNELL UNIVERSITY

RUTH M. ALEXANDER
COLORADO STATE UNIVERSITY

D. C. HEATH AND COMPANY
Lexington, Massachusetts   Toronto

Address editorial correspondence to:

D. C. Heath and Company
125 Spring Street
Lexington, MA 02173

Acquisitions: James Miller
Development: Pat Wakeley
Editorial Production: Carolyn Ingalls
Design: Jan Shapiro
Photo Research: Mary Lang
Production Coordination: Charles Dutton
Permissions: Margaret Roll

PHOTO CREDITS: **Page 121:** *Plan of a nineteenth-century farmhouse.* Reprinted from *Greek Revival Architecture in America,* by Talbot Hamlin, 1944, Dover Press. **Page 178:** *A temperance broadside.* Archive Photos. **Page 261:** *Suffrage parade held in New York City, May 6, 1912.* The Granger Collection. **Page 304:** *Female clerks and their customers in a busy dry-goods and leather-goods store, 1915.* The Bettman Archive. **Page 378:** *African-American women training to become auto mechanics in 1943.* Reprinted from the Collections of the Library of Congress. **Page 408:** *A couple at a New Orleans lesbian bar in the early 1950s.* Courtesy of the Lesbian Herstory Archives/Lesbian Herstory Educational Foundation, Inc. From the Blue Lunden Collection, New Orleans early 1950s. **Page 450:** *A demonstration sponsored by the Congress of Racial Equality (CORE).* Bruce Davidson/Magnum. **Page 503:** *A demonstration by anti-abortion activists outside an abortion clinic.* © 1992 Maggie Boys.

Published simultaneously in Canada.

Printed in the United States of America.

International Standard Book Number: 0–669–35390–6

Library of Congress Catalog Card Number: 95–68039

10 9 8 7

For Grael and Lia
and
for Genny Nicole and Natalie

Preface

The first books on women's history published in the United States appeared in the mid-nineteenth century; yet as a subject of serious scholarly inquiry, the field is barely three decades old. For generations the only authors who concerned themselves with women's past were women with no formal training in the discipline of history. Until the mid-1960s graduate education in history was dominated by men who showed little interest in studying the history of the other sex.

But that pattern was to change dramatically when two interrelated developments had an enormous impact on the practice of history in this country. First, the modern feminist movement erupted in the general turmoil of that most turbulent decade, the sixties, and women pressed for equality with men in all areas of life. Second, appreciable numbers of women began to enter the history profession, partly as a result of new employment opportunities that had become available to them. The history that these first young women historians studied in graduate school was defined within traditional parameters, focusing on politics, diplomacy, and intellectual life. Yet historians' views of the past are always affected by their experiences in the present. The demonstrations, riots, and iconoclastic atmosphere of the 1960s helped to create a revolution in the way history was studied, bringing to the fore questions about ordinary people, their families, and their work lives in what has come to be called the "new social history."

The earliest works of social history, like those written on more traditional topics, concerned themselves exclusively with men. But by the mid-1970s an increasing number of books and articles on women's experiences, most of them written by young female historians, began to appear in print. A new field was being born: courses on the subject proliferated in undergraduate and graduate curricula, journals were founded to publish articles on the new subject, and women's studies programs were organized, most with a strong historical component. At long last, graduate and undergraduate women could study the history of their own sex in a formal educational setting, and men could learn the history of women just as women had long studied the history of men.

Today the field of American women's history is a lively one, full of fervent debates and hotly contested disputes. The essays and documents in this book, like those that appear in other books in this series, are intended to introduce the student to the most interesting and fundamental of those arguments. Currently, there is widespread agreement on basic interpretations of many important subjects in American women's history—the history of women's education and the role of women in the nation's religious life, to name two examples. Accordingly, those issues are not central to this collection, although they are discussed in some of the selections. Rather, this book focuses on interpretive dialogues, that is, subjects on which historians disagree. Sometimes the authors whose works are included here draw diametrically opposing conclusions from the same material; on other occasions they approach questions from diverse perspectives, and thereby emphasize different aspects of women's experiences. In either case, the historians are engaging in perhaps their most important professional function: learning from and challenging each other's viewpoints in order to arrive at a better, more complete, and more accurate understanding of the past.

For this second edition, we have located examples of the latest work in women's history, at the same time reflecting the current trend toward a more multicultural approach. In addition to essays on African- and Euro-American women, this edition includes recent scholarship on Native Americans, Latina-Americans, Asian-Americans, and other ethnic groups. The resulting selections bring into sharp focus the differences and similarities in women's experiences across lines of race and class.

Each chapter opens with a brief introduction. There follows a selection of pertinent documents, and then two or three essays examining the subject. All writings are aimed at allowing readers to reach their own conclusions about the most appropriate interpretations.

We are grateful to colleagues who reviewed our plans for this edition and offered many helpful suggestions: Gail Bederman, University of Notre Dame; Kathleen C. Berkeley, University of North Carolina at Wilmington; Sarah Deutsch, Clark University; Nancy M. Forestell, Queen's University; Jane Hunter, Lewis and Clark College; Carol F. Karlsen, University of Michigan; Molly Ladd-Taylor, Carleton College; Sarah Stage, University of California–Riverside.

For help in locating and copying documents and essays for this collection, we wish to thank A. Paige Shipman, Tracy Brady, and Andrea Russo. Ruth Alexander also acknowledges financial assistance from a Professional Development Grant from the College of Liberal Arts at Colorado State University. Both authors are also grateful for the editorial asssistance offered by Sylvia Mallory and Pat Wakeley at D. C. Heath.

M. B. N.
R. M. A.

Contents

CHAPTER 7
Varieties of Nineteenth-Century Activism
Page 161

CHAPTER 8
Women in the Nineteenth- and Twentieth-Century West
Page 189

Defining Women's History

Historians of women, unlike those scholars who work in more conventional fields, must confront a novel and challenging problem: defining what they are doing and why they are doing it. Every student of history automatically accepts the proposition that war, politics, diplomacy, and the other aspects of life that have fallen primarily within the purview of men are important subjects for research. Women's activities, however, traditionally have been devalued in European and American societies, and women have but rarely assumed leadership roles in national political or economic life. Why, then, should we study women's history? Why is it important for us to learn about women's past experiences? Given the racial, ethnic, religious, and class differences among American women, is it even possible to write about them as a unified group? Women's historians have had to address questions such as these.

✳ E S S A Y S

The three essays reprinted here represent attempts to answer such inquiries. In 1975, Gerda Lerner of the University of Wisconsin, a pioneer in the field of women's history, made one of the first systematic efforts to criticize traditional approaches to the topic and to sketch out possible alternative ways of thinking about it. Nearly two decades later, Gisela Bock, a German historian, critically examined the dichotomous thinking that had come to characterize women's historians' debates on key interpretative issues. At about the same time, Evelyn Brooks Higginbotham of Harvard University pointed out that most works in American "women's" history focused solely on whites, while most works in American "black" history focused solely on men. What, she asked, does that mean for African-American women?

Placing Women in History

GERDA LERNER

In the brief span of five years in which American historians have begun to develop women's history as an independent field, they have sought to find a conceptual framework and a methodology appropriate to the task.

Gerda Lerner, "Placing Women in History: Definitions and Challenges," *Feminist Studies,* III, no. 1–2 (fall 1975), 5–14. Reprinted by permission of Gerda Lerner.

The first level at which historians, trained in traditional history, approach women's history is by writing the history of "women worthies" or "compensatory history." Who are the women missing from history? Who are the women of achievement and what did they achieve? The resulting history of "notable women" does not tell us much about those activities in which most women engaged, nor does it tell us about the significance of women's activities to society as a whole. The history of notable women is the history of exceptional, even deviant women, and does not describe the experience and history of the mass of women. This insight is a refinement of an awareness of class differences in history: Women of different classes have different historical experiences. To comprehend the full complexity of society at a given stage of its development, it is essential to take account of such differences. . . .

The next level of conceptualizing women's history has been "contribution history": describing women's contribution to, their status in, and their oppression by male-defined society. Under this category we find a variety of questions being asked: What have women contributed to abolition, to reform, to the Progressive movement, to the labor movement, to the New Deal? The movement in question stands in the foreground of inquiry; women made a "contribution" to it; the contribution is judged first of all with respect to its effect on that movement and secondly by standards appropriate to men.

The ways in which women were aided and affected by the work of these "great women," the ways in which they themselves grew into feminist awareness, are ignored. Jane Addams' enormous contribution in creating a supporting female network and new structures for living are subordinated to her role as a Progressive, or to an interpretation which regards her as merely representative of a group of frustrated college-trained women with no place to go. In other words, a deviant from male-defined norms. Margaret Sanger is seen merely as the founder of the birth control movement, not as a woman raising a revolutionary challenge to the centuries-old practice by which the bodies and lives of women are dominated and ruled by man-made laws. In the labor movement, women are described as "also there" or as problems. Their essential role on behalf of themselves and of other women is seldom considered a central theme in writing their history. Women are the outgroup, Simone de Beauvoir's "other."

Another set of questions concern oppression and its opposite, the struggle for women's rights. Who oppressed women and how were they oppressed? How did they respond to such oppression?

Such questions have yielded detailed and very valuable accounts of economic or social oppression, and of the various organizational, political ways in which women as a group have fought such oppression. Judging from the results, it is clear that to ask the question — why and how were women victimized — has its usefulness. We learn what society or individuals or classes of people have done to women, and we learn how women themselves have reacted to conditions imposed upon them. While inferior status and oppressive restraints were no doubt aspects of women's historical experience, and should be so recorded, the limitation of this approach is that it makes it appear either that women were largely passive or that, at the most, they reacted to male pressures or to the restraints of patriarchal society.

Such inquiry fails to elicit the positive and essential way in which women have functioned in history. Mary Beard was the first to point out that the ongoing and continuing contribution of women to the development of human culture cannot be found by treating them only as victims of oppression. I have in my own work learned that it is far more useful to deal with this question as one aspect of women's history, but never to regard it as the *central* aspect of women's history. Essentially, treating women as victims of oppression once again places them in a male-defined conceptual framework: oppressed, victimized by standards and values established by men. The true history of women is the history of their ongoing functioning in that male-defined world, *on their own terms*. The question of oppression does not elicit that story, and is therefore a tool of limited usefulness to the historian.

A major focus of women's history has been on women's-rights struggles, especially the winning of suffrage, on organizational and institutional history of the women's movements, and on its leaders. This, again, is an important aspect of women's history, but it cannot and should not be its central concern. . . .

"Contribution" history is an important stage in the creation of a true history of women. The monographic work which such inquiries produce is essential to the development of more complex and sophisticated questions, but it is well to keep the limitations of such inquiry in mind. When all is said and done, what we have mostly done in writing contribution history is to describe what men in the past told women to do and what men in the past thought women should be. This is just another way of saying that historians of women's history have so far used a traditional conceptual framework. Essentially, they have applied questions from traditional history to women, and tried to fit women's past into the empty spaces of historical scholarship. The limitation of such work is that it deals with women in male-defined society and tries to fit them into the categories and value systems which consider *man* the measure of significance. Perhaps it would be useful to refer to this level of work as "transitional women's history," seeing it as an inevitable step in the development of new criteria and concepts.

Another methodological question which arises frequently concerns the connection between women's history and other recently emerging fields. Why is women's history not simply an aspect of "good" social history? Are women not part of the anonymous in history? Are they not oppressed the same way as racial or class or ethnic groups have been oppressed? Are they not marginal and akin in most respects to minorities? The answers to these questions are not simple. It is obvious that there has already been rich cross-fertilization between the new social history and women's history, but it has not been nor should it be a case of subsuming women's history under the larger and already respectable field of social history.

Yes, women are part of the anonymous in history, but unlike them, they are also and always have been part of the ruling elite. They are oppressed, but not quite like either racial or ethnic groups, though some of them are. They are subordinate and exploited, but not quite like lower classes, though some of them are. We have not yet really solved the problems of definition, but it can be suggested that the key to understanding women's history is in accepting — painful though that may be — that it is the history of the *majority* of mankind. Women are essentially different from all the above categories, because they are the majority now and always have been at least half of mankind, and because their subjection to patriarchal institutions antedates all other oppression and has outlasted all economic and social changes in recorded history.

Social history methodology is very useful for women's history, but it must be placed within a different conceptual framework. For example, historians working in family history ask a great many questions pertaining to women, but family history is not in itself women's history. It is no longer sufficient to view women mainly as members of families. Family history has neglected by and large to deal with unmarried and widowed women. In its applications to specific monographic studies, such as the work of Philip Greven, family history has been used to describe the relationships of fathers and sons and the property arrangements between them. The relationships of fathers to daughters and mothers to their children have been ignored. The complex family-support patterns, for example, whereby the work and wages of daughters are used to support the education of brothers and to maintain aged parents, while that of sons is not so used, have been ignored. . . .

I learned in studying the history of black women and the black family that relatively high status for women within the family does not signify "matriarchy" or "power for women," since black women are not only members of families, but persons functioning in a larger society. The status of persons is determined not in one area of their functioning, such as within the family, but in several. The decisive historical fact about women is that the *areas* of their functioning, not only their status *within* those areas, have been determined by men. The effect on the consciousness of women has been pervasive. It is one of the decisive aspects of their history, and any analysis which does not take this complexity into consideration must be inadequate.

Then there is the impact of demographic techniques, the study of large aggregates of anonymous people by computer technology based on census data, public documents, property records. Demographic techniques have led to insights which are very useful for women's history. They have yielded revealing data on fertility fluctuations, on changes in illegitimacy patterns and sex ratios, and aggregate studies of life cycles. . . .

The compensatory questions raised by women's history specialists are proving interesting and valuable in a variety of fields. It is perfectly understandable that after centuries of neglect of the role of women in history, compensatory questions and those concerning woman's contribution will and must be asked. In the process of answering such questions it is important to keep in mind the inevitable limitation of the answers they yield. Not the least of these limitations is that this approach tends to separate the work and activities of women from those of men, even where they were essentially connected. As yet, synthesis is lacking. For example, the rich history of the abolition movement has been told as though women played a marginal, auxiliary, and at times mainly disruptive role in it. Yet female antislavery societies outnumbered male societies; women abolitionists largely financed the movement with their fundraising activities, did much of the work of propaganda-writing in and distribution of newspapers and magazines. The enormous political significance of women-organized petition campaigns remains unrecorded. Most importantly, no historical work has as yet taken the organizational work of female abolitionists seriously as an integral part of the antislavery movement.

Slowly, as the field has matured, historians of women's history have become dissatisfied with old questions and old methods, and have come up with new ways of approaching historical material. They have, for example, begun to ask about the actual *experience* of women in the past. This is obviously different from a description of the condition of women written from the perspective of male sources, and leads one to the use of women's letters, diaries, autobiographies, and oral history sources. This shift from male-oriented to female-oriented consciousness is most important and leads to challenging new interpretations.

Historians of women's history have studied female sexuality and its regulation from the female point of view, making imaginative use of such sources as medical textbooks, diaries, and case histories of hospital patients. Questions concerning women's experience have led to studies of birth control, as it affects women and as an issue expressing cultural and symbolic values; of the physical conditions to which women are prone, such as menarche and pregnancy and women's ailments; of customs, attitudes, and fashions affecting women's health and women's life experience. Historians are now exploring the impact of female bonding, of female friendship and homosexual relations, and the experience of women in groups, such as women in utopian communities, in women's clubs and settlement houses. There has been an interest in the possibility that women's century-long preoccupation with birth and with the care of the sick and dying have led to some specific female rituals.

Women's history has already presented a challenge to some basic assumptions historians make. While most historians are aware of the fact that their findings are not value-free and are trained to check their biases by a variety of methods, they are as yet quite unaware of their own sexist bias and, more importantly, of the sexist bias which pervades the value system, the culture, and the very language within which they work.

Women's history presents a challenge to the periodization of traditional history. The periods in which basic changes occur in society and which historians have commonly regarded as turning points for all historical development, are not necessarily the same for men as for women. This is not surprising when we consider that the traditional time frame in history has been derived from political history. Women have been the one group in history longest excluded from political power as they have, by and large, been excluded from military decision making. Thus the irrelevance of periodization based on military and political developments to their historical experience should have been predictable. . . .

What kind of periodization might be substituted for the periodization of traditional history, in order for it to be applicable to women? The answer depends largely on the conceptual framework in which the historian works. Many historians of women's history, in their search for a unifying framework, have tended to use the Marxist or neo-Marxist model supplied by Juliet Mitchell and recently elaborated by Sheila Rowbotham. The important fact, says Mitchell, which distinguished the past of women from that of men is precisely that until very recently sexuality and reproduction were inevitably linked for women, while they were not so linked for men. Similarly, child-bearing and child-rearing were inevitably linked for women and still are so linked. Women's freedom depends on breaking those links. Using Mitchell's categories we can and should ask of each historical period: What happened to the link between sexuality and reproduction? What happened to the link between child-bearing and child-rearing? Important changes in the status of women occur when it becomes possible through the availability of birth control information and technology to sever sexuality from inevitable motherhood. However, it may be the case that it is not the availability and distribution of birth control information and technology so much as the level of medical and health care which are the determinants of change. That is, when infant mortality decreases, so that raising every child to adulthood becomes the normal expectation of parents, family size declines.

The above case illustrates the difficulty that has vexed historians of women's history in trying to locate a periodization more appropriate to women. Working in different fields and specialties, many historians have observed that the transition from agricultural to industrializing society and then again the transition to fully developed industrial society entails important changes affecting women and the family. Changes in relations of production affect women's status as family members and as workers. Later, shifts in the mode of production affect the kinds of occupations women can enter and their status within them. Major shifts in health care and technological development, related to industrialization, also affect the lives of women. It is not too difficult to discern such patterns and to conclude that there must be a causal relationship between changes in the mode of production and the status of women. Here, the Marxist model seems to offer an immediately satisfying solution, especially if, following Mitchell, "sexuality" as a factor is added to such factors as class. But in the case of women, just as in the case of racial castes, ideology and prescription internalized by both women and men, seem to be as much a causative factor as are material changes in production relations. Does the entry of lower-class women into industrial production really bring them closer to "liberation"? In the absence of institutional changes such as the right to abortion and safe contraception, altered child-rearing arrangements, and varied options for sexual expression, changes in economic relations may become oppressive. Unless such changes are accompanied by changes in consciousness, which in turn result in institutional changes, they do not favorably affect the lives of women.

Is smaller family size the result of "domestic freedom" of choice exercised by women, the freedom of choice exercised by men, the ideologically buttressed coercion of institutions in the service of an economic class? Is it liberating for women, for men, or for corporations? This raises another difficult question: What about the relationship of upper-class to lower-class women? To what extent is the relative advance in the status of upper-class women predicated on the status loss of lower-class women? Examples of this are: the liberation of the middle-class American housewife in the mid-nineteenth century through the availability of cheap black or immigrant domestic workers; the liberation of the twentieth-century housewife from incessant drudgery in the home through agricultural stoop labor and the food-processing industry, both employing low paid female workers.

Is periodization then dependent as much on class as on gender? This question is just one of several which challenge the universalist assumptions of all previous historical categories. I cannot provide an answer, but I think the questions themselves point us in the right direction.

It appears to me that all conceptual models of history hitherto developed have only limited usefulness for women's history, since all are based on the assumptions of a patriarchal ordering of values. . . .

I raised the question of a conceptual framework for dealing with women's history in 1969, reasoning from the assumption that women were a subgroup in history. Neither caste, class, nor race quite fit the model for describing us. I have now come to the conclusion that the idea that women are some kind of a subgroup or particular is wrong. It will not do — there are just too many of us. No single framework, no single factor, four-factor or eight-factor explanation can serve to contain all that the history of women is. Picture, if you can, an attempt to organize the history of men by using four factors. It will not work; neither will it work for women.

Women are and always have been at least half of mankind and most of the time have been the majority of mankind. Their culturally determined and psychologically internalized marginality seems to be what makes their historical experience essentially different from that of men. But men have defined their experience as history and have left women out. At this time, as during earlier periods of feminist activity, women are urged to fit into the empty spaces, assuming their traditional marginal, "subgroup" status. But the truth is that history, as written and perceived up to now, is the history of a minority, who may well turn out to be the "subgroup." In order to write a new history worthy of the name, we will have to recognize that no single methodology and conceptual framework can fit the complexities of the historical experience of all women.

The first stage of "transitional history" may be to add some new categories to the general categories by which historians organize their material: sexuality, reproduction, the link between child-bearing and child-rearing; role indoctrination; sexual values and myths; female consciousness. Further, all of these need to be analysed, taking factors of race, class, ethnicity and, possibly, religion into consideration. What we have here is not a single framework for dealing with women in history, but new questions to all of universal history.

The next stage may be to explore the possibility that what we call women's history may actually be the study of a separate women's culture. Such a culture would include not only the separate occupations, status, experiences, and rituals of women but also their consciousness, which internalizes patriarchal assumptions. In some cases, it would include the tensions created in that culture between the prescribed patriarchal assumptions and women's efforts to attain autonomy and emancipation. . . .

A following stage may develop a synthesis: a history of the dialectic, the tensions between the two cultures, male and female. Such a synthesis could be based on close comparative study of given periods in which the historical experience of men is compared to that of women, their tensions and interactions being as much the subject of study as their differences. Only after a series of such detailed studies can we hope to find the parameters by which to define the new universal history. My guess is that no one conceptual framework will fit so complex a subject.

Methods are tools for analysis — some of us will stick with one tool, some of us will reach for different tools as we need them. For women, the problem really is that we must acquire not only the confidence needed for using tools, but for making new ones to fit our needs. We should do so relying on our learned skills and our rational scepticism of handed-down doctrine. The recognition that we had been de-nied our history came to many of us as a staggering flash of insight, which altered our consciousness irretrievably. We have come a long way since then. The next step is to face, once and for all and with all its complex consequences, that women are the majority of mankind and have been essential to the making of history. Thus, all history as we now know it, is merely prehistory. Only a new history firmly based on this recognition and equally concerned with men, women, the establishment and the passing away of patriarchy, can lay claim to being a truly universal history.

Challenging Dichotomies in Women's History

GISELA BOCK

Women's history has come a long way. Some twenty years ago, Gerda Lerner wrote that 'the striking fact about the historiography of women is the general neglect of the subject by historians'. Historical scholarship was far from 'objective' or 'uni-versal', because it was based on male experience, placed men at the centre and as a measure of all things human, thereby leaving out half of humankind. In the past two decades, the situation has changed considerably. In an enormous (and enormously growing) body of scholarship women have been rendered visible. They have been placed at the centre, and what women do, have to do, and want to do has been re-evaluated in view of social, political and cultural change, of an improvement in women's situations and, more generally, in terms of a change towards more free-dom and justice. More precisely, what has been rendered historically visible by making women a subject of research was, in the first place, their subjection. In the second place, however, it was their subjectivity — because women are not only vic-tims, but also actively shape their own lives, society and history.

Much of this research was carried out in the context of three conceptual or the-oretical frameworks that have been used by many feminist scholars, particularly historians, in the past two decades and which will be outlined in the first section of this paper. These frameworks point to three dichotomies in traditional thought on gender relations, and all of them have been not only used, but also profoundly chal-lenged. The second section will illustrate three further dichotomies which, in the de-velopment of modern women's history, have emerged more recently and which presently seem to dominate and direct women's studies. . . .

1. Nature versus culture. It was mainly in the United States in the early 1970s that the relation of the sexes was discussed in terms of the relation, or rather dichotomy, between 'nature and nurture' or 'nature and culture'. Men and their activities had been seen as culture and of cultural value, whereas women and their activities had been seen as natural, outside of history and society, always the same and therefore not worthy of scholarly, political or theoretical interest and inquiry. Moreover, it was the relations between the sexes, and most particularly their relations of power

Gisela Bock, "Challenging Dichotomies: Perspectives on Women's History," in *Writing Women's His-tory: International Perspectives,* ed. Karen Offen et. al, 1991, pp. 1–12, 15–17. Reprinted by permission of Indiana University Press.

and subjection, that had been attributed to nature. 'Nature', in this context, most often meant sexuality between men and women, women's bodies and their capacity for pregnancy and motherhood. Fatherhood, however, was usually seen not as natural but as 'social'. Female scholars challenged this traditional dichotomy. They argued that what 'nature' really meant in this discourse was a devaluation of everything that women stood for, that '"nature" always has a social meaning', that both 'nature' and 'culture' meant different things at different times, in different places and to the different sexes, and that women's bodies and bodily capacities were not always and everywhere seen as disabilities, but also as a basis for certain kinds of informal power and public activities. The nature/culture dichotomy was recognised as a specific and perhaps specifically Western way of expressing the hierarchies between the sexes. The binary terms of this dichotomy only apparently refer to antagonistic and independent terms; but in fact, they refer to a hierarchy of social realities and cultural meanings, between strongly interdependent terms. In other words: no such nature without such culture, and no such culture without such nature. One of the linguistic results of such insights in women's history is that the term 'nature' is now almost always placed in quotation marks. . . .

2. Work versus family. A second theoretical framework for rendering women visible, and for dismantling their identification with the merely natural, unchanging and therefore uninteresting, was the issue of their distinctive patterns of work. The discussion around it had its origins more in the European than in the American context, particularly in Italy, Britain, Germany and France. What had been seen as nature was now seen as work: bearing, rearing and caring for children, looking after the breadwinner-husband and after other family members. To call this activity 'work' meant to challenge the dichotomy 'work and family' (because the family may mean work to women), but also 'work and leisure' (because men's leisure may be women's work), and 'working men and supported wives' (because wives support men through their work). It meant questioning the view that work is only that which is done for pay. Women have always worked, and unpaid work was and is women's work. Obviously, men's work is valued more highly than women's work. In theoretical and economic terms, it has been demonstrated that women's work was overlooked by male theoreticians of work and the economy and why this happened; accordingly the value or 'productivity' of domestic work came to be discussed. . . .

The sexual division of labour was found to be not just a division, but a hierarchy of labour; and not just one of labour but, primarily, a sexual division of value and rewards. The lower value of women's work continues — through economic and cultural mediation — in employment outside the home. Here, where women have always worked, they earned only 50 per cent to 80 per cent of men's earnings in the nineteenth and twentieth centuries in western countries, with variations over time and space. . . .

The apparent dichotomy between 'work and family', between men as workers and women as 'non-workers', turns out to be one between paid and unpaid work, between underpaid and decently paid work, between the superior and inferior value of men's and women's work respectively. The underlying assumption of mutually exclusive superiority and inferiority seems to be another common feature of such gender-linked dichotomies. The challenge posed by women's studies to this opposition is obviously linked to political and economic challenges to pay women's as yet unpaid work, to raise their earnings in low-pay jobs, and to admit more women to well-paid professions. It has also led to some linguistic changes. Even though, in the English language, the terms 'working women' and working mothers' are still reserved for employed women only, and non-employed women are still often called 'non-working', the terms 'work and family' are now often replaced by 'paid and unpaid work'. . . .

3. Public versus private. A third conceptual framework of women's history has been the relation between the public and the private, or the political and the personal, or the sphere of power and the domestic sphere. Traditional political theory has seen them, again, as a dichotomy of mutually exclusive terms, identified with women's 'sphere' and men's 'world'. Women's studies have profoundly challenged this view, pointing out its inadequacy for understanding politics and society. The slogan 'the personal is political' indicated that the issue of power is not confined to 'high politics', but also appears in sexual relations. Men inhabit, and rule within both spheres, whereas women's proper place was seen to be only in the domestic sphere and in her subjection to father or husband. This means, on the one hand, the dichotomy is not one between two autonomous, symmetrical and equivalent spheres, but rather a complex relation between domination and subordination, between power and powerlessness. On the other hand, women's studies have shown that the public 'world' was essentially based on the domestic 'sphere'. Male workers, male politicians and male scholars perform their tasks only because they are born, reared and cared for by women's labour. The boundaries between public and private shift significantly over time and cross-culturally, as in the historical transition between private charity and public assistance, in both of which women played important roles. . . .

Women's history has also discovered that what is perceived as 'private' by some may be seen as 'public' by others. The domestic tasks of bearing and rearing children, for instance, were proclaimed as being of public importance by many women in the early women's movement. They requested that it be re-evaluated, and many of them based their demand for equal political citizenship precisely on this vision of the 'separate sphere', understood not as a dichotomy of mutually exclusive and hierarchical terms, but as a source of equal rights and responsibilities of the female sex in respect to civil society. On this basis, they did not so much challenge the sexual division of labour, as the sexual division of power. . . .

These three dichotomies seem to have some important characteristics in common. They are eminently gender-linked, and as such they have distant roots in European and western traditions of gender perception. They have been taken up and used as crucial conceptual frameworks in the newly emerging women's history of the past decades, and simultaneously their long-standing apparent validity for the perception of gender relations has been thoroughly challenged. This challenge concerned the analysis, historicisation and deconstruction of the character and meaning of these three dual categories, as well as the links between them, and it questioned the traditional assumption that these dichotomies were expressions — natural and necessary expressions — of sexual difference.

The question has been raised as to whether these dichotomies are just a few examples among many similar binary oppositions and dualistic modes of western thought in general, or whether their gender-linked character makes them very special. . . . But it seems that, whenever they are used for describing gender relations, they do not refer so much to separate, autonomous, independent, equivalent dual spheres, as to relations of hierarchy: hierarchies of spheres, meanings, values, of inferiority and superiority, of subordination and power; in other words, to relations where 'culture' subjects 'nature', the world of 'work' reigns over that of the 'family', the 'political' dominates the 'private'. . . .

Somehow, ironically, the same process by which women became historically (and not only historically) visible through the critique of these contradictories has also led to a number of new dichotomies of which little or nothing was heard during the first phase of women's studies, and which later came to the fore within the context of feminist scholarship itself. In part, they are the result of past attempts to resolve the earlier binary modes with the help of new concepts and theoretical frameworks. It seems that future strategies for women's history lie precisely, and once more, in the possibility and necessity of challenging these newer dichotomies.

1. Sex versus gender. The concept 'gender' has been introduced into women's history and women's studies in the 1970s as a social, cultural, political and historical category, in order to express the insight that women's subordination, inferiority and powerlessness are not dictated by nature, but are social, cultural, political and historical constructions. Whereas 'gender' had previously referred mainly to linguistic-grammatical constructions, it now became a major theoretical framework. One of the reasons for its success in replacing the word 'sex' has been the insistence that the study of women does not only deal with sexuality, wifehood and motherhood, but with women in all walks of life. Women's studies do not only concern half of humankind, but all of it, because it is not only women who are gendered beings, but also men who are therefore far from representing universal humanity. Consequently, 'men's history' and 'men's studies' which analyse men as 'men' have emerged. The concept of 'gender' radicalised and universalized the efforts to make women visible, and the insight that gender is a basic, though flexible structure of society meant that women's and gender studies concern, in principle, any field or object of historical (and non-historical) scholarship.

But the new terminology has also brought to the fore major problems. They result from the fact that the concept of gender has been introduced in the form of a dichotomy. It distinguishes categorically between gender and sex, 'sex' to be understood as 'biological' and 'gender' as 'social' or cultural, and both are seen as combined in a 'sex/gender system' where 'raw biological sex' is somehow transformed into 'social gender'. The dichotomous structure of the pair had been evident since the late 1950s when, even before being taken up by feminist scholarship, it came to be theorised by male scholars who studied intersexuals and transsexuals. But this dichotomy between the 'biological' and the 'social' does not resolve but only restates the old nature versus culture quarrel. Again, it relegates the dimension of women's body, sexuality, motherhood and physiological sexual difference to a supposedly pre-social sphere, and it resolves even less the question of precisely what part of women's experience and activity is 'biological' and what part 'social' or 'cultural'. . . .

In this situation, it is not the concept of gender that should be challenged — as some feminist historians seem to prefer at present — but the linguistic and theoretical dichotomy of sex and gender. Particularly in history, the humanities and social sciences, it might be challenged through using 'gender' in a comprehensive sense which may include both the physiological and the cultural dimension, and using 'sex' in the same sense as 'gender', thus leaving space for continuities instead of polarities of meaning.

2. Equality versus difference. The problems of the sex/gender dichotomy are closely related to those of another dichotomy with which we are faced today in a new way and in an international debate which has taken on different shapes and phases in different countries: that of 'equality versus difference'. Women's studies have largely relied on the concept of 'sexual' or 'gender equality' as an analytical tool, and physiological 'difference' has been played down as insignificant because it has so often been used to justify discriminatory treatment of women. In this perspective, it has been demanded that women be treated in the same way as men, as if they were men, and that new laws and reforms be formulated in gender-neutral terms . . . , thus eliminating sexual difference and rendering masculinity and femininity politically irrelevant. Other feminist scholars, however, argue that burning issues such as rape, abortion or wife-battering cannot be dealt with adequately in gender-neutral terms; that female 'difference', physiological as well as social, should not be erased but recognised, in historical, philosophical and legal terms; that it has never had a chance to develop autonomous political and cultural forms other than in social niches and in opposition to dominant cultures; that emphasis should be laid on a critical evaluation of men's distinctive needs and activities and that women's distinctive needs and activities should be valued, thus opening alternatives both to female inferiority and to women's assimilation to men. . . .

Some scholars tend to believe that the dichotomy 'equality versus difference' is simply a false dichotomy, more the result of misunderstandings than of insight. But others insist on the mutually exclusive character of the relation between 'equality' and 'difference', and therefore on the necessity of an either/or choice. The historian Joan Hoff-Wilson urges that a decision be made, particularly by feminist leaders, between either 'equality between the sexes based on prevailing masculine societal norms' or 'justice between the sexes based on a recognition of equal, but different socialised patterns of behavior'. On the other hand, the historian Joan Scott considers this to be 'an impossible choice', and she questions precisely the dichotomy itself. I also believe that it is unacceptable, among other reasons because both the 'difference dilemma' ('difference' being used, overtly or implicitly, to confirm women's inferiority in relation to men) and the 'equality dilemma' ('equality' being used, overtly or implicitly, to erase gender difference in view of women's assimilation to male societal norms) are far from being sufficiently explored. Such an exploration should be put on the agenda for future women's history. Why is it, for instance, that 'equality' and 'justice' seem to complement each other in the case of men, but be opposed to each other in the case of women? Why is it that 'difference' is only attributed to one half of humankind and not to the other? Why is it that 'equality' is so intimately bound up with 'fraternity', but not with sisterhood, since the French Revolution but also in earlier political thought?

Again, the only way forward seems to be to challenge the dichotomy itself, and to do so by analysing and dismantling the sexist construction of difference as well as of equality. . . .

3. Integration versus autonomy. An analogous argument may be appropriate in regard to the problems of the 'integration' or 'autonomy' of women's studies in respect to scholarship at large, and of women in respect to academic institutions. Despite the expansion of women's studies, and even though it is now occasionally admitted as a 'sub-disciplinary specialisation', its impact on and integration in the academic disciplines have remained minimal, and what has been called 'mainstreaming' is still far from being implemented, even though there are important differences here as to countries and disciplines. . . .

Clearly, women's studies need to be recognised as an integral part of scholarship at large. But such 'mainstreaming' may also risk being drawn into a dynamic that makes women invisible again. There are now a number of cases where 'gender history' is being opposed, in a dichotomous way, to 'women's history', and where chairs in 'women's history' are strongly opposed, but chairs in 'gender history' are welcome. As an institutional problem, the latter situation may be dealt with according to institutional circumstances, but the theoretical problem remains, largely due to a specific definition of 'gender' which excludes sexual 'difference', meaning women, by classifying it as 'biological' and therefore as socially and historically irrelevant. In such a view, the radical promise of gender history as an extension of women's history risks being subverted by the reduction of the history of women, once again, to a mere appendix of an allegedly more 'generic' gender history. Again, women are not considered to be an equally universal subject as are other, and male-centred subjects.

Therefore, women's history also requires autonomy from male-dominated scholarship, in institutional and particularly in intellectual terms, in order to develop its full potential. But 'autonomy', another virtue central to the heritage of the Renaissance and the Enlightenment, also needs to be redefined. In practice, the difficult question is to recognize the fine line, which is also a profound divide, between autonomy and segregation, the ghetto in which women's studies often find themselves. It seems that the problem 'autonomy versus integration' cannot be adequately dealt with through terminological distinctions, between women's history, feminist history, and gender history. . . .

Challenging dichotomies seems to be a major issue on the scholarly as well as the political agenda of women's and gender history, and of women's studies more broadly. The act of challenging requires, of course, further study of the precise character of the opposing categories, of the particularities and dynamics of the dichotomous relationship, and of the form and character of the challenge itself.

As to the nature of gender-based dichotomies, there is obviously a significant difference between the first set of three which have been mentioned in the earlier section of this paper, and the latter set of three. This difference reflects, among other things, the increasingly complex character of the categories under which gender relations are being considered and studied. The dichotomies nature/culture, paid/unpaid work, public/private were constructed in alignment with a fixed divide between women and men, the ostensibly internally homogeneous categories on each side of which pointing either to women or to men. In the case of sex/gender, equality/difference, integration/autonomy, however, both (apparently) opposing terms refer to both sexes. We are therefore not dealing just with relations between the sexes, but with relations between relational categories; and not just with (apparent) contradictories between women and men, but with opposing or apparently opposing conceptualisations and practices of gender relations. Hence, women's studies and the search for new visions of gender has led us — despite, or rather because of sometimes profoundly different approaches — to at least one common ground: gender issues are issues which concern complex human relations, relations both between the sexes and within the sexes.

And what could or should be the character of the challenge? It requires continuous work on the dismantling, historicisation, and deconstruction of the apparently given meanings of the various categories. I believe that it also implies the rejection of mutually exclusive hierarchies, and especially of either/or solutions, in favour of as-well-as solutions. . . . In the case of the two latter dilemmas, we may particularly need to challenge their mutual exclusiveness and claim 'equality in difference' and 'difference in equality', 'autonomy in integration' and 'integration in autonomy'. For both of them one might object, and it has been objected, that women cannot have their cake and eat it too. But for too long, women have baked the cake and taken only the smallest slice to eat for themselves.

Afro-American Women in History

EVELYN BROOKS HIGGINBOTHAM

'Ah wanted to preach a great sermon about colored women sittin' on high, but they wasn't no pulpit for me.' This line from Zora Neale Hurston's *Their Eyes Were Watching God* expresses the frustration of Nanny, the black grandmother who never realized the fulfillment of her dreams of 'whut a woman oughta be and to do.' Racism and poverty had silenced her and left her no opportunity or means to voice, much less realize, her message to the world. Like Nanny, the story of black American womanhood has been denied a 'pulpit' for far too long. It was not until the mid-1970s that scholars began to notice the omission of black women in historical literature. Even today, with the plethora of publications in Afro-American and women's history, the black woman's voice goes largely unheard. The sound of silence, which resonates throughout much of the scholarship on Afro-Americans and women, reflects the failure to recognize black women's history as not only an identifiable field of inquiry in its own right, but as an integral part of Afro-American, American, and women's history.

Writing black women into history is critical in illuminating the relation of both

Evelyn Brooks Higginbotham, "Beyond the Sound of Silence: African-American Women in History" from *Gender and History*, I, no. 1 (spring 1989), pp. 50–63. Reprinted by permission of Basil Blackwell Publishers.

Afro-American and women's history to American history. Both Afro-Americans and women reflect the complicated dialectic of being integrally part of the larger American story, while also being quite distinguishable and apart from it. Both Afro-Americans and women find meaning and self-identity in the American past and in American culture, and yet they each claim a cultural uniqueness and separate consciousness. Afro-American history and women's history have shared similar historiographic trends throughout the twentieth century. Each has depended heavily upon the conventional sub-disciplines, e.g., political, economic, and social history, for periodization, conceptual frameworks, and methodologies. Yet each has made its own unique methodological contributions as well. Both have suffered from the weakness of omission. Afro-American history has failed to address gender issues adequately, while women's history has similarly failed to address questions of race. . . .

Women's history, like black history, came to life during the early twentieth century, but it came of age during the politically charged 1960s and early 1970s. In certain respects, the study of women has followed a historiographic course similar to that of black history. It has striven to fill the female gaps in the American story by integrating women into political and social histories. It has devoted entire textbooks to the subject of women's achievements. It has revised misconceptions and chronicled woman's struggle for equality. Women's history has benefited especially from social history's focus on the invisible and anonymous masses in society and has exploited its quantitative and interdisciplinary methods in examining female life cycles, labour force participation rates, and household and family structures.

Influenced by the concept of 'cultural separatism' — especially as utilized in studies of slave culture — historians of women have sought to identify a female culture and consciousness divorced from male points of reference and have explored hitherto uninvestigated, even unimagined, topics and sources related to the private world of women. Most important, in their formulation of the gender system as a set of social relations that interact and intersect with class and race relations, historians of women have made a valuable and unique methodological contribution. These varied historiographic trends notwithstanding, women's history has suffered from a racial bias. Criticized for its white, middle-class, and northeastern emphasis, it has just begun to write black women into its blossoming field of literature.

Although published work on black women remains sparse, articles and books increase yearly and now exist in sufficient number to reveal the different and conflicting voices of the black female experience. The conflicting voices usher from the paradoxical nature of the black woman's identity — of being simultaneously black and female, black and American, and American and female. By focusing on black women within the Afro-American context and including them in studies on American womanhood, historians will discover the importance of black women to both black and women's history. It is in addressing the conflicting voices of black womanhood that historians will ultimately unveil the too-often obscured dialectical relationship between women's and American history and between Afro-American and American history.

The theme of double jeopardy marks the starting point for all literature on black women. To be black and female carries the dual burden of racial and sexual oppression. Most historians assert the primacy of race as opposed to gender when identifying the objective context for the black female experience and black women's subjective perceptions of it. . . .

Historians of black women call into question the concept of a universal woman-hood by underscoring the unity of white men and women in determining American racial thought and policy. The white suffragists' vision of representative govern-ment excluded black women and black men alike. Their discrimination against black suffragists, along with their vacillation between silence and vocal support for the southern states' disfranchisement of black male voters, exposed their goal as being equality with white men only. In this regard, the white suffragists remained an integral part of the dominant American culture.

Social histories focusing on women's lives provide another source for observ-ing racial differences. Again, black women defy dominant American patterns. Such studies employ an arsenal of statistics to disclose racial disparities in household structures, workforce participation rates, and types of occupation. The more sophis-ticated social histories place black women against the backdrop of contrasting pat-terns among various white ethnic groups and introduce cultural factors to explain these differences. . . . Proponents of cultural difference deny that any one culture embraces both black and white women, while they simultaneously question a racial identity that does not account for gender differences. Shaped by African traditions and American socio-economic forces, black women are described as perceiving and experiencing their lives in ways distinguishable from both white women and black men. . . .

Research on slave women . . . highlights cultural difference and finds the exis-tence of a black female culture and consciousness to be anchored in the reality of daily work for black women. Black women worked, for the most part, either in gender-specific employment or in female-segregated groups within types of em-ployment that engaged both sexes. Except for harvesting time, when male and fe-male worked side by side, male gangs commonly plowed and female ones hoed. However, a noticeable number of women plowed and performed other physically arduous tasks associated with masculine strength. On the other hand, the positions of cook, mid-wife, and seamstress — all female jobs — commanded respect in the quarters. Since slave women worked largely in sexually segregated groups during the course of the day, they shared a world in which they developed their own crite-ria and value system for ranking and ordering themselves. The private world of slave women afforded, too, a sense of interdependence and cooperation that encour-aged female self-esteem both individually and collectively and helped mitigate the dehumanizing aspects of slavery. . . .

The preponderant emphasis on differences between black and white women testifies to the overarching historical reality of racist oppression and the exclusion of blacks from a large part of American life. Yet, the acknowledgement of this re-alty does not negate the bicultural voice that also articulates the values of the domi-nant society. A singular focus on racial difference misses the bicultural aspects of the black woman's existence. It avoids understanding her as both black and American.

Black women have historically lived in a community whose collective behav-iour derived not only from Afro-American traditions, but also from the values and social behaviour of the dominant American society. The case for cultural difference is strongest, although not beyond challenge, for the slave period, as slave narratives themselves reveal. . . .

The bicultural tensions heightened dramatically after emancipation. . . . Although slavery prescribed the black community to a 'cultural world whose dictates and values were accepted with a minimum of ambivalence and questioning, or inhibiting self-consciousness,' freedom introduced new and alternate standards, namely those of the dominant American society. The new standards, promoted by Yankee missionaries, black schools and colleges, and black churches, set the process of biculturation in motion. Schools, churches, and many black leaders taught that individual advancement, as well as the advancement of the entire black community demanded a lifestyle that stood at odds with many of the older black cultural traditions. Gaining respect, even justice, from white America required changes in religious beliefs, speech patterns, and also in gender roles and relations.

In the self-conscious as well as sub-conscious acceptance of dominant American values, many blacks increasingly linked the new values with upward mobility and the old with backwardness. Even the masses, held down by poverty and racial oppression, deemed certain mainstream values and behaviour as proper and correct, despite their inability to manifest them in practice. [This] is the same 'double consciousness' of which [W.E.B.] Du Bois wrote so eloquently at the dawn of the twentieth century: 'One ever feels his twoness, — an American, a Negro; two souls, two thoughts, two unreconciled strivings; two warring ideals in one dark body, whose dogged strength alone keeps it from being torn asunder.'

My own work on the women's movement in the black Baptist church between 1880 and 1920 exposes the class dimension of biculturation and the decisive participation of women missionaries in the dissemination and internalization of middle-class values among and by countless poor and uneducated blacks. Despite the racial segregation, disfranchisement, and violence of the late nineteenth-century South, women's societies — called conventions by black Baptists — influenced some blacks to aspire to and even achieve upward mobility, but they influenced many more to make financial sacrifices, limit personal consumption, and channel their meager resources to the support of the educational and other self-help institutions of their race. . . .

If the concept of biculturation informs the black woman's identity as a black American, it simultaneously shapes her identity as an American woman. In the immediate post–Civil War South, black families sought the withdrawal of mothers and wives from the workforce in order to attend to their own households. The attempt on the part of blacks to practice gender roles prevalent among white Americans met with a hostile response from white Union army officers, planters, and Freedmen's Bureau agents, who viewed black women's domesticity not as an ideal but as an 'evil of female loaferism.' Economic necessity soon returned these women to the fields and kitchens of the South, but this reversal does not imply a rejection of their preference for domesticity. . . .

Ex-slaves were quick to idealize the role of man as provider and woman as homemaker, even though both were forced to work. . . . Indeed, Afro-Americans protested the racist reality that forced so many of their women into the full-time jobs of cleaning and caring for white women's homes and children. This reality served as a constant reminder of the inability of black men to earn a 'man's' wage. Racial restrictions and job ceilings denied them the same 'breadwinner' self-image that white husbands enjoyed. Implicit in their idealization of domesticity seemed to be the reinstatement of dignity to black manhood and womanhood.

The visible assimilation or, at least, psychological allegiance to the sexual behaviour and attitudes of white middle-class America conveys the class-specific context of gender relations within the black community. Unquestioningly, discussions of class differences among blacks become inherently problematic, because of the difficulty in establishing objective definitions that are useful beyond the slavery period. Until recently racism and poverty skewed income and occupational levels so drastically that sociologists relied heavily upon values and behaviour as additional criteria for discerning blacks who maintained or aspired to middle-class status from those who practiced alternative lifestyles. Thus social scientists as well as members of the black community, in general, focused on adherence to bourgeois standards of respectability and morality in designating classes.

Gender relations constitute one of the important variables, although not the only one, traditionally used to establish attitudinal and behavioural criteria for class differences among blacks. Nineteenth and early twentieth century leaders rarely alluded to income or occupation when referring, as they frequently did, to the 'better class of Negroes.' Domestic servants could be included, and some were cited in this category, for it comprised all who were hardworking, religious, clean, and, so far as sex was concerned, respectful of the dominant society's manners and morals.

The club movement among middle-class black women during the late nineteenth century constituted an effort to win greater respectability for black womanhood through the uplift of black working women. 'Lifting as we climb,' the motto of the National Association of Colored Women, reveals the black middle-class woman's commitment to her working-class sister, but also to dominant American assumptions regarding the benefits of upward mobility. . . . Given the economic realities, many black women sought to emulate mainstream female roles, codes of dress, and public behaviour as best they could, for they linked assimilation with self-respect and racial progress. It is not uncommon for oppressed peoples to adopt the values of their oppressors for reasons of their own. The shared acceptance of the dominant society's normative gender roles forged the link between black and white missionary women and permitted their cooperative work through religious and educational institutions. . . .

. . . At specific historical moments, black women have borne discrimination that was peculiar to their gender. The ratification of the Fifteenth Amendment, for instance, accentuated discrimination against the black woman as woman. During Reconstruction black women shared their men's ecstasy and optimism, but not their right to wield the ballot. Like all American women, they stood as spectators, not as recipients of an expanding democracy. Black women rejoiced to hear the voices of their men resound from the lowest local offices in the South to the halls of the United States Congress, and yet they, as women, remained on the margins of representative government. Sojourner Truth, an outspoken critic of the unequal political rights of black men and women, expressed her displeasure with the limitations of the Fifteenth Amendment: 'There is a great stir about the colored men getting their rights, but not a word about the colored women; and if colored men get their rights, and not colored women theirs, you see the colored men will be masters over the women, and it will be just as bad as it was before.'

> Black clubwomen and countless numbers in church societies championed woman's suffrage in the early twentieth century. Studies . . . clearly exhibit the importance of the vote to black women. Divisions in women's political and reform work reflected the very real barrier of white racism; however, parallels and cooperative efforts, which also existed between black and white women's organizations, reflected commonalities and shared interests among women regardless of race. . . .

Writing black women into history carries scholarship beyond the silence of the past, while ultimately weaving a more intricate, yet more honest narrative of women, Afro-Americans, and this nation as a whole. Studies of Afro-American women, when taken together, tell a story of gender and racial oppression, but also one of new dimensions of cultural autonomy, cooperation, supportive bonding, and survival strategies. The inclusion of black women holds the key to recognizing and analyzing American social systems and social relations in all their permutations of race, class, and gender. Attention is thereby called to the interaction and intersection of gender, race, and class, and their roles — as sets of social relations — in both determining and being determined by power relations.

The relation of gender to power is at the core of women's history; yet factors of class and race make any generalization regarding womanhood's common oppression impossible. The relation of race to power remains central to Afro-American history, but gender and class preclude a monolithic black community as well. Studies of black women help to dispel the silence and correct imbalances in both Afro-American and women's history. By so doing, they also help to explain the contradictory relationship of women and blacks to the American experience.

FURTHER READING

Gretchen Bataile, ed., *Native American Women: A Biographical Dictionary* (1992)
Carol Ruth Berkin and Mary Beth Norton, eds., *Women of America: A History* (1979)
Carl Degler, *At Odds: Women and the Family in America from the Revolution to the Present* (1980)
Ellen DuBois and Vicki Ruiz, eds., *Unequal Sisters: A Multicultural Reader in American Women's History* (1994)
Sara Evans, *Born for Liberty* (1989)
Paula Giddings, *When and Where I Enter: The Impact of Black Women on Race and Sex in America* (1984)
Evelyn Brooks Higginbotham, "African-American Women's History and the Metalanguage of Race," *Signs,* 17 (1991–1992), 251–274
Edward and Janet James, eds., *Notable American Women 1607–1950* (1971)
Joan Kelly, *Women, History, and Theory* (1984)
Linda Kerber, "Separate Spheres, Female Worlds, Woman's Place: The Rhetoric of Women's History," *Journal of American History,* 75 (1988–1989), 3–39
Gerda Lerner, *The Majority Finds Its Past* (1979)
Alfredo Mirande and Evangelina Enriquez, *La Chicana* (1979)
Dorothy C. Salem, ed., *African American Women: A Biographical Dictionary* (1992)
Joan W. Scott, *Gender and the Politics of History* (1988)
Barbara Sicherman, ed., *Notable American Women: The Modern Period* (1980)
Nancy Woloch, *Women and the American Experience* (1984)

The Impact of Christianity
on Native American Women

The historical study of Native American women prior to and in the early years of European contact is a field still in its infancy. To date, few book-length accounts of the topic have appeared, and even articles are relatively sparse in number. The paucity of scholarship stems not from lack of interest but largely from the difficulty of doing research on the subject. Since the indigenous people of North America encountered by the English and the French had no written language of their own, the vast majority of surviving accounts of these encounters between the two cultures exists only in the words of Europeans. Such sources reflect the bias of the authors, who were in the main elite, well-educated men with specific goals — usually to convert the Indians, exploit their labor, or appropriate their lands. The documents, accordingly, must be read creatively and with great care in order to avoid making the same cultural preconceptions as the men who produced them.

Even so, in the past two decades scholars have begun to ask a series of important questions about the European invaders' impact on the indigenous inhabitants of North America. These range from the general — How large was the precontact population of the continent, and why was it so quickly reduced after the Europeans' arrival? — to the specific — What was the fate of particular tribal or language groups? Still more recently, gender-differentiated inquiries have been raised: What were the roles of women in precontact Indian societies? How did those roles change as Europeans gradually asserted their control over the northeastern quadrant of the continent during the 150 years between their arrival and the American Revolution?

There has been little agreement on the answer to one key question in particular: What impact did Christianity have on Native American women? Roman Catholic missionaries were active in New France, and missionaries of several Protestant denominations sporadically proselytized the indigenous people in regions of North America claimed by England. Historians have argued both sides — that Indian women were especially resistant to Christianity or that they were especially receptive to its message. Most scholars, admittedly, agree with the first thesis, but the second does have its adherents. Those who contend that conversion to Christianity had a negative, even oppressive, effect on native women must find ways to explain why so many became active in Catholic and Protestant congregations. And those who view the process of women's conversion in a more positive light must deal with the fact that most scholars today believe that Native American women had a high standing in precontact societies. Why, then, would women abandon traditional beliefs to convert to Christianity, a religious system that subordinated women to men? As of yet, neither side appears to have adequately handled the arguments against it. That fact might well suggest that the questions historians are asking need to be reformulated.

❋ D O C U M E N T S

Among the first Europeans to attempt to convert the native peoples of North America to Christianity were Roman Catholic priests in New France, most notably members of the Society of Jesus, or Jesuits. From the early seventeenth century until New France fell to the English in 1759, the Jesuits worked tirelessly to spread Catholic doctrine among the tribes who lived north of the St. Lawrence River, in what is now Canada. The first two documents, which report on Native American women's social role and their resistance to the missionaries' message, are drawn from a published collection known as the *Jesuit Relations* — the priests' regular reports to their superiors in France on the progress of their conversion efforts. The third document, the brief official record of the adultery trial of an Algonkian woman in Massachusetts Bay in 1668, shows that the settlers of English North America sought to impose their definitions of morality on their Indian neighbors. The fourth document, a set of extracts from an English missionary's account of the Christian converts on the island of Martha's Vineyard, movingly describes the sincere piety of some Indian women. Taken together, the documents illustrate the complexity of female Native Americans' reactions to the Christian religion brought to their continent by its European invaders.

Father Le Jeune on the Importance of Native American Women, 1633

I see that it is absolutely necessary to teach the girls as well as the boys, and that we shall do nothing or very little, unless some good household has the care of this sex; for the boys that we shall have reared in the knowledge of God, when they marry Savage girls or women accustomed to wandering in the woods, will, as their husbands, be compelled to follow them and thus fall back into barbarism, or to leave them, another evil full of danger.

On the first day of April, the Captain of the Algonquains came to see us.

. . . I asked him if he had a son, and if he would not give him to us to be educated. He asked me how many children I wanted, and [said] that I already had two. I told him that in time I should perhaps feed twenty. He was astonished. "Wilt thou clothe so many as well?" asked he. I answered him that we would not take them until we had the means to clothe them. He replied that he would be very glad to give us his son, but that his wife did not wish to do so. The women have great power here. A man may promise you something, and, if he does not keep his promise, he thinks he is sufficiently excused when he tells you that his wife did not wish to do it. I told him then that he was the master, and that in France women do not rule their husbands.

Native Women Resist the Jesuits, 1640

They [Native American men] resolved to call together the women, to urge them to be instructed and to receive holy Baptism. Accordingly, they were brought together, and the young people also. The best of it was that they preached to them so well that the following day some of these poor women, encountering Father de Quen, said to him, "Where is such a Father? we have come to beg him to baptize us. Yesterday the men summoned us to a Council, the first time that women have ever entered one; but they treated us so rudely that we were greatly astonished. 'It is you women,' they said to us, 'who are the cause of all our misfortunes, — it is you who keep the demons among us. You do not urge to be baptized; you must not be satisfied to ask this favor only once from the Fathers, you must importune them. You are lazy about going to prayers; when you pass before the cross, you never salute it; you wish to be independent. Now know that you will obey your husbands; and you young people, you will obey your parents and our Captains; and, if any fail to do so, we have concluded to give them nothing to eat.'" This is a part of the sermon of these new Preachers, who, in my opinion, are so much the more wonderful as they are new and very far removed from the Savage methods of action. I believe, indeed, that they will not all at once enter into this great submissiveness that they promise themselves; but it will be in this point as in others, they will embrace it little by little. A young woman having fled, shortly after these elections, into the woods, not wishing to obey her husband, the Captains had her searched for, and came to ask us, if, having found her, it would not be well to chain her by one foot; and if it would be enough to make her pass four days and four nights without eating, as penance for her fault.

The Trial of Sarah Ahhaton in Massachusetts, 1668

Whereas Sarah Ahaton [*sic*], an Indian squa, is now in prison for adultery, & there being severall considerations about it, wherein much difficulty appeares, it is ordered, that this case be heard by the Generall Court on 27 instant October, at one of the clocke.

The Court at the time sent for the said Sarah Ahaton out of prison, & being at the barr, & hearing what was produced ag[ains]t her, upon the question relating to the said Sarah Ahatons confession of committing adultery with Joseph, an Indian, whither on what hath been heard, as the case is circumstanced, she should be put to death, it was resolved on the negative; and it is further ordered, that the said Sarah Ahaton shall, on the 29th instant, stand on the gallowes after the lecture in Boston, with a roape about hir necke one hower, & that then the marshall generall shall cause her to be tooke doune & returned to prison, & committed to the Indian constable of Naticke, who, on a publick day, by order from Capt. Gookin, shall severely whip hir, not exceeding thirty stripes, & that she pay all charges for the prosecution, to be allowed by Capt. Gookin, (hir whiping to be deferred till after the time of hir delivery, if she be with child, as is reported).

Experience Mayhew Describes the Pious Wampanoag Women of Martha's Vineyard, 1727

The number of *Women* truly fearing God, has by some been thought to exceed that of *Men* so doing; but whether the Observation will generally hold true or not, I shall not now inquire. However, it seems to be a Truth with respect to our *Indians,* so far as my Knowledge of them extends, that there have been, and are a greater number of their *Women* appearing pious than of the *Men* among them. . . .

[Rebeccah Sissetom] appeared sober, and well disposed from her very Childhood, was obedient to her Parents, and not so much given to Vanity as most Children are.

Having been taught to read while she was young, she appeared to delight in her Book. She seemed also to delight in going to Meetings; and, being about ten Years old when her Mother was admitted to full Communion in the Church of Christ, she her self manifested a Desire of being baptized before the same was proposed to her, and was accordingly admitted to the Privilege, being first examined, and found to understand the Nature of the baptismal Covenant, as well as willing to give her Consent to it.

After this she frequently discoursed of the things of God and another Life, and this in such a manner as shewed a becoming Seriousness, and manifested a Desire of obtaining that Knowledge which is necessary to Salvation, and also a great Concern that she might not fall short of eternal Life. . . .

[Hannah Nohnosoo] join'd early to the Church already mentioned, and was a Member of it in full Communion, I suppose, at least forty Years before she died; in all which time, I cannot learn that she was ever guilty of any scandalous Evil whatsoever, but constantly behav'd her self as became a good Christian, so as to adorn the Doctrine of God her Saviour in all things.

She was really, and not by Profession only, a praying Woman, praying always when there were proper Occasions for it; as in her own Family when she was a Widow and her Children lived with her; and afterwards in the Houses wherein she lived with others, when there were none present for whom it might be more proper. And she always manifested a Love and Zeal for the House and Ordinances of God, not in her Discourses only, but in her constant and serious Attendance on them. . . .

Having very considerable Skill in some of the Distempers to which human Bodies are subject, and in the Nature of many of those Herbs and Plants which were proper Remedies against them, she often did good by her Medicines among her Neighbours, especially the poorer sort of them, whom she readily served without asking them any thing for what she did for them. . . . Several Women, some *English* and some *Indians,* being divers Years after Marriage without the Blessing of Children, having barren Wombs and dry Breasts, which Persons in a married State are scarce ever pleased with, some of these Women applying themselves to the good old *Hannah* of whom I am now speaking, for help in Case that thus afflicted them, have soon after become joyful Mothers of Children; for which Comfort, under God, they have been oblig'd to her. . . .

[Jerusha Ompan] seemed to have the Fear of God in her Heart, while she was but a young Girl, was very dutiful to her Parents, and was not known to be given to any Vice. She never much affected going to Huskings and Weddings, and if at any time she went to them, she would be sure to come home seasonably, not tarrying too long, as the Generality of Persons did. . . .

She was about 29 Years old before she dy'd; and tho she had had some Offers of Marriage made to her, yet she would accept none of them, alledging to her Friends as the reason of her Refusal, that of the Apostle in the first Epistle to the *Corinthians, Chap.* vii. *The unmarried Woman careth for the Things of the Lord, &c.* . . .

[Hannah Tiler] was as bad by Nature as any others, so the former part of her Life was no better ordered than the Lives of Persons in a State of Nature generally be. . . . [Her husband] lived but viciously before he married her, and continued so to do for some Years afterward. He would frequently have his drunken Fits. . . .

But the Woman being at length convinced of the great Evil there is in the Sin of Drunkenness, resolved that she would forsake it, and God helped her so to do; so that she overcame her Temptations to that Vice, and lived in that regard very temperately: but being her self in that Particular reformed, and Drunkenness now becoming exceeding offensive to her, she could not bear with it in others, and therefore could not forbear talking too angrily to her Husband when she saw him guilty of that Crime; and this was an Occasion of sore Contentions betwixt them. . . .

Being thus reform'd in her Life, she made a publick Profession of Religion, and joined her self to the Church of Christ about nine or ten Years before that wherein she died; during all which time, she walked, as far as I can understand, very blamelessly, ordering her Conversation as did become the Gospel. . . .

Accordingly she, after some time, did so far overcome his Evil by her Goodness, that he carried himself more kindly to her than formerly he had done; and appeared to become religious, took some care about the Instruction of his Children, and made a publick Profession of Faith and Repentance, joining himself to the Church of Christ. . . .

❇ E S S A Y S

The first essay, by Carol Devens, a professor at Central Michigan University, focuses on the Jesuits' mission to New France. Asking whether Indian men and women responded differently to the priests' message, Devens argues that, unlike men, women were more resistant to Christianity and to the new trading economy fostered by the insatiable European demand for furs. She finds the women's stance understandable, even laudable, and contends that their high standing in Indian society deteriorated considerably after contact with Europeans and their religion. In the second essay, by contrast, James P. Ronda of the University of Tulsa emphasizes the positive impact of Christianity on the Wampanoag people of Martha's Vineyard island. Admitting that the island might have been an exception to a more general pattern of resistance, he nevertheless thinks it significant that so many women there were attracted to Christian precepts. This essay is an excerpt from a longer article that examines more fully the experience of men, women, and children. An examination of a single incident — the adultery prosecution of Sarah Ahhaton in 1668 — forms the core of the third essay, by Ann Marie Plane, a young historian who teaches at the University of California at Santa Barbara. Plane's detailed analysis of this case suggests that the question of

Christianity's impact on Native American women might be more complicated than either Devens or Ronda seems willing to admit.

Resistance to Christianity by the Native Women of New France

CAROL DEVENS

"'It is you women,'" charged the men, "' . . . who are the cause of all our misfortunes, — it is you who keep the demons among us. You do not urge to be baptized; you must not be satisfied to ask this favor only once from the Fathers, you must importune them. You are lazy about going to prayers; when you pass before the cross, you never salute it; you wish to be independent. Now know that you will obey your husbands.'" With this angry accusation the Christian men of a Montagnais Indian band in New France, frustrated by the persistence of traditional religion in their community, identified women as the major obstacle to the group's conversion. The band had been under the direct influence of the French since a Jesuit priest convinced the survivors of the 1639–40 smallpox epidemic to accompany him from their small camp at Three Rivers to the St. Joseph mission at Sillery. There the French sheltered and provided for them, and resident Christian Indians demanded their conversion. Whether the women of the group eventually capitulated was not noted by the priest who recorded the incident. He did remark that at least one woman fled into the forest rather than submit. The men, believing that the women's independence and apparent lack of interest in Christianity had divided the group, resolved that should she be captured, they would chain and starve her as punishment.

The Montagnais women's opposition vividly illustrates the pervasiveness of women's resistance in "domiciled" Indian groups to the conversion efforts of seventeenth-century missionaries. The conflict between the men and women of St. Joseph's indicated more than the men's need of a scapegoat for their troubles. The episode revealed religious and social tensions between the sexes in a native community; and it foreshadowed similar discord among Indian groups throughout New France. Men and women diverged in their receptivity to Christianity and in how they confronted the changes triggered by European intrusion. Essentially, they found themselves holding different expectations and faced with different options. The men's decision to adopt Catholicism and a sedentary lifestyle would seem to reflect an unwillingness or inability on their part to continue their traditional functions as nomadic hunters. Women, the men's accusations implied, had for some time opposed the imposition of alien Christian values and gender roles, and supported a subsistence pattern which fostered their status and authority.

Conversion placed unaccustomed restrictions upon women. The French socioeconomic structure and belief system distinctly favored men. The Christian message of the priests stressed the authority of the male in society and the family. The

Carol Devens, "Separate Confrontations: Gender as a Factor in Indian Adaptation to European Colonization in New France," *American Quarterly,* vol. 38 (1986), Gary Kulik, Ed., pp. 461–80. Reprinted by permission of The Johns Hopkins University Press, Baltimore/London.

trading system itself was one in which men dealt with men. Many women did not willingly accept the imposition of European-defined sex roles and their resistance was expressed in their reluctance to convert. This resistance — related to social and economic changes as well as religious factors — became a divisive force in many native communities.

Similar ruptures among other nomadic hunting-gathering groups in eastern Canada suggest a pattern of native response to ongoing contact with seventeenth-century missionaries and traders. Using a regional rather than tribal approach, the experiences of the Montagnais-Naskapi, Algonquin, and Ojibwa who occupied the area from the Labrador Peninsula to Lake Winnipeg can be considered. Groups from among these bands chose to settle in villages near French missions, generally for protection from enemy bands or to recuperate from the devastation of epidemics. It is these "domiciled" Indians who form the basis of this study. The extent to which the ideology, subsistence activities, and material culture of these people resembled one another makes it possible to consider their interaction with Europeans as analogous situations. Sources from the period such as the *Jesuit Relations,* journals, and travel accounts of explorers and traders provide a wealth of information on native customs and on their reactions to Europeans. Despite certain ethnocentric biases these sources can be evaluated against modern ethnological data to furnish a portrait of precontact relationships between the sexes.

The striking feature of such a profile is the sexual division which permeated all aspects of life — rituals, authority, production and reproductive activities, spatial arrangements, and food distribution — and profoundly influenced the manner in which women and men dealt with the vicissitudes of daily living. In a physical and ideological sense, each sex was an integral yet autonomous part of the social and productive unit. Male and female had complementary functions which seldom overlapped so that, as one missionary noted, "The women know what they are to do, and the men also; and one never meddles with the work of the other. The men make the frames of their canoes, and the women sew the bark with willow withes or similar wood. The men shape the wood of the raquettes [snowshoes], and the women do the sewing on them. Men go hunting, and kill the animals; and the women go after them, skin them, and clean the hides." "To live among us without a wife," one man explained, "is to live without help, without home, and to be always wandering."

Rituals and ideology complemented the separation of responsibility and authority. Men, and male rituals, were oriented to the bush. Males actively participated in camp life, but their primary productive role was hunting large game and furbearers. A man's value to his group was based largely on his contributions as a hunter, and his authority and respect rested on his skills. Success in the chase depended on the cooperation of animal spirits and the guidance of supernatural "helpers" gained through vision quests or dreaming. Men moved between the bush and the camp yet governed neither, for animal spirits "owned" the bush and women controlled the camp. Men's activities required little cooperative effort, with the exception of warring and divination, and they generally worked individually or in very small groups. Their identities as hunters forced a degree of physical isolation from the group upon them. Hunting removed them from the camp for a number of days, perhaps weeks, as they tracked game or checked traps. Moreover, a hunter's relationship with supernaturals vital to the chase was a highly individual one which he was compelled to maintain on his own.

Women worked apart from men, either within the commensal unit or in groups. The communal nature of their work allowed them frequent interaction with one another. They fished and hunted small game in the vicinity of the encampment, thus providing a large portion of the daily staple. Women controlled the apportionment and distribution of meat which men had obtained. After a successful hunt, men informed the women of the kill and the game became the women's to butcher and process as they saw fit. After spending the winter of 1633–34 in the bush with a Montagnais band, Paul Le Jeune, head of the Jesuit mission, described this transferral with amazement: "Men leave the arrangement of the household to the women, without interfering with them; they cut, and decide, and give away [meat] as they please, without making the husband angry." A woman's distribution of meat to families within the group simultaneously acknowledged her autonomy and control of particular resources while reinforcing a sense of community and interdependence between households.

Women were responsible as well for the processing of hides and for the making of clothing and tools. Men received such items in return for the meat which they provided. Women also controlled the assignment of living space and the selection of campsites. Childbearing, too, was a highly valued activity. Children were wanted and cherished, and were needed for the parents' support in old age. "The father and mother draw the morsel from the mouth if the child asks for it," commented one observer, "They love their children greatly." Raising and training children occupied an important place in women's activities; after a child was weaned at the age of two or three its care became a communal effort in which all women participated.

Women's ritual activities, like their practical ones, were separate from those of men. References to specific female beliefs and customs are obscure in the French records since the practices the Jesuits recorded were usually the hunting rites of men or the shamanistic rituals performed by both sexes. Le Jeune and others did note, however, that women had certain special foods, held separate feasts, and performed dances quite different from those of men. Le Jeune also remarked that women had a special spiritual potency, manifested during menses and childbirth. Female spiritual power was innate, unlike the "helpers" upon whom men depended.

The separate rituals and attributes of the sexes suggest that male and female had distinct spiritual identities in traditional ideology. This system recognized the autonomy of male and female by emphasizing their different needs and concerns. Such division was not disruptive, however, countered as it was by the complementary nature of women's and men's social and productive activities. Instead, the different aspects combined in a vital symmetry upon which the perpetuation of the community depended. . . .

The confrontation between men and women of St. Joseph's at Sillery was by no means an isolated incident. Indeed, the Jesuits recorded similar episodes of resistance throughout New France. The missionary effort became a divisive force in many native communities because women and men reacted to the Jesuit assault in very different ways. Men more often seemed receptive to European religion and customs. At first the Jesuits consciously chose to focus their proselytizing on men and boys, alternating attacks on male hunting and divination rituals with blandishments of the comforts and virtue of life as a Christian man.

Modesty and convenience combined to encourage the priests to avoid unnecessary contact with women. Le Jeune decided that "in regard to the women, it is not becoming for us to receive them into our houses," and so barred them from participation in most religious instruction. The priests expected women to convert as a matter of course, if only because the "Neophytes" needed Christian wives to eliminate the temptation of backsliding. Christian men who married pagan girls, Le Jeune feared, would "as their husbands, be compelled to follow them and thus fall back onto barbarism or to leave them, another evil full of danger." While women converts were essential for the priests to fulfill their goal of establishing sedentary villages based on the nuclear family structure, the Jesuits planned initially to leave the instruction of females to chance or to male converts.

To the missionaries' dismay, women declined conversion and stressed the importance of older rituals and practices. Priests and converts alike faced women's scorn when they flouted tradition. When Christians warned that eternal damnation awaited those who clung to heathen practices, the women had short patience. The Baron Lahontan, traveling through New France in the late seventeenth century, reported a very divided response to the Jesuits' exhortations that "a Fire is Kindled in the other World to Torment 'em forever. . . . To such Remonstrances," he found, "the Men reply, 'That's Admirable'; and the Women usually tell the Good Fathers in a deriding way, 'That if their Threats be well grounded, the Mountains of the other World must consist of the Ashes of souls.'"

Year after year the Jesuits recorded incidents of women's resistance throughout the Canadian mission. Le Jeune recounted that one convert's wife, "a rough and wild creature, who gives a great deal of trouble to the poor man," refused to consider conversion when her husband insisted he must have a Christian wife. The priest described the man's anxiety over the situation: "'You have told me that those who do evil are very often incited to it by Demons; alas!' said he, 'then I am always with some Demon, for my wife is always angry; I fear that the Demons she keeps in my cabin are perverting the good that I received in holy Baptism.'" The fellow confided that she had even hurled a knife at him during an argument over her refusal to convert. The woman spurned his efforts and mocked his faith in Christianity. "'Dost thou not see that we are all dying since they told us to pray to God?'" she asked. "'Where are thy relatives? Where are mine? the most of them are dead; it is no longer a time to believe.'" Other male converts had similarly difficult times convincing their wives to become Christians. Women continued to retain many customary social and religious values and men became increasingly aggressive and punitive in their attempts to secure conversions. . . .

The women . . . were responding to the gradual redefinition of social and religious identities and status, a result both of French assaults on native culture and of environmental changes. Indian communities had been weakened structurally by imported epidemic diseases and the extermination of peltry animals through overhunting. Many were shaken by the shamans' inability to fight the epidemics or to replenish the animal population. Missionaries' efforts to impose their values on native groups capitalized on this vulnerability. The introduction of alien cultural values into communities already exhausted by inexplicable changes and newly settled near missions or trading centers altered traditional social relationships, in particular those between the sexes.

The French who first set out to bring European religion and culture to the Indians encountered a system of balanced yet autonomous gender roles which baffled and sometimes horrified them. They dealt with this problem by assigning natives a place within the western scheme of gender relations. When the French observed the camp-oriented activities of women they assumed that the sexual division of labor indicated status divisions as well, as it did in Europe. They based this supposition in part on French concepts of labor: women's food processing, tool making, and camp tasks were manual labor and thus drudgery. Noting that men hunted large game — an activity reserved for the privileged in Europe — while women generally remained near the camp, one early missionary concluded that the women's "duties and positions are those of slaves, laborers and beasts of burden" — hardly the most tempting targets for a conversion effort. . . .

Native women's power in the family and community amazed the French. Le Clercq explained that "the men leave the arrangements of the housekeeping to the women, and do not interfere with them. . . . I can say that I have never seen the head of the wigwam where I was living ask of his wife what had become of the meat of moose and of beaver. . . . " Le Jeune described more exactly what disturbed him about native marriage when he related an incident in which he tried to persuade a headman to enroll his son in mission school. The man insisted that he must defer to his wife's wish that the child remain at home. "The women have great power here," the priest reported. "A man may promise you something, and, if he does not keep his promise, he thinks he is sufficiently excused when he tells you that his wife did not wish to do it. I told him then that he was the master, and that in France women do not rule their husbands." By the good Father's standards, the relationship between the sexes in New France was definitely askew. He as well as others encouraged male converts to assert their wills and exact obedience from their spouses.

To the French the disturbing aspects of native marital relations paled beside those of their amorous affairs. Women and men controlled their own pre- and post-marital sexual activities. Among the Ojibwa, Lahontan recalled, "a Young Woman is allow'd to do what she pleases; let her Conduct be what it will, neither Father nor Mother, Brother nor Sister can pretend to control her. A Young Woman, say they, is Master of her own Body, and by her Natural Right of Liberty is free to do what she pleases." Although most missionaries and travelers agreed that the Micmac generally were monogamous and favored premarital chastity, on the whole they found the natives' sexual mores shocking. A description sent by Father Allouex in 1667 from the Ottawa mission clearly conveys his horror at their practices: "The fountain-head of their Religion is libertinism; and all these various sacrifices end ordinarily in debauches, indecent dances, and shameful acts of concubinage. All the devotion of the men is directed toward securing many wives, and changing them whenever they choose; that of the women, toward leaving their husbands; and that of the girls, toward a life of profligacy."

The Fathers found the ease with which Indian couples obtained divorce equally distressing. "The stability of marriage is one of the most perplexing questions in the conversion and settlement of the Savages" wrote Vimont, head of the missions after Le Jeune, "we have much difficulty in obtaining and maintaining it." And Pierre

Boucher, several times governor of the Three Rivers settlement and a resident of New France from 1635 until 1717, observed that "divorce is not an odious thing among them [*sic*] Indians. . . . for when a woman wishes to put away her husband, she has only to tell him to leave the house, and he goes out of it without another word. . . . " In fact, most Indians found divorce quite acceptable if a couple had a hostile or unsatisfying relationship. Women felt free to leave spouses who were poor or lazy hunters or who were otherwise not adequate mates.

To the Jesuits this situation was untenable. The priests clearly understood that if native Christian communities were to develop successfully sexual freedom, divorce, and polygamy had to be eliminated. By 1638 they had decided that dispensing land and money might be the most effective inducement to marital fidelity, "for a husband will not so readily leave a wife who brings him a respectable dowry; and a woman, having her possessions near our French settlements, will not readily leave them, any more than her husband" — or so they hoped. The missionaries worked hard to get women to accept monogamy since they were convinced that "it was not honorable for a woman to love anyone else except her husband." They often had to rely on male converts to enforce observation of this alien practice, however. In one notable instance, zealous Christians at Sillery captured a woman who had left her husband and, with the French Governor's approval, imprisoned her without food, fire, or cover in early January. Women, particularly non-Christians, resisted the change because it was not to their advantage. They undoubtedly wanted to retain control over their sexual activities. Moreover, women objected to monogamy for more practical reasons. A Montagnais convert told Le Jeune that "since I have been preaching among them that a man should not have more than one wife, I have not been well received by the women; for, since they are more numerous than the men, if a man can only marry one of them, the others will have to suffer. Therefore this doctrine is not according to their liking."

To be sure, some women apparently accepted the Jesuits' teachings. For most of them, however, conversion seems to have been a protective measure aimed at preserving social and religious autonomy when outright resistance proved dangerous. They may have converted for the sake of their families, striking a bargain with the Christian God to save a sick one's life. Some, such as the young woman whom Le Jeune recommended to the dungeon, decided that Catholicism was preferable to flogging or imprisonment — an understandable choice. It is likely that in many instances conversion decreased the pressures applied to a band by the French and alleviated tensions which arose in communities such as St. Joseph's from conflict over religious allegiances. Quite possibly, superficial observance of Christian practices enabled women to divert attention from themselves.

If converted, women tended to interpret and manipulate Christianity to serve their own needs. They continued to emphasize the sexual dichotomy and female autonomy which had distinguished precolonial society. Catholic mysticism proved a useful tool for this. Le Clercq, describing the activities of certain Micmac converts who emulated the missionaries, was surprised by the number of women involved. Moreover, he expressed concern at how they were able to increase their authority in the community: "These, in usurping the quality and the name of *religieuses,* say certain prayers in their own fashion, and affect a manner of living more reserved than that of the commonalty of Indians, who allow themselves to be dazzled by the glamour of a false and ridiculous devotion. They look upon these women as extraordinary persons, who they believe to hold converse, to speak familiarly, and to hold communication with the sun, which they have all adored as their divinity." By the 1670s a virtual cult of the Virgin developed in some mission communities as women converts focused their ritual attention on that consummate symbol of femaleness in Catholic ideology. The Ursuline convents — the ultimate separate institution for females within the Church — became gathering places for converted native women. There they continued to stress the values of female autonomy, now in a format acceptable to the demands of the missionaries.

In evaluating the changes which occurred in women's roles and status it is essential to consider the virtually symbiotic association of religion and economics in the colonization of New France. Missionaries were not facing virgin country when they set out to evangelize the *sauvages*. A fundamental economic transformation already had begun as market-oriented trapping gradually replaced subsistence hunting-gathering. This shift preceded the mission effort, and paved the way for it. . . .

French merchants were interested primarily in acquiring the furs obtained by men rather than the small game, tools, utensils, or clothing procured or produced by women. "They deal principally in Beavers," another Jesuit, Charles Lalemont, observed, "in which they find their greatest profit." For groups directly participating in the trade, fur hunting and trapping gradually became the major activity of most men. Furs were made the medium of exchange for trade goods, and daily and seasonal life for all increasingly revolved around the trade. Although Indians were eager for ornaments and trinkets, most of the items given in exchange by the French were tools and weapons intended to facilitate trapping, and they did so at the expense of subsistence hunting. . . .

The introduction of and growing dependence on European goods obtainable primarily with furs not only reoriented male hunting patterns; it altered or removed many female productive activities. . . . Items whose manufacture had previously constituted some of women's most important productive activities were being replaced with European merchandise. Whereas women had been responsible for processing skins and transforming them into garments, hunters now exchanged furs for clothing. "Now that they trade with the French for capes, blankets, cloths, and shirts," Le Jeune reported, "there are many who use them." Although natives did not, of course, immediately buy all of their clothing from the French, ready-made goods may have seemed a convenient substitute for time-consuming manufacture of native dress. They also made it possible for women to spend more time instead readying furs for market. As a result, the significance of women's direct contribution to the community welfare diminished as their relationship to the disposal of furs changed.

The orientation of many female tasks began to shift from the creation of a useful end product, such as clothing or tools, to assistance in the preparation of furs. Awls and bodkins which might have been used for sewing coats or breechclouts instead enabled a woman to stretch more furs and stretch them faster. Women were undeniably vital to the production of the furs which Europeans sought so eagerly —

their scraping, stretching, and tanning of skins was essential to the process. They did not participate as producers in their own right, however, but were becoming auxiliaries to the trapping process. . . .

Increased dependence on European foodstuffs was another factor which influenced native women's activities. Their food procuring — fishing, hunting small game, and gathering — was crucial to the aboriginal economy. After the introduction of European food items women continued to gather nuts and berries when available, and to fish, but the importance of these subsistence foods decreased as French food became more accessible. When Le Jeune listed the foods which had been a routine part of the diet of the Montagnais band he wintered with in 1633–34, he included in his notes that "they get from our French People galette, or sea biscuit, bread, prunes, peas, roots, figs, and the like." Women's direct contribution to communal and family well-being diminished as dried peas, bread, and biscuits became common fare acquired by the trapper in exchange for his furs. . . .

The economic and technological developments which created this imbalance were obscured by the immediate benefits of the tools or trade goods which accompanied them. Furthermore, the gradual nature of these changes made it improbable that Indians would respond directly to them. Missionary activities, however, were a part of these developments which were not disguised by more momentous external events. Because the priests' efforts obviously were aimed at changing established beliefs and social organization they were a dimension of the transformations that was clearly visible to the Indians. In particular, the Jesuits' attempts to form Christian communities provided a focal point for the reactions of native men and women to the changes affecting them.

Christianity and European culture appear to have attracted men, especially those involved in the fur trade, for practical and spiritual reasons. The fact that men initially were the target of the priests and traders' solicitations undoubtedly contributed to their greater receptivity. Familiarity alone may eventually have made the new religion acceptable to many. More significantly, conversion placed the individual in the good graces of the clergy and the French colonial government. Christians had a decided advantage in terms of access to French goods and protection. When conversion was complemented by settlement in a mission village, a "Neophyte's" base of trapping operations was then located strategically near the source of trade. Proximity to the missionaries was a further asset in that it was they who legitimized the men's newly elevated position within domiciled groups. The priests expected men, as members of a European-patterned community, to exercise authority over women, the family, and political affairs, such as they were. Sedentary life made the imposition of this new pattern possible by breaking groups into nuclear families which functioned independently of one another. . . .

It is provocative that Christianity apparently appealed to men who no longer identified themselves primarily as hunters. In precontact culture the hunt had been more than a routine productive activity — it was virtually a religious vocation and not easily abandoned, one would suspect, for the more prosaic labor of trapping for exchange. Economic and status motivation alone cannot account for the shift from pagan hunter to Christian trapper. Hunting had provided the very foundation of a man's social and religious identity. It seems likely that a spiritual crisis may have been the culminating factor in a man's decision to convert. Indeed, throughout their

Relations the Jesuits noted that men complained that the old religion was not working for them; they had lost touch with the supernaturals and animal guardians upon which they depended. . . . Alienated from their traditional source of self-definition by forces which they could not rationalize, men appear to have found in Christianity a reasonable substitute.

Women, however, were reluctant to accept either the new religion or its followers. They apparently perceived little advantage in Christianity and found instead that it imposed unfamiliar and unwelcome limitations on them. The reciprocity and interdependence previously governing the relationships between men and women were missing from the patriarchal order of the *reserves.* Missionaries worked to establish a hierarchy which rested upon stratified gender roles and status — a reflection of their own class-bound understanding of French social order. Priests and colonial officials deliberately and persistently stressed the importance of male authority in the community and family, and women's obligation to obedience. The settled life and nuclear family pattern advocated by the Jesuits as the means to civilizing the Indians undoubtedly encouraged the breakdown of the flexible, multifamily units which were apparently based on matrilocal principles. This further weakened women's position in the community. When male converts accepted this system and acted accordingly, women stood to lose status and self-determination.

Another important influence on women's reception of Christianity seems to have been that their personal spiritual development did not depend on individual rapport with supernaturals. While they too must have been disturbed by the failure of the shamans' power, women themselves were not susceptible to the disruption of relationships with "helpers" as men were. Their source of spiritual strength was internal, less vulnerable. It is my contention that they did not need the replacement offered by Christianity. Moreover, while Christianity attracted men with its emphasis on individualism, it may have alienated women for the same reason. Women's orientation in precontact culture necessarily had been more communal than that of men. Many of their activities were performed in groups and they collectively controlled the camp area. They formed a ritual community as well which the imposition of Christian practices and beliefs apparently threatened. One can speculate that in their efforts to establish Christian nuclear families the Jesuits were not unaware that by isolating women from one another and decreasing their cooperative and ritual activities they might undermine female opposition to conversion. . . .

Women's resistance to Christianity — and all that faith represented — in seventeenth-century New France can be seen as a rational strategy designed to preserve a way of life which maximized female autonomy and authority. In the face of changes which threatened to deprive them of social, economic, and ritual significance women stressed customs which reinforced older beliefs dependent on reciprocity between the sexes. Their success in this effort cannot be measured by their often marginal positions in the colonized communities which developed around missions and trading posts. It must be considered internally, in the context of the very survival of Indian societies. It seems likely that women's adherence to "traditional" ways strengthened in the course of their confrontation with missionaries and converts. In effect, their efforts to protect their interests as women may have created a vehicle which ensured the persistence of native culture and ideology through women's identity.

The Attractions of Christianity for the Native Women of Martha's Vineyard

JAMES P. RONDA

. . . Studies of New England missions have emphasized either the culturally destructive effects of conversion or native resistance to the gospel. While many Puritan missionaries demanded what amounted to cultural suicide from their converts, we must not overlook the possibility of genuine conversion on the part of Indians searching for spiritual meaning in an increasingly hostile world. So long as the mission did not demand immediate and radical cultural change, there was a fair chance that Indians would accept substantial portions of the Christian message. The vital, self-sufficient Christian Indian communities and churches of Martha's Vineyard testify to the actuality of becoming a faithful Christian while remaining no less an Indian.

In numbers of Indians and English, and in relations between the peoples, Martha's Vineyard was substantially different from the mainland. When Thomas Mayhew, Jr., began missionary work among Indian islanders in the 1640s, the Wampanoag population was at least fifteen hundred and may have been as high as three thousand. At the same time, the English numbered about sixty-five, all living at the east end of the island. Although reduced by disease, natives clearly outnumbered English folk throughout the seventeenth century. On the eve of King Philip's War there were only one hundred eighty English settlers while the Wampanoag population was well over one thousand. Fragmentary census records show that whites did not become the majority on the island until the 1720s. On the mainland, the mission was part of a wider attack on Indian land and leadership mounted by a large and well-armed English population, but Thomas Mayhew's preaching had no such resources or ambitions. His efforts had little success until 1645, when an epidemic swept the island and the failure of the powwows to cure the sick touched off a rapid series of conversions. Most important, the mission did not insist upon sudden cultural change. Mayhew and the very small English population could not compel Indians to follow John Eliot's demand that natives must "have visible civility before they can rightly enjoy visible sanctities in ecclesiastical communion." No codes required Vineyard Indians to cut their hair, wear English clothing, give up customary mourning ceremonies, or attend church meetings. It was in this more permissive environment, as Indian congregations and praying towns rose and flourished, that political power and cultural leadership remained in Wampanoag hands. Study of the Martha's Vineyard faithful reveals Christianity Indianized as well as Indians Christianized. William Simmons has aptly characterized Indian Christianity on the island as "the most profound social conversion to occur anywhere in New England."

Only on Martha's Vineyard can the process by which Indian converts transformed Christianity to suit native cultural needs be traced through four generations.

James P. Ronda, "Generations of Faith: The Christian Indians of Martha's Vineyard," *William and Mary Quarterly,* 3d ser, vol. 38 (1981), pp. 369–72, 379–80, 383–88, 390–91, 394. Reprinted by permission of William and Mary Quarterly and the author.

That tracing is possible because a substantial body of biographies of Martha's Vineyard converts exists for the period 1642–1722. This evidence is unlike any other compendium of convert stories in mission literature. The narratives in the *Jesuit Relations,* the confessions of faith in the Eliot tracts, and the testimonies of converts in the Moravian records all suffer from stereotyped language and missionary ghostwriting. Though some of those narratives contain such vivid phrases as "I am as a dead man in my soul, and desire to live," and "God broke my head," they only rarely and dimly exhibit Indians as active shapers of their own lives and thoughts. Only for Martha's Vineyard do we have multi-generational records that allow us to view the dynamics of conversion and community over a long period.

These records are contained in Experience Mayhew's *Indian Converts,* the product of a lifetime of direct contact with Martha's Vineyard Indian Christians. Grandson of Thomas Mayhew, Jr., Experience was born on the island in 1673, spoke Wampanoag, and knew most of the people whose stories he wrote. In the early 1720s he began to collect material for capsule biographies of Christian Indians. *Indian Converts* is a kind of oral history assembled by an informed observer with a sharp eye for detail and a keen ear for arresting tales. Mayhew composed 126 biographies, touching 208 Indians in at least sixteen family lineages. Although primarily concerned with the lives of the godly and the good, he did not fail to note their frailties. . . .

Conversion on Martha's Vineyard most often followed family lines. *Indian Converts* shows that as early as the 1650s Christian Indian families were perpetuating the faith within their lineages. Mayhew took pains to trace the gospel pedigree in many such families. . . .

On Martha's Vineyard, Christian Indian families faithfully propagated the gospel from generation to generation. Those Indians, like their Puritan counterparts, maintained that Christian family life was essential to prepare the heart for an infusion of grace. But the converts on the island were more than clusters of praying Indian families. They were members of genuine communities and churches with Wampanoag clerical and lay leadership. The presence of that native leadership over a long period illustrates the strength of Christian Indian culture, a culture secure and confident enough to sustain its own corporate life without depending on English sources. Cotton Mather and other preachers made occasional forays to the island, but the day-to-day spiritual lives of Indian Christians were fully in the hands of native pastors, ruling elders, home-devotion leaders, discoursers, catechists, and musicians. . . .

While Indian laymen filled the English offices of ruling elder and deacon, the special needs of converts for regular religious instruction required a new lay post, that of discourser. Discoursers were lay preachers who served in family worship and also filled pulpits when regular preachers were unavailable. Two of the most prominent were Noquittompany, discourser at Christiantown and father of the preacher Isaac Ompany, and Abiah Paaonit, wife of Chilmark pastor Elisha Paaonit. . . . Abiah Paaonit was an especially effective discourser among Indian women. Women concerned about faith and practice often visited her, and she would "lay her work aside that she might sit and discourse with them." Assuring his readers that these were not occasions for idle gossip, Mayhew insisted that Paaonit's talks "were not vain and frothy, but such as were good for the use of edifying, and might administer grace to the hearers." . . .

While men served as ruling elders and deacons, the lay tradition also provided important roles for women. Abiah Paaonit was by no means unique as an active lay leader. Margaret Osooit of Gay Head, for example, often met with Indian women troubled by personal wrong-doing or family difficulty, and "she would not willingly leave them till she brought them to a confession of their faults, sometimes with tears, and to engage to endeavor to reform what was amiss in them." Momchquannum of Edgartown was one of many literate converts who regularly catechized young Indians. She sought out boys and girls and "frequently admonished [them] for their faults, and excited [them] to their duty."

The activities of Sarah Cowkeeper are worthy of special note because this woman made a substantial contribution to the life of the Indian Christian community. She was a long-time member of the Edgartown Indian church and was known for her industry and piety. Because she lived on a main road into Edgartown, travellers often spent the night in her home. Taking her Christianity seriously, Cowkeeper regularly visited and fed the sick, though she herself was poor. The rituals of charity were very much a part of her faith, despite the fact that she had to clothe and feed her own large family. In addition, Mayhew made special mention of "the care she took of poor fatherless and motherless children; when she heard of any such under suffering circumstances, she used to fetch them to her own house, and . . . keep them till they could in some other way he provided for." When her family complained, she replied that God would provide food and care for all. Sarah Cowkeeper's Christian commitment gave added dimension to her Indian name, Assannooshque, "woman that is a giver of victuals."

Assannooshque and her spiritual sisters were part of a sizable group of Indian Christian women on Martha's Vineyard. Indeed, so many Wampanoag women were active Christians that Experience Mayhew found "a greater number of women appearing pious than of the men among them." In *Indian Converts* he offered the biographies of thirty-seven "good women," most of whom were second- or third-generation Christians. Mayhew was able to glean information about the ages at conversion of thirty-three women, finding that fourteen waited until they were adults to join churches, while nineteen had a childhood conversion experience of some kind. Mayhew reported that seventeen of the thirty-seven women were literate. Most important for the future of the Christian Indian communities, twenty-four of these "good women" were instrumental in converting their children. Though Mayhew was either unwilling or unable to suggest reasons why so many Indian women were attracted to the gospel, that attraction appears to have had four main sources.

The Christianity preached by Thomas Mayhew, Jr., and his Indian successors tended to elevate and honor the roles and tasks of Indian women. The wife-mother-housekeeper functions were given special value in a public way unknown in pre-contact Wampanoag life. Experience Mayhew's glowing description of Hepzibah Assaquanhut expresses an ideal that emphasized the self-worth and importance of women in families. Assaquanhut "was a good wife. . . , being a discreet and chaste keeper at home, and one that loved her husband and children, being also very obedient to him; and was one that labored diligently with her hands, to provide necessaries for the family." This description of the ideal Christian Indian woman is more complex than it appears. The gospel, as preached to and by Indian women, held that what women did in their lives was an act of virtue and worship as well as duty. Thus Abigail Ahhunnut, who outlived three husbands, found favor with the body of Indian believers because "she was such a wife to them all, as whoso finds, finds a good thing, and obtains favor of the Lord." Like Ahhunnut, Mary Coshomon's patient relationship with her husband won esteem among Indian Christians. "She was remarkable," reported Mayhew, "for her dutiful carriage towards her husband, even showing him great reverence and respect; and when he was guilty of any miscarriage, she would bring no railing accusations against him, but would in a very submissive manner advise and entreat him."

An Indian Christian woman's faithful performance of household tasks was also noted and praised. Industry in the wigwam became not simply a domestic duty but a service to God. Clean and orderly homes were pointed to as marks of a godly and sober woman. Mayhew's catalogue of the interior of Sarah Hannit's wigwam has more than passing ethnographic interest. "The fair and large *wigwam* wherein she with her husband lived, was a great part of it her own work; the mats, or platted straw, flags and rushes with which it was covered, being wrought by her own hands; and those of them that appeared within side the house, were neatly embroidered with the inner barks of walnut trees artificially softened, and dyed several colors for that end."

If Christianity had attracted Indian women by valuing their traditional roles, it had even stronger appeal for women with special abilities. Articulate and literate women like Abiah Paaonit and Margaret Osooit found the Indian church and community a supportive arena for their ready minds and quick wits. When male powwows were discredited during the epidemics of the 1640s, the way was opened for Christian women healers. Most prominent of these was Hannah Nohnosoo, an herb doctor with a large practice among both Indian and English islanders. Like her powwow predecessors, Nohnosoo believed that the efficacy of her medicine depended on a proper relationship with supernatural forces. When asked if she could cure a certain disease, she replied, "I do not know but I may, if it please God to bless means for that end." Her patients included both Wampanoag and English women who were "divers years after marriage without the blessing of children, having barren wombs and dry breasts, which persons in a married state are scarce ever pleased with." Mayhew claimed that after Hannah Nohnosoo's ministrations, these women became "joyful mothers of children, for which comfort, under God, they have been obliged to her."

Nohnosoo's Chilmark neighbor Hannah Ahhunnut also possessed abilities that combined Christian faith and medical skill. Ahhunnut regularly visited the sick, bringing them food and herbal medications. Like Hannah Nohnosoo, she believed that prayer was an essential to healing; her sickroom visits combined applications medicinal and spiritual. One of Hannah Ahhunnut's most valued skills was her experience as a midwife. She was sent for whenever a birth was expected to be especially dangerous. By methods as much religious as medical, she brought Christian comfort and encouragement while aiding in the delivery.

From the time of Thomas Mayhew, Jr., Christianity on the island was closely linked to formal schooling for converts. Educational opportunities extended to Indian women proved a powerful incentive for both conversion and continued Christian affiliation. The Indian churches promoted literacy among women and gave educated women a place to use their learning. Of the thirty-seven women in *Indian Converts,* seventeen were literate. Indian women clearly prized learning. Rebecca Sissetom, who was taught to read as a child, "appeared to delight in her book." Sarah Hannit struggled to read her favorite book, an Algonkian translation of William Perkins's *Six Principles of Religion.* Women who knew how to read wanted to pass on the skill to their children. Abigail Kesoehaut "loved to read in good books and after she was married, and had some children, (not being nigh any school) she did herself teach them to read, and did otherwise carefully instruct them." Few could match the zeal for learning displayed by Jerusha Ompan. An unmarried daughter in a large family, she labored under a heavy burden of household duties. Denied time to read during the day, "she would not ordinarily fail of reading in the night, and for that end always used to be provided with something to make a light withal."

Christianity attracted Indian women by honoring their traditional tasks, rewarding their special abilities, and offering them educational opportunities. Indian churches also provided certain women with special support and solace in the face of a steadily worsening social problem. By the 1680s, alcoholism and the violence bred of excessive drinking had become epidemic among island Indian males. Native preachers lashed out at the abuse of alcohol, describing alcoholics as members of "the drinking tribe." Mayhew called heavy drinking "the National Sin of our Indians." Alcoholism was a serious problem even among Christian Indian men. Some eleven of the thirty-seven males in Mayhew's section on "good men" either had had or were continuing to have difficulties with alcohol. Immoderate drinking caused tension and violence within many Indian families.

The experiences of two women, Hannah Tiler and Hannah Sissetom, suggest ways by which Indian Christianity prepared women to deal with alcoholic and often abusive husbands. Hannah Tiler of Edgartown was the child of Christian parents. But in her case such nurture did not produce the desired results; Experience Mayhew found that young Hannah "was as bad by nature as any other." Her marriage to a vicious drunkard further threatened her wavering faith. According to Mayhew, her husband "would frequently have his drunken fits, and was often very contentious in them." Husband and wife became caught in a ceaseless round of drinking sprees and fierce arguments. Finally convinced that the cycle had to be broken, Hannah Tiler turned to Christian friends in the Edgartown Indian congregation for support and advice. At first she sharply criticized her husband for his drinking but soon discovered that "this was an occasion of sore contentions betwixt them." Counselled by fellow Christians to use gentler means, she tried "mild entreaties and a good carriage." Although this approach proved equally ineffective, "she found peace in it, and God helped her, in this way of well-doing, to cast all her care on him."

Experience Mayhew recorded the tempestuous marriage of Hannah and Haukkings Sissetom with an almost clinical fascination. Hannah was raised by an English family on the island; Haukkings was part of the Christian Sissetom lineage. The placid first years of their marriage were marked by regular family worship and steady attendance at the Edgartown Indian church. However, Haukkings developed "such an excessive lust after strong drink that he was frequently overcome by it," spent his wages on hot liquors, and thus reduced his family to poverty. Confronted with his failings by both his wife and members of the congregation, "he sometimes appeared to be under great convictions" and seemed prepared to reform. But these resolutions were short-lived; "the temptation prevailed too much against him, and sometimes overcame him." Urged by her English neighbors to employ stiff words and strong measures, Hannah replied that she had tried but found that such efforts only angered her husband. With children to feed and instruct, she turned to the Indian church and the Christian Sissetoms. The solution suggested by the Sissetom family and approved by the church was to have Haukkings's mother live with the family. Mayhew reported that the older Sissetom woman was "very kind and obliging" to Hannah, "endeavoring to comfort her under all her trials." . . .

An essential part of the Christian gospel for Indian islanders was a new identity, one that did not deny all aspects of native culture but offered membership in God's tribe. Worship in Indian churches and life among believing neighbors powerfully strengthened the sense of Christian commitment and solidarity. . . . What emerged from preaching, worship, and corporate rituals was an image of the ideal Christian Indian. Shaped as much by Indian cultural needs as by English Puritan requirements, the ideal called for charity, prudence, industry, temperance, family worship, and attendance at public meeting, as well as belief in the gospel message. This Christian identity did not represent a radical break with the traditional past. Communal ceremonies for healing and charity were rooted in Wampanoag culture. Being part of God's tribe at once preserved and extended those ancient values, while giving them a fresh rationale.

The rise of Christian family lineages gave an added dimension to conversion and new identity. Some Indians in Eliot's mainland mission rejected Christianity because they did not want to renounce family and kinship ties. Such renunciations were not necessary on Martha's Vineyard. An Indian child or adult could convert or profess the faith within a supportive Christian family. The presence of many Christian lines offered Indian believers emotional shelter and a sense of belonging. Because identity had always been linked to kinship, it was possible to know who one was as a Christian Indian without stepping outside family relationships. . . .

Lawrence W. Levine has written that "culture is not a fixed condition but a process: the product of interaction between the past and the present. Its toughness and resiliency are determined not by a culture's ability to withstand change, which indeed may be a sign of stagnation not life, but its ability to react creatively and responsively to the realities of a new situation." The Indian Christians of Martha's Vineyard demonstrated just that sort of toughness and resiliency. Many Indian islanders used Christianity to revitalize their lives in a world growing more and more unfriendly. That one could be a Christian and still live in a wigwam and bear a traditional name was not doubted by the Martha's Vineyard faithful. One of those faithful was Old Katherine, a basket maker at Edgartown. She exemplifies that blending of Indian tradition and Christian commitment. Old Katherine was devoted to public worship services, which "she attended with very great constancy and seriousness." She was equally devoted to charity. Whenever she heard that a neighbor needed extra money for food, she would spend long hours making additional baskets for sale to English villagers. Even when she grew old and "was but meanly clothed," she continued to travel long distances for sabbath observances. In the coldest storms of winter she made her way to meeting with a dedication that astounded her friends. Old Katherine, like many other Martha's Vineyard Indian Christians, found that the rituals of her faith gave shape and meaning to her life. She remains a witness to the vitality of a culture that was simultaneously Christian and Indian.

The Adultery Trial of Sarah Ahhaton

ANN MARIE PLANE

One day in October of 1668, an Indian woman named Sarah Ahhaton sat before an Englishman and, through an interpreter, told the story of how she came to be unfaithful to her husband. Her account details the whole affair — from the suspicions and beatings which weakened her love for her husband, to the attentions of Joseph, a married man in her town. Sarah Ahhaton's odyssey led her away from her home in the small "praying town" of Punkapoag, or Packemit, the present-day Canton, Massachusetts. She left behind her husband, William Ahhaton, the son of a local leader, who served both as an interpreter and as the native Christian minister. Sarah Ahhaton fled to Mount Hope, the home of the Indian leader Metacom (King Philip), who would launch his anti-English rebellion, or King Philip's War, in just a few years. After an absence of several days, she found her way back, brought home by a seemingly troubled conscience, and threw herself on the mercy of God and men. While Sarah Ahhaton did not face the death penalty for her "crime," she did suffer imprisonment and punishment before being allowed to return to her husband. Certainly the surviving deposition describes the complexity of human sexual relationships, and Ahhaton's troubles touch themes not unfamiliar to modern readers. But Sarah Ahhaton's deposition transcends the level of individual history. As an official document, created through a process of questioning by an Englishman with the aid of an interpreter, Sarah Ahhaton's story is a social artifact. More than one woman's story, this text bears witness to changes within Indian communities, revealing the tensions of life in what one historian has termed "the Indians' New World."

By the year 1668, Massachusetts Indians certainly lived in a "New World." Involvement in the English economy had changed Indian social relations forever. Further, English missionizing attempted to control and shape the most intimate aspects of these Indians' lives. Whatever "marriage" might have meant for the precontact Massachusett, the English defined it as a life-long commitment. In the new colonial world, Sarah Ahhaton's actions constituted the crime of adultery, the penalty for which could be death. Her deposition reveals remnants of indigenous ways of forming intimate relationships. At the same time, the very creation of this text exposes significant changes in the gender relations of colonial-era native society. By looking

---

Ann Marie Plane, "'The Examination of Sarah Ahhaton: The Politics of Adultery in an Indian Town of Seventeenth-Century Massachusetts," in Peter Benes, ed., *Algonkians of New England Past and Present*, Boston University Press, 1993, pp. 1–12.

closely at Sarah Ahhaton's story, we can explore the meaning of native marriage as it was constructed over time and by a society under stress. Further, in this new world, even marital problems became part of a symbolic struggle between Indians' accommodation or resistance to colonial authority. "Personal" and "political" realms interconnected, calling into question many of our revered notions of separate private and public spheres. The study of Sarah Ahhaton's odyssey reveals the complex ways in which the "personal" experiences of Massachusett men and women can illuminate the more "political" story of their domination by the English.

Sarah Ahhaton had been married for about ten years before she saw any sign of trouble. She and William had four children, all of whom were still alive in 1668. Their small Indian town, Punkapoag, was described in 1674 as having not more than "twelve families," or about "sixty souls." But beginning two years earlier, there had been "some differences and jealousies between them. . . . " Sarah explained that she had been approached by three of the older women in the town. These three, the mother and the aunt of Joseph "(an indian whom since shee comited folly with-all)" and the wife of the one called Wachennakin, told her "that her husband did love and keepe company with other women. . . . " She did not believe their rumours, "but loved her husband still." All would have remained well, we must suppose, except that her husband began to grow jealous of her. In February of 1667/8 he "chardged her that shee loved other men & kept them company. . . . " Although she pleaded that she was innocent, he "did beat her severall times, as som other indians of the place do know. . . . " His suspicions "without cause . . . did weaken and alienate her former affections to him: from this occasion did spring her sinne and misery."

At planting time, "Shee was brought before Waban the Ruler . . . who told her that hee was informed that shee did somtimes speak alone with Joseph a married man of packemit and that her husband william Ahhaton was offended thereat. . . . " Waban ordered her to avoid being alone with Joseph. But in a few weeks, "about weeding time," she was at the Indian court "at the house of squamock the ruler," along with her husband. "Joseph called her out of the house privatly" and told her that "his unkel william" had told him that she was to be whipped for having disobeyed Waban's earlier orders. Joseph "advised her to hide her selfe in som secret place. . . . " That night she "was by his advise & appointment directed to goe to his mothers wigwam. . . . " There Joseph's mother hid her "in a corner of her wigwam in the night time & in the day time guided her to a swampe neare the wigwam where shee hid herself. . . . " The older woman provided Sarah with food and helped her in this way for three days. Once during this time, Joseph came to the swamp to see her, accompanied by his mother.

After three days of concealment in the swamp, Sarah Ahhaton took action to resolve her crisis. She left her hiding place, "alone and traveld to wamesitt [another Christian Indian town, to the north of Punkapoag] neer Pawtuckett, wher her father and mother lived." She told her parents of her plight, and "when they understood her tale," they, "with some other friends came downe wth her to packemit, & by their endeavor a reconsiliation was made between her & her husband; then shee continued wth her husband about seaven or 8 weekes untill about hilling time." But such peace was not to last. When her husband was away from home, "at the sea-side," the fateful sin occurred: "Joseph came to her wigwam & by his intisements obtained her consent & lay wth her once thn." After this transgression, Sarah said that Joseph "& his mother . . . advised her to withdraw herselfe & go to Phillips wigwam Sachem of mount hope neare Secunck where shee should bee entertained. . . . " She listened to their "evel councel . . . & so went away to the place aforsaid where shee was entertained & two or 3 daies after shee was there Joseph came to her & there kept her company & lay wth her several times. . . . "

Unfortunately, we cannot know why Sarah Ahhaton returned to face her punishment. Her deposition never mentions what happened to her children during this crisis. It seems unlikely that she hid them with her; more probably they remained behind at Punkapoag in the care of kinsmen or friends, perhaps encouraging her return. But she explains her return as due to her troubled heart: "It pleased God to smite her hurt wth the sense of her sinne, & shee could not bee at quiet in her mind, untill shee resolved to come away from the said Joseph . . . and to returne home. . . . " She was passed from Packemit to the judgment of Waban at Natick. The Indian ruler sent her on to the Indians' overseer, Captain Gookin, who committed her to prison. After giving her deposition on 24 October, she was tried before the General Court on 27 October. She was found guilty and ordered to stand on the gallows in Boston with a noose around her neck for one hour on the twenty-ninth, a Sunday, after the morning church services, so that godly Bostonians would see her punishment. To send a deterrent message to her Indian neighbors, she was to be "severly" whipped on a public day in Natick by the Indian constable on the orders of Captain Gookin. This part of the punishment, however, was to be deferred until after the delivery of her child. The sentence, which seems severe, perhaps was due to her race and the need to deter other potential offenders. . . .

[Her] account suggests native strategies for restoring marital harmony. Before any adultery had been committed, she took refuge at her parents' house. With some friends her mother and father accompanied her back to Packemit and managed to negotiate a reconciliation between their daughter and her husband William. Who were the "friends" who also participated in this renewal of the marriage contract? The text unfortunately gives no clue, but probably they were high-status community members, whose presence at the negotiations would remind both William and Sarah Ahhaton of their responsibilities to each other and to their families. . . .

It is not clear why these measures were not enough for Sarah Ahhaton, but perhaps the answer lies in the political dynamics of her situation. What business was William Ahhaton attending to at the seaside when the adultery occurred? Perhaps he was on some regular part of the subsistence rounds. But because of his frequent role as interpreter and as a petitioner representing the Punkapoag community to the English, Ahhaton may have been on some business or trade related to the English settlements. Further, after the "adultery," Sarah Ahhaton did not run to her family; rather she chose to protect herself — and for protection she ran to the heart of the Indian resistance, away from her acculturated husband and the community of converts. . . .

That she ran to this place under the advice not only of Joseph, but also of his mother, adds a "political" dimension to the older women's involvement. Sarah's account suggests that the three women may have been stirring up discord between Sarah and William. Her troubles began, in her view, when the older women approached her with news of William's infidelities. Throughout the crisis Joseph's mother reappears again and again, taking an active part in the intrigues. Perhaps Joseph's mother's role can be explained simply as part of the normal mechanisms of community life. But Sarah Ahhaton may have been a target of attention by individuals opposing her husband and the English. The symbolism of a minister's wife turning her back on her husband, the English, and the Christian faith may have been important to the traditionalists who surrounded Metacom on the Rhode Island border. The older women in the community may have been aiding the anti-English cause by turning older social roles to new political purposes.

However, it would be a distortion to suggest too deep a split between converts and traditionalists. Christian conversion and English domination did not always subvert local systems of authority; in fact the opposite often occurred. The governments of the "praying towns" retained important continuities to the precontact native world. Native sachems and their relations often continued traditional roles within new offices as ministers and justices of the peace. In Punkapoag, William Ahhaton himself appears to have been part of this leadership, . . . described as a member of the "Council or Wisemen" to the sachem. . . .

If Metacom's allies saw symbolic value in this story, presumably English magistrates did as well. A woman, sexually "deviant," opposed her husband. She ran to the anti-English forces, out of the domain of English control and away from the converted Indians who were directly subject to colonial authority. She committed a great sin in opposition to "civilized" English laws. But all of these threatening oppositions were resolved happily in the end of the tale in which "it pleased God to smite her hurt with the sense of her sinne," leading her to abandon her wicked ways and cast herself before the English magistrates and her husband, repentant and ready to submit herself to the authority of both the magistrates and her husband, no matter how unjustly that authority might manifest itself. Sarah Ahhaton's lover apparently escaped any judgment of his actions. Presumably he melted away into the pagan Indian community of Mount Hope, beyond the reach of Massachusetts colonial authorities. . . .

As the symbolism of this English court document reveals, the tensions of the Indians' new world included a gendered dimension in the conflicts between traditionalist and assimilationist elements. This gendered conflict is inextricably linked to the political conflict of resistance or accommodation and potentially functioned on several levels — in the subconscious fears of English authorities and in new struggles between Indians old and young, male and female, over the definition of gender relations. The dynamic of Sarah Ahhaton's story pits the English-aligned, male authority of William Ahhaton, Waban, and Squamock against the female, subversive traditionalism of Joseph's mother, his aunt, and Wachennakin's wife. Sarah moves back and forth between these two worlds. Her movements are revealing of the changes in women's status in the Indians' "New World."

While scholars have recently stressed the syncretic nature of native Christianity, it must not be forgotten that conversion and the concurrent socio-economic domination brought many changes in terms of both gender relations and other facets of daily life. Through the new demands of an apparently genuine Christian conscience, Sarah Ahhaton accepted the definition of her unfaithfulness as a capital crime and accepted an individual responsibility for her actions. She acknowledged "that if the Governor and magistrates will spare her life," she would "love her husband & continue faithfull to him during her life yea although hee should beat her againe and suspect her of falsneses to him without cause, yet shee doth acknowledge it to bee her duty to suffer it & to pray for her husband & to love him still." Some recent scholarship on Indian conversion has stressed that the traditional roles of native women were valued more highly by converts than by traditionalists. James Ronda espouses this view. . . .

But Sarah Ahhaton's tale shows the double-edged nature of Anglo-Christian teachings. Even as missionaries were preaching against practices they saw as cruel abuses of women, they were subverting native mechanisms for restraining truly abusive behavior and eliminating women's abilities to change marital partners. Sarah Ahhaton's husband, after all, was one of the most acculturated, Christianized figures in the village; and yet, contrary to Christian teaching, he engaged in wife-beating and possible extramarital sexual relations. He even brought his own wife into court in an attempt to restrain her rebellious behavior. Apparently, Indian women had been used to much greater autonomy than their English counterparts. And yet English domination restricted this autonomy. Sometimes husbands exercised their newfound patriarchal authority to commit the worst abuses of English marriage rather than its better aspects preached by the missionaries.

To a modern eye the ending is the most puzzling portion of Sarah Ahhaton's story. Why did she return? This essay has suggested as reasons the curious absence of her children from the narrative and the possibility of her loneliness once removed from the village in which she had spent her last twelve years. Yet these are mere speculations. The best course, then, is to take Sarah Ahhaton's story at its face value and look deeply into the "shame, greife and Sorrow of hart" which drew her back to Packemit and to the judgment of her husband and the Indian and English authorities. She confessed that "shee well knew & considered before shee returned her danger & that shee had broken the law of God & man & deserved Death: but yet shee resolved to returne againe and to cast her selfe at the feet of the Governor & magistrates desiring mercy. . . . " She was drawn back because "shee could not bee at quiet in her mind. . . . " Her motives must have been powerful; like any good Puritan woman, she realized that her sin came from "the abundant evell that is in her hart. . . . " As no other explanations were offered, Sarah Ahhaton must be taken at her word. Surely her heart was troubled. She found herself confused, away from friends and familiar surroundings, and unable to reject her husband of twelve years and the Christian teachings of at least that length of time.

In the end, Ahhaton could not go through with her "divorce" because it would be un-Christian. In a question put to Sarah regarding the current state of her marriage, she answered that "her husband hath manefested himself to her as willing againe to receve [?] her if the Court please to pardon her." Indeed, William Ahhaton had already come to her and "layne wth her . . . once in the prison about a month since. . . . " And, as noted in the first lines of her deposition, she remained pregnant with his child, "about six months gonne." This Indian couple appeared ready to renew a marriage which had not been saved even by the intervention of Sarah's family and friends. Perhaps, during her sojourn at Mount Hope, Sarah Ahhaton realized the nature of her new world. There was more to the new social order than the subordination of native women by colonial authorities. Instead of this simple dichotomy, when we look closely at this episode of colonial history we see a complex web of individuals. Each player made his or her own accommodations to the new demands upon them, creating through their actions a new sort of gender relations and a new meaning for native "marriage." All of them — Sarah Ahhaton, her husband Joseph, and the older women — played out their personal relations in a newly politicized field. Sarah experienced the implications of her choices through a new religious belief. As much as her story reveals the distinctiveness of native communities, it also shows the ways in which native marriage was being remade in a new, English mold. The text which tells Sarah Ahhaton's story is a complex production of a particular social moment. Through her examination, we can see the complex intertwining of old and new ways of life and of the personal and political choices made by one Massachusett woman.

※ *F U R T H E R   R E A D I N G*

Karen Anderson, *Chain Her By One Foot: The Subjugation of Native Women in Seventeenth-Century New France* (1991)

James Axtell, ed., *The Indian Peoples of Eastern America: A Documentary History of the Sexes* (1981)

James Axtell, *The Invasion Within: The Contest of Cultures in Colonial North America* (1985)

Philip Barbour, *Pocahontas and Her World* (1970)

Henry Bowden, *American Indians and Christian Missions: Studies in Cultural Conflict* (1981)

Kathryn Holland Braund, "Guardians of Tradition and Handmaidens to Change: Women's Roles in Creek Economic and Social Life during the Eighteenth Century," *American Indian Quarterly,* XIV (1990), 239–253

Judith K. Brown, "Economic Organization and the Position of Women among the Iroquois," *Ethnohistory,* XVII (Winter-Spring 1970), 151–167

John Demos, *The Unredeemed Captive: A Family Story from Early America* (1994)

Carol Devens, *Countering Colonization: Native American Women and Great Lakes Missions, 1630–1900* (1992)

Robert Grumet, "Sunksquaws, Shamans, and Tradeswomen: Middle Atlantic Coastal Algonkian Women during the Seventeenth and Eighteenth Centuries," in Mona Étienne and Eleanor Leacock, eds., *Women and Colonization: Anthropological Perspectives* (1980), 43–62

Ramón Gutíerrez, *When Jesus Came, the Corn Mothers Went Away: Marriage, Sexuality, and Power in New Mexico, 1500–1846* (1991)

Joan Jensen, "Native American Women and Agriculture: A Seneca Case Study," *Sex Roles,* III (1977), 423–441

CHAPTER
3

Witchcraft
in Seventeenth-Century America

The Salem witchcraft crisis of 1692–1693, in which a small number of adolescent girls and young women accused hundreds of older women (and a few men) of having bewitched them, has long fascinated Americans, providing material for innumerable books, plays, movies, and television productions. To twentieth-century Americans, the belief in witchcraft that permeated the seventeenth-century colonies is difficult to explain or understand; perhaps that is why the Salem episode has attracted so much attention. For those interested in studying women's experiences, of course, witchcraft incidents are particularly intriguing. The vast majority of suspected witches were female, and so, too, were many of their accusers. Although colonial women rarely played a role on the public stage, in witchcraft cases they were the primary actors. What accounts for their prominence under these peculiar circumstances?

To answer that question, the Salem crisis must be placed into its proper historical and cultural context. People in the early modern world believed in witchcraft because it offered a rationale for events that otherwise seemed random and unfathomable. In the absence of modern scientific knowledge about such natural phenomena as storms and diseases and of clear explanations for accidents of various sorts, the evil actions of a witch could provide a ready answer to a person or community inquiring about the causes of a disaster.

Therefore, witchcraft accusations — and some large-scale "witch hunts" — were not uncommon in Europe between the early fourteenth and late seventeenth centuries (1300 to 1700). In short, the immigrants to the colonies came from a culture in which belief in witchcraft was widespread and in which accusations could result in formal prosecutions and executions. Recent research has demonstrated that the Salem incident, though the largest and most important witch hunt in New England, was just one of a number of such episodes in the American colonies.

But why were witches women? Admittedly, historians have not yet answered that question entirely satisfactorily. Certain observations can be made. Women gave birth to new life and seemed to have the potential to take life away. Western culture viewed women as less rational than men, more linked to the "natural" world, in which magic held sway. Men, who dominated European society, defined the characteristics of a "proper woman," as one who was submissive and accepted a

46

subordinate position; the stereotypical witch, usually described as an aggressive and threatening older woman, represented the antithesis of this image. These broad categories need further refinement, and historians are looking closely at the women who were accused of practicing witchcraft in order to identify the crucial characteristics that set them apart from their contemporaries and made them a target for accusations.

※ D O C U M E N T S

In 1654, in a little-known incident, an old woman traveling on a ship en route to Maryland was executed as a witch. She was killed because the sailors and some of the passengers believed that a storm that had afflicted them for weeks had been caused by a malevolent power. The first two documents here give three different accounts of that incident. The first is Father Francis Fitzherbert's account of the voyage, which mentions the incident but allows for the possibility that the old woman was not guilty. In the second selection, the testimonies of two witnesses betray confusion about how to take responsibility for the situation while on board the ship. At about the same time, Mistress Elizabeth Godman, a contentious woman who lived in the New Haven Colony, was likewise suspected of witchcraft. However, unlike the woman executed at sea, the legal system afforded her some protection against her accusers. The second group of documents are the records of a slander suit Mistress Godman filed against a number of persons in 1653, and the proceedings at her 1655 trial for witchcraft. These accounts reveal the personal characteristics and behaviors common to many of the women accused of practicing witchcraft in seventeenth-century New England.

The Execution of a Witch at Sea, 1654

Account of Father Francis Fitzherbert's Voyage to Maryland

Four ships sailed together from England, which a fearful storm overtook, when carried beyond the Western Isles, and the ship in which the Father was carried, the violent waves so shattered, that, springing a leak by the continued violence of the sea, it almost filled its hold. But in carrying away and exhausting the water, the men, four at a time, not only of the ship's crew but of the passengers, every one in his turn, sweated at the great pump in ceaseless labor, day and night.

Wherefore, having changed their course, their intention was to make sail towards the island, which the English call Barbados; but it could be accomplished by no art, by no labor; then the design was, having abandoned the ship and its freight, to commit themselves to the long boat. But the sea, swelling with adverse winds, and the huge mountainous waves, forbade. Many a form of death presenting itself to the minds of all, the habit of terror, now grown familiar, had almost excluded the fear of death. The tempest lasted two months in all, whence the opinion arose, that it was not raised by the violence of the sea or atmosphere, but was occasioned by the malevolence of witches. Forthwith they seize a little old woman suspected of sorcery; and after examining her with the strictest scrutiny, guilty or not guilty, they slay her, suspected of this very heinous sin. The corpse, and whatever belonged to her, they cast into the sea. But the winds did not thus remit their violence, or the raging sea its threatenings. To the troubles of the storm, sickness was added, which having spread to almost every person, carried off not a few. Nevertheless, the Father remained untouched by all the contagion, and unharmed, except that in working and exercising at the pump too laboriously, he contracted a slight fever of a few days' continuance. Having passed through multiplied dangers, at length, by the favor of God, the ship, contrary to the expectation of all, reached the port of Maryland.

The Testimonies of Two Witnesses

The Deposition of mr Henry Corbyn of London Merchant aged about 25 years, Sworne and Examined in the Province of Maryland before the Governour & Councell there (whose Names are hereunto Subscribed) the 23ᵗʰ day of June Anno Domini 1654. Saith

That at Sea upon his this Deponents Voyage hither in the Ship called the Charity of London mʳ John Bosworth being Master and about a fortnight or three weeks before the Said Ships arrivall in this Province of Maryland, or before A Rumour amongst the Seamen was very frequent, that one Mary Lee then aboard the Said Ship was a witch, the Said Seamen Confidently affirming the Same upon her own deportment and discourse, and then more Earnestly then before Importuned the Said Master that a tryall might be had of her which he the Said Master, mʳ Bosworth refused, but re-solved (as he Expressed to put her ashore upon the Barmudoes) but Cross winds prevented and the Ship grew daily more Leaky almost to desparation and the Chiefe Seamen often declared their Resolution of Leaving her if an opportunity offerred it Self which aforesaid Reasons put the Master upon a Consultation with mʳ Chip-sham and this Deponent, and it was thought fitt, Considering our Said Condition to Satisifie the Seamen in a way of trying her according to the Usuall Custome in that kind whether She were a witch or Not and Endeavoured by way of delay to have the Commanders of other Ships aboard but Stormy weather prevented, In the Interime two of the Seamen apprehended her without order and Searched her and found Some Signall or Marke of a witch upon her, and then calling the Master mʳ Chip-sham and this Deponent with others to See it afterwards made her fast to the Cap-stall betwixt decks, And in the Morning the Signall was Shrunk into her body for the Most part, And an Examination was thereupon importuned by the Seamen which this Deponent was desired to take whereupon She confessed as by her Con-fession appeareth, And upon that the Seamen Importuned the Said Master to put her to Death which it Seemed he was unwilling to doe, and went into his Cabbinn, but being more Vehemently pressed to it, he tould them they might doe what they would and went into his Cabbinn, and Sometime before they were about that Action he desired this deponᵗ to acquaint them that they Should doe no more then what they Should Justifie which they Said they would doe by laying all their hands in generall to the Execution of her, All which herein before Expressed or the Same in Effect this Deponᵗ averreth upon his oath to be true, And further Sayth not

William Stone　　　　　Sworne before us the　　　　　Henry Corbyne
Tho: Hatton　　　　　　day and year above written
Job Chandler

The Deposition of ffrancis Darby Gent Aged about 39 yeares Sworne and Examined in the Province of Maryland before the Governour and Councell there whose Names are hereunto Subscribed the 23 day of June Anno Domini 1654. Saith

That at Sea upon the Voyage hither about a fortnight or three weeks before the Arrivall of the Ship called the Charity of London in this Province of Maryland, whereof m^r John Bosworth was then Master and upon the Same day that one Mary Lee was put to Death aboard the Said Ship as a witch he the Said m^r Bosworth Seeing him this Deponent backward to Assist in the Examination of her asked this Depon^t why? and tould him that he was perplext about the busieness Seeing he did not know how he might doe it by the Law of England afterwards this deponent being present in the Round house heard the Said m^r Bosworth give Order that nothing Should be done concerning the Said Mary Lee without Speaking first with him, and after She was put to Death or Executed to the best of this Deponents remembrance he Said he knew nothing of it, And this Deponent Saith that the Said Bosworth was in the inner room of the Round house, he this deponent being in the next room at the time they treated about the busieness And this Depon^t could not perceive any thing either by word or Deed whereby he gave order for her Execution or putting to Death and after this he Commanded they Should doe Nothing without his Order and alsoe after the Execution, expressed he knew not of it for that this Deponent hearing these words (She is dead) ran out and asked who was dead, and it was replyed the witch then this Deponent Entred the next Room and Said they have hanged her and he the Said Bosworth thereupon as it were Speaking with trouble in a high Voyce replyed he knew not of it All which herein before Expressed or the Same in Effect this Deponent averreth upon his oath to be true, And further Sayth not.

Sworne before us the day and   Francis Darby
Yare abovewritten
    William Stone
    Tho: Hatton
    Job Chandler

The Trials of a Witch

Elizabeth Godman *v.* Goodwife Larremore, *et al., 1653*

The Examination of Elizabeth Godman, May 21th, 1653

Elizabeth Godman made complainte of M^r. Goodyeare, M^ris. Goodyeare, M^r. Hooke, M^ris. Hooke, M^ris. Bishop, M^ris. Atwater, Hanah & Elizabeth Lamberton, and Mary Miles, M^ris. Atwaters maide, that they have suspected her for a witch; she was now asked what she had against M^r. Hooke and M^ris. Hooke; she said she heard they had something against her aboute their soone. M^r. Hooke said hee was not w^thout feares, and hee had reasons for it; first he said it wrought suspition in his minde because shee was shut out at M^r. Atwaters upon suspition, and hee was troubled in his sleepe aboute witches when his boye, was sicke, wch was in a verey strang manner, and hee looked upon her as a mallitious one, and prepared to that

mischeife, and she would be often speaking aboute witches and rather justifye them
then condemne them; she said why doe they provoake them, why doe they not let
them come into the church. Another time she was speaking of witches w^thout any
occasion given her, and said if they accused her for a witch she would have them to
the governor, she would trounce them. . . .

M^r. Hooke further said, that he hath heard that they that are adicted that way
would hardly be kept away from ye houses where they doe mischeife, and so it was
wth her when his boy was sicke, she would not be kept away from him, nor gott
away when she was there, and one time M^ris. Hooke bid her goe away, and thrust
her from ye boye, but she turned againe and said she would looke on him. M^ris.
Goodyeare said that one time she questioned wth Elizabeth Godman aboute y^e
boyes sickness, and said what thinke you of him, is he not strangly handled, she replyed, what, doe you thinke hee is bewitched; M^ris. Goodyeare said nay I will keepe
my thoughts to myselfe, but in time God will discover. . . .

M^r. Hooke further said, that when M^r. Bishop was married, M^ris. Godman
came to his house much troubled, so as he thought it might be from some affection
to him, and he asked her, she said yes; now it is suspitious that so soone as they
were contracted M^ris. Byshop fell into verey strang fitts wch hath continewed at
times ever since, and much suspition there is that she hath bine the cause of the loss
of M^ris. Byshops children, for she could tell when M^ris. Bishop was to be brought to
bedd, and hath given out that she kills her children wth longing, because she longs
for every thing she sees, wch M^ris. Bishop denies. . . .

The 24th of May, 1653

M^ris. Godman being examined, (M^r. Davenport being present,) she was asked why
she said M^ris. Bishop longed allmost for every thing she see, and when she could
not have it, that was the cause of her fainting fitts and ye loss of her chilldren; she
said she heard something of M^ris. Hooke to that purpose, that she longed for pease,
but M^ris. Hooke being sent for denyed that ever she told her so, and Jane Hooke
being present said M^ris. Godman told her that M^ris. Bishop was much given to longing and that was the reason she lost her chilldren, and Hanah Lamberton said M^ris.
Godman told her so also, and M^ris. Bishop said another woman in ye towne told her
that she had heard M^ris. Godman say as much, so that she could not denye it; she
was told she hath much inquired after the time of M^ris. Bishops delivery of her
chilldren, and would speake of it so as M^ris. Goodyeare and her daughters marveled
how she could know, and Hanah Lamberton one time told her mother that M^ris.
Godman kept her sisters count; she was asked the reason of this and of her saying
M^ris. Bishop was so given to longing as it was a meanes to lose her chilldren when
it was not so; she said she could give no reason, then she was told it was a high slander upon M^ris. Bishop, she said she can say nothing but must lye under it. . . .

June 16, 1653

Goodwife Thorp complained that M^ris. Godman came to her house and asked to buy
some chickens, she said she had none to sell, M^ris. Godman said will you give them
all, so she went away, and she thought then that if this woman was naught as folkes

suspect, may be she will smite my chickens, and quickly after one chicken dyed, and she remembred she had heard if they were bewitched they would consume w^{t}hin, and she opened it and it was consumed in ye gisard to water & wormes, and divers others of them droped, and now they are missing and it is likely dead, and she never saw either hen or chicken that was so consumed w^{t}hin w^{t}h wormes. M^{ris}. Godman said goodwife Tichenor had a whole brood so, and M^{ris}. Hooke had some so, but for M^{ris}. Hookes it was contradicted presently. This goodwife Thorp thought good to declare that it may be considered w^{t}h other things.

Court of Magistrates, New Haven, August 4, 1653

M^{ris}. Elizabeth Godman accused goodwife Larremore that one time when she saw her come in at goodman Whitnels she said so soone as she saw her she thought of a witch. Goodwife Larremore said that one time she had spoken to that purpose at M^r. Hookes, and her ground was because M^r. Davenport aboute that time had occasion in his ministry to speake of witches, and showed that a froward discontented frame of spirit was a subject fitt for ye Devill to worke upon in that way, and she looked upon M^{rs}. Godman to be of such a frame of spirit, but for saying so at goodman Whitnels she denyes it. M^{ris}. Godman said, goodman Whitnels maid can testify it. The maid was sent, and when she came she said she heard M^{ris}. Godman and good-wife Larremore a talking, and she thinkes she heard goodwife Larremore say she thought of a witch in ye Bay when she see M^{ris}. Godman. Goodwife Larremore fur-ther said that M^{ris}. Godman had her before the governor for this, and the governor asked her if she thought M^{ris}. Godman was a witch, and she answered no.

M^{ris}. Godman was told she hath warned to the court divers psons, viz^d: M^r. Goodyeare, M^{ris}. Goodyeare, M^r. Hooke, M^{ris}. Hooke, M^{ris}. Atwater, Hanah & Elizabeth Lamberton, goodwife Larremore, goodwife Thorpe, &c., and was asked what she hath to charge them w^{t}h, she said they had given out speeches that made folkes thinke she was a witch, and first she charged M^{ris}. Atwater to be ye cause of all, and to cleere things desired a wrighting might be read w^{c}h was taken in way of examination before ye magistrate, (and is hereafter entred,) wherein sundrie things concerning M^{ris}. Atwater is specifyed w^{c}h were now more fully spoken to, and she further said that M^{ris}. Atwater had said that she thought she was a witch and that Hobbamocke [the devil] was her husband, but could prove nothing, though she was told that she was beforehand warned to prepare her witnesses ready, w^{c}h she hath not done, if she have any. After sundrie of the passages in ye wrighting were read, she was asked if these things did not give just ground of suspition to all that heard them that she was a witch. She confessed they did, but said if she spake such things as is in M^r. Hookes relation she was not herselfe. She was told she need not say, if she spake them, for she did at the governo^{r}s before many witnesses confess them all as her words, though she made the same excuse that she was not in a right minde; but M^{ris}. Hooke now testifyed she was in a sober frame and spake in a deliberate way, as ordinarily she is at other times. Beside what is in the paper, M^{ris}. Godman was remembred of a passage spoken of at the governo^{r}s aboute M^r. Goodyeares falling into a swonding fitt after hee had spoken something one night in the exposi-tion of a chapter, w^{c}h she (being present) liked not but said it was against her, and as soone as M^r. Goodyeare had done duties she flung out of the roome in a discontented way and cast a fierce looke upon M^r. Goodyeare as she went out, and imediately M^r. Goodyeare (though well before) fell into a swond, and beside her notorious lying in this buisnes, for being asked how she came to know this, she said she was present, yet M^r. Goodyeare, M^{ris}. Goodyeare, Hanah and Elizabeth Lamberton all affirme she was not in ye roome but gone up into the chamber.

After the agitation of these things the court declared to M^{ris}. Godman, as their judgment and sentence in this case, that she hath unjustly called heither the severall persons before named, being she can prove nothing against them, and that her cariage doth justly render her suspitious of witchcraft, wch she herselfe in so many words confesseth, therefore the court wisheth her to looke to her carriage hereafter, for it further proofe come, these passages will not be forgotten, and therefore gave her charge not to goe in an offensive way to folkes houses in a rayling manner as it seemes she hath done, but that she keepe her place and medle wth her owne buisnes.

New Haven *v.* Elizabeth Godman, *1655*

New Haven Town Court, August 7, 1655

Elizabeth Godman was called before the Court, and told that she lies under suspition for witchcraft, as she knowes, the grounds of which were examined in a former Court, and by herselfe confessed to be just grounds of suspition, wch passages were now read, and to these some more are since added, wch are now to be declared:. . .

Goodwife Thorpe informed the Court that concerning something aboute chickens she had formerly declared, wch was now read, after wch she one time had some speech wth M^{ris}. Evance aboute this woman, and through the weakness of her faith she began to doubt that may be she would hurt her cowes, and that day one of her cowes fell sick in the herd, so as the keeper said he thought she would have dyed, but at night when she came into the yard was well and continewed so, but would never give milk nor bring calfe after that; therfore they bought another cow, that they might have some breed, but that cast calfe also; after that they gott another, and she continewed well aboute a fortnight, but then began to pine away and would give no milke and would sweat so as she would be all of a water wher-ever she lay, wthout or wthin; then she thought ther was some thing more then ordinary in it, and could not but thinke that she was bewitched. . . . Aboute a weeke after, she went by M^r. Goodyeares, and there was Eliza: Godman pulling cherries in ye streete; she said, how doth Goody Thorpe? I am behoulden to Goody Thorpe above all the weomen in the Towne: she would have had me to the gallowes for a few chickens; and gnashed and grinned wth her teeth in a strang manner, wch she confesseth was true, but owned nothing about ye cowes. . . .

Allen Ball informed the Court that one time Eliza Godman came to his house and asked his wife for some butter-milke; she refused, and bid her be gone, she cared not for her company: she replyed, what, you will save it for your piggs, but it will doe them no good; and after this his piggs all but one dyed, one after another, but the cause he knowes not. . . .

These things being declared, the Court told Elizabeth Godman that they have considered them wth her former miscariages, and see cause to Order that she be committed to prison, ther to abide the Courts pleasure, but because the matter is of weight, and the crime whereof she is suspected capitall, therefore she is to answer it at the Court of Magistrats in October next.

Court of Magistrates, New Haven, October 17, 1655

Elizabeth Godman was called before the court and told that upon grounds formerly declared, wch stand upon record, she by her owne confession remaines under suspition for witchcraft, and one more is now added, and that is, that one time this last summer, comeing to M^r. Hookes to beg some beare, was at first denyed, but after, she was offered some by his daughter which stood ready drawne, but she refused it and would have some newly drawne, wch she had, yet went away in a muttering discontented manner, and after this, that night, though the beare was good and fresh, yet the next morning was hott, soure and ill tasted, yea so hott as the barrell was warme w^{t}hout side, and when they opened the bung it steemed forth; they brewed againe and it was so also, and so continewed foure or five times, one after another.

She brought divers persons to the court that they might say something to cleere her, and much time was spent in hearing them, but to litle purpose, the grounds of suspition remaining full as strong as before and she found full of lying, wherfore the court declared unto her that though the evidenc is not sufficient as yet to take away her life, yet the suspitions are cleere and many, wch she cannot by all the meanes she hath used, free herselfe from, therfore she must forbeare from goeing from house to house to give offenc, and cary it orderly in the family where she is, wch if she doe not, she will cause the court to comitt her to prison againe, & that she doe now presently upon her freedom give securitie for her good behaviour; and she did now before the court ingage fifty pound of her estate that is in M^r. Goodyeares hand, for her good behaviour, wch is further to be cleered next court, when M^r. Goodyeare is at home.

※ *E S S A Y S*

Two recent books on witchcraft present sharply differing interpretations of the sorts of women most likely to be accused of that crime in seventeenth-century New England. The first essay is from the book by John Putnam Demos, a professor at Yale University who is descended from the Putnam family of Salem, active accusers in the 1692–1693 crisis. Demos contends that witches were likely to be low-status widows with few or no children. The second selection, from the book by Carol Karlsen of the University of Michigan, agrees that witches were likely to be childless widows but puts a very different interpretation on their childlessness. Demos argues that a lack of children would make women relatively powerless and anomalous in a society in which five or six children per woman were the norm. Karlsen, by contrast, focuses on the women's lack of sons, brothers, or other male relatives to inherit the family's lands. This, she argues, made such women potentially *powerful* and threatening in a society in which females were supposed to be subordinate to males and in which they did not usually own real estate. Thus these women were disproportionately represented among those accused of being witches.

The Poor and Powerless Witch

JOHN PUTNAM DEMOS

To investigate the witches as a biographical type is no easy task. With rare exceptions the record of their experience is scattered and fragmentary. Much of the surviving evidence derives from their various trial proceedings; in short, we can visualize them quite fully as *suspects,* but only here and there in other aspects of their lives. We lack, most especially, a chance to approach them directly, to hear their side of their own story. Most of what we do hear comes to us second- or third-hand, and from obviously hostile sources.

It is hard enough simply to count their number. Indeed, it is impossible to compile a complete roster of all those involved. We shall be dealing in what follows with 114 individual suspects. Of these people 81 were subject to some form of legal action for their supposed witchcraft, i.e., "examination" by magistrates and/or full-fledged prosecution. Another 15 were not, so far as we know, formally accused in court; however, their status as suspects is apparent from actions — for slander — which they themselves initiated. A final group of 18 (some not identified by name) are mentioned elsewhere in writings from the period.

Yet these figures certainly *under*-represent the total of witchcraft suspects in seventeenth-century New England. The court records are riddled with gaps and defects; it is possible, even probable, that important cases have been entirely lost from sight. . . .

But if our list of 114 is only the tip, its substantive and structural features still merit investigation. There is no reason to imagine any considerable difference between the known witches and their unknown counterparts. The former are presented here, as a group, in their leading biographical characteristics. Their (1) sex and (2) age have an obvious claim to attention. Thence the focus moves, successively, to their (3) background and early life, (4) marital and child-bearing status, (5) pattern of family relationships, (6) overall record of social and/or criminal "deviance," (7) occupational history, and (8) social and economic position. A final question concerns their (9) personal style and character, and their specific experiences as witches — that is, as objects of formal and informal sanction at the hands of their cultural peers.

Sex

There was no intrinsic reason why one sex should have been more heavily represented among New England witches than the other. The prevailing definitions of witchcraft — the performance of *maleficium* and "familiarity with the Devil" — made no apparent distinctions as to gender. Yet the predominance of women among those actually accused is a historical commonplace — and is confirmed by the present findings.

Females outnumbered males by a ratio of roughly 4:1. These proportions ob-

Abridged from *Entertaining Satan: Witchcraft and the Culture of Early New England,* 57–94, by John Putnam Demos. Copyright © 1982 by Oxford University Press, Inc. Reprinted by permission.

tained, with some minor variations, across both time and space. Furthermore, they likely *under*state the association of women and witchcraft, as can be seen from a closer look at the males accused. Of the twenty-two men on the list, eleven were accused together with a woman. Nine of these were husbands of female witches, the other two were religious associates (*protégés* of the notorious Anne Hutchinson). There is good reason to think that in most, if not all, such cases the woman was the primary suspect, with the man becoming implicated through a literal process of guilt by association. Indeed this pattern conformed to a widely prevalent assumption that the transmission of witchcraft would follow the lines of family or close friendship. (There were at least two instances when a woman-witch joined in the charges against her own husband.) . . .

An easy hypothesis — perhaps too easy — would make of witchcraft a single plank in a platform of "sexist" oppression. Presumably, the threat of being charged as a witch might serve to constrain the behavior of women. Those who asserted themselves too openly or forcibly could expect a summons to court, and risked incurring the ultimate sanction of death itself. Hence the dominance of *men* would be underscored in both symbolic and practical terms. Male dominance was, of course, an assumed principle in traditional society — including the society of early New England. Men controlled political life; they alone could vote and hold public office. Men were also leaders in religion, as pastors and elders of local congregations. Men owned the bulk of personal property (though women had some rights and protections). Furthermore, the values of the culture affirmed the "headship" of men in marital and family relations and their greater "wisdom" in everyday affairs. Certainly, then, the uneven distribution of witchcraft accusations and their special bearing on the lives of women were consistent with sex-roles generally.

But was there *more* to this than simple consistency? Did the larger matrix of social relations enclose some dynamic principle that would energize actual "witch-hunting" so as to hold women down? On this the evidence — at least from early New England — seems doubtful. There is little sign of generalized (or "structural") conflict between the sexes. Male dominance of public affairs was scarcely an issue, and in private life there was considerable scope for female initiative. Considered overall, the relations of men and women were less constrained by differences of role and status than would be the case for most later generations of Americans. It is true that many of the suspects displayed qualities of assertiveness and aggressiveness beyond what the culture deemed proper. But these displays were not directed at men as such; often enough the targets were other women. Moreover, no single line in the extant materials raises the issue of sex-defined patterns of authority. Thus, if witches were at some level protesters against male oppression, they themselves seem to have been unconscious of the fact. As much could be said of the accusers, in their (putative) impulse to dominate.

Two possible exceptions should be noticed here. Anne Hutchinson was suspected of performing witchcraft, during and after her involvement with "antinomianism." And the ecclesiastical proceedings against her affirmed, among other things, the "natural" subordination of women to male authority. (Said Governor Winthrop at one point: "We do not mean to discourse with those of your sex.") Similarly, the convicted witch Anne Hibbens had been "cast out" of the Boston church for a variety of reasons, including this one: "she hath [violated] . . . the rule of the

Apostle in usurping authority over him whom God hath made her head and husband." (According to John Cotton, the pastor, "some do think she doth but make a wisp of her husband.") Yet even in these cases there was no clear line of connection between the (alleged) witchcraft and the flouting of conventional sex-roles. With Mrs. Hutchinson heresy remained the central issue throughout. With Mrs. Hibbens many years elapsed between her trial of excommunication (1640) and her conviction for witchcraft (1656). It is also well to remember numerous other New England women who would seem to qualify as sex-role "deviants." Their sins were many and various — assault on magistrates and constables, "wicked carriage and speeches" toward husbands, physical violence against husbands (and others), sexual harassment and abuse of men — yet most of them would never fall prey to charges of witchcraft.

And one final point in this connection: a large portion of witchcraft charges were brought against women *by* other women. Thus, if the fear of witchcraft expressed a deep strain of misogyny, it was something in which both sexes shared. It was also something in which other cultures have quite generally shared. . . .

Age

How old were the accused? At what age did their careers as suspected witches begin? These questions are difficult to answer with precision, in many individual cases; but it is possible to create an aggregate picture by analyzing a broad sample of age-estimates. . . .

The results converge on one time of life in particular: what we would call "midlife," or simply "middle age." The years of the forties and fifties account for the great mass of accused witches, whether considered at the time of prosecution (67 percent) or of earliest known suspicion (82 percent). It seems necessary to emphasize these figures in order to counteract the now familiar stereotype which makes witches out to be old. In fact, they were not old, either by their standards or by ours. (One victim, in her fits, was asked pointedly about the age of her spectral tormentors, and "she answered neither old nor young.") Contrary (once again) to currently prevalent understandings, the New Englanders construed the chronology of aging in terms not very different from our own. Their laws, their prescriptive writings, and their personal behavior expressed a common belief that old age begins at sixty. All but a handful of the witches were younger than this. Indeed, substantial majorities of both the groups considered above were age fifty or less (72 percent of the general sample, and 78 percent of the "major suspects"). . . .

One can scarcely avoid asking *why* this should have been so. What, for a start, was the meaning of midlife in that time and that cultural context? One point seems immediately apparent: midlife was *not* seen as one of several stages in a fully rounded "life-cycle." Early Americans spoke easily and frequently of "childhood," "youth," and "old age" — but not of "middle age." The term and (presumably) the concept, so familiar to us today, had little place in the lives of our forebears centuries ago. Instead of constituting a stage, midlife meant simply manhood (or womanhood) itself. Here was a *general* standard, against which childhood and youth, on the one side, and old age, on the other, were measured as deviations. Early life was preparatory; later life brought decline. The key element in midlife — as defined, for example, by the Puritan poet Anne Bradstreet — was the exercise of power, the use of fully developed capacity. The danger was *mis*use of power, the besetting sin an excess of "vaulting ambition." In fact, these conventions gave an accurate reflection of experience and behavior. In the average life the years from forty to sixty enclosed a high point of wealth, of prestige, of responsibility for self and others. This pattern can be demonstrated most clearly for *men* in midlife (from tax-lists, inventories, records of office-holding, and the like); but it must have obtained for women as well. A middle-aged woman was likely, for one thing, to have a full complement of children in her care and under her personal authority. The numbers involved could well reach eight or ten, and in some families there would be additional dependents — servants, apprentices, other children "bound out" in conditions of fosterage. With female dependents the authority of the "mistress" was particularly extensive; significantly, it appeared as an issue in at least one of the witchcraft cases. Listen to the words of Mercy Short, "in her fits" and addressing her spectral tormentors:

> What's that? Must the younger women, do ye say, hearken to the elder? They must be another sort of elder women than you then! They must not be elder witches, I am sure. Pray, do you for once hearken to me!

Beyond the cultural insistence that others "hearken" to her, a woman in midlife would enjoy considerable prestige in her village or neighborhood. She was likely by this time to be a church member — and, if her husband was well to do, to have a front-row seat in the meeting-house. Indeed, her status reflected her husband's quite generally, and his was probably higher than at any time previous. The point, in sum, is this. Midlife was associated, in theory and in fact, with power over others. Witchcraft was a special (albeit malign) instance of power over others. Ergo: most accused witches were themselves persons in midlife.

If this seems a bit too simple, there are indeed some additional — and complicating — factors. The accused were not, on the whole, well positioned socially. Their personal access to power and authority was, if anything, below the average for their age-group. They can therefore be viewed as representative of midlife status only in a very generalized sense. Perhaps it was the discrepancy between midlife norms and their own individual circumstances that made them seem plausible as suspects. Perhaps a middle-aged person who was poorly situated (relative to peers) could be presumed to want "power" — and, in some cases, to seek it by any means that came to hand.

To suggest this is to acknowledge elements of *dis*advantage — of deficit and loss — in generating suspicions of witchcraft. And one more such element must be mentioned, at least speculatively. Most of the accused were middle-aged women; as such they were subject to the menopausal "change of life." The old phrase sounds quaint and slightly off-key to modern ears, but in traditional society menopause brought more — at least more tangible — change than is the usual case nowadays. Its effects embraced biology, psychology, and social position, in roughly equal measure. This process will need further, and fuller, consideration in relation to the putative victims of witchcraft; for the moment we simply underscore its meaning as loss of function. The generative "power" of most women was by midlife visibly manifest in a houseful of children; yet that same power came suddenly to an end. There was a gap here between one mode of experience and another — past versus present — an additional kind of unsettling discrepancy. Was it, then, coincidental that witches appeared to direct their malice especially toward infants and very young children?. . .

Background

The most severe of all the deficiencies in the source materials relate to the early life of the witches. In what circumstances did they grow up? Was there something distinctive about their various families of origin? Were they orphaned, sent out into servitude, subject to illness, raised by disabled or insensitive parents, to any extent beyond the average for their cultural peers? Unfortunately, the material to answer such questions is not extant. . . .

Other elements of "background" deserve investigation. Were the witches anomalous in their ethnic and/or religious heritage? On this the evidence is clearer, and it supports a negative answer overall. An early suspect in the Hartford trials of 1662–63 was Dutch — Judith Varlet, daughter of a merchant and relative by marriage of Governor Peter Stuyvesant of New Netherland. (A leading victim in the case was given to "Dutch-toned discourse," when overtaken by fits.) The widow Glover, convicted and executed at Boston in 1688, was Irish and Catholic, and at her trial could speak only in Gaelic. Elizabeth Garlick of Easthampton apparently had one Huguenot parent. And Mary Parsons was the wife of a "papist" before her ill-starred second marriage and trial for witchcraft at Springfield. But otherwise the witches seem to have been of solidly English stock and mostly "Puritan" religion. . . .

Marriage and Child-Bearing

But what of the families in which witches lived as adults, the families they helped to create as spouses and parents? The results on this point seem generally unremarkable: there are no clear departures from the pattern of the culture at large. The portion of widows (10 percent) looks normal for the age-group most centrally involved, given the prevailing demographic regime. The never-marrieds (another 10 percent) include those few young men who virtually courted suspicion and also the several children of witches accused by "association." (John Godfrey was the only person past "youth" in this particular sub-group.) There was but one divorcée.

In sum, most witches were married persons (with spouses still living) when brought under suspicion. Most, indeed, had been married only once. Four were definitely, and two probably, in a second marriage; one had been married (also widowed) twice previously. Perhaps a few others belong in the previously married group, assuming some lost evidence; however, this would not alter the total picture. Again, the witches seem little different in their marital situation from their cultural peers.

As part of their marriages the accused would, of course, expect to bear and rear children. But in this their actual experience may have differed somewhat from the norm. The pertinent data (vital records, genealogies, and the like) are flawed at many points, and conclusions must be qualified accordingly. Still, with that understood, we may ponder the following. It appears that nearly one in six of the witches was childless — twice the rate that obtained in the population at large. Moreover, those who *did* bear children may have experienced lower-than-normal fecundity (and/or success in raising children to adulthood). In numerous cases (23 out of 62) the procedure of family reconstitution yields but one or two clearly identifiable off-spring. Meanwhile, relatively few cases (7 of 62) can be associated with large complements of children, i.e., six or more per family. Fuller evidence would surely change these figures, reducing the former and raising the latter; but it would take a quite massive shift to bring the witches into line with the child-bearing and child-rearing norms of the time.

Connections between witchcraft and children emerge at many points in the extant record: children thought to have been made ill, or murdered, by witchcraft; mothers apparently bewitched while bearing or nursing children; witches alleged to suckle "imps" (in implicit parody of normal maternal function); witches observed to take a special (and suspicious) interest in other people's children; witches found to be predominantly of menopausal age and status; and so on. Thus the witches' own child-bearing (and child-rearing) is a matter of considerable interest. And if they were indeed relatively ill-favored and unsuccessful in this respect, their liability to witch-charges becomes, by so much, easier to understand.

Family Relationships

There is another, quite different way in which the witches may have been atypical. Briefly summarized, their domestic experience was often marred by trouble and conflict. Sometimes the witch and her (his) spouse squared off as antagonists. Jane Collins was brought to court not only for witchcraft but also for "railing" at her husband and calling him "gurley-gutted Devil." Bridget Oliver and her husband Thomas were tried, convicted, and punished for "fighting with each other," a decade before Bridget's first trial for witchcraft. (A neighbor deposed that she had "several times been called . . . to hear their complaints one of the other, and . . . further [that] she saw Goodwife Oliver's face at one time bloody and at other times black and blue, . . . and [Goodman] Oliver complained that his wife had given him several blows.") The witchcraft trials of Mary and Hugh Parsons called forth much testimony as to their marital difficulties. Mary was alleged to have spoken "very harsh things against him before his face . . . such things as are not ordinary for persons to speak one of another." Hugh, for his part, "never feared either to grieve or displease his wife any time"; once, by his own admission, he "took up a block [of wood] and made as if . . . [to] throw it at her head." A second Mary Parsons also quarreled frequently with her husband. The estrangement between Sarah Dibble and *her* husband was so bitter that he actively encouraged suspicions of her witchcraft; moreover, his general "carriage" toward her was "most inhumane, [e.g.] beating of her so that he caused the blood to settle in several places of her body." There was similar evidence about other suspects, including several of those tried at Salem.

In some cases the lines of conflict ran between parents and children. The Marblehead witch Jane James was chronically at odds with her son Erasmus; at least once the county court undertook an official arbitration of their differences. (On a separate occasion the same court examined and fined Erasmus "for giving his mother abusive language and carriage.") The witchcraft charges against William Graves seem to have developed out of a long-standing dispute with his daughter and son-in-law. Susannah Martin's household was disrupted by violent quarrels between her husband and son; the latter was brought to court and convicted of "high misdemeanors" in "abusing of his father, and throwing him down, and taking away his clothes."

This material cannot meaningfully be quantified; in too many cases the surviving evidence does not extend to any part of the suspect's domestic experience. But what does survive seems striking, if only by way of "impressionism." Harmony in human relations was a touchstone of value for early New Englanders, and nowhere more so than in families. A "peaceable" household was seen as the foundation of all social order. Hence domestic disharmony would invite unfavorable notice from neighbors and peers. A woman from Dorchester, Massachusetts, called to court in a lawsuit filed by her son, expressed the underlying issue with candor and clarity: "it is no small trouble of mind to me that there should be such recording up [of] family weaknesses, to the dishonor of God and grief of one another, and I had rather go many paces backward to cover shame than one inch forward to discover any." Yet the lives of witches — we are speculating — were often crossed with "family weaknesses." And perhaps these belonged to the matrix of factors in which particular suspicions originated.

Such weaknesses may have held other significance as well. The troubles in Rachel Clinton's family left her isolated and exposed to a variety of personal misadventures: her sheer vulnerability made a central theme in her story. Rachel was doubtless an extreme case, but not a wholly atypical one. Conflict with spouse, siblings, children had the effect of neutralizing one's natural allies and defenders, if not of turning them outright into adversaries. The *absence* of family was also a form of weakness. Widowhood may not by itself have invited suspicions of witchcraft; yet where suspicions formed on other grounds, it could become a serious disadvantage. Case materials from the trials of the widows Godman (New Haven), Holman (Cambridge), Hale (Boston), and Glover (Boston) implicitly underscore their vulnerable position.

The experience of Anne Hibbens (Boston) is particularly suggestive this way. Mrs. Hibbens had arrived in New England with her husband William in the early 1630s. Almost at once William established himself as an important and exemplary member of the community: a merchant, a magistrate, a member of the Court of Assistants. But Anne made a different impression. In 1640 she suffered admonition, then excommunication, from the Boston church; a still-extant transcript of the proceedings reveals most vividly her troubled relations with neighbors and peers. In 1656 she was tried in criminal court — and convicted — and executed — for witchcraft. The long interval between these two dates invites attention; and there is a third date to notice as well, 1654, when William Hibbens died. It seems likely, in short, that William's influence served for many years to shield her from the full force of her neighbors' animosity. But with his passing she was finally, and mortally, exposed.

Crime

Witchcraft was itself a crime, and witches were criminals of a special sort. Were they also criminals of other — more ordinary — sorts? Were they as a group disproportionately represented within the ranks of all defendants in court proceedings?

Was there possibly some implicit affinity between witchcraft and other categories of crime?

Again, the extant records do not yield fully adequate information. Some 41 of the accused can be definitely associated with other (and prior) criminal proceedings; the remaining 73 *cannot* be so associated. The difficulty is that many in the latter group can scarcely be traced at all beyond their alleged involvement with witchcraft. Still, the total of 41 offenders is a considerable number, which serves to establish a minimum "crime rate" — of 36 percent — for the witches as a whole. Clearly, moreover, this is only a minimum. To concentrate on witches for whom there is some evidence of *ongoing* experience is to reduce the "at risk" population to no more than 65. (The latter, in short, form a sub-sample among the accused whose offences might plausibly have left some trace in the records; the rest are biographical phantoms in a more complete sense.) This adjustment yields an alternative rate (of offenders/witches) of some 63 percent.

The two figures, 36 and 63 percent, may be viewed as lower and upper bounds for the actual rate, and their midpoint as a "best guess" response to the central question. In short, approximately one half of the people accused of practicing witchcraft were also charged with the commission of other crimes. But was this a notably large fraction, in relation to the community at large? Unfortunately, there are no fully developed studies of criminal behavior in early America to provide firm standards of comparison, only scattershot impressions and partial analyses of two specific communities included in the current investigation. The latter may be summarized in a sentence. The overall "crime rate" — defined as a percentage of the total population charged with committing crimes at some point in a lifetime — was on the order of 10 to 20 percent.[*] Thus, even allowing for the possibility of substantial error, the link between witchcraft and other crime does look strong.

There is more to ask about the other crime, particularly about its substantive range and distribution. Taken altogether, the witches accounted for fifty-two separate actions at court (apart from the witchcraft itself). . . . Crimes of assaultive speech and theft are dramatically highlighted here. Together they account for 61 percent of all charges pressed against the witches, as opposed to 35 percent for the larger sample. Moreover, the fact that accused witches were predominantly female suggests a refinement in the sample population. If men were excluded — if, in short, the comparison involves witches versus *women* offenders generally — then the disparity becomes even larger, 61 percent and 27 percent.

Are there reasons why persons previously charged with theft and/or assaultive speech might be found, to a disproportionate extent, in the ranks of accused witches? Was there something which these two categories of offense shared (so to say) with witchcraft? Such questions point to the meaning of witchcraft in the minds of its supposed (or potential) victims. But consider what is common to crimes of theft and assaultive speech themselves. The element of loss, of undue and unfair taking away, seems patent in the former case, but it is — or was for early New Englanders — equally central to the latter one as well. Slander, for example,

---

[*]The rate for *women only* was much lower, perhaps in the vicinity of 5 percent. And this may be a better "control group" for present purposes, since most witches were female. If so, the disparity between witch-behavior and prevailing norms appears even more pronounced.

meant the loss of good name, of "face," of reputation, and thus was a matter of utmost importance. (The evidence against one alleged slanderer, who would later be charged as a witch, was summarized as follows: "She hath *taken away* their [i.e., the plaintiffs'] names and credits . . . which is *as precious as life itself.*" [Emphasis added.]) "Filthy speeches" was a somewhat looser designation, but in most specific instances it described a similar threat. Even "lying" — a third category of crime, notably salient for witches — can be joined to this line of interpretation. A lie was, in a sense, a theft of truth, and seemed especially dangerous when directed toward other persons.

In sum, each of these crimes carried the inner meaning of theft. And so did witchcraft. Theft of property, theft of health (and sometimes of life), theft of competence, theft of will, theft of self: such was *maleficium*, the habitual activity of witches.

Occupations

. . . "Jane Hawkins, of Boston, midwife . . . " "Isabel Babson, of Gloucester, midwife . . . " "Wayborough Gatchell, of Marblehead, midwife . . . "; here was a special *woman's* occupation. That midwife and witch were sometimes (often?) the same person has long been supposed by historians; hence the evidence, for individual cases, deserves a most careful review. In fact, only two people in the entire suspect-group can be plausibly associated with the regular practice of midwifery. Otherwise the witches were not midwives, at least in a formal sense. It is clear, moreover, that scores of midwives carried out their duties, in many towns and through many years, without ever being touched by imputations of witchcraft.

However, this does not entirely dispose of the issue at hand. Witchcraft charges often did revolve in a special way around episodes of childbirth, and some of the accused were thought to have shown inordinate (and sinister) interest in the fate of the very young. Thus, for example, Eunice Cole of Hampton aroused suspicion by trying to intrude at the childbed (later deathbed) of her alleged victims. Others among the accused pressed medicines and advice on expectant or newly delivered mothers, or, alternatively, sought to take from the same quarter. Some may have displayed special skills in attending at childbirth, even without being recognized officially as midwives. (When Elizabeth Morse was tried for witchcraft, witnesses described her part in the delivery of a neighbor. First, she was deliberately kept away. Then, as "strong labor . . . continued . . . without any hopeful appearance," she was "desired to come" — but declined, evidently miffed at not being asked sooner. Eventually she relented, "and so at last . . . went, and quickly after her coming the woman was delivered.") Perhaps, at bottom, there was a link of antipathy: the midwife *versus* the witch, life-giving and life-taking, opposite faces of the same coin.

Recent scholarship of English witchcraft has spotlighted the activities of so-called "cunning folk." These were local practitioners of magic who specialized in finding lost property, foretelling the future, and (most especially) treating illness. Usually they sided with moral order and justice; often enough their diagnoses served to "discover" witchcraft as the cause of particular sufferings. Yet their powers were mysterious and frightening: charms, incantations, herbal potions, a kind of second sight — all in exotic combination. Inevitably, it seemed, some of them would be tempted to apply such powers in the cause of evil. Thus they might move from the role of "discoverer" to that of suspect — in short, from witch-doctor to witch.

Were there also "cunning folk" among the transplanted Englishmen of North America? The extant evidence seems, at first sight, to yield a negative answer. There is little sign that individual persons achieved (or wanted) a public reputation of this sort, as was plainly the case in the mother country. The nomenclature itself rarely appears, and then only as a form of name-calling. ("What?" exclaimed one man of Goody Morse; "Is she a witch, or a cunning woman?") Almost certainly, the religious establishment of early New England set itself against such practice. Puritan leaders, on both sides of the Atlantic, associated it with the Devil — and, on this side, their views carried decisive influence.

And yet, while "cunning folk" did not present themselves as such, some of their ways (and character) may have survived in at least attenuated forms. For within the ranks of witches were several — perhaps many — women of singular aptitude for "healing." Not "physicians," not midwives, and not (publicly) identified by the pejorative term "cunning," they nonetheless proffered their services in the treatment of personal illness. For example: the widow Hale of Boston (twice a target of witchcraft proceedings) ran a kind of lodging-house where sick persons came for rest and "nursing." Anna Edmunds of Lynn (presented for witchcraft in 1673) was known locally as a "doctor woman"; references to her practice span at least two decades. (One prolonged court case showed her in implicit competition with a Boston physician. The physician had tried, and failed, to cure a young girl with a badly infected leg; and when the girl's parents turned next to Goody Edmunds he vowed to "swallow a firebrand" if her treatment proved successful.) Elizabeth Garlick of Easthampton prescribed "dockweeds" and other herbal remedies for sick neighbors. Katherine Harrison played a similar part at Wethersfield; her therapies included "diet, drink, and plasters." A woman of Boston, not identified but suspected in the "affliction" of Margaret Rule, "had frequently cured very painful hurts by muttering over them certain charms." . . .

What this and other evidence does make clear is a key association: between efforts of curing, on the one hand, and the "black arts" of witchcraft, on the other. Opposite though they seemed in formal terms, in practice they were (sometimes) tightly linked. "Power" in either direction could be suddenly reversed. We cannot discover how many New England women may have tried their hand at doctoring, but we know that some who did so brought down on themselves a terrible suspicion. Among the various occupations of premodern society this one was particularly full of hope — and of peril.

Social Position

There is a long-standing, and reasonably well attested, view of early America that makes the settlers solidly middle-class. To be sure, the notion of "class" is somewhat misleading when applied to the seventeenth century; "status" would be a better term in context. But "middle" does seem the right sort of qualifier. The movement of people from England to America included few from either the lowest or the highest ranks of traditional society — few, that is, from among the laboring poor (or the truly destitute) and fewer still from the nobility and upper gentry. Yet, with that understood, one cannot fail to notice how the middle range became itself divided and graded by lines of preference. The "planting" of New England yielded its own array of leaders and followers, of more and less fortunate citizens. Social distinction remained important, vitally so, to the orderly life of communities. . . .

The sorting attempted here posits three broad social groups — "high" (I), "middle" (II), and "low" (III) — of roughly equal size. Of course, all such categories are a matter of contrivance, conforming to no specific historical reality; but they do help to arrange the material for analysis.

Within our working roster of accused witches, some eighty-six can be classified according to this scheme. (For the other twenty-eight there is too little evidence to permit a judgement.) A substantial majority can be assigned directly to one or another of the basic rank-groups. Eighteen more occupy marginal positions (i.e., *between* groups), while seven seem distinctive in their mobility (up or down) and are on that account held for a separate category. . . . Witches were recruited, to a greatly disproportionate extent, among the most humble, least powerful of New England's citizens. As a matter of statistical probabilities, persons at the bottom of the sorting-scale were many times more likely to be accused and prosecuted than their counterparts at the top. Moreover, when the results of such accusation are figured in, the difference looks stronger still. Among all the suspects in categories I, I/II, and II, only one was a *convicted* witch. (And of the remainder, few, if any, were seriously threatened by the actions taken against them.) The accused in categories II/III and III present quite another picture. Indeed they account for all convictions save the one above noted, and for the great bulk of completed trials.

Finally, the "mobile" group deserves special consideration. Five of them started life in a top-category position and ended near the bottom (e.g., Rachel Clinton). Two experienced equivalent change but in the opposite direction. None was convicted; all but one, however, were subject to full-scale prosecution. (Moreover, five were tried more than once.) In short, the mobile group, while not numerous, included people whose "witchcraft" was taken very seriously. To interpret this finding is difficult, without comparable information about the population at large. But there is the suggestion here of a significant relationship: between life-change and witchcraft, between mobility and lurking danger. Perhaps mobility seemed a threat to traditional values and order. And if so, it may well have been personally threatening to the individuals involved. As they rose or fell, moving en route past their more stable peers, they must at the least have seemed conspicuous. But perhaps they seemed *suspect* as well. To mark them as witches would, then, be a way of defending society itself.

Character

With the witches' sex, age, personal background, family life, propensity to crime, occupations, and social position all accounted for (as best we can manage), there yet remains one category which may be the most important of all. What were these people like — as people? What range of motive, of style, and of behavior would they typically exhibit? Can the scattered artifacts of their separate careers be made to yield a composite portrait, a model, so to speak, of witch-character? . . .

Witchcraft was *defined* in reference to conflict; and most charges of witchcraft grew out of specific episodes of conflict. Hence it should not be surprising that the suspects, as individuals, were notably active that way. . . .

What follows is a motley assemblage of taunts, threats, and curses attributed to one or another suspect:

Mercy Disborough did say that it should be pressed, heaped, and running over to her.

He [Hugh Parsons] said unto me, "Gammer, you need not have said anything. I spoke not to you, but I shall remember you when you little think on it.

She [Goodwife Jane Walford] said I had better have done it; that my sorrow was great already, and it should be greater — for I was going a great journey, but should never come there.

She [Elizabeth Godman] said, "How doth Goody Thorp? I am beholden to Goody Thorp above all the women in the town; she would have had me to the gallows for a few chickens."

Mercy Disborough told him that she would make him as bare as a bird's tail.

Then said he [Hugh Parsons], "If you will not abate it [i.e., a certain debt in corn] it shall be but as lent. It shall do you no good. It shall be but as wild fire in your house, and as a moth in your clothes." And these threatening speeches he uttered with much anger.

Goodwife Cole said that if this deponent's calves did eat any of her grass, she wished it might poison or choke them. . . .

Some suspects appeared to favor witchcraft and its alleged practitioners. Elizabeth Godman "would be often speaking about witches . . . without any occasion . . . and [would] rather justify them than condemn them"; indeed, "she said, 'why do they provoke them? why do they not let them come into the church?'" When her neighbor, Mrs. Goodyear, expressed confidence that God would ultimately "discover" and punish witches, "for I never knew a witch to die in their bed," Mrs. Godman disagreed. "You mistake," she said, "for a great many die and go to the grave in an orderly way." Hugh Parsons was suspected of holding similar views. According to his wife he could "not abide that anything should be spoken against witches." Indeed the two of them quarreled while discussing a witch trial in another community: Hugh was allegedly angered "because she wished the ruin of all witches." There were, in addition, postures of support for particular suspects (e.g., Alice Stratton for Margaret Jones, Elizabeth Seager for Goodwife Ayres, Mary Staples for Goodwife Knapp), which would also invite unfavorable notice.

Some of these statements and postures serve to raise a further question. Was the impulse to provoke others through leading references to witchcraft a manifestation of some larger characterological disturbance? Here, indeed, is the germ of an old supposition, that witches have usually been deranged persons, insane or at least deeply eccentric. For New England the situation was largely otherwise. . . .

Conclusion

From this long and somewhat tortuous exercise in prosopography a rough composite finally emerges. To recapitulate, the typical witch:

1. was female.
2. was of middle age (i.e., between forty and sixty years old).
3. was of English (and "Puritan") background.
4. was married, but was more likely (than the general population) to have few children — or none at all.
5. was frequently involved in trouble and conflict with other family members.
6. had been accused, on some previous occasion, of committing crimes — most especially theft, slander, or other forms of assaultive speech.
7. was more likely (than the general population) to have professed and practiced a medical vocation, i.e., "doctoring" on a local, quite informal basis.
8. was of relatively low social position.
9. was abrasive in style, contentious in character — and stubbornly resilient in the face of adversity.

The Potentially Powerful Witch

CAROL F. KARLSEN

Most observers now agree that witches in the villages and towns of late sixteenth-and early seventeenth-century England tended to be poor. They were not usually the poorest women in their communities, one historian has argued; they were the "moderately poor." Rarely were relief recipients suspect; rather it was those just above them on the economic ladder, "like the woman who felt she ought to get poor relief, but was denied it." This example brings to mind New England's Eunice Cole, who once berated Hampton selectmen for refusing her aid when, she insisted, a man no worse off than she was receiving it.

Eunice Cole's experience also suggests the difficulty in evaluating the class position of the accused. Commonly used class indicators such as the amount of property owned, yearly income, occupation, and political offices held are almost useless in analyzing the positions of women during the colonial period. While early New England women surely shared in the material benefits and social status of their fathers, husbands, and even sons, most were economically dependent on the male members of their families throughout their lives. Only a small proportion of these women owned property outright, and even though they participated actively in the productive work of their communities, their labor did not translate into financial independence or economic power. Any income generated by married women belonged by law to their husbands, and because occupations open to women were few and wages meager, women alone could only rarely support themselves. Their material condition, moreover, could easily change with an alteration in their marital status. William Cole, with an estate at his death of £41 after debts, might be counted among the "moderately poor," as might Eunice Cole when he was alive. But the refusal of the authorities to recognize the earlier transfer of this estate from husband

Reprinted from "The Economic Basis of Witchcraft," Chapter 3 of *The Devil in the Shape of a Woman: Witchcraft in Colonial New England*, 77–83, 102–116, by Carol F. Karlsen, by permission of the author and W.W. Norton & Co., Inc. Copyright © 1987 by Carol F. Karlsen.

to wife ensured, among other things, that as a widow Eunice Cole was among the poorest of New England's poor.

The distinction between the economic circumstances of wife and widow here may not seem particularly significant, but in other cases the problem is more complicated. How, for instance, do we classify the witch Ann Doliver? The daughter of prominent Salem minister John Higginson, who was well above most of his neighbors in wealth and social status, she was also the deserted wife of William Dolliver, and lived out her life without the support of a husband, dependent first on her father and then on the town for her maintenance. Even if we were willing to assume that the accused shared the class position of their male relatives, the lack of information on so many of the families of witches makes it impossible to locate even the males on an economic scale.

Despite conceptual problems and sparse evidence, it is clear that poor women, both the destitute and those with access to some resources, were surely represented, and very probably overrepresented, among the New England accused. Perhaps 20 percent of accused women, including both Eunice Cole and Ann Dolliver, were either impoverished or living at a level of bare subsistence when they were accused. Some, like thirty-seven-year-old Abigail Somes, worked as servants a substantial portion of their adult lives. Some supported themselves and their families with various kinds of temporary labor such as nursing infants, caring for sick neighbors, taking in washing and sewing, or harvesting crops. A few, most notably Tituba, the first person accused during the Salem outbreak, were slaves. Others, like the once-prosperous Sarah Good of Wenham and Salem, and the never-very-well-off Ruth Wilford of Haverhill, found themselves reduced to abject poverty by the death of a parent or a change in their own marital status. Accused witches came before local magistrates requesting permission to sell family land in order to support themselves, to submit claims against their children or executors of their former husbands' estates for nonpayment of the widow's lawful share of the estate, or simply to ask for food and fuel from the town selectmen. Because they could not pay the costs of their trials or jail terms, several were forced to remain in prison after courts acquitted them. The familiar stereotype of the witch as an indigent woman who resorted to begging for her survival is hardly an inaccurate picture of some of New England's accused.

Still, the poor account for only a minority of the women accused. Even without precise economic indicators, it is clear that women from all levels of society were vulnerable to accusation. If witches in early modern England can accurately be described as "moderately poor," then New Englanders deviated sharply from their ancestors in their ideas about which women were witches. Wives, daughters, and widows of "middling" farmers, artisans, and mariners were regularly accused, and (although much less often) so too were women belonging to the gentry class. The accused were addressed as Goodwife (or Goody) and as the more honorific Mrs. or Mistress, as well as by their first names.

Prosecution was a different matter. Unless they were single or widowed, accused women from wealthy families — families with estates valued at more than £500 — could be fairly confident that the accusations would be ignored by the authorities or deflected by their husbands through suits for slander against their accusers. Even during the Salem outbreak, when several women married to wealthy men were arrested, most managed to escape to the safety of other colonies through their husbands' influence. Married women from moderately well-off families — families with estates valued at between roughly £200 and £500 — did not always escape prosecution so easily, but neither do they seem, as a group, to have been as vulnerable as their less prosperous counterparts. When only married women are considered, women in families with estates worth less than £200 seem significantly overrepresented among *convicted* witches — a pattern which suggests that economic position was a more important factor to judges and juries than to the community as a whole in its role as accuser.

Without a husband to act on behalf of the accused, wealth alone rarely provided women with protection against prosecution. Boston's Ann Hibbens, New Haven's Elizabeth Godman, and Wethersfield's Katherine Harrison, all women alone, were tried as witches despite sizeable estates. In contrast, the accusations against women like Hannah Griswold of Saybrook, Connecticut, Elizabeth Blackleach of Hartford, and Margaret Gifford of Salem, all wives of prosperous men when they were accused, were simply not taken seriously by the courts. The most notable exception to this pattern is the obliviousness of the Salem judges to repeated accusations against Margaret Thatcher, widow of one of the richest merchants in Boston and principal heir to her father's considerable fortune. Her unusual wealth and social status may have kept her out of jail in 1692, but more likely it was her position as mother-in-law to Jonathan Corwin, one of the Salem magistrates, that accounts for her particular immunity.

Economic considerations, then, do appear to have been at work in the New England witchcraft cases. But the issue was not simply the relative poverty — or wealth — of accused witches or their families. It was the special position of most accused witches vis-à-vis their society's rules for transferring wealth from one generation to another. To explain why their position was so unusual, we must turn first to New England's system of inheritance.

Inheritance is normally thought of as the transmission of property at death, but in New England, as in other agricultural societies, adult children received part of their father's accumulated estates prior to his death, usually at the time they married. Thus the inheritance system included both pre-mortem endowments and post-mortem distributions. While no laws compelled fathers to settle part of their estates on their children as marriage portions, it was customary to do so. Marriages were, among other things, economic arrangements, and young people could not benefit from these arrangements unless their fathers provided them with the means to set up households and earn their livelihoods. Sons' portions tended to be land, whereas daughters commonly received movable goods and/or money. The exact value of these endowments varied according to a father's wealth and inclination, but it appears that as a general rule the father of the young woman settled on the couple roughly half as much as the father of the young man.

Custom, not law, also guided the distribution of a man's property at his death, but with two important exceptions. First, a man's widow, if he left one, was legally entitled "by way of dower" to one-third part of his real property, "to have and injoy for term of her natural life." She was expected to support herself with the profits of this property, but since she held only a life interest in it, she had to see that she did not "strip or waste" it. None of the immovable estate could be sold, unless necessary for her or her children's maintenance, and then only with the permission of the court. A man might will his wife more than a third of his real property — but not less. Only if the woman came before the court to renounce her dower right publicly, and then only if the court approved, could this principle be waived. In the form of her "thirds," dower was meant to provide for a woman's support in widowhood. The inviolability of dower protected the widow from the claims of her children against the estate and protected the community from the potential burden of her care.

The second way in which law determined inheritance patterns had to do specifically with intestate cases. If a man died without leaving a will, several principles governed the division of his property. The widow's thirds, of course, were to be laid out first. Unless "just cause" could be shown for some other distribution, the other two-thirds were to be divided among the surviving children, both male and female. A double portion was to go to the eldest son, and single portions to his sisters and younger brothers. If there were no sons, the law stipulated that the estate was to be shared equally by the daughters. In cases where any or all of the children had not yet come of age, their portions were to be held by their mother or by a court-appointed guardian until they reached their majorities or married. What remained of the widow's thirds at her death was to be divided among the surviving children, in the same proportions as the other two-thirds.

Although bound to conform to laws concerning the widow's thirds, men who wrote wills were not legally required to follow the principles of inheritance laid out in intestate cases. Individual men had the right to decide for themselves who would ultimately inherit their property. As we shall see later, will-writers did sometimes deviate sharply from these guidelines, but the majority seem to have adhered closely (though not always precisely) to the custom of leaving a double portion to the eldest son. Beyond that, New England men seem generally to have agreed to a system of partible inheritance, with both sons and daughters inheriting.

When these rules were followed, property ownership and control generally devolved upon men. Neither the widow's dower nor, for the most part, the daughter's right to inherit signified more than *access to* property. For widows, the law was clear that dower allowed for "use" only. For inheriting daughters who were married, the separate but inheritance-related principle of coverture applied. Under English common law, "feme covert" stipulated that married women had no right to own property — indeed, upon marriage, "the very being or legal existence of the woman is suspended." Personal property which a married daughter inherited from her father, either as dowry or as a post-mortem bequest, immediately became the legal possession of her husband, who could exert full powers of ownership over it. A married daughter who inherited land from her father retained title to the land, which her husband could not sell without her consent. On her husband's death such land became the property of her children, but during his life her husband was entitled to the use and profits of it, and his wife could not devise it to her children by will. The property of an inheriting daughter who was single seems to have been held "for improvement" for her until she was married, when it became her dowry.

This is not to say that women did not benefit when they inherited property. A sizeable inheritance could provide a woman with a materially better life; if single or widowed, inheriting women enjoyed better chances for an economically advantageous marriage or remarriage. But inheritance did not normally bring women the independent economic power it brought men.

The rules of inheritance were not always followed, however. In some cases, individual men decided not to conform to customary practices; instead, they employed one of several legal devices to give much larger shares of their estates to their wives or daughters, many times for disposal at their own discretion. Occasionally, the magistrates themselves allowed the estate to be distributed in some other fashion. Or, most commonly, the absence of male heirs in families made conformity impossible. In all three exceptions to inheritance customs, but most particularly the last, the women who stood to benefit economically also assumed a position of unusual vulnerability. They, and in many instances their daughters, became prime targets for witchcraft accusations. . . .

A substantial majority of New England's accused females were women without brothers, women with daughters but no sons, or women in marriages with no children at all. Of the 267 accused females, enough is known about 158 to identify them as either having or not having brothers or sons to inherit: only sixty-two of the 158 (39 percent) did, whereas ninety-six (61 percent) did not. More striking, *once accused,* women without brothers or sons were even more likely than women with brothers or sons to be tried, convicted, and executed: women from families without male heirs made up 64 percent of the females prosecuted, 76 percent of those who were found guilty, and 89 percent of those who were executed.

These figures must be read with care, however, for two reasons. First, eighteen of the sixty-two accused females who *had* brothers or sons to inherit were themselves daughters and granddaughters of women who did not. If these eighteen females, most of whom were young women or girls, were accused because their neighbors believed that their mothers and grandmothers passed their witchcraft on to them, then they form a somewhat ambiguous group. Since they all had brothers to inherit, it would be inaccurate to exclude them from this category, yet including them understates the extent to which inheritance-related concerns were at issue in witchcraft accusations. At the same time, the large number of cases in which the fertility and mortality patterns of witches' families are unknown (109 of the 267 accused females in New England) makes it impossible to assess precisely the proportion of women among the accused who did not have brothers or sons. . . .

Numbers alone, however, do not tell the whole story. More remains to be said about what happened to these inheriting or potentially inheriting women, both before and after they were accused of witchcraft.

It was not unusual for women in families without male heirs to be accused of witchcraft shortly after the deaths of fathers, husbands, brothers, or sons. Katherine Harrison, Susanna Martin, Joan Penney, and Martha Carrier all exemplify this pattern. So too does elderly Ann Hibbens of Boston, whose execution in 1656 seems to have had a profound enough effect on some of her peers to influence the outcome of subsequent trials for years to come. Hibbens had three sons from her first marriage, all of whom lived in England; but she had no children by her husband William Hibbens, with whom she had come to Massachusetts in the 1630s. William died in 1654; Ann was brought to trial two years later. Although her husband's will has not survived, he apparently left a substantial portion (if not all) of his property directly to her: when she wrote her own will shortly before her execution, Ann Hibbens was in full possession of a £344 estate, most of which she bequeathed to her sons in England.

Similarly, less than two years elapsed between the death of Gloucester's William Vinson and the imprisonment of his widow Rachel in 1692. Two children, a son and a daughter, had been born to the marriage, but the son had died in 1675. Though William Vinson had had four sons (and three daughters) by a previous marriage, the sons were all dead by 1683. In his will, which he wrote in 1684, before he was certain that his last son had been lost at sea, William left his whole £180 estate to Rachel for her life, stipulating that she could sell part of the lands and cattle if she found herself in need of resources. After Rachel's death, "in Case" his son John "be Living and returne home agayne," William said, most of the estate was to be divided between John and their daughter Abigail. If John did not return, both shares were to be Abigail's.

Bridget Oliver (later Bridget Bishop) was brought into court on witchcraft charges less than a year after the death of her husband Thomas Oliver in 1679. He had died intestate, but since the estate was worth less than £40 after debts, and since Bridget had a child to raise, the court gave her all but £3 of it during her lifetime, stipulating that she could sell a ten-acre lot "towards paying the debts and her present supply." Twenty shillings went to each of her husband's two sons by his first wife, and twenty shillings to the Olivers' twelve-year-old daughter Christian, the only child of their marriage.

In other cases, many years passed between the death of the crucial male relative and the moment when a formal witchcraft complaint was filed. Twenty years had elapsed, for instance, between the death of Adam Hawkes of Lynn and the arrest of his widow and daughter. Adam had died in 1672, at the age of sixty-four, just three years after his marriage to the much-younger Sarah Hooper and less than a year after the birth of their daughter Sarah. He had died without leaving a will, but his two principal heirs — his widow and his son John from his first marriage — said they were aware of Adam's intentions concerning his £772 estate. The magistrates responsible for distributing Adam's property took their word, allowing "certain articles of agreement" between the two to form the basis of the distribution. As a result, the elder Sarah came into full possession of 188 acres of land and one-third of Adam's movable property. Her daughter was awarded £90, "to be paid five pounds every two years until forty pounds is paid, and the fifty pounds at age or marriage."

It was just about the time young Sarah was due to receive her marriage portion that she and her mother, then Sarah Wardwell, were accused of witchcraft. Named with them as witches were the elder Sarah's second husband, carpenter Samuel Wardwell, their nineteen-year-old daughter Mercy, and the mother, two sisters, and brother of Francis Johnson, the younger Sarah's husband-to-be. It is not clear whether when Sarah Hawkes became Sarah Johnson she received the balance of her inheritance, but £36 of Sarah and Samuel Wardwell's property was seized by the authorities in 1692. Massachusetts passed a law at the height of the Salem outbreak providing attainder for "conjuration, witchcraft and dealing with evil and wicked spirits." Attainder meant the loss of civil, inheritance, and property rights for persons like Sarah Wardwell who had been sentenced to death. Not until 1711 was restitution made to Sarah Wardwell's children. . . .

Not all witches from families without male heirs were accused of conspiring with the Devil *after* they had come into their inheritances. On the contrary, some were accused prior to the death of the crucial male relative, many times before it was clear who would inherit. Eunice Cole was one of these women. Another was Martha Corey of Salem, who was accused of witchcraft in 1692 while her husband was still alive. Giles Corey had been married twice before and had several daughters by the time he married the widow Martha Rich, probably in the 1680s. With no sons to inherit, Giles's substantial land holdings would, his neighbors might have assumed, be passed on to his wife and daughters. Alice Parker, who may have been Giles's daughter from a former marriage, also came before the magistrates as a witch in 1692, as did Giles himself. Martha Corey and Alice Parker maintained their innocence and were hanged. Giles Corey, in an apparently futile attempt to preserve his whole estate for his heirs, refused to respond to the indictment. To force him to enter a plea, he was tortured: successively heavier weights were placed on his body until he was pressed to death.

What seems especially significant here is that most accused witches whose husbands were still alive were, like their counterparts who were widows and spinsters, over forty years of age — and therefore unlikely if not unable to produce male heirs. Indeed, the fact that witchcraft accusations were rarely taken seriously by the community until the accused stopped bearing children takes on a special meaning when it is juxtaposed with the anomalous position of inheriting women or potentially inheriting women in New England's social structure.

Witches in families without male heirs sometimes had been dispossessed of part or all of their inheritances before — sometimes long before — they were formally charged with witchcraft. Few of these women, however, accepted disinheritance with equanimity. Rather, like Susanna Martin, they took their battles to court, casting themselves in the role of public challengers to the system of male inheritance. In most instances, the authorities sided with their antagonists.

The experience of Rachel Clinton of Ipswich is instructive. As one of five daughters in line to inherit the "above £500" estate of their father, Richard Haffield, Rachel had been reduced to abject poverty at least eighteen years before she came before county magistrates in 1687 as a witch. Richard Haffield had bequeathed £30 to each of his daughters just before his death in 1639, but since Rachel was only ten at the time, and her sister Ruth only seven, he stipulated that their shares were to be paid "as they shall com to the age of sixteen yeares old." While he had not made other bequests, he made his wife Martha executrix, and so the unencumbered portions of the estate were legally at her disposal. In 1652, since Rachel and Ruth were still unmarried (Rachel was twenty-three at the time), local magistrates ordered Martha Haffield to pay one of her sons-in-law, Richard Coy, the £60 still due Rachel and Ruth, to "improve their legacy."

When Martha Haffield wrote her own will in 1662, six years before her death, she bequeathed the still-single Rachel the family farm, valued at £300, with the proviso that she share the income it produced with her sisters, Ruth (now Ruth White) and Martha Coy. The household goods were to be divided among the three. Martha had effectively disinherited her two oldest children (children of her husband's first marriage) with ten shillings apiece. This will, though legal, would never be honored. In 1666, the county court put the whole Haffield estate into the hands of Ruth's husband, Thomas White, whom they named as Martha Haffield's guardian and whom they empowered to "receive and recover her estate." They declared Martha Haffield "non compos mentis."

The issue that seems to have precipitated this court action was Rachel's marriage to Lawrence Clinton several months before. Lawrence was an indentured servant and fourteen years younger than his wife. Perhaps even more offensive to community standards, Rachel had purchased Lawrence's freedom for £21, with money she said her mother had given her. Once Thomas White had control of the Haffield estate, he immediately sued Lawrence's former master, Robert Cross, for return of the £21.

Several issues were raised in the almost four years of litigation that followed, but arguments focused on the legality of Rachel's access to and use of the money. Never explicitly mentioned by White, but clearly more important to him than the £21, was Rachel's sizeable inheritance. For Rachel, the stakes were obvious: "my brother [in-law] White . . . is a cheaten Rogue," she insisted, "and [he] goese about to undoe mee. He keeps my portion from me, and strives to git all that I have." The case was complicated by a number of factors, including Lawrence Clinton's desertion of his wife. White did at last gain full control of the Haffield estate, however, and retained it for the rest of his life.

Martha Haffield died in 1668. Shortly before, Rachel, then thirty-nine, had been forced to petition the court for relief, "being destitute of money and friends and skill in matters of Law." The house where she and her mother had lived, she said, had been sold by White, and its contents seized. Even her marriage portion, she averred, was still withheld from her "under pretence of emprovement." Giving up her attempt to claim her inheritance, she subsequently tried to make her estranged husband support her. Though the court made several halfhearted attempts to compel Lawrence to live with his wife, or at least to maintain her, by 1681 they had tired of the effort: "Rachel Clinton, desiring that her husband provide for her, was allowed 20 shillings," they declared, "she to demand no more of him." No doubt Rachel's adulterous involvement with other men influenced the court's decision, although Lawrence's sexual behavior had been even more flagrant. In 1677, Rachel had petitioned for, but had been denied, a divorce. When she appealed again in late 1681, it was granted her. From then on, she was a ward of the town. In 1687, and again in 1692, she was accused of malefic witchcraft. The second time she was tried and convicted. . . .

Aside from these many women who lived or had lived in families without male heirs, there were at least a dozen other witches who, despite the presence of brothers and sons, came into much larger shares of estates than their neighbors would have expected. In some cases, these women gained full control over the disposition of property. We know about these women because their fathers, husbands, or other relatives left wills, because the women themselves wrote wills, or because male relatives who felt cheated out of their customary shares fought in the courts for more favorable arrangements.

Grace Boulter of Hampton, one of several children of Richard Swain, is one of these women. Grace was accused of witchcraft in 1680, along with her thirty-two-year-old daughter, Mary Prescott. Twenty years earlier, in 1660, just prior to his removal to Nantucket, Grace's father had deeded a substantial portion of his Hampton property to her and her husband Nathaniel, some of which he gave directly to her.

Another witch in this group is Jane James of Marblehead, who left an estate at her death in 1669 which was valued at £85. While it is not clear how she came into possession of it, the property had not belonged to her husband Erasmus, who had died in 1660, though it did play a significant role in a controversy between her son and son-in-law over their rightful shares of both Erasmus's and Jane's estates. Between 1650 and her death in 1669, Jane was accused of witchcraft at least three times by her Marblehead neighbors.

A third woman, Margaret Scott of Rowley, had been left most of her husband Benjamin's small estate in 1671. The land and most of the cattle were hers only "dureing hir widowhood," but approximately one-third of the estate was "to be wholy hir owne." Margaret did not remarry. By the time she was executed as a witch in 1692, twenty-one years after her husband's death, she was seventy-five years old and little remained of the estate for the next generation to inherit.

In each of these last few cases, the women came into property through the decision of a father or husband. Only occasionally, however, do we find the courts putting property directly into the hands of women subsequently accused of witchcraft. Mary English's mother, Elinor Hollingworth, was one of these exceptions. In this situation, as in the others, the unusual decision of the magistrates can be attributed to the small size of the estate involved. These particular inheriting women were widows, usually with young children to support.

Looking back over the lives of these many women — most particularly those who did not have brothers or sons to inherit — we begin to understand the complexity of the economic dimension of New England witchcraft. Only rarely does the actual trial testimony indicate that economic power was even at issue. Nevertheless it is there, recurring with a telling persistence once we look beyond what was explicitly said about these women as witches. Inheritance disputes surface frequently enough in witchcraft cases, cropping up as part of the general context even when no direct link between the dispute and the charge is discernible, to suggest the fears that underlay most accusations. No matter how deeply entrenched the principle of male inheritance, no matter how carefully written the laws that protected it, it was impossible to insure that all families had male offspring. The women who stood to benefit from these demographic "accidents" account for most of New England's female witches.

The amount of property in question was not the crucial factor in the way these women were viewed or treated by their neighbors, however. Women of widely varying economic circumstances were vulnerable to accusation and even to conviction. Neither was there a direct line from accuser to material beneficiary of the accusation: others in the community did sometimes profit personally from the losses sustained by these women (Rachel Clinton's brother-in-law, Thomas White, comes to mind), but only rarely did the gain accrue to the accusers themselves. Indeed, occasionally there was no direct temporal connection: in some instances several decades passed between the creation of the key economic conditions and the charge of witchcraft; the charge in other cases even anticipated the development of those conditions.

Finally, inheriting or potentially inheriting women were vulnerable to witch-craft accusations not only during the Salem outbreak, but from the time of the first formal accusations in New England at least until the end of the century. Despite sketchy information on the lives of New England's early witches, it appears that Alice Young, Mary Johnson, Margaret Jones, Joan Carrington, and Mary Parsons, all of whom were executed in the late 1640s and early 1650s, were women without sons when the accusations were lodged. Elizabeth Godman, brought into court at least twice on witchcraft charges in the 1650s, had neither brothers nor sons. Decade by decade, the pattern continued. Only Antinomian and Quaker women, against whom accusations never generated much support, were, as a group, exempt from it.

The Salem outbreak created only a slight wrinkle in this established fabric of suspicion. If daughters, husbands, and sons of witches were more vulnerable to dan-ger in 1692 than they had been previously, they were mostly the daughters, hus-bands, and sons of inheriting or potentially inheriting women. As the outbreak spread, it drew into its orbit increasing numbers of women, "unlikely" witches in that they were married to well-off and influential men, but familiar figures to some of their neighbors nonetheless. What the impoverished Sarah Good had in common with Mary Phips, wife of Massachusetts's governor, was what Eunice Cole had in common with Katherine Harrison, and what Mehitabel Downing had in common with Ann Hibbens. However varied their backgrounds and economic positions, as women without brothers or women without sons, they stood in the way of the or-derly transmission of property from one generation of males to another.

※ *F U R T H E R   R E A D I N G*

Paul Boyer and Stephen Nissenbaum, *Salem Possessed* (1974)
Richard Godbeer, *The Devil's Dominion: Magic and Religion in Early New England* (1992)
Larry Gragg, *The Salem Witch Crisis* (1992)
Chadwick Hansen, *Witchcraft at Salem* (1969)
Joseph Klaits, *Servants of Satan: The Age of the Witch Hunt* (1985)
Christina Larner, *Enemies of God: The Witch-hunt in Scotland* (1981)
———, *Witchcraft and Religion* (1984)
Brian Levack, *The Witch-Hunt in Early Modern Europe* (1987)
Bernard Rosenthal, *Salem Story: Reading the Witch Trials of 1692* (1993)
Marion Starkey, *The Devil in Massachusetts* (1950)
Keith Thomas, *Religion and the Decline of Magic* (1971)
Richard Weisman, *Witchcraft, Magic, and Religion in 17th-Century Massachusetts* (1984)

The Impact
of the American Revolution

In many ways the American Revolution changed the course of history for the residents of what had been Britain's mainland North American colonies. In 1774 the settlers were colonials — subjects of a monarchy based thousands of miles across the Atlantic and participants in a traditional political system. Less than a decade later these successful revolutionaries, now Americans, were the founders of an independent republic and the first colonists in history to win their freedom and establish their own nation.

Such dramatic events, it could be argued, impinged primarily on men, not women. After all, men alone fought in the armies, voted in the new republic's elections, drafted state and national constitutions, and served in legislative bodies. Women traditionally did not take part in politics; their domain was the household, whereas the public world was defined exclusively as the men's arena. Did the revolution, then, affect women? If so, did it have different effects on black women than it did on white women? Or can the revolution be safely ignored by historians of women because it held so little meaning for their subjects?

❋ D O C U M E N T S

In March 1776, recognizing that the United States, which had already been at war with Britain for nearly a year, would soon declare independence, Abigail Adams wrote to her congressman husband, John, in Philadelphia, reminding him to "remember the ladies" in the nation's "new code of laws." She thus initiated the first known exchange in American history on the subject of women's rights. The Adamses' comments on the matter comprise the first set of documents. The second document dates from 1780: After the Americans had suffered one of their worst defeats of the war at Charleston, South Carolina, a Pennsylvanian named Esther DeBerdt Reed published a broadside, "The Sentiments of an American Woman," proposing a nationwide Ladies Association to contribute to the welfare of the troops. In the third document, dated many years after the revolution, Sarah Osborn, who had traveled with her husband and the American army, recalled her experiences when she applied for a government pension in 1837. The fourth document is Thomas Jefferson's laconic description of what happened to the slaves from his plantations who ran off to join the invading British forces in 1781.

Abigail and John Adams's "Remember the Ladies" Letters, 1776

Abigail Adams to John Adams:

Braintree March 31 1776

I long to hear that you have declared an independancy — and by the way in the new Code of Laws which I suppose it will be necessary for you to make I desire you would Remember the Ladies, and be more generous and favourable to them than your ancestors. Do not put such unlimited power into the hands of the Husbands. Remember all Men would be tyrants if they could. If perticuliar care and attention is not paid to the Laidies we are determined to foment a Rebelion, and will not hold ourselves bound by any Laws in which we have no voice, or Representation.

That your Sex are Naturally Tyrannical is a Truth so thoroughly established as to admit of no dispute, but such of you as wish to be happy willingly give up the harsh title of Master for the more tender and endearing one of Friend. Why then, not put it out of the power of the vicious and the Lawless to use us with cruelty and in-dignity with impunity. Men of Sense in all Ages abhor those customs which treat us only as the vassals of your Sex. Regard us then as Beings placed by providence under your protection and in immitation of the Supreem Being make use of that power only for our happiness.

John to Abigail:

Ap. 14. 1776

As to Declarations of Independency, be patient. Read our Privateering Laws, and our Commercial Laws. What signifies a Word.

As to your extraordinary Code of Laws, I cannot but laugh. We have been told that our Struggle has loosened the bands of Government every where. That Children and Apprentices were disobedient — that schools and Colledges were grown turbu-lent — that Indians slighted their Guardians and Negroes grew insolent to their Masters. But your Letter was the first Intimation that another Tribe more numerous and powerfull than all the rest were grown discontented. — This is rather too coarse a Compliment but you are so saucy, I wont blot it out.

Depend upon it, We know better than to repeal our Masculine systems. Altho they are in full Force, you know they are little more than Theory. We dare not exert our Power in its full Latitude. We are obliged to go fair, and softly, and in Practice you know We are the subjects. We have only the Name of Masters, and rather than give up this, which would compleatly subject Us to the Despotism of the Peticoat, I

Reprinted by permission of the publishers from *The Book of Abigail and John: Selected Letters of the Adams Family 1762–1784,* edited by L.H. Butterfield, Cambridge, Mass.: Harvard University Press, Copyright © 1975 by the Massachusetts Historical Society.

hope General Washington, and all our brave Heroes would fight. I am sure every good Politician would plot, as long as he would against Despotism, Empire, Monarchy, Aristocracy, Oligarchy, or Ochlocracy, — A fine Story indeed. I begin to think the Ministry as deep as they are wicked. After stirring up Tories, Landjobbers, Trimmers, Bigots, Canadians, Indians, Negroes, Hanoverians, Hessians, Russians, Irish Roman Catholicks, Scotch Renegadoes, at last they have stimulated the   to demand new Priviledges and threaten to rebell.

Abigail to John:

B[raintre]e May 7 1776

I can not say that I think you very generous to the Ladies, for whilst you are proclaiming peace and good will to Men, Emancipating all Nations, you insist upon retaining an absolute power over Wives. But you must remember that Arbitrary power is like most other things which are very hard, very liable to be broken — and notwithstanding all your wise Laws and Maxims we have it in our power not only to free our selves but to subdue our Masters, and without violence throw both your natural and legal authority at our feet —

> "Charm by accepting, by submitting sway
> Yet have our Humour most when we obey."

The Sentiments of an American Woman, 1780

On the commencement of actual war, the Women of America manifested a firm resolution to contribute as much as could depend on them, to the deliverance of their country. Animated by the purest patriotism, they are sensible of sorrow at this day, in not offering more than barren wishes for the success of so glorious a Revolution. They aspire to render themselves more really useful; and this sentiment is universal from the north to the south of the Thirteen United States. Our ambition is kindled by the fame of those heroines of antiquity, who have rendered their sex illustrious, and have proved to the universe, that, if the weakness of our Constitution, if opinion and manners did not forbid us to march to glory by the same paths as the Men, we should at least equal, and sometimes surpass them in our love for the public good. I glory in all that which my sex has done great and commendable. I call to mind with enthusiasm and with admiration, all those acts of courage, of constancy and patriotism, which history has transmitted to us: The people favoured by Heaven, preserved from destruction by the virtues, the zeal and the revolution of Deborah, of Judith, of Esther! The fortitude of the mother of the Macchabees, in giving up her sons to die before her eyes: Rome saved from the fury of a victorious enemy by the efforts of Volumnia, and other Roman Ladies: So many famous sieges where the Women have been seen forgeting the weakness of their sex, building new walls, digging trenches with their feeble hands, furnishing arms to their defenders, they themselves darting the missile weapons on the enemy, resigning the ornaments of their apparel, and their fortune, to fill the public treasury, and to hasten the deliverance of their country; burying themselves under its ruins; throwing themselves into the flames rather than submit to the disgrace of humiliation before a proud enemy.

Born for liberty, disdaining to bear the irons of a tyrannic Government, we associate ourselves to the grandeur of those Sovereigns, cherished and revered, who have held with so much splendour the scepter of the greatest States, The Batildas, the Elizabeths, the Maries, the Catharines, who have extended the empire of liberty, and contented to reign by sweetness and justice, have broken the chains of slavery, forged by tyrants in the times of ignorance and barbarity. The Spanish Women, do they not make, at this moment, the most patriotic sacrifices, to encrease the means of victory in the hands of their Sovereign. He is a friend to the French Nation. They are our allies. We call to mind, doubly interested, that it was a French Maid who kindled up amongst her fellow-citizens, the flame of patriotism buried under long misfortunes: It was the Maid of Orleans who drove from the kingdom of France the ancestors of those same British, whose odious yoke we have just shaken off; and whom it is necessary that we drive from this Continent.

But I must limit myself to the recollection of this small number of atchievements. Who knows if persons disposed to censure, and sometimes too severely with regard to us, may not disapprove our appearing acquainted even with the actions of which our sex boasts? We are at least certain, that he cannot be a good citizen who will not applaud our efforts for the relief of the armies which defend our lives, our possessions, our liberty? The situation of our soldiery has been represented to me; the evils inseparable from war, and the firm and generous spirit which has enabled them to support these. But it has been said, that they may apprehend, that, in the course of a long war, the view of their distresses may be lost, and their services be forgotten. Forgotten! never; I can answer in the name of all my sex. Brave Americans, your disinterestedness, your courage, and your constancy will always be dear to America, as long as she shall preserve her virtue.

We know that at a distance from the theatre of war, if we enjoy any tranquility, it is the fruit of your watchings, your labours, your dangers. If I live happy in the midst of my family; if my husband cultivates his field, and reaps his harvest in peace; if, surrounded with my children, I myself nourish the youngest, and press it to my bosom, without being affraid of seeing myself separated from it, by a ferocious enemy; if the house in which we dwell; if our barns, our orchards are safe at the present time from the hands of those incendiaries, it is to you that we owe it. And shall we hesitate to evidence to you our gratitude? Shall we hesitate to wear a cloathing more simple; hair dressed less elegant, while at the price of this small privation, we shall deserve your benedictions, Who, amongst us, will not renounce with the highest pleasure, those vain ornaments, when she shall consider that the valiant defenders of America will be able to draw some advantage from the money which she may have laid out in these; that they will be better defended from the rigours of the seasons, that after their painful toils, they will receive some extraordinary and unexpected relief; that these presents will perhaps be valued by them at a greater price, when they will have it in their power to say: *This is the offering of the Ladies.* The time is arrived to display the same sentiments which animated us at the beginning of the Revolution, when we renounced the use of teas, however agreeable to our taste, rather than receive them from our persecutors; when we made it appear to them that we placed former necessaries in the rank of superfluities, when our liberty was interested; when our republican and laborious hands spun the flax, prepared the linen intended for the use of our soldiers; when exiles and fugitives we supported with courage all the evils which are the concomitants of war. Let us not lose a moment; let us be engaged to offer the homage of our gratitude at the altar of military valour, and you, our brave deliverers, while mercenary slaves combat to cause you to share with them, the irons with which they are loaded, receive with a free hand our offering, the purest which can be presented to your virtue,

By an AMERICAN WOMAN
[Esther DeBerdt Reed]

Sarah Osborn's Narrative, 1837

That she was married to Aaron Osborn, who was a soldier during the Revolutionary War. That her first aquaintance with said Osborn commenced in Albany, in the state of New York, during the hard winter of 1780. That deponent then resided at the house of one John Willis, a blacksmith in said city. That said Osborn came down there from Fort Stanwix and went to work at the business of blacksmithing for said Willis and continued working at intervals for a period of perhaps two months. Said Osborn then informed deponent that he had first enlisted at Goshen in Orange County, New York. That he had been in the service for three years, deponent thinks, about one year of that time at Fort Stanwix, and that his time was out. And, under an assurance that he would go to Goshen with her, she married him at the house of said Willis during the time he was there as above mentioned, to wit, in January 1780. . . .

That after deponent had married said Osborn, he informed her that he was returned during the war, and that he desired deponent to go with him. Deponent declined until she was informed by Captain Gregg that her husband should be put on the commissary guard, and that she should have the means of conveyance either in a wagon or on horseback. That deponent then in the same winter season in sleighs accompanied her husband and the forces under command of Captain Gregg on the east side of the Hudson river to Fishkill, then crossed the river and went down to West Point. . . .

Deponent further says that she and her husband remained at West Point till the departure of the army for the South, a term of perhaps one year and a half, but she cannot be positive as to the length of time. While at West Point, deponent lived at Lieutenant Foot's, who kept a boardinghouse. Deponent was employed in washing and sewing for the soldiers. Her said husband was employed about the camp. . . .

When the army were about to leave West Point and go south, they crossed over the river to Robinson's Farms and remained there for a length of time to induce the belief, as deponent understood, that they were going to take up quarters there, whereas they recrossed the river in the nighttime into the Jerseys and traveled all night in a direct course for Philadelphia. Deponent was part of the time on horse-

Sarah Osborn, Narrative, 1837, in John Dann, ed., *The Revolution Remembered,* 1980, pp. 241–246, The University of Chicago Press.

back and part of the time in a wagon. Deponent's said husband was still serving as one of the commissary's guard. . . .

They continued their march to Philadelphia, deponent on horseback through the streets, and arrived at a place towards the Schuylkill where the British had burnt some houses, where they encamped for the afternoon and night. Being out of bread, deponent was employed in baking the afternoon and evening. Deponent recollects no females but Sergeant Lamberson's and Lieutenant Forman's wives and a colored woman by the name of Letta. The Quaker ladies who came round urged deponent to stay, but her husband said, "No, he could not leave her behind." Accordingly, next day they continued their march from day to day till they arrived at Baltimore, where deponent and her said husband and the forces under command of General Clinton, Captain Gregg, and several other officers, all of whom she does not recollect, embarked on board a vessel and sailed down the Chesapeake. There were several vessels along, and deponent was in the foremost. . . . They continued sail until they had got up the St. James River as far as the tide would carry them, about twelve miles from the mouth, and then landed, and the tide being spent, they had a fine time catching sea lobsters, which they ate.

They, however, marched immediately for a place called Williamsburg, as she thinks, deponent alternately on horseback and on foot. There arrived, they remained two days till the army all came in by land and then marched for Yorktown, or Little York as it was then called. The York troops were posted at the right, the Connecticut troops next, and the French to the left. In about one day or less than a day, they reached the place of encampment about one mile from Yorktown. Deponent was on foot and the other females above named and her said husband still on the commissary's guard. Deponent's attention was arrested by the appearance of a large plain between them and Yorktown and an entrenchment thrown up. She also saw a number of dead Negroes lying round their encampment, whom she understood the British had driven out of the town and left to starve, or were first starved and then thrown out. Deponent took her stand just back of the American tents, say about a mile from the town, and busied herself washing, mending, and cooking for the soldiers, in which she was assisted by the other females; some men washed their own clothing. She heard the roar of the artillery for a number of days, and the last night the Americans threw up entrenchments, it was a misty, foggy night, rather wet but not rainy. Every soldier threw up for himself, as she understood, and she afterwards saw and went into the entrenchments. Deponent's said husband was there throwing up entrenchments, and deponent cooked and carried in beef, and bread, and coffee (in a gallon pot) to the soldiers in the entrenchment.

On one occasion when deponent was thus employed carrying in provisions, she met General Washington, who asked her if she "was not afraid of the cannonballs?"

She replied, "No, the bullets would not cheat the gallows," that "It would not do for the men to fight and starve too."

They dug entrenchments nearer and nearer to Yorktown every night or two till the last. While digging that, the enemy fired very heavy till about nine o'clock next morning, then stopped, and the drums from the enemy beat excessively. . . .

All at once the officers hurrahed and swung their hats, and deponent asked them, "What is the matter now?"

One of them replied, "Are not you soldier enough to know what it means?"

Deponent replied, "No."

They then replied, "The British have surrendered."

Deponent, having provisions ready, carried the same down to the entrenchments that morning, and four of the soldiers whom she was in the habit of cooking for ate their breakfasts.

Deponent stood on one side of the road and the American officers upon the other side when the British officers came out of the town and rode up to the American officers and delivered up [their swords, which the deponent] thinks were returned again, and the British officers rode right on before the army, who marched out beating and playing a melancholy tune, their drums covered with black handkerchiefs and their fifes with black ribbands tied around them, into an old field and there grounded their arms and then returned into town again to await their destiny. . . .

On going into town, she noticed two dead Negroes lying by the market house. She had the curiosity to go into a large building that stood nearby, and there she noticed the cupboards smashed to pieces and china dishes and other ware strewed around upon the floor, and among the rest a pewter cover to a hot basin that had a handle on it. She picked it up, supposing it to belong to the British, but the governor came in and claimed it as his, but said he would have the name of giving it away as it was the last one of twelve that he could see, and accordingly presented it to deponent, and she afterwards brought it home with her to Orange County and sold it for old pewter, which she has a hundred times regretted.

Thomas Jefferson's Slaves Join the British, 1781

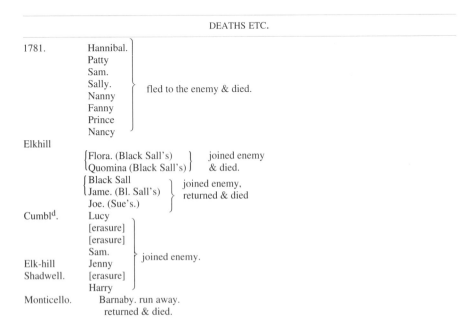

		DEATHS ETC.
1781.	Hannibal. Patty Sam. Sally. Nanny Fanny Prince Nancy	fled to the enemy & died.
Elkhill		
	Flora. (Black Sall's) Quomina (Black Sall's)	joined enemy & died.
	Black Sall Jame. (Bl. Sall's) Joe. (Sue's.)	joined enemy, returned & died
Cumbl^d.	Lucy [erasure] [erasure] Sam.	joined enemy.
Elk-hill Shadwell.	Jenny [erasure] Harry	
Monticello.	Barnaby. run away. returned & died.	

Elkhill.   York.
               Isabel.
               Jack.   } caught small pox
               Hanah's child.   from enemy & died.
               Phoebe's child

[note Judy & Nat of Elkhill, Will & Robin of Shadwell joined the enemy, but came back again & lived.
so did Isabel, Hannibal's daughter. aftwds given to A.S. Jefferson.]

Elk-hill   Branford
               Sue. Sue's daur.

                                   caught the camp
                                 } fever from the
                                   negroes who
Monticello   Old Jenny   returned: & died
Elk-hill   Phoebe (Sue's) } 1782
               Nanny (Tom's)

✳ *E S S A Y S*

In 1976, Joan Hoff of Indiana University posited that the effect of the American Revolution
on white women, if there could be said to be an effect, was chiefly negative. The war, she argued, brought few or no benefits to women, whose prewar situation was so circumscribed
that they could not take advantage of the opportunities that had opened up for their male contemporaries. After reading hundreds of women's and men's letters and diaries from the
period, however, Mary Beth Norton reached the opposite conclusion, contending in her 1980
book *Liberty's Daughters* that the revolution was, to a limited extent, "liberating" for white
women and for some black men and women as well. More recently, Jacqueline Jones, who
teaches history at Brandeis University, focused her attention on enslaved women and
concluded that for them the revolution had decidedly mixed results.

The Negative Impact of the American Revolution on White Women

JOAN HOFF

I will argue that certain types of female functions, leading either to the well-known
exploitation of working women or to the ornamental middle-class housewife of the
nineteenth century, were abetted by the American Revolution, although not caused
by it.

This occurred because the functional opportunities open to women between
1700 and 1800 were too limited to allow them to make the transition in attitudes
necessary to insure high status performance in the newly emerging nation. In other
words, before 1776 women did not participate enough in conflicts over land, religion, taxes, local politics, or commercial transactions. They simply had not come into
contact with enough worldly diversity to be prepared for a changing, pluralistic,

Excerpts from Joan Hoff-Wilson, "The Illusion of Change: Women and the American Revolution," in
Alfred Young, ed., *The American Revolution: Explorations in the History of American Radicalism,*
386–401, 419–431. Copyright 1976 by Northern Illinois University Press. Reprinted with permission of
the publisher.

modern society. Women of the postrevolutionary generation had little choice but to fill those low status functions prescribed by the small minority of American males who *were* prepared for modernization by enough diverse activities and experiences.

As a result, the American Revolution produced no significant benefits for American women. This same generalization can be made for other powerless groups in the colonies — native Americans, blacks, probably most propertyless white males, and indentured servants. Although these people together with women made up the vast majority of colonial population, they could not take advantage of the overthrow of British rule to better their own positions, as did the white, propertied males who controlled economics, politics, and culture. By no means did all members of these subordinate groups support the patriot cause, and those who did, even among whites, were not automatically accorded personal liberation when national liberation was won. This is a common phenomenon of revolution within subcultures which, because of sex, race, or other forms of discrimination or deprivation of the members, are not far enough along in the process toward modernization to express their dissatisfaction or frustration through effectively organized action.

Given the political and socioeconomic limitations of the American Revolution, this lack of positive societal change in the lives of women and other deprived colonials is to be expected. It is also not surprising that until recently most historians of the period have been content to concentrate their research efforts on the increased benefits of Lockean liberalism that accrued to a relatively small percent of all Americans and to ignore the increased sexism and racism exhibited by this privileged group both during and after the Revolution. They have also tended to ignore the various ways in which the experience of the Revolution either hastened or retarded certain long-term eighteenth-century trends already affecting women.

What has been called in England and Europe "the transformation of the female in bourgeois culture" also took place in America between 1700 and 1800. This process would have occurred with or without a declaration of independence from England. It produced a class of American bourgeoises who clearly resembled the group of middle-class women evident in England a century earlier. However, the changing societal conditions leading up to this transformation in American women were much more complex than they had been for seventeenth-century British women because of the unique roles, that is, functions, that colonial women had originally played in the settlement and development of the New World. The American Revolution was simply one event among many in this century-long process of change. It was a process that ultimately produced two distinct classes of women in the United States — those who worked to varying degrees exclusively in their homes and those who worked both inside and outside of their homes. . . .

It is true, however, for most of the period up to 1750 that conditions *out of necessity* increased the functional independence and importance of all women. By this I mean that much of the alleged freedom from sexism of colonial women was due to their initial numerical scarcity and the critical labor shortage in the New World throughout the seventeenth and eighteenth centuries. Such increased reproductive roles (economic as well as biological) reflected the logic of necessity and *not any fundamental change* in the sexist, patriarchal attitudes that had been transplanted from Europe. Based on two types of scarcity (sex and labor), which were not to last, these enhanced functions of colonial women diminished as the commercial and agricultural economy became more specialized and the population grew.

A gradual "embourgeoisement" of colonial culture accompanied this preindustrial trend toward modern capitalism. It limited the number of high status roles for eighteenth-century American women just as it had for seventeenth-century English and European women. Alice Clark, Margaret George, Natalie Zemon Davis, and Jane Abray have all argued convincingly that as socioeconomic capitalist organization takes place, it closes many opportunities normally open to women both inside and outside of the family unit in precapitalist times. The decline in the status of women that accompanied the appearance of bourgeois modernity in England, according to Margaret George, "was not merely a relative decline. Precapitalist woman was not simply relatively eclipsed by the great leap forward of the male achiever; she suffered rather, an absolute setback."

In the New World this process took longer but was no less debilitating. Before 1800 it was both complicated and hindered by the existence of a severe labor shortage and religious as well as secular exhortations against the sins of idleness and vanity. Thus, colonial conditions demanded that all able-bodied men, women, and children work, and so the ornamental, middle-class woman existed more in theory than in practice.

The labor shortage that plagued colonial America placed a premium on women's work inside and outside the home, particularly during the war-related periods of economic dislocation between 1750 and 1815. And there is no doubt that home industry was basic to American development both before and after 1776. It is also true that there was no sharp delineation between the economic needs of the community and the work carried on within the preindustrial family until after the middle of the eighteenth century. Woman's role as a household manager was a basic and integral part of the early political economy of the colonies. Hence she occupied a position of unprecedented importance and equality within the socioeconomic unit of the family.

As important as this function of women in the home was, from earliest colonial times, it nonetheless represented a division of labor based on sex-role stereotyping carried over from England. Men normally engaged in agricultural production; women engaged in domestic gardening and home manufacturing — only slave women worked in the fields. Even in those areas of Massachusetts and Pennsylvania that originally granted females allotments of land, the vestiges of this practice soon disappeared, and subsequent public divisions "simply denied the independent economic existence of women." While equality never extended outside the home in the colonial era, there was little likelihood that women felt useless or alienated because of the importance and demanding nature of their domestic responsibilities.

In the seventeenth and eighteenth centuries spinning and weaving were the primary types of home production for women and children (of both sexes). This economic function was considered so important that legal and moral sanctions were developed to insure it. For example, labor laws were passed, compulsory spinning schools were established "for the education of children of the poor," and women were told that their virtue could be measured in yards of yarn. So from the beginning there was a sex, and to a lesser degree a class and educational, bias built into colonial production of cloth, since no formal apprenticeship was required for learning the trade of spinning and weaving.

It has also been recognized that prerevolutionary boycotts of English goods after 1763 and later during the war increased the importance of female production of textiles both in the home and in the early piecework factory system. By mid-1776 in Philadelphia, for example, 4,000 women and children reportedly were spinning under the "putting out system" for local textile plants. . . .

American living standards fluctuated with the unequal prosperity that was especially related to wars. Those engaging in craft production and commerce were particularly hard hit after 1750, first by the deflation and depression following the French and Indian War (1754–1763), and then by the War for Independence. In fact, not only were the decades immediately preceding and following the American Revolution ones of economic dislocation, but the entire period between 1775 and 1815 has been characterized as one of "arrested social and economic development." These trends, combined with increased specialization, particularly with the appearance of a nascent factory system, "initiated a decline in the economic and social position of many sections of the artisan class." Thus with the exception of the innkeeping and tavern business, all of the other primary economic occupations of city women were negatively affected by the periodic fluctuations in the commercial economy between 1763 and 1812.

Women artisans and shopkeepers probably suffered most during times of economic crisis because of their greater difficulty in obtaining credit from merchants. Although research into their plight has been neglected, the documents are there — in the records of merchant houses showing women entrepreneurs paying their debts for goods and craft materials by transferring their own records of indebtedness, and in court records showing an increased number of single women, especially widows sued for their debts, or in public records of the increased number of bankrupt women who ended up on poor relief lists or in debtors' prisons or who were forced to become indentured servants or earn an independent living during hard times.

It was also a difficult time for household spinners and weavers, about whom a few more facts are known. First, this all-important economic function increasingly reflected class distinctions. In 1763 one British governor estimated that only the poor wore homespun clothes, while more affluent Americans bought English imports. Second, it was primarily poor women of the northern and middle colonies who engaged in spinning and weaving for pay (often in the form of credit rather than cash), while black slave women and white female indentured servants performed the same function in the South. Naturally women in all frontier areas had no recourse but to make their own clothing. Beginning with the first boycotts of British goods in the 1760s, women of all classes were urged to make and wear homespun. Several additional "manufactory houses" were established as early as 1764 in major cities specifically for the employment of poor women. Direct appeals to patriotism and virtue were used very successfully to get wealthier women to engage in arduous home-spinning drives, but probably only for short periods of time.

Thus all classes of women were actively recruited into domestic textile production by male patriots with such pleas as, "In this time of public distress you have each of you an opportunity not only to help to sustain your families, but likewise to call your mite into the treasury of the public good." They were further urged to "cease trifling their time away [and] prudently employ it in learning the use of the spinning wheel." Beyond any doubt the most well-known appeal was the widely reprinted 9 November 1767 statement of advice to the "Daughters of Liberty" which first appeared in the *Massachusetts Gazette*. It read in part:

> First then throw aside your high top knots of pride
> Wear none but your own country linen.
> Of economy boast. Let your pride be the most
> To show cloaths of your make and spinning.

Peak periods in prerevolutionary spinning and weaving were reached during every major boycott from 1765 to 1777. But the war and inflation proved disruptive. For example, we know that the United Company of Philadelphia for Promoting American Manufactures, which employed 500 of the City's 4,000 women and children spinning at home, expired between 1777 and 1787, when it was revived. The record of similar organizations elsewhere was equally erratic.

It is common for developing countries with a labor shortage to utilize technological means to meet production demands. After the war, the new republic proved no exception, as the inefficiency and insufficiency of household spinners became apparent. Ultimately the "putting out" system was replaced entirely by the factory that employed the same women and children who had formerly been household spinners. It took the entire first half of the nineteenth century before this process was completed, and when it was, it turned out to be at the expense of the social and economic status of female workers. . . .

Why didn't the experiences of the Revolution result in changing the political consciousness of women? Part of the answer lies in the socialized attitudes among female members of the revolutionary generation that set them apart from their male contemporaries. Their attitudes had been molded by the modernization trends encountered by most women in the course of the eighteenth century. Out of the necessity wrought by the struggle with England, women performed certain tasks that appeared revolutionary in nature, just as they had performed nonfamilial tasks out of necessity throughout the colonial period. But this seemingly revolutionary behavior is not necessarily proof of the acceptance of abstract revolutionary principles.

Despite their participation in greater economic specialization, despite their experiences with a slightly smaller conjugal household where power relations were changing, despite a limited expansion of the legal rights and somewhat improved educational opportunities for free, white women, the revolutionary generation of females were less prepared than most men for the modern implications of independence. Their distinctly different experiential level, combined with the intellectually and psychologically limiting impact of the Great Awakening and the Enlightenment on women, literally made it impossible for even the best educated females to understand the political intent or principles behind the inflated rhetoric of the revolutionary era. Words like virtue, veracity, morality, tyranny, and corruption were ultimately given public political meanings by male revolutionary leaders that were incomprehensible or, more likely, misunderstood by most women.

As the rhetoric of the revolution began to assume dynamic, emotional proportions, its obsession with "virtue" versus "corruption" struck a particularly responsive chord among literate women, as evidenced for example, in their patriotic statements as individuals and in groups when supporting the boycott of English goods between 1765 and 1774. While these statements are impressive both in number and intensity of feeling, it can be questioned whether the idea of taking "their country back on the path of virtue" and away from "the oppression of corrupt outside forces" was understood in the same way by female and male patriots, when even men of varying Whig persuasions could not agree on them. Virtue and morality for the vast majority of Americans, but particularly women, do not appear to have had the modernizing implications of pluralistic individualism, that is, of the "acceptance of diversity, the commitment to individual action in pursuit of individual goals, the conception of politics as an arena where these goals contest and the awareness of a national government which is at once the course of political power and the framework for an orderly clash of interest." These are characteristics of "modern man."

How does one prove such a generalization about attitudes behind the behavior of women during the Revolution? Few poor white and black women left records revealing how they felt about the war. Such women, whether Loyalists or patriots, conveyed their sentiments silently with their physical labor. Among the more articulate and educated women there is written testimony to at least an initial sense of pride and importance involved in their participation in the war effort. Thus a young Connecticut woman named Abigail Foote wrote in her diary in 1775 that carding two pounds of whole wool had made her feel "Nationly," while others recorded their contributions in similarly patriotic terms.

But the question remains: did their supportive actions prepare them to accept a vision of society anywhere near the version ultimately conveyed by James Madison's Federalist Number Ten in the fight over the Constitution of 1787? To date there is little evidence that this type of sophisticated political thought was present, either in the writings of women about the Revolution and its results or in the appeals made to them during or immediately following the war. From the popular 1767 statement of advice to the Daughters of Liberty to the 1787 one urging women to use "their influence over their husbands, brothers and sons to draw them from those dreams of liberty under a simple democratical form of government, which are so unfriendly to . . . order and decency," it is difficult to conclude that women were being prepared to understand the political ramifications of the Revolution.

The same lack of political astuteness appears to underlie even the least traditional and most overtly political activities of women, such as the fifty-one who signed the anti-tea declaration in Edenton, North Carolina, on 25 October 1774 (later immortalized in a London cartoon). The same could be said of the more than 500 Boston women who agreed on 31 January 1770 to support the radical male boycott of tea; of the Daughters of Liberty in general; and of the 1,600 Philadelphia women who raised 7,500 dollars in gold for the Continental Army. Even Mercy Otis Warren never perceived the modern political system that evolved from the Revolution. Instead she viewed the war and its aftermath as the "instrument of Providence that sparked a world movement, changing thought and habit of men to complete the divine plan for human happiness" largely through the practice of virtue.

Perhaps the most important aspect of the supportive activities among women for the patriot cause was the increase in class and social distinctions they symbolized. For example, it appears unlikely that poor white or black women joined Daughters of Liberty groups, actively boycotted English goods, or participated in any significant numbers in those associations of "Ladies of the highest rank and influence," who raised money and supplies for the Continental Army. On the contrary, it may well have been primarily "young female spinsters" from prominent families and well-to-do widows and wives who could afford the time or the luxury of such highly publicized activities. The vast majority, however, of middle-class female patriots (and, for that matter, Loyalists), whether single or married, performed such necessary volunteer roles as seamstresses, nurses, hostesses, and sometime spies, whenever the fighting shifted to their locales, without any undue fanfare or praise.

The same is true of poorer women, with one important difference: they had no choice. They had all they could do to survive, and although this did lead a few of them to become military heroines, they could not afford the luxury of either "disinterested patriotism" or the detached self-interest and indulgences that some of the richer women exhibited. The very poorest, particularly those in urban areas, had no resources to fall back on when confronted with the personal or economic traumas caused by the War for Independence. As noted above, this was especially evident in the case of women wage earners who, regardless of race or class, had apparently always received lower pay than free men or hired-out male slaves, and who had suffered severely from runaway inflation during the war. Women's services were more likely to be paid for in Continental currency than with specie. Fees for male "doctors," for example, according to one Maryland family account book, were made in specie payment after the middle of 1780, while midwives had to accept the depreciated Continental currency for a longer period of time. Thus, the American Revolution hastened the appearance of greater class-based activities among "daughters of the new republic," with poor women undertaking the least desirable tasks and suffering most from the inflationary spiral that plagued the whole country. It is easy to imagine the impact that inflation had on the rural and urban poor, but it even affected those middle- and upper middle-class women who were left at home to manage businesses, estates, plantations, or farms. Their activities often meant the difference between bankruptcy and solvency for male revolutionary leaders.

Probably the classic example of housewifely efficiency and economic shrewdness is found in Abigail's management of the Adams's family and farm during John's long absences. But in this respect Abigail Adams stands in direct contrast to the women in the lives of other leading revolutionaries like Jefferson, Madison, and Monroe — all of whom were bankrupt by public service in part because their wives were not as capable at land management as she was. This even proved true of the most outspoken of all revolutionary wives, Mercy Otis Warren. Numerous lesser well-known women, however, proved equal to the increased domestic responsibilities placed upon them. Only the utterly impoverished could not resort to the traditional colonial task of household manager.

As the months of fighting lengthened into years, more and more poverty-stricken women left home to join their husbands, lovers, fathers, or other male relatives in the army encampments. Once there, distinctions between traditional male and female roles broke down. While a certain number of free white and black slave women were needed to mend, wash, and cook for officers and care for the sick and wounded, most enlisted men and their women took care of themselves and fought beside each other on many occasions. Moreover, unlike the English, German, and French commanders, American military leaders were often morally offended or embarrassed by the presence of these unfortunate and destitute women, "their hair flying, their brows beady with the heat, their belongings slung over one sholder [sic], chattering and yelling in sluttish shrills as they went and spitting in the gutters."

This puritanical, hostile attitude on the part of patriot army officers toward such a common military phenomenon insured that camp followers of the American forces were less systematically provided for than those of foreign troops. Aside from its class overtones (after all Martha Washington, Catherine Greene, and Lucy Knox were accepted as respectable camp followers), it is difficult to explain this American attitude, except that in the prevailing righteous rhetoric of the Revolution and of later historians these women were misrepresented as little better than prostitutes. In reality they were the inarticulate, invisible poor whose story remains to be told from existing pension records based on oral testimony. At any rate there is pathos and irony in the well-preserved image of Martha Washington, who visited her husband at Valley Forge during the disastrous winter of 1777–1778, copying routine military communiques and presiding over a sewing circle of other officers' wives, while the scores of combat-hardened women, who died along with their enlisted men, have been conveniently forgotten.

These camp followers, as well as the women who stayed at home, complained about their plight privately and publicly, and on occasion they rioted and looted for foodstuffs. Women rioting for bread or other staples never became a significant or even a particularly common revolutionary act in the New World as it did in Europe, largely because of the absence of any long-term, abject poverty on the part of even the poorest colonials. The most likely exception to this generalization came during the extreme inflation that accompanied the war. Then there is indeed some evidence of what can be called popular price control activity by groups of women who had a definite sense of what were fair or legitimate marketing practices. At the moment we have concrete evidence of only a half-dozen seemingly spontaneous instances of "a corps of female infantry" attacking merchants. Other examples will probably be discovered as more serious research into the "moral economy of the crowd" is undertaken by American historians.

What is interesting about the few known cases is that the women involved in some of them did not simply appear to be destitute camp followers passing through towns stripping the dead and looting at random for food. A few at least were women "with Silk gownes on," who were offering to buy sugar, salt, flour, or coffee for a reasonable price with Continental currency. When a certain merchant insisted on payment with specie or with an unreasonable amount of paper money, the women then, and only then, insisted on "taking" his goods at their price. These appear, therefore, to be isolated examples of collective behavior by women where there was, at the least, a very strongly held cultural notion of a moral economy.

Nevertheless, there is still no clear indication of an appreciable change in the political consciousness of such women. Perhaps it was because even the poorest who took part in popular price control actions primarily did so, like the Citoyennes Républicaines Révolutionnaires during the French Revolution, out of an immediate concern for feeding themselves and their children and not for feminist reasons growing out of their age-old economic plight as women in a patriarchal society. In addition, except for camp followers and female vagabonds, the principal concern of most members of this generation of primarily rural women remained the home and their functions there. During the home-spinning drives and during the war when their men were away, their domestic and agricultural duties became all the more demanding, but not consciousness-raising. . . .

Lastly, in explaining the failure of the equalitarian ideals of the Revolution to bear even limited fruit for women, one must analyze the narrow ideological parameters of even those few who advocated women's rights, persons such as Abigail Adams, Judith Sargent Murray, Elizabeth Southgate Bowne, Elizabeth Drinker, and Mercy Otis Warren.

These women . . . were not feminists. Like most of the better organized, but no less unsuccessful Républicaines of France, they seldom, if ever, aspired to complete equality with men except in terms of education. Moreover, none challenged the institution of marriage or defined themselves "as other than mothers and potential mothers." They simply could not conceive of a society whose standards were not set by male, patriarchal institutions, nor should they be expected to have done so. Instead of demanding equal rights, the most articulate and politically conscious American women of this generation asked at most for privileges and at least for favors — not for an absolute expansion of their legal or political functions, which they considered beyond their proper womanly sphere. Man was indeed the measure of equality to these women, and given their societal conditioning, such status was beyond their conception of themselves as individuals.

Ironically it is this same sense of their "proper sphere" that explains why the most educated female patriots did not feel obliged to organize to demand more from the Founding Fathers. It is usually overlooked that in the famous letter of 31 March 1776 where Abigail asks John Adams to "Remember the Ladies," she justified this mild request for "more generous and favourable" treatment on the grounds that married women were then subjected to the "unlimited power" of their husbands. She was not asking him for the right to vote, only for some legal protection of wives from abuses under common law practices. "Regard us then," she pleaded with her husband, "as Beings placed by providence under your protection and in imitation of the Supreme Being make use of that power only for our happiness." Despite an earlier statement in this letter about the "Ladies" being "determined to foment a Rebellion" and refusing to be "bound by any Laws in which we have no voice, or Representation," Abigail Adams was not in any sense demanding legal, let alone political or individual, equality with men at the beginning of the American Revolution. If anything, her concept of the separateness of the two different spheres in which men and women operated was accentuated by the war and the subsequent trials of the new republic between 1776 and 1800.

This idea that men and women existed in two separate spheres or orbits was commonly accepted in the last half of the eighteenth century as one of the natural laws of the universe. While European Enlightenment theories adhered strictly to the inferiority of the natural sphere that women occupied, in colonial America they were tacitly challenged and modified by experience — as were so many other aspects of natural law doctrines. On the other hand, the degree to which educated, upper-class women in particular thought that their sphere of activity was in fact equal, and the degree to which it actually was accorded such status by the male-dominated culture, is all important. Historians have tended to place greater emphasis on the former rather than the latter, with misleading results about the importance of the roles played by both colonial and revolutionary women.

It is true that Abigail Adams was an extremely independent-minded person who firmly criticized books by foreign authors who subordinated the female sphere to that of the male. Writing to her sister Elizabeth Shaw Peabody in 1799, she said that "I will never consent to have our sex considered in an inferior point of light. Let each planet shine in their own orbit, God and nature designed it so — if man is Lord, woman is *Lordess* — that is what I contend for." Thus, when her husband was away she deemed it was within her proper sphere to act as head of the household on all matters, including the decision to have her children inoculated against smallpox without his permission. At the same time, however, she always deferred to his ambitions and his inherent superiority, because the equality of their two separate orbits did not make them equal as individuals. In general Abigail Adams and other women of her class accepted the notion that while they were mentally equal to men their sphere of activity was entirely private in nature, except on those occasions when they substituted for their absent husbands. "Government of States and Kingdoms, tho' God knows badly enough managed," she asserted in 1796, "I am willing should be solely administered by the lords of creation. I should contend for Domestic Government, and think that best administered by the female." Such a strong belief in equal, but separate, spheres is indeed admirable for the times, but it should not be confused with feminism. . . .

Only unusual male feminists like Thomas Paine asked that women be accorded "the sweets of public esteem" and "an equal right to praise." It was Paine — not the female patriots — who also took advantage of American revolutionary conditions to attack the institution of marriage. Later, in the 1790s, only a few isolated women in the United States supported Mary Wollstonecraft's demand for the right to public as well as private fulfillment on the grounds that "private duties are never properly fulfilled unless the understanding enlarges the heart and that public virtue is only an aggregate of private. . . ." Her criticisms of marital bondage were never seriously considered by American women in this postrevolutionary decade.

The reasons for this unresponsiveness to the feminism of both Paine and Wollstonecraft are complex, for it was not only opposed by the sexist Founding Fathers, but by most women. Again we must ask — why?

The physical and mental hardships that most women had endured during the war continued to varying degrees in the economic dislocation that followed in its wake. Sheer personal survival, not rising social or material expectations, dominated the thinking and activities of lower and even some middle- and upper-class women. Probably more important, the few well-educated American women, fortunate to have the leisure to reflect, clearly realized the discrepancy that had occurred between the theory and practice of virtue in the course of the war and its aftermath. While it was discouraging for them to view the corruption of morals of the society at large and particularly among men in public life, they could take some satisfaction in the greater consistency between the theory and practice of virtue in their own private lives. Such postrevolutionary women found their familial duties and homosocial relationships untainted by the corruption of public life. They considered themselves most fortunate and they *were*, compared to their nineteenth-century descendants, who had to pay a much higher price for similar virtuous consistency and spiritual purity.

It was natural, therefore, for the educated among this generation to express disillusionment with politics, as they saw republican principles corrupted or distorted, and then to enter a stage of relative quiescence that marked the beginning of the transitional period between their war-related activities and a later generation of female reformers who emerged in the 1830s. They cannot be held responsible for not realizing the full extent of the potentially debilitating features of their withdrawal to the safety of modern domesticity — where virtue becomes its own punishment instead of reward.

A final factor that helps to explain the absence of feminism in the behavior of women during the Revolution and in their attitudes afterward is related to the demographic changes that were taking place within the family unit between 1760 and 1800. Middle- and upper-class women were increasingly subjected to foreign and domestic literature stressing standards of femininity that had not inhibited the conduct of their colonial ancestors. While the rhetoric of this new literature was that of the Enlightenment, its message was that of romantic love, glamorized dependence, idealized motherhood, and sentimentalized children within the ever-narrowing realm of family life. At poorer levels of society a new family pattern was emerging as parental control broke down, and ultimately these two trends would merge, leaving all women in lower status domestic roles than they had once occupied.

In general it appears that the American Revolution retarded those societal conditions that had given colonial women their unique function and status in society, while it promoted those that were leading toward the gradual "embourgeoisement" of late eighteenth-century women. By 1800 their economic and legal privileges were curtailed; their recent revolutionary activity minimized or simply ignored; their future interest in politics discouraged; and their domestic roles extolled, but increasingly limited.

Moreover, at the highest *and* lowest levels of society this revolutionary generation of women was left with misleading assumptions: certain educated women believing strongly in the hope that immediate improvement for themselves and their children would come with educational reform, and some lower-class women believing that improvement would come through work in the "manufactories." Both admitted, according to Mercy Otis Warren, that their "appointed subordination" to men was natural, if for no other reason than "for the sake of Order in Families." Neither could be expected to anticipate that this notion would limit their participation in, and understanding of, an emerging modern nation because the actual (as opposed to idealized) value accorded their postrevolutionary activities was not yet apparent.

A few, like Priscilla Mason, the valedictorian of the 1793 graduating class of the Young Ladies' Academy of Philadelphia, might demand an equal education with men and exhort women to break out of their traditional sphere, but most ended up agreeing with Eliza Southgate Bowne when she concluded her defense of education for women by saying: "I believe I must give up all pretension to *profundity*, for

I am much more at home in my female character." And the dominant male leadership of the 1790s could not have agreed more.

For women, the American Revolution was over before it ever began. Their "disinterested" patriotism (or disloyalty, as the case may be) was accorded identical treatment by male revolutionaries following the war: conscious neglect of female rights combined with subtle educational and economic exploitation. The end result was increased loss of function and authentic status for all women whether they were on or under the proverbial pedestal.

The Positive Impact of the American Revolution on White Women

MARY BETH NORTON

Women could hardly have remained aloof from the events of the 1760s and early 1770s even had they so desired, for, like male Americans, they witnessed the escalating violence of the prerevolutionary decade. Into their letters and diary entries — which had previously been devoted exclusively to private affairs — crept descriptions of Stamp Act riots and "Rejoicings" at the law's repeal, accounts of solemn fast-day observances, and reports of crowd actions aimed at silencing dissidents. The young Boston shopkeeper Betsy Cuming, for instance, was visiting a sick friend one day in 1769 when she heard "a voilint Skreeming Kill him Kill him" and looked out the window to see John Mein, a printer whose publications had enraged the radicals, being chased by a large crowd armed with sticks and guns. Later that evening Betsy watched "ful a thousand Man & boys" dragging around the city "a Kart [on which] a Man was Exibited as . . . in a Gore of Blod." At first Betsy believed Mein had been caught, but she then learned that the victim was an unfortunate customs informer who had fallen into the crowd's hands after Mein made a successful escape.

Betsy herself confronted an angry group of Bostonians only a few weeks later. She and her sister Anne had just unpacked a new shipment of English goods when "the Comitey wated" on them, accusing them of violating the nonimportation agreement. "I told them we have never antred into eney agreement not to import for it was verry trifling owr Business," Betsy explained to her friend and financial backer Elizabeth Murray Smith. She charged the committeemen with trying "to inger two industrious Girls who ware Striving in an honest way to Git there Bread," resolutely ignoring their threat to publish her name in the newspaper as an enemy to America. In the end, Betsy and Anne discovered, the publicity "Spirits up our Friends to Purchess from us," and they informed Mrs. Smith that they ended the year with "mor custom then before."

Despite their bravado the Cuming sisters had learned an important political lesson: persons with their conservative beliefs were no longer welcome in Massachusetts. As a result, they emigrated to Nova Scotia when the British army evacuated

From *Liberty's Daughters: The Revolutionary Experience of American Women, 1750–1800*, by Mary Beth Norton. Copyright © 1980 by Mary Beth Norton. Reprinted with permission of HarperCollins Publishers, Inc.

Boston in 1776. Patriot women, too, learned lessons of partisanship. Instead of being the targets of crowds, they actively participated in them. They marched in ritual processions, harassed female loyalists, and, during the war, seized essential supplies from merchants whom they believed to be monopolistic hoarders. In addition, they prepared food for militia musters and, in the early days of September 1774 — when the New England militia gathered in Cambridge in response to a false rumor that British troops were mounting an attack on the populace — they were reported by one observer to have "surpassed the Men for Eagerness & Spirit in the Defense of Liberty by Arms." As he rode along the road to Boston, he recounted later, he saw "at every house Women & Children making Cartridges, running Bullets, making Wallets, baking Biscuit, crying & bemoaning & at the same time animating their Husbands & Sons to fight for their Liberties, tho' not knowing whether they should ever see them again."

The activism of female patriots found particular expression in their support of the colonial boycott of tea and other items taxed by the Townshend Act of 1767. Male leaders recognized that they needed women's cooperation to ensure that Americans would comply with the request to forgo the use of tea and luxury goods until the act was repealed. Accordingly, newspaper essays urged women to participate in the boycott, and American editors frequently praised those females who refused to drink foreign Bohea tea, substituting instead coffee or local herbal teas. . . .

In a marked departure from the tradition of feminine noninvolvement in public affairs, women occasionally formalized their agreements not to purchase or consume imported tea. Most notably, the *Boston Evening Post* reported in February 1770 that more than three hundred "Mistresses of Families" had promised to "totally abstain" from the use of tea, "Sickness excepted." Their statement showed that they understood the meaning of their acts: the women spoke of their desire to "save this abused Country from Ruin and Slavery" at a time when their "invaluable Rights and Privileges are attacked in an unconstitutional and most alarming Manner." In the South, groups of women went even further by associating themselves generally with nonimportation policies, not confining their attention to the tea issue alone. The meeting satirized in the famous British cartoon of the so-called Edenton Ladies' Tea Party fell into this category. The agreement signed in October 1774 by fifty-one female North Carolinians — among them two sisters and a cousin of Hannah Johnston Iredell — did not mention tea. Instead, the women declared their "sincere adherence" to the resolves of the provincial congress and proclaimed it their "duty" to do "every thing as far as lies in our power" to support the "publick good."

This apparently simple statement had unprecedented implications. The Edenton women were not only asserting their right to acquiesce in political measures, but they were also taking upon themselves a "duty" to work for the common good. Never before had female Americans formally shouldered the responsibility of a public role, never before had they claimed a voice — even a compliant one — in public policy. Accordingly, the Edenton statement marked an important turning point in American women's political perceptions, signaling the start of a process through which they would eventually come to regard themselves as participants in the polity rather than as females with purely private concerns.

Yet the North Carolina meeting and the change it embodied aroused amusement among men. The same tongue-in-cheek attitude evident in the satirical drawing of the grotesque "Ladies" was voiced by the Englishman Arthur Iredell in a letter to his emigrant brother James. He had read about the Edenton agreement in the newspapers, Arthur wrote, inquiring whether his sister-in-law Hannah's relatives were involved in the protest. "Is there a Female Congress at Edenton too?" he continued. "I hope not," for "Ladies . . . have ever, since the Amazonian Era, been esteemed the most formidable Enemies." If they choose to attack men, "each wound They give is Mortal. . . . The more we strive to conquer them, the more are Conquerd!"

Iredell thus transformed a serious political gesture that must have been full of meaning for the participants into an occasion for a traditional reference to women's covert power over men. Like many of his male contemporaries, he dismissed the first stirrings of political awareness among American women as a joke, refusing to recognize the ways in which their concept of their role was changing. In an Englishman, such blindness was understandable, but the similar failure of perception among American men must be attributed to a resolute insistence that females remain in their proper place. The male leaders of the boycott movement needed feminine cooperation, but they wanted to set the limits of women's activism. They did not expect, or approve, signs of feminine autonomy.

Nowhere was this made clearer than in a well-known exchange between Abigail and John Adams. . . . Abigail asked her husband in March 1776 to ensure that the new nation's legal code included protection for wives against the "Naturally Tyrannical" tendencies of their spouses. In reply John declared, "I cannot but laugh" at "your extraordinary Code of Laws." Falling back upon the same cliché employed by Arthur Iredell, he commented, "[O]ur Masculine systems . . . are little more than Theory. . . . In Practice you know We are the subjects. We have only the Name of Masters." Adams, like Iredell, failed to come to terms with the implications of the issues raised by the growing interest in politics among colonial women. He could deal with his wife's display of independent thought only by refusing to take it seriously.

American men's inability to perceive the alterations that were occurring in their womenfolk's self-conceptions was undoubtedly heightened by the superficially conventional character of feminine contributions to the protest movement. Women participating in the boycott simply made different decisions about what items to purchase and consume; they did not move beyond the boundaries of the feminine sphere. Likewise, when colonial leaders began to emphasize the importance of producing homespun as a substitute for English cloth, they did not ask women to take on an "unfeminine" task: quite the contrary, for spinning was the very role symbolic of femininity itself. But once the context had changed, so too did women's understanding of the meaning of their traditional tasks. . . .

The first months of 1769 brought an explosion in the newspaper coverage of women's activities, especially in New England. Stories about spinning bees, which had been both rare and relegated to back pages, suddenly became numerous and prominently featured. The *Boston Evening Post,* which carried only one previous account of female domestic industry, printed twenty-eight articles on the subject between May and December 1769, and devoted most of its front page on May 29 to an enumeration of these examples of female patriotism. The editor prefaced his extensive treatment of women's endeavors with an enthusiastic assessment of their significance: "[T]he industry and frugality of American ladies must exalt their character in the Eyes of the World and serve to show how greatly they are contributing to bring about the political salvation of a whole Continent."

It is impossible to know whether the increased coverage of spinning bees in 1769 indicated that women's activities expanded at precisely that time, or whether the more lengthy, detailed, and numerous stories merely represented the printers' new interest in such efforts. But one fact is unquestionable: the ritualized gatherings attended by women often termed Daughters of Liberty carried vital symbolic meaning both to the participants and to the editors who reported their accomplishments.

The meetings, or at least the descriptions of them, fell into a uniform pattern. Early in the morning, a group of eminently respectable young ladies (sometimes as many as one hundred, but normally twenty to forty), all of them dressed in homespun, would meet at the home of the local minister. There they would spend the day at their wheels, all the while engaging in enlightening conversation. When they stopped to eat, they had "American produce prepared which was more agreeable to them than any foreign Dainties and Delicacies," and, of course, they drank local herbal tea. At nightfall, they would present their output to the clergyman, who might then deliver a sermon on an appropriate theme. For example, the Reverend Jedidiah Jewell, of Rowley, Massachusetts, preached from Romans 12:2, "Not slothful in business, fervent in spirit, serving the Lord," and the Reverend John Cleaveland of Ipswich told the seventy-seven spinners gathered at his house, "[T]he women might recover to this country the full and free enjoyment of all our rights, properties and privileges (which is more than the men have been able to do)" by consuming only American produce and manufacturing their own clothes.

The entire community became involved in the women's activities. Large numbers of spectators — Ezra Stiles estimated that six hundred persons watched the bee held at his house in 1769 — encouraged the spinners in their work, supplied them with appropriate American foodstuffs, and sometimes provided entertainment. The occasional adoption of a match format, in which the women competed against each other in quality and quantity, must have further spurred their industry. And they must have gloried in being the center of attention, if only for the day. In reporting a Long Island spinning bee, the *Boston Evening Post* captured the spirit of the occasion with an expression of hope that "the ladies, while they vie with each other in skill and industry in their profitable employment, may vie with the men in contributing to the preservation and prosperity of their country and equally share in the honor of it."

"Equally share in the honor of it": the idea must have been exceedingly attractive to any eighteenth-century American woman raised in an environment that had previously devalued both her and her domestic sphere. Those involved in the home manufacture movement therefore took great pride in their newfound status, demonstrating that fact unequivocally when satirical essayists cast aspersions on their character.

Late in 1767, "Mr. Squibo" of Boston joked that the spinners were so patriotic they consumed only "New-England Rum . . . the principal and almost only manufacture of this country." Shortly thereafter, "A Young American" hinted that women discussed only "such triffling subjects as Dress, Scandal and Detraction" during their spinning bees. Three female Bostonians responded angrily to both

letters, which they declared had "scandalously insulted" American women. Denying that gossip engrossed their thoughts or that rum filled their glasses, they pronounced themselves so committed to the patriot cause that they would even endure
the unmerited ridicule of "the little wits and foplings of the present day" in order to
continue their efforts. "Inferior in abusive sarcasm, in personal invective, in low
wit, we glory to be," they concluded; "but inferior in veracity, honesty, sincerity,
love of virtue, of liberty and of our country, we would not willingly be to any." Significantly, the Bostonians made a special point of noting that women had been "addressed as persons of consequence, in the present economical regulations." They
thereby revealed the novelty and importance of that designation in their own minds.
Having become established as "persons of consequence" in American society,
women would not relinquish that position without a fight.

The formal spinning groups had a value more symbolic than real. They do not
seem to have met regularly, and in most cases their output appears to have been donated to the clergyman for his personal use. The women might not even have consistently called themselves Daughters of Liberty, for many newspaper accounts did
not employ that phrase at all. But if the actual production of homespun did not motivate the meetings, they were nonetheless purposeful. The public attention focused
on organized spinning bees helped to dramatize the pleas for industry and frugality
in colonial households, making a political statement comparable to men's ostenta-
tious wearing of homespun on public occasions during the same years. The spinning
bees were ideological showcases: they were intended to convince American women
that they could render essential contributions to the struggle against Britain, and to
encourage them to engage in increased cloth production in the privacy of their own
homes. Sometimes the newspaper accounts made this instructional function quite
explicit. The fact that many of the participants came from "as *good families* as any
in town," one editor remarked, showed that "it was no longer a disgrace for one of
our fair sex to be catched at a spinning wheel." . . .

Wives of ardent patriots and loyalists alike were left alone for varying lengths
of time while their spouses served in the army or, in the case of loyalists, took
refuge behind the British lines. Although women could stay with their soldier husbands and earn their own keep by serving as army cooks, nurses, or laundresses,
most did not find this an attractive alternative. Life in the military camps was hard,
and army commanders, while recognizing that female laborers did essential work,
tended to regard them as a hindrance rather than an asset. Only in rare cases — such
as the time when the laundresses attached to General Anthony Wayne's regiment
staged a strike in order to ensure that they would be adequately paid — were camp
followers able to ameliorate their living and working conditions. Consequently,
most women who joined the army probably did so from necessity, lacking any other
means of support during their husbands' absence.

At least, though, patriot women had a choice. For the most part, loyalists were
not so fortunate. From the day they and their spouses revealed their loyalty to the
Crown, their fate was sealed. Like other eighteenth-century women, their lives had
focused on their homes, but because of their political beliefs they lost not only those
homes but also most of their possessions, and they had to flee to alien lands as well.
Understandably, they often had difficulty coping with their problems. Only those
women who had had some experience beyond the household prior to the war were

able to manage their affairs in exile in England, Canada, or the West Indies with more than a modicum of success.

Female loyalists' claims petitions are particularly notable because the women frequently commented on their lack of a network of friends and relatives. The laments convey a sense of an entire familiar world that had been irretrievably lost. Many women submitted claims after the deadline, each giving a similar reason in her request for special consideration: there had been "no person to advise her how to proceed," she "was destitute of advice and Assistance," or "she had nobody to advise with & that she did not know how to do it." Even when some of a woman loyalist's friends were also exiles her situation was little better; as one southerner pointed out to the claims commission, "[T]hose Friends and Acquaintances to whom under other circumstances she could look up to for comfort and Assistance are equally involved in the Calamities which overwhelm" her. . . .

The importance of friendship networks and a familiar environment for women left alone is further confirmed when the focus shifts from widowed loyalists to the patriots who called themselves temporary widows — those women whose husbands had joined the American army. In contrast to the distressed, disconsolate refugee loyalists, who often complained of their inability to deal effectively with their difficulties, patriot women who managed the family property in the absence of their menfolk tended to find the experience a positive one. Although they had to shoulder a myriad of new responsibilities, they did so within a well-known and fully understood context: that of their own households. Accordingly, aided by friends and relatives, they gained a new sense of confidence in themselves and their abilities as they learned to handle aspects of the family affairs that had previously fallen solely within their husbands' purview. And the men, in turn, developed a new appreciation of their wives' contributions to the family's welfare. . . .

Patriot men found it difficult to avoid service in the militia or the Continental Army. They accordingly had to leave their wives behind to take charge of their affairs for months or years at a time. Most sets of wartime correspondence that survive today come from the families of officers or congressmen — in other words, from those patriots of some wealth or prominence who also tended to experience the longest separations — but the scattered evidence available for couples of lesser standing suggests that the same process was at work in poor, middling, and well-to-do households alike. As the months and years passed, women became more expert in their handling of business matters and their husbands simultaneously more accustomed to relying on their judgment.

A standard pattern emerges from the sequences of letters, some of which will shortly be examined in greater detail. Initially, the absent husband instructed his wife to depend upon male friends and relatives for advice and assistance. In 1776, for example, Edward Hand, a Pennsylvania officer, told his wife, Kitty, to have one neighbor invest money for her and to ask another to estimate the value of two horses he had sent home for sale. Women, for their part, hesitated to venture into new areas. "In some particulars I have been really puzzled how to act," a South Carolinian informed her spouse, a private soldier; and in 1777 Esther Reed, asking Joseph whether she should plant some flax, explained, "[A]s I am not famous for making good Bargains in things out of my Sphere I shall put it off as long as possible, in hopes you may be at home before it is too late."

But as time went on, women learned more about the family's finances while at the same time their husbands' knowledge became increasingly outdated and remote. Accordingly, whereas men's letters early in the war were filled with specific orders, later correspondence typically contained statements like these: "I Can't give any Other Directions About Home more than what I have Done but must Leave all to your good Management" (1779); "Apply [the money] to such as you think proper" (1780); draw on a neighbor for "any Sums you may choose, for providing things necessary & comfortable for yourself & the little Folks & Family for the approaching Season, in doing which I am sure you will use the greatest discretion" (1779). By the same token, women's letters showed their increasing familiarity with business and their willingness to act independently of their husbands' directions. . . .

The diary of the Philadelphian Sally Logan Fisher provides an especially illuminating example of this process. Thomas Fisher was among the Quakers arrested and sent into exile in Virginia by the patriots just prior to the British conquest of Philadelphia in September 1777. Then nearly eight months pregnant with her daughter Hannah, Sally at first found "this fiery triall" almost more than she could bear. Nine days after the men had been forcibly carried off, she commented, "I feel forlorn & desolate, & the World appears like a dreary Desart, almost without any visible protecting Hand to gaurd us from the ravenous Wolves & Lions that prowl about for prey." Sally became so depressed that she failed to write in her diary for several weeks, and when she resumed her daily entries in mid-October she observed, "[N]o future Days however calm & tranquil they may prove, can ever make me forget my misery at this time."

Soon thereafter, though, Mrs. Fisher became too busy to be able to allow herself the luxury of debilitating depression. A long entry on November 1 reflected her changed role in its detailed attention to household financial affairs and at the same time signaled the end of her period of incapacitating despair. "I have to think & provide every thing for my Family, at a time when it is so difficult to provide anything, at almost any price, & cares of many kinds to engage my attention," she wrote revealingly. After Hannah's birth six days later Sally remarked, "[I have] been enabled to bear up thro' every triall & difficulty far beyond what I could have expected." Although in succeeding months she continued to lament Tommy's absence, her later reflections differed significantly from her first reaction to her situation. Instead of dwelling upon her despondency, Sally wrote of "the fond, the delightfull Hope" that her husband would return to love her as before. "Oh my beloved, how Ardently, how tenderly how Affectionately, I feel myself thine," she effused in February 1778, describing "the anxiety I feel for thee, the longing desire to be with thee, & the impatience I feel to tell thee I am all thy own" — but not indicating any sense of an inability to cope with problems in his absence. When Tommy returned in late April 1778, she welcomed him gladly, but she did not revert completely to her former role of ignorance about monetary matters. Her diary subsequently noted several consultations with him about household finances, a subject they had not discussed before his exile.

Although Mary Bartlett, the wife of a New Hampshire congressman, left no similar record of her feelings about her husband's extended stays in Philadelphia during the war, she nevertheless subtly disclosed the fact that her role had undergone a comparable change. When Josiah Bartlett first went to Congress in the fall of 1775, he told Mary he hoped she would have "no Great trouble about my out Door affairs," and he continued to write to her about "my farming Business." In 1776 she accepted his terminology, reporting on "Your farming business," but during Josiah's second stint in Congress in 1778 that phrase became "our farming business" in her letters. No longer was the farm simply "his": she had now invested too much effort in it for that. The distinction between male and female spheres she had once accepted without question had been blurred by her own experience.

Although Josiah Bartlett's persistent use of "my farm" implies that he did not recognize the way in which his wife's role had altered, other patriot men separated from their spouses for long periods revealed changing attitudes toward their womenfolk in their correspondence. The differences are especially apparent in the case of a New Englander, Timothy Pickering, because he began with a severely limited conception of his wife's capability. . . .

Pickering adopted a patronizing tone in his early letters to his wife, Rebecca White. In November 1775, before their marriage, he told her he wanted to "instruct" her and went on to quote the same poem other Americans cited in discussions of children's education: " 'Tis a 'Delightful task to rear the tender thought, / To teach the fair idea how to shoot.' " Like a father teaching a daughter, he encouraged her to write to him, saying, "[F]requent writing will improve your hand." Unremarkably, Pickering's condescension continued during the early years of their marriage, after he had joined the Continental Army's quartermaster corps. When he sent home a lame horse in June 1777, he told her to consult male friends "for advice and direction" in caring for it, then apologized for asking her to undertake a task that was "entirely out of [her] sphere." Even his praise contained an evident patronizing note. "Your conduct in domestic affairs gives me the highest satisfaction," he told her in July 1778, spoiling it by adding, "even if you had done wrong I could not find fault; because I know in every action you aim at the best good of our little family: and knowing this: it would be cruel and unreasonable to blame you." In other words, he was telling her she would be judged on the basis of her intentions, not her actual performance, because he feared she could not meet the higher standard.

For the Pickerings matters changed in October 1780 after Rebecca acted as Timothy's agent in a complex arrangement for the repayment of a debt. "I am very glad you made me fully acquainted with it," she told him. "It is a satisfaction to me to pa[r]take of any thing that gives you Concern. I know my Dear you would make me happy in telling me any thing that had a tendency to make you so." After the successful resolution of the debt problem and her verbalization of her desire to assist him with their financial affairs, Timothy began to rely more heavily upon her. When the family rented a farm in 1782, she ably shouldered the responsibility for managing it despite her fears of "not being acquainted with farming business." Five years later, after they had moved to the frontier community of Wilkes-Barre, Pennsylvania, and Timothy's post required him to be in Philadelphia, she not only supervised the building of their new house but also oversaw the harvest, all the while nursing their newest baby. Timothy continued to apologize for the burdens he was placing on her (as well he should have), but he no longer mentioned her "sphere." Rebecca Pickering, like Mary Bartlett before her, began to speak in her letters of "our business" and "our crops." Timothy had already revealed his new attitude as early as August 1783: "This war which has so often & long separated us, has taught me how to value you," he told her then. . . .

The war dissolved some of the distinctions between masculine and feminine traits. Women who would previously have risked criticism if they abandoned their "natural" feminine timidity now found themselves praised for doing just that. The line between male and female behavior, once apparently so impenetrable, became less well defined. It by no means disappeared, but requisite adjustments to wartime conditions brought a new recognition of the fact that traditional sex roles did not provide adequate guidelines for conduct under all circumstances. When Betsy Ambler Brent looked back on her youth from the perspective of 1810, she observed, "[N]ecessity taught us to use exertions which our girls of the present day know nothing of. We Were forced to industry to appear genteely, to study Manners to supply the place of Education, and to endeavor by amiable and agreeable conduct to make amends for the loss of fortune."

The realization that they had been equally affected by the war led some women to expect equal treatment thereafter and, on occasion, to apply to their own circumstances the general principles promulgated by the revolutionaries. "I have Don as much to Carrey on the warr as meney that Sett Now at ye healm of government & No Notice taken of me," complained the New Jersey widow Rachel Wells as she protested to the Continental Congress in 1786 about a technicality that deprived her of interest payments on the money she had invested in state bonds during the war. "If she did not fight She throw in all her mite which bought ye Sogers food & Clothing & Let them have Blankets," she explained, asking only for the "justice" due her. "Others gits their Intrust & why then a poor old widow be put of[f]?" Mrs. Wells asked. "Now gentlemen is this Liberty?"

Mary Willing Byrd's social standing was much higher than that of Rachel Wells, but she advanced a similar argument when she contended in 1781 that Virginia had treated her unfairly. She claimed the right to redress of grievances "as a female, as the parent of eight children, as a virtuous citizen, as a friend to my Country, and as a person, who never violated the laws of her Country." Byrd's recital of her qualifications was peculiarly feminine in its attention to her sex and her role as a parent (no man would have included such items on a list describing himself), but it was also sexless in its references to her patriotism and her character as a "virtuous citizen." In developing the implications of the latter term, Byrd arrived at her most important point. "I have paid my taxes and have not been Personally, or Virtually represented," she observed. "My property is taken from me and I have no redress."

The echoes of revolutionary ideology were deliberate. Mary Byrd wanted the men she addressed to think about the issue of her status as a woman, and she adopted the revolutionaries' own language in order to make her point. The same tactic was employed by Abigail Adams in her most famous exchange with her husband.

In March 1776, after admonishing John to "Remember the Ladies" and to offer them legal protection from "the unlimited power" of their husbands, Abigail issued a warning in terms that John must have found exceedingly familiar. "If perticular care and attention is not paid to the Laidies," Abigail declared, "we are determined to foment a Rebellion, and will not hold ourselves bound by any Laws in which we have no voice, or Representation." On one level, she was speaking tongue-in-cheek; she did not mean her husband to take the threat seriously. Yet she chose to make a significant observation about women's inferior legal status by putting a standard argument to new use and by applying to the position of women striking phraseology previously employed only in the male world of politics. Like Mary Willing Byrd, Abigail Adams thus demonstrated an unusual sensitivity to the possible egalitarian resonances of revolutionary ideology and showed an awareness of implications that seem to have escaped the notice of American men.

The Mixed Legacy of the American Revolution for Black Women

JACQUELINE JONES

For the historian, race, as a socially defined category of human relationships, should constitute a central consideration in exploring the self-evident truths of this country's past. More specifically, during the era of the American Revolution, the status of all black women differed in fundamental ways from the status of all white women. Together, slave women and men endured the agony of bondage, and together blacks, both enslaved and free, struggled to form families that eventually served as the foundation of a distinctive Afro-American culture. The military conflict between loyalists and rebels intensified physical hardship among blacks, while the ensuing social and economic turmoil afforded some of their race the opportunities for a basic kind of freedom that white women and men — for all their rhetoric about the evils of tyranny — already enjoyed. Therefore, any discussion of the war's impact on American women must first highlight racial factors before dealing with issues related to class, regional, ethnic, and religious diversity in the late eighteenth-century population.

Yet within the confines of the slave system, and within the boundaries of their own households and communities, black women shouldered burdens that set them apart from their menfolk. In the period from 1750 to 1800, the nature and extent of these burdens varied according to whether a woman was African- or American-born; whether she lived in the North or South, in a town or rural area; whether she toiled in the swampy South Carolina lowcountry or on a Virginia wheat farm. This is not to suggest that black women suffered more than black men under the oppressive weight of the racial caste system, only that gender considerations played a significant role in shaping the task assignments parceled out to blacks by slaveholders, and in shaping the way blacks structured relationships among themselves. . . .

The ordeal of black women as wives, mothers, and workers encapsulates all the ironies and tensions that marked the history of slavery during the era of the American Revolution. In their efforts to create and preserve a viable family life, these women sought to balance caution and daring, fear and hope, as they reacted to the peculiar matrix of individual circumstances. Regardless of their work and family status in Boston, on a small farm in Pennsylvania, on George Washington's plantation, or in the South Carolina lowcountry, they saw freedom through the prism of family life. Consequently they perceived this revolutionary idea in ways fundamentally

---

Jacqueline Jones, "Race, Sex, and Self-Evident Truths: The Status of Slave Women during the Era of the American Revolution," in *Women in the Age of the American Revolution,* edited by Ronald Hoffman and Peter J. Albert, pp. 296–98, 324–34 (Charlottesville: Virginia 1989). Used by permission of the University Press of Virginia.

different from the white men who tried to claim the War for Independence as their own, and from the white women who remained so awkwardly suspended between their racial prerogatives on the one hand and gender and class liabilities on the other. Caught in the crossfire of sexual and racial oppression, black women contributed to the definition of liberation in these turbulent times. Indeed, through their modest everyday struggles, these wives and mothers offered a vision of freedom that was, by virtue of its consistency and fairness, more enduring than the one articulated so eloquently by the Founding Fathers. . . .

The political unrest and wartime devastation that marked the Revolutionary era brought into focus all the contradictions implicit in the emerging democratic republic of slaveholders and their allies. Masters found themselves confronted by their own demands for liberty and reacted accordingly, either by manumitting their slaves or by fighting ever more tenaciously to enforce black subordination. These conflicting impulses among the white elite helped to shape the experiences of black women during this period of upheaval, but so too did the economic transformations wrought by armed conflict and incipient nation-building. For their part, slaves seized the initiative whenever an opportune moment presented itself and fought their own battles for self-determination as field hands, refugees, and liberators of their own kin. Finally, black women's family responsibilities as wives and mothers remained constant even as the Revolution gave their productive abilities a new political significance. . . .

For the bulk of slave women located on southern plantations, the war entailed both physical suffering and great latitude for personal action. Forced to make do with less in the way of food, clothing, and other basic supplies, white southerners considered the daily needs of their slaves to be a low priority (especially after 1778, when fighting engulfed the region). At least some whites fulfilled the prediction of the patriot who railed against runaway slave men seeking protection from the British: "The aged, the infirm, the women and children, are still to remain the property of the masters, masters who will be provoked to severity, should part of their slaves desert them." Untold numbers of slave women felt the wrath of "an enraged and injured people" desperate to keep the upper hand at home as well as on the battlefield.

The women who remained with their masters gave whites cause enough for alarm. Thomas Pinckney's depleted South Carolina plantation consisted primarily of mothers and children in 1779, but they proved no more tractable than the male slaves who had already deserted; according to the white man, the slave women "pay no attention" to the overseer. Residing on another estate, Pinckney's mother commiserated with him, noting that she had lost control over her servants, "for they all do now as they please everywhere." As the war raged near her North Carolina estate in 1781, another mistress complained bitterly about the insolent Sarah: "She never came near me till after repeated messages yesterday to come and Iron a few clothes. . . . She made shift to creep here and then was very impudent." Such recalcitrance could provoke some whites to violence, others to reluctant indulgence. A Baltimore slaveholder urged his overseer not to upset the slave Ruth, or "she will run off, for she is an arch bitch."

Slaveholders might try to brutalize, cajole, or bribe black women into submission, but they could not escape the fact that they needed every available worker. The estimated 55,000 slaves who absconded, and many others pressed into service by the colonists and British alike, left some areas of the South bereft of field hands and thus devastated by food shortages. Planters who sought to institute a system of household cloth production reserved the positions of spinners and weavers for black women and girls, a sexual division of labor shaped in part by the now critical lack of male laborers. The rebels were not about to let gender considerations interfere with their exploitation of black labor in this time of crisis, and southern states often sought to buy, hire, or impress slaves of both sexes for use on public works projects. For example, in 1780 the Board of Trade of Virginia purchased twenty-six blacks (among them three women) to work in its tanneries, ironworks, boatyards, and army hospitals. The intense demand for unskilled labor during the war, exacerbated by a temporary halt in the foreign slave trade, endangered the well-being of free blacks, as well as slave women. In 1778 Ann Driggus of North Carolina suffered a beating at the hands of two men who then kidnapped four of her children in order to sell them.

Increased demands on their productive energies, combined with the confusion produced by wartime, prompted slave women to seek safety with the enemies of their master, whether rebel or loyalist. According to Gerald W. Mullin and other historians, family ties assumed even greater significance as a source of motivation among runaways, compared to the colonial period, perhaps reflecting more favorable conditions for flight and for beginning a new life elsewhere with kinfolk. Moreover, Mary Beth Norton has suggested that "although a majority of runaways were male, women apparently sought freedom in greater numbers [that is, proportion] during the war than in peacetime." Evidence from scattered sources reveals that up to a third of all wartime refugees were female, compared to the 10 percent or so of runaways listed in colonial newspapers who were female. Panic-stricken, patriot law-enforcement officials condemned to hard labor, executed, or sold to the West Indies those women and men who failed in their bid for freedom.

Benjamin Quarles has estimated that 5,000 black men served in the patriot armed forces, including the Continental army and navy, and state militias. This figure includes slaves who deserted their loyalist owners to fight with the rebels, and free blacks (almost all in the North) who volunteered for duty. But a far larger number of blacks perceived their best interests to lie with the British, a conviction no doubt encouraged early on by Virginia's royal governor Lord Dunmore, who in 1775 promised to liberate all the slaves of patriots who joined his army. As a slaveholder, Dunmore promoted policies that reflected the opportunistic attitude of the British toward blacks in general; they were considered worthy of decent treatment only insofar as they furthered the king's cause as soldiers, manual laborers, or insurgents who deprived the colonists of much needed labor. According to Sylvia Frey, British authorities showed little inclination to offer refuge to the slaves of loyalists. Dunmore himself refused sanctuary to runaways whom he could not readily use in his current military campaigns.

As might be expected, few slave women found a haven behind British lines. Army camps along the coast of Virginia were crowded and disease-ridden, with black people of both sexes and all ages suffering from exposure, hunger, and smallpox. The grisly image of a child seeking nourishment from the breast of its dead mother on Gwynne Island in 1776 conveys the bitter reality of black life — and death — in refugee camps. The image itself is also a reminder of the unique forms of oppression that impelled slave women to flee their owners' plantations and the lack of concern for their plight among officials on either side of the conflict. Few white women had cause to risk so much during the war. . . .

The black people evacuated with British troops after the war faced an uncertain future indeed. At least 15,000 black women and men left the country aboard British ships that sailed from Savannah, Charleston, and New York; some were self-defined loyalists, others served loyalist masters, and still others hoped to benefit from British efforts to deprive their conquerors of personal property. The wide range of experiences that awaited individual women — a lifetime of slavery in the West Indies; a struggle to survive in the fledgling British colony of Sierra Leone; or a new beginning of health, safety, and freedom in Nova Scotia — mirrored the crosscurrents of hardship and liberation that characterized the status of slave women during the Revolutionary War.

Thus the black fight for independence proceeded apace, whenever formerly compliant slave women suddenly turned "sassy" and defiant or abandoned their master's household, either to cast their lot with the British or slip as self-freed persons into the anonymity of urban life. A more formal (though no less difficult) route to freedom lay through the state courts and legislatures and through the efforts of free blacks to buy and then emancipate their own kin. . . .

Within three decades of the war's end, all of the northern states had provided for emancipation, although some enacted gradual provisions that left thousands of blacks in slavery for years to come. For example, according to New York's law of 1799, the daughters born to slave women after that date were to be bound (like indentured servants or apprentices) to the mother's master for twenty-five years, sons for twenty-eight years. . . . Two points are relevant to this issue: first, the most far-reaching antislavery legislation was enacted by northerners, who had the least to lose financially from their altruism; and second, the burden of transition from a slave to free black population fell most heavily on mothers whose offspring perpetuated the system of bondage. . . .

Regardless of how they obtained their freedom, black women shared common goals: to consolidate family members, keep their households intact, and provide for the material welfare of dependents. . . . Many newly freed blacks (and runaways) from the upper South and rural areas migrated to northern towns. This movement gradually produced an unbalanced urban sex ratio in favor of women (the reverse of the colonial pattern), probably because single women found it easier to support a family in the city than on the countryside. . . . Although they might now labor for wages, the vast majority continued to perform the same services they had for whites under slavery — cooking, washing clothes, cleaning, serving, and tending white children. The fact of freedom did not affect the racial caste system as it related to the social division of labor.

In the 1780s and 1790s, free and slave women together actively participated in the creation of an "institutional core" for Afro-American life — the formation of churches, schools, and benevolent societies separate and distinct from those of whites, blending an African heritage with American political realities. Although several historians have described in detail the emergence of black organized religion after the war, the role of women in that story remains untold. . . .

During these years the exhilaration of freedom experienced by some black women contrasted mightily with the plight of many more who remained condemned to slavery. . . . Masters fully appreciated a self-replenishing labor force, but their efforts each year to grow as much cotton as humanly possible worked to the detriment of childbearing females. Most white men did not fully comprehend the connection between overwork and high miscarriage and infant mortality rates; the result was untold pain and grief for slave mothers. As the institution of bondage renewed itself, so too did the drive for hegemony among ambitious men on the make as well as among the sons of Revolutionary-era slaveholders — a drive that held sacred the tenet of private property (no matter what its form) and eventually provoked a war far bloodier than the rebellion of 1776. While their free sisters kept alive the spirit of Afro-American community autonomy, black mothers and wives in the Cotton South would continue to eat the bitter fruit borne of a white man's political and economic revolution. . . .

❋ F U R T H E R   R E A D I N G

Ruth H. Bloch, "American Feminine Ideals in Transition: The Rise of the Moral Mother, 1785–1815," *Feminist Studies*, IV, No. 2 (June 1978), 100–126

———, "The Gendered Meanings of Virtue in Revolutionary America," *Signs*, XIII (1987), 37–58

Richard and Joy Buel, *The Way of Duty: A Woman and Her Family in Revolutionary America* (1984)

Nancy Cott, "Divorce and the Changing Status of Women in Massachusetts," *William and Mary Quarterly*, 3rd Ser., XXXIII (1976), 586–614

Linda Grant DePauw and Conover Hunt, *"Remember the Ladies": Women in America 1750–1815* (1976)

Edith Gelles, *Portia: The World of Abigail Adams* (1992)

Joan R. Gundersen, "Independence, Citizenship, and the American Revolution," *Signs*, XIII (1987), 59–77

Ronald Hoffman and Peter Albert, eds., *Women in the Age of the American Revolution* (1989)

Linda K. Kerber, *Women of the Republic* (1980)

Barbara Lacey, "Women in the Era of the American Revolution: The Case of Norwich, Connecticut," *New England Quarterly*, LIII (1980), 527–543

Jan Lewis, "The Republican Wife: Virtue and Seduction in the Early Republic," *William and Mary Quarterly*, 3rd Ser., XLIV (1987), 689–721

Mary Beth Norton, "Eighteenth-Century American Women in Peace and War: The Case of the Loyalists," *William and Mary Quarterly*, 3rd Ser., XXXIII (1976), 386–409

CHAPTER
5

The Cult of Domesticity

If one concept seems essential to understanding the circumstances of middle-class white women in nineteenth-century America, that concept is "the cult of domesticity," the phrase historians have coined to describe the ideology, advanced in thousands of publications over many decades, of woman's place in society. Woman's proper sphere was the home, commentators agreed; females were uniquely suited to raise children, care for the needs of their menfolk, and devote their lives to creating a nurturing home environment. Women were inherently more pious, gentle, instinctive, and submissive than men, it was argued; therefore, they had no place in the world outside the home. It was believed that women should concentrate their energies on running their households, not on seeking to enter the world of men by agitating for the vote or for other modes of participation in public life. This ideal was so pervasive that it affected other races and classes of women as well as the white, middle-class women it primarily targeted.

Yet the cult of domesticity, seemingly confining, subverted its own intent. If women were so uniquely suited to caring for young children, some contended, then they should do so as teachers in schools as well as in their own homes. If women were naturally religious, then they should join foreign missions and work in domestic charitable organizations. If their lives and roles were so different from those of men, then, logically, they could form close, long-lasting relationships with other women — relationships that another era might deem "lesbian."

Ever since the dimensions of the cult of domesticity and its inherent ambiguities were first explored by historians, they have been arguing over where to place the emphasis — on the limitations of domestic ideology, or on the opportunities it opened to creative and innovative women who understood how to turn its tenets to their advantage. That question is by no means resolved, nor has the meaning of domesticity for females who were neither white nor middle class been fully analyzed.

❋ DOCUMENTS

In 1850, Lydia H. Sigourney, one of the most popular female authors of the nineteenth century, published a book entitled *Whisper to a Bride,* which included the first document in this chapter, a sentimental discourse on "Home." Five years earlier, *Godey's Lady's Book,* the most widely read women's magazine of the time, printed the second document, a statement on the importance of the mother's role, probably written by the magazine's editor, Sarah Josepha Hale. One of the many middle-class women who made up the audience for such magazines and books was Sarah Alden Ripley, who frequently exchanged letters with her female relatives and friends; the third document consists of several extracts from her correspondence. The fourth and fifth documents trace the growing impact of the cult of domesticity on the Indians of the southeastern United States: The Indian agent Benjamin Hawkins recounted a 1796 conversation with some Creek women, and the Council of the Cherokee Nation adopted laws designed to bring tribal practices more fully into accordance with white Americans' ideas of womanhood while still retaining some Cherokee customs.

Lydia H. Sigourney's "Home," 1850

Home! — sweet word and musical! — keytone of the heart, at whose melody, as by the harp of Orpheus, all the trees in its garden are moved, holy word! refuge from sadness, and despair, best type of that eternal rest, for which we look, when the journey of life is ended!

Home, — blessed spot! — for which the sick yearn, and the stranger sigheth, among people of a strange speech, where none taketh him by the hand, who seeth casements glimmer through the evening storm, and firesides sparkle, — but not for him! . . .

Blessed Bride, — thou art about to enter this sanctuary, and to become a priestess at its altar. When thy foot first presseth its threshold, ask in thy secret soul, wisdom from above, to make the place of thy rest, fair and holy.

Bring with thee the perennial flowers of a pure affection; and however humble may be thine abode, beautify it by neatness, and order, and the ministries of love. Desire that it shall be thine own, and choose not to dwell under the roof of another, that thou mayest avoid care.

In the thronged hotel, a married man hath not his true pre-eminence. At the table of another, he misseth the honor that belongeth unto the head of a household. He is subordinate, and may not show that hospitality which God commendeth.

For his sake, therefore, acquaint thyself with the knowledge that appertaineth unto a wife and a housekeeper. If thou art deficient in this knowledge, rest not, till thou hast acquired it. It cometh readily to an attentive mind, and groweth with experience.

He, who chose thee, above all others, to bear his name, and to share his fortunes, hath a right to expect of thee such knowledge. Defraud him not, by continuing in ignorance, nor make thy beloved a stranger to the comforts of home, that thou mayst fold thy hands in indolence.

For the Apostle hath said, that "no man liveth unto himself." More especially should a woman, when she hath promised to be no longer her own, renounce self, as the aim of her existence. . . .

Consider the sphere in which thou art placed, as the one in which God willeth thee to be; and show kindness, and do good to all, according to thine ability.

Count thy husband's relatives as thy own; and if he hath parents show them the respect and tenderness of a true daughter. Be grateful to them for the culture of his virtue, whose fruits thou art gathering, and under the shadow of whose branches thou dost repose in peace.

Should his, or thine own parents, reside under the same roof with thee, give thanks for the privilege. For so thou mayest have opportunity to repay some portion of the affection of their cradle-watchings, and tender care, and patience of hope.

Whatever service their feeble years may require, render willingly, and with a cheerful countenance. Covet their prayers more than gold; and by filial piety, win their blessing. . . .

Forgive me, Oh Bride, if in the time of thy joy, I have spoken too gravely unto thee of life's cares. Yet in these very cares lies the secret of woman's happiness, more than in the haunts of pleasure, or the giddiness of mirth.

And in thy faithful efforts to make home beautiful and holy, the wings of guardian spirits shall enfold thy bosom, and give thee strength from above.

"Maternal Instruction," 1845

It takes a long time for the world to grow wise. Men have been busying themselves these six thousand years nearly to improve society. They have framed systems of philosophy and government, and conferred on their own sex all the advantages which power, wealth and knowledge could bestow. They have founded colleges and institutions of learning without number, and provided themselves teachers of every art and science; and, after all, the mass of mankind are very ignorant and very wicked. Wherefore is this? Because the *mother,* whom God constituted the first teacher of every human being, has been degraded by men from her high office; or, what is the same thing, been denied those privileges of education which only can enable her to discharge her duty to her children with discretion and effect. God created the woman as a *help-meet* for man in every situation; and while he, in his pride, rejects her assistance in his intellectual and moral career, he never will succeed to improve his nature and reach that perfection in knowledge, virtue and happiness, which his faculties are constituted to attain.

If half the effort and expense had been directed to enlighten and improve the minds of females which have been lavished on the other sex, we should now have a very different state of society. Wherever a woman is found excelling in judgment and knowledge, either by natural genius or from better opportunities, do we not see her children also excel? Search the records of history, and see if it can be found that a great and wise man ever descended from a weak and foolish mother. So sure and apparent is this maternal influence, that it has passed into an axiom of philosophy, it is acknowledged by the greatest and wisest of men; and yet, strange to say, the inference which ought to follow, namely, that in attempting to improve society, the first, most careful and continued efforts should be to raise the standard of female education, and qualify woman to become the educator of her children, has never yet been acted upon by any legislators, or acknowledged and tested by any philanthropists.

What is true of the maternal influence respecting sons is, perhaps, more important in the training of daughters. The fashionable schools are a poor substitute for such example and instruction as a thoroughly educated and right principled mother would bestow on her daughters. The best schools in the world will not, in and of themselves, make fine women. The tone of *family education* and of society needs to be raised. This can never be done till greater value is set on the cultivated female intellect. Young ladies must be inspired with high moral principles, noble aims, and a spirit of self-improvement to become what they ought to be. Maternal instruction is the purest and safest means of opening the fountain of knowledge to the young mind.

Sarah Alden Ripley's Letters, 1809–1810 and 1859

To Mary Emerson, c. 1809:

Dear, Dear Mary, —

I am afraid you will hear no more about satiety and disgust of life. With every rising dawn your idea is associated. The day no longer presents in prospect an unvaried tasteless round of domestic duties. Bright gleams of hope illumine the dull perspective. The mellow rays of the declining sun sweep the chords of love. Oh that they ceased to vibrate with the gentle touch! Your idea intrudes too often on the hallowed hours. But it will not be always thus. The affection whose object is so pure, so heavenly, cannot, will not, forever militate with devotion. Once convinced the chains are riveted, suspicion, dread to have disgusted or offended, will give place to calm reposing satisfaction. How delightful the thought that our religion sanctions friendship! How does worldliness dry up every spring of pure affection, chill every generous, glowing emotion! I was bantered a little at tea about violent romantic attachments. I was bold in the defense of disinterested friendship. My mother considers it a delusion, innocent as to its object, rather dangerous as to its effects, making me unsteady, as she terms it. But you told me once you hated sentimental epistles. May everything that can make life's journey pleasant be yours in perfection!

To Miss Allyn, 1810:

Miss Emerson has left Boston for an uncertain time. You know how I dislike writing; yet I have already written to her. It was the condition on which I am to expect her letters; and if they are of as much benefit to me as I hope her society has been, I shall be abundantly compensated. Do not be jealous of her, my best friend. My affection for you and her are very different: there is too much of reverential respect mingled with the former to admit of that unreserved confidence which is so strong a bond of union between *us*. Can an acquaintance of a few months, where there is disparity of years and difference in pursuits, be weighed in the balance with a friendship of years, cemented by union in studies as well as sentiment?

To Mary Emerson, 1810:

Dear Mary, —

I have just received your valuable letter, and would answer it while warm with gratitude for the affectionate interest it expresses in my welfare. Your caution against an undue devotion to literary pursuits is, I fear, too necessary. Perhaps not more time is allotted to them than conscience would permit for innocent amusements. But their dominion over the affections is the danger. I fear, if called to relinquish them entirely or desert some positive duty, the sacrifice would be made with reluctance. Yet, when I experience how much more easy is the transition to serious meditation from an evening spent in study than one spent in society, where vanity may have been excited or pride flattered, I am inclined to consider them, if not directly tending to produce, at least not unfavorable to, piety. How ready we are to excuse a favorite passion! It is my constant prayer that my affections may be purified, and with advantages for improvement my sphere of usefulness may also be enlarged. My friend, I should not write thus to any one but yourself. I am almost ashamed when I see that I have as yet been the only subject. Do tell me if you think me vain or presuming.

. . . You are the only person who ever thought me of any consequence, and I am pretty well convinced other folks are more than half right. I want you to love me, but you must do as you please about it.

To Sophia Bradford, Her Sister-in-Law, 1859:

Dear Sophia, —

Can there be a possible chance that I may never look upon your dear face again! Am I to stand on the declivity of life, while one after another drops from my side of those who have been so long parts of myself? You are the vision of my nights; you appear to me for the first time in the little parlor of the house in South Street, a graceful and bright being of sixteen or seventeen, with a becoming straw hat and a most agreeable smile. I still see the corner of the room where you sat, though I see nothing else connected with the visit. Then the scene changes to your uncle Blake's, where I found you one morning practicing on the guitar before the family had arisen from their beds. After your closer connection with us as a family, our interviews so crowd together in the background of the past that I am kept awake as if solving a mathematical problem to arrange them in their proper time and place as they press in confusion upon the scene. How much we enjoyed those evening rides to Cambridge, to the house you had planned and built, where we forgot, for an hour or two, the school bondage of home! How much you did to soften the pillow of decline and death for the father I loved and respected so much! How can I recall or arrange the happy meetings we have had together as a family in Waltham or Lowell! How much you were to dear Margaret! How much Martha has always enjoyed, and still enjoys, your society! Do you wonder that I should desire to see you now? Still, I should not be willing to see you at the risk of exciting and doing you harm. So I will try to content myself with thinking of you with hope when I can. But sorrow, not hope, is the color of old age.

Your Sister.

Benjamin Hawkins Talks to Creek Women, 1796

I had a long conversation with them on the situation and circumstances as it respected their labour, and inquired to know what they made and what they wished, in aid of their own exertions. They informed me they performed almost all the labour, the men assisted but little and that in the corn. They generally made a plenty of corn and sweet potatoes and pumpkins. They made beans, ground peas, cymblins, gourds, watermelons, musmelons, collards and onions. They made great use of beans in their bread.

They wanted principally salt, that they used but little from necessity, and where they were able to supply themselves plentifully with meat, they were unable to preserve it for the want of salt. They raised hogs, some cattle, and a great many poultry.

If they could be directed how to turn their labour to account like the white people, they should be contented, they made sugar, had raised some cotton, and manufactured their baskets, sifters, pots and earthen pans. Their men hunted in the proper season and aided them with the skins in providing cloathes and blankets, such as I saw, but this was not sufficient to make them comfortable and the poor old men, women and children were under the necessity of sleeping as I saw them in their town house.

They in the morning told me that many men had been sent into their nation to their chiefs but I was the first who thought it worth while to examine into the situation of the women. I had addressed myself to them, and talked freely and fondly to them, and they were sure I meant to better their condition. They would follow my advise.

Laws of the Cherokee Nation, 1819, 1825, 1829

November 1819

Resolved by the National Committee and Council, That any white man who shall hereafter take a Cherokee woman to wife be required to marry her legally by a minister of the gospel or other authorized person, after procuring license from the National Clerk for that purpose, before he shall be entitled and admitted to the privilege of citizenship, and in order to avoid imposition on the part of any white man,

Resolved, That any white man who shall marry a Cherokee woman, the property of the woman so marry, shall not be subject to the disposal of her husband, contrary to her consent, and any white man so married and parting from his wife without just provication, shall forfeit and pay to his wife such sum or sums, as may be adjudged to her by the National Committee and Council for said breach of marriage, and be deprived of citizenship, and it is also resolved, that it shall not be lawful for any white man to have more than one wife, and it is also recommended that all others should also have but one wife hereafter. By order of the National Committee.

JNO. ROSS, Pres't N. Com.

his

Approved — PATH ⋈ KILLER,

mark

CHAS. R. HICKS.

A. McCOY, Clerk.

November 1825

Where a person possessing property and dies intestate, and having a wife and children, the property of the deceased, shall be equally divided among his lawful and acknowledged children, allowing the widow an equal share with the children, after all just debts of the deceased shall have been paid, by those obtaining letters of administration, agreeably to law, and in case the deceased leave a wife without children, then, in that case, the widow shall be entitled to receive one fourth of the estate, after said estate shall have been freed from incumbrance of all just and lawful demands, and the residue of the estate to go to his nearest kin, and in case a woman claiming and having exclusive right to property dies and leaving a husband and children, her property shall revert to her children and husband, in the same manner as above stated and provided for. . . .

The section embraced in the law regulating marriages between white men and Cherokee women, and making it unlawful for whitemen to have more than one wife, and recommending all others, also, to have but one wife, be, and the same is, hereby amended, so that it shall not be lawful hereafter, for any person or persons whatsoever, to have more than one wife.

> JNO. ROSS, Pres't N. Com.
> MAJOR RIDGE, Speaker.
> his
> Approved — PATH   KILLER,
> mark
> CH. R. HICKS.

A. McCOY, clerk N. Com.
E. BOUDINOTT, clerk N. Council.

November 1829

Whereas, It has long been an established custom in this Nation and admitted by the courts as law, yet never committed to writing, that the property of Cherokee women after their marriage cannot be disposed of by their husbands, or levied upon by an officer to satisfy a debt of the husband's contracting, contrary to her will and consent, and disposable only at her option — therefore,

Resolved by the National Committee and Council, in General Council Convened, That the property of Cherokee, and other women, citizens of this Nation, after their marriage shall not be taken or disposed of in any manner contrary to her consent, for the purpose of satisfying a debt contracted by her husband, nor shall the property of the husband be liable to seizure, or otherwise to satisfy the debts contracted by the wife. . . .

> Approved — JNO. ROSS.

※ *E S S A Y S*

In 1966, Barbara Welter of Hunter College was the first scholar to examine scores of books and magazines that were aimed at a middle-class, nineteenth-century female audience. Her study outlined in detail the dimensions of what she called the "cult of true womanhood," now more frequently termed the cult of domesticity. Welter decried the effects of the limited definition of woman's sphere. Nine years later, however, Carroll Smith-Rosenberg of the University of Pennsylvania celebrated the positive aspects of this definition, those characteristics that brought women together into a specifically female world. Still more recently, Theda Perdue, who teaches at the University of Kentucky, studied the impact of the cult of domesticity on southern Indian women, primarily Cherokees, whose traditional roles were very different from those outlined in domestic ideology.

The Cult of True Womanhood, 1820–1860

BARBARA WELTER

The nineteenth-century American man was a busy builder of bridges and railroads, at work long hours in a materialistic society. The religious values of his forebears were neglected in practice if not in intent, and he occasionally felt some guilt that he had turned this new land, this temple of the chosen people, into one vast counting-house. But he could salve his conscience by reflecting that he had left behind a hostage, not only to fortune, but to all the values which he held so dear and treated so lightly. Woman, in the cult of True Womanhood presented by the women's magazines, gift annuals and religious literature of the nineteenth century, was the hostage in the home. In a society where values changed frequently, where fortunes rose and fell with frightening rapidity, where social and economic mobility provided instability as well as hope, one thing at least remained the same — a true woman was a true woman, wherever she was found. If anyone, male or female, dared to tamper with the complex of virtues which made up True Womanhood, he was damned immediately as an enemy of God, of civilization and of the Republic. It was a fearful obligation, a solemn responsibility, which the nineteenth-century American woman had — to uphold the pillars of the temple with her frail white hand.

The attributes of True Womanhood, by which a woman judged herself and was judged by her husband, her neighbors and society could be divided into four cardinal virtues — piety, purity, submissiveness and domesticity. Put them all together and they spelled mother, daughter, sister, wife — woman. Without them, no matter whether there was fame, achievement or wealth, all was ashes. With them she was promised happiness and power.

Religion or piety was the core of woman's virtue, the source of her strength. Young men looking for a mate were cautioned to search first for piety, for if that were there, all else would follow. Religion belonged to woman by divine right, a gift of God and nature. This "peculiar susceptibility" to religion was given her for a reason: "the vestal flame of piety, lighted up by Heaven in the breast of woman" would throw its beams into the naughty world of men. So far would its candle power reach that the "Universe might be Enlightened, Improved, and Harmonized by WOMAN!!" She would be another, better Eve, working in cooperation with the Redeemer, bringing the world back "from its revolt and sin." The world would be

Barbara Welter, "The Cult of True Womanhood: 1820–1860," *American Quarterly,* XVIII (1966), 151–174, copyright 1966, American Studies Association.

reclaimed for God through her suffering, for "God increased the cares and sorrows of woman, that she might be sooner constrained to accept the terms of salvation." A popular poem by Mrs. Frances Osgood, "The Triumph of the Spiritual Over the Sensual" expressed just this sentiment, woman's purifying passionless love bringing an erring man back to Christ.

Dr. Charles Meigs, explaining to a graduating class of medical students why women were naturally religious, said that "hers is a pious mind. Her confiding nature leads her more readily than men to accept the proffered grace of the Gospel." Caleb Atwater, Esq., writing in *The Ladies' Repository,* saw the hand of the Lord in female piety: "Religion is exactly what a woman needs, for it gives her that dignity that best suits her dependence." And Mrs. John Sandford, who had no very high opinion of her sex, agreed thoroughly: "Religion is just what woman needs. Without it she is ever restless or unhappy. . . . " Mrs. Sandford and the others did not speak only of that restlessness of the human heart, which St. Augustine notes, that can only find its peace in God. They spoke rather of religion as a kind of tranquilizer for the many undefined longings which swept even the most pious young girl, and about which it was better to pray than to think.

One reason religion was valued was that it did not take a woman away from her "proper sphere," her home. Unlike participation in other societies or movements, church work would not make her less domestic or submissive, less a True Woman. In religious vineyards, said the *Young Ladies' Literary and Missionary Report,* "you may labor without the apprehension of detracting from the charms of feminine delicacy." Mrs. S. L. Dagg, writing from her chapter of the Society in Tuscaloosa, Alabama, was equally reassuring: "As no sensible woman will suffer her intellectual pursuits to clash with her domestic duties" she should concentrate on religious work "which promotes these very duties."

The women's seminaries aimed at aiding women to be religious, as well as accomplished. Mt. Holyoke's catalogue promised to make female education "a handmaid to the Gospel and an efficient auxiliary in the great task of renovating the world." The Young Ladies' Seminary at Bordentown, New Jersey, declared its most important function to be "the forming of a sound and virtuous character." In Keene, New Hampshire, the Seminary tried to instill a "consistent and useful character" in its students, to enable them in this life to be "a good friend, wife and mother" but more important, to qualify them for "the enjoyment of Celestial Happiness in the life to come." And Joseph M' D. Mathews, Principal of Oakland Female Seminary in Hillsborough, Ohio, believed that "female education should be preeminently religious."

If religion was so vital to a woman, irreligion was almost too awful to contemplate. Women were warned not to let their literary or intellectual pursuits take them away from God. Sarah Josepha Hale spoke darkly of those who, like Margaret Fuller, threw away the "One True Book" for others, open to error. Mrs. Hale used the unfortunate Miss Fuller as fateful proof that "the greater the intellectual force, the greater and more fatal the errors into which women fall who wander from the Rock of Salvation, Christ the Saviour. . . . "

One gentleman, writing on "Female Irreligion" reminded his readers that "Man may make himself a brute, and does so very often, but can woman brutify herself to his level — the lowest level of human nature — without exerting special wonder?"

Fanny Wright, because she was godless, "was no woman, mother though she be." A few years ago, he recalls, such women would have been whipped. In any case, "woman never looks lovelier than in her reverence for religion" and, conversely, "female irreligion is the most revolting feature in human character."

Purity was as essential as piety to a young woman, its absence as unnatural and unfeminine. Without it she was, in fact, no woman at all, but a member of some lower order. A "fallen woman" was a "fallen angel," unworthy of the celestial company of her sex. To contemplate the loss of purity brought tears; to be guilty of such a crime, in the women's magazines at least, brought madness or death. Even the language of the flowers had bitter words for it: a dried white rose symbolized "Death Preferable to Loss of Innocence." The marriage night was the single great event of a woman's life, when she bestowed her greatest treasure upon her husband, and from that time on was completely dependent upon him, an empty vessel, without legal or emotional existence of her own.

Therefore all True Women were urged, in the strongest possible terms, to maintain their virtue, although men, being by nature more sensual than they, would try to assault it. Thomas Branagan admitted in *The Excellency of the Female Character Vindicated* that his sex would sin and sin again, they could not help it, but woman, stronger and purer, must not give in and let man "take liberties incompatible with her delicacy." "If you do," Branagan addressed his gentle reader, "You will be left in silent sadness to bewail your credulity, imbecility, duplicity, and premature prostitution."

Mrs. Eliza Farrar, in *The Young Lady's Friend,* gave practical logistics to avoid trouble: "Sit not with another in a place that is too narrow; read not out of the same book; let not your eagerness to see anything induce you to place your head close to another person's."

If such good advice was ignored the consequences were terrible and inexorable. In *Girlhood and Womanhood: Or Sketches of My Schoolmates,* by Mrs. A. J. Graves (a kind of mid-nineteenth-century *The Group*), the bad ends of a boarding school class of girls are scrupulously recorded. The worst end of all is reserved for "Amelia Dorrington: The Lost One." Amelia died in the almshouse "the wretched victim of depravity and intemperance" and all because her mother had let her be "high-spirited not prudent." These girlish high spirits had been misinterpreted by a young man, with disastrous results. Amelia's "thoughtless levity" was "followed by a total loss of virtuous principle" and Mrs. Graves editorializes that "the coldest reserve is more admirable in a woman a man wishes to make his wife, than the least approach to undue familiarity."

A popular and often-reprinted story by Fanny Forester told the sad tale of "Lucy Dutton." Lucy "with the seal of innocence upon her heart, and a rose-leaf on her cheek" came out of her vine-covered cottage and ran into a city slicker. "And Lucy was beautiful and trusting, and thoughtless: and he was gay, selfish and profligate. Needs the story to be told? . . . Nay, censor, Lucy was a child — consider how young, how very untaught — oh! her innocence was no match for the sophistry of a gay, city youth! Spring came and shame was stamped upon the cottage at the foot of the hill." The baby died; Lucy went mad at the funeral and finally died herself. "Poor, poor Lucy Dutton! The grave is a blessed couch and pillow to the wretched. Rest thee there, poor Lucy!" The frequency with which derangement follows loss of virtue suggests the exquisite sensibility of woman, and the possibility that, in the women's magazines at least, her intellect was geared to her hymen, not her brain. . . .

Purity, considered as a moral imperative, set up a dilemma which was hard to resolve. Woman must preserve her virtue until marriage and marriage was necessary for her happiness. Yet marriage was, literally, an end to innocence. She was told not to question this dilemma, but simply to accept it.

Submission was perhaps the most feminine virtue expected of women. Men were supposed to be religious, although they rarely had time for it, and supposed to be pure, although it came awfully hard to them, but men were the movers, the doers, the actors. Women were the passive, submissive responders. The order of dialogue was, of course, fixed in Heaven. Man was "woman's superior by God's appointment, if not in intellectual dowry, at least by official decree." Therefore, as Charles Elliott argued in *The Ladies' Repository,* she should submit to him "for the sake of good order at least." In *The Ladies Companion* a young wife was quoted approvingly as saying that she did not think woman should "feel and act for herself" because "When, next to God, her husband is not the tribunal to which her heart and intellect appeals — the golden bowl of affection is broken." Women were warned that if they tampered with this quality they tampered with the order of the Universe.

The Young Lady's Book summarized the necessity of the passive virtues in its readers' lives: "It is, however, certain, that in whatever situation of life a woman is placed from her cradle to her grave, a spirit of obedience and submission, pliability of temper, and humility of mind, are required from her."

Woman understood her position if she was the right kind of woman, a true woman. "She feels herself weak and timid. She needs a protector," declared George Burnap, in his lectures on *The Sphere and Duties of Woman.* "She is in a measure dependent. She asks for wisdom, constancy, firmness, perseverance, and she is willing to repay it all by the surrender of the full treasure of her affections. Woman despises in man every thing like herself except a tender heart. It is enough that she is effeminate and weak; she does not want another like herself." Or put even more strongly by Mrs. Sandford: "A really sensible woman feels her dependence. She does what she can, but she is conscious of inferiority, and therefore grateful for support." . . .

The true woman's place was unquestionably by her own fireside — as daughter, sister, but most of all as wife and mother. Therefore domesticity was among the virtues most prized by the women's magazines. "As society is constituted," wrote Mrs. S. E. Farley, on the "Domestic and Social Claims on Woman," "the true dignity and beauty of the female character seem to consist in a right understanding and faithful and cheerful performance of social and family duties." Sacred Scripture reenforced social pressure: "St. Paul knew what was best for women when he advised them to be domestic," said Mrs. Sandford. "There is composure at home; there is something sedative in the duties which home involves. It affords security not only from the world, but from delusions and errors of every kind."

From her home woman performed her great task of bringing men back to God. *The Young Ladies' Class Book* was sure that "the domestic fireside is the great guardian of society against the excesses of human passions." *The Lady at Home* expressed its convictions in its very title and concluded that "even if we cannot reform the world in a moment, we can begin the work by reforming ourselves and our households — It is woman's mission. Let her not look away from her own little family circle for the means of producing moral and social reforms, but begin at home."

Home was supposed to be a cheerful place, so that brothers, husbands and sons would not go elsewhere in search of a good time. Woman was expected to dispense comfort and cheer. In writing the biography of Margaret Mercer (every inch a true woman) her biographer (male) notes: "She never forgot that it is the peculiar province of woman to minister to the comfort, and promote the happiness, first, of those most nearly allied to her, and then of those, who by the Providence of God are placed in a state of dependence upon her." Many other essays in the women's journals showed woman as comforter: "Woman, Man's Best Friend," "Woman, the Greatest Social Benefit," "Woman, A Being to Come Home To," "The Wife: Source of Comfort and the Spring of Joy." . . .

In the home women were not only the highest adornment of civilization, but they were supposed to keep busy at morally uplifting tasks. Fortunately most of housework, if looked at in true womanly fashion, could be regarded as uplifting. Mrs. Sigourney extolled its virtues: "The science of housekeeping affords exercise for the judgment and energy, ready recollection, and patient self-possession, that are the characteristics of a superior mind." According to Mrs. Farrar, making beds was good exercise, the repetitiveness of routine tasks inculcated patience and perseverance, and proper management of the home was a surprisingly complex art: "There is more to be learned about pouring out tea and coffee, than most young ladies are willing to believe." Godey's went so far as to suggest coyly, in "Learning vs. Housewifery" that the two were complementary, not opposed: chemistry could be utilized in cooking, geometry in dividing cloth, and phrenology in discovering talent in children. . . .

The debate over women's education posed the question of whether a "finished" education detracted from the practice of housewifely arts. Again it proved to be a case of semantics, for a true woman's education was never "finished" until she was instructed in the gentle science of homemaking. Helen Irving, writing on "Literary Women," made it very clear that if women invoked the muse, it was as a genie of the household lamp. "If the necessities of her position require these duties at her hands, she will perform them nonetheless cheerfully, that she knows herself capable of higher things." The literary woman must conform to the same standards as any other woman: "That her home shall be made a loving place of rest and joy and comfort for those who are dear to her, will be the first wish of every true woman's heart." Mrs. Ann Stephens told women who wrote to make sure they did not sacrifice one domestic duty. "As for genius, make it a domestic plant. Let its roots strike deep in your house. . . . "

The fear of "blue stockings" (the eighteenth-century male's term of derision for educated or literary women) need not persist for nineteenth-century American men. The magazines presented spurious dialogues in which bachelors were convinced of their fallacy in fearing educated wives. One such dialogue took place between a young man and his female cousin. Ernest deprecates learned ladies ("A *Woman* is far more lovable than a *philosopher*") but Alice refutes him with the beautiful example of their Aunt Barbara who "although she *has* perpetrated the heinous crime of writing some half dozen folios" is still a model of "the spirit of feminine gentleness." His memory prodded, Ernest concedes that, by George, there was a woman: "When I last had a cold she not only made me a bottle of cough syrup, but when I complained of nothing new to read, set to work and wrote some twenty stanzas on consumption."

The magazines were filled with domestic tragedies in which spoiled young girls learned that when there was a hungry man to feed French and china painting were not helpful. According to these stories many a marriage is jeopardized because the wife has not learned to keep house. Harriet Beecher Stowe wrote a sprightly piece of personal experience for *Godey's,* ridiculing her own bad housekeeping as a bride. She used the same theme in a story "The Only Daughter," in which the pampered beauty learns the facts of domestic life from a rather difficult source, her mother-in-law. Mrs. Hamilton tells Caroline in the sweetest way possible to shape up in the kitchen, reserving her rebuke for her son: "You are her husband — her guide — her protector — now see what you can do," she admonishes him. "Give her credit for every effort: treat her faults with tenderness; encourage and praise whenever you can, and depend upon it, you will see another woman in her." He is properly masterful, she properly domestic and in a few months Caroline is making lumpless gravy and keeping up with the darning. Domestic tranquility has been restored and the young wife moralizes: "Bring up a girl to feel that she has a responsible part to bear in promoting the happiness of the family, and you make a reflecting being of her at once, and remove that lightness and frivolity of character which makes her shrink from graver studies." These stories end with the heroine drying her hands on her apron and vowing that *her* daughter will be properly educated. . . .

Marriage was seen not only in terms of service but as an increase in authority for woman. Burnap concluded that marriage improves the female character "not only because it puts her under the best possible tuition, that of the affections, and affords scope to her active energies, but because it gives her higher aims, and a more dignified position." *The Lady's Amaranth* saw it as a balance of power: "The man bears rule over his wife's person and conduct. She bears rule over his inclinations: he governs by law; she by persuasion. . . . The empire of the woman is an empire of softness . . . her commands are caresses, her menaces are tears."

Woman should marry, but not for money. She should choose only the high road of true love and not truckle to the values of a materialistic society. A story "Marrying for Money" (subtlety was not the strong point of the ladies' magazines) depicts Gertrude, the heroine, rueing the day she made her crass choice: "It is a terrible thing to live without love. . . . A woman who dares marry for aught but the purest affection, calls down the just judgments of heaven upon her head."

The corollary to marriage, with or without true love, was motherhood, which added another dimension to her usefulness and her prestige. It also anchored her even more firmly to the home. "My Friend," wrote Mrs. Sigourney, "If in becoming a mother, you have reached the climax of your happiness, you have also taken a higher place in the scale of being . . . you have gained an increase of power." The Rev. J. N. Danforth pleaded in *The Ladies' Casket,* "Oh, mother, acquit thyself well in thy humble sphere, for thou mayest affect the world." A true woman naturally loved her children; to suggest otherwise was monstrous.

America depended upon her mothers to raise up a whole generation of Christian statesmen who could say "all that I am I owe to my angel mother." The mothers must do the inculcating of virtue since the fathers, alas, were too busy chasing the dollar. Or as *The Ladies' Companion* put it more effusively, the father "weary with the heat and burden of life's summer day, or trampling with unwilling foot the decaying leaves of life's autumn, has forgotten the sympathies of life's joyous springtime. . . . The acquisition of wealth, the advancement of his children in worldly honor — these are his self-imposed tasks." It was his wife who formed "the infant mind as yet untainted by contact with evil . . . like wax beneath the plastic hand of the mother." . . .

The American woman had her choice — she could define her rights in the way of the women's magazines and insure them by the practice of the requisite virtues, or she could go outside the home, seeking other rewards than love. It was a decision

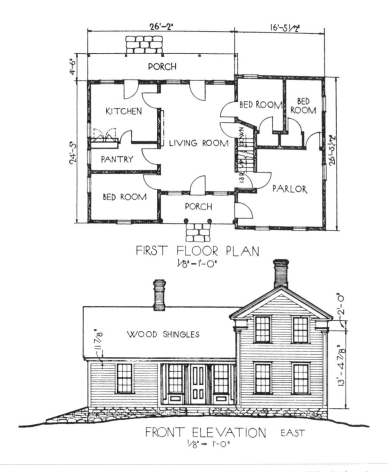

Plan of a nineteenth-century farmhouse. By the 1840s, when this Illinois farmhouse was designed, the demands of the cult of domesticity were such that even this modest rural dwelling contained a parlor — a room used solely for formal entertaining and for the display of genteel possessions.

on which, she was told, everything in her world depended. "Yours it is to determine," the Rev. Mr. Stearns solemnly warned from the pulpit, "whether the beautiful order of society . . . shall continue as it has been" or whether "society shall break up and become a chaos of disjointed and unsightly elements." If she chose to listen to other voices than those of her proper mentors, sought other rooms than those of her home, she lost both her happiness and her power — "that almost magic power, which, in her proper sphere, she now wields over the destinies of the world."

But even while the women's magazines and related literature encouraged this ideal of the perfect woman, forces were at work in the nineteenth century which impelled woman herself to change, to play a more creative role in society. The movements for social reform, westward migration, missionary activity, utopian communities, industrialism, the Civil War — all called forth responses from woman which differed from those she was trained to believe were hers by nature and divine decree. The very perfection of True Womanhood, moreover, carried within itself the seeds of its own destruction. For if woman was so very little less than the angels, she should surely take a more active part in running the world, especially since men were making such a hash of things. . . .

The Female World of Love and Ritual

CARROLL SMITH-ROSENBERG

The female friendship of the nineteenth century, the long-lived, intimate, loving friendship between two women, is an excellent example of the type of historical phenomenon that most historians know something about, few have thought much about, and virtually no one has written about. It is one aspect of the female experience which, consciously or unconsciously, we have chosen to ignore. Yet an abundance of manuscript evidence suggests that eighteenth- and nineteenth-century women routinely formed emotional ties with other women. Such deeply felt same-sex friendships were casually accepted in American society. Indeed, from at least the late eighteenth through the mid-nineteenth century, a female world of varied and yet highly structured relationships appears to have been an essential aspect of American society. These relationships ranged from the supportive love of sisters, through the enthusiasms of adolescent girls, to sensual avowals of love by mature women. It was a world in which men made but a shadowy appearance.

Defining and analyzing same-sex relationships involves the historian in deeply problematical questions of method and interpretation. This is especially true since historians, influenced by Freud's libidinal theory, have discussed these relationships almost exclusively within the context of individual psychosexual development or, to be more explicit, psychopathology. Seeing same-sex relationships in terms of a dichotomy between normal and abnormal, they have sought the origins of such apparent deviance in childhood or adolescent trauma and detected the symptoms of "latent" homosexuality in the lives of both those who later became "overtly" homo-

Extracts from Carroll Smith-Rosenberg, "The Female World of Love and Ritual: Relations between Women in Nineteenth-Century America," *Signs,* I (1975), 1–29. Reprinted by permission of The University of Chicago Press.

sexual and those who did not. Yet theories concerning the nature and origins of same-sex relationships are frequently contradictory or based on questionable or arbitrary data. In recent years such hypotheses have been subjected to criticism, both from within and without the psychological professions. Historians who seek to work within a psychological framework, therefore, are faced with two hard questions: Do sound psychodynamic theories concerning the nature and origins of same-sex relationships exist? If so, does the historical datum exist which would permit the use of such dynamic models?

I would like to suggest an alternative approach to female friendships — one that would view them within a cultural and social setting rather than from an exclusively individual psychosexual perspective. Only by thus altering our approach will we be in the position to evaluate the appropriateness of particular dynamic interpretations. Intimate friendships between men and men and women and women existed in a larger world of social relations and social values. To interpret such friendships more fully, one must relate them to the structure of the American family and to the nature of sex-role divisions and of male-female relations, both within the family and in society generally. The female friendship must not be seen in isolation; it must be analyzed as one aspect of women's overall relations with one another. The ties between mothers and daughters, sisters, female cousins, and friends, at all stages of the female life cycle, constitute the most suggestive framework the historian can use to begin an analysis of intimacy and affection between women. Such an analysis would not only emphasize general cultural patterns rather than the internal dynamics of a particular family or childhood; it would shift the focus of the study from a concern with deviance to that of defining configurations of legitimate behavioral norms and options. . . .

Several factors in American society between the mid-eighteenth and the mid-nineteenth centuries may well have permitted women to form a variety of close emotional relationships with other women. American society was characterized in large part by rigid gender-role differentiation within the family and within society as a whole, leading to the emotional segregation of women and men. The roles of daughter and mother shaded imperceptibly and ineluctably into each other, while the biological realities of frequent pregnancies, childbirth, nursing, and menopause bound women together in physical and emotional intimacy. It was within just such a social framework, I would argue, that a specifically female world did indeed develop, a world built around a generic and unself-conscious pattern of single-sex or homosocial networks. These supportive networks were institutionalized in social conventions or rituals that accompanied virtually every important event in a woman's life, from birth to death. Such female relationships were frequently supported and paralleled by severe social restrictions on intimacy between young men and women. Within such a world of emotional richness and complexity, devotion to and love of other women became a plausible and socially accepted form of human interaction.

An abundance of printed and manuscript sources exists to support such a hypothesis. Etiquette books, advice books on child-rearing, religious sermons, guides to young men and young women, medical texts, and school curricula all suggest that late-eighteenth- and most nineteenth-century Americans assumed the existence of a world composed of distinctly male and female spheres, spheres determined by the immutable laws of God and nature. The unpublished letters and diaries of Americans during this same period concur, detailing the existence of sexually segregated worlds inhabited by human beings with different values, expectations, and personalities. Contacts between men and women frequently partook of a formality and stiffness quite alien to twentieth-century America, and which today we tend to define as "Victorian." Women, however, did not form an isolated and oppressed subcategory in male society. Their letters and diaries indicate that women's sphere had an essential integrity and dignity that grew out of women's shared experiences and mutual affection and that, despite the profound changes that affected American social structure and institutions between the 1760s and the 1870s, retained a constancy and predictability. The ways in which women thought of and interacted with one another remained unchanged. Continuity, not discontinuity, characterized this female world. . . .

Friends did not form isolated dyads but were normally part of highly integrated networks. Knowing one another, perhaps related to one another, they played a central role in holding communities and kin systems together. Especially when families became geographically mobile, women's long visits to one another and their frequent letters filled with discussions of marriages and births, illnesses and deaths, descriptions of growing children, and reminiscences of times and people past provided an important sense of continuity in a rapidly changing society. Central to this female world was an inner core of kin. The ties between sisters, first cousins, aunts, and nieces provided the underlying structure upon which groups of friends and their network of female relatives clustered. Although most of the women within this sample would appear to be living within isolated nuclear families, the emotional ties between nonresidential kin were deep and binding and provided one of the fundamental existential realities of women's lives. Twenty years after Parke Lewis Butler moved with her husband to Louisiana, she sent her two daughters back to Virginia to attend school, live with their grandmother and aunt, and be integrated back into Virginia society. The constant letters between Maria Inskeep and Fanny Hampton, sisters separated in their early twenties when Maria moved with her husband from New Jersey to Louisiana, held their families together, making it possible for their daughters to feel a part of their cousins' network of friends and interests. The Ripley daughters, growing up in western Massachusetts in the early 1800s, spent months each year with their mother's sister and her family in distant Boston; these female cousins and their network of friends exchanged gossip-filled letters and gradually formed deeply loving and dependent ties.

Women frequently spent their days within the social confines of such extended families. Sisters-in-law visited one another and, in some families, seemed to spend more time with one another than with their husbands. First cousins cared for one another's babies — for weeks or even months in times of sickness or childbirth. Sisters helped one another with housework, shopped and sewed for one another. Geographic separation was borne with difficulty. A sister's absence for even a week or two could cause loneliness and depression and would be bridged by frequent letters. Sibling rivalry was hardly unknown, but with separation or illness the theme of deep affection and dependency re-emerged.

Sisterly bonds continued across a lifetime. In her old age, a rural Quaker matron, Martha Jefferis, wrote to her daughter Anne concerning her own half-sister,

Phoebe: "In sister Phoebe I have a real friend — she studies my comfort and waits on me like a child. . . . She is exceedingly kind and this to all other homes (set aside yours) I would prefer — it is next to being with a daughter." Phoebe's own letters confirmed Martha's evaluation of her feelings. "Thou knowest my dear sister," Phoebe wrote, "there is no one . . . that exactly feels [for] thee as I do, for I think without boasting I can truly say that my desire is for thee."

Such women, whether friends or relatives, assumed an emotional centrality in one another's lives. In their diaries and letters they wrote of the joy and contentment they felt in one another's company, their sense of isolation and despair when apart. The regularity of their correspondence underlines the sincerity of such words. Women named their daughters after one another and sought to integrate dear friends into their lives after marriage. As one young bride wrote to an old friend shortly after her marriage, "I want to see you and talk with you and feel that we are united by the same bonds of sympathy and congeniality as ever." After years of friendship, one aging woman wrote of another, "Time cannot destroy the fascination of her manner . . . her voice is music to the ear. . . . " Women made elaborate presents for one another, ranging from the Quakers' frugal pies and breads to painted velvet bags and phantom bouquets. When a friend died, their grief was deeply felt: Martha Jefferis was unable to write to her daughter for three weeks because of the sorrow she felt at the death of a dear friend, and such distress was not unusual. A generation earlier, a young Massachusetts farm woman filled pages of her diary with her grief at the death of her "dearest friend" and transcribed the letters of condolence other women sent her. She marked the anniversary of Rachel's death each year in her diary, contrasting her faithfulness with that of Rachel's husband, who had soon remarried.

These female friendships served a number of emotional functions. Within this secure and empathetic world women could share sorrows, anxieties, and joys, confident that other women had experienced similar emotions. One mid-nineteenth-century rural matron, in a letter to her daughter, discussed this particular aspect of women's friendships: "To have such a friend as thyself to look to and sympathize with her — and enter into all her little needs and in whose bosom she could with freedom pour forth her joys and sorrows — such a friend would very much relieve the tedium of many a wearisome hour. . . . " A generation later Molly more informally underscored the importance of this same function in a letter to Helena: "Suppose I come down . . . [and] spend Sunday with you quietly," she wrote Helena, " . . . that means talking all the time until you are relieved of all your latest troubles, and I of mine. . . . " These were frequently troubles that apparently no man could understand. When Anne Jefferis Sheppard was first married, she and her older sister Edith (who then lived with Anne) wrote in detail to their mother of the severe depression and anxiety they experienced. Moses Sheppard, Anne's husband, added cheerful postscripts to the sisters' letters — which he had clearly not read — remarking on Anne's and Edith's contentment. Theirs was an emotional world to which he had little access.

This was, as well, a female world in which hostility and criticism of other women were discouraged, and thus a milieu in which women could develop a sense of inner security and self-esteem. As one young woman wrote to her mother's long-time friend: "I cannot sufficiently thank you for the kind unvaried affection &

indulgence you have ever shown and expressed both by words and actions for me. . . . Happy would it be did all the world view me as you do, through the medium of kindness and forbearance." They valued one another. Women, who had little status or power in the larger world of male concerns, possessed status and power in the lives and worlds of other women.

An intimate mother-daughter relationship lay at the heart of this female world. The diaries and letters of both mothers and daughters attest to their closeness and mutual emotional dependency. Daughters routinely discussed their mothers' health and activities with their own friends, expressed anxiety when their mothers were ill and concern for their cares. Expressions of hostility which we would today consider routine on the part of both mothers and daughters seem to have been uncommon indeed. On the contrary, this sample of families indicates that the normal relationship between mother and daughter was one of sympathy and understanding. Only sickness or great geographic distance was allowed to cause extended separation. When marriage did result in such separation, both viewed the distance between them with distress. Something of this sympathy and love between mothers and daughters is evident in a letter Sarah Alden Ripley, at age sixty-nine, wrote her youngest and recently married daughter: "You do not know how much I miss you, not only when I struggle in and out of my mortal envelop and pump my nightly potation and no longer pour into your sympathizing ear my senile gossip, but all the day I muse away, since the sound of your voice no longer rouses me to sympathy with your joys or sorrows. . . . You cannot know how much I miss your affectionate demonstrations." A dozen aging mothers in this sample of over thirty families echoed her sentiments.

Central to these mother-daughter relations is what might be described as an apprenticeship system. In those families where the daughter followed the mother into a life of traditional domesticity, mothers and other older women had carefully trained daughters in the arts of housewifery and motherhood. Such training undoubtedly occurred throughout a girl's childhood but became more systematized, almost ritualistic, in the years following the end of her formal education and before her marriage. At this time a girl either returned home from boarding school or no longer divided her time between home and school. Rather, she devoted her energies to two tasks: mastering new domestic skills and participating in the visiting and social activities necessary to finding a husband. Under the careful supervision of their mothers and of older female relatives, such late-adolescent girls temporarily took over the household management from their mothers, tended their young nieces and nephews, and helped in childbirth, nursing, and weaning. Such experiences tied the generations together in shared skills and emotional interaction. . . .

At some point in adolescence, the young girl began to move outside the matrix of her mother's support group to develop a network of her own. Among the middle class, at least, this transition toward what was at the same time both a limited autonomy and a repetition of her mother's life seemed to have most frequently coincided with a girl's going to school. Indeed, education appears to have played a crucial role in the lives of most of the families in this study. Attending school for a few months, for a year, or longer was common even among daughters of relatively poor families, while middle-class girls routinely spent at least a year in boarding school. These school years ordinarily marked a girl's first separation from home. They served to wean the daughter from her home, to train her in the essential social graces, and, ultimately, to help introduce her into the marriage market. It was not infrequently a trying emotional experience for both mother and daughter.

In this process of leaving one home and adjusting to another, the mother's friends and relatives played a key transitional role. Such older women routinely accepted the role of foster mother; they supervised the young girl's deportment, monitored her health, and introduced her to their own network of female friends and kin. Not infrequently, women who had been friends from their own school years arranged to send their daughters to the same school, so that the girls might form bonds paralleling those their mothers had made. For years Molly and Helena wrote of their daughters' meeting and worried over each other's children. When Molly finally brought her daughter east to school, their first act on reaching New York was to meet Helena and her daughters. Elizabeth Bordley Gibson virtually adopted the daughters of her school chum, Eleanor Custis Lewis. The Lewis daughters soon began to write Elizabeth Gibson letters with the salutation "Dearest Mama." Eleuthera DuPont, attending boarding school in Philadelphia at roughly the same time as the Lewis girls, developed a parallel relationship with her mother's friend, Elizabeth McKie Smith. Eleuthera went to the same school as and became a close friend of the Smith girls, and eventually married their first cousin. During this period she routinely called Mrs. Smith "Mother." Indeed, Eleuthera so internalized the sense of having two mothers that she casually wrote her sisters of her "Mamma's" visits at her "mother's" house — that is, at Mrs. Smith's.

Even more important to this process of maturation than their mother's friends were the female friends young women made at school. Young girls helped one another overcome homesickness and endure the crises of adolescence. They gossiped about beaux, incorporated one another into their own kinship systems, and attended and gave teas and balls together. Older girls in boarding school "adopted" younger ones, who called them "Mother." Dear friends might indeed continue this pattern of adoption and mothering throughout their lives; one woman might routinely assume the nurturing role of pseudo-mother, the other the dependency role of daughter. The pseudo-mother performed for the other woman all the services we normally associate with mothers; she went to absurd lengths to purchase items her "daughter" could have obtained from other sources, gave advice, and functioned as an idealized figure in her "daughter's" imagination. Helena played such a role for Molly, as did Sarah for Jeannie. Elizabeth Bordley Gibson bought almost all Eleanor Parke Custis Lewis's necessities — from shoes and corset covers to bedding and harp strings — and sent them from Philadelphia to Virginia, a procedure that sometimes took months. Eleanor frequently asked Elizabeth to take back her purchases, have them redone, and argue with shopkeepers about prices. These were favors automatically asked and complied with. Anne Jefferis Sheppard made the analogy very explicitly in a letter to her own mother written shortly after Anne's marriage, when she was feeling depressed about their separation: "Mary Paulen is truly kind, almost acts the part of a mother and tries to aid and *comfort me*, and also to *lighten my new cares.*"

A comparison of the references to men and women in these young women's letters is striking. Boys were obviously indispensable to the elaborate courtship ritual girls engaged in. In these teen-age letters and diaries, however, boys appear distant and warded off — an effect produced both by the girl's sense of bonding and by a highly developed and deprecatory whimsy. Girls joked among themselves about the conceit, poor looks, or affectations of suitors. Rarely, especially in the eighteenth and early nineteenth centuries, were favorable remarks exchanged. Indeed, although hostility and criticism of other women were so rare as to seem almost tabooed, young women permitted themselves to express a great deal of hostility toward peer-group men. If unacceptable suitors appeared, girls might even band together to harass them. When one such unfortunate came to court Sophie DuPont, she hid in her room, first sending her sister Eleuthera to entertain him and then dispatching a number of urgent notes to her neighboring sister-in-law, cousins, and a visiting friend, who all came to Sophie's support. A wild female romp ensued, ending only when Sophie banged into a door, lacerated her nose, and retired, with her female cohorts, to bed. Her brother and the presumably disconcerted suitor were left alone. These were not the antics of teen-agers but of women in their early and mid-twenties.

Even if young men were acceptable suitors, girls referred to them formally and obliquely: "The last week I received the unexpected intelligence of the arrival of a friend in Boston," Sarah Ripley wrote in her diary of the young man to whom she had been engaged for years and whom she would shortly marry. Harriet Manigault assiduously kept a lively and gossipy diary during the three years preceding her marriage, yet did not once comment upon her own engagement or, indeed, make any personal references to her fiancé — who was never identified as such but always referred to as Mr. Wilcox. The point is not that these young women were hostile to young men. Far from it: they sought marriage and domesticity. Yet in these letters and diaries men appear as an other or out group, segregated into different schools, supported by their own male network of friends and kin, socialized to different behavior, and coached to a proper formality in courtship behavior. As a consequence, relations between young women and men frequently lacked the spontaneity and emotional intimacy that characterized the young girls' ties to one another. . . .

Marriage followed adolescence. With increasing frequency in the nineteenth century, marriage involved a girl's traumatic removal from her mother and her mother's network. It involved, as well, adjustment to a husband, who, because he was male, came to marriage with both a different world view and vastly different experiences. Not surprisingly, marriage was an event surrounded by supportive, almost ritualistic, practices. (Weddings are one of the last female rituals remaining in twentieth-century America.) Young women routinely spent the months preceding their marriage almost exclusively with other women — at neighborhood sewing bees and quilting parties or in a round of visits to geographically distant friends and relatives. Ostensibly they went to receive assistance in the practical preparations for their new homes — sewing and quilting trousseaux and linen — but, of equal importance, they appear to have gained emotional support and reassurance. Sarah Ripley spent over a month with friends and relatives in Boston and Hingham before her wedding; Parke Custis Lewis exchanged visits with her aunts and first cousins throughout Virginia. Anne Jefferis, who married with some hesitation, spent virtually half a year in endless visiting with cousins, aunts, and friends. Despite their reassurance and support, however, she would not marry Moses Sheppard until her sister Edith and her cousin Rebecca moved into the groom's home, met his friends, and explored his personality. The wedding did not take place until Edith wrote to Anne, "I can say in truth I am entirely willing thou shouldst follow him even away in the Jersey sands believing if thou are not happy in thy future home it will not be any fault on his part. . . . "

Sisters, cousins, and friends frequently accompanied newlyweds on their wedding night and wedding trip, which often involved additional family visiting. Such extensive visits presumably served to wean the daughter from her family of origin. As such they often contained a note of ambivalence. Nelly Custis, for example, reported homesickness and loneliness on her wedding trip. "I left my Beloved and revered Grandmamma with sincere regret," she wrote Elizabeth Bordley. "It was some time before I could feel reconciled to traveling without her." Perhaps they also functioned to reassure the young woman herself, and her friends and kin, that though marriage might alter it would not destroy old bonds of intimacy and familiarity.

Married life too was structured about a host of female rituals. Childbirth, especially the birth of the first child, became virtually a *rite de passage,* with a lengthy seclusion of the woman before and after delivery, severe restrictions on her activities, and finally a dramatic re-emergence. This seclusion was supervised by mothers, sisters, and loving friends. Nursing and weaning involved the advice and assistance of female friends and relatives. So did miscarriage. Death, like birth, was structured around elaborate, unisexed rituals. When Nelly Parke Custis Lewis rushed to nurse her daughter who was critically ill while away at school, Nelly received support, not from her husband, who remained on their plantation, but from her old school friend Elizabeth Bordley. Elizabeth aided Nelly in caring for her dying daughter, cared for Nelly's other children, played a major role in making arrangements for the elaborate funeral (which the father did not attend), and frequently visited the girl's grave at the mother's request. For years Elizabeth continued to be the confidante of Nelly's anguished recollections of her lost daughter. These memories, Nelly's letters make clear, were for Elizabeth alone. "Mr. L. knows nothing of this" was a frequent comment. Virtually every collection of letters and diaries in my sample contained evidence of women turning to one another for comfort when facing the frequent and unavoidable deaths of the eighteenth and nineteenth centuries. While mourning for her father's death, Sophie DuPont received eloquent letters and visits of condolence — all from women. No man wrote or visited Sophie to offer sympathy at her father's death. Among rural Pennsylvania Quakers, death and mourning rituals assumed an even more extreme same-sex form, with men or women largely barred from the deathbeds of the other sex. Women relatives and friends slept with the dying woman, nursed her, and prepared her body for burial.

Eighteenth- and nineteenth-century women thus lived in emotional proximity to one another. Friendships and intimacies followed the biological ebb and flow of women's lives. Marriage and pregnancy, childbirth and weaning, sickness and death, involved physical and psychic trauma which comfort and sympathy made easier to bear. Intense bonds of love and intimacy bound together those women who, offering one another aid and sympathy, shared such stressful moments.

These bonds were often physical as well as emotional. An undeniably romantic and even sensual note frequently marked female relationships. This theme, significant throughout the stages of a woman's life, surfaced first during adolescence. As one teen-ager from a struggling pioneer family in the Ohio Valley wrote in her diary in 1808, "I laid with my dear R[ebecca] and a glorious good talk we had until about 4[A.M.] — O how hard I do *love* her. . . . " Only a few years later, Bostonian Eunice Callender carved her initials and Sarah Ripley's into a favorite tree, along with a pledge of eternal love, and then waited breathlessly for Sarah to discover and respond to her declaration of affection. The response appears to have been affirmative. A half-century later, urbane and sophisticated Katherine Wharton commented upon meeting an old school chum: "She was a great pet of mine at school & I thought as I watched her light figure how often I had held her in my arms — how dear she had once been to me." Katie maintained a long, intimate friendship with another girl. When a young man began to court this friend seriously, Katie commented in her diary that she had never realized "how deeply I loved Eng and how fully." She wrote over and over again in that entry, "Indeed I love her!," and only with great reluctance left the city that summer, since it meant also leaving Eng with Eng's new suitor.

Peggy Emlen, a Quaker adolescent in Philadelphia in the 1760s, expressed similar feelings about her first cousin, Sally Logan. The girls sent love poems to each other (not unlike the ones Elizabeth Bordley wrote to Nelly Custis a generation later), took long, solitary walks together, and even haunted the empty house of the other when one was out of town. Indeed, Sally's absences from Philadelphia caused Peggy acute unhappiness. So strong were Peggy's feelings that her brothers began to tease her about her affection for Sally and threatened to steal Sally's letters, much to both girls' alarm. In one letter that Peggy wrote the absent Sally, she elaborately described the depth and nature of her feelings:

> I have not words to express my impatience to see My Dear Cousin, what would I not give just now for an hours sweet conversation with her, it seems as if I had a thousand things to say to thee, yet when I see thee, everything will be forgot thro' joy. . . . I have a very great friendship for several Girls yet it dont give me so much uneasiness at being absent from them as from thee. . . . [Let us] go and spend a day down at our place together and there unmolested enjoy each others company.

Sarah Alden Ripley, a young, highly educated woman, formed a similar intense relationship, in this instance with a woman somewhat older than herself. The immediate bond of friendship rested on their atypically intense scholarly interests, but it soon involved strong emotions, at least on Sarah's part. "Friendship," she wrote Mary Emerson, "is fast twining about her willing captive the silken hands of dependence, a dependence so sweet who would renounce it for the apathy of self-sufficiency?" Subsequent letters became far more emotional, almost conspiratorial. Mary visited Sarah secretly in her room, or the two women crept away from family and friends to meet in a nearby wood. Sarah became jealous of Mary's other young woman friends. Mary's trips away from Boston also thrust Sarah into periods of anguished depression. Interestingly, the letters detailing their love were not destroyed but were preserved and even reprinted in a eulogistic biography of Sarah Alden Ripley. . . .

How, then, can we ultimately interpret these long-lived intimate female relationships and integrate them into our understanding of Victorian sexuality? Their ambivalent and romantic rhetoric presents us with an ultimate puzzle: the relationship along the spectrum of human emotions between love, sensuality, and sexuality.

One is tempted, as I have remarked, to compare Molly, Peggy, or Sophie's relationship with the friendships adolescent girls in the twentieth century routinely form — close friendships of great emotional intensity. Helena Deutsch and Clara Thompson have both described these friendships as emotionally necessary to a girl's psychosexual development. But, they warn, such friendships might shade into adolescent and postadolescent homosexuality.

It is possible to speculate that in the twentieth century a number of cultural taboos evolved to cut short the homosocial ties of girlhood and to impel the emerging women of thirteen or fourteen toward heterosexual relationships. In contrast, nineteenth-century American society did not taboo close female relationships but, rather, recognized them as a socially viable form of human contact — and, as such, acceptable throughout a woman's life. Indeed, it was not these homosocial ties that were inhibited but, rather, heterosexual learnings. While closeness, freedom of emotional expression, and uninhibited physical contact characterized women's relationships with one another, the opposite was frequently true of male-female relationships. One could thus argue that within such a world of female support, intimacy, and ritual it was only to be expected that adult women would turn trustingly and lovingly to one another. It was a behavior they had observed and learned since childhood. A different type of emotional landscape existed in the nineteenth century, one in which Molly and Helena's love became a natural development.

Of perhaps equal significance are the implications we can garner from this framework for the understanding of heterosexual marriages in the nineteenth century. If men and women grew up, as they did, in relatively homogeneous and segregated sexual groups, then marriage represented a major problem in adjustment. From this perspective we could interpret much of the emotional stiffness and distance that we associate with Victorian marriage as a structural consequence of contemporary sex-role differentiation and gender-role socialization. With marriage both women and men had to adjust to life with a person who was, in essence, a member of an alien group.

I have thus far substituted a cultural or psychosocial for a psychosexual interpretation of women's emotional bonding. But there are psychosexual implications in this model which I think it only fair to make more explicit. Despite Sigmund Freud's insistence on the bisexuality of us all, or the recent American Psychiatric Association decision on homosexuality, many psychiatrists today tend explicitly or implicitly to view homosexuality as a totally alien or pathological behavior — as totally unlike heterosexuality. I suspect that in essence they may have adopted an explanatory model similar to the one used in discussing schizophrenia. As a psychiatrist can speak of schizophrenia and of a borderline schizophrenic personality as both ultimately and fundamentally different from a normal or a neurotic personality, so they also think of both homosexuality and latent homosexuality as states totally different from heterosexuality. With this rapidly dichotomous model of assumption, "latent homosexuality" becomes the indication of a disease in progress — seeds of a pathology which belie the reality of an individual's heterosexuality.

Yet, at the same time, we are well aware that cultural values can affect choices in the gender of a person's sexual partner. We, for instance, do not necessarily consider homosexual-object choice among men in prison, on shipboard, or in boarding schools a necessary indication of pathology. I would urge that we expand this relativistic model and hypothesize that a number of cultures might well tolerate or even encourage diversity in sexual and nonsexual relations. Based on my research into this nineteenth-century world of female intimacy, I would further suggest that, rather than seeing a gulf between the normal and the abnormal, we view sexual and emotional impulses as part of a continuum or spectrum of affect gradations strongly affected by cultural norms and arrangements, a continuum influenced in part by observed and thus learned behavior. At one end of the continuum lies committed heterosexuality, at the other uncompromising homosexuality; between, a wide latitude of emotions and sexual feelings. Certain cultures and environments permit individuals a great deal of freedom in moving across this spectrum. I would like to suggest that the nineteenth century was such a cultural environment. That is, the supposedly repressive and destructive Victorian sexual ethos may have been more flexible and responsive to the needs of particular individuals than those of the mid-twentieth century.

Southern Indians and the Cult of True Womanhood

THEDA PERDUE

Southern Indians stand apart culturally and historically from other native Americans. Building of temple mounds, an elaborate ceremonial life, a complex belief system, riverine agriculture, and matrilineal descent characterized their aboriginal culture. Southern Indians embraced European culture with such enthusiasm and success that they came to be known as the "five civilized tribes." They acquired this sobriquet in the half-century after the ratification of the United States Constitution, a time when many southern Indians came to believe that their physical survival depended on adopting an Anglo-American lifestyle and value system. These Indians gradually abandoned hunting and subsistence agriculture, the practice of blood vengeance, their traditional religious beliefs and practices, and other aspects of their aboriginal way of life. Some individual Indians succeeded so well that they became culturally indistinguishable from their white neighbors. They owned large plantations, operated successful businesses, attended Christian churches, promoted formal legal and judicial systems, and wrote and conversed in the English language.

An integral part of this cultural transformation was a redefinition of gender roles. Just as men could no longer follow their aboriginal pursuits of hunting and warfare, women could no longer behave in what was perceived to be a "savage" or "degraded" way. Instead, they had to attempt to conform to an Anglo-American ideal characterized by purity, piety, domesticity, and submissiveness. By the second quarter of the nineteenth century, the glorification of this ideal had become so pervasive in American society that the historian Barbara Welter has called it the cult of true womanhood." . . .

Theda Perdue, "Southern Indians and the Cult of True Womanhood," in Walter J. Fraser, et al., eds., *The Web of Southern Social Relations,* 1985, pp. 35–51. Reprinted by permission of The University of Georgia Press.

Traditionally southern Indians had a very different view of womanhood. Indian women occupied a separate sphere from that of men, but they had considerable economic, political, and social importance. While men hunted and went to war, women collected firewood, made pottery and baskets, sewed clothes, cared for children, and cooked the family's food. These tasks certainly fell within the nineteenth-century definition of domesticity, but the sphere of Indian women extended beyond home and hearth to encompass economic activities that seemed far less appropriate to their sex. In particular, women farmed in a society that depended primarily on agriculture for subsistence, and women performed most of the manual labor with men assisting only in clearing fields and planting corn. . . .

. . . [Women] received formal recognition for their economic contribution and they controlled the fruit of their labor. In the Green Corn Ceremony, the southern Indians' most important religious event, women ritually presented the new crop, which was sacrificed to the fire, and when Europeans occasionally purchased corn from Indians in the eighteenth century, they bought it from women. . . . Southern Indians distinguished between the sexes on other than merely biological grounds. Women were women not only because they could bear children but also because they farmed, and men who farmed came to be regarded sexually as women. Men hunted, therefore, because hunting was intrinsically linked to male sexuality; women farmed because farming was one of the characteristics that made them women.

The matrilocal residence pattern of southern Indians probably contributed to the association of women and agriculture. A man lived in the household of his wife's lineage, and buildings, garden plots, and sections of the village's common field belonged to her lineage. A man had no proprietary interest in the homestead where he lived with his wife or in the land his wife farmed. Nor was a husband necessarily a permanent resident in the household of his wife's lineage. Polygamy was common, and he might divide his time between the lineages of his wives. Furthermore, southeastern Indians frequently terminated their marriages, and in the event of divorce, a man simply left his wife's household and returned to his mother's house and his own lineage. Because southeastern Indians were also matrilineal, that is, they traced kinship only through the female line, children belonged to the mother's lineage and clan rather than to the father's, and when divorce occurred, they invariably remained with their mothers. Men, therefore, had no claim on the houses they lived in or the children they fathered. . . .

Women in southern Indian tribes did have considerable sexual freedom. Except for restraints regarding incest and menstrual taboos, Indian women were relatively free in choosing sexual partners, engaging in intercourse, and dissolving relationships. All southern Indians condoned premarital sex and divorce, which were actually female or male prerogatives, but attitudes toward adultery varied from one tribe to another. . . .

Although all southern Indians had certain common characteristics — they were matrilineal and matrilocal, women farmed, and both sexes enjoyed some sexual freedom — Cherokee women had the highest degree of power and personal autonomy. The trader James Adair maintained that the Cherokees "have been a considerable while under a petticoat-government." In Cherokee society, women spoke in council and determined the fate of war captives. Some even went on the warpath and earned a special title, "War Woman." In fact, Cherokee women were probably as far from the "true women" of the early nineteenth-century ideal as any women Anglo-Americans encountered on the continent. When the United States government and Protestant missionaries undertook the "civilization" of native Americans in the late eighteenth century, however, the Cherokees proved to be the most adept at transforming their society. Because the Cherokees provide the greatest contrast between the aboriginal role of women and the role that emerged in the early nineteenth century as a consequence of civilization, I will examine the impact of the cult of true womanhood on the status of Cherokee women. . . .

In a letter of 1796, George Washington advised the Cherokees to raise cattle, hogs, and sheep. He pointed out that they could increase the amount of corn they produced by using plows and that they could also cultivate wheat and other grains. Apparently addressing the letter to the men, Washington continued: "To these you will easily add flax and cotton which you may dispose of to the White people, or have it made up by your own women into clothing for yourselves. Your wives and daughters can soon learn to spin and weave." Washington apparently knew nothing about traditional gender roles, and the agents he sent usually had little sympathy for the Indian division of labor. They provided plows to the men and instructed them in clearing fields, tilling soil, and building fences. Women received cotton cards, spinning wheels, and looms.

The women, politically ignored in the eighteenth century and bypassed in the earlier hunting economy, welcomed the opportunity to profit from contact with whites. In 1796, agent Benjamin Hawkins met with a group of Cherokee women and explained the government's plan. He reported to Washington that "they rejoiced much at what they had heard and hoped it would prove true, that they had made some cotton, and would make more and follow the instruction of the agent and the advice of the President." According to a Cherokee account, the women proved far more receptive to the civilization program than the men. . . .

Cultural change came more easily . . . among Cherokees who already had adopted the acquisitive, materialistic value system of white Americans. Turning from an economy based on hunting, they took advantage of the government's program and invested in privately owned agricultural improvements and commercial enterprises. They quickly became an economic elite separated from the majority of Cherokees by their wealth and by their desire to emulate whites. In the early nineteenth century, members of this economic elite rose to positions of leadership in the Cherokee Nation because of the ease and effectiveness with which they dealt with United States officials. Gradually they transformed Cherokee political institutions into replicas of those of the United States. This elite expected Cherokee women to conform to the ideals of the cult of true womanhood. . . .

Cherokees learned to be true women primarily through the work of Protestant missionaries whom tribal leaders welcomed to the nation. . . .

Mission schools provided an elementary education for girls as well as boys. Either single women or the wives of male missionaries usually taught the girls, but all students studied the same academic subjects, which included reading, writing, spelling, arithmetic, geography, and history. Examinations took place annually and were attended by parents. The teachers questioned students in their academic subjects as well as Bible history, catechism, and hymns, and "the girls showed specimens of knitting, spinning, mending, and fine needlework."

Mastery of the domestic arts was an essential part of the girls' education because, according to one missionary, "all the females need is a proper education to be qualified to fill any of the relations or stations of domestic life." The children at the mission schools performed a variety of tasks, and the division of labor approximated that in a typical Anglo-American farming family. The boys chopped wood and plowed fields, and the girls milked, set tables, cooked meals, washed dishes, sewed clothing, knitted, quilted, did laundry, and cleaned the houses. Because their fathers were wealthy, many students were not accustomed to such menial labor. Missionaries endeavored to convince them that "the charge of the kitchen and the mission table" was not degrading but was instead a "most important station," which taught them "industry and economy."

The great advantage of teaching Cherokee girls "industry and economy" was the influence they might exert in their own homes. . . . Although missionaries and students expected the domestic arts learned in the mission schools to improve the parental home, they believed that the primary benefit would be to the homes the girls themselves established. Missionary Sophia Sawyer specifically hoped to "raise the female character in the Nation" so that "Cherokee gentlemen" could find young women "sufficiently educated for companions." In 1832 missionaries could report with satisfaction that the girls who had married "make good housewives and useful members of society."

The marriages missionaries had in mind were not the Cherokees' traditional polygamous or serial marriages. . . . Although the Cherokee elite accepted most tenets of Western civilization, some balked at abandoning the practice of polygamy. . . . They recognized the desirability of monogamous unions, however, encouraged others to enter into them, and sent their children to mission schools where they were taught that polygamy was immoral. . . .

Achieving "moral deportment" at the mission schools was no simple matter, but missionaries considered the teaching of New England sexual mores to be one of their chief responsibilities. According to some reports, they enjoyed success. In 1822, American Board missionaries reported: "Mr. Hall thinks the moral influence of the school has been considerable. . . . The intercourse between the young of both sexes was shamefully loose. Boys & girls in their teens would strip & go into bathe, or play ball together naked. They would also use the most disgustingly indecent language, without the least sense of shame. But, when better instructed, they became reserved and modest." . . .

The girls' appearance was another concern of the missionaries. Ann Paine related an attempt to correct the daughter of a particularly prominent Cherokee: "Altho' her parents supplied her with good clothes, she was careless and indifferent about her appearance. — I often urged her attention to these things and offered as a motive her obligation to set a good example to her nation as the daughter of their chief. Told her how the young ladies of the North were taught to govern their manners and tempers and of their attention to personal appearance. She never appeared more mortified than in hearing of her superiority of birth, and of the attention she ought to pay to her personal appearance." Paine soon had "the satisfaction of witnessing her rapid improvement." . . .

In addition to a neat, feminine appearance, respectable men presumably also admired piety in young women and probably expected them to be more pious than they themselves were. The missionaries clearly believed that the female students in mission schools were more serious about religion than the male students, and they encouraged this emotion. . . . The girls at the mission station . . . organized a society to raise money to send missionaires into heathen lands. The American Board agreed to pay them for clothing they made, and they in turn donated the money to mission work. They also sold their handwork to local Cherokee women. The piety of the girls extended beyond the school and into the community. Once a month, neighboring women would gather at the mission for a prayer meeting "that missionary labors may be blessed." One missionary reported with satisfaction that "the females have a praying society which is well attended, and they begin to do something by way of benevolence." . . .

Although the feminine ideal of purity, piety, submissiveness, and domesticity did not immediately filter down to the mass of Cherokees, the nation's leaders came to expect these qualities in women. Therefore, the influence of the cult of true womanhood probably far exceeded the modest number of women trained in mission schools. The Cherokee leaders helped create a new sphere for women by passing legislation that undermined matrilineal kinship and excluded women from the political process. In the first recorded Cherokee law of 1808, the national council, which apparently included no women, established a police force "to give their protection to children as heirs to their father's property, and to the widow's share." Subsequent legislation gave further recognition to patrilineal descent and to the patriarchial family structure common among men of wealth. In 1825 the council extended citizenship to the children of white women who had married Cherokee men, another act that formally reordered descent. Legislation further isolated women by prohibiting polygamy and denied women the right to limit the size of their families by outlawing the traditional practice of infanticide. In 1826 the council decided to call a constitutional convention to draw up a governing document for the tribe. According to legislation that provided for the election of delegates to the convention, "No person but a free male citizen who is full grown shall be entitled to vote." Not suprisingly, when the convention met and drafted a constitution patterned after that of the United States, women could neither vote nor hold office. The only provisions in the Cherokee legal code reminiscent of the power and prestige enjoyed by aboriginal women were laws that protected the property rights of married women and prohibited their husbands from disposing of their property without consent. . . .

Of all the southern tribes, the Cherokees provide the sharpest contrast between the traditional role of women and the role they were expected to assume in the early nineteenth century. In this period, the Cherokees excluded women, who originally had participated in tribal governance, from the political arena. Women in other tribes had been less active politically; consequently, their status did not change as dramatically. All southern nations, however, did move toward legally replacing matrilineal with patrilineal descent and restricting the autonomy of women. . . . Although these changes occurred at different rates among southern Indians, women began to fade from economic and political life in the early nineteenth century. Just as the traditional female occupation, farming, became commercially viable, men took over and women became only secondarily involved in subsistence. Women, of course, still had their homes and families, but their families soon became their husbands' families, and domesticity brought influence, not power. Similarly, purity and piety seemed almost anachronistic in a culture and age that tended to value the material above the spiritual. . . .

This separate sphere in which Indian women increasingly lived in the nineteenth century could hardly give rise to a women's rights movement, as some historians have suggested it did among white women, because true womanhood came to be associated with civilization and progress. Any challenge to the precepts of the cult of true womanhood could be interpreted as a reversion to savagery. Ironically, by the end of the century, some white Americans had come to view the traditional status of Indian women in a far more favorable light. In 1892 the author of an article in the *Albany Law Review* applauded the revision of property laws in the United States to protect the rights of married women and noted that such a progressive practice had long existed among the Choctaw and other southern Indians. This practice, however, was only a remnant of a female role that had been economically productive, politically powerful, and socially significant but had been sacrificed to the cult of true womanhood.

※ *F U R T H E R   R E A D I N G*

Lee Virginia Chambers-Schiller, *Liberty, A Better Husband: Single Women in America, The Generations of 1780–1840* (1984)

Frances B. Cogan, *All-American Girl: The Ideal of Womanhood in Mid-Nineteenth Century America* (1989)

Nancy Cott, *The Bonds of Womanhood* (1977)

Ann Douglas, *The Feminization of American Culture* (1977)

John Mack Faragher, *Women and Men on the Overland Trail* (1979)

Harvey Green, *The Light of the Home: An Intimate View of the Lives of Women in Victorian America* (1983)

Karen Halttunen, *Confidence Men and Painted Women: A Study of Middle-Class Culture in America, 1830–1870* (1982)

Julie Jeffrey, *Frontier Women: The Trans-Mississippi West, 1840–1880* (1979)

Mary Kelley, *Private Woman, Public Stage: Literary Domesticity in Nineteenth-Century America* (1984)

Suzanne Lebsock, *The Free Women of Petersburg* (1984)

Jane Nylander, *Our Own Snug Fireside: Images of the New England Home, 1760–1860* (1993)

Mary P. Ryan, *Cradle of the Middle Class: The Family in Oneida County, New York, 1790–1865* (1981)

Kathryn Kish Sklar, *Catharine Beecher* (1973)

Carroll Smith-Rosenberg, *Disorderly Conduct: Visions of Gender in Victorian America* (1985)

CHAPTER
6

The Lives of Enslaved Women

Historians who study the experience of African-Americans under slavery are currently engaged in a heated debate on the extent to which bondspeople were able to carve out areas of autonomy for themselves within an admittedly oppressive system. The dispute dates back to the 1950s, when such scholars as Stanley Elkins published books emphasizing enslaved blacks' lack of control over their lives. The tide turned in the 1970s, when most scholars took the opposite approach, describing the ways in which slaves were able to create rich familial, cultural, and religious lives for themselves despite their bondage. Such writers stressed African-Americans' success at resisting slaveholders; they assessed the character of the lives of those in the slave quarters as if they were independent of outside forces, and paid little attention to whites' powerful hold on their human chattel.

Now the pendulum has swung back the other way, and some historians are once again emphasizing the oppressive nature of the slave system in the American South during the antebellum years. In this new wave of scholarship, a discussion of gender differences within the slave experience plays a major role. What were the conditions of slavery for women? Can an examination of women's unique experiences under slavery offer useful evidence about the oppressiveness of the system of slavery as a whole?

Regardless of how they answer these questions, historians are constrained by the nature of the sources available to them. Only a few slaves were literate, and just a small number of these produced accounts of their experiences. Accordingly, many of the major pieces of surviving evidence are the letters, diaries, and plantation records of white slaveholders, and these must be used with extreme caution because of their inherent bias. Historians can also rely on slave narratives collected in the 1930s by researchers from the Federal Writers' Project, who traveled through the South talking with aged African-Americans about their lives before emancipation. But since the youngest interviewees were already in their late seventies by this time, researchers must always be aware that the memories of old persons can be faulty and that the stories told by these elderly ex-slaves were probably influenced by the race and sex of the person who interviewed them.

The first three documents are all narratives of former slaves. The first, the recollections of Cornelia, a Tennessean, was collected by a researcher from Fisk University. The other two come from work done by the Federal Writers' Project: The second selection is an interview with Rose Williams, of Texas, and the third is an interview with Fannie Moore, who grew up in South Carolina. The last document consists of two letters from literate slave wives to their husbands; they are rare, direct, contemporary testimonies of the anguish of women forcibly separated from their spouses through sale.

Cornelia's Life on a Tennessee Farm

I began to exist in the year 1844, in a small town in Tennessee. Eden, Tennessee, was between Nashville and Memphis. . . .

I was the personal property of Mr. Jennings, who was a well-polished southern man. He was portly in build, lively in step, and dignified in manner. Mr. Jennings was a good man. There was no disputing that. . . .

Master Jennings had a small farm. We did not cultivate any cotton; we raised corn, oats, hay and fruits. Most of Master Jennings' slaves were hired out. He had four families of slaves, that is, Aunt Caroline's family, Uncle Tom's family, Uncle Dave's family, and the family of which I was a member. None of these others were related by blood to us. My father had several brothers who lived on other places.

Aunt Caroline, a big mulatto woman, was very quiet and good-natured. I don't remember ever hearing her fuss. Each family had a cabin, and there were but four cabins on the place. Aunt Mary, my mother's aunt, stayed with us in our cabin. She had never married or had any children.

My mother was the smartest black woman in Eden. She was as quick as a flash of lightning, and whatever she did could not be done better. She could do anything. She cooked, washed, ironed, spun, nursed and labored in the field. She made as good a field hand as she did a cook. I have heard Master Jennings say to his wife, "Fannie has her faults, but she can outwork my nigger in the country. I'd bet my life on that."

My mother certainly had her faults as a slave. She was very different in nature from Aunt Caroline. Ma fussed, fought, and kicked all the time. I tell you, she was a demon. She said that she wouldn't be whipped, and when she fussed, all Eden must have known it. She was loud and boisterous, and it seemed to me that you could hear her a mile away. Father was often the prey of her high temper. With all her ability for work, she did not make a good slave. She was too high-spirited and independent. I tell you, she was a captain.

The one doctrine of my mother's teaching which was branded upon my senses was that I should never let anyone abuse me. "I'll kill you, gal, if you don't stand up

"Cornelia," in Bert S. Loewenberg and Ruth Bogin, eds., *Black Women in Nineteenth-Century American Life,* pp. 48–53, 1976. Reprinted by permission of Fisk University Library and The Pennsylvania State University Press.

for yourself," she would say. "Fight, and if you can't fight, kick; if you can't kick, then bite." Ma was generally willing to work, but if she didn't feel like doing something, none could make her do it. At least, the Jennings couldn't make, or didn't make her. . . .

I was the oldest child. My mother had three other children by the time I was about six years old. It was at this age that I remember the almost daily talks of my mother on the cruelty of slavery. I would say nothing to her, but I was thinking all the time that slavery did not seem so cruel. Master and Mistress Jennings were not mean to my mother. It was she who was mean to them. . . .

One day my mother's temper ran wild. For some reason Mistress Jennings struck her with a stick. Ma struck back and a fight followed. Mr. Jennings was not at home and the children became frightened and ran upstairs. For half hour they wrestled in the kitchen. Mistress, seeing that she could not get the better of ma, ran out in the road, with ma right on her heels. In the road, my mother flew into her again. The thought seemed to race across my mother's mind to tear mistress' clothing off her body. She suddenly began to tear Mistress Jennings' clothes off. She caught hold, pulled, ripped and tore. Poor mistress was nearly naked when the storekeeper got to them and pulled ma off.

"Why, Fannie, what do you mean by that?" he asked.

"Why I'll kill her, I'll kill her dead if she ever strikes me again."

I have never been able to find out the why of the whole thing. My mother was in a rage for two days, and when pa asked her about it and told her that she shouldn't have done it, it was all that Aunt Caroline could do to keep her from giving him the same dose of medicine.

"No explaining necessary. You are chicken-livered, and you couldn't understand." That was all ma would say about it.

Pa heard Mr. Jennings say that Fannie would have to be whipped by law. He told ma. Two mornings afterwards, two men came in at the big gate, one with a long lash in his hand. I was in the yard and I hoped they couldn't find ma. To my surprise, I saw her running around the house, straight in the direction of the men. She must have seen them coming. I should have known that she wouldn't hide. She knew what they were coming for, and she intended to meet them halfway. She swooped upon them like a hawk on chickens. I believe they were afraid of her or thought she was crazy. One man had a long beard which she grabbed with one hand, and the lash with the other. Her body was made strong with madness. She was a good match for them. Mr. Jennings came and pulled her away. I don't know what would have happened if he hadn't come at that moment, for one man had already pulled his gun out. Ma did not see the gun until Mr. Jennings came up. On catching sight of it, she said, "Use your gun, use it and blow my brains out if you will."

Master sent her to the cabin and he talked with the man for a long time. I had watched the whole scene with hands calmly clasped in front of me. I felt no urge to do anything but look on.

That evening Mistress Jennings came down to the cabin. She stopped at the door and called my mother. Ma came out.

"Well, Fannie," she said, "I'll have to send you away. You won't be whipped, and I'm afraid you'll get killed. They have to knock you down like a beef."

"I'll go to hell or anywhere else, but I won't be whipped," ma answered. . . .

About a week later, she called me and told me that she and pa were going to leave me the next day, that they were going to Memphis. She didn't know for how long.

"But don't be abused, Puss." She always called me Puss. My right name was Cornelia. I cannot tell in words the feelings I had at that time. My sorrow knew no bound. My very soul seemed to cry out, "Gone, gone, gone forever." I cried until my eyes looked like balls of fire. I felt for the first time in my life that I had been abused. How cruel it was to take my mother and father from me, I thought. My mother had been right. Slavery was cruel, so very cruel.

Thus my mother and father were hired to Tennessee. The next morning they were to leave. I saw ma working around with the baby under her arms as if it had been a bundle of some kind. Pa came up to the cabin with an old mare for ma to ride, and an old mule for himself. Mr. Jennings was with him.

"Fannie, leave the baby with Aunt Mary," said Mr. Jennings very quietly.

At this, ma took the baby by its feet, a foot in each hand, and with the baby's head swinging downward, she vowed to smash its brains out before she'd leave it. Tears were streaming down her face. It was seldom that ma cried, and everyone knew that she meant every word. Ma took her baby with her.

With ma gone, there was no excitement around the place. Aunt Mary was old and very steady in her ways; Aunt Caroline was naturally quiet, and so were all the rest. I didn't have much to do around the place, and I thought about ma more than anyone around there knew. Yes, ma had been right. Slavery was chuck full of cruelty and abuse. During this time I decided to follow my mother's example. I intended to fight, and if I couldn't fight I'd kick; and if I couldn't kick, I'd bite. The children from the big house played with my brothers, but I got out of the bunch. I stopped playing with them. I didn't care about them, so why play with them. At different times I got into scraps with them. Everyone began to say, "Cornelia is the spit of her mother. She is going to be just like Fannie." And I delighted in hearing this. I wanted to be like ma now.

An uneventful year passed. I was destined to be happily surprised by the return of my mother and father. They came one day, and found me sitting by the roadside in a sort of trance. I had not seen them approaching; neither was I aware of their presence until ma spoke. Truly, I had been thinking of ma and pa at the time. I had dreams of seeing them again, but I thought that I would have to go to them. I could hardly believe that ma and pa were standing before my very eyes. I asked myself if I was still dreaming. No, I was not dreaming. They were standing over me. Ma was speaking to me.

"Puss, we've come back, me and pa, and we've come to stay."

"Oh, Ma," I exclaimed, "I was a praying to see you."

She and pa embraced and caressed me for a long time. . . .

Ma had on new clothes, and a pair of beautiful earrings. She told Aunt Mary that she stayed in Memphis one year without a whipping or a cross word.

Rose Williams's Forced Marriage in Texas

What I say am the facts. If I's one day old, I's way over ninety, and I's born in Bell County, right here in Texas, and am owned by Massa William Black. He owns Mammy and Pappy, too. Massa Black has a big plantation, but he has more niggers than he need for work on that place, 'cause he am a nigger trader. He trade and buy and sell all the time.

Massa Black am awful cruel, and he whip the colored folks and works 'em hard and feed 'em poorly. We-uns have for rations the corn meal and milk and 'lasses and some beans and peas and meat once a week. We-uns have to work in the field every day from daylight 'til dark, and on Sunday we-uns do us washing. Church? Shucks, we-uns don't know what that mean.

I has the correct memorandum of when the war start. Massa Black sold we-uns right then. Mammy and Pappy powerful glad to git sold, and they and I is put on the block with 'bout ten other niggers. When we-uns gits to the trading block, there lots of white folks there what come to look us over. One man shows the interest in Pappy. Him named Hawkins. He talk to Pappy, and Pappy talk to him and say, "Them my woman and childs. Please buy all of us and have mercy on we-uns." Massa Hawkins say, "That gal am a likely-looking nigger; she am portly and strong. But three am more than I wants, I guesses."

The sale start, and 'fore long Pappy am put on the block. Massa Hawkins wins the bid for Pappy, and when Mammy am put on the block, he wins the bid for her. Then there am three or four other niggers sold before my time comes. Then Massa Black calls me to the block, and the auction man say, "What am I offer for this portly, strong young wench. She's never been 'bused and will make the good breeder."

I wants to hear Massa Hawkins bid, but him say nothing. Two other men am bidding 'gainst each other, and I sure has the worriment. There am tears coming down my cheeks' cause I's being sold to some man that would make separation from my mammy. One man bids $500, and the auction man ask, "Do I hear more? She am gwine at $500." Then someone say, "$525," and the auction man say, "She am sold for $525 to Massa Hawkins." Am I glad and 'cited! Why, I's quivering all over.

Massa Hawkins takes we-uns to his place, and it am a nice plantation. Lots better than Massa Black's. There is 'bout fifty niggers what is growed and lots of children. The first thing Massa do when we-uns gits home am give we-uns rations and a cabin. You must believe this nigger when I says them rations a feast for us. There plenty meat and tea and coffee and white flour. I's never tasted white flour and coffee, and Mammy fix some biscuits and coffee. Well, the biscuits was yum, yum, yum to me, but the coffee I doesn't like.

The quarters am pretty good. There am twelve cabins all made from logs and a table and some benches and bunks for sleeping and a fireplace for cooking and the heat. There am no floor, just the ground.

Massa Hawkins am good to he niggers and not force 'em work too hard. There am as much difference 'tween him and Old Massa Black in the way of treatment as 'twixt the Lord and the devil. Massa Hawkins 'lows he niggers have reasonable parties and go fishing, but we-uns am never tooken to church and has no books for larning. There am no education for the niggers.

There am one thing Massa Hawkins does to me what I can't shunt from my mind. I knows he don't do it for meanness, but I always holds it 'gainst him. What he done am force me to live with that nigger, Rufus, 'gainst my wants.

After I been at he place 'bout a year, the massa come to me and say, "You gwine live with Rufus in that cabin over yonder. Go fix it for living." I's 'bout sixteen year old and has no larning, and I's just ignomus child. I's thought that him mean for me to tend the cabin for Rufus and some other niggers. Well, that am start the pestigation for me.

I's took charge of the cabin after work am done and fixes supper. Now, I don't like that Rufus, 'cause he a bully. He am big and 'cause he so, he think everybody do what him say. We-uns has supper, then I goes here and there talking, till I's ready for sleep, and then I gits in the bunk. After I's in, that nigger come crawl in the bunk with me 'fore I knows it. I says, "What you means, you fool nigger?" He say for me to hush the mouth. "This am my bunk, too," he say.

"You's teched in the head. Git out," I's told him, and I puts the feet 'gainst him and give him a shove, and out he go on the floor 'fore he know what I's doing. That nigger jump up and he mad. He look like the wild bear. He starts for the bunk, and I jumps quick for the poker. It am 'bout three feet long, and when he comes at me I lets him have it over the head. Did that nigger stop in he tracks? I's say he did. He looks at me steady for a minute, and you could tell he thinking hard. Then he go and set on the bench and say, "Just wait. You thinks it am smart, but you am foolish in the head. They's gwine larn you something."

"Hush your big mouth and stay 'way from this nigger, that all I wants," I say, and just sets and hold that poker in the hand. He just sets, looking like the bull. There we-uns sets and sets for 'bout an hour, and then he go out, and I bars the door.

The next day I goes to the missy and tells her what Rufus wants, and Missy say that am the massa's wishes. She say, "You am the portly gal, and Rufus am the portly man. The massa wants you-uns for to bring forth portly children."

I's thinking 'bout what the missy say, but say to myself, "I's not gwine live with that Rufus." That night when him come in the cabin, I grabs the poker and sits on the bench and says, "Git 'way from me, nigger, 'fore I bust your brains out and stomp on them." He say nothing and git out.

The next day the massa call me and tell me, "Woman, I's pay big money for you, and I's done that for the cause I wants you to raise me childrens. I's put you to live with Rufus for that purpose. Now, if you doesn't want whipping at the stake, you do what I wants."

I thinks 'bout Massa buying me offen the block and saving me from being separated from my folks and 'bout being whipped at the stake. There it am. What am I's to do? So I 'cides to do as the massa wish, and so I yields. . . .

I never marries, 'cause one 'sperience am 'nough for this nigger. After what I does for the massa, I's never wants no truck with any man. The Lord forgive this colored woman, but he have to 'scuse me and look for some others for to 'plenish the earth.

Fannie Moore's Memories of a South Carolina Childhood

Nowadays when I heah folks a'growlin an' a'grumblin bout not habbin this an' that I jes think what would they done effen they be brought up on de Moore plantation. De Moore plantation b'long to Marse Jim Moore, in Moore, South Carolina. De

Moores had own de same plantation and de same niggers and dey children for yeahs back. . . .

Marse Jim own de bigges' plantation in de whole country. Jes thousands acres ob lan'. An de ole Tiger Ribber a'runnin' right through de middle ob de plantation. On one side ob de ribber stood de big house, whar de white folks lib and on the other side stood de quarters. De big house was a purty thing all painted white, a standin' in a patch o' oak trees. . . .

De quarters jes long row o' cabins daubed wif dirt. Ever one in de family lib in one big room. In one end was a big fireplace. Dis had to heat de cabin and do de cookin' too. We cooked in a big pot hung on a rod over de fire and bake de co'n pone in de ashes or else put it in de skillet and cover de lid wif coals. We allus hab plenty wood to keep us warm. Dat is ef we hab time to get it outen de woods.

My granny she cook for us chillens while our mammy away in de fiel. Dey wasn't much cookin to do. Jes make co'n pone and bring in de milk. She hab big wooden bowl wif enough wooden spoons to go 'roun'. She put de milk in de bowl and break it up. Den she put de bowl in de middle of de flo' an' all de chillun grab a spoon.

My mammy she work in de fiel' all day and piece and quilt all night. Den she hab to spin enough thread to make four cuts for de white fo'ks ebber night. Why sometime I nebber to go bed. Hab to hold de light for her to see by. She hab to piece quilts for de white folks too. Why dey is a scar on my arm yet where my brother let de pine drip on me. Rich pine war all de light we ebber hab. My brother was a holdin' de pine so's I can help mammy tack de quilt and he go to sleep and let it drop.

I never see how my mammy stan' sech ha'd work. She stan' up fo' her chillun tho'. De ol' overseeah he hate my mammy, case she fight him for beatin' her chillun. Why she git more whuppins for dat den anythin' else. She hab twelve chillun. . . .

My mammy grieve lots over brothah George, who die wif de fever. Granny she doctah him as bes' she could, evah time she git way from de white folks kitchen. My mammy nevah git chance to see him, 'cept when she git home in de evenin'. George he jes lie. One day I look at him an' he had sech a peaceful look on his face, I think he sleep and jes let him lone. Long in de evenin' I think I try to wake him. I touch him on de face, but he was dead. Mammy nebber know til she come at night. Pore mammy she kneel by de bed an' cry her heart out'. Ol' uncle Allen, he make pine box for him an' carry him to de graveyard over on de hill. My mammy jes plow and cry as she watch 'em put George in de groun'.

Two Letters from Enslaved Wives, 1840 and 1852

Richmond Va. october 27 1840

Dear Husband —

this is the third letter that I have written to you, and have not received any from you; and dont no the reason that I have not received any from you. I think very hard of it. the trader has been here three times to Look at me. I wish that you would try to see if you can get any one to buy me up there. if you dont come down here this Sunday, perhaps you wont see me anymore. give my love to them all, and tell them all that perhaps I shan't see you any more. give my love to your mother in particular, and to mamy wines, and to aunt betsy, and all the children; tell Jane and Mother they must come down a fortnight before christmas. I wish to see you all, but I expect I never shall see you all — never no more.

I remain your Dear and affectionate Wife,
Sargry Brown.

Charlottesville Oct. 8, 1852

Dear Husband   I write you a letter to let you know of my distress   my master has sold Albert to a trader on Monday court day and myself and other child is for sale also and I want you to let [me] hear from you very soon   before next cort if you can   I don't know when   I don't want you to wait till Christmas

I want you to tell Dr. Hamilton your master if either will buy me they can attend to it know and then I can go afterwards

I don't want a trader to get me   they asked me if I had got any person to buy me and I told them no   they told me to the court house too   they never put me up   A man buy the name of brady bought albert and is gone   I don't know whare   they say he lives in scottsville   my things is in several places   some is in stanton and if I would be sold I don't know what will become of them   I don't expect to meet with the luck to get that way till I am quite heart sick   nothing more   I am and ever will be your kind wife

Marie Perkins

❋ E S S A Y S

In the first essay, Christie Farnham, who teaches at Iowa State University, interprets the daily lives of slave women in light of the African past, and explicitly discusses twentieth-century commentaries on contemporary African-American family life. Emphasizing that women's work and the organization of families under the slave system did not differ greatly from their ancestors' West African experience, she stresses enslaved women's ability to control certain aspects of their lives. In the second essay, Thelma Jennings, a retired history professor, reaches a different conclusion by relying heavily on the Federal Writers' Project slave narratives. Uncovering substantial evidence that women were sexually exploited by slaveholders, she contends that many bondswomen's personal lives were severely disrupted by their masters' attempts to reduce them to concubinage or to force them to bear as many children as possible. Which historian makes the stronger case? Is the history of enslaved families relevant to the lives of African-Americans in the 1990s?

The Position of Women in the Slave Family

CHRISTIE FARNHAM

The question of dominance in the black family became a national issue in 1965 with the publication of *The Negro Family in America: The Case for National Action,* by Daniel Patrick Moynihan, who attributed the problems of the black urban poor to a

Christie Farnham, "Sapphire? The Issue of Dominance in the Slave Family, 1830–1865," in Carol Groneman and Mary Beth Norton, eds., *To Toil the Livelong Day": America's Women at Work.* Copyright © 1987, pp. 68–83. Used by permission of the publisher, Cornell University Press.

"tangle of pathology" resulting from the "disorganization" of the black family. The term "disorganization," by which Moynihan meant the presence of female-headed households whose origins he claimed to find in slavery, is significant. It is a value-laden term that has become part of the jargon of social science; it implies that female-headed households are inherently disorderly because there is no male to impose his authority over the woman and her children. Female-headed households constituted for Moynihan *ipso facto* evidence of the existence of matriarchy and were by definition contrary to nature, since "the very essence of the male animal, from the bantam rooster to the four-star general, is to strut." This report is but the most prominent example of what has been termed the pathological school of black family studies, which accepts the white, middle-class nuclear family as the norm and assumes that all groups should assimilate its values. From this perspective the black family is seen as deviant, being characterized by high rates of illegitimacy, the absence of fathers, and welfare dependency — all of which are thought to undermine female–male relationships and produce adverse effects on the personality development of the children. These views have come under increasing attack from scholars with a commitment to a pluralistic society, such as R. H. Hill and Andrew Billingsley, who emphasize the strengths of the black family, especially its coping strategies in a racist society. However, the growth of female-headed families from 17.6 percent in 1950 to 40.2 percent in 1980 (compared with 8.5 and 14.6 percent for whites) — in conjunction with statistics showing that "a Black child is twice as likely as a white child to live with neither parent, three times as likely as a white child to be born to a teenage mother, seven times as likely to have parents who separate, and three times as likely to see his or her father die" — has kept the question of dominance in the black family alive more than twenty years after Moynihan first focused national attention on this issue.

However, the question of power relationships in the slave family cannot be understood apart from the African context, particularly as it affected women's work roles. Although earlier scholars rejected Melville Herskovits' emphasis on African cultural transfers, there is now a general consensus that, whereas links to African culture are not nearly so strong among Afro-Americans as among their counterparts in Latin America, such retentions are nevertheless not only numerous but fundamental to the formation of Afro-American culture. Contemporary scholars have delineated an important substratum of African retentions in such areas as music, dance, religion, folklore, and family life.

African societies were many and varied; therefore, generalizations must be made with caution. Nevertheless, there appears to have been a basic similarity in family structures. Whether they were organized as matrilineages or patrilineages, Niara Sudarkasa makes the case for a fundamental distinction between African forms consisting of extended families — built around consanguineal cores of same-sex adult siblings with their spouses and children, living together in compounds — and Euro-American patterns of isolated households based on the husband-wife-children bond. She terms this distinction the difference between consanguinity and conjugality. Although the nuclear family may not have been so typical as it was once thought to be, these two models are useful for highlighting cultural differences that influenced the development of the black family under slavery.

One of the most important differences to flow from these two models lies in the work roles of women. Most African societies were polygynous. A bride moved into the compound of her husband's kin or her husband moved into hers. In either case the lineage or kin group was of paramount importance. It was lineage elders, not husbands, who parceled out farmland to women for their individual use. Although in some parts of West Africa both men and women engaged in agriculture, elsewhere in the region, as well as in most areas to the south, farming was considered women's work. In short, there is no reason to suspect that in precolonial times women did not perform most of the agricultural labor.

Women's role in cultivation derived from a sexual division of labor that assigned women the responsibility for feeding their husbands and children. Since the land was given to women for their own use, the surplus they produced often belonged to them. For example, a French missionary to the eighteenth-century Bakongo living north of the Zaire River described how "each woman has her own hut, fields, gardens, and slaves over which the husband has no rights after she takes care of his needs." Such customs continued into the nineteenth century. A German, describing the Bakongo living on the Loango coast, observed that "when they have satisfied the needs of their husband, the produce that remains from the fields and from animal husbandry is their own." During that same period it is reported that the Bakalai women of Gabon "are expected to feed their husbands . . . but to what is left or not needed of the fruits thus raised the men have no right. The women sell and keep for themselves the articles received." Where women controlled the agricultural surplus, internal trade markets came to form a central part of their world. Maintaining property and profits separate from those of their husbands facilitated a tradition of female entrepreneurship in which a few women even achieved wealth and status.

The fact that the women of the compound were numerous and bound together by intimate ties facilitated organization in support of common interests. Women of the villages and towns, all wives of a local lineage, usually formed associations. The Igbo women of eighteenth-century Onitsha, for example, organized for the purpose of regulating trade, arranging the cooking for village meetings, and the like. Strength in numbers also provided them with some leverage in female-male relationships, enabling them to insist upon the proper treatment of wives.

Polygyny, women's organizations, and the support extended by one's blood kin tended to dilute the emotional importance of marriage, which was essentially an economic transaction between two families rather than a love match that established an all-encompassing relationship, as in the conjugal model. Although some societies, like the Hausa of present-day Nigeria, required virginity in brides, most accepted premarital sex. The overarching concern of the lineage for perpetuation and the strength that numbers bring gave procreation a central focus in African life. Sterility was a calamity. The primacy of lineage and the organization of family life into collectivities of blood relatives and their spouses also meant that childbearing lacked the exclusivity attached to the conjugal model. Although biological parents had the primary responsibility for their children, there were no rigid boundaries; the parenting role was exercised by all adults, and children were taught to identify themselves as daughters and sons of the lineage rather than as cousins.

The work roles of women and the sexual division of labor are in marked contrast to those of the conjugal model, whose characteristics were sharpened during the Victorian period under consideration and idealized in what Barbara Welter has termed the "cult of true womanhood," which emphasized piety, purity, submissiveness, and domesticity. The nuclear family epitomized the notion of exclusivity. Spouses were emotionally dependent on each other; resources were pooled and decisions made jointly or by the husband for the entire unit. Wives were isolated in the home, often separated from close kin and bearing sole responsibility for child care; husbands were providers and protectors, mediating between the home and the outside world. In striking contrast to the African view of sex as normal and healthy was the Victorian ambivalence, tinged with guilt and burdened with a Western cultural heritage that tended to dichotomize women into two types: the good, who were pure and passionless like the Virgin Mary; and the bad, who were sinful and seductive like Eve.

Separate decision-making, property, and incomes, combined with the power that resided in women's organizations and the allies available in natal villages, provided the traditional African woman with the space to be self-reliant. Self-reliance should never be confused with equality between the sexes, however. Although many traditional societies operated with dual sex systems in which each sex managed its own affairs and maintained its own hierarchies of power and position, such systems were meant to be complementary, not parallel — which says nothing about the relative balance of power and prestige between women and men. Separate is not equal. In general, the world that women inhabited offered labor-intensive work that largely involved taking care of the physical needs of men and children. That this work was organized and regulated by the women themselves does not erase the subordinate character of the enterprise.

What happened when the consanguineal and conjugal models collided on American plantations? Reaction to the Moynihan report had the positive effect of spurring research into the slave family. Although conscious attempts were made to avoid the previous error of viewing the black family through the prism of white middle-class norms, the thrust of the research has been an effort to refute Moynihan's position by documenting the presence of males in the household. The major factor underlying this approach seems to have been a desire to substantiate the importance of the family in Afro-American culture and to attack the negative stereotype of blacks as promiscuous. Laudable as these goals are, they have had the unfortunate effect of trivializing the importance of the female-headed household.

The most important study to respond to Moynihan's allegations is Herbert Gutman's book *The Black Family in Slavery and Freedom, 1750–1925*. Documenting premarital sexual norms and naming patterns, Gutman demonstrates that Afro-American culture was not a mimetic version of white forms. He also presents evidence of a shockingly high rate of forced separations. However, he does not use this high rate to support Moynihan's contention that the separation of spouses by planters resulted in a legacy of family disorganization. On the contrary, he counters this finding with evidence demonstrating that most slaves lived in double-headed families, thereby emphasizing how slaves clung to this form of family organization despite the exigencies of the slave system.

The term "double-headed," however, calls forth an image similar to that of the two-parent nuclear family and obscures the fact that many men were not the biological fathers of all the children present in the family. Such usage avoids the issue of serial monogamy, yet serial monogamy can produce at least temporary and often permanent female-headed households. Gutman seems to share Moynihan's view that female-headed families are aberrant. When he finds, for example, that "nearly one in five children born in families that started before 1855 grew up in households headed by women who had all their children by unnamed fathers" on the Stirling plantation in Louisiana, he considers the situation "important" but "far from common." Since some of these women had large families and were never sold, these facts suggest to him that "far from revealing the legitimacy of the single-parent household, such behavior may have represented deviation from the community's norm." Nevertheless, he also finds evidence of female-headed households elsewhere — for example, eight of them on the Bennehan-Cameron plantation were established before 1830. And 9 percent of those who fled to Camp Becker during the Civil War listed themselves as single parents — and some of them were in their thirties, not teenage mothers living with their families of origin. Gutman's study attempts to demonstrate the continuance of double-headed families into the twentieth century, but although he insists that the "typical black household . . . had in it two parents," he again documents numerous exceptions.

Recent research demonstrates the ubiquitousness of female-headed families in northern urban areas in the late nineteenth century, and a newly discovered 1878 survey of a portion of Dinwiddie County, Virginia, provides evidence that serial monogamy and the presence of children from pre- and extramarital unions were characteristic of the post-Emancipation family. Figures from this survey show that of those who had been married during slavery, 29.8 percent had been married more than once and 7 percent more than twice. These statistics are virtually identical to those indicating that by 1878 31.1 percent married more than once and 7.7 percent more than twice, thus demonstrating that serial marriage was common in slave times and remained substantially unchanged after emancipation. A study of ex-slave narratives finds that 18 percent remembered having lived in single-parent households. This finding is corroborated by Paul D. Escott's work, which shows that one-fifth of the ex-slaves interviewed reported having experienced at least partial breakup of their families. Orville Vernon Burton finds in his study of slavery in Edgefield, South Carolina, that "there was an accepted pattern of divorce among the slaves: long periods of relations between two slaves were replaced by alliances with others." He estimates the frequency of such divorce at 25 percent. Although Burton places little importance on African retentions as an explanation for slave society's acceptance of "divorce," the fact that it was practiced within a dominant culture to which divorce was anathema, whereas traditional African societies accepted the practice, argues for African continuities. Furthermore, since it is unlikely that both spouses would find new mates simultaneously, the potential for the formation of significant numbers of female-headed households is obvious. Thus the existence of such households is sufficiently extensive to warrant their inclusion among Afro-American cultural institutions.

There are two difficulties in dealing with female-headed households: the definition of the term and the significance of the form. Are only those households to be included in which the women never married? But since slave marriages had no legal standing, what constitutes a marriage? Despite more than fifteen years of feminist scholarship, the female-headed family has yet to be viewed as a significant institution under slavery. Contemporary scholars of all persuasions have regarded the female-headed family as transitory: a young woman will soon "settle" into marriage, giving her children a father; teenage mothers remain with their families of origin until marriage, so there is a father figure present to provide a role model; if a woman is widowed or separated from her spouse, her previous marriage constitutes evidence that she does not reject the institution. Those instances of women who never married — such as the mother of William Wells Brown, who had seven children by seven men, both black and white — are dismissed as aberrant cases that existed for the benefit of the master.

Susanne Lebsock has taken a different view of female-headed families among free blacks in antebellum Petersburg, Virginia, half of whose households were headed by women. She sees this phenomenon as a rational response to the fact that single women retained ownership of their property, whereas married women's property reverted to their husbands: "The possibility remains that some free black women valued their relative equality and did their best to maintain it." The large numbers of female-headed families under slavery indicate that for some women the maintenance of a single-parent family was an inventive approach to conditions common to the slave system and represented an expansion of women's choices. Obviously, slavery was a brutal and coercive system, and the concept of choice does not apply to those spouses torn asunder by death or forced separation, nor does it imply that the available choices included an ideal one. Nevertheless, in a system where basic needs were provided by the master, the option of heading a family offered a small measure of autonomy that some women may have found preferable to other possible arrangements. To see this choice as aberrant is to interpret female-headed families within an androcentric framework and to ignore the attempts of some women to enlarge the confines of the cage of slavery.

If female heads of households have been cast as matriarchs, the wives in double-headed families have not altogether escaped a similar charge of being "Sapphires." Named after the wife of the Kingfish on the popular *Amos 'n' Andy* radio show of the 1930s, Sapphires wore the pants in the family and treated men with contempt. Stanley M. Elkins, for example, analyzed the slave family as one in which the " 'real' father was virtually without authority over his child, since discipline, parental responsibility, and control of rewards and punishments all rested in other hands." Thus the role of the slave mother was more important than that of the father. Since the father could not protect his family from the lash, Elkins saw the cardinal components of the conjugal family's conception of manhood — provision and protection — as being undermined. But Africans did not view manhood in those terms. The lineage was the basic means of protection, and women themselves had a large role in providing for the family through their obligation to raise food. Yet if one conceptualizes the black family in terms of the nuclear middle-class white family, the slave mother is seen to slip into the power vacuum created by the emasculating effects of the slave system on the father, in consequence of which her power is unnaturally enhanced.

This view of the emasculated male which was popularized by Moynihan resulted in a particularly angry reaction, coming as it did in the midst of the Black Power movement, a movement which emphasized self-defense and pride in manhood. To counteract this interpretation, scholars sensitive to black nationalism have searched for evidence of male supremacy in both precolonial African and antebellum American societies. John Blassingame characterizes African societies as patri-archal; but, accepting the view of manhood which requires men to provide for and protect their families, he emphasizes the efforts fathers made to furnish their cabins and supplement the family diet through barter and hunting. Nevertheless, their sta-tus within the family, which Blassingame sees as resting on the authority of the hus-band over his wife and children, was reduced by slavery: "They could no longer ex-ercise the same power over their families as they did in Africa." The bedrock of such a conception of manhood is the determination to stand and fight, which leads Blassingame to describe the plantation as "a battlefield where slaves fought masters for physical and psychological survival. Although unlettered, unarmed, and out-numbered, slaves fought in various ways to preserve their *manhood*" (emphasis mine). Thus, for Blassingame, Sapphire is banished, and the slave experience be-comes synonymous with the male experience.

The feminist movement began to impinge upon this conceptualization of the problem of dominance in the 1970s, with curious results. Eugene Genovese, for ex-ample, describes cornshucking parties in *Roll, Jordan, Roll: The World the Slaves Made.* Slaves gathered from neighboring plantations for an evening of feasting, singing, and storytelling designed to make the mountain of corn disappear faster. The men did the shucking and were served by the women. Since Genovese can find no evidence that the women complained about being excluded from the party, he concludes that "they seem to have grasped the opportunity to underscore a division of labor and authority in the family and support the pretensions of their men." He believes that "on whatever level of consciousness" — his explanation for the lack of explicit documentation — women attempted "to strengthen their men's self-esteem and to defer to their leadership." He concludes that "what has usually been viewed as a debilitating female supremacy was in fact a closer approximation to a healthy sexual equality than was possible for whites." Unlike Blassingame, who agrees with Elkins that husbands had lost some of their power under slavery and consequently struggled to rise to a position of parity with their wives, Genovese sees the wives as being conscious, at some level, of their unseemly superiority and therefore as at-tempting to reduce themselves to the level of their husbands by becoming deferen-tial and increasing the division of labor in slave society.

By 1979, Blassingame had joined Genovese in viewing the slave family as es-sentially egalitarian in structure. He extolled "the transportation of African familial roles [which] led to the creation of America's first democratic family in the quar-ters, where men and women shared authority and responsibility." Thus, in the short space of about a decade, the picture of the slave family changed from one in which the wife exceeded her husband in power and authority to a situation characterized by egalitarian relationships. This new-found democratic family was based largely on evidence drawn from the labor force participation of black women: from the be-ginning of slavery most female slaves had been agricultural laborers, doing even such heavy work as plowing, cutting wood, and building fences, roads, and canals. This interpretation of the family may have been influenced by the movement of American women into the work force in ever larger numbers in the 1970s and by the emphasis of the women's movement on the right of women to enter previously male-dominated professions. Many analyses in anthropology and other disciplines delineated the split between the public and private spheres of life, demonstrating

how power and prestige inhered in the public sphere, from which women were traditionally excluded.

However, the field was not a forum for slave power, either female or male. Furthermore, the fact that women worked in both the public and private spheres — that
is, the field and the house — whereas men were active primarily in only one, the
field, did not represent equality. Scholars have recently attempted to rectify this
analysis by constructing the notion of the egalitarian slave family on a two-way
movement in the division of labor. Angela Davis insists that not only did women
labor in the fields but "men executed important domestic duties"; thus "the salient
theme emerging from domestic life in the slave quarters is one of sexual equality."
She points to the fact that "men would sometimes work in the cabin and women
might tend the garden and perhaps even join the hunt." The argument that women
gardened and hunted is but another instance of women participating in what white
society considered to be men's work. The reverse situation — men working in the
home — is but a "sometimes" activity. Thomas Webber makes the most ambitious
attempt to document the presence of males in the domestic sphere. He concludes
that "while it is true that in most slave households women did the cooking, washing,
sewing, and cleaning and men did the gardening, constructing, and hunting, roles
were reversed often enough to suggest this was more a convenient division of labor
than an expression of a societal norm that favored one sex over the other." He fails
to explain, however, on what grounds he considers the assignment of household
tasks to women to be "more convenient."

The ex-slave narratives make abundantly clear that women had responsibility
for what has traditionally been seen as women's work. There is no evidence, for example, that men engaged in spinning, a job that occupied much of the women's time
in the evenings. More typical of the life of the ordinary slave woman is the description by the former slave Henry Baker: ". . . de wimmin plowed jes lack de men. On
Wednesday night dey had tuh wash en aftuh dey washed dey had tuh cook suppah.
De nex' mornin' dey would get wid de men en dey had tuh cook breakfus 'fore dey
went tuh de fiel' en had tuh cook dinner [the noon meal] at de same time en take hit
wid 'em." Even husbands in cross-owner marriages, who saw their wives only on
weekends, did not do their own laundry. A white man living in Georgia described
how, on "Saturday night, the roads were . . . filled with men on their way to the
'wife house,' each pedestrian or horseman bearing his bag of soiled clothes." The
movement of women into agricultural labor did not engender egalitarian relationships, since the public sphere (if such it can be termed) was a source of neither
wealth nor power. Although women took pride in their strength and competence,
their labor in the public sphere meant double duty, not power parity.

Sarah Fitzpatrick, a slave born in Alabama in 1838, observed: "Love is a
won'erful thing. A mother al'ays loves her chillun. Don't care whut dey do. Dey
may do 'rong but it's stil' her chile. Den dere is de love uv'va 'oman fer her man,
but it ain't nut'in lack a mother's love fer her chillun. I loves a man when he treats
me right but I ain't never had no graveyard love fer no man." Inasmuch as protection and provision were not as salient to the concept of manhood in the consanguineal model as they were in the conjugal model, it is unlikely that slaves brought
from Africa insisted upon these qualities in a relationship. The slave experience it-

self inhibited the development of this conception, since shelter and basic provisions were provided by the masters, who also controlled to a large extent the use of physical force on the plantation. Thus there is little in the historical record to indicate that slave women considered their husbands to be unmanly. With no property to transmit or lineages to maintain, it is reasonable to suppose that companionship became a major attribute in the choice of a spouse. This may have been less true of men, however, since both consanguineal and conjugal models require women to take care of their husband's physical needs. Robert Smalls, a former slave, explained to a congressional committee that in slavery "the colored men in taking wives always do so in reference to the service the women will render."

Della Promise, a resident of rural Macon County, Alabama, explained in the early 1900s that "everybody don't git married, and if I can't git the one I want I don't want to git married. I never seen but one boy I thought I could marry, and me and him had ways too much alike, and I knowed we couldn't git along, so I just has my chillun and raises 'em myself." Della Promise was exercising an option that some white professional women have only recently begun to choose. Although not universally applauded, the decision of single white professional women to raise families alone is sometimes seen as a positive approach to the problem of the paucity of men in their age and status categories, whereas the same choice by some black women — under slavery and later — has been castigated. Certainly, to be the female head of a family was not the ideal of slave society any more than it is the ideal of today's white professional women. But slaves, perhaps more than others, recognized that life is not always ideal. Of course, for many women — such as those separated from spouses by force or death — circumstances, not choice, brought them to the heads of their families. Nevertheless, a significant if small number of women appear to have chosen not to marry at all.

Black women were able to develop the alternative of female-headed families when it seemed in their interest to do so, given the constraints of slavery, because neither the slave community nor the planter class raised sanctions against it. The female-headed family, while different from the matricentric cell of the polygynous African family, was sufficiently similar in physical structure — a woman and her children living together in a separate residence — that this phenomenon would not have appeared altogether alien to slave society.

Despite occasional instances of polygamy, this form of marriage did not take root in America; nevertheless, the consanguineal model formed a general perspective toward marriage and family which could become the basis of patterns of behavior developed to meet the exigencies of slavery. Of these, the prime example is the fictive kin networks, which provided slaves — many of them torn from their blood relatives — with feelings of belonging and the protection previously provided by the lineage.

The development of a unique Afro-American culture grew out of attempts to retain what was feasible from African values and institutions. In the process, new forms were created. Female-headed families were viable under slavery because the planter provided the cabin, clothing, and food rations. Slave women understood that this arrangement was not a gift; they knew that their labor paid for their upkeep and that their children increased the value of their masters' estates. Since African women fed their families and Afro-American women continued to be agricultural laborers, the fact that slave women were ultimately responsible for feeding their children would not have seemed inappropriate.

Female-headed families were also viable in terms of child care, since the fictive kinship system, designed in part to replace the lineages of West African society, continued the practice of the socialization of children by the group rather than by parents alone. All adults felt some responsibility for the children on the plantation, and this arrangement had the added benefit of providing male role models in abundance. Furthermore, child-care arrangements were imposed upon all mothers, not just single heads of families, so that women would be free to labor in the fields. The designation of elderly women and other children to provide child care while the mothers worked removed a major obstacle that contemporary working mothers face. In fact, it was this very communal nature of the socialization of children — especially the assistance of grandmothers in caring for children resulting from the custom of prebridal pregnancy, and the assistance of older women while younger ones worked in the field — that made it possible to split off sexual relations from reproduction, much as access to the pill has separated sex from pregnancy in contemporary American society, thereby facilitating a change in sexual mores.

Blassingame points out that premarital sex was accepted among many African peoples as a normal part of courtship. Although the religious significance of sex was lost in the move to the American slave system, and Christianization developed ambivalent attitudes toward sex outside of marriage for many, the belief remained that sex is a natural act largely unconnected with sin. Such a view of sexuality permitted the slave community to be more accepting of female-headed families than was possible in white society. Although null evidence is seldom reported, the fact that slave communities did not shun such women or their children supports this interpretation of slave society. In fact, their full inclusion in the community argues strongly for the acceptance of this family form.

If female-headed families did not seem totally alien or threatening to Afro-American slave society, neither did they disturb the rationale for slavery developed by the master class. Reproduction, however achieved, added to a planter's wealth. Furthermore, the female-headed family did not adversely affect the labor supply, since female heads of families were forced to work in the fields or big house in the same manner as wives. Finally, slave indifference to the white middle-class standards of female purity idealized by Victorian America appeared to corroborate negative stereotypes of black women as promiscuous, thereby making it easier for white women as well as white men to blame the exploitation of black women on the victims.

It is useful to compare the development of the female-headed family under slavery with the development of a similarly small population of single white women in America during the nineteenth century. Because the norms of white middle-class society insisted on celibacy outside of marriage, these women were never in a position to become heads of families — a tragic deprivation for some of them. The prevalent animosity toward self-reliant women required them to accept Victorian notions of purity and self-sacrifice. It was only by extending these ideals to society generally, in what has been termed social housekeeping, that they were able to maintain a precarious existence. Slave women, on the other hand, through the redefinition of certain West African cultural forms that also meshed with the interests of the planter class, were able to raise a family alone. Unmarried white women, despite the image of single blessedness, were trivialized by a society that mocked them as man-hating old maids whom no man found attractive, but there is nothing in the historical record to indicate that the slave community treated female heads of families as pariahs or stigmatized their children as the illegitimate fruit of illicit unions.

"Sapphire" and "matriarch" are derogatory labels that have in common the image of women "lording it" over men. Yet black women in both double-headed and female-headed families were slaves to a double work load — both field and domestic labor. Perhaps what is so threatening, especially to a society based on conjugality, is not their power and privilege (for they had little) but their self-reliance, for self-reliance implies not so much ruling over men as the ability to manage without them.

The Sexual Exploitation of African-American Slave Women

THELMA JENNINGS

Because they were slaves, African-American women were affected by the rule of the patriarch in more ways and to a greater degree than the white women in the Big House. The size of the food allotment, brutal whippings, slave sales, and numerous other variables influenced the bondwoman's view of the patriarchy. Yet because she was a woman, her view, like that of the white woman, was also gender related. . . . This essay will, therefore, deal only with the bondwomen's perspective from the viewpoint of gender, using twentieth-century interviews with female ex-slaves who were at least twelve or thirteen years of age at the time of emancipation. Of the 514 women in this category, 205, or almost forty percent, made comments of this nature. Undoubtedly, the reluctance of ex-bondwomen to discuss such private matters, especially with white men and women, accounts for the fact that the number was not larger. A sample of fifty-eight male slave interviews in the same category was made for comparison; twenty-seven, or 46.55 percent, made gender-related comments. Likewise, a sample of contemporary testimony for both women and men was used. Compared to the Works Progress Administration narratives, contemporary testimony offers a great deal less evidence of sexual exploitation. The men outnumber the women even more than in the WPA narratives.

Female bondage was more severe than male bondage because these women had to bear children and cope with sexual abuse in addition to doing the work assigned to them, work that was often similar in type and quantity to that of male slaves. When it was profitable to exploit women as if they were men in the work force, slaveholders regarded female slaves, in effect, as genderless. But when they could be exploited in ways designed only for women, they were exclusively female — subordinate and unequal to all men. Bondwomen realized the white patriarch had

Thelma Jennings, " 'Us Colored Women Had To Go Through A Plenty': Sexual Exploitation of African-American Slave Women," from *Journal of Women's History,* I (1990), pp. 45–66. Reprinted by permission of Journal of Women's History.

the *power* to force them to mate with whomever he chose, to reproduce or suffer the consequences, to limit the time spent with their children, and even to sell them and their children.

From the beginning of adolescence, females were subject to their master's desire for them to reproduce because increasing the number of slaves meant profits to him. Intervention in the process of procreation, either through subtle or forceful means, became an integral part of the sexual exploitation of bondwomen. Numerous women testified that all owners wanted slaves to have a goodly number of children. . . .

Generally speaking, slaveowners dictated the rules governing slave unions. Whether the woman was allowed to mate with a man who chose her or had one forced upon her by the master was crucial. Phobe Henderson vowed that her master had nothing to do with bringing Phobe and her husband together. She guessed that God did it since they fell in love. . . . Though Rose Williams' master treated his slaves well, he forced Rose to live with an African-American against her desires. She always held this against him. Rose's master told her to live with Rufus, a man she considered a bully. At first, Rose resisted and went to her mistress who explained the master's wishes. "Yous am de portly gal and Rufus am de portly man," Missus told Rose. "De massa wants 'you-uns for to bring forth portly chillen." Rose remained adamant until her master told her, "Woman, I'se pay big money for yous an' I'se done dat fo' de cause I'se wants yous to raise me chilluns. I'se put you to live wid Rufus fo' dat pu'pose. Now if yous don't want to be whupped at the stake, yous do w'at I'se want." After the war, Rose never married. "One 'sperience am 'nough fo' dis nigger," she explained. "Aftah w'at I'se do fo' de Marster, I'se never want any truck wid any man." . . .

Interference with sexual activities in such a direct manner as in the case of Rose and Rufus constituted slave breeding by some slaveowners. Considerable controversy exists among historians on the nature and extent of slave breeding. . . . [Most] discussions of slave breeding are strictly economic in focus — an increase in *quantity* for *profits*. No mention is made of *quality* or the improvement of the species; there is no hint at the practice of eugenics. In his quantitative analysis of the slave narratives, Paul Escott briefly discusses the interference of masters with the sexual activities of slaves. He enumerates several different types of slave breeding: rewards to good breeders or sale of barren women, directed pairings often between "fine and stout" individuals, the use of stock men, and the elimination of "runty" males as fathers. Most of these types of slave breeding represent a crude form of eugenics. Though Escott cites a few examples in such cases, he does not include an explicit discussion of the eugenics of slave breeding. . . .

When we turn our attention to the female interviewees in this study, we note that only twenty-five (4.86 percent) commented on slave breeding as outlined by Escott. However, six of the fifty-eight male interviewees (10.34 percent) in the sample made such comments. Only one slave (male) in the contemporary sample noted slave breeding. What is quite significant is that six of the twenty-five women and four of the six men made remarks that specifically indicated "eugenic manipulation." . . .

Some bondwomen revealed bitter resentment in very frank, pathetic terms. Katie Darling said her master would pick out "a po'tly man and a po'tly gal" and just "put 'em together because what he wanted was the stock." Slave weddings on Annie Row's place were compared to "de weddin' 'tween de cows and de bull" because "dey wants bigger niggers an' dey mates to suits demse'ves." In discussing the mating of men and women on her plantation, Polly Shine said "this never suited us much but we had to do just like our Masers made us, as we could not do any other way." Refusals would only result in whippings and "mean" treatment. . . .

Slave breeding made it very difficult for couples to establish stable family relationships. Describing the cruelty of her master, Louisa Everett said he mated slaves indiscriminately without any regard for family unions. If the master thought a certain man and woman might have strong, healthy offspring, he forced them to have sexual relations even though they were married to other slaves. In case either one showed any reluctance, the master would make the couple consummate this relation in his presence. . . . On Mary Ingram's plantation, the master made the decision on who could and could not get married. "Him select de po'tly and p'lific women, and de po'tly man, and use sich for de breeder an' de father ob de women's chilluns." The women selected were not allowed to marry and "de womens have nothin' to says 'bout de'rangement." . . .

One thing that distinguished a "good master" from a bad one in the slaves' eyes was his attitude toward marriage. It is impossible to determine how many couples had their marriage solemnized "officially" by a preacher or the master himself or how many simply jumped the broom. It is clear, however, that bondwomen who had a big wedding with a minister spoke with pride of the event. Lou Williams recalled, "I'se had a 'spectable weddin' 'cause Miss she say I was her nursemaid. De preacher he reads and I was all dressed up in white clothes and sech a supper we never had." Lou claimed she had the best white folks in the state of Maryland. Tempie Durham, dressed in white, was married on the front porch of the Big House by the black preacher of the plantation church. Tempie also spoke highly of her master and mistress. When interviewed in her early nineties, Nancy King related that she was married in a church two miles off the place by a white preacher. Her owners were "good" to their slaves and "didn' disfigure" them as some were known to do. These examples and others in the narratives indicate that a respectable wedding by a minister, black or white, definitely affected an ex-bondwomen's view of the patriarch, who often was described as a "good" master. . . .

Whether for black or white, the importance of prenatal care was not well understood; and, for both, childbirth was a dangerous procedure. Slaveowners faced a conflict of interests. They deplored the loss of time granted to a pregnant field worker, yet they faced the possibility of the loss of both mother and child if she were forced to work too long and too hard. The two objectives, immediate profits and long-term economic considerations, therefore, clashed at times. In their eagerness for profits, most slaveowners apparently agreed with the Mississippi planter who declared that "labor is conducive to health; a healthy woman will rear most children." Though they were aware to some extent that very hard work was not beneficial, they placed the blame for the loss of slave babies on their mothers, who were often accused of smothering their infants. Slaveowners also sometimes blamed the pregnant bondwomen for miscarriages that increased during the cotton boom years. . . .

Overseers and drivers were responsible for much of the physical abuse of pregnant women, but masters were also guilty at times. Without some explanation, such abuse is incomprehensible. The basic reason — immediate profits — that accounts for long hours of overwork also explains the use of violent methods to achieve a productive work force. Masters often suspected bondwomen of shamming and feigning illness. They became impatient with the slower work of pregnant women. In their eagerness for a bumper crop, they were determined to discipline pregnant women, as well as other workers, who failed to do the work expected of them. Undoubtedly, the patriarchal desire to show authority also accounts for some of the physical abuse. Moreover, there was unfortunately a trace of sadism in some slaveowners, as well as overseers and drivers, which was directed against the weaker members of the slave community — pregnant women, children, and the elderly. Thwarted in their desires to discipline a strong male, these slaveowners punished the pregnant women who fell behind with their work. Driven by impulse, masters in a fit of anger also punished pregnant women without ever thinking of the dangerous consequences for them and their unborn children. . . .

Given the pressure to reproduce for the master's profit at a time when childbirth was dangerous and children could be sold at the master's whim, we can readily understand why bondwomen would have reason to practice birth control and abortion and to induce miscarriages. Such practices may be seen as a form of passive resistance, depriving owners of what they demanded from bondwomen. . . . Forced by her master to marry a man she hated, Mary Gaffney at first refused to let him touch her, but he told the master who then whipped Mary. That night, then, she let her husband have his way. "Maser was going to raise him a lot more slaves, but still I cheated Maser." Mary had no babies, and her owner wondered what was wrong. She said she chewed cotton roots and was careful not to let her master catch her. After freedom, Mary had five children. Anna Lee claimed that female slaves had started chewing cotton roots to keep from having babies. If slavery had lasted much longer, there would have been only old ones left as "we had done quit breeding." Another Texas woman said women could cause a miscarriage by taking calomel, turpentine, and indigo. . . .

Soon after giving birth, most slave mothers usually had to trust the care of their babies to someone else in order to return to the fields. From that time on, the contact they had with their children during the day was limited by the rule of the patriarch who did not consider their maternal needs and feelings, his primary motive being profit. In most cases, an old slave woman took care of the babies and small children. Larger plantations had nurseries and hospitals; smaller places used an old slave woman's house. Young slave girls also cared for the children. The image of patriarchal society with happy, contented slaves dims when we read the words of Elvira Boles, who had to work very hard. "Don' evvy thing but split rails. I've cut timber — evvy thing a man could do." But she hated to leave her baby when working. "I'd leave mah baby cryin' in the yard and I'd be cryin', but I couldn't stay." As Louisa Everett pointed out, slave women had no time for their own children. Sometimes they were further deprived of what little time they did have by being forced to care for white children. Rachel Sullivan told her interviewer that as a young girl she took care of some black children while their mother served as wet nurse for a white woman. What this slave woman must have felt one can only imagine. . . .

In all probability, slave infants and children did receive fairly good physical care as measured by the standards of the time. After all, it was in the owners' best interests to see that they developed into strong, healthy adults to be used as workers and breeders or to be sold. It must be noted that knowledge of such things as diet, sanitation, and medical treatment was very limited. House flies, for example, were a menace to the whites as well as the slaves. Moreover, owners often seemed more concerned about unborn children than pregnant women. The former represented future investment. For the highest return, the labor of pregnant women and nursing mothers should, however, be utilized in the present, while they were making their contribution to the future. This also explains why owners were careful in regulating nursing periods.

Bondwomen were not only forced to live with males of their own race but were also forced to have sexual relations with white men. . . . Of the 514 female slaves selected for this study, sixty-three, or 12.26 percent commented on interracial sex. Twenty-two of this number (35 percent) were directly involved; that is, their fathers were white men and/or they had given birth to one or more mulatto children. The number was probably much higher. Escott has shown that the sex and race of the interviewer influenced the frequency of all ex-slaves' revelations concerning miscegenation. It is reasonable to believe that some freedwomen were reticent, except with a black woman interviewer. According to both white and black sources, *forced* interracial sex was much more frequent than slave breeding. In only one instance did an interviewee state that some bondwomen were not forced. She told her Fisk University interviewer that "all the colored women didn't have to have white men, some did it because they wanted to and some were forced. They had a horror of going to Mississippi and they would do anything to keep from it."

Regardless of the number involved, the freedwomen clearly indicate, as did white women, that crossing the racial barrier was a source of discontent. The difference, however, was that the bondwomen were the victims. Only slave breeding could compare with forced interracial sex in the extent of pain and humiliation they caused. Although male slaves were subjected to forced sex as stock men, in the case of miscegenation, only the bondwomen could be subjected to the white man's passion. . . .

Thirty-six of the interviewees who commented on miscegenation, or 57 percent, noted that the master himself was guilty of interracial sex. . . . Moreover, nine of the sixty-three interviewees who commented on interracial sex claimed the master or his son as father (14.28 percent). None treated their paternity as unusual. Alice Marshall explained that her mother was "a very light woman who never got beat" and was "kinda favorite wid de white folks." When asked about her father, Alice replied, "Well, I reckon I oughter not to tell dat, but it ain' my shame. 'Twas ole massa. . . . He's my father. Chile, dat was ev'y day happenin's in dem days." . . . The master-father of Amy Patterson ran a kind of agency through which he collected slaves and yearly sold them to dealers or hired them out to other people. He promised Amy's mother he would never sell their mulatto child, but later he decided to sell all his slaves and move to another place. At first he refused to sell his daughter, but he finally sold Amy to her mother's new master because of the grief of mother and daughter. Amy's stinging remark, disguised as a question, was "when a father can sell his own child, humiliate his own daughter by auctioning her on the slave block, what good could be expected where such practices were allowed?" . . .

How could a white father ignore his own flesh and blood and even sell his off-spring? The first reason is the ideology of race. Children with even a drop of African blood were not considered members of the white family. Only offspring of a man with his white wife were family and legitimate heirs to carry on his name. Moreover, some white men did not feel responsible for the mulatto children they fathered since, according to their justification, the black, promiscuous Jezebel had initiated the sexual relationship. Sex and race were further intertwined with capital. Slave offspring could increase the labor force or add money to the master's pockets if he sold them. . . .

Female bondage was not only different from male bondage, it was more severe as a result of sexual exploitation. Twentieth-century interviews and contemporary autobiographies of black women narrate sexual abuse and sufferings "peculiarly their own." Male slave testimony confirms the bondwomen's perspective. Throughout the South, slaveowners required bondwomen to reproduce for their profit in addition to working as long and often as hard as male slaves. The master's attitude, often insensitive and cavalier, was deeply disturbing on such matters as choice of mates, marriage, pregnancy, and child care. Some bondwomen were even subjected to breeding. Moreover, they knew they could become victims of the white man's sexual desires any time. Anne Firor Scott has described the resulting "widespread discontent" among white women; bondwomen responded in different ways, depending on temperament and circumstances. Most acquiesced in an effort to prevent themselves or family members from being beaten or sold. Others reacted violently but with little success, which caused greater pain, such as whippings and sale. Many of them seethed with resentment and bitterness, which perhaps they passed on to their children. Undoubtedly, they experienced both mental anguish and physical pain as a result of the selfish desires of the white patriarch, but they just went "on hopin' that things" wouldn't "be that way always."

※ *F U R T H E R   R E A D I N G*

Barbara Bush, *Slave Women in Caribbean Society, 1650–1832* (1990)

Catherine Clinton, *The Plantation Mistress* (1982)

Angela Y. Davis, *Women, Race, and Class* (1981)

Elizabeth Fox-Genovese, *Within the Plantation Household: Black and White Women of the Old South* (1988)

Herbert S. Gutman, *The Black Family in Slavery and Freedom, 1750–1925* (1976)

Jacqueline Jones, *Labor of Love, Labor of Sorrow: Black Women, Work and the Family from Slavery to the Present* (1985)

Gerda Lerner, ed., *Black Women in White America* (1972)

Sally McMillan, *Southern Women: Black and White in the Old South* (1991)

Filomina Chioma Steady, ed., *The Black Woman Cross-Culturally* (1981)

Deborah Gray White, *Ar'n't I a Woman? Female Slaves in the Plantation South* (1985)

Varieties

of Nineteenth-Century Activism

The antebellum years (the 1820s through the 1850s) witnessed a novel phenomenon
in American history: the creation of a wide variety of women's organizations.
Unprecedented prior to the Ladies Association of 1780, innumerable women's
groups were founded after the turn of the century. At first, they focused primarily
on charitable and self-help activities — aiding widows and orphans or establishing
discussion groups for young mothers concerned about childrearing. Later, they
branched out into other areas, pursuing broader goals. Female industrial workers
in the new textile mills attempted to win better wages and working conditions by
organizing "turn-outs," actions later known as strikes; middle-class women attacked
prostitution; middle- and working-class women advocated temperance in the consumption of alcohol; and some northern women eagerly joined the female auxiliaries
established by the male-dominated societies that sought the abolition of slavery.
Finally, by the late 1840s a few women began to promote their own cause, formally
calling for "women's rights."

Historians have long inquired into the origins of these proliferating organizations, asking about the identity and motives of their members, the methods and
aims of their leaders, and the reasons for their successes or failures. One key
question is their relationship to the precepts of the cult of domesticity, examined in
Chapter 5. Did these groups embody domestic ideology, or did they challenge it?
What were their goals, and what methods did they adopt in their attempts to reach
those goals?

❊ D O C U M E N T S

The Lowell Offering, a magazine produced by the women who worked in the textile mills,
often carried essays that young women had written about their experiences. The first
document, an essay from the issue of December 1840, suggests the novelty of the work in
which the women in the mills were engaged. Mary Paul, an operative at a Lowell, Massachusetts, mill in the 1840s, wrote letters home describing her life in the mills; some of them
comprise the second document. Taken together, these first items help to explain why female

mill workers engaged in collective action. The third document, from late 1841, is an excerpt from an address given by the secretary of a Martha Washington society in New York City when she presented a temperance banner to the men of a fire company. Expressing a very different view of woman's role from that held by Martha Washingtonians, the "Declaration of Sentiments" adopted by the Seneca Falls convention in 1848 is the fourth document reprinted here. The best-known of the nineteenth-century statements calling for women's rights, this document even demanded the right to vote, a radical request for the time. Not all female activists supported suffrage demands, however. Notable among the nay-sayers were Catharine Beecher and her novelist sister, Harriet Beecher Stowe, who in 1869 included an antisuffrage statement in their best-selling book, *The American Woman's Home*; this is the fifth document.

"Defence of Factory Girls," 1840

"She has worked in a factory, is sufficient to damn to infamy the most worthy and virtuous girl."

So says Mr. Orestes A. Brownson; and either this horrible assertion is true, or Mr. Brownson is a slanderer. I assert that it is *not* true, and Mr. B. may consider himself called up to prove his words, if he can. . . .

And whom has Mr. Brownson slandered? A class of girls who in this city alone are numbered by thousands, and who collect in many of our smaller towns by hundreds; girls who generally come from quiet country homes, where their minds and manners have been formed under the eyes of the worthy sons of the Pilgrims, and their virtuous partners, and who return again to become the wives of the free intelligent yeomanry of New England, and the mothers of quite a proportion of our future republicans. Think, for a moment, how many of the next generation are to spring from mothers doomed in infamy? "Ah," it may be replied, "Mr. Brownson acknowledges that you may still be worthy and virtuous." Then we must be a set of worthy and virtuous idiots, for no virtuous girl of common sense would choose for an occupation one that would consign her to infamy. . . .

Whence has arisen the degree of prejudice which has existed against factory girls, I cannot tell; but we often hear the condition of the factory population of England, and the station which the operatives hold in society there, referred to as descriptive of *our* condition. As well might it be said, as say the *nobility* of England, that *labor itself* is disgraceful, and that all who work should be consigned to contempt, if not to infamy. And again: it has been asserted that to put ourselves under the influence and restraints of corporate bodies, is contrary to the spirit of our institutions, and to that love of independence which we ought to cherish. There is a spirit of independence which is averse to social life itself; and I would advise all who wish to cherish it, to go far beyond the Rocky Mountains, and hold communion with none but the untamed Indian, and the wild beast of the forest. We are under restraints, but they are voluntarily assumed; and we are at liberty to withdraw from them, whenever they become galling or irksome.

Neither have I ever discovered that any restraints were imposed upon us, but those which were necessary for the peace and comfort of the whole, and for the promotion of the design for which we are collected, namely, to get money, as much of it and as fast as we can; and it is because our toil is so unremitting, that the wages of factory girls are higher than those of females engaged in most other occupations. It is these wages which, in spite of toil, restraint, discomfort, and prejudice, have drawn so many worthy, virtuous, intelligent, and well-educated girls to Lowell, and other factories; and it is the wages which are in a great degree to decide the characters of the factory girls as a class. . . . The avails of factory labor are now greater than those of many domestics, seamstresses, and school-teachers; and strange would it be, if in money-loving New England, one of the most lucrative female employments should be rejected because it is toilsome, or because some people are prejudiced against it. Yankee girls have too much *independence* for *that*.

But it may be remarked, "You certainly cannot mean to intimate, that all factory girls are virtuous, intelligent," &c. No, I do not; and Lowell would be a stranger place than it has ever been represented, if among eight thousand girls there were none of the ignorant and depraved. Calumniators have asserted, that *all* were vile, because they knew *some* to be so; and the sins of *a few* have been visited upon *the many*. While the mass of the worthy and virtuous have been unnoticed, in the even tenor of their way, the evil deeds of a few individuals have been trumpeted abroad, and they have been regarded as specimens of factory girls. It has been said, that factory girls are not thought as much of any where else as they are in Lowell. If this be true, I am very glad of it; it is quite to our credit to be most respected where we are best known. Still, I presume, there are girls here who are a disgrace to the city, to their sex, and to humanity. But *they* do not fix the tone of public sentiment, and their morals are not the standard. . . . Our well filled churches and lecture halls, and the high character of our clergymen and lecturers, will testify that the state of morals and intelligence is not low.

Mr. Brownson, I suppose, would not judge of our moral characters by our church-going tendencies; but as many do, a word on this subject may not be amiss. That there are many in Lowell who do not regularly attend any meeting; is as true as the correspondent of the Boston Times once represented it; but for this there are various reasons. There are many who come here for but a short time, and who are willing for a while to forego every usual privilege, that they may carry back to their homes the greatest possible sum they can save. There are widows earning money for the maintenance and education of their children; there are daughters providing for their aged and destitute parents; and there are widows, single women, and girls, endeavoring to obtain the wherewithal to furnish some other home than a factory boarding-house. Pew rent, and the dress which custom has wrongly rendered essential, are expenses which they cannot afford, and they spend their Sabbaths in rest, reading, and meditation. There may also be many other motives to prevent a regular attendance at church, besides a disinclination to gratify and cultivate the moral sentiments.

There have also been nice calculations made, as to the small proportion which the amount of money deposited in the Savings Bank bears to that earned in the city; but this is not all that is saved. Some is deposited in Banks at other places, and some is put into the hands of personal friends. Still, much that is earned is immediately, though not foolishly, spent. Much that none but the parties concerned will ever know of, goes to procure comforts and necessaries for some lowly home, and a great deal is spent for public benevolent purposes. The fifteen hundred dollars which were collected in one day for Missionary purposes by a single denomination in our city, though it may speak of what Mrs. Gilman calls the "too great tendency to overflow in female benevolence," certainly does not tell of hearts sullied by vice, or souls steeped in infamy. And it is pleasing to view the interest which so many of the factory girls take in the social and religious institutions of this place, who do not call Lowell aught but a temporary home. Many of them stay here longer than they otherwise would, because these institutions have become so dear to them, and the letters which they send here after they do leave, show that the interest was too strong to be easily eradicated. I have known those who left homes of comfort and competence, that they might here enjoy religious privileges which country towns would not afford them. And the Lowell Offering may prove to all who will read it, that there are girls here whose education and intellect place them above the necessity of pursuing an avocation which will inevitably connect them with the ignorant and vicious. . . .

Mary Paul's Letters, 1845–1848

[Woodstock, Vt.] Saturday Sept. 13th 1845

Dear Father . . .

I want you to consent to let me go to Lowell if you can. I think it would be much better for me than to stay about here. I could earn more to begin with than I can any where about here. I am in need of clothes which I cannot get if I stay about here and for that reason I want to go to Lowell or some other place. We all think if I could go with some steady girl that I might do well. I want you to think of it and make up your mind. Mercy Jane Griffith is going to start in four or five weeks. Aunt Miller and Aunt Sarah think it would be a good chance for me to go if you would consent — which I want you to do if possible. I want to see you and talk with you about it. . . .

Mary

Lowell Nov 20th 1845

Dear Father

An opportunity now presents itself which I improve in writing to you. I started for this place at the time I talked of which was Thursday. . . . On Saturday after I got here Luthera Griffith went round with me to find a place but we were unsuccessful. On Monday we started again and were more successful. We found a place in a spinning room and the next morning I went to work. I like very well have 50 cts first payment increasing every payment as I get along in work have a first rate overseer and a very good boarding place. I work on the Lawrence Corporation. Mill is No 2 spinning room. . . . It cost me $3.25 to come. Stage fare was $3.00 and lodging at Windsor, 25 cts. Had to pay only 25 cts for board for 9 days after I got here before I went into the mill. Had 2.50 left with which I got a bonnet and some other small articles. . . .

excuse bad writing and mistakes
This from your own daughter
Mary

Thomas Dublin, ed., "Letters of Mary Paul, 1845–1848," in *Farm to Factory*, 1981, pp. 100–109, copyright © 1981 Columbia University Press. Used by permission.

Lowell Dec 21st 1845

Dear Father

I received your letter on Thursday the 14th with much pleasure. I am well which is one comfort. My life and health are spared while others are cut off. Last Thursday one girl fell down and broke her neck which caused instant death. She was going in or coming out of the mill and slipped down it being very icy. The same day a man was killed by the [railroad] cars. Another had nearly all of his ribs broken. Another was nearly killed by falling down and having a bale of cotton fall on him. Last Tuesday we were paid. In all I had six dollars and sixty cents paid $4.68 for board. With the rest I got me a pair of rubbers and a pair of 50.cts shoes. Next payment I am to have a dollar a week beside my board. We have not had much snow the deepest being not more than 4 inches. It has been very warm for winter.

Perhaps you would like something about our regulations about going in and coming out of the mill. At 5 o'clock in the morning the bell rings for the folks to get up and get breakfast. At half past six it rings for the girls to get up and at seven they are called into the mill. At half past 12 we have dinner are called back again at one and stay till half past seven. I get along very well with my work. I can doff as fast as any girl in our room. I think I shall have frames before long. The usual time allowed for learning is six months but I think I shall have frames before I have been in three as I get along so fast. I think that the factory is the best place for me and if any girl wants employment I advise them to come to Lowell. . . .

This from
Mary S Paul

Lowell April 12th 1846

Dear Father

You wanted to know what I am doing. I am at work in a spinning room and tending four sides of warp which is one girls work. The overseer tells me that he never had a girl get along better than I do and that he will do the best he can by me. I stand it well, though they tell me that I am growing very poor. I was paid nine shillings a week last payment and am to have more this one. . . .

I have a very good boarding place have enough to eat and that which is good enough. The girls are all kind and obliging. The girls that I room with are all from Vermont and good girls too. Now I will tell you about our rules at the boarding house. We have none in particular except that we have to go to bed about 10. o'clock. At half past 4 in the morning the bell rings for us to get up and at five for us to go into the mill. At seven we are called out to breakfast are allowed half an hour between bells and the same at noon till the first of May when we have three quarters [of an hour] till the first of September. We have dinner at half past 12 and supper at seven. . . .

Yours affectionately
Mary S Paul

Lowell Nov 5th 1848

Dear Father

Doubtless you have been looking for a letter from me all the week past. I would have written but wished to find whether I should be able to stand it — to do the work that I am now doing. I was unable to get my old place in the cloth room on the

Suffolk or on any other corporation. I next tried the dressrooms on the Lawrence Cor[poration], but did not succe[e]d in getting a place. I almost concluded to give up and go back to Claremont, but thought I would try once more. So I went to my old overseer on the Tremont Cor. I had no idea that he would want one, but he *did*, and I went to work last Tuesday — warping — the same work I used to do.

It is *very* hard indeed and sometimes I think I shall not be able to endure it. I never worked so hard in my life but perhaps I shall get used to it. I shall try hard to do so for there is no other work that I can do unless I spin and that I shall not undertake on any account. I presume you have heard before this that the wages are to be reduced on the 20th of this month. It is *true* and there seems to be a good deal of excitement on the subject but I can not tell what will be the consequence. The companies pretend they are losing immense sums every *day* and therefore they are obliged to lessen the wages, but this seems perfectly absurd to me for they are constantly making *repairs* and it seems to me that this would not be if there were really any danger of their being obliged to *stop* the mills.

It is very difficult for any one to get into the mill on any corporation. All seem to be very full of help. I expect to be paid about two dollars a week but it will be dearly earned. I cannot tell how it is but never since I have worked in the mill have I been so very tired as I have for the last week but it may be owing to the long rest I have had for the last six months. . . .

(Monday Eve) I have been to work today and think I shall manage to get along with the work. I am not so tired as I was last week. I have not yet found out what wages I shall get but presume they will be about $2.00 per week exclusive of board. . . .

Write soon. Yours affectionately
Mary S Paul

Miss Mary Downing's Address to Fire Engine Company 18, New York City, 1841

When the sable curtain of night is drawn around us, and we are quietly reposing on our pillow, who is it that is first to hear the sound of yonder "alarm bell" as it tolls off the burning district? Is it not the fireman? . . . When the building is wrapt in flames, who is first to hazard his life to save the inmates from the most distressing of all deaths? It is the fireman. If such be your worth; if such your praiseworthy acts; if such your danger, should you not be temperate men? Then go forth in a mighty phalanx — go forth and rear the standard of temperance — show to your fellow firemen that you can brave the severest storm of winter or bask in the sultry heat of summer without the use of intoxicating drinks. And now, members of Union Co. No. 18, as a token of our respect and approbation of your course, we, the members of the Lady Howard Temperance Society, present you with the first Fireman's Banner that was ever unfurled in the city of New York. May it long wave in triumph over your heads, and may Heaven forbid that you should ever prove recreant to the high trust we have reposed in you.

The "Declaration of Sentiments"
of the Seneca Falls Convention, 1848

When, in the course of human events, it becomes necessary for one portion of the family of man to assume among the people of the earth a position different from that which they have hitherto occupied, but one to which the laws of nature and of nature's God entitle them, a decent respect to the opinions of mankind requires that they should declare the causes that impel them to such a course.

We hold these truths to be self-evident: that all men and women are created equal; that they are endowed by their Creator with certain inalienable rights; that among these are life, liberty, and the pursuit of happiness; that to secure these rights governments are instituted, deriving their just powers from the consent of the governed. Whenever any form of government becomes destructive of these ends, it is the right of those who suffer from it to refuse allegiance to it, and to insist upon the institution of a new government, laying its foundation on such principles, and organizing its powers in such form, as to them shall seem most likely to effect their safety and happiness. Prudence, indeed, will dictate that governments long established should not be changed for light and transient causes; and accordingly all experience hath shown that mankind are more disposed to suffer, while evils are sufferable, than to right themselves by abolishing the forms to which they were accustomed. But when a long train of abuses and usurpations, pursuing invariably the same object evinces a design to reduce them under absolute despotism, it is their duty to throw off such government, and to provide new guards for their future security. Such has been the patient sufferance of the women under this government, and such is now the necessity which constraints them to demand the equal situation to which they are entitled.

The history of mankind is a history of repeated injuries and usurpations on the part of man toward woman, having in direct object the establishment of an absolute tyranny over her. To prove this, let facts be submitted to a candid world.

He has never permitted her to exercise her inalienable right to the elective franchise.

He has compelled her to submit to laws, in the formation of which she had no voice.

He has withheld from her rights which are given to the most ignorant and degraded men — both natives and foreigners.

Having deprived her of this first right of a citizen, the elective franchise. thereby leaving her without representation in the halls of legislation, he has oppressed her on all sides.

He has made her, if married, in the eye of the law, civilly dead.

He has taken from her all right in property, even to the wages she earns.

He has made her, morally, an irresponsible being, as she can commit many crimes with impunity, provided they be done in the presence of her husband. In the covenant of marriage, she is compelled to promise obedience to her husband, he becoming, to all intents and purposes, her master — the law giving him power to deprive her of her liberty, and to administer chastisement.

He has so framed the laws of divorce, as to what shall be the proper causes, and in case of separation, to whom the guardianship of the children shall be given, as to be wholly regardless of the happiness of women — the law, in all cases, going upon a false supposition of the supremacy of man, and giving all power into his hands.

After depriving her of all rights as a married woman, if single, and the owner of property, he has taxed her to support a government which recognizes her only when her property can be made profitable to it.

He has monopolized nearly all the profitable employments, and from those she is permitted to follow, she receives but a scanty remuneration. He closes against her all the avenues to wealth and distinction which he considers most honorable to himself. As a teacher of theology, medicine, or law, she is not known.

He has denied her the facilities for obtaining a thorough education, all colleges being closed against her.

He allows her in Church, as well as State, but a subordinate position, claiming Apostolic authority for her exclusion from the ministry, and, with some exceptions, from any public participation in the affairs of the Church.

He has created a false public sentiment by giving to the world a different code of morals for men and women, by which moral delinquencies which exclude women from society, are not only tolerated, but deemed of little account in man.

He has usurped the prerogative of Jehovah himself, claiming it as his right to assign for her a sphere of action, when that belongs to her conscience and to her God.

He has endeavored, in every way that he could, to destroy her confidence in her own powers, to lessen her self-respect, and to make her willing to lead a dependent and abject life.

Now, in view of this entire disfranchisement of one-half the people of this country, their social and religious degradation — in view of the unjust laws above mentioned, and because women do feel themselves aggrieved, oppressed, and fraudulently deprived of their most sacred rights, we insist that they have immediate admission to all the rights and privileges which belong to them as citizens of the United States.

In entering upon the great work before us, we anticipate no small amount of misconception, misrepresentation, and ridicule; but we shall use every instrumentality within our power to effect our object. We shall employ agents, circulate tracts, petition the State and National legislatures, and endeavor to enlist the pulpit and the press in our behalf. We hope this Convention will be followed by a series of Conventions embracing every part of the country.

Catharine Beecher and Harriet Beecher Stowe on Why Women Should Not Seek the Vote, 1869

Many intelligent and benevolent persons imagine that the grand remedy for the heavy evils that oppress our sex is to introduce woman to political power and office, to make her a party in primary political meetings, in political caucuses, and in the scramble and fight for political offices; thus bringing into this dangerous *melée* the distinctive tempting power of her sex. Who can look at this new danger without dismay? . . .

Let us suppose that our friends have gained the ballot and the powers of office: are there any real beneficent measures for our sex, which they would enforce by law and penalties, that fathers, brothers, and husbands would not grant to a united petition of our sex, or even to a majority of the wise and good? Would these not confer what the wives, mothers, and sisters deemed best for themselves and the children they are to train, very much sooner than they would give power and office to our sex to enforce these advantages by law? Would it not be a wiser thing to *ask* for what we need, before trying so circuitous and dangerous a method? God has given to man the physical power, so that all that woman may gain, either by petitions or by ballot, will be the gift of love or of duty; and the ballot never will be accorded till benevolent and conscientious men are the majority — a millennial point far beyond our present ken.

※ *ESSAYS*

The first essay, by Thomas Dublin, a history professor at Binghamton University, examines the experiences of female workers in the textile mills of Lowell, Massachusetts, and their sporadic organizational efforts. In the second essay, Ruth M. Alexander, who teaches at Colorado State University, looks closely at a lower-class women's temperance society, the Martha Washingtonians. She argues that historians have incorrectly seen temperance as a middle-class phenomenon, and contends that working-class women reinterpreted the cult of domesticity to suit their own purposes. Finally, Steven Beuchler, a social scientist, describes the origins of the women's rights movement, positing that it was not — as commonly believed — wholly an offshoot of abolitionism.

Women Workers in the Lowell Mills

THOMAS DUBLIN

In the years before 1850 the textile mills of Lowell, Massachusetts were a celebrated economic and cultural attraction. Foreign visitors invariably included them on their American tours. Interest was prompted by the massive scale of these mills, the astonishing productivity of the power-driven machinery, and the fact that women comprised most of the workforce. Visitors were struck by the newness of both mills and city as well as by the culture of the female operatives. The scene stood in sharp contrast to the gloomy mill towns of the English industrial revolution.

Lowell, was, in fact, an impressive accomplishment. In 1820, there had been no city at all — only a dozen family farms along the Merrimack River in East Chelmsford. In 1821, however, a group of Boston capitalists purchased land and water rights along the river and a nearby canal, and began to build a major textile manufacturing center. Opening two years later, the first factory employed Yankee women recruited from the nearby countryside. Additional mills were constructed until, by

---

Thomas Dublin, "Women, Work, and Protest in the Early Lowell Mills: The Oppressing Hand of Avarice Would Enslave Us," *Labor History*, XVI (1975), pp. 99–116. Reprinted by permission.

1840, ten textile corporations with thirty-two mills valued at more than ten million dollars lined the banks of the river and nearby canals. Adjacent to the mills were rows of company boarding houses and tenements which accommodated most of the eight thousand factory operatives.

As Lowell expanded, and became the nation's largest textile manufacturing center, the experiences of women operatives changed as well. The increasing number of firms in Lowell and in the other mill towns brought the pressure of competition. Overproduction became a problem and the prices of finished cloth decreased. The high profits of the early years declined and so, too, did conditions for the mill operatives. Wages were reduced and the pace of work within the mills was stepped up. Women operatives did not accept these changes without protest. In 1834 and 1836 they went on strike to protest wage cuts, and between 1843 and 1848 they mounted petition campaigns aimed at reducing the hours of labor in the mills.

These labor protests in early Lowell contribute to our understanding of the response of workers to the growth of industrial capitalism in the first half of the nineteenth century. They indicate the importance of values and attitudes dating back to an earlier period and also the transformation of these values in a new setting.

The major factor in the rise of a new consciousness among operatives in Lowell was the development of a close-knit community among women working in the mills. The structure of work and the nature of housing contributed to the growth of this community. The existence of community among women, in turn, was an important element in the repeated labor protests of the period. . . .

The textile corporations made provisions to ease the adjustment of new operatives. Newcomers were not immediately expected to fit into the mill's regular work routine. They were at first assigned work as sparehands and were paid a daily wage independent of the quantity of work they turned out. As a sparehand, the newcomer worked with an experienced hand who instructed her in the intricacies of the job. The sparehand spelled her partner for short stretches of time, and occasionally took the place of an absentee. One woman described the learning process in a letter reprinted in the *Offering*:

> Well, I went into the mill, and was put to learn with a very patient girl. . . . You cannot think how odd everything seems. . . . They set me to threading shuttles, and tying weaver's knots, and such things, and now I have improved so that I can take care of one loom. I could take care of two if only I had eyes in the back part of my head. . . .

After the passage of some weeks or months, when she could handle the normal complement of machinery — two looms for weavers during the 1830s — and when a regular operative departed, leaving an opening, the sparehand moved into a regular job. . . .

Living conditions also contributed to the development of community among female operatives. Most women working in the Lowell mills of these years were housed in company boarding houses. In July 1836, for example, more than 73 percent of females employed by the Hamilton Company resided in company housing adjacent to the mills. Almost three-fourths of them, therefore, lived and worked with each other. Furthermore, the work schedule was such that women had little opportunity to interact with those not living in company dwellings. They worked, in these years, an average of 73 hours a week. Their work day ended at 7:00 or 7:30

P.M., and in the hours between supper and the 10:00 curfew imposed by management on residents of company boarding houses there was little time to spend with friends living "off the corporation."

Women in the boarding houses lived in close quarters, a factor that also played a role in the growth of community. A typical boarding house accommodated twenty-five young women, generally crowded four to eight in a bedroom. There was little possibility of privacy within the dwelling, and pressure to conform to group standards was very strong (as will be discussed below). The community of operatives which developed in the mills, it follows, carried over into life at home as well.

The boarding house became a central institution in the lives of Lowell's female operatives in these years, but it was particularly important in the initial integration of newcomers into urban industrial life. Upon first leaving her rural home for work in Lowell, a woman entered a setting very different from anything she had previously known. One operative, writing in the *Offering*, described the feelings of a fictional character: ". . . the first entrance into a factory boarding house seemed something dreadful. The room looked strange and comfortless, and the women cold and heartless; and when she sat down to the supper table, where among more than twenty girls, all but one were strangers, she could not eat a mouthful."

In the boarding house, the newcomer took the first steps in the process which transformed her from an "outsider" into an accepted member of the community of women operatives.

Recruitment of newcomers into the mills and their initial hiring was mediated through the boarding house system. Women generally did not travel to Lowell for the first time entirely on their own. They usually came because they knew someone — an older sister, cousin, or friend — who had already worked in Lowell. The scene described above was a lonely one — but the newcomer did know at least one boarder among the twenty seated around the supper table. The Hamilton Company Register Books indicate that numerous pairs of operatives, having the same surname and coming from the same town in northern New England, lived in the same boarding houses. If the newcomer was not accompanied by a friend or relative, she was usually directed to "Number 20, Hamilton Company," or to a similar address of one of the other corporations where her acquaintance lived. Her first contact with fellow operatives generally came in the boarding houses and not in the mills. Given the personal nature of recruitment in this period, therefore, newcomers usually had the company and support of a friend or relative in their first adjustment to Lowell.

Like recruitment, the initial hiring was a personal process. Once settled in the boarding house a newcomer had to find a job. She would generally go to the mills with her friend or with the boarding house keeper who would introduce her to an overseer in one of the rooms. If he had an opening, she might start work immediately. More likely, the overseer would know of an opening elsewhere in the mill, or would suggest that something would probably develop within a few days. In one story in the *Offering*, a newcomer worked on some quilts for her house keeper, thereby earning her board while she waited for a job opening.

Upon entering the boarding house, the newcomer came under pressure to conform with the standards of the community of operatives. Stories in the *Offering* indicate that newcomers at first stood out from the group in terms of their speech and dress. Over time, they dropped the peculiar "twang" in their speech which so amused experienced hands. Similarly, they purchased clothing more in keeping with urban than rural styles. It was an unusual and strongwilled individual who could work and live among her fellow operatives and not conform, at least outwardly, to the customs and values of this larger community.

The boarding houses were the centers of social life for women operatives after their long days in the mills. There they ate their meals, rested, talked, sewed, wrote letters, read books and magazines. From among fellow workers and boarders they found friends who accompanied them to shops, to Lyceum lectures, to church and church-sponsored events. On Sundays or holidays, they often took walks along the canals or out into the nearby countryside. The community of women operatives, in sum, developed in a setting where women worked and lived together, twenty-four hours a day.

Given the all-pervasiveness of this community, one would expect it to exert strong pressures on those who did not conform to group standards. Such appears to have been the case. . . .

To the extent that women could not have completely private lives in the boarding houses, they probably had to conform to group norms, whether these involved speech, clothing, relations with men, or attitudes toward the ten-hour day. Group pressure to conform, so important to the community of women in early Lowell, played a significant role in the collective response of women to changing conditions in the mills.

In addition to the structure of work and housing in Lowell, a third factor, the homogeneity of the mill workforce, contributed to the development of community among female operatives. In this period the mill workforce was homogeneous in terms of sex, nativity, and age. Payroll and other records of the Hamilton Company reveal that more than 85 per cent of those employed in July, 1836, were women and that over 96 per cent were native-born. Furthermore, over 80 per cent of the female workforce was between the ages of 15 and 30 years old; and only ten per cent was under 15 or over 40.

Workforce homogeneity takes on particular significance in the context of work structure and the nature of worker housing. These three factors combined meant that women operatives had little interaction with men during their daily lives. Men and women did not perform the same work in the mills, and generally did not even labor in the same rooms. Men worked in the picking and initial carding processes, in the repair shop and on the watchforce, and filled all supervisory positions in the mills. Women held all sparehand and regular operative jobs in drawing, speeding, spinning, weaving and dressing. A typical room in the mill employed eighty women tending machinery, with two men overseeing the work and two boys assisting them. Women had little contact with men other than their supervisors in the course of the working day. After work, women returned to their boarding houses, where once again there were few men. Women, then, worked and lived in a predominantly female setting.

Ethnically the workforce was also homogeneous. Immigrants formed only 3.4 per cent of those employed at Hamilton in July, 1836. In addition, they comprised only 3 per cent of residents in Hamilton company housing. The community of women operatives was composed of women of New England stock drawn from the hill-country farms surrounding Lowell. Consequently, when experienced hands made fun of the speech and dress of newcomers, it was understood that they, too, had been "rusty" or "rustic" upon first coming to Lowell. This common background was another element shared by women workers in early Lowell.

The work structure, the workers' housing, and workforce homogeneity were the major elements which contributed to the growth of community among Lowell's women operatives. To best understand the larger implications of community it is necessary to examine the labor protests of this period. For in these struggles, the new values and attitudes which developed in the community of women operatives are most visible.

In February, 1834, 800 of Lowell's women operatives "turned-out" — went on strike — to protest a proposed reduction in their wages. They marched to numerous mills in an effort to induce others to join them; and, at an outdoor rally, they petitioned others to "discontinue their labors until terms of reconciliation are made. Their petition concluded:

> Resolved, That we will not go back into the mills to work unless our wages are continued . . . as they have been.
>   Resolved, That none of us will go back, unless they receive us all as one.
>   Resolved, That if any have not money enough to carry them home, they shall be supplied.

The strike proved to be a brief and failed to reverse the proposed wage reductions. Turning-out on a Friday, the striking women were paid their back wages on Saturday, and by the middle of the next week had returned to work or left town. Within a week of the turn-out, the mills were running near capacity.

This first strike in Lowell is important not because it failed or succeeded, but simply because it took place. In an era in which women had to overcome opposition simply to work in the mills, it is remarkable that they would further overstep the accepted middle-class bounds of female propriety by participating in a public protest. The agents of the textile mills certainly considered the turn-out unfeminine. . . .

Certainly a prime motive for the strike was outrage at the social implications of the wage cuts. In a statement of principles accompanying the petition which was circulated among operatives, women expressed well the sense of themselves which prompted their protest of these wage cuts:

UNION IS POWER

> Our present object is to have union and exertion, and we remain in possession of our unquestionable rights. We circulate this paper wishing to obtain the names of all who imbibe the spirit of our Patriotic Ancestors, who preferred privation to bondage, and parted with all that renders life desirable — and even life itself — to procure independence for their children. The oppressing hand of avarice would enslave us, and to gain their object, they gravely tell us of the pressure of the time, this we are already sensible of, and deplore it. If any are in want of assistance, the Ladies will be compassionate and assist them; but we prefer to have the disposing of our charities in our own hands; and as we are free, we would remain in possession of what kind Providence has bestowed upon us; and remain daughters of freeman still.

At several points in the proclamation the women drew on their Yankee heritage. Connecting their turn-out with the efforts of their "Patriotic Ancestors" to secure independence from England, they interpreted the wage cuts as an effort to "enslave" them — to deprive them of their independent status as "daughters of freemen."

Though very general and rhetorical, the statement of these women does suggest their sense of self, of their own worth and dignity. Elsewhere, they expressed the conviction that they were the social equals of the overseers, indeed of the millowners themselves. The wage cuts, however, struck at this assertion of social equality. These reductions made it clear that the operatives were subordinate to their employers, rather than equal partners in a contract binding on both parties. By turning-out the women emphatically denied that they were subordinates; but by returning to work the next week, they demonstrated that in economic terms they were no match for their corporate superiors.

In point of fact, these Yankee operatives were subordinate in early Lowell's social and economic order, but they never consciously accepted this status. Their refusal to do so became evident whenever the mill owners attempted to exercise the power they possessed. This fundamental contradiction between the objective status of operatives and their consciousness of it was at the root of the 1834 turn-out and of subsequent labor protests in Lowell before 1850. The corporations could build mills, create thousands of jobs, and recruit women to fill them. Nevertheless, they bought only the workers' labor power, and then only for as long as these workers chose to stay. Women could always return to their rural homes, and they had a sense of their own worth and dignity, factors limiting the actions of management.

Women operatives viewed the wage cuts as a threat to their economic independence. This independence had two related dimensions. First, the women were self-supporting while they worked in the mills and, consequently, were independent of their families back home. Second, they were able to save out of their monthly earnings and could then leave the mills for the old homestead whenever they so desired. In effect, they were not totally dependent upon mill work. Their independence was based largely on the high level of wages in the mills. They could support themselves and still save enough to return home periodically. The wage cuts threatened to deny them this outlet, substituting instead the prospect of total dependence on mill work. Small wonder, then, there was alarm that "the oppressing hand of avarice would enslave us." To be forced, out of economic necessity, to lifelong labor in the mills would have indeed seemed like slavery. The Yankee operatives spoke directly to the fear of a dependency based on impoverishment when offering to assist any women workers who "have not money enough to carry them home." Wage reductions, however, offered only the *prospect* of a future dependence on mill employment. By striking, the women asserted their actual economic independence of the mills and their determination to remain "daughters of freemen still."

While the women's traditional conception of themselves as independent daughters of freeman played a major role in the turn-out, this factor acting alone would not necessarily have triggered the 1834 strike. It would have led women as individuals to quit work and return to their rural homes. But the turn-out was a collective protest. When it was announced that wage reductions were being considered, women began to hold meetings in the mills during meal breaks in order to assess tactical possibilities. Their turn-out began at one mill when the agent discharged a woman who had presided at such a meeting. Their procession through the streets passed by other mills, expressing a conscious effort to enlist as much support as possible for their cause. At a mass meeting, the women drew up a resolution which insisted that none be discharged for their participation in the turn-out. This strike, then, was a collective response to the proposed wage cuts — made possible because women had come to form a "community" of operatives in the mill, rather than simply a group of individual workers. The existence of such a tight-knit community turned individual opposition to the wage cuts into a collective protest.

In October, 1836, women again went on strike. This second turn-out was similar to the first in several respects. Its immediate cause was also a wage reduction; marches and a large outdoor rally were organized; again, like the earlier protest, the basic goal was not achieved; the corporations refused to restore wages; and operatives either left Lowell or returned to work at the new rates.

Despite these surface similarities between the turn-outs, there were some real differences. One involved scale: over 1500 operatives turned out in 1836, compared to only 800 earlier. Moreover, the second strike lasted much longer than the first. In 1834 operatives stayed out for only a few days; in 1836, the mills ran far below capacity for several months. Two weeks after the second turn-out began, a mill agent reported that only a fifth of the strikers had returned to work: "The rest manifest *good 'spunk'* as they call it." Several days later he described the impact of the continuing strike on operations in his mills: "we must be feeble for months to come as probably not less than 250 of our former scanty supply of help have left town." These lines read in sharp contrast to the optimistic reports of agents following the turn-out in February, 1834.

Differences between the two turn-outs were not limited to the increased scale and duration of the later one. Women displayed a much higher degree of organization in 1836 than earlier. To co-ordinate strike activities, they formed a Factory Girls' Association. According to one historian, membership in the short-lived association reached 2500 at its height. The larger organization among women was reflected in the tactics employed. Strikers, according to one mill agent, were able to halt production to a greater extent than numbers alone could explain; and, he complained, although some operatives were willing to work, "it has been impossible to give employment to many who remained." He attributed this difficulty to the strikers' tactics: "This was in many instances no doubt the result of calculation and contrivance. After the original turn-out they [the operatives] would assail a particular room — as for instance, all the warpers, or all the warp spinners, or all the speeder and stretcher girls, and this would close the mill as effectually as if all the girls in the mill had left."

Now giving more thought than they had in 1834 to the specific tactics of the turn-out, the women made a deliberate effort to shut down the mills in order to win their demands. They attempted to persuade less committed operatives, concentrating on those in crucial departments within the mill. Such tactics anticipated those of skilled mulespinners and loomfixers who went out on strike in the 1880s and 1890s.

In their organization of a Factory Girl's Association and in their efforts to shut down the mills, the female operatives revealed that they had been changed by their industrial experience. Increasingly, they acted not simply as "daughters of freemen" offended by the impositions of the textile corporations, but also as industrial workers intent on improving their position within the mills.

There was a decline in protest among women in the Lowell mills following these early strike defeats. During the 1837–1843 depression, textile corporations twice reduced wages without evoking a collective response from operatives. Because of the frequency of production cutbacks and lay-offs in these years, workers probably accepted the mill agents' contention that they had to reduce wages or close entirely. But with the return of prosperity and the expansion of production in the mid-1840s, there were renewed labor protests among women. Their actions paralleled those of working men and reflected fluctuations in the business cycle. Prosperity itself did not prompt turn-outs, but it evidently facilitated collective actions by women operatives.

In contrast to the protests of the previous decade, the struggles now were primarily political. Women did not turn-out in the 1840s; rather, they mounted annual petition campaigns calling on the State legislature to limit the hours of labor within the mills. These campaigns reached their height in 1845 and 1846, when 2,000 and 5,000 operatives respectively signed petitions. Unable to curb the wage cuts, or the speed-up and stretch-out imposed by mill owners, operatives sought to mitigate the consequences of these changes by reducing the length of the working day. Having been defeated earlier in economic struggles, they now sought to achieve their new goal through political action. The Ten Hour Movement, seen in these terms, was a logical outgrowth of the unsuccessful turn-outs of the previous decade. Like the earlier struggles, the Ten Hour Movement was an assertion of the dignity of operatives and an attempt to maintain that dignity under the changing conditions of industrial capitalism. . . .

The women's Ten Hour Movement, like the earlier turn-outs, was based in part on the participants' sense of their own worth and dignity as daughters of freemen. At the same time, however, [it] also indicated the growth of a new consciousness. It reflected a mounting feeling of community among women operatives and a realization that their interests and those of their employers were not identical, that they had to rely on themselves and not on corporate benevolence to achieve a reduction in the hours of labor. One woman, in an open letter to a State legislator, expressed this rejection of middle-class paternalism: "Bad as is the condition of so many women, it would be much worse if they had nothing but your boasted protection to rely upon; but they have at last learnt the lesson which a bitter experience teaches, that not to those who style themselves their 'natural protectors' are they to look for the needful help, but to the strong and resolute of their own sex." Such an attitude, underlying the self-organizing of women in the ten-hour petition campaigns, was clearly the product of the industrial experience in Lowell.

Both the early turn-outs and the Ten Hour Movement were, as noted above, in large measure dependent upon the existence of a close-knit community of women operatives. Such a community was based on the work structure, the nature of worker housing, and workforce homogeneity. Women were drawn together by the initial job training of newcomers; by the informal work sharing among experienced hands, by living in company boarding houses, by sharing religious, educational, and social activities in their leisure hours. Working and living in a new and alien setting, they came to rely upon one another for friendship and support. Understandably, a community feeling developed among them.

This evolving community as well as the common cultural traditions which Yankee women carried into Lowell were major elements that governed their response to changing mill conditions. The pre-industrial tradition of independence and self-respect made them particularly sensitive to management labor policies. The sense of community enabled them to transform their individual opposition to wage cuts and to the increasing pace of work into public protest. In these labor struggles women operatives expressed a new consciousness of their rights both as workers and as women. Such a consciousness, like the community of women itself, was one product of Lowell's industrial revolution.

The experiences of Lowell women before 1850 present a fascinating picture of the contradictory impact of industrial capitalism. Repeated labor protests reveal that female operatives felt the demands of mill employment to be oppressive. At the same time, however, the mills provided women with work outside of the home and family, thereby offering them an unprecedented opportunity. That they came to challenge employer paternalism was a direct consequence of the increasing opportunities offered them in these years. The Lowell mills both exploited and liberated women in ways unknown to the pre-industrial political economy.

The Martha Washingtonians

RUTH M. ALEXANDER

Throughout the winter and spring of 1842, the women of the Ladies Chelsea Temperance Benevolent Society visited the houses, alleys, and streets of their Manhattan neighborhood searching for families and individuals who suffered from the ravages of alcohol. Led by "Directress" Bowrason, a butcher's wife, the Chelsea devotees of the Washingtonian temperance movement offered cash, clothing, and the message of abstinence from alcohol to impoverished inebriates. Among those aided were three women "restored" to sobriety by the actions of the female Washingtonians. The first woman was destitute, drunk, "nearly naked," and "sick from exposure" when members of the society found her. She was persuaded to take the pledge of total abstinence, food and medical care were provided for her, and society members helped her find employment and board. Later she became a "worthy member" of the organization. The second, a young woman who was destitute and "without friends," took the pledge and was clothed, boarded, and assisted in obtaining work with a sympathetic family. The third, a mother so poor and drunken that local authorities had taken her children from her, was able to resume care of her family after receiving help from the Washingtonian women.

News of these striking transformations may have caused admiration and amazement among those who read of the society's work in the pages of the *Olive*

Ruth M. Alexander, "'We Are Engaged as a Band of Sisters': Class and Domesticity in the Washingtonian Temperance Movement, 1840–1850," *Journal of American History*, LXXV (1988–89), pp. 763–85. Reprinted by permission of Journal of American History.

A temperance broadside. This broadside distributed by a temperance organization simultaneously envisioned a harmonious family and enumerated the dangers of "the Traffic in Intoxicating Liquors." The consumption of alcohol, the flyer implied through its jarring conjunction of the pleasant scene and the list of negative consequences, would destroy orderly families, nations, and even civilization itself.

Plant and Ladies' Temperance Advocate, a monthly newspaper dedicated to women's "systematic and persevering exertions" in aid of the Washingtonian temperance movement. But lest the sympathetic readers of the *Olive Plant* be overawed by the successes of the Chelsea women, the society's report ended with the modest claim, "We have not any cases of thrilling interest. . . . Our tale will be unvarnished, we have no disposition to shine."

Feminine modesty, charity, the "rescue" of destitute or degraded females, and attentiveness to the reform of personal habits, all evident in the report from the Ladies' Chelsea Temperance Benevolent Society, were common features of the reform efforts spearheaded by middle-class women during the nineteenth century. In the antebellum era thousands of wives from the homes of merchants, manufacturers, professionals, and politicians left well-appointed parlors, nurseries, and kitchens to champion benevolent and reform causes. Numerous historians have asserted that this enthusiastic activism was inspired in part by middle-class women's adherence to the tenets of domesticity — an ideology that sharply differentiated the "public" world of men from the "private" world of women and yet ultimately prompted many matrons to take their message of moral probity into the temperance, moral reform, antislavery, and woman's rights movements.

However, the Washingtonian cause, to which the Chelsea society claimed loyalty, drew its constituents largely from the working and lower middle classes. Its most visible leaders were skilled artisans newly converted to the cause of total abstinence, and Washingtonianism marked the first time that American women of relatively low rank joined and played a prominent role in reform. The thousands of women who established Martha Washington societies in the 1840s throughout the Northeast and Midwest were, like Mrs. Bowrason, primarily from the homes of laborers, artisans, shopkeepers, and clerks. As one contemporary observer of the Marthas in New York and New Jersey wrote, their societies were "composed mostly of women whose earthly comforts are derived mainly from the labor of their own hands." Later in the decade the temperance benevolent societies disbanded, yet women of the working and lower middle classes remained active in the cause and organized new temperance mutual benefit societies. Women of higher status and privilege were not absent from the movement, especially in small cities and towns, but the leadership of most female Washingtonian societies was probably in the hands of women of humble background and social standing. What motivated such women to join the temperance cause? How are we to interpret their sentiments and their activism?

The deleterious effects of alcohol within the family setting may have been the principal concern of the women who joined the Washingtonian movement. Certainly that was true in New York State, one of the most active and well documented centers of Washingtonianism, and the region upon which this study is largely based. Many Martha Washingtonian societies were auxiliaries to men's societies, with family ties bringing men and women into the movement. Moreover, the *Olive Plant's* editor noted that female Washingtonians were often the wives and daughters of reformed inebriates, and that Washingtonian meetings were "deeply affecting, especially where women have been seen urging their husbands to come up and sign the pledge." . . .

The women who joined the Washingtonian movement during its first phase, from approximately 1840 to 1843, dedicated themselves to four principal tasks in aid of the cause. Their temperance benevolent societies sought to provide material aid to those in want and to persuade both hardened and moderate drinkers to sign the pledge of total abstinence. They offered instruction to mothers to prevent them from leading their offspring to intemperate habits. Finally, the Martha Washingtonians took messages of inspiration and moral fortitude to recently reformed groups of young men. In each task, Washingtonian women revealed their deep absorption in the affairs of the home and the conviction that the use of alcohol was inimical to family happiness.

The early Martha Washingtonians declared that their foremost duty was to provide reforming inebriates with material aid. Society members gathered as often as once a week to sew and repair clothing, and they distributed garments, furniture, bedding and cash in a constant round of visits to the homes of the newly abstinent. A few groups formed primitive employment agencies that helped reformed men and women locate jobs with employers who supported the Washingtonian movement and were themselves temperate. Underlying Washingtonian women's material assistance was the belief that alcoholic men and women were unfit to support or properly care for their families. Personal experience and observation had shown them that inebriates and their loved ones lived in conditions of "wretchedness and despair." . . .

Second, like Washingtonian men, the Marthas sought to bring the pledge of total abstinence to those who still used alcohol. The women's societies were particularly concerned with reclaiming inebriates of their own sex, thereby laying the foundation for the "moral resurrection" of homes "previously given to vice and cruelty." Many Martha Washingtonian societies claimed large numbers of formerly alcoholic women as members, including some "inveterate cases." . . . [Such] efforts to rehabilitate alcoholic females rested on the conviction that it was women's duty to establish order and stability in the domestic setting. They also demonstrated profound faith in the plasticity of the female character. In telling of a woman who had successfully reformed after twenty years as a drunkard, one society asked, "to whom could she have appealed had there been no similar association?" Washingtonian women were willing to accept previously intemperate women into their ranks as full members, believing that even an utterly degraded woman might be identified with, comforted, and redeemed. . . .

Concern for the well-being of families and children also prompted Washingtonian women to attempt to teach mothers to overcome the "deeply rooted . . . prejudices and propensities" that might endanger their children's future happiness. As charity visitors they urged mothers to set a healthful example to their children by pledging "not to use or provide for other's use, directly or indirectly, as an article of entertainment of beverage, any intoxicating liquors." Martha Washingtonians were also active in the formation of juvenile temperance societies that flourished in New York, Massachusetts, and Connecticut. . . .

Washingtonian women's fourth field of activity — inspirational work — reflected the primacy of their concern for the family. . . . Unfurling banners that proclaimed Let the Rising Generation Be a Temperate One or Our Cause Is Righteous and Will Prevail, Martha Washingtonians took the message of abstinence to gatherings of Washingtonian men or, more often, to volunteer fire companies. Fire fighters were generally young men of socioeconomic backgrounds similar to those of the Washingtonians. In many cases they were newcomers to the city, independent of their families for the first time, and "at the most reckless and excitable stage of life." Urban fire companies functioned as social fraternities, but they were notorious for the "riotous and disorderly" conduct of their members. Moreover, they enjoyed the "sport" of fire fighting so much that they were of dubious value in protecting property.

Despite their poor reputation, youthful fire fighters won the interest, rather than the scorn, of Martha Washingtonians. Believing that the companies encouraged intemperance, Washingtonian women acted as surrogate mothers and intervened to save impressionable young men from becoming fixed in habits that would surely produce misery for them and their families. As the Wallabout Martha Washingtonian Society of Brooklyn declared in presenting a silk and tasseled banner to Engine Company No. 12,

> To you and your honorable company we now surrender the keeping of this momento; take it as proof of the interest we feel in your moral welfare, and whenever the armies of Temperance are summoned to the bloodless combat, rally around it, and bear it proudly there. . . .

The activism and rhetoric of the early Martha Washingtonians attests to their belief in the centrality of women's role in nurturing and protecting the family. The Washingtonian emphasis on women's maternal and moral responsibilities paralleled values and behaviors of the nineteenth century's new middle class. Yet that emphasis had been forcefully shaped, not by domestic privacy and comfort, but by familiarity with poverty, insecurity, and violence. It reflected Washingtonian women's precarious dependence on men who might squander their meager but much-needed earnings at the corner tavern or turn on their families with a drunkard's wrath. Washingtonian domesticity was inspired too by the responsibility that the Marthas felt for children who might lose all protection if their mothers gave in to the temptations of drink.

Yet if Washingtonian women's domesticity was shaped by fear and urgency, it was also inspired by a fundamental desire to reaffirm what they perceived as the normative, traditional, and reciprocal obligations of men and women in artisan and laboring households. Washingtonian women were convinced that as wives and mothers they could not afford to remain silent while men, struggling to protect jobs, skills, and status in a changing economy, succumbed to the temporary pleasures of drink. Ultimately, Washingtonian domesticity rested on the conviction that if workingmen were to continue to be dutiful breadwinners, women must take responsibility for "keeping the morals of our brothers." . . .

As early as 1842, the Washingtonian movement showed signs of weakening as it was beset with internal disputes over its inexperienced leaders, lack of organization, alienation of elite temperance and religious leaders, and "low-class" social affairs. The resolve of many new abstainers wore thin and most societies suffered from high rates of "backsliding." . . . Washingtonian men and women soon began to regroup, forming mutual benefit societies that adopted strict rules regarding the admission and day-to-day behavior of their members. Giving up their efforts to rescue the unreformed, they concentrated on providing support to those who had already demonstrated a basic, if still somewhat faltering, commitment to the pledge. Women were less frequently called upon to seek out and extend aid and sympathy to destitute drunkards, and most female Washingtonians gave up their charitable work and banner presentations. Instead, they turned their attention to a closer scrutiny of behavior within their own societies and within the ranks of the movement as a whole. . . .

The new groups had three basic functions: to care for one another in illness and at the hour of death, to advance the cause of temperance by fostering female unity, and to organize excursions and entertainments for the enjoyment of all adherents to cold-water principles. These concerns appear quite different from those of the early Martha Washingtonians, but underlying both was a persistent dedication to the protection of home and family against the misfortunes that haunted the working and lower middle classes. . . .

The seriousness with which the women's mutual benefit societies regarded their duty to provide illness and death benefits to dues-paying members in good standing is revealed in their printed advertisements and reports. Weekly notices in the back pages of the *Pearl* disclosed the precise amount that each society had collected, and if the society was fortunate enough to have an account, the name of the bank in which savings were kept and the rate at which interest accrued. The handful of annual reports published by the *Pearl* specified dues collected, benefits and other expenses paid, and "balances on hand." They showed that societies could expect to spend at least one-half of their yearly savings on direct benefit disbursements.

Societies gave little justification for their monetary benefits in the temperance press, but the significance of the benefits must have been well understood. They permitted women of little means a degree of self-sufficiency and a hedge against disaster that were otherwise unavailable. . . .

Female unity was the centerpiece of the mutual benefit societies, even when it was not required by the illness or death of a member. Washingtonian women had come to understand female unity as the foundation of domesticity and as a preventive to intemperance, poverty, and suffering. It was not a mere social contrivance, but rather the product of deliberately cultivated moral virtues. By "improving [their] social and moral condition, and elevating the female character," members would achieve "unity of action, and advance the cause of Virtue, Love, and Temperance.". . .

The earliest Martha Washingtonian societies had no requirements for membership save a willingness to sign the pledge of total abstinence. But in the temperance mutual benefit societies (both male and female) members were also required to be of "good moral standing" and in good health. Men had to show proof of ability to earn a living; women had to show visible means of support. The standards were not taken lightly, for without them the societies would have been unable to collect regular dues and offer benefits. The strict standards also gave Washingtonian women ground rules for judging their own behavior and the character and behavior of others. . . .

Finally, the female mutual benefit societies took charge of organizing temperance recreation for members of local societies, both male and female, and their families. The women were talented social directors, and [their newspapers] were filled with announcements and reports of banquets, performances by temperance choirs, boating excursions, and temperance festivals in and around New York City. . . . An immediate concern of Washingtonian women was to retain oversight over men who, without the watchful eye and steadying hand of women, might "relapse" into intemperance and again be unable to provide for their families. Their carefully engineered social events, mixed gatherings of women and men (and sometimes children) that replaced the all-male affairs of the early Washingtonians, made oversight possible and relapse less likely. . . .

The history of the Martha Washingtonians adds welcome subtlety to our understanding of the connections between domesticity, class, and reform in antebellum America. The language of domesticity played a critical role in bringing Washingtonian women to an awareness of their social and economic standing, and to an appreciation of the kinds of leverage that they might realistically use to redress their grievances. Washingtonian women were preoccupied with the meaning of gender, with an assessment of their special duties as women in the home and the community. Their sharp focus on gender permitted both a penetrating analysis of the particular effects of alcoholism on female dependency and the family circle and an acute awareness of the special vulnerability of the working and lower middle classes to the destructive power of drink. . . .

Yet to argue that Washingtonian women simply embraced middle-class standards or to conclude that nineteenth-century domesticity was essentially a middle-class construct is to ignore the actual operation of domesticity within the Washingtonian movement. Washingtonian women actively interpreted the meanings of gender and domesticity and elaborated a domestic ideology rooted in the exigencies of working-class and lower middle-class families and communities. They successfully combined a domestic ideology with Washingtonian faith in the fundamental worth of artisans and laborers and in the capacity of workingmen to join with one another and their families for the purposes of self-improvement. They were not prevented by lack of wealth or obscurity of rank from finding positive affirmation in domesticity, neither were they prevented from molding it to answer to their particular circumstances. That Washingtonian women appear to have found more certainty in gender than in class identity, to have compensated for economic insecurity and wifely dependence by elaborating and laying heavy emphasis on normative gender behaviors, does not point to a betrayal of class origins. Rather it suggests the immediacy of the family in their daily lives, and their less-than-constant exposure to social or working situations in which class relations were of decisive importance. The activism of Washingtonian women is evidence of the power of domestic ideology, the viability of a domestic model for women who had little material security, and of the fluidity of concepts of domesticity in antebellum life.

The Origins of the Women's Rights Movement

STEVEN BUECHLER

. . . Of all the proximate causes identified in discussions of the origins of the women's rights movement, the abolitionist movement seems to be the most frequently mentioned. Many commentators have observed that while not all

Steven M. Buechler, *Women's Movements in the United States*, pp. 17–23, copyright © 1990 by Steven M. Buechler. Reprinted by permission of Rutgers University Press.

abolitionists supported women's rights, many women's rights advocates had prior experience in the abolitionist movement, and they drew on these experiences as they formulated and pursued the goals of the early women's rights movement. Beyond a basic agreement on the fact that the women's movement somehow emerged from the abolitionist movement, however, there is room for competing interpretations of the exact dynamics involved in this process.

The involvement of women in the abolitionist movement was evident almost from its beginnings. Also evident from the beginning was a tension over the appropriate role of women in the antislavery effort. When the American Anti-Slavery Society was formed in Philadelphia in 1833, women were allowed to attend the meeting and to speak, but they were not allowed to join the society or to sign its founding document. In response, women formed the Philadelphia Female Anti-Slavery Society. Four years later, a National Female Anti-Slavery Society met in New York with eighty-one delegates from twelve states. By 1840, women allied with the Garrisonian wing of the abolitionist movement had won positions within the American Anti-Slavery Society. However, when they traveled to the World Anti-Slavery Convention in London to act as delegates of the American Society, they were not recognized or seated, because they were women. These incidents, and others like them, reflect a dialectic of opposition that was a crucial legacy of the abolitionist movement for later feminist mobilization. In this dialectic, women who worked for abolition in ways that overstepped the normative boundaries of feminine behavior were opposed both by some abolitionists and by the larger society for their efforts. This opposition thematized the issue of gender, which became a mobilizing issue for some female abolitionists who went on to organize around the issue of women's rights both within and eventually outside of the abolitionist movement.

In this process, the role of the Garrisonian wing of the abolitionist movement was critical. By stressing individual conscience rather than religious authority as the basis for action, and by criticizing clerical support of slavery, Garrisonian abolitionism created a path from pious activism to political activism that many women in the movement followed. It was at this point that some abolitionist women stepped over the line that defined appropriate feminine behavior and provoked an oppositional response from the more conventional abolitionist movement. For these reasons, the abolitionist movement may be regarded as a more important forerunner of the women's rights movement than the temperance movement, even if the latter attracted larger numbers of women. Despite their numbers, women's temperance activism tended to remain only nascently feminist; it did not openly challenge the boundaries of normative female behavior. Women in the abolitionist movement did increasingly challenge those boundaries, contributing to the dialectic of opposition that helped to generate a women's rights movement.

As this dialectic unfolded, some abolitionist women began to address the issue of women's rights alongside antislavery. Sarah and Angelina Grimké are the best-known figures to move in this direction, but they were followed by a number of others. In one study of "feminist-abolitionists" as a distinct group set off from earlier antislavery advocates and later woman suffragists, Blanche Hersh traces the careers of over fifty women who worked for the twin causes of abolitionism and women's rights in this important phase in both movements. By arguing that women were enslaved in ways that paralleled the oppression of blacks and required a parallel movement for their emancipation, these women were the first to formulate what

William Chafe has termed the analogy of race and sex. In Hersch's interpretation, most feminist-abolitionists came to their feminism after their struggles within the abolitionist movement; by this logic, women's consciousness of their own oppression was underdeveloped until they became active in seeking the emancipation of another group and saw the parallels between the enslavement of blacks and the oppression of women. . . .

Hersch's interpretation is part of a larger argument that identifies the abolitionist movement as critical to the emergence of the women's movement in a number of ways. In this argument, the abolitionist movement is seen as providing women with the organizational experience, the oratorical skills, the leadership abilities, the ideological rhetoric, the political analysis, and the social consciousness to address their own subordination in their own movement. This argument raises a key question in understanding the origins of the women's rights movement: What was the precise role played by the abolitionist movement in the generation of the women's rights movement that followed on its heels?

At least two answers to this question are possible, and they may be framed in terms of sociological theories of social movements. For the older tradition of movement analysis, the origins of movements are to be sought both in background factors like structural strain and in processes that give rise to grievances that then become the basis of mobilization. For this approach, the role of abolitionism would be important primarily because it created the grievances that then stimulated the mobilization of the women's rights movement. The grievances emerged only with the understanding of the dynamics of slavery, which women acquired via abolitionism and then generalized to their own situation through the analogy of race and sex. For the newer tradition of movement analysis, the origins of movements have more to do with the shifting opportunities for mobilizing resources to sustain a movement. In this view, grievances are assumed to have a long-standing history that predates the emergence of the social movement, and to be secondary because grievances themselves are not sufficient to launch a social movement. For this approach, the role of abolitionism would be important primarily for the resources it provided to women who already had a keen sense of their grievances as women but had previously lacked the resources necessary to respond effectively to their situation.

While it is undeniable that the abolitionist movement provided important resources to women for the mobilization of a women's rights movement, it is debatable whether a consciousness of their own oppression was one of these resources. Close analysis of the generation of feminist-abolitionists does not support the idea that this entire group underwent a uniform process of consciousness-raising about women's subordination only after their work in the antislavery cause. This thesis seems especially weak in the cases of prominent leaders such as Lucy Stone, Elizabeth Cady Stanton, and Susan B. Anthony. Each traveled a different route, but none traveled the hypothesized one toward involvement in the early women's rights movement. Stone and Stanton's feminist sympathies predated their involvement in abolitionism, while Anthony's experiences as a teacher and a temperance worker were most important in leading her into the women's rights movement. While some women doubtless came to the women's rights movement because of a raised consciousness derived from the antislavery movement, this thesis seems unable to account for the important leadership cadre of the early women's movement.

These considerations support Ellen DuBois's claim that "women's discontent with their position was as much cause as effect of their involvement with the anti-slavery movement." In terms of social movement theory, these considerations suggest that feminist grievances were a long-standing reality for many women and not a new revelation as a result of their antislavery work. Consistent with the claims of resource mobilization theory, however, grievances alone do not suffice to generate a social movement, and that is why a women's rights movement did not emerge any earlier despite preexisting discontent. If DuBois is right, that discontent motivated some women to participate in the major emanicipatory social movement of the late 1830s and 1840s: the abolitionist movement, and its Garrisonian wing in particular. As a result of participation in the abolitionist movement, some women gained access to other mobilization resources, which were vital to generating a women's movement. In DuBois's perspective, these resources included an escape from clerical authority, an egalitarian ideology, and a theory of social change.

As they participated in the abolitionist cause, novice female reformers acquired important skills in speaking, organizing, and agitating for social change at the very same time that they encountered resistance to their participation in the abolitionist cause. As a result of preexisting grievances, new access to resources, and an internal dialectic of opposition, the issue of women's rights was increasingly discussed from abolitionist platforms throughout the 1840s. These dynamics culminated in 1848 with the well-known Seneca Falls women's rights convention, which drafted a Declaration of Sentiments and Principles that formally launched the women's rights movement. While the precise timing of this convention concerns the biographies of the women involved in calling the convention, the year 1848 is a significant reminder that the women's rights movement began in a social climate of agitation and reform at home and a political climate of revolutionary social change in Europe. Both nationally and internationally, such reform and revolutionary movements created important social and political space for other movements, including women's rights, to build a foundation. Such movement space is yet another resource that some movements bequeath to others as part of the dynamics of social reform and change.

The Seneca Falls convention addressed a broad spectrum of issues, including women's economic position, legal status, occupational possibilities, educational opportunities, familial roles, and political disenfranchisement. After 1848, numerous women's rights conventions were held in various locations until the Civil War. The conventions disseminated and popularized ideas about women's rights through the network provided by the abolitionist movement and by female antislavery societies in particular. At the same time that it facilitated the spread of these ideas, however, the abolitionist movement inhibited the development of women's rights organizations by providing an existing organizational network. Hence, the abolitionist movement nurtured an emergent women's rights ideology while constricting women's independent organizational development. As a result, no major women's rights organizations or associations were formed despite a dozen years of agitation leading up to the Civil War.

This organizational time lag revives the dilemma of defining social movements and thereby dating their origins. If movements are defined on the basis of distinct sentiments, then the women's movement may be dated from the early to mid-1840s. If movements are defined on the basis of networks of people acting on distinct sentiments, then the women's movement may be dated from the series of women's rights conventions initiated at Seneca Falls in 1848 and continuing over the next dozen years. If movements are defined on the basis of independent movement organizations, however, then the women's movement must be dated from the formation of the national woman suffrage organizations, which appeared only after the Civil War.

The emergence of an organizationally independent women's rights movement is the final chapter in the long history of the relations between the antislavery and women's rights causes. During the Civil War, women activists put aside their agenda and concentrated on supporting the war effort and the abolitionist cause. When the Thirteenth Amendment to abolish slavery was proposed in 1863, Susan B. Anthony and Elizabeth Cady Stanton formed the National Woman's Loyal League and collected nearly four hundred thousand signatures on petitions urging Congress to pass the amendment. With passage and subsequent ratification of the amendment in December 1865, the legal status of black men and women became more analogous to that of white women: members of each group were recognized as citizens but were still lacking basic civil liberties enjoyed by white male citizens. Many women who had worked for both abolitionism and women's rights thus came to see this moment as the perfect opportunity to broaden democracy and extend justice by enfranchising black men and women as well as white women, and they began to push for a broadly oriented constitutional amendment to implement this goal.

The response of male abolitionists and Radical Republicans, who had won a major victory with the Thirteenth Amendment and sensed another in the offing, was a major disappointment to women's rights advocates. The male reformers argued that it was "the Negro's hour" and that it would be too risky to link the goal of black suffrage and civil rights with that of female suffrage; this strategy called for immediate work on black rights with vague promises of subsequent effort on behalf of female suffrage. Without female enfranchisement, "the Negro's hour" really meant black *male* suffrage, a principle embodied in the proposed Fourteenth Amendment, which specified voting as a male right. Stanton and Anthony resisted this version of the amendment and fought vigorously for one that would extend suffrage to black men, black women, and white women. Toward this end, they organized the American Equal Rights Association to seek a broad extension of voting rights under the rubric of "universal suffrage." Despite these efforts, the Fourteenth Amendment passed with its reference to voting as a male right, thereby writing a sexual distinction on voting rights into the Constitution for the first time.

The incomplete nature of the Fourteenth Amendment necessitated the Fifteenth Amendment to securely guarantee black male voting rights. Once again, feminists sought to bring the issues of black and female suffrage together as one universal reform, only to be met with the stubborn refusal of abolitionists and Republicans to take their call for universal suffrage seriously. As the Republicans prepared to fight the Democrats over black enfranchisement, some women came to feel that the "hypocrisy of Democrats serves us a better purpose in the present emergency than does the treachery of Republicans," and they joined Democratic resistance to black enfranchisement because Republicans refused to seek female enfranchisement at the same time. In an increasingly complex political battle structured by race, gender, and partisan politics, women's rights advocates thus split over the relative priority of black rights and women's rights, with Lucy Stone and Henry Blackwell reluctantly acquiescing to the Republican strategy and Susan B. Anthony and Elizabeth Cady Stanton rejecting Republican "treachery" and seeking a different political base for pursuing women's rights.

The struggles around black rights and women's rights after the Civil War are a powerful example of how the politics of race and the politics of gender can be used by dominant groups as a divide-and-conquer strategy. To Republicans seeking to implement a Reconstruction program, black rights had an instrumental value that women's rights did not have, and that is part of the explanation for the "Negro's hour" strategy. For women's rights advocates, this was a bitter lesson, and one that provoked racist reactions on the part of some white women about extending voting rights to black men but not to white women. In the end, the abolitionist movement, which had contributed to the emergence of a women's rights ideology through an earlier dialectic of opposition, also contributed to the appearance of women's rights organizations through a later dialectic of opposition in the context of Reconstruction politics. In 1869, two national woman suffrage organizations appeared. The National Woman Suffrage Association (NWSA), founded in May by Anthony and Stanton, and the American Woman Suffrage Association (AWSA), founded in November by Stone and Blackwell, signify the end of the tumultuous relationship between abolitionism and women's rights and the beginning of an organizationally independent women's movement in the United States.

❊ F U R T H E R R E A D I N G

Barbara Berg, *The Remembered Gate: Origins of American Feminism* (1978)

Mary H. Blewett, *Men, Women, and Work: A Study of Class, Gender, and Protest in the Nineteenth-Century New England Shoe Industry* (1988)

Jeanne Boydston et al., *The Limits of Sisterhood: The Beecher Sisters of Women's Rights and Woman's Sphere* (1988)

Thomas Dublin, *Women at Work: The Transformation of Work and Community in Lowell, Massachusetts, 1820–1860* (1979)

Ellen DuBois, *Feminism and Suffrage: The Emergence of an Independent Women's Movement in America, 1848–1869* (1978)

Barbara Epstein, *The Politics of Domesticity: Women, Evangelism, and Temperance in Nineteenth-Century America* (1980)

Lori D. Ginzberg, *Women and the Work of Benevolence: Morality, Politics, and Class in the Nineteenth-Century United States* (1990)

Elisabeth Griffith, *In Her Own Right: The Life of Elizabeth Cady Stanton* (1984)

Blanche Hersch, *The Slavery of Sex: Feminist-Abolitionists in Nineteenth-Century America* (1978)

Nancy Hewitt, *Women's Activism and Social Change: Rochester, New York, 1822–1872* (1984)

Teresa Anne Murphy, *Ten Hours Labor: Religion, Reform, and Gender in Early New England* (1992)

Kathryn Kish Sklar, *Catharine Beecher* (1973)

Shirley J. Yee, *Black Women Abolitionists: A Study in Activism, 1828–1860* (1992)

Jean Fagan Yellin, *Women and Sisters: The Antislavery Feminists in American Culture* (1990)

CHAPTER
8

Women in the Nineteenth-
and Twentieth-Century West

During the nineteenth century, the American West became a place of discord and violence as Anglos, Native Americans, Hispanics, and others competed — on highly unequal terms — for access to western lands and resources. Later, as the nineteenth century turned into the twentieth, disparate cultural communities struggled to coexist in the post-"frontier" West; straightforward stories of Anglo "conquest" mingled with complex histories of exploitation, negotiation, and exchange.

In this multicultural setting, women's experiences were shaped simultaneously by gender and ethnicity. Thus while thousands of nineteenth-century tribal women witnessed the destruction of their traditional cultures and suffered encounters with arrogant whites who believed them to be less than "true women," countless Anglo women experienced the loneliness and hardship that came with trying to transplant, to unfamiliar soil, the ideals and social practices of the country's eastern or midwestern communities.

As these examples suggest, the West was a place where women of diverse backgrounds encountered tragedy, deprivation, and loss of status or identity. Yet it was also a place where women struggled to retain cherished cultural traditions and to prosper amid persistent disadvantage and rapid change. How well did these women succeed? What does the historical record tell us about the impact of continental migration and cross-cultural contact on the roles, status, and self-perceptions of Native American, Hispanic, and Anglo women in the nineteenth- and twentieth-century West? Under what circumstances did women of different racial or ethnic communities sustain a diminution of social standing and power? And when were such women able to advance their interests by negotiating across cultural or gender boundaries?

❈ D O C U M E N T S

The first document, written in 1862, is a letter penned by an anonymous individual to a small California newspaper, denouncing the rape of elderly Indian women in Tehama County by a party of U.S. Army soldiers who had been sent to that locale to protect white settlers. In the

189

second document, Mrs. A. M. Green, a white native of Pennsylvania, describes the self-pity and desolation she felt on moving to Colorado's Union Colony with her ambitious young husband and two small children in 1870. By way of contrast, Sadie Martin, another white migrant, relates in the third document her cheerful adjustment to the rigors of life in the Arizona desert in the late 1880s. Notable too are Sadie's affable yet belittling comments about her Indian neighbors. By the twentieth century, Native Americans throughout the West had had much exposure to Anglo culture, especially through schooling and employment; in the fourth document, Helen Sekaquaptewa, a Hopi, recounts the difficulties in trying to combine Anglo and Hopi rituals during her wedding to Emory, a fellow Hopi, in Hotevilla, Arizona, in 1919. The fifth document, dating from 1912, reveals the prejudice toward Hispanics that was common even among educated whites at the turn of the century; it excerpts a report by a Stanford University labor expert on Mexican-American communities in the southwestern United States. In the last document, Jesusita Aragon, a Hispanic single mother, describes her life in 1950s Las Vegas, New Mexico: how determined she was to send her children to high school and how she combined factory work with midwifery.

A Citizen Protests the Rape of Indian Women in California, 1862

Editor *Beacon:* — It is well known that there is, or has been, a body of soldiers in this county for several weeks past, for the avowed object of defending and protecting the citizens of the county against Indian depredations. . . .

On Friday night a party of these soldiers visited the ranch of Col. Washington, and made themselves annoying to the Indians in the rancheria. This party was small, only three, as reported.

Saturday night, the 4th of October, 1862, was made memorable by the visit of a portion of this command, headed, aided and abetted by the commanding officer, Lieut. ———— , (or some one assuming his title,) to the farm of Col. Washington, and to the rancheria of peaceful and domesticated Indians resident thereon. Not one of the soldiers, private or Lieutenant, (or pretended Lieutenant, if such he was,) called at the farm house, but rode by and entered the Indian rancheria, with demands for Indian women, for the purpose of prostitution! They were requested to leave and ordered off the place. They answered they would do as they pleased, as they had the power. They were then told that it was true they were the strongest, and no force at hand was sufficient to contend with them, and they were left in the Indian rancheria. Most of the young squaws in the rancheria had by this time ran off and concealed themselves, and were beyond the reach and brutal grasp of the ravishers. They, however, were to be satiated, and like brutes dragged the old, decrepit "tar-heads" forth, and as many as three of the soldiers, in rapid succession, had forced intercourse with old squaws. Such was the conduct of the portion of the command of Co. E, on the night of the 4th of October, 1862, who visited the Indian rancheria at the Old Mill Place, about 3 miles from N. L. headquarters.

It is but proper, after consulting with those who are acquainted with the outrage, to say that the Lieut. (or pretended Lieut., if such he was,) did not arrive at the scene of action until after the larger portion of his men were on the ground — But it is absolutely certain that he was there — that he put his horse in the stable to hay, and then prowled around and through the Indian rancherias in quest of some squaw.

Whether he found a fit subject upon which to practice his virtuous and civilizing purposes, the writer is not informed. He, however, saddled up and left the scene of moral exploit about daylight.

In justice to decency, humanity and civilization, these brutes should be punished. It is due to the honor, the reputation, the chivalry of the army of the United States, that the insignia of rank and position should be torn from the person of the Lieutenant (if it was he who was there,) as an officer unworthy its trust and confidence.

Mrs. A. M. Green's Account of Frontier Life, 1887

Of the founder of this place I have nothing to say except that I regret the sad manner in which he came to his death, for I really believe he was a very pure minded man, and one who sought the good of his fellow beings. After securing several lots in the new town, we pitched our tent, which was almost daily blown to the ground. To say that I was homesick, discouraged and lonely, is but a faint description of my feelings.

It was one of those terrible gloomy days that I sat in my lonely tent with my baby, Frank, in my arms, who was crying from the effects produced by the sands of the American desert, while beside my knee stood my little Sisy, (as we called her) trying to comfort her brother by saying: "Don't cry, F'ankie, we is all going back to grandpa's pitty soon, ain't we, mamma?" Not receiving an immediate answer from me, she raised her eyes to mine, from which gushed a fountain of burning tears. "Don't cry, mamma," said she; "sing to F'ank like you always does, and he will stop crying." I obeyed the child's request. . . .

As I closed my song the curtain raised and my husband entered, sank wearily on a three-legged stool and took up our little five-year-old, placed her upon his tired knee and then addressed me thus: "Well, dear, how do you get along to-day? I see the tent hasn't blown down." I attempted to answer in the negative, but failed, the meaning of which he comprehended in a moment. Notwithstanding any vain attempts to conceal my emotion, he pressed to his sad heart the little change which he held in his arms, saying in a low voice: "Darling little one, you and your poor mamma have hard times, don't you?" Then turning to me, he said: "Annie, I am very sorry for you. If I had compelled you to come to this country I could never forgive myself; as it is, I feel that you reflect on me." By this time I had regained my speech and endeavored with all my might, mind and strength to convince him to the contrary. Whether I succeeded or not I never knew, but I resolved there and then to cultivate a cheerful disposition, which I believe has prolonged my life, for, at the rate I was going into despair at that time, I could not have retained my reason six months' longer, and doubtless the brittle thread of life would have been snapped long ere this. O how thankful I am that I still live to love, work and care for those whom to me are dearer than life itself! If I have one wish above another in this world, it is that I may live a long and useful life. . . .

The 7th of July was Sabbath, and in those days I was usually found under the droppings of the sanctuary, for, though there was not a church in the town, we had regular services every Sabbath in the Union Colony Hall; but this morning I felt so depressed in spirits that I dispensed with going, and busied myself in writing to those for whom my heart panted continually. I had finished my third letter, closing up with a fervent prayer to Him whom I had been taught to believe would hear and answer the prayer of faith, for the preservation of my life, and also for those to whom I had been writing, until we should meet again (?) when the word *never, never,* sounded in my ear, and penetrated my aching heart with an arrow, the effect of which I feel to this day. At that moment my little girl approached me bearing in her hand the picture of her who loved me first and best on earth. I took it from the child, pressed it to my quivering lips, and cried: Oh, God, bereave me not of her! Until this time I had not ventured to open our album, but now that the ice was broken, I looked it through while tears gushed from my eyes. During this terrible emotion my husband returned from church, and again found me in tears and deep sorrow. This added pain to his already desponding heart. "Annie," said he, with a self-reproaching look, and in a pathetic tone which I shall never forget, "do you know you are killing me?" "I thought," he continued, "you had resolved to cultivate a more cheerful disposition; this will not do; it is cruel in the extreme for me to compel you to remain where you are so unhappy." My heart bounded for joy; and then, my pulse stood still to listen for the much longed for sentence, — we will go home; but, alas! it came in the singular number; "you must go home." "What!" I cried, "go without you, no, never;" and I repeat those words to-day; and ever shall, so long as circumstances control my husband's freedom. Again I resolved to try and be cheerful, but, my resolution and promise were but to be broken in less than twenty-four hours. On this occasion the physician was summoned and my disease pronounced mountain fever, from which I recovered, after an illness of six weeks. During all my affliction I had answered each letter from home without intimating that I was out of health, until the shortness of my communications excited their attention, and they demanded an explanation, which I was obliged to give.

It was now August, but oh! how different from any one which I had ever witnessed. Not a tree, plant nor shrub on which to rest my weary eye, to break the monotony of the sand beds and cactus of the Great American Desert. My attention was often called to the grandeur of the snow capped Rocky Mountains, towering toward the skies; and although I sometimes feigned an appreciation of their beauty in order to coincide with my other half, who displayed much anxiety to have me admire something in Colorado, I speak the truth when I say that the sun, moon, or stars never put on that brilliant appearance in my western home as they did in the land of my nativity. . . .

Sadie Martin's Memories of Desert Life, 1888

It was early on the morning of the 22nd of August, 1888, when my train rolled into the most desolate little town I had ever seen or ever expected to see. Nevertheless my heart was beating high as I was to meet my husband, who had preceded me to Arizona five months before. As I stepped from the train I could hardly realize that

Sadie Martin, "My Desert Memories," typed manuscript, Arizona Historical Society Library, 1939.

the young man coming toward me was my John. He was as dark as an Indian and only his height, eagerness, and familiar smile made me recognize him. . . .

We reached the ranch about sundown, tired, warm and hungry and were met by the members of the family who had preceded us. My! What a sight I was — my face burned to a deep and unbecoming red and down my left arm were three rows of blisters in the design of the lace in my sleeve. It was so good to have that sun go down and to take a long cool drink of delicious water from the great Mexican olla — a porous clay vessel, which was kept cool by a covering of wet gunny sacks. There was no ice on the desert, but I was soon to find that we could keep our milk and butter cool and sweet, by wrapping damp cloths around the receptacles that held them and setting them in the air. And as we were everlastingly thirsty it was a relief to find there would be no dearth of cooling drinks.

The family consisted of John's father, mother and brother and four or five Indian helpers. These were the first Indians I had ever seen and I must say I was greatly disappointed. Of course, I was not exactly expecting to see war paint and feathers, but I was hardly prepared for such harmless looking creatures in overalls. One of them had a light blue handkerchief draped around his neck in picturesque fashion and was grinning in an embarrassed way. They told me afterwards that he had been to school at the Yuma reservation, that his experience there had rather dissatisfied him with life among his own people and he was the laziest one of the lazy bunch.

I found that the family was living in the tents Father had used at the Toltec camp and were quite comfortable while the cabin of cottonwood logs (cut from the river bottom) was being built for a permanent home. . . .

Our great interest was the building of this log house. The Indians of the Yuma Apache tribe were there for the purpose of "chinking" and "mudding," as they called it, and for making adobes for the fire-places. The one in charge was named Steve and he had been a scout in one of the Indian wars and was mentioned in some of Captain King's novels. His father was one of the old timers — no overalls for him — nothing but a "gee string." His skin was like wrinkled leather. I was quite pleased to find him, as he more nearly typified what I was expecting to see in the way of an Indian. . . .

And now, after I had been there only three days, I was to experience my first sand storm. When the desert does things, it seems to do them in a great big way. It may only have been doing what it conceived to be its duty, but sometimes I have felt that back of it all there was a sort of resentment toward human beings who dared to come in there and meddle around in a puny way, to make things more comfortable for themselves. The longer I lived there, the more I felt this Spirit of the desert, sometimes benign, but often the opposite, as though it must make up for those heavenly days of smiling sunshine by a tremendous blast which would show those humans their absurd insignificance. . . .

We were indeed glad when the house was finished and I think we were in it by October. It was such a comfortable, rambling house (if only a log one) with a dirt roof. . . . The folks had cots, tables, chairs, etc., which they had used at camp, and the boys made other things that we needed until we could have our furniture shipped out from Iowa. . . .

There were few settlers in the valley at that time and it would be two or three months at a time that Mother and I would not see another white woman. Men would stop in often and sometimes Indians would come around — the squaws appearing without a sound and put their faces against the window pane to peek in at us. It took me some time to get used to this, but they were quite friendly and meant no harm and really were just as curious about us and our methods of living as we were about them. After a few years, they moved their tepees nearer us, as the men worked on the ranches and the women washed for us. What a boon that was for the boys, who up to this time, had insisted on doing the rubbing for us, which John said was the hardest work a woman could do. He was always considerate and helpful, so that life was well worth living even under such conditions. I was extremely lonely at times, but through it all felt that I had much to be thankful for. . . .

Helen Sekaquaptewa's Wedding, 1919

About halfway through the rites, our consciences troubled us, because we felt the Hopi way was not quite right. We decided to get a license and be married legally. Emory told his folks what we wanted to do. He made application to the agency at Keams Canyon, and a marriage license was obtained by mail from Holbrook, the nearest county seat. It took about a week. In the afternoon that the license came, I went to my father's house in Hotevilla; Emory went with me. I just walked in and told my father that I was going to be married by license that night and had come to get my clothes. I could feel the disapproval of my father and my sister as I gathered the things I was going to wear. I just could not stay there and get dressed. I took my clothes and went to one of the school teachers, and she let me dress in her house.

I was married in a white batiste dress, which was my pride and joy. I had earned the money and bought the material and made the dress in domestic art class in the Phoenix school. It had lace insertion set in bow knots around the gathered skirt, on the flared sleeves, and on the collar. My teacher had entered it in the State Fair, and I got second prize on it. . . .

We were married in the evening on February 14, 1919, in the living room of the home of Mr. Anderson, principal of the school in Hotevilla, by Reverend Dirkson of the Mennonite Mission. Emory's people, including some of his cousins, came to the ceremony. The teachers served some refreshments and gave us some little presents and a room where we could spend the night. In the morning they served a wedding breakfast, and then we went back to finish the tribal wedding rites at Bacabi. . . .

When the weaving was finished the men took the robes from the looms and brought them into the house to be tried on. A border of sixteen running stitches in red was embroidered in the two corners, suggesting a limit of sixteen children, the most a person should have, and four stitches in each of the other two corners in orange, suggesting a minimum number of children. The white moccasins with leggings in one piece were finished just in time to be put on with the rest of the outfit. It was by then evening; food was placed before the guests and everyone ate again. (Hopis do not invite you to eat. They set the food before you, and the food invites.)

The next morning before sunup, Susie led the others in clothing me, first washing my hair. Everyone admired the bride, and I was now ready to go back to my father's house. A line of white cornmeal was sprinkled on the ground, pointing the way. There was a lot of snow on the ground, so they wrapped rags over my white moccasins so I wouldn't get them wet or muddy. Emory's people went with me out of the village and over the little hill back to my home in Hotevilla. Emory did not go with me this time. How I wished that my own dear mother could be there to meet me. The sun was just coming up when we got to my father's house. Verlie opened the door, and my father thanked them for the beautiful bridal apparel that would make his daughter eligible to enter the world of the hereafter. Thus ends the wedding ritual. . . .

The groom may follow the bride to her home as soon as he likes. Some go right away, some wait a long time before claiming their brides. Emory came over after a few days and stayed a couple of nights, but I could see that the tension and hostility was hard on him; too many children, too little room, not even a room to ourselves. After my going through all that ceremony just to please my family, my sister was still so hostile that I felt neither wanted nor welcome.

One day, about a month after we were married, when no one was at home, I felt that I could not stand it another minute. I gathered and packed my belongings, as many as I could carry, returning later for the rest of them, and went to the house where Emory lived near the [Hotevilla] school. He was at his work teaching shop when I got there. I cleaned up the house and had a meal cooked when he came home, and we were real happy. Soon afterward I got a job teaching beginners in the school. It was hard to get teachers there because it was so isolated.

Samuel Bryan Reports on Mexican Immigrants in the United States, 1912

Comparatively few people in the United States have any conception of the extent to which Mexicans are entering this country each year, of their geographical distribution, or of their relative importance in the various industries in which they are employed after their arrival. Nor are the social problems resulting from the influx of Mexicans fully appreciated by many persons who are not acquainted with the situation at first hand. This is primarily because the attention of students of the race problem has been focused upon the more important development of European and eastern Asiatic immigration to the eastern states, and upon Chinese, Japanese, and East Indian immigration to the Pacific coast. Other factors in diverting attention from Mexican immigration have been the relatively non-competitive character of their employment in certain parts of the country, and the lack of adequate data with regard to their numbers. . . .

In the arid regions of the border states where they have always been employed and where the majority of them still live, the Mexicans come into little direct competition with other races, and no problems of importance result from their presence. But within the last decade their area of employment has expanded greatly. They are now used as section hands as far east as Chicago and as far north as Wyoming. Moreover, they are now employed to a considerable extent in the coal mines of Colorado and New Mexico, in the ore mines of Colorado and Arizona, in the smelters of Arizona, in the cement factories of Colorado and California, in the beet-sugar industry of the last mentioned states, and in fruit growing and canning in California. In these localities they have at many points come into direct competition with other races, and their low standards have acted as a check upon the progress of the more assertive of these.

Where they are employed in other industries, the same wage discrimination against them as was noted in the case of railroad employees is generally apparent where the work is done on an hour basis, but no discrimination exists in the matter of rates for piece-work. As piece-workers in the fruit canneries and in the sugar-beet industry the proverbial sluggishness of the Mexicans prevents them from earning as much as the members of other races. In the citrus fruit industry their treatment varies with the locality. In some instances they are paid the same as the "whites" — in others the same as the Japanese, according to the class with which they share the field of employment. The data gathered by the Immigration Commission show that although the earnings of Mexicans employed in the other industries are somewhat higher than those of the Mexican section hands, they are with few exceptions noticeably lower than the earnings of Japanese, Italians, and members of the various Slavic races who are similarly employed. This is true in the case of smelting, ore mining, coal mining, and sugar refining. Specific instances of the use of Mexicans to curb the demands of other races are found in the sugar-beet industry of central California, where they were introduced for the purpose of showing the Japanese laborers that they were not indispensable, and in the same industry in Colorado, where they were used in a similar way against the German-Russians. Moreover, Mexicans have been employed as strike-breakers in the coal mines of Colorado and New Mexico, and in one instance in the shops of one important railroad system.

Socially and politically the presence of large numbers of Mexicans in this country gives rise to serious problems. The reports of the Immigration Commission show that they lack ambition, are to a very large extent illiterate in their native language, are slow to learn English, and in most cases show no political interest. In some instances, however, they have been organized to serve the purposes of political bosses, as for example in Phoenix, Arizona. Although more of them are married and have their families with them than is the case among the south European immigrants, they are unsettled as a class, move readily from place to place, and do not acquire or lease land to any extent. But their most unfavorable characteristic is their inclination to form colonies and live in a clannish manner. Wherever a considerable group of Mexicans are employed, they live together, if possible, and associate very little with members of other races. In the mining towns and other small industrial communities they live ordinarily in rude adobe huts outside of the town limits. As section hands they of course live as the members of the other races have done, in freight cars fitted with windows and bunks, or in rough shacks along the line of the railroad. In the cities their colonization has become a menace. . . . In Los Angeles the housing problem centers largely in the cleaning up or demolition of the Mexican "house courts," which have become the breeding ground of disease and crime, and which have now attracted a considerable population of immigrants of other races. . . .

As is to be expected under the circumstances, the proportion of criminals and paupers among the Mexicans is noticeably greater than among the other foreign-born or among the natives. In Los Angeles county, California, the Mexicans comprised 11.4 per cent of the total number of persons bound over for felonies in 1907. In 1908 and 1909 the percentages were 12.6 and 13.4, respectively. . . . In both Arizona and California the offenses for which they were committed were in the large majority of cases traceable to gambling or excessive drinking. Most of the serious trouble with Mexicans, however, arises from quarrels among themselves which interfere very little with the white population.

In the matter of poor relief, Mexican families were concerned in 11.7 per cent of the cases dealt with by the Associated Charities of Los Angeles in 1908. The proportion has increased since that time, and in 1910 it was estimated that Mexicans comprised fully one-third of those given relief from this source. . . .

In conclusion it should be recognized that although the Mexicans have proved to be efficient laborers in certain industries, and have afforded a cheap and elastic labor supply for the southwestern United States, the evils to the community at large which their presence in large numbers almost invariably brings may more than overbalance their desirable qualities. Their low standards of living and of morals, their illiteracy, their utter lack of proper political interest, the retarding effect of their employment upon the wage scale of the more progressive races, and finally their tendency to colonize in urban centers, with evil results, combine to stamp them as a rather undesirable class of residents.

Jesusita Aragon, Midwife and Factory Worker in New Mexico, 1950s

I lived in Trujillo with my three kids until Ernesto was ready to start high school. There were good neighbors and everything in Trujillo, but the school just goes to eighth grade, and I want my kids to go to high school.

I wanted to go to high school myself, but they didn't want to bring me here. I used to talk and talk to them about it, but they say, "No, we can't. That's all, we can't." So I stop asking them, but it's important that Ernesto and Dolores and Ben go.

So in 1952 I sell the wood in my house and pay a neighbor to move me to Las Vegas [New Mexico]. . . .

When I first came here I washed for people and ironed and cleaned houses and

From Fran Leeper Buss, *La Partera: Story of a Midwife*, 1980, pp. 54–59, University of Michigan Press. Reprinted by permission of the publisher.

cleaned doctors' offices too. . . . Yes, back then I have to clean too many houses, and I have to wash the floors on my hands and knees. It was hard work then; now everything is easy. They have vacuum cleaners, and you are not kneeling down.

Dolores helps me so much during the times when I work in Las Vegas. She takes all the care of our house while I work on my jobs. She's a good girl and doesn't get into trouble.

One day I quit cleaning and I went to work at the parachute factory on the plaza. There were 475 of us, mostly ladies and a few men and our three bosses. Our three bosses were men. I work there eleven years, for a long time, until they close the factory.

I do many things at the factory. I rip, I cut, I sew, I darn. . . . They like my work at the parachute factory. When my boss asks me to stay two or three hours after work, overtime, I never say no; I never say no. Sometimes I didn't get off work until 11:00 at night. Yes, and then I have to go at 6:00 in the morning, but I was young and strong.

Sometimes I would leave to deliver babies, and one time somebody from another town came to get me almost as soon as I go to work. So, I asked my boss if I could go, and he said, "Go ahead."

I wasn't at the lady's too long, the birth came a little fast, but it was far, and when I came back my time card wasn't there to be punched like the others. Everybody calls me and says, "Jesusita, they're going to send you home; they're going to fire you. You were gone too long."

I said, "Well, I can't help it," and then I turned and looked to the window where my boss was in the office, and he called me to him with his hand.

And I feel bad. You know how it is when you need the money, when you need to work. So I tell my friends, "Goodbye, girls."

Then my boss said, "Come here, Jessie. Where did you go?"

I don't know, I was afraid to tell him the truth because I said, "If I tell him the truth he won't give me any more work." . . .

"OK, OK," he says. "Here is your card, punch it and go to work on those pieces. I can't send you home because I like your work; you do everything I tell you." . . .

I still go out to deliver babies, and one day he says, "Jessie, I want to know, why do you go out so often."

I don't know what he thinks of me, so I get my license out of my pocket and show it to him.

"Why didn't you tell me? I was ready to fire you, to send you back three times."

"Well, if you send me home I can look for another job."

"No, that's OK, and you can go out when they need you." So, he never bothers me again. When somebody goes to the office and asks for me, my boss goes and stands by me and says, "Somebody needs you better; you have another baby."

And they let the ladies who are pregnant work, to the last minute, and you know what he says, "You don't have to quit; here is Jesusita." And when they're to lift a heavy box or something, he says, "No, don't do it," and he looks for something easier for them to do. . . .

Yes, we had a good boss in those days, but I worked hard too. . . .

※ *E S S A Y S*

The effects of Hispanic and Anglo settlement on Indian family life in California during the late eighteenth and nineteenth centuries are described by Albert L. Hurtado of Arizona State University in the first essay. Hispanic settlers married Native Americans and sought to convert Indian couples to Catholicism; Anglos opposed "amalgamation," however, and instead tried to impose racial segregation. Both patterns of settlement threatened the security of Native American women and the integrity of their families. In the second essay, Yale University's John Mack Faragher explores the lives of white men and women on the Overland trail in the mid-nineteenth century, emphasizing the "separate worlds" of the sexes and women's lack of social authority on the long and lonely trip out west. Finding different meaning in the separation of the sexes, Sarah Deutsch of Clark University argues, in the last essay, that Hispanic women in northern New Mexico adapted creatively to interaction with Anglos during the late nineteenth century by assuming the vital task of preserving village life and community traditions, while Hispanic men migrated seasonally to Colorado to work in the Anglo-owned sugar beet industry. However, as entire families moved permanently to the Anglo north in the 1920s and 1930s, Hispanic women lost their status relative to Hispanic men and suffered from narrowing social and economic opportunities. What might Deutsch have found had she carried her study of Hispanic women in Colorado beyond the 1930s?

Culture and Family on the California Frontier

ALBERT L. HURTADO

In the 1850s good California farmland was hard to come by. Much of it had been taken up in the 1840s, when the Mexican government had granted huge parcels to settlers; squatters took most of the rest during the gold rush. James Kilgore was fortunate to have an unencumbered claim to agricultural land on the eastern side of the Sacramento Valley, yet he relinquished it to a young married man because he wanted "to see this country settled up with families." Apparently Kilgore had an extraordinary attachment to the domestic institution that Victorians held most dear, but he might have acted out of farsighted self-interest as well: the family had a strong influence on the Anglo-American frontier. Families brought stability, growth, and white civilization to Indian country. The more quickly families settled the country, the faster prosperity, cities, and sundry opportunities would follow. But not just any families would do. Kilgore meant to see a white family occupy his claim. If he had intended otherwise, he could have turned over the land to one of the Indian families who lived nearby. He would not do so, of course, because Indians lacked the racial and cultural qualifications he had in mind.

If settlement by families had been the sole criterion of a civilized territory, California would have been one of the most civilized places in the trans-Mississippi West before the turn of the eighteenth century. With three hundred thousand native people, California was one of the most heavily populated places in North America. But it was not common for men like Kilgore to think of Indians as family members. White frontiersmen saw them as primitive tribal folk, lacking the sentimental domestic affections that marked Victorian society. Yet family ties bound native people to each other, to their communities, and to the land. Family bonds defined social, political, and economic relationships in native cultures and were of paramount importance to Indian personal and corporate life. Tragically, the arrival of family-oriented people from other cultures threatened the network of kinship that had supported native society and survival for untold generations.

The Indian family fit into an elaborate set of social relationships that varied by tribe and locality. . . . For most California Indians, kinship defined the individual's place within the community and family associations suffused every aspect of life. Elites, commoners, poor, and sometimes slaves inherited their status, although it was possible to better one's position by a propitious marriage or by gaining wealth. Because northwestern tribes in particular emphasized acquisitiveness, most marriages in this culture area occurred within economic and social ranks, tending to stabilize economic and power relationships. . . .

Kinship was important to the daily lives of ordinary people. Families controlled particular hunting and gathering areas; individuals accumulated, shared, or traded resources according to familial associations. . . . Throughout California, kinship determined the nature of trading and ordinarily removed the profit motive from the transactions. Marriage and kinship influenced the social structure of each ranchería, depending on tribal customs. Communities were composed of extended residence groups that were linked by family ties. The Yokuts supplemented blood relations with moieties that connected them to a special totem animal such as the eagle or coyote. Children belonged to their father's moiety and were forbidden to kill their totem animal. . . . Moreover, totemic affiliations affected blood ties because an individual had to marry someone from another moiety.

Given the significance and complexity of kin and moiety relationships, marriage was an extremely important institution, governed according to strict rules. Unions were prohibited if a couple was related within three to five generations, depending on tribal affiliation. Consequently, men had to look for eligible wives outside their tribelet, and women had to leave their home communities when they married. Because kinship was so important, the departing women formed important new links for their families and communities, strengthening the system of reciprocity that girded native California. . . .

California's native household economy was based on hunting and gathering according to a sexual division of labor. Men hunted, fished, and — after the advent of white settlement — raided livestock herds. . . . As important as the male activities were, women did more work and provided the plant foods that comprised the bulk of the Indian diet. The acorn was a staple food, and although men assisted in gathering acorns, women ground them to flour and leached the tannic acid from the meal. In season, women collected grass seeds, roots, pine nuts, berries, and other foods, prepared them, and stored the surplus against lean times. Basket making was also a female task, and elaborate twined pieces, sometimes adorned with precious feathers and shell beads, were esteemed items of trade. All California tribes prized hardworking, productive women.

By bearing children — their most important contribution to Indian society — women created the human resources necessary to sustain their communities. . . .

Under ordinary conditions the Indian family was flexible, productive, and viable, but when placed under demographic stress it proved highly vulnerable.

When Spanish settlers began to arrive in California in 1769, they brought with them family customs that were well adapted to frontier circumstances. American conditions, especially the lack of Iberian women, modified the ideal Hispanic family in several ways and, as we shall see, impinged on Indian family traditions, with baleful consequences for the latter.

The family was the solid foundation of Spanish-American society. The husband was a patriarch who theoretically controlled all the family's important business. While he went out into the world, his wife took charge of the household, managing child rearing and domestic activities. During most of the colonial era the role of the family was to serve social and economic ends rather than to exemplify romantic love. Especially among the wealthy classes, parents often tried to arrange marriages that would enhance family fortunes, and young couples usually sought their parents' permission to marry. . . .

. . . As among Indians, important families were allied through marriage and such unions were ordinarily considered a matter of duty for the partners. Masculine passion was reserved for prostitutes and mistresses, if they could be afforded. On the other hand, Hispanic culture supposed that wives should be little interested in sexual relations, engaging in sex only for procreation and reserving their love for their children. Brides were supposed to approach the marriage bed with their maidenheads intact, so families strove to protect the virginity of daughters and sisters and the honor of wives — and thus their husbands — by confining them to the home, out of the reach of virile males.

With few exceptions, men were the household's primary economic providers, although women's economic contribution in the form of maintenance, food preparation, and child rearing were by no means inconsiderable. It was expensive to maintain the ideal Hispanic family, and poor people simply could not afford to rigorously confine women's activities to the home. Among the lower classes women baked, sewed, and acted as herbal healers (*curanderas*). As a rule, men and women tried to marry as high above their own class as circumstances might permit. The bride's family usually paid a dowry to the husband, but in colonial Peru wealthy *conquistadores* sometimes reversed this procedure so that they could marry women of higher rank than themselves. Regardless of the riches he obtained in the New World, only marriage into the upper classes would confer the highest possible status to the Hispanic frontiersman. . . .

The family that evolved in Hispanic America was not merely a frontier replica of an Iberian model. . . . Early in the conquest of the Americas, the shortage of Spanish women led not only to illegitimate sexual liaisons but to marriages as well. Throughout the Spanish Empire frequent intermarriage along with illicit unions created a substantial mixed blood *mestizo* population. . . .

Amalgamation in the California borderlands did not mean that Indian and Spanish cultures united on an equal footing. On the contrary, Hispanic Catholic values were meant to supplant native ways. As elsewhere in Spanish America, the Franciscan missions aimed to eliminate marriage and family customs repugnant to Spaniards and the Church. The mission could control only Indians who were under its authority, and Indians were at first slow to volunteer for Christian instruction. As elsewhere in the Western Hemisphere, the Spanish advance was accompanied by epidemic diseases that decimated native populations, and the new pastoral economy disrupted native lifeways. Disease, death, and hunger caused native people to question the efficacy of their old traditions and enhanced the appeal of mission life. By 1785 five thousand Indians had become mission neophytes. Twenty years later there were twenty thousand neophytes in a mission system that eventually expanded to twenty-one establishments, all located near the coast between Sonoma and San Diego.

The missions converted Indians to habits of industry as well as Catholic piety. . . . The mission functioned as a magnet, drawing Indian workers who established and maintained settlements where labor was otherwise scarce. This was particularly true in California. Since the non-Indian population of Hispanic California never exceeded thirty-five hundred, the missions and Indian labor were the basis for California's economy. Neophytes constructed the buildings, herded the cattle, worked the fields, and did whatever was required to keep the missions running. The Franciscan establishments became the paramount economic institutions of the colony, controlling most of the land and an Indian labor force of many thousands.

To control Indian and Spanish sexual behavior at the missions, single women were locked in sleeping rooms at night. Nocturnal cloistering protected the women's chastity and this made them desirable spouses, but it also made them more susceptible to the infectious diseases that swept through the missions from time to time, killing thousands. Franciscan missionaries were anxious to eliminate polygyny and legitimize native marriages with appropriate Catholic ceremonies. Once these marriages were solemnized, divorce became nearly impossible, although widows and widowers were encouraged to remarry.

Eight northern California missions recorded more than twenty-three hundred marriages between Indians who had previously been joined by native customs, and over five thousand new Indian unions. . . . Not only did marriages bind Indian couples to the mission, but Christian Indian parents baptized their children in the Church, increasing the neophyte population with Indians whose links with native culture were weaker than their parents'. By 1834 more than seven thousand Indians had received baptism at six northern California missions. . . .

Indian interracial marriages were uncommon in California, producing fewer than one hundred children, according to northern California mission records. Mexican Californians preferred to marry among themselves, but californio men had illicit sexual liaisons with native women. Franciscan padres often complained that soldiers molested Indian women. Few statistics reflect the extent of casual sex, but contemporary accounts indicate that such liaisons must have been common. The rapid spread of venereal diseases among Indian people was one result of unregulated sexual intercourse. Syphilis was especially devastating; it either killed Indians outright or lowered their resistance to other diseases, often with mortal effects. Women were particularly vulnerable in childbirth, and a mother's death usually resulted in the loss of the infant. Measles, diphtheria, and smallpox likewise caused high mortality rates in the neophyte population, but Spanish frontier family customs and sexual behavior also contributed to native population decline and reduced fertility rates among neophytes. Thus, Hispanic families displaced native families by a long process of attrition. . . . The traditional Indian family was a major casualty on the Spanish borderland frontier.

Anglo families also brought well-defined traditions to California. As in Hispanic society, Anglo families were based on the conjugal couple and their children; the husband was the head of the household and the woman's place ideally was in the home. Men were supposed to support and protect their families and theoretically their wives were pure, pious, and domestic. Men confronted the world; women shunned it for household life. Anglo-Americans believed that this sexual dichotomy was fitting because men and women had different natures: males were virile, strong, worldly, coarse, competitive, and forward; women were demure, retiring, passive, spiritual, and maternal. Man's role was to subdue the world; women were supposed to civilize it. In the early years of the nineteenth century a woman could own property, but it became her husband's after she married. Divorce was difficult to obtain and the husband usually retained the children. Some marriages, no doubt, were convenient alliances for combining family fortunes, but the romantic ideal was to marry a loving companion, regardless of social class and economic considerations. Extramarital sex was not condoned, although brothels were common enough to indicate that the ideal was not always attained.

The family was basic to the Anglo-American westward movement. In the earliest stages single males went to the frontier. Unlike the Spanish, whose settlements were made according to royal decree, Anglos pushed beyond settled areas on their own initiative and were reluctant to bring women with them until they gained a secure foothold in the new land. Once established, Anglo men looked for spouses and usually returned to settled areas to find them. Since Anglo tradition did not encourage interracial marriages, Indian women were not considered acceptable mates. Fur traders were the only notable exception to this rule, yet they sometimes abandoned their marriages to Indians after the country was settled and white women became available.

Anglo frontier women were extraordinarily fertile and large families were the rule. Unfortunately, the level of health care was so primitive that death in childbirth was an ordinary occurrence. A grieving husband with a cabin full of children remarried as soon as possible, and commonly his new wife produced more offspring. High birthrates and immigration populated frontier areas. As land became scarce and expensive and landless sons moved on to the next frontier where land was readily available, the frontier process was repeated.

Anglo women on the frontier did more than bear children and keep the home fires burning. They pitched in to help with the dozens of chores necessary to operate a family farm in a new country. Whether spinning thread, making clothes, tending a garden, or raising children, frontier women were assets to their husbands and to their communities. . . . That is why Anglo men returned to settled areas to find brides. Women provided not only emotional and social stability, but economic contributions as well. Hence, the family was an engine for frontier advancement, casting forth westering sons who came back periodically to take away the excess of unmarried daughters. This dynamic was in force from colonial times until the end of the nineteenth century.

As for Indian families, the United States favored moving them away from settled areas to Indian country, where Indian Office bureaucrats and humanitarians supposedly would teach them Christianity and civilized ways. The transformation of native traditions was the goal of Anglo humanitarians, but it was not a prerequisite for their settlements. Indeed, the elimination of Indians from settled areas was a distinguishing characteristic of the Anglo frontier. . . . In California, however, complete racial segregation was impossible and Anglos had to adjust to a closer association with Indians. . . .

Between 1820 and 1860 . . . Anglos accommodated to Mexican California, Indian labor, and even miscegenation. But in asserting control over California, they quickly reestablished their old family customs as they adapted new technology and labor arrangements. By 1860 Anglo families far exceeded native and Hispanic families in numbers and power, and the newcomers viewed their position with a sense of self-satisfaction that was common in the age of Manifest Destiny. In 1864 Fannie Reading, the wife of the Anglo pioneer Pierson B. Reading, described the wheat harvest for her mother back east. In one week twenty-two men, a steam engine, threshing machine, two heading machines, two wagons, and twenty-two horses would finish a job that used to take up to three months and require the services of scores of Indians. . . . The arrival of steam-powered threshers, horse-driven headers, and other innovations reduced the need for Indian agricultural labor and inexorably diminished an important source of subsistence for Indian families. But Indian survival was not Fannie Reading's concern. . . . In California she lived a leisured but rustic life in the north end of the Sacramento Valley, attended parties, feted guests, doted on her children, and vacationed near Mount Lassen. Her domestic duties were eased by Indian servants and two native nurses.

Fannie's family attachments and household life were in many ways typical of middle-class Victorian women. Her sentimental love for her husband, children, and kin were much in keeping for a woman of her status and background. That she never inquired — in writing, at least — into the family lives of her domestic help also speaks of the cultural blindness and class presumptions that were common to women of southern birth. People of color were born to serve whites in the world of Fannie's youth. If Fannie thoughtlessly accepted the exploitation of people who were not white, she was hardly alone. . . .

The Separate Worlds of Men and Women on the Overland Trail

JOHN MACK FARAGHER

Midwestern society had a developed sense of gender distinction. The existence of a strict division of labor and separate cultural character models for men and women suggests that significant portions of men's and women's time were spent in the

---

From John Mack Faragher, "The Separate Worlds of Men and Women," Chapter five in *Women and Men on the Overland Trail,* Copyright © 1979. Reprinted by permission of Yale University Press.

company of their own sex. Indeed, despite the importance of the family, midwestern society contained separate sexual worlds for men and women, each with its own separate bundle of behaviors and beliefs, each understood and appropriated by the right sex only. . . .

[The] situation on the trail was no different, really, from life at home. The isolation of women in their homes was a social fact introduced by the division of labor, but it was further reinforced by the settlement patterns of the Midwest. In 1840, in the Sangamon River farming country of Illinois, for instance, there were only about eight people per square mile. . . . The homes were not built in proximity to each other; each was isolated on its separate farmstead. . . .

This residential isolation severely limited the social opportunities for women. Men's responsibilities allowed them to lay up their ploughs or hoes for the day and ride or walk out to visit the neighbors or frequent the village store, but women, with their more or less constant responsibilities at home, especially the care of the children, could not be so casual. The single most important distinction between the social and cultural worlds of men and women was the isolation and immobility of wives compared to husbands.

The public world, culture and society outside the family, was the world of men. The Midwest was first and foremost a society of farmers who for most of the year were locked into isolated and solitary work on their family homesteads; at these times public life was accordingly slow, almost nonexistent. But at other times, and on other occasions, neighboring men came together in cooperative work. . . . Logrollings were a first chance for the neighboring men to get together after the winter and break the social monotony that had prevailed since the close of the previous hunting season. These were not only workdays but celebrations of male strength and physical prowess as well. "Each man vied with the other to show his strength. It meant much in those days to be considered the strongest man of the neighborhood." . . . In those days before mechanical reapers, neighboring men circulated to one another's farms, bringing in the hay and wheat, cradling, binding, and mowing in gangs. . . . A few weeks later one or more farmers were sure to hold a cornhusking where the men worked into the night with much rivalry, competition, and heavy whiskey drinking. . . . Occasionally men came together when needed for a cabin raising, where much the same competitive and boisterous spirit prevailed. . . .

Men rode in to mill their grain or corn, to trade surpluses in corn or pork for goods at the stores, to have their wool carded or their skins tanned and made into shoes, to call on the craftsmen, and generally to meet their neighbors and socialize. The village was the hub of country life in northern Sangamon County, the little general stores the center of village life. "Throughout the day shoppers and gossipers came and went, or lounged on its porch, reading mail, exchanging news, or talking crops and politics." . . . The common denominator of the male experience was boasting and boisterous competition, the settlement of disputes by resort to force, and the promotion of the hail-fellow feeling that fostered necessary social cooperation. . . .

Politics was perhaps the most refined of the common male pursuits, and the midwestern countryside "seethed with politics." At the local level, politics and social life were woven from the same yarn, spun on the wheel of male social life. Talking politics, defining the important issues — nearly all of them of local significance — was a constant habit. On election day each man stepped forward at the polls as his name was called and shouted out his preferred candidate to the huzzahs or catcalls of his fellowmen. Election day was a local holiday; local Indians called it the day of the "big drunk." . . . In their elections, male heads of household chose male representatives to make policy for, to administer, and to sanction the social and economic order of the midwestern patriarchy. The masculine state was the capstone of male control of the public world. . . .

This male public world of cooperative farm labor, village social life, politics, and the state was a world from which women were absent. . . . The one public event that women claimed as their own was the religious meeting. Throughout much of Indiana and Illinois, churches were few and far between, so the few dedicated churchgoers met in schools or farmhouses. Annual camp meetings, a tradition through the thirties and forties, were a way to prevent serious backsliding. When it was camp-meeting time, work was put aside and a family might camp out for a few days of vacation. The simple cold meals freed women from most of their cooking chores, and it was one of the only times of the year when wives were free from housework. Women responded by getting into the thick of the meeting; it was often the women who were most prone to emotionalism, who would "get the jerks." . . .

In contrast to men, women's social relationships were mostly within their families. A certain number of family kin usually remained settled in one area, and for women the relationships among sisters and cross-generational feminine kin provided them with their social contacts. . . . Thus was women's world structured around the intimate events of family and personal life, events experienced not alone but within the circle of feminine kin and neighbors. Women's world was marked by qualities of personal intensity and inter-subjectivity.

In Adams County, Illinois, the mass of advice directed toward the common problems of women reflected the sympathy women felt for one another. . . . Granny women or midwives were storehouses of this wisdom of the feminine life cycle and were consulted by community women in matters of contraception, abortion, and miscarriage as well as menstrual problems. Most important, grannies, and women in general, were holders of the secrets of birth and obstetrics. . . . By the same token, men (the public) had almost no role to play in the elaborate feminine rituals of birth. . . .

Women were much more self-consciously aware of the life and care of the body than were men. Women's personal lives, unlike men's, were shaped by passage through a series of character-defining life-cycle events of bodily change. The terrible toll of miscarriage, infant mortality, and maternal mortality certainly impressed mothers with the close conjuncture of death and the genesis of life. In addition, their responsibilities for infant care and the maintenance of family health made women most conscious of the problems of health. On the basis of such concerns women built an enormous lore concerning health and health care. Midwestern farm wives continued in the centuries-old tradition that placed women in the role of administratrix of folk medicines. Given the state of the healing profession even as late as 1850, it may have been a distinct advantage that doctors were scarce in the Midwest. Home gardens included herbs for folk remedies, and women seemed to know substantially more than men the value of wild plants and Indian concoctions. The principle was "every disease has a herb that cures it."

It was from these common bases — the experience of being a woman, of childbirth and motherhood, of healer and nurse — that a specific female culture took form. Just as men were united in competitive action, women too shared a unique view of the world, a common culture.

Moreover, this common culture was given meaning beyond the family in the social relationships neighboring women enjoyed with one another. Although the opportunities for social contact were severely limited in the Midwest, nonetheless women had occasion to come together. There was a female side to the work bees, for instance; at logrollings, cabin raisings, cornhuskings and the like, visiting wives joined the hostess in the kitchen to prepare the midday meal. . . . The ritual of the kitchen complemented the male ritual of the field. . . .

In the context of these separate sexual worlds the experience of men and women on the trail looks very familiar. For men the trip was a continuation and extension of their social lives at home. The grand encampment outside the jumping-off place replaced the logrolling as the opening social event of the year. Men reproduced their own experience when they organized the trains and parties, so the society of the trail most resembled local militias and local politics. Electioneering for trail office was complete with the panoply of midwestern democracy: campaigning, speechmaking, demonstrating, and patriotic displays. . . . The male camaraderie of country life, in fact, was exaggerated by the dangers and excitements of the trail. "Men were drawn together on the plains as in every day walks of life," William Thompson remembered, "only the bonds were closer and far more enduring. The very dangers through which they passed together rendered the ties more lasting." . . . Truly one of the great attractions of the trip was the notion of spending the entire spring and summer "in the rough" with the boys, away from the routines of farm work. Trail work was hard, to be sure, but farm drudgery held none of this romantic allure. . . .

In some ways, then, the trip across the plains fulfilled male dreams of camaraderie, action, and achievement. For women the experience was perceived in quite another way. First, there was no relief from the daily drudgery of women's work. To be fair, the work so familiar at home was the same on the trail, only more difficult and more frustrating — as any mother who has tried roadside camping with a family of children can testify. The burden of work, however, took second place to the disruption the emigration brought to women's social and cultural lives. Women constructed a social life on the trail, but in their diaries and recollections they demonstrated a deep regret at their inability to sustain close and deep attachments with other women. Men by habit participated in a cultural life that abounded in outward forms of sociability, and they found it relatively easy to adapt to life on the trail. Women, whose cultural needs were traditionally met in closer quarters, with an intensity that could survive periods of isolation, found the superficial relations of the trail inadequate; for them, the trip was a lonely experience.

The failure of the more organized trains was a bitter disappointment to women who had benefited from the number of families — and women — the trains brought together. Women traveling alone with their husbands and children, in the catch-as-catch-can manner of the trail, always had to be on the lookout for female company. Watching for women became a central preoccupation: July 18, 1853, a group of packers passed by, "no women but twenty men in the camp"; July 19, "twenty one men, well armed, but no ladies." Each day the survey was made. When two parties with womenfolk happened into each other's company, the women often pressured their men to travel together. . . .

But since men usually saw little reason to slow or quicken their own pace to match that of strangers, more often women had to be content with the fleeting contact they made with other women along their way. . . .

Brief contacts were not always all women had. If several women found themselves traveling together, or if a family party included a number of female kin, they would visit together as they traveled along, perhaps walking in a group "talking over our home life back in 'the states,' telling of the loved ones left behind, voicing our hopes for the future in the far west and even whispering a little friendly gossip of emigrant life." . . .

Perhaps women's most important relations with each other were expressed in the sisterhood of the sickbed. Women took it upon themselves to act in nurturant and nursing roles for the sick and injured about them, most especially for stricken women. . . . This was even more the case with childbirth, when men were absolutely incapacitated and women in fine fettle. Woman's work continued on the trail, and childbirth was no exception to the rule. . . . But at delivery women wanted women to assist: what woman was prepared and willing to be alone, with just her husband? If there was no sister in camp, men desperately rode ahead or back looking for a surrogate midwife or doctor. . . .

. . . With childbirth suddenly upon them, men, too, understood the importance of women's relationships with women. But for women there was no forgetting at any time; the need was only more desperate at delivery. Women were haunted by the fear that the trauma of leaving home would be repeated in the loss of whatever feminine company they had been able to find along the way. . . .

The loneliness, isolation and dread of loss that women felt frequently brought to mind friends they had left behind. "How often I have thought of my dear friend Mary E. Ballard," Harriet Cummings confided. "How earnestly do I pray that she may be happy and that she may never know sorrow and care. How I would like to see her and hers." "This is a beautiful morning," Esther McMillan Hanna wrote. "I think of home and the dear ones there; each day I am getting farther from them." Agnes Stewart, desperately missing her lifelong friend Martha, wondered "whether it is my nature to love so well, or because I have no one else to love, I do not know. But one thing I do know; I miss you more than I can find words to express."

This catalogue of women's laments could be continued for pages, so vocal were women about their disrupted relationships. It is the contrast with men, however, that is most striking. In their diaries most family men accompanied by their wives were virtually silent about the loneliness or isolation they must have felt. But then men were by no means short on company; there were always other men on the road. More importantly, men were on familiar ground, easily able to communicate with strangers through the silent languages of male competitions and solidarities, if not casual conversation. Women, on the other hand, were living out a male-constructed enterprise with little control over its social terms. What feminine relations they could construct existed only at male pleasure. The anguish women expressed was a measure of the importance that same-sex relations held for them, and of how much they needed their own autonomous context for living out those relationships.

Hispanic Women and Intercultural Relations in New Mexico and Colorado

SARAH DEUTSCH

At the turn of the century, the part women played in intercultural relations — in assimilation, acculturation, or resistance — was perfectly obvious to those who studied the question with an eye to Americanization. Women ruled the home. They governed a private world to which they gave outside forces, in this case Americanizers, only limited access. In addition, the women alone, in the eyes of these officials, cared for the young children and shaped the values, habits, and desires of the next generation. In the twin temporal kingdoms of present and future, as guardians of the present home and as mothers of the future generation, they held the primary power to influence their cultural complex.

Many current scholars, like their predecessors, have seen women as crucial to intercultural relations chiefly in their capacity as mothers and guardians of the hereditary culture. Some historians depict women as builders of cultural bridges either between generations or between ethnic groups. Alternatively, women are portrayed as barriers, resisting Americanization, or even as burdens on their own ethnic groups, preventing rapid assimilation and upward mobility as defined by the dominant culture. Other historians have abandoned the traditional attempt to define women in these terms and, instead, look more closely at women's economic activities. These historians describe women's work patterns as part of a family economy and strategy but usually stop short of examining the implications that changes in those patterns had for women and for the group as a whole as it struggled to survive in an intercultural arena.

This article reassesses women's part in the dynamics of cultural interaction, focusing on Hispanic women in Colorado and northern New Mexico. Written histories of village Hispanic women or rural Chicanas are still rare, and of Chicanas or Hispanic women in Colorado virtually nonexistent.* The mushrooming contemporary scholarship on Chicanos concentrates instead on the urban experience from 1850 to 1930. It indicates that many urban Chicanas worked for wages and headed households, but it assumes that this pattern of activity — outside the home and with some measure of autonomy — stands in contrast to women's lives in the villages.

Sarah Deutsch, "Women and Intercultural Relations: The Case of Hispanic New Mexico and Colorado" from *Signs: Journal of Women in Culture and Society* 12 (Summer 1987), pp. 719–739. Reprinted by permission of the University of Chicago Press.
*"Hispanic" and "Spanish American" refer to Spanish-speaking, Spanish-surnamed, and/or Spanish-heritage people whose ancestors had settled in Colorado and New Mexico before the U.S. conquest. "Chicanos" and "Chicanas" encompass as well the more recent Mexican migrants and immigrants. . . .

My research on Hispanic-Anglo relations in northern New Mexico and Colorado from 1880 to 1940 undermines the assumptions that Hispanic village women were more subordinated in the village than outside it and that they found the move north to Anglo areas and cities a liberating experience. In other words, the common wisdom will not do. A better understanding of Hispanic women's experience in the village is central, it turns out, to our understanding of the Hispanic experience in Hispanic-Anglo relations anywhere.

In the Hispanic world of northern New Mexico's communal villages, a sexual division of labor and production laid the foundation on which villagers built their strategies for interaction with the Anglo world that surrounded them by the end of the nineteenth century. In the villages, women's activities regarding community networks, land, and production grew in importance as male migration out of the villages for wage work became increasingly vital to village survival. But when entire Hispanic families migrated and settled in enclaves away from the villages, the balance between women's and men's activities shifted. The process by which women's experiences, so central to village life, became isolated and peripheral the closer women moved to Anglo towns and farms, is inextricably bound to the transformation of social and economic relationships wrought by Anglo-Hispanic contact. Taken together, the changes in those relations across time and space tell us much about how village households could and could not use their production patterns to maintain some cultural autonomy while at the same time taking advantage of economic opportunities offered by a rival culture. . . .

Nestled among relatively inaccessible mountains, northern New Mexico's villages seemed to many changeless and idyllic. Yet as mines, railroads, and commercial agricultural enterprises encompassed the region in the 1880s, as Anglo courts legalized the dispossession of villages in the loss of communal lands, and as taxes and cash demands rose, increasingly men migrated seasonally out of the villages in search of wage work. Through at least the 1930s, these migrants provided the majority of Spanish-speaking labor for the mines, railroads, and farms of Colorado and New Mexico. Despite the migration and the increasing Anglo presence in the region, the villages remained distinctively Hispanic. The social organization of the villages and, in particular, the activities of women, help explain this resilience. For as the men migrated, their participation in the village began to shrink until the women's world and the world of the village began to merge. . . .

Northern New Mexico's Hispanic villages had long survived by a mixture of pastoral and irrigated agricultural activities, along with a modest but absolutely essential amount of external trade that was gradually replaced by seasonal wage labor as barriers to trade rose. This was an economy, in the arid mountains, requiring a substantial amount of communal labor — for both agricultural and stock production — and an economy also dependent on communal rights regarding pasturage and water.

The norm among village households was a complete or extended family headed by a married couple. . . . In a household with adult men and women, men earned some cash through trade or seasonal labor and raised grain crops and livestock, while women raised produce, including cash-earning items such as chili and eggs. When one or other of the partners was missing, whether through divorce, death, or desertion, the household became lopsided and difficult to keep afloat. Men and women both owned property, inheriting it equally; community property in marriage was the rule, and husbands left property to wives, not eldest sons. Yet widows and widowers remarried at about the same high rates. As heads of households, single men appeared no more frequently than single women. Single heads of household of either sex tended to live with siblings or nieces or nephews given to them by generous relatives to redress the imbalance of age and sex in their household.

While women and men both demonstrated this desire to multiply attachments to the group, for women there were particular and increasing hazards in remaining unattached. Despite the fact that Hispanic women bought and sold property, homesteaded, conducted business, and let sheep out on shares independently, men had greater access to the cash economy: they could migrate out of the village in search of seasonal labor in local mining ventures, on railroad tracks, or herding other people's sheep or cattle. Not one of these cash-earning jobs in the Anglo sector was open to women. . . .

. . . Limited as most women were to such low-paying professions as sewing and taking in laundry, women who were left without sufficient property or sufficient numbers of male wage earners in their household had a far lower earning potential than did men. . . . If widowed or divorced women owned their own property and had grown sons to help work it, they could sustain themselves as heads of families, but divorced or widowed women with young children seldom could sustain an independent existence. They relied on exchange with and the kindness of relatives and neighbors.

It is possible to see, in the light of their greater vulnerability to poverty and their greater stake in supportive networks outside marriage, women's particular part in constructing the sense of community so vital to the survival of the Hispanic villages. They did have, after all, and always have had a hand even in the literal construction of the community. Men made the adobes and built basic structures, but women did all the plastering, inside and out, for their homes and for common buildings, and they built adobe ovens and fireplaces. . . .

Women, also, to a greater extent than did men, nurtured the human networks of the village. Often fourteen different visitors would come to one home, some returning three or four times in a single afternoon. Women also maintained the links with kin in other villages, sometimes journeying with the whole family, sometimes alone, sometimes for several weeks at a time. These links maintained connections with coparents, grandparents, or trustworthy foster parents for the children in case of economic disaster. They provided farm labor in old age, widowhood, or illness, and employment (usually for payment in goods rather than cash). The maintenance of community ties thus became a means to ensure the welfare of oneself and one's family.

Perhaps the most fundamental work of women was one more obviously allied to maintenance and to women's place in Hispanic society; it centered around food. Hispanic women were responsible for the "garden," a plot of irrigated land usually closer to the house than were the fields of grain. This garden produced more and more of the food consumed by the family as Anglo and Hispanic speculators, railroads, and national parks acquired the grazing lands necessary for livestock production. Women controlled this garden land totally. It provided them with an autonomous base, a source of subsistence independent of but not in competition with men. . . .

Food, as a woman's own product to dispose of as she wished, became intimately bound to her virtue, and a woman's treatment of it defined her character both as a woman (one worthy to be a mother) and as a member of a communal village. Women did not belong to the community simply as dependents whose place there was determined by the behavior of their nearest male relative. They belonged as producers, and it was in part through the distribution of their own produce that they held a place in their own right.

Women also produced food for exchange. For example, one woman "sold" her cheese "to the village people who did not have cows or goats of their own." But she sold it within an informal women's exchange network bartering cornmeal, flour, or homemade soap for the cheese. . . . Trading for cash — outside the village almost by definition since there was virtually no cash in circulation there, and certainly outside a woman's network of community and kin — usually remained in the hands of either husbands or male relatives. This delegation of the cash nexus to men would acquire new meaning when whole families migrated to Anglo areas.

Meanwhile, food remained distinct from other products women and men produced, and there were separate peripheries to its legitimate sale. It was more like village land, whose preferred buyers were always relatives, than like, for example, weavings or sheep. A woman from Cordova rejected the opportunity to sell her homemade ice cream through a local merchant. "It would be dishonest to sell food you make in your home for profit at a store," she explained. Her husband concurred, "She is right, because to make food is part of our life as a family and to start selling that is to say that we have nothing that is *ours* . . . better to have less money and feel we own ourselves, than more and feel at the mercy of so many strangers." Exchange for trade, even cash sales if sold by the producer, retained the intimate connection between producer and subsistence product and retained the producer's control over that product. By introducing a middleman, one lost control of one's virtue. Women's production of food, like women's creation of neighborhood, was thus both imbued with the communalism of the village and vital to it. . . .

Both Anglos and Hispanics noted the relatively rapid spread of "American" bedsteads, tables, chairs, sewing machines, and cooking stoves into Hispanic homes after 1880, paid for by the men's earnings from newly available wage jobs. They noted this technological cross-cultural contact, but they gave less notice to the concommitant extension of women's work in the village. That women often enjoyed the new technology, in particular the cookstoves, is not in dispute. In 1901 two women were sufficiently attached to the same cookstove to bring a case to court. But the changes in women's labor were not limited to their work within the home. When men left the village for wage work each spring, the women were left with the care of the men's crops. The women were moving from a shared position at the village center as village producer to sole tenancy. . . .

. . . The cash the migrants brought home to the villages paid taxes and permitted such modern necessities as gable or corrugated iron roofs and school supplies despite depleted resources. Without the work of the women in the villages, however, without adapting the sexual division of labor to new strategies made necessary by cross-cultural contact, the Hispanic villages, as such, could not have survived. . . . In a village increasingly divided into village women and migrant men, women's activities sustained the community physically and spiritually. The integrative function of women grew in importance, and increasingly women provided the ongoing principle, the continuity for the village. Through the work of women, Hispanics could maintain an area where they retained control over the development of their own culture, selected artifacts from the Anglo world, and continued their patterns of communal networking and exchange outside of direct Anglo contact, despite loss of overall economic and political dominance. So completely, in fact, had village life come to devolve on these women by the end of the 1920s that one Hispanic male recalled, "When the men came back, they were kind of like guests."

This tightly bound economic balancing act worked for the villages and their migrant men, but it would fall apart when whole families moved to the Anglo-dominated city or the Anglo rural north, to Denver or northern Colorado's beet fields, as they did increasingly during the 1920s. In these northern Anglo areas, Hispanic women experienced a new marginality. Differences in the social structure of Anglo communities and restrictions on Hispanic landowning there inhibited the ability of women to play the same vital economic role they had played in the village.

Hispanics in sugar beet growing areas of northern Colorado found it difficult if not impossible to make the traditional progression from laborer to tenant to farm owner. Landowners hesitated to lease farms to Hispanics. Largely restricted, as a result, to seasonal beet labor, the migrants arrived at a time when land values had escalated while wages had not and when the move to ownership by anyone had generally dwindled. Yet without owning productive land, it would be difficult for Hispanics to convert new settlements in the north into stable villages. Even town lots were not easily acquired. Restrictive covenants and low wages kept Hispanics on the margins in northern towns. The state's largest beet sugar company, Great Western Sugar, with its company-financed colonies for Hispanic labor, did not discourage this state of affairs. Rather, the colonies epitomized the effort to preserve a system that identified Hispanics as a perpetual and distinct laboring force. Their one- or two-room distinctive adobe structures stood on lots devoid of shade, sufficient water, or farmland, a mile or two outside Anglo towns, or literally across the tracks.

Women in this setting could not produce enough food to feed their families. Hispanic women in northern Colorado planted gardens when they could, but with over half the women working in the beet fields, even in the relatively rare instances when they had suitable land and water, they did not have the time to tend vegetables, so often they planted flowers instead. Fewer than 2 percent of Hispanic families working in the beet fields in northern Colorado produced a major part of their own food, and at least 33 percent had no gardens at all.

. . . In the Hispanic villages, women had measured their value by their ability to provide and prepare food, both for their own and for neighboring families. As in other societies, food was more than sustenance; it carried emotional freight, bound villagers to one another, and defined their relations. Change in this arena would eventually shake all others. Women would have to find new ways to measure their value. As with the men, their relationship to the land and to what it produced, a relationship that had provided the key to village membership, had changed.

Membership in the community, like women's own value, would have to be defined in other ways.

The community itself was none too easy for women to find. Its elusiveness became most evident at childbirth. Midwives, essential and respected members of villages, moved north in the same way other women did, as members of beet-working families. But as such, they, too, became highly transient, here one year, gone the next. Some Hispanic women turned instead to free county clinics when they opened in the 1930s, but they found them a mixed blessing. It was "much better" during birth because they had ether for the pain, but much harder afterward. In New Mexico, relatives and neighbors had gathered round. All helped. In the north, remembered one mother, "we didn't have nobody to do anything for us so we had to work up to the minute we had kids and then up immediately, no women around to help." . . .

Without the communal and exchanged labor of the village, the comradeship of women in childbirth, the power bases of the garden and of the village itself, Hispanic women in northern Colorado found their place in society altered indeed. Thoroughly dependent on a money economy, Chicanas in northern Colorado did not find in wage labor, when they could get it, a satisfactory replacement for their gardens as a means, or for their villages as an end. Performing agricultural labor for wages, unlike the nonwage labor in the garden or the village fields, provided neither the status of ownership nor even necessarily control of income produced. The farmer contracted with and paid the husband and not the wife for the family's labor.

Moreover, there was little in the off-season jobs available to them that would advance the status of Hispanic women in either the Hispanic or the Anglo society. The winter occupations open to the women were even more limited and poorly paid than those open to Hispanic men. Only about one-tenth of the Chicanos with winter wage work were mothers, and while the men with winter employment averaged sixty dollars a month income, the women averaged half of that. Domestic service, the largest category of jobs open to Chicanas, paid as much as ten or twelve dollars per week in Denver, but Maria Chavez remembered cleaning houses for fifty cents a day in the beet areas of Wyoming. And not all employers looked kindly on Chicana domestics, as one Spanish American girl, a U.S. citizen working her way through school, recalled: "A woman to whom I applied for work when I first came to x —— said, 'People of your nationality are just terrible; I can't stand them, they're so crude, lazy, and so uncultured.'"

Hispanic women in Anglo areas virtually were left, of the entire panoply of their village activities, with the home alone. In contrast, the male realm of wage earning and external relations took on an ever-increasing importance. Hispanic men in the Anglo north, too, faced limited opportunities and options, and male/ female relations in terms of decision-making and respect within marriage did not necessarily change, at least not immediately. But the Hispanic women had lost ground within the Hispanic community as well as in the larger community, for they continued, after all, as inferior wage earners, and now wage earning had become the only means to an autonomous base. The balance within the Hispanic community had altered.

Anglo women, too, had a role to play in this intercultural equation. . . . Over 200 unaccompanied Anglo women missionaries had come to claim the Hispanic villages for Protestant America between 1900 and 1914 alone, and in the Anglo north, social workers and settlement house residents were simply missionaries by another name.

Anglo women, like Anglo men, sought to fit Hispanic women into roles Anglos had designed for them. They envisioned them not as semiautonomous property owners who worked outside the house as well as within it and who lived with a relatively flexible sexual division of labor. Instead, they saw Hispanic women either as women thrust by circumstance and improvident men outside their true role (in the home) or as martyrs to domestic ignorance, their bad housekeeping making them slovenly and impoverished. From the missionaries in the village to social workers in Denver, these middle-class Anglo women sought to transform Hispanic women into ideal domestic servants and proper housewives capable of Americanizing Hispanic men. . . .

The assumption on the part of Americanizers that women functioned as cultural guardians ensured women, both Anglo and Chicana, a central role in the process of Americanization. They would comprise both teacher and pupil. Such Americanization, however, was limited in what it offered Chicanas. Improved domestic care and the ability to speak English in and of themselves would not move Chicanas from margin to center in Anglo society and would certainly not return them to the center of Hispanic society. Even their job of cultural transmission was work on the margin of both cultures, at the boundary between them, and so provided them with a central place in neither.

Increasingly at the center of village life, Hispanic women found the move north anything but liberating. Both men and women settling permanently in the Anglo north suffered from narrowed opportunities, but among Hispanics in the north, women found that their activities declined in significance relative to the men's. Contrary to what many sociologists and other observers believed, this marginality of Hispanic women in the north was not something carried with them from the villages, but the result of adapting to life in a new, an Anglo, setting. In a sense, this development was an Americanization of gender roles. It echoed the experiences of U.S. women during nineteenth-century industrialization as well as those of immigrant groups at the turn of the century. Arenas of female authority — such as food production, nonwage work, and kin and community affairs — for Chicanas became as they were in Anglo society, increasingly peripheral to the main concerns of subsistence in a centralized, male-dominated, and cash economy. For Hispanic women and men alike, a move into Anglo areas to the north afforded a loss of status, but for the women, full integration into the Anglo community would not remedy that loss. . . .

The changes in the balance between women's and men's activities brought about by cross-cultural relations affected not only the Hispanic women or the nature of the Hispanic family, for the village's sexual division of labor had sustained the entire group and their cultural autonomy. As varied sources of income diminished, as Hispanics came to rely solely on the men's wages, the autonomy of the community diminished also. Bereft of their autonomous base, Hispanic women in the north could not provide the stability that permitted forays into the cash economy to coexist with an autonomous cultural base. In Hispanic villages, the autonomy of women and the autonomy of the community had depended on each other. It was the work of the village women that made it possible for a time to exploit the exchange between Anglo and Hispanic economies. The Hispanic settlements in Anglo areas could not recreate this system.

※ *F U R T H E R   R E A D I N G*

Susan Armitage and Betsy Jameson, eds., *The Women's West* (1987)

Barbara Babcock and Nancy J. Parezo, *Daughters of the Desert: Women Anthropologists and the Native American Southwest, 1880–1980: An Illustrated Catalogue* (1980)

Anne M. Butler, *Daughters of Joy, Sisters of Mercy: Prostitutes in the American West, 1865–1890* (1985)

Adelaida R. Del Castillo, ed., *Between Borders: Essays on Mexicana/Chicana History* (1990)

Deborah Fink, *Agrarian Women: Wives and Mothers in Rural Nebraska, 1880–1940* (1992)

Ramon A. Gutiérrez, *When Jesus Came the Corn Mothers Went Away: Marriage, Sexuality, and Power in New Mexico, 1500–1846* (1991)

Joan M. Jensen and Darlis A. Miller, "The Gentle Tamers Revisited: New Approaches to the History of Women in the American West," *Pacific Historical Review* XLIX (1980), 173–213

Annette Kolodny, *The Land Before Her: Fantasy and Experience of the American Frontiers, 1630–1860* (1984)

K. Tsianina Lomawaima, *They Called It Prairie Light: The Story of Chilocco Indian School* (1994)

Patricia Preciado Martin, *Songs My Mother Sang to Me: An Oral History of Mexican-American Women* (1992)

Valerie J. Matsumoto, *Farming the Home Place: A Japanese American Community in California, 1919–1982* (1993)

Devon A. Mihesuah, *Cultivating the Rosebuds: The Education of Women at the Cherokee Female Seminary* (1993)

Peggy Pascoe, *Relations of Rescue: The Search for Female Moral Authority in the American West, 1874–1939* (1990)

Vicki Ruiz, *Cannery Women, Cannery Lives: Mexican Women, Unionization, and the California Food Processing Industry, 1930–1950* (1987)

Lillian Schlissel, Vicki L. Ruiz, and Janice Monk, eds., *Western Women: Their Land, Their Lives* (1988)

Sylvia Van Kirk, *Many Tender Ties: Women in Fur Trade Society, 1670–1870* (1980)

Patricia Zavella, *Women's Work and Chicano Families: Cannery Workers of the Santa Cruz Valley* (1987)

Zitkala-Sa, *American Indian Stories* (1985)

Victorian Sexuality

Nineteenth-century Americans — especially physicians — produced an abundance of literature on sexual behavior. Much of this literature was meant to advise ordinary middle-class men and women on proper sexual conduct, but physicians also wrote innumerable scientific articles on sexual "diseases" and "perversions" to be read by their medical colleagues. Regardless of whether it was directed toward a lay audience or toward specialists, however, most of this literature contended that the "true woman" felt little or no sexual passion and that she engaged in sex only for reproduction. It was only the morally degraded woman or the "pathological" female who felt strong sexual desire, these experts claimed. By contrast, these same writers did acknowledge men's sexual desires. Nonetheless, they promoted the view that masturbation and frequent sexual intercourse impaired men's health and destroyed their careers. Initially concerned only with sexual relations between men and women, during the second half of the nineteenth century physicians began to study same-sex relations, invariably labelling them as abnormal. The primary message of this sexual advice literature was, then, that both men and women should restrict themselves to moderate sexual activity, within the confines of marriage.

The significance of the nineteenth-century literature on sexual behavior has long been a source of debate and speculation among historians. Is it possible that this literature faithfully reflects the thinking and behavioral norms of the white middle class? Did physicians carry the views that they expressed in their written tracts into the examining rooms and homes in which they received patients? If so, to what effect? And what about working-class Americans, or black women and men who were held as slaves? Under what circumstances did women of different backgrounds elude or transgress Victorian precepts of sexuality in their relations with men? Finally, how did women of the Victorian era view passion toward members of their own sex?

❋ *D O C U M E N T S*

In the first document, written in 1839, the American Female Moral Reform Society uses individual case histories and medical opinion to warn mothers about the dangers that masturbation posed for children of both genders. Twenty years later, Dr. William Sanger interviewed two thousand female prostitutes in New York City as part of his research on why women entered the sex trade. Refusing to believe the women who cited "inclination" as their primary motivation, Sanger declared in his book (excerpted as the second document) that sexual aggression was highly unusual in women, even prostitutes. In 1883, Drs. J. C. Shaw and G. N. Ferris brought the case of a young woman with "abnormal" feelings for other women to the attention of their medical colleagues; this case appears as the third document. In the fourth document, taken from a speech delivered in 1907, Dr. Carlton C. Frederick summarizes his opinions on female "nymphomania" — views developed over the course of a lengthy career in medicine and fully representative of the medical orthodoxy of the day. Challenging these views, Dr. Elizabeth Blackwell argues in the fifth document, which is from 1902, that sexual desire is normal in women but that "awkward" husbands and ill health keep many wives from engaging willingly in sexual intercourse. In the 1890s, Clelia Duel Mosher, a doctor, began asking some of her female patients about their sexual practices. Although she never formally analyzed her findings, historians have come to rely heavily on her survey of forty-five women; four extracts from longer questionnaires comprise the sixth document. M. Carey Thomas, later president of Bryn Mawr College, recorded in a journal she kept in the 1870s, while attending school and then Cornell University, her thoughts about her love for other young women; some extracts from her journal make up the seventh selection. Finally, in a document taken from her autobiography, Harriet Jacobs describes the sexual practices and sexual abuses common in the slave South. The variety present in these documents suggests significant discrepancies between the dominant attitudes toward sex in the era's prescriptive literature and the actual attitudes and behavior of nineteenth-century women.

A Warning to Mothers from the Female
Moral Reform Society, 1839

BELOVED SISTERS,

Will you permit an associated band, most of whom share responsibilities similar to your own, and know with yourselves the deep yearnings of maternal love, to call your attention, for a few moments, to a forbidding, but most important subject. Be assured that nothing but the fixed conviction that it is a subject affecting the temporal and eternal well-being of the young immortals committed to your care, would induce us to commend it to your consideration through the Press. We refer to a species of licentiousness from which neither age nor sex is exempt; a vice that has done its work of ruin, physical, mental, and moral, when no eye but that of Omniscience could behold it, a vice that has been practised in ten thousand instances, without a correct knowledge of its consequences, or its guilt, until it has paved the way for the most revolting excesses in crime. . . .

Recently it has pleased, our Heavenly Father to bring before our minds a flood of light, by which we have been solemnly convinced, that in nine cases out of ten, "solitary vice" [masturbation] is the first cause of social licentiousness, and the foundation and hidden source of the present corrupt state of society. . . .

The dangers to which all classes of the rising generation are exposed, are great beyond expression, they are dangers, too, that may stain the soul with guilt, and yet elude the vigilance of the most watchful parent, unless obviated *from the cradle,* by proper training and correct instruction. . . .

"A pupil in a select school, a child but ten years of age, confessed to her teacher, that she had been guilty of the sin alluded to for years, although she had never been taught it, and knew not that any one living practised it but herself. Her mind was fast sinking, she was wholly unable to reckon even small sums. This child had been religiously educated, but she was reared where the table was made a snare. Rich and high seasoned food, and abundance of dainties were given her, bathing was neglected, and a precocious development of the passions, and their consequent indulgence, was, in this case, the result."

"A child, under 12 years of age, whose morals in every respect had been carefully guarded, and who had never, except in one instance, been exposed, to the influence of an evil associate; on being questioned by her mother, confessed with tears that the sin had been taught her by the suspected individual."

"A son of a highly respectable physician, under three years of age, with no teacher but depraved instinct, had become so addicted to this pernicious habit, that the mother was obliged to provide a close night dress, and watch his waking hours with unceasing care.". . .

"A theological student, of superior mind and high attainments, deservedly beloved by numerous friends, and eminently fitted to be the centre of attraction in the highest circles of refinement, became a subject of this debasing vice. Presently his health failed, and abused reason deserted his throne. He was carried from the seminary to his friends, a maniac, and after lingering a few days, was ushered into the presence of his Judge."

A physician, who has long had an extensive practice in this city, confidently affirms that most of the young men in feeble health, who go south, to escape or recover from consumption, are the victims of this body and soul-destroying sin. . . .

Dr. William Sanger Questions Women on Their Reasons for Entering Prostitution, 1859

Question. WHAT WAS THE CAUSE OF YOUR BECOMING A PROSTITUTE?

CAUSES	NUMBERS
Inclination	513
Destitution	525
Seduced and abandoned	258
Drink, and the desire to drink	181
Ill-treatment of parents, relatives, or husbands	164
As an easy life	124
Bad company	84
Persuaded by prostitutes	71
Too idle to work	29
Violated	27
Seduced on board emigrant ships	16
" in emigrant boarding houses	8
Total	2000

This question is probably the most important of the series, as the replies lay open to a considerable extent those hidden springs of evil which have hitherto been known only from their results. First in order stands the reply "Inclination," which can only be understood as meaning a voluntary resort to prostitution in order to gratify the sexual passions. Five hundred and thirteen women, more than one fourth of the gross number, give this as their reason. If their representations were borne out by facts, it would make the task of grappling with the vice a most arduous one, and afford very slight grounds to hope for any amelioration; but it is imagined that the circumstances which induced the ruin of most of those who gave the answer will prove that, if a positive inclination to vice was the proximate cause of the fall, it was but the result of other and controlling influences. In itself such an answer would imply an innate depravity, a want of true womanly feeling, which is actually incredible. The force of desire can neither be denied nor disputed, but still in the bosoms of most females that force exists in a slumbering state until aroused by some outside influences. No woman can understand its power until some positive cause of excitement exists. What is sufficient to awaken the dormant passion is a question that admits innumerable answers. Acquaintance with the opposite sex, particularly if extended so far as to become a reciprocal affection, will tend to this; so will the companionship of females who have yielded to its power; and so will the excitement of intoxication. But it must be repeated, and most decidedly, that without these or some other equally stimulating cause, the full force of sexual desire is seldom known to a virtuous woman. In the male sex nature has provided a more susceptible organization than in females, apparently with the beneficent design of repressing those evils which must result from mutual appetite equally felt by both. In other words, man is the *aggressive* animal, so far as sexual desire is involved. Were it otherwise, and the passions in both sexes equal, illegitimacy and prostitution would be far more rife in our midst than at present. . . .

Two Doctors Describe a Case of Perverted Sexual Instinct in a Young Female, 1883

CASE. 5. — A Jewish servant-girl, twenty-eight years old, went of her own free will to an asylum; said she felt sick and miserable, and wished to die. She had a great passion for a female friend; recognized the same as abnormal, but could not repress it; wished to be helped. Patient's mother died of consumption, and in her later years had been quite demented. No further hereditary history obtained. As a child she was careless, mischievous; did not learn readily; played almost exclusively with boys; menstruated at twelve and a half years irregularly, profusely, and with pain. About this time experienced a preference for girls, particular ones who attracted her by the expression of their eyes; followed the chosen ones all over; blushed when she spoke to them; was jealous when they spoke to others; when she kissed them, experienced a voluptuous sensation in her genital organs. This desire occurred shortly before and after the menses; when masturbating, thought of the loved girl. As she grew older, was shown some attention by men; had offers of marriage, but she would have nothing to do with them; was not interested in men, and at times experienced a real disgust for them. But her love for girls increased in intensity; was not content to kiss and hug them, but wished to sleep with them and handle their sexual organs. When resisted by them she became very much excited; finally recognized the fact that they did not feel as she did, and began to think she was sick; neglected her work; would stand still gazing in one direction; became very unhappy; attempted to drown herself. The suppression of her desire made her finally so unhappy that medical advice was sought. Physically, patient corresponded to the female type: breasts well developed, genital organs quite normal, uterus in normal position; some asymmetry of the face. Patient complains of headache, dizziness, backache, pain in pit of stomach, and loss of sleep and appetite. In the institution was restless, depressed, worked but little; fell in love with a nurse and a childish patient; wished to embrace them and sleep with them; menstruated twice without trouble; improved very much; went home; did fairly well after another short exacerbation during which she attempted to drown herself. . . .

Carlton C. Frederick, M. D., on the Manifestations of Nymphomania, 1907

The sexual instinct is not so common in woman as it is in man. With the latter it is, under normal conditions of health and vigor, an ever-present, powerful impulse to procreation. Sexual desire is entirely absent in a much larger number of women than is generally supposed. If present it is ordinarily not so strong as it is in man. If a woman has in her makeup the sexual instinct to the ordinary degree, that impulse is only aroused by the man she loves, and for no other has she that feeling. There is a small percentage of women in whom it is very strong, but relatively to the whole number the percentage is small. . . . Fortunate it is for the morals of humanity that woman generally is not so constituted sexually as is man, otherwise, as has been aptly said, this world would be one vast brothel. Surely, to the influence of woman we must look for the standard of moral tone, however high that may be. . . .

Nymphomania is an excessive development of sexual desire in the female, manifesting itself in various ways dependent upon the mental status, moral sense, environment, or social scale of the individual. . . . Masturbation is probably one of its most prominent manifestations. . . . In general, women who have practised masturbation long are not satisfied by normal sexual indulgence, although the desire which they have may lead them to such indulgence. . . . This is the rule with sexual perverts of all kinds — the normal act is not one of gratification, or they would not be perverts.

Nymphomaniacs, especially among the insane and mildly insane, are liable to resort to exposure of their persons or by lascivious movements in presence of men, and thus invite coitus. But among those not insane such acts are seldom openly indulged in, but secretly they are often shameless. All sorts of degenerate practices are followed by some. One of the most frequent is tribadism — the so-called "Lesbian Love," which consists in various degenerate acts between two women in order to stimulate the sexual orgasm. Not an uncommon practice is the fondling of the genitalia of small boys and babies and contact of the same. In fact, the numbers and variations of practices are so various that it would take pages to mention them. . . .

Elizabeth Blackwell, M.D., on Sexual Feelings in Women, 1902

. . . Those who deny sexual feeling to women, or consider it so light a thing as hardly to be taken into account in social arrangements, confound appetite and passion; they quite lose sight of this immense spiritual force of attraction, which is distinctly human sexual power, and which exists in so very large a proportion in the womanly nature. The impulse towards maternity is an inexorable but beneficent law of woman's nature, and it is a law of sex. . . .

The affectionate husbands of refined women often remark that their wives do not regard the distinctively sexual act with the same intoxicating physical enjoyment that they themselves feel, and they draw the conclusion that the wife possesses no sexual passion. A delicate wife will often confide to her medical adviser (who may be treating her for some special suffering) that at the very time when marriage love seems to unite them most closely, when her husband's welcome kisses and caresses seem to bring them into profound union, comes an act which mentally separates them, and which may be either indifferent or repugnant to her. But it must be understood that it is not the special act necessary for parentage which is the measure of the compound moral and physical power of sexual passion; it is the profound attraction of one nature to the other which marks passion, and delight in kiss and caress — the love-touch — is physical sexual expression as much as the special act of the male.

It is well known that terror or pain in either sex will temporarily destroy all physical pleasure. In married life, injury from childbirth, or brutal or awkward conjugal approaches, may cause unavoidable shrinking from sexual congress, often wrongly attributed to absence of sexual passion. But the severe and compound suffering experienced by many widows who were strongly attached to their lost partners is also well known to the physician, and this is not simply a mental loss that they feel, but an immense physical deprivation. It is a loss which all the senses suffer by the physical as well as moral void which death has created.

Although physical sexual pleasure is not attached exclusively, or in woman chiefly, to the act of coition, it is also a well-established fact that in healthy, loving women, uninjured by the too frequent lesions which result from childbirth, increasing physical satisfaction attaches to the ultimate physical expression of love. A repose and general well-being results from this natural occasional intercourse, whilst the total deprivation of it produces irritability. . . .

This power of sex in women is strikingly shown in the enormous influence which they exert upon men for evil. It is not the cold beauty of a statue which enthrals and holds so many men in terrible fascination; it is the living, active power of sexual life embodied in its separate overpowering female phase. The immeasurable depth of degradation into which those women fall, whose sex is thoroughly debased, who have intensified the physical instincts of the brute by the mental power for evil possessed by the human being, indicates the mighty character of sexual power over the nature of woman for corruption. It is also a measure of what the ennobling power of passion may be.

Happily in all civilized countries there is a natural reserve in relation to sexual matters which indicates the reverence with which this high social power of our human nature should be regarded. It is a sign of something wrong in education, or in the social state, when matters which concern the subject of sex are discussed with the same freedom and boldness as other matters. This subject should neither be a topic of idle gossip, of unreserved publicity, nor of cynical display. . . .

Each sex has its own stern battle to fight in resisting temptation, in walking resolutely towards the higher aim of life. . . .

Extracts from the Mosher Survey, 1892–1913

Number 1

(Respondent Number 1 was twenty-five when interviewed in 1892. A former music teacher, she had been married for two and one-half years and had one child, age six months.)

What knowledge of Sexual Physiology had you before marriage?
Knew process of ovulation & menstruation in fairly well-defined way. [Hence] knew when conception was likely to take place & why. Very little about male sexual physiology. Knew, in regard to intercourse, condition of man at time [hence] necessity also need of self-control; danger of its occurring too often; time when woman was supposed to desire intercourse, if ever; best time for conception, as regards health of mother & child; several means of preventing conception. Realized little how important it is to a man and how much self-control it may entail. Did not suppose it was often desired by women. Considered that it sh'd be regulated largely by the woman.

Did conception occur by choice or by accident?
Accident.

Habit of intercourse? Average number of times per month?
Two or three times. Before conception, once or at most twice per month.

Was intercourse held during pregnancy?
No.
>*Did you desire it at this period?*
>Occasionally during first months. Not at all, during last half — or more.

At other times have you any desire for intercourse?
Yes.
>*How often?*
>Once or twice a month.
>*At what time in relation to your menses?*
>Immediately after. Occasionally just before — and rarely at some other time. Except in 1st case, it is scarcely ever except when there is some outside exciting cause.

Is intercourse agreeable to you or not?
Usually.

Do you always have a venereal orgasm?
No.

What do you believe to be the purpose of intercourse?
  Necessity to the man?
  Yes.
  To the woman?
  No.
  Reproduction?
  Yes. Primarily.

Have you ever used any means to prevent conception? If so, what? What was the effect on your health?
Thin rubber covering for man. Depended on so-called "safety week" at first.
  I have not perceived any effect on my health.

Number 10

(Respondent Number 10 was twenty-six, married for two and one-half years, when interviewed in 1894. She had two children.)

What knowledge of sexual physiology had you before marriage?
Very slight.
  How did you obtain it?
  Mostly from *Tokology* [a popular sexual guide].

Did conception occur by choice or accident?
First conception by choice. Second by accident.

Habit of intercourse, average number of times?
1st time 5 months after marriage. Then not until 7 mos. after our first child was born. After that twice a week usually.

Was intercourse held during pregnancy? If so, how often?
Not during first pregnancy. Yes during second pregnancy. Once or twice a week until 6th or 7th month. Not after that.
  Had you any desire for it during this period?
  Yes, at times.

At other times have you any desire for intercourse?
Yes.
  At what time in relation to your menses?
  Immediately after menstruation.

Is intercourse agreeable to you or not?
Yes.

Do you always have a venereal orgasm?
No, but usually.
  When you do,
  Effect immediately afterwards?
  I think there is more exhaustion.

What do you believe to be the true purpose of intercourse?
  Necessity to the man? to woman?
No. [The woman's single negative response applied to both sexes.]
  Pleasure?
Not solely.
  Reproduction?
  What other reasons beside reproduction are sufficient to warrant intercourse?
I think to the man and woman married from love, it may be used *temperately*, as one of the highest manifestations of love, granted us by our Creator.

Have you ever used any means to prevent conception?
Yes.
  If so, what?
Sulphate of zinc. It is not infallible.
  Effect on your health?
None.

What, to you, would be an ideal habit?
Occasional intercourse, with control over conception (?), everything to be absolutely mutual.

Number 35

(Respondent Number 35 was interviewed in 1897, when she was fifty-three. She had had six children and six miscarriages — twelve pregnancies in all — during more than twenty-eight years of marriage.)

What knowledge of sexual physiology had you before marriage?
Slight from girls. Mother taught her that such things were not only not talked about but also not thought of. School child at 14 told [her] what intercourse was. [She] was shocked and didn't believe it.

Habit of intercourse, average number of times per week?
[Average once a week,] sometimes oftener, sometimes less often.

Was intercourse held during pregnancy? If so, how often?
About average. Not so often during last 2 mo.
  Had you any desire for it during this period?
  [Often] more desire than at other times, and she needed it. "Nothing would ease my nervous condition but that."

At other times have you any desire for intercourse?
Yes. Very soon after period, [it is] more agreeable. Sometimes just before [period]. Much of time could have blotted [it] out and never missed it. Then another time wanted it. [She prefers intercourse] when not too tired, just before and just after [menses].

Is intercourse agreeable to you or not?
Yes, when not too tired & conditions are right.

Do you always have a venereal orgasm?
Always when she desires. Many times not.
> *When you do,*
> *Effect immediately afterwards?*
> Sleepy, relaxed, less nervous, good.
> *Effect next day?*
> Feels well.
> *When you do not,*
> *Effect immediately afterwards?*
> Nervous, strung up, not sleepy.
> *Effect next day?*
> No effect.

What do you believe to be the true purpose of intercourse?
> *Necessity to man? to woman?*
> [Yes] Because many [who are] unmarried are too nervous & do not recognize what the cause is.
> *Pleasure?*
> [Yes] for purpose of bringing about [reproduction].
> *Reproduction?*
> [Yes] highest purpose.
> *What other reasons beside reproduction are sufficient to warrant intercourse?*
> Individual health: a normal desire and a rational use of it tends to keep people healthier.

Have you ever used any means to prevent conception? If so, what?
Withdrawal sometimes.
> *Effect on your health?*
> None in either [husband or wife?]

What, to you, would be an ideal habit?
Once a week or [once every] ten days. When both want it.

Number 44

(Respondent No. 44 was forty-two when interviewed in 1913. She had had two children and two miscarriages. The length of time she had been married was not recorded.)

What knowledge of sexual physiology had you before marriage? (b) How did you obtain it?
No knowledge. Did not know what marriage meant.

1st intercourse how long after marriage?
2 or 3 days after marriage.

Did conception occur by choice or accident?
1st by choice. All others accidental.

Habit of intercourse, average number of times per week?
Formerly 2 [times] weekly. Now once in 2–3 wks. Depends on whether they have leisure.

Was intercourse held during pregnancy? If so, how often?
Rarely with 1st [child] during [entire pregnancy]. Not with 2nd [child].
   Had you any desire for it during this period?
   With 2nd one yes, not with 1st.

At other times have you any desire for intercourse?
Yes.
   At what time in relation to your menses?
   Following or preceding menstruation.

Is intercourse agreeable to you or not?
Yes.

Do you always have a venereal orgasm?
No. Conscious of suppression on part of woman. Time reaction slower.
   When you do,
   Effect immediately afterwards?
   Rests better when she has orgasm. Temperamental uplift.
   When you do not,
   Effect immediately afterwards?
   Very little difference.

What do you believe to be the true purpose of intercourse?
   Necessity to man?
   Yes.
   To woman?
   Yes.
   Pleasure?
   Very strong. Psychological 2nd.
   Reproduction?
   Yes 1st.
   What other reasons beside reproduction are sufficient to warrant intercourse?
   If women enjoyed intercourse, the demands on them would be much less. Males
   [have] less desire when [they are] more perfectly satisfied. Intellectual work on
   part of husband — less leisure. [Intercourse produces] oneness [and is] uplifting
   like music. [There is] very little that is animal about it. The comradeship of it.
   [Remainder of response is unintelligible.]

Have you ever used any means to prevent conception? a) if so, what?
After known miscarriage because husband did not wish her to conceive again until
she was strong. Douches of bichloride.
   Effect on your health?
   No effect.

What, to you, would be an ideal habit?
When desired by both.

M. Carey Thomas on Loving Other Women, 1872–1877

March 14 [1872]

The first of this month I got my allowance[:]$5.00 a month for ribbons, cuffs, collars, etc. Rex has one too. Oh Bessie and I have changed our names. I call her Rex and she calls me Rush and I suppose we'll call each other by them all our lives.

Yesterday was the Sewing Meeting, the last one I guess, and we had a real nice time, none of those horrid boys nor Lea [?] were there, and so after the supper we went up in the Meeting house by ourselves.

It was so still. . . . We walked up and down the aisle, we talked of what we wanted to be and do and formed plans how after we had come home from Vassar having taken bright honors we would do everything, we would devote ourselves to study and live together, have a library with all the splendid books, with a bright wood fire always burning, dark crimson curtains and furniture, great big easy chairs where we could sit lost in books for days together, a great large table covered with papers for we would be authors. Adjoining this should be a laboratory where far into the night we would pour over Crucibles, mixing our mystic engredients and perhaps making discoveries which should effect the whole world and there we would live loving each other so and urge each other on to every high and noble deed or action and all who passed should say "Their example arouses me, their books enoble me, their deeds inspire me and behold they are women!" Of course, these were only the wildest fancies, but oh if only some of them might come true. Why can't two girls love each other and live together and help each other in life's struggle just as well as a man and a woman! But I suppose one of us'll have to go and fall in love or something or other horrid. The more I see of lovers the more thoroughly I despise the whole lot so I don't think it will be me at any rate.

April 27

. . . Now I must give my thoughts on things in general. 1st Anna — I like her ever so much. She is just too nice for any thing. She is real smart and interested in every thing. Next to Rex she is the jolliest girl I know. . . . I think I must feel towards Anna for instance like a boy would for I admire her so not any particular thing but just an undefined sense of admiration and then I like to touch her and the other morning I woke up and she was asleep and I admired her hair so much that I kissed it. I never felt it so much with any body else.

[Spring 1873]

I took up my journal today though with the intention of writing about a friendship of last term in case it should never be renewed that at least I may have *some* remembrance. It was with Libbie Conkey — we got acquainted how I hardly know. The girls said we "smashed" on each other or "made love," I don't know. I only know it was elegant—she called me "her boy," her "liebe knabe" and she was my "Elsie." . . .

June 12, 1877

. . . Well I began to see more and more of Miss H. She got in the habit of coming

The papers of M. Carey Thomas (microfilm reels #1 & #2), Bryn Mawr College Archives.

and reading me her mother's letters and of bidding me good night. We used to go and study some time in Caskadilla woods and when it would get dark we would sit under her blue shawl and talk. Then we came across Swinburne's "Atlanta in Calydon" and Miss Hicks would come in in her wrapper after I was in bed and we would read it out loud and we learned several of the choruses. One night we had stopped reading later than usual and obeying a sudden impulse I turned to her and asked "do you love me?" She threw her arms around me and whispered "I love you passionately." She did not go home that night and we talked and talked. She told me she had been praying that I might care for her. That was the beginning and from that time, it was the Fall of '75 till June '77, we have been inseparable. I put this all down because I cannot understand it. I am sure it is not best for people to care about each other so much. . . .

In fact I just fell in love with her and I did it gradually too (not that adoring worship I had for Libbie, nor the equal fun and earnest loving devoted friendship Carrie and I have) but that Atlanta night I knew I did not care as much as she did and so it went on, I getting fonder and fonder of her until it was as I say — all the time against my better judgment and yet I cannot tell why it was, she is lovely, in many, many ways much better than I am.

Harriet Jacobs on Interracial Sex in the Slave South, 1861

. . . No pen can give an adequate description of the all-pervading corruption produced by slavery. The slave girl is reared in an atmosphere of licentiousness and fear. The lash and the foul talk of her master and his sons are her teachers. When she is fourteen or fifteen, her owner, or his sons, or the overseer, or perhaps all of them, begin to bribe her with presents. If these fail to accomplish their purpose, she is whipped or starved into submission to their will. She may have had religious principles inculcated by some pious mother or grandmother, or some good mistress; she may have a lover, whose good opinion and peace of mind are dear to her heart; or the profligate men who have power over her may be exceedingly odious to her. But resistance is hopeless. . . .

. . . Nor do the master's daughters always escape. . . . The white daughters early hear their parents quarreling about some female slave. Their curiosity is excited, and they soon learn the cause. They are attended by the young slave girls whom their father has corrupted; and they hear such talk as should never meet youthful ears, or any other ears. They know that the women slaves are subject to their father's authority in all things; and in some cases they exercise the same authority over the men slaves. I have myself seen the master of such a household whose head was bowed down in shame; for it was known in the neighborhood that his daughter had selected one of the meanest slaves on his plantation to be the father of his first grandchild. She did not make her advances to her equals, nor even to her father's more intelligent servants. She selected the most brutalized, over whom her authority could be exercised with less fear of exposure. Her father, half frantic with rage, sought to revenge himself on the offending black man; but his daughter, foreseeing the storm that would arise, had given him free papers, and sent him out of the state.

In such cases the infant is smothered, or sent where it is never seen by any who know its history. But if the white parent is the *father,* instead of the mother, the offspring are unblushingly reared for the market. . . .

You may believe what I say; for I write only that whereof I know. I was twenty-one years in that cage of obscene birds. I can testify, from my own experience and observation, that slavery is a curse to the whites as well as to the blacks. It makes the white fathers cruel and sensual; and the sons violent and licentious; it contaminates the daughters, and makes the wives wretched. And as for the colored race, it needs an abler pen than mine to describe the extremity of their sufferings, the depth of their degradation. . . .

※ E S S A Y S

In the first essay, Carol Groneman of John Jay College explores the development, during the second half of the nineteenth century, of physicians' views and treatment of "nymphomania" — a disease classification that became broad enough to group together prostitutes, lesbians, and women who actively sought intercourse with their husbands. Groneman argues that the medical world's construction of the nymphomania classification reflected physicians' fears that American women were growing too independent and finding too many opportunities for sexual experience. In the second essay, Princeton University's Christine Stansell examines the lives of young women who became prostitutes in New York City in the 1850s, the same decade in which William Sanger conducted his study of prostitution. Rejecting Sanger's attempt to portray prostitutes as the miserable victims of moral degradation, Stansell argues that they were young women from poor families who used prostitution to challenge both the sexual double standard and their economic dependency on men. Prostitution was a risky choice, but a choice nonetheless for women living in a world already fraught with suffering and inequity. The last essay, by Martha Hodes of New York University, explores the illicit sexual relations between black men and white slaveholding women in the plantation South. The white women who engaged in these relations willfully defied the sexual standards of the day; yet in doing so they coerced and exploited the black men who became their sexual partners.

Nymphomania: Physicians and Female Sexuality in Victorian America

CAROL GRONEMAN

The term *nymphomania* resonates with a sense of the insatiable sexuality of women, devouring, depraved, diseased. It conjures up an aggressively sexual female who both terrifies and titillates men. Surrounded by myth, hyperbole, and fantasy, the twentieth-century notion of a nymphomaniac is embedded in the popular culture: referred to in films, novels, music videos, and sex-addiction manuals, as well as in locker rooms and boardrooms. In the nineteenth century, however, nymphomania was believed to be a specific organic disease, classifiable, with an assumed set of

Carol Groneman, "Nymphomania: The Historical Construction of Female Sexuality," *Signs: Journal of Women in Culture and Society 19* (Winter 1994), pp. 337–367. Reprinted by permission of the University of Chicago Press.

symptoms, causes, and treatments. Like alcoholism, kleptomania, and pyromania — diseases that were identified in the mid-nineteenth century — a diagnosis of nymphomania was based on exhibited behavior. "Excessive" female sexual desire is, however, a much more ambiguous concept than habitual drunkenness, shoplifting, or setting fires. Consider the following cases of nymphomania diagnosed in the second half of the nineteenth century.

"Mrs. B.," age twenty-four and married to a much older man, sought the help of Dr. Horatio Storer, a gynecologist and the future president of the American Medical Association, because of lascivious dreams. He reported that she "can hardly meet or converse with a gentleman but that the next night she fancies she has intercourse with him, . . . though thinks she would at once repel an improper advance on the part of any man." In fact, she "enjoys intercourse greatly" (with her husband) and has had sex with him nightly for the seven years of their marriage. The husband "has of late complained that he found physical obstruction to intercourse on her part, though she thinks it rather an increasing failure by him in erection." In this "Case of Nymphomania," Storer directed Mrs. B. to separate temporarily from her husband as well as to restrict her intake of meat and abstain from brandy and all stimulants to lessen her sexual desire, to replace the feather mattress and pillows with ones made of hair to limit the sensual quality of her sleep, and to take cold enemas and sponge baths and swab her vagina with borax solution to cool her passions. "If she continued in her present habits of indulgence," Storer argued, "it would probably become necessary to send her to an asylum." . . .

In another case, the mother of a seventeen-year-old girl contacted Dr. John Tompkins Walton in 1856 because the girl, Catherine, was having "a fit." "This paroxysm," according to Walton, "was peculiar and specific . . . in the lascivious leer of her eye and lips, the contortions of her mouth and tongue, the insanity of lust which disfigured [her], . . . as well as in the positions she assumed and the movements which could not be restrained." He judged her to be "in a condition of ungovernable sexual excitement" and was convinced that the primary cause of the disease was seated in her "animal organization," which he deduced from her small eyes, large, broad nose and chin, thick lips, and the disproportionate size of the posterior portion of her head. (An enlarged cerebellum was believed by some doctors to indicate increased "amativeness" or sexual desire.) Moralism and science — and class bias — combined in Walton's belief that Catherine was infected by "the exposure and contagion incident to several families living in one house, with a hydrant and watercloset shared by all the court, and [by] the immorality of the youths who lounged about the place." Ultimately, the girl admitted that she was a "wanton" and that her sexual appetite was insatiable. Walton rendered her "emasculate for a time" (although he does not describe his method), prescribed a vegetable diet, various drugs, cold hip baths, and leeches to the perineum.

The case description continued with the cryptic statement that Catherine was later intercepted in *coitu;* paroxysms and additional treatment followed. Although the doctor assured her that he would "render her sexually fit to assume the duties of a wife whenever such services were needed," Catherine denounced him more than once during this time for "having destroyed her virility." Seven months after the beginning of treatment, Dr. Walton concluded that the girl "has no inclination to resume her old habits, and renew the disease."

Yet another case of nymphomania, reported in 1895, was that of "Mrs. L.," thirty-five years old, married with three children. Reflecting the influence of Richard von Krafft-Ebing's major work on the classification of psychopathology published in 1886, Dr. L. M. Phillips of Penn Yann, New York, diagnosed Mrs. L.'s problem as "acquired anaesthesia sexualis episodiac . . . [seemingly] . . . paranoia erotisa episodiac manifesting itself as nymphomania." It seems that Mrs. L. attended a New York theater party where a fashionable *tableau vivant* took place in which women posed seminude as living statues. Filled with disgust but also fascinated, Mrs. L. returned repeatedly that night to the room where the living statues displayed themselves. Following this experience, she lost interest in sex with her husband for two years, then recovered it for eighteen months, during which time "it burned with such intensity that it very nearly wrecked the physical well-being" of the couple. She repeated these episodes of asexuality and "sexual pyrotechnics" over the ensuing six years before seeking the doctor's help. Phillips found no physical abnormalities — describing Mrs. L. as a "perfect woman" — and instead relied on a psychopathological diagnosis in which he argued that the psychosexual sphere of the brain and spinal cord had been indelibly imprinted with a hypnotic suggestive impression. In effect, Mrs. L. was compelled by this image to return to the attractive, yet repellant, scene, thus inducing nymphomania. Phillips did not describe the treatment he provided Mrs. L. but did state that she would have developed brain disease if she had not sought his help. While his diagnosis foreshadowed the twentieth-century shift from a strictly organic to a more psychological explanation of nymphomania, it also hearkened back to the Renaissance belief that madness could occur when an impression of the unattainable beloved became seared upon the brain.

This amazing confusion about the nature of nymphomania can be found throughout more than one hundred case studies . . . published in American and European medical journals and texts from the late eighteenth to the early twentieth centuries. Nymphomania is variously described as too much coitus (either wanting it or having it), too much desire, and too much masturbation. Simultaneously, it was seen as a symptom, a cause, and a disease in its own right. Its etiologies, symptoms, and treatments often overlapped with those of erotomania, hysteria, hysteroepilepsy, and ovariomania, despite doctors' attempts to classify each as a distinct "disease." . . .

To further complicate the study of this disease, certain kinds of behavior were labeled nymphomania that today would be associated with psychosis, such as incessant and uncontrolled masturbation, lewd and lascivious tearing of clothes, and public display of the genitals. . . .

At the same time, however, and sometimes even in the same case studies, nineteenth- and early twentieth-century European and American doctors also diagnosed as nymphomaniacs women whose "symptoms" consisted of committing adultery, flirting, being divorced, or feeling more passionate than their husbands. Physicians writing for a popular audience diagnosed nymphomania in those women who actively tried to attract men by wearing perfume, adorning themselves, or talking of marriage.

In the late nineteenth century, therefore, even minor transgressions of the social strictures that defined "feminine" modesty could be classified as diseased. A convergence of several factors helps to explain this medicalization of female behavior. Starting in the late eighteenth century, woman's nature was increasingly defined as inextricably bound up with her reproductive organs. This supposedly objective, scientific "fact" created the new framework within which physicians and other authorities found justifications for the limitations of women's social and economic roles. It was thought only natural that women would and should find their fulfillment solely in taking on the roles of wives and mothers.

But the changing realities of women's lives in the second half of the nineteenth century contradicted this formulation. Contrary to their presumed natural passivity, modesty, and domesticity, women were demanding greater access to education, engaging in public debate over issues of prostitution and women's rights, joining the workforce in growing numbers, and marrying later — or not at all — and having fewer children. Although medical and other authorities hoped to define femaleness as fixed and static, it was in fact unstable and fluid.

This paradox was augmented by the contradictions implicit in the Victorian construction of female sexual desire. Women — that is to say white, middle-class women — were supposed to be naturally modest and sexually passive (although not passionless), awaiting the awakening of desire in response to the approaches of men.* And yet, sympathetic medical observers recognized the reality of female heterosexual desire, occasionally bemoaning the effects of the necessary strictures placed on young girls, unmarried women, and widows.

These tensions and contradictions are highlighted in the physicians' case studies of nymphomania. The concept of nymphomania constructs a female sexuality that is totally out of control, both literally and figuratively: out of the control of Mrs. B., Catherine, and Mrs. L.; out of the control of their husbands, mothers, and doctors; and out of the control of the "natural laws" that supposedly determined women's passive response to male desire. This disease — defined as the extreme end of the sexual spectrum — embodied Victorian fears of the dangers of even the smallest transgressions, particularly among middle-class women whose conventional roles as daughters, wives, and mothers were perceived as a necessary bastion against the uncertainties of a changing society.

Within this theoretical context, gynecology emerged as a medical specialty in the second half of the nineteenth century by focusing particular attention on the generative organs as the source of most women's diseases. In addition, an increasing medical interest in perversion and deviance and a growing fear by many in the medical profession that these abnormal behaviors and desires were hereditary and incurable led to attempts to organize, classify, and thus gain some control over a

---

*Medical theories reflect the class and racial stereotypes of the period. In Europe and the United States, black and lower-class women in general, and in the United States, African-American and immigrant women in particular, were seen by the Victorian middle and upper classes as more promiscuous, animal-like, and unrestrained than white middle-class women. What appears to us as a contradiction between the Victorians' biological construction of "woman" as controlled by her reproductive organs (thus all women would presumably be the same) and the distinctions they drew between middle- and lower-class and black and white women was explained in light of evolutionary theory. The "more highly evolved" white middle-class woman was thought to be more civilized, refined, and moral and consequently to have less sexual desire. Scientific theory was called upon to support these notions; for example, ethnographical, anatomical, phrenological, and other studies of "primitive" societies were used to support arguments about these distinctions. . . .

myriad of newly defined psychopathologies, including diseases such as nymphomania. . . .

Notions of insane love — accompanied by symptoms of uncontrolled sexuality and/or pining away for love — are as old as medical theory. In *On the Diseases of Young Women,* Hippocrates described the melancholy madness that could consume young girls and recommended marriage as the cure. The second-century Greek physician Galen believed that uterine fury occurred particularly among young widows whose loss of sexual fulfillment could drive them to madness. Clinical observations of nymphomania or *furor uterinus,* as it was more likely to be called until the seventeenth century, were discussed by medical theorists as early as the fifteenth century, and numerous medical school dissertations and scholarly texts examining the disease appeared in the sixteenth and seventeenth centuries. Cases of *furor uterinus* were reported in Italy, France, Spain, Portugal, Germany, and England during these centuries.

One of the clearest early definitions of the disease can be found in the works of the Italian physician Girolamo Mercuriale, a major contributor to sixteenth-century gynecological studies. According to him, *furor uterinus* was an "immoderate burning in the genital area of the female, caused by the surging of hot vapor, bringing about an erection of the clitoris. Because of this burning sensation women were thought to be driven insane." Other physicians, such as Pieter van Foreest, whose works were often quoted during the sixteenth century, pointed to the "corrupted imagination" and to the brain alone as the seat of the furor caused by insane love. . . .

Up to the Renaissance, physicians had contended that lovesickness was a disease almost exclusively afflicting noblemen; throughout the period, most of the victims discussed in the few detailed case studies of sexual excitement were men. . . . Gradually, the focus of the diseases of morbid love began to shift toward women. . . . Enlightenment discourses on the rationality of man, as distinct from women's irrational nature, may have contributed to this shift toward locating love madness in women and femininity. Whatever the reasons for this change, by the nineteenth century insane love in its various forms was much more likely to be associated with women.

. . . Sweeping changes in the assumptions about female sexuality occurred in the Western world in the late eighteenth and nineteenth centuries. Well into the eighteenth century, both popular notions and medical understanding retained vestiges of the belief that women were as passionate, lewd, and lascivious as men were. While some doctors had begun to question whether female orgasm was necessary for pregnancy, the popular assumption that female pleasure and fertility were connected remained intact. And yet by the nineteenth century, an ideology was firmly established: women by nature were less sexually desirous than men; the wifely and maternal role dominated their identity.

Some historians argue that the rise of evangelical Christianity in the late eighteenth century helped to transform attitudes about female sexuality, encouraging an ideology of female "passionlessness." The revitalized churches demanded moral restraint of women as evidence of their noble character. Women themselves, these theories suggest, adopted this link between passionlessness and moral superiority as a means of enhancing their status, gaining some control over their lives, and, ultimately, expanding their opportunities.

Economic factors also contributed to this transformation. The development of urban industrial capitalism leading to a separation of work from home resulted in a hardening of the divisions between men's and women's roles, particularly among the middle classes. This growing sexual division of labor was underscored by medical-scientific theories that posited the naturalness of this divide by arguing that women's passive nature left her ill-equipped for the rough and tumble, competitive public world of work and politics. Thus, women's too delicate nervous systems, monthly "illness," smaller brains, and specific reproductive organs all made it unhealthy — indeed unnatural — for women to work, write, vote, go to college, or participate in the public arena.

At the same time, according to several recent historical studies, a new representation of the female as profoundly different from the male was promulgated. From the Ancient period to the eighteenth century, they argue, the female body was seen simply as an inferior male body, one whose genitals had not descended because of lack of heat. This one-sex model mirrored the cosmological understanding of the social order. As that world view was transformed by revolutions, both scientific and political, a new model of the body that posited difference rather than sameness was created. Profoundly suspicious of passion, Enlightment and post-Revolutionary writers argued that women had less sexual desire than men and thus were uniquely suited to be a civilizing force; male passion would be controlled by the strength of woman's moral virtue.

Treatments prescribed for nymphomania also underwent major changes. Renaissance doctors, working within the context of humoral medicine, treated *furor uterinus* with bleeding, purges, emetics, and a variety of herbal medicines to restore equilibrium to the body's elements. Bleeding would draw off the noxious and excess humors or remove the "obstruction" caused by too much blood, restore harmony to the body, and cure the disease. . . .

In the late eighteenth century, . . . virtuous living was more likely to be prescribed, for both men and women, as the necessary anodyne to the diseases of insane love. In a treatise titled *Nymphomania, or a Dissertation concerning the Furor Uterinus,* translated into English in 1775, an obscure French doctor, M. D. T. Bienville, stated emphatically that too much pleasure and high living, rich sauces, and spiced meat made the "blood too abundant" and thus indulgent women were much more likely to succumb to the disease of insane love. The emphasis on the consequences of luxurious living suggests that Bienville was particularly concerned about warning middle-class women not to yield to the excesses of the upper classes. . . .

Bienville's work provides a link between earlier notions of uterine fury and nineteenth-century conceptions of the disease in its greater focus on the nervous system, with less attention paid to the theory of an imbalance of the humors as the cause of insane love. Later in the nineteenth century, a link between the genitals and the brain via the nervous system (through the spinal column) was posited as a more scientific explanation than the earlier notion of vapors rising from the uterus to the brain.

This still did not satisfactorily explain the "seat" or specific location of the disease — the brain or the genitals — and debates over this issue continued throughout the nineteenth century. On the one hand, neurologists, anatomists, phrenologists, and others looked for an organic cause of nymphomania in the brain. Their attempts to establish somatic causes in cerebral lesions, changes in the brain's blood vessels, a thickening of the cranial bones, or overexcited nerve fibers generally came to naught. . . .

On the other hand, especially in the second half of the nineteenth century, the relatively young and growing medical specialization of gynecology reversed the focus from the brain to the genitals. Diseased ovaries or disordered menstruation, gynecologists argued, could lead to injury of the nervous system and of the brain and thus to mental illness. Furthermore, because the etiology of many female disorders, such as nymphomania, was so uncertain, gynecologists searched for a sign, or a symptom, that could clearly identify the disease. Redness, soreness, or itching of the genitals was often noted, but in particular, an enlarged clitoris or labia was believed to be the preeminent indicator of female lasciviousness. A woman's body would yield evidence of behavior to the trained eye of the physician that the woman herself might deny. In this way, gynecology was able to lay claim to a unique role in the diagnosis and treatment of female disease. . . .

The diets, drugs, bloodletting, cold baths, or moral treatments of the neurologists, alienists (psychiatrists), and other physicians had not provided a cure for nymphomania, hysteria, and the other diseases connected to women's sexuality in the nineteenth century. Gynecology, attempting to consolidate its professional status, offered a new and controversial treatment for certain of these diseases — gynecological surgery. The underlying assumption that women were dominated by their reproductive organs led some physicians to blame virtually all women's diseases and complaints on disorders of these organs. . . .

In addition to "normal ovariotomy" or oophorectomy (terms generally associated with removal of nondiseased ovaries), other gynecological surgery, such as excision of the clitoris and/or the labia, was also recommended in cases diagnosed as excessive sexual desire. . . .

The efficacy of gynecological surgery for nervous and mental disorders, including nymphomania, was both praised and condemned at major medical congresses and in the pages of leading medical journals throughout the last two decades of the nineteenth century. Not surprisingly, gynecologists were generally more enthusiastic about the operation than were neurologists, psychiatrists, and other physicians. . . . Within gynecological circles, however, the indiscriminate use of oophorectomy was condemned by many. . . .

The debates surrounding the treatment of nymphomania starkly reveal the tensions and ambiguities implicit in the representations of female sexuality and the nature of female desire. One part of the controversy centered on what effect the removal of ovaries would have on women as women. This question was fraught with contradiction: if the productive role in society for which women were biologically determined was motherhood, then removal of the ovaries essentially eliminated woman's reason for being. On the other hand, because the disease of nymphomania raised fears that the intensity of sexual desire would lead a woman to lose all self-control and modesty, some physicians argued that oophorectomy was justified. . . .

Another part of the argument over oophorectomy centered on the nature of sexual desire itself. Contrary to the twentieth-century popular notion that the Victorians perceived women as asexual, most nineteenth-century doctors assumed that women's sexual desire was natural, albeit more limited than men's. What would happen to this sexual desire after the ovaries were removed? Some argued that oophorectomy did not eliminate desire, claiming that desire resided in the nervous system, not the ovaries. . . . Other physicians argued strenuously that oophorectomy "unsexed" women, using terms like "spaying" for the operation. A scathing criticism of the surgical operation was offered by T. Spencer Wells: "But would anyone strip off the penis for a stricture or a gonorrhea, or castrate a man because he had a hydrocele? [an accumulation of fluid in the scrotum], or was a moral delinquent?"

The medical establishment's lack of consensus makes clear that psychogynecological surgery was not based on a scientific, proven understanding of its effects. Rather, this method of treatment reflected the confluence of a particular construction of the female, the development of "safe" and anesthetized surgery, and the desire by gynecologists to consolidate their professional position by establishing themselves as the experts who could diagnosis, treat, and cure these elusive female disorders. . . .

In the latter part of the nineteenth century, the classification (and creation) by Krafft-Ebing and others of a wide variety of psychopathologies, such as sadism, masochism, lesbianism, nymphomania, and satyriasis — combined with the theory that these "perversions" were inheritable — contributed to a climate in which sexual dangers were thought to be rampant. Rather than focus on the sexually deviant act itself, Krafft-Ebing and other sexologists began to look to the very character of the person. A nymphomaniac, like a homosexual, was increasingly seen as a particular type of deviant, one whose pathology would be inherited by her daughters. Older notions of moderation-is-best gave way to anxiety that deviance and perversion would be passed on by defective genes, ineradicably marking the nervous system of the next generation.

Female sexual desire was believed to be particularly dangerous: women were more easily overwhelmed by the power of their sexual passion because they were closer to nature and thus more volatile and irrational than men. According to one doctor, "when they are touched and excited, a time arrived when, though not intending to sin, they lost all physical control over themselves." Women's potential for explosive sexuality jeopardized the self-discipline and control of desire that the Victorian middle class asserted were the mainstays of civilization. Throughout these discussions, women were presented not only as metaphorically dangerous — to the family, to the moral order, to civilization itself — but literally dangerous as well. Some doctors argued that a nymphomaniac would not just seduce a man but would overpower him and actually force him to satisfy her sexual desires. Female sexuality was thus understood in terms of the male sexual act, a kind of reverse rape fantasy.

Physicians' own anxieties about the nature of sexuality — theirs and their patients' — were brought into sharp focus in these debates. One form this took was warnings to other doctors about the female patient as "seductress": a nymphomaniac who sought to entice the physician into a gynecological exam, demanding that a speculum or a catheter be inserted as a means of sexual gratification. Physicians claimed that these women resorted to remarkable subterfuges to induce handling of the sexual organs, one of the most frequent of which was a pretense of urine retention. In addition, doctors described "hair pins, pencils, crochet needles, small keys, bits of bone, of tobacco pipes, of glass tubing, etc. etc." lodged in the bladder or urethra. Many of the doctors assumed the women were using these objects, and the subsequent gynecological examination, as a means of sexual excitement. None of the physicians suggested that sexual abuse or attempted abortion might be responsible; they saw these women as temptresses, not victims.

Decoding these cases is difficult. It is not implausible that a few women did approach doctors in this manner; others likely came seeking treatment for gynecological problems and were unfairly perceived to be acting lasciviously. Certainly the gynecologists' representation of the female patient as seducer reflected anxiety on the part of the physicians. Like male midwives in an earlier period, gynecologists were perceived by husbands and fathers as potential ravishers of their wives and daughters. Turning this idea on its head, the gynecologists claimed that they were the victims, preyed upon by wanton women patients. . . . The ideological assumptions of the period . . . imagined that female desire was passive and latent, connected to true love, marriage, and motherhood. A woman's strong physical response to a doctor's touching the clitoris or labia, or her vaginal contractions upon insertion of a speculum, were interpreted by some as the signs of excessive sexuality, indicative of a masturbator or a nymphomaniac.

By the late nineteenth century, physicians tended to group all sexualized women together: nymphomaniacs, lesbians, and prostitutes. . . . According to the gynecologist Carlton Frederick, "All sorts of degenerate practices are followed by some [nymphomaniacs]. One of the most frequent is tribadism — the so-called 'Lesbian Love,' which consists in various degenerate acts between two women in order to stimulate the sexual orgasm." . . .

Nymphomaniacs were driven to prostitution to satisfy their desires; prostitutes were often lesbians. According to the New York gynecologist Bernard Talmey, "It is known that Lesbianism is very prevalent among the prostitutes of Paris. . . . One-fourth of all the prostitutes in Paris serve as tribadists for the rich women who patronize public houses."

Just as physicians assumed that an enlarged clitoris was the sign of nymphomaniacs and prostitutes, they drew attention to hypertrophy of the lesbian's clitoris, which was used, many believed, like a penis in the "imitation of coitus." This construction vividly illustrates the physicians' inability to conceive of the sexual act in any way other than a male, heterosexual model. Indeed, it was the presumed "inversion" of gender role by the "masculine" partner in a lesbian couple that most troubled the Victorians. . . .

By the late nineteenth and early twentieth centuries, discussions about nymphomania reflected increasing concern over the "New Woman's" greater independence and potential opportunity for sexual experience. Commentators feared the "proletarianization of sexuality" — that is, that middle- and upper-class women who left the safe confines of home to work or attend school would become like working-class women, who were perceived as inordinately lustful and as sexual opportunists. . . .

Furthermore, some authors began to focus on the potential "masculinization" of women who stepped outside the boundaries of family and home. Career women, feminists, educated women who did not marry — a growing number at the turn of the century — were taking on male roles and potentially acquiring the "masculine" trait of aggressive sexual behavior. This concern about women's masculinization coincided with the development of new psychoanalytic theories that reasserted the essential passivity of female sexuality and underscored the notion that a mature, fulfilling sexual experience for a woman could only be achieved through vaginal orgasm in heterosexual intercourse. Eventually, those women who did not experience vaginal orgasm but maintained their sexual focus and excitement in the clitoris would be diagnosed by psychoanalysts as "frigid."

These new psychodynamic theories opened the way for an understanding of nymphomania as a symptom of a disordered psyche rather than as a biological disease. But they also allowed for a new interpretation of appropriate female sexuality, one in which the threat of a woman's being labeled "not a real woman" could be used to control women's sexual behavior, to shape it in the image of male pleasure, that is, vaginal orgasm.

This shift from a physiological to a psychological explanation of nymphomania during the twentieth century, with all its ramifications, remains to be explored. . . . In a future study, I plan to explore nymphomania and the relationship between twentieth-century biological and psychological theories, new constructions of the nature of women, and the changing realities of women's lives.

Working Women and Prostitution in Nineteenth-Century New York

CHRISTINE STANSELL

As urban reformers and writers told it, no tale of working-class life was more chilling in its revelations of vice than the prostitute's. From the 1830s on, prostitutes flitted wraithlike across the pages of urban social commentary, a class of women rendered human only by the occasional penitent in their ranks. Prostitutes had long been familiar to New Yorkers, but between 1830 and 1860 women "on the town" became the subject of a sustained social commentary. By the 1850s, urban prostitution was troubling enough to lead city fathers to lend the services of their police force in aiding William Sanger in conducting a massive investigation. Dr. Sanger's report, the compendious *History of Prostitution,* represents the coming of age of prostitution as a social "problem" in America, and its integration into the new discourse of secular urban reform.

The very fact that reformers . . . were thinking about prostitution had to do with tensions over gender relations and female sexuality. . . . The alarm over prostitution was one response to the growing social and sexual distance that working-class women — especially working-class daughters — were traveling from patriarchal regulation. . . .

In 1818, when the city watch published its latest statistics on crime, the authorities took a complacent view of prostitution. Although the numbers of known prostitutes and bawdy houses in the city had doubled in a dozen years, they reported, the women and their patrons had never been more quiet and law-abiding. In subsequent

Christine Stansell, *City of Women: Sex and Class in New York, 1789–1860* (Chicago: University of Illinois Press, 1987), 171–192.

years, an offensive against urban vice put an end to such laissez-faire attitudes. After 1831, when the evangelical women of New York's Magdalene Society first took up the battle to banish prostitution from the city, denunciations of what was purported to be an urgent problem became common currency among moral reformers and public authorities. . . . By 1855, public concern was sufficiently strong to move the aldermen to commission William Sanger to conduct a statistical investigation in New York of the kind Parent-Duchâtelet had published for Paris in 1836. Sanger's researches confirmed to him and to his public (as such researches often do) that the city was indeed prey to an "enormous vice." It was, he gravely concluded, "a fact beyond question that this vice is attaining a position and extent in this community which cannot be viewed without alarm." . . .

What disturbed observers was not just the number of women who bargained with men for sex, but the identity of those women. For if the numbers of known professional prostitutes were not growing disproportionally, those of casual prostitutes — girls or women who turned to prostitution temporarily or episodically to supplement other kinds of livelihoods — probably were. Moreover, the entire context of the transaction was changing, as prostitution moved out of the bawdy houses of the poor into cosmopolitan public spaces like Broadway. "It no longer confines itself to secrecy and darkness," lamented Sanger, "but boldly strikes through our most thronged and elegant thoroughfares."

. . . Since prostitution was not a statutory offense, there was no legal pressure to conceal it. By 1857 William Sanger could catalogue a wide range of establishments catering to prostitution. "Parlor houses," clustered near the elegant hotels on Broadway, were the most respectable, frequented by gentlemen; the second-class brothels served clerks and "the higher class of mechanics." In some theaters, prostitutes solicited and consorted with patrons in the notorious third tier, reserved for their use. . . . Except for the parlor and bawdy houses, however, the trade was informal rather than organized; that is, a woman could easily ply it on her own outside a brothel. Prostitution was still a street trade of independent workers; pimps were a phenomenon of the early twentieth century, a consequence of the onset of serious police harassment. . . .

There were specialized services as well. In the 1840s, a nascent commercial sex trade began to offer variegated sexual experiences beyond the prostitute's bed, mostly to gentlemen. The sex trade was centered in the area between City Hall Park, the commercial heart of the city, and the Five Points. There, crime and amusement rubbed elbows, laboring people mixed with gentlemen and the quick scam flourished. Visitors and men about town could, within an easy walk from most places of business, gain entrance to dance halls featuring naked performers, brothels with child prostitutes, eating places decorated with pornographic paintings, pornographic book shops and "model artist" shows, where naked women arranged themselves in edifying tableaux from literature and art (Susannah and the Elders, for example) — as well as a variety of facilities for having sex. The network of sexual experiences for sale was certainly troubling evidence of the centrality of sex to metropolitan life; indeed, its presence in the most cosmopolitan areas of the city was one indication of just how closely a particular kind of sex (bourgeois men with working-class women) was linked to an evolving mode of sophisticated urbanity. . . .

For laboring people as well as bourgeois moralists, prostitution was closely linked to "ruin," a state of affairs to be avoided at all costs. But while bourgeois men and women viewed ruin as the consequence of prostitution, working-class people reversed the terms. It was ruin, occasioned by a familial or economic calamity (for women the two were synonymous), that precipitated the "fall" into prostitution. The disasters that afflicted women's lives — male desertion, widowhood, single motherhood — propelled adult women into prostitution as a comparatively easy way to earn a living. The prospect of prostitution was, like the possibility of these other misfortunes, a part of everyday life: a contingency remote to the blessed, the strong and the fortunate, right around the corner for the weak and the unlucky. Prostitution was neither a tragic fate, as moralists viewed it (and continue to view it), nor an act of defiance, but a way of getting by, of making the best of bad luck.

Prostitution was indeed, as reformers liked to point out, tied to the female labor market. Women on their own earned such low wages that in order to survive, they often supplemented waged employment with casual prostitution. There is a good deal of information on this practice in the 1850s because William Sanger asked about it. "A large number of females," he observed, "earn so small wages that a temporary cessation of their business, or being a short time out of a situation, is sufficient to reduce them to absolute distress." . . .

Many of the women with whom Sanger and his police interviewers talked had turned to prostitution as the closest employment at hand after suddenly losing male support. . . . "My husband deserted me and four children. I had no means to live." "My husband eloped with another woman. I support the child." "I came to this city, from Illinois, with my husband. When we got here he deserted me. I have two children dependent on me." These were the painful female actualities from which popular culture would fashion its own morality tales of sexual victimization and depravity. . . .

Yet ultimately Sanger's survey yields a very different picture than his own preferred one of the victim of circumstance, the distressed needle-woman and the deserted wife at starvation's door. . . . When Sanger asked his subjects their reasons for taking up prostitution, over a quarter — a number almost equal to those who cited "destitution" — gave "inclination" as their answer. "Inclination," whatever its moral connotations, still indicated some element of choice within the context of other alternatives. "C. M.: while virtuous, this girl had visited dance-houses, where she became acquainted with prostitutes, who persuaded her that they led an easy, merry life." "S. C.: this girl's inclination arose from a love of liquor." "E. C. left her husband, and became a prostitute willingly, in order to obtain intoxicating liquors which had been refused her at home."

The historical issues are complicated. One can imagine a sullen woman trapped in the virtual jail that was the Blackwell's Island venereal disease hospital, flinging cynical answers — "drink," "amusement" — to the good doctor's questions as those most likely to shock him or to appeal to the preconceptions she sensed in him. But although this may have been true in some encounters, the dynamic between the doctor and his subject is an unlikely explanation of why so many women rejected a paradigm of victimization (which, if anything, Sanger himself promoted) for answers that stressed their own agency in entering prostitution. . . .

Of course we cannot separate such answers from the economic difficulties laboring women faced. But structural factors alone cannot clarify why some women took up prostitution and others in similar straits did not. Nor can they illuminate the histories of women who entered prostitution from comparatively secure economic positions. . . . It is possible to see from Sanger's statistics that while a substantial proportion of prostitutes came from the ranks of unskilled immigrants, as one might expect, a large number did not. Even more significantly, a sizable group of women (73) had fathers in the elite artisanal trades — ship carpentry, butchering, silversmithing — and a scattering (49) claimed to be daughters of professional men — physicians, lawyers and clergymen. Still others came from small property-owning families in the city and country, the daughters of shopkeepers, millers and blacksmiths.

Sanger threw up his hands over an array of data that defied his preconceptions. . . . But the range of family circumstances is confounding only if one assumes that indigence was the major cause of prostitution. In fact, a variety of factors led women into the trade. The daughter of a prosperous ship carpenter could end up on the streets because she was orphaned and left to support herself; she could also use prostitution as a way to escape a harsh father's rule. A country girl, abandoned by a suitor, might go on the town because she knew no other way to earn her bread, or because she was determined to stay in the city rather than return to the farm. A married woman might even hazard the prospects of a hand-to-mouth independence, supported in part by prostitution, rather than submit to a drunken and abusive spouse. . . .

For working-class women, the pressures of daily life took the form both of need and desire: the need for subsistence, the desire for change. Either could be urgent enough to push a girl or woman into that shady zone not too many steps removed from the daily routines in which she was raised. The resemblance of prostitution to other ways of dealing with men suggests why, for many poor women, selling themselves was not a radical departure into alien territory.

It was in large part the involvement of young girls in prostitution — or more important, the relationship to the family that juvenile prostitution signified — that brought prostitution to public attention in the 1850s. . . . Adolescents and young women found casual prostitution inviting as metropolitan life made it an increasingly viable choice for working girls. Casual prostitution bordered on working-class youth culture: both provided some tenuous autonomy from family life. . . .

Prostitution was by no means a happy choice, but it did have advantages that could override those of other, more respectable employments. The advantages were in part monetary, since prostitution paid quite well. The gains could amount to a week or even a month's earnings for a learner, a servant or a street seller; for girls helping their mothers keep house or working in some kind of semi-indentured learning arrangement, money from men might be the only available source of cash. . . . The serving girl Harriet Newbury, a country girl from Pennsylvania, came into a windfall of luck in 1828 when a navy captain gave her ten dollars each time they had intercourse. These were gentlemen's prices. Prostitution with workingmen yielded smaller gains, "trifling things" — a few shillings, a meal or admission to the theater. But even to sell oneself for a shilling was to earn in an hour what a seamstress earned in a day in the 1830s.

. . . Who were the men who created the demand for young girls' sexual services? . . . Certainly gentlemen had money for such pleasures, and Victorian men could use sex with prostitutes to satisfy longings they could not express to their supposedly asexual wives. . . . However, the erotic sensibilities of workingmen were also involved. Juvenile prostitution stemmed not just from class encounters but from the everyday relations of men and girls in working-class neighborhoods. Rape trials, one source of information about illicit sexuality, show that sex with girl children was woven into the fabric of life in the tenements and the streets: out-of-the-ordinary, but not extraordinary. . . .

The men who made sexual advances to girls were not interlopers lurking at the edges of ordinary life, but those familiar from daily routines: lodgers, grocers (who encountered girls when they came into their stores on errands) and occasionally fathers. Sometimes the objects of their attentions could be very young. For the men, taboos against sexual involvement with children seem to have been weak; in court, they often alluded to their actions as a legitimate and benign, if slightly illicit, kind of play. . . . Roughhousing, teasing, fondling and horseplay were the same tokens of affection that men gave to children in the normal course of things. Similarly, the favors men offered in exchange for sexual compliance — pennies and candy — were what they dispensed in daily life to garner children's affection. Men's erotic attention to girls, then, was not a discrete and pathological phenomenon but a practice that existed on the fringes of "normal" male sexuality.

Child molestation could blur into juvenile prostitution. The pennies a man offered to a girl to keep quiet about his furtive fumblings were not dissimilar to the prostitute's price. Adult prostitutes were also highly visible throughout the city, and their presence taught girls something about sexual exchange. . . . For the great majority of girls, however, it was not the example of adult prostitutes that led them into "ruin" but the immediate incentive of contact with interested men. Laboring girls ran across male invitations in the course of their daily rounds — street selling, scavenging, running errands for mothers or mistresses, in walking home from work, in their workplaces and neighborhoods and on the sophisticated reaches of Broadway. Opportunities proliferated as New York's expanding industry and commerce provided a range of customers extending well beyond the traditional clientele of wealthy rakes and sailors. Country storekeepers in town on business, gentlemen travelers, lonely clerks and workingmen were among those who propositioned girls on the street.

Men made the offers, but girls also sought them out. "Walking out" in groups, hanging about corners, flirting with passersby, and generally being "impudent & saucy to men" (as parents committing a girl to the House of Refuge described it) could lead to prostitution. The vigilant John McDowall at watch on fashionable Broadway observed "females of thirteen and fourteen walking the streets without a protector, until some pretended gentleman gives them a nod, and takes their arm, and escorts them to houses of assignation." . . .

City life allowed such girls to find a wide range of customers and to travel far enough to thwart their mothers' vigilance. Early experiences with men, which girls may have shared round with their peers, perhaps bequeathed a bit of knowledge and shrewdness; perhaps the streets taught them how to turn sexual vulnerability to their own uses. To be sure, there were no reliable means of artificial contraception; only later, with the vulcanization of rubber, did condoms become part of the prostitute's equipment. Any sexually active girl would have risked an illegitimate pregnancy, attended by moral and financial burdens that could bring her to the edge of "ruin."

Nonetheless, there were ways to practice birth control. Most likely, a girl engaging in sexual barter stopped short of sexual intercourse, allowing the man instead to ejaculate between her legs, the client's customary privilege in the nineteenth century. Recipes for abortifacients and suppositories . . . probably circulated among young women. If other measures failed, abortions, provided by midwives and "irregular" physicians (as those outside the medical establishment were called), were widely available in American cities. Indeed, ferreting out abortions — both medically induced and self-induced — was a major task of the city coroner. In 1849, the chief official of public health in the city reported that stillbirths were increasing at an alarming rate, and he concluded darkly that the role of "crime and recklessness" — that is, abortion — in this phenomenon "dare not be expressed"

To us now, and to commentators then, selling one's body for a shilling might seem an act imbued with hopelessness and pathos. Such an understanding, however, neglects the fact that this was a society in which many men still saw coerced sex as their prerogative. In this context, the prostitute's price was not a surrender to male sexual exploitation but a way of turning a unilateral relationship into a reciprocal one. If this education in self-reliance was grim, the lessons in the consequences of heterosexual dependency were often no less so.

Prostitution offered more than money to girls. Its liaisons were one important way they could escape from or evade their families. For young girls, the milieu of casual prostitution, of walking out, could provide a halfway station to the urban youth culture to which they aspired. For older girls, casual prostitution could finance the fancy clothes and high times that were the entrée to that culture. For all ages, support from lovers and clients could be critical in structuring a life apart from the family.

Prostitution and casual sex provided the resources for girls to live on their own in boardinghouses or houses of assignation — a privilege that most workingwomen would not win until after the First World War. Before factory work began to offer a more respectable alternative, sex was one of the only ways to finance such an arrangement. The working-class room of one's own offered a girl escape from a father's drunken abuse or a mother's nagging, the privilege of seeing "as much company as she wished" and the ability to keep her earnings for herself. Sanger touched on this aspect when he identified "ill treatment" in the family as one of the primary reasons girls went into prostitution. The testimony he collected bears witness to the relationship between youthful prostitution and the relations of the household: "My parents wanted me to marry an old man, and I refused. I had a very unhappy home afterward." "My step-mother ill-used me." "My mother ill-treated me." "My father accused me of being a prostitute when I was innocent. He would give me no clothes to wear." "I had no work, and went home. My father was a drunkard, and ill-treated me and the rest of the family." Sexuality offered a way out. . . .

A girl's ability to engage quietly in casual prostitution or sexual bartering depended largely on whether she used streetwalking openly to defy her obligations to her family. She might earn a little money now and then from casual liaisons; as long as she hid the luxuries she gained thereby and continued to earn her keep at home, she might evade suspicion. But part of the allure of prostitution was precisely the chance it offered to break free of work and authority. The "ruin" working people feared for their girls was not sexual activity alone, but sex coupled with irresponsibility; the defiance of the claims of the family went hand in hand with working-class conceptions of immorality. Parents became alarmed and angered, for example, when their girls moved about from one servant's position to another without consulting them. They saw such independent ways as a prelude to trouble. Sometimes the girl had changed to a place in a "bad house," a dance hall or house of assignation where the temptation to dabble in prostitution would have been nearly irresistible. Sometimes, however, the girl provoked her parents' wrath simply by shifting from one place to another. . . .

Fancy dress also played into prostitution. As in the cases of domestic servants and factory girls, fancy dress signified a rejection of proper feminine behavior and duties. For the girls who donned fine clothes, dress was an emblem of an estimable erotic maturity, a way to carry about the full identity of the adult, and a sign of admission into heterosexual courting. Virtuous girls, who gave over their wages to their families, had no money to spare for such frivolities; from a responsible perspective, fancy dress was a token of selfish gratification at the expense of family needs. . . .

Country girls from New England and upstate New York were also open to the inducements of prostitution in the city. Refugees from the monotony and discipline of rural life, they were drawn by the initial excitement of the life, its sociability and novel comforts. Rachel Near, for instance, came from Poughkeepsie to New York in 1835 to learn the trade of tailoressing from her sister. About three months after she arrived she ran into another Poughkeepsie girl on the street whom a man was supporting in a house of assignation. "She persuaded her to go into her House, which was neatly furnished by her ill gotten gain, and asked her to come and live with her, and persuaded her until she consented to do so." There Rachel met a Dr. Johnson, visiting the city from Albany, who supported her in style for six weeks, and she supplemented her earnings from him with visits to a bawdy house "where she used to get from 5 to 7 $ pr night, some weeks she used to make 40 & 45$." . . .

Rural courtships often played a part in urban prostitution. . . . Courtship was a gamble; elopement, the possibility of rape and male mobility made it all the more treacherous. Country girls were especially vulnerable to the process whereby desertion led to prostitution. Sanger found that 440 of his subjects were farmers' daughters. Left alone in the city, often without friends to help them, country girls sometimes had no choice but to turn to the streets for their bread. The sanctions of rural communities gave some protection to young women, but once they isolated themselves from neighbors, family and other women, they could find themselves caught in an escalating series of circumstances in which intercourse, voluntary or involuntary, led to prostitution. . . . However, we should avoid interpreting prostitution as a desperate measure. It could also be an act of shrewdness, prompted by a woman's comprehension of the power relations in which she found herself. . . . But it would also be wrong to cast prostitution as a deliberate bid for control; mostly, farm girls — like their urban peers — just wanted to live on their own. . . .

The money and perquisites from casual prostitution opened up a world beyond the pinched life of the tenements, the metropolitan milieu of fashion and comfort. Every day girls viewed this world from the streets, as if in the audience of a theater: the elaborate bonnets in shop windows, the silk dresses in the Broadway promenade, the rich food behind the windows of glittering eating places. Bonnets, fancy aprons, silk handkerchiefs, pastries were poor girls' treasures, coveted emblems of felicity and style. There were serious drawbacks to prostitution: venereal disease, physical abuse, the pain of early intercourse and the ever-present prospect of pregnancy. While the road back to respectable marriage was not irrevocably closed, it must have been rocky, the reproaches and contempt of kin and neighbors a burden to bear. Still, casual prostitution offered many their best chance for some kind of autonomy — even for that most rare acquisition for a poor girl, a room of her own. . . .

The urgency that discussions of prostitution took on in the 1850s indicates just how disturbing youthful female independence could be in a society structured culturally on women's dependence on the household. In the public spaces of New York, as well as in domestic service and on the Bowery, the evidence of girls' circumvention of family discipline was deeply troubling, especially (but not exclusively) to people who saw the family as woman's *only* proper place and asexuality as a cardinal tenet of femininity. The stress on the female reprobate's active pursuit of her appetites was the reformers' rendition of an obvious fact of youthful prostitution: It was not solely the resort of hopelessness and misery. . . .

We are still too much influenced by the Victorians' view of prostitution as utter degradation to accept easily any interpretation that stresses the opportunities commercial sex provided to women rather than the victimization it entailed. Caution is certainly justified. Prostitution was a relationship that grew directly from the double standard and men's subordination of women. It carried legal, physical and moral hazards for women but involved few, if any, consequences for men. Whatever its pleasures, they were momentary; its rewards were fleeting and its troubles were grave. But then, the same could be said of other aspects of laboring women's relations with men. Prostitution was one of a number of choices fraught with hardship and moral ambiguity. . . .

A Brief Dialogue on Illicit Sex Between White Women and Black Men in the Slave South

MARTHA HODES

In the wartime and Reconstruction climate of social upheaval in the American South, sex between white women and black men became a highly charged political issue, spurring whites to a level of public violence unknown under slavery. The subject of sex between white women and black men entered the national political arena during the Civil War in the presidential election campaign of 1864. It was then that the Democratic party coined the pejorative term "miscegenation" (from the Latin *miscere,* "to mix"; and *genus,* race) and asserted that Lincoln's Republican party advocated sex and marriage across the color line. . . .

Democratic politicians also brought the specter of sex between white women and black men into wartime and Reconstruction congressional debates about such

Martha Hodes, "Wartime Dialogues on Illicit Sex: White Women and Black Men," in Catherine Clinton and Nina Silber, eds., *Divided Houses: Gender and the Civil War* (New York and Oxford: Oxford University Press, 1992), 232–242.

issues as integrated transportation and schools and black suffrage. In an 1864 Senate exchange about the exclusion of blacks from Washington, D.C., railroad cars, for example, one Maryland Democrat introduced the point that a white woman marrying a black man would provoke a "trembling, anxious, depressing, harassing, crushing fear" on the part of the woman's male family members. . . . Thus did white southern politicians begin to conflate the newly won political power of black men with the issue of black male sexuality. With the advent of emancipation, southern whites who sought to maintain a racial hierarchy began systematically to invoke the idea that black men posed a grave sexual threat to white women.

White communities in the antebellum South that had been forced to contend with sexual liaisons between white women and black men (in the forms of bastardy or adultery, for example) had rarely given the black men a chance to tell their own stories. The men were not always named in legal documents and, if named, were rarely consulted for the public record. During the tremendous social chaos of the Civil War years, however, the voices of black men on the subject of sex with white women entered the historical record in the chronicles of the national government.

"I will tell you a fact that I have never seen alluded to publicly, and I suppose a man would be scouted who should allude to it publicly; but my relations with colored people have led me to believe that there is a large amount of intercourse between white women and colored men." So Captain Richard J. Hinton, an ardent white abolitionist who commanded black troops during the Civil War, testified in Washington, D. C., in 1863. Captain Hinton spoke before the American Freedmen's Inquiry Commission (AFIC) which had been formed under the War Department of Congress to address the incorporation of emancipated slaves into American society. The AFIC, composed of three white anti-slavery men, would ultimately propose the establishment of the Freedmen's Bureau to assist former slaves in the transition to free labor.

Captain Hinton was not the only witness to tell the wartime commission that white women and black men in the South had sex. . . . James Redpath, another white abolitionist and a self-described revolutionary, had traveled through the South during the 1850s to talk with black residents. . . . Testifying before the AFIC, . . . Redpath first elaborated on the depravity of white men who sexually exploited slave women, prompting one of the commissioners to ask: "Well sir, among such a universal system of libertinage what is the effect upon white women?" Of his black informants, Redpath said: "I have often heard them talking and laughing about the numerous cases that have occurred in which white women have had colored children." One black man told Redpath that "it was just as common for colored men to have connection with white women, as for white men to have to do with colored women." . . . Redpath relayed an episode of a white woman "of good family" in Mobile, Alabama, who carried on an affair with a slave, had sex with him on the morning of her wedding, and bore his child nine months later. Redpath concluded: "[T]here is a great deal more of this than the public suspect." . . .

Richard Hinton told the AFIC in no uncertain terms that white women in the South sought out sex with black men. A black Mississippi River steamboat steward named Patrick H. Miner (he was the son of a white plantation owner in New Orleans, and a graduate of Oberlin College) told Hinton about the women of a particular white family. According to Miner, "the colored men on that river knew that the women of the Ward family of Louisville, Kentucky, were in the habit of having the stewards, or other fine looking fellows, sleep with them when they were on the boats." Miner also relayed a personal anecdote about a Ward woman who, when on Miner's boat, had offered him five dollars and "told him to come to her house at Louisville on a certain day, giving him particular directions as to the door at which he was to knock." Upon arrival, Miner was "shown to the room adjoining her bed-room," where he waited until he had to return to work. Although the rendezvous never took place, Miner "had no doubt that she wanted him to have connection with her." Another story offered by Hinton concerned the Missouri frontier where white settlers from North Carolina and Tennessee had grown richer; the daughters in these families were envious of their brothers who "got a flashy education, which they completed in the slave quarters and the bar-room." As Hinton understood it: "The girls knew that their brothers were sleeping with the chambermaids, or other servants, and I don't see how it could be otherwise than that they too should give loose to their passions." Redpath had heard similar stories. When pressed on how liaisons with white women came to pass, one black man had told Redpath: " 'I will tell you how it is here. I will go up with the towels, and when I go into the room the woman will keep following me with her eyes, until I take notice of it, and one thing leads to another. Others will take hold of me and pull me on to the sofa, and others will stick out their foot and ask one to tie their boot, and I will take hold of their foot, and say "what a pretty foot!" ' "

Most antebellum documents regarding liaisons between white women and black men concern women from the servant or yeoman classes, women whose families did not command the social authority to stay out of court for transgressions such as bastardy or adultery. The narratives of the black men as recorded in the wartime testimony, on the other hand, also concern illicit liaisons with planters' daughters or plantation mistresses, and specifically illuminate the phenomenon of the sexual coercion of black men by white women. . . . In southern slave society, men of the planter classes ruled, but white women of slaveholding families also commanded power over slaves, both female and male. While scholars have documented the sexual exploitation of black women by white men, the voices of black men, recorded during the Civil War years, point to a consequence of slave society that has remained unexplored.

"I have never yet found a bright looking colored man, whose confidence I have won," Hinton said, "who has not told me of instances where he has been compelled, either by his mistress, or by white women of the same class, to have connection with them." . . . A former slave . . . told Hinton about his experiences with his forty-year-old widowed mistress. The man, who had been "brought up in the family," said he had "never had anything to do with his mistress until after her husband died," but that almost a year into her widowhood, the woman "ordered him to sleep with her, and he did regularly."

A black underground railroad agent named Captain Matthews told Hinton about another black man who relayed that "a young girl got him out in the woods and told him she would declare he attempted to force her, if he didn't have connection with her." The black steward, Patrick Miner, told Hinton "several cases of the same kind." Although the class status of the women in these last incidents remained unspecified, poorer white women might not have attempted such a threat. Those who held authority in antebellum southern communities were likely to consider white women outside the planter classes to be the depraved agents of their illicit liaisons with black men. White women of the planter classes, however, were protected by an ideology of white female virtue. Redpath asked one black man who had spoken of sexual liaisons with planter-class women: "'Do you dare to make advances?'" to which the man answered, "'No, we know too much for that.'" Of the white daughters on the Missouri frontier, Hinton said: "It was a great deal safer for them to have one of these colored fellows than a white man." This point was corroborated by one of Redpath's informants, who pointed out: "'If I have connection with a white girl she knows that if she takes precautions she is safe, for if I should tell I should be murdered by her father, her brother, or herself.'"

During Hinton's testimony, one of the commissioners prompted him: "But the consequences are terrible to the negro if found out?" When Hinton agreed, the commissioner asked: "What are the consequences to the woman if found out?" to which Hinton replied: "They generally brush it up." This testimony is supported by an antebellum North Carolina case in which a white woman had local justices of the peace record an oath that the father of her bastard child was white, when many people knew that the father had been one of the family's slaves. Planter-class white women were also more likely to have access to effective birth control, as indicated by the words of Redpath's informant about taking precautions. The black man who had been ordered to sleep with his widowed mistress told Hinton that the woman had "procured some of those French articles, that are used to prevent the consequences of sexual intercourse," a reference to condoms. Another black man had told Redpath that white women (of more well-to-do families) and black men had sex "because the thing can be so easily concealed. The woman has only to avoid being impregnated, and it is all safe." . . .

Questions about agency and consent are difficult to untangle in a slave society. If a coerced slave man complied with a white woman, that compliance was in some measure strategic; and just as some black women chose to risk fending off white men, some black men who were propositioned also chose to risk refusal. At the same time, the wartime testimony before the AFIC points to well-guarded circles of black men, both free and slave, as one arena in which black men expressed defiance about sex with white women. Recall the words of the steamboat steward Patrick Miner, who said that black men who worked on the Mississippi River shared information among themselves about the desires of certain white women to "sleep with them." Recall Redpath's words about his informants, who were slaves in the 1850s: "I have often heard them talking and laughing about the numerous cases that have occurred in which white women have had colored children." Even if Hinton and Redpath were exaggerating their roles as insiders, there is no reason to doubt that black men traded information and laughed together about their defiance of law and taboo.

Moreover, the possibility of men like Hinton and Redpath having fabricated their testimony before the AFIC is contradicted by more direct, if rarer, records of black voices. In her 1861 autobiography, for example, fugitive slave Harriet Jacobs wrote of planters' daughters: "They know that the women slaves are subject to their father's authority in all things; and in some cases they exercise the same authority over the men slaves. I have myself seen the master of such a household whose head was bowed down in shame; for it was known in the neighborhood that his daughter had selected one of the meanest slaves on his plantation to be the father of his first grandchild." . . . If there were such a thing as a consensual sexual relationship between a black man, either slave or free, and a white woman, black men talking to white abolitionists like Hinton and Redpath may have crafted their narratives as stories of coercion in order to present themselves as innocent participants in such legal and social transgressions. Yet stories of reluctance and resistance, even if crafted for white ears, would not have been fabricated out of imagination alone; rather, their tellers would be drawing upon dynamics that they knew to exist between white women and black men. Although we have no way of knowing how common or uncommon were scenarios such as those the black men described to Hinton and Redpath, their words uncover a ground of coercion in the slave South that lurked as a possibility regardless of how often it was acted upon.

While dominant white southern ideology about female sexuality exempted planter-class women from convictions of depravity, northerners were less convinced of this distinction among the white women of the South. The theme of profligacy among white southerners of all classes was common in northern antislavery thought, and Hinton and other witnesses before the AFIC unmistakably drew upon this tradition in their wartime testimony. Hinton's portrayal of all southern white women was one of total licentiousness. "The complete demoralization of the South is astonishing," he told the commissioners. "I have seen white women who call themselves ladies, stand on the street and call minor officers, as they were passing by, 'sons of bitches,' 'God damn' them, and use all such phrases; and I have never been to any locality where the officers and men, who were so disposed, did not sleep with all the women around." . . . In one printed report, commissioner Samuel Howe wrote . . . "The subject is repulsive, but whoever examines critically the evidence of the social conditions of the Slave States, sees that the vaunted superior virtue of the Southern women is mere boast and sham." . . .

The wartime testimony also indicates that black convictions about the sexuality of southern white women were in accord with those of white northerners. The sentiments of a black man who had fled the South for Canada were likely shared by others; the town's white mayor reported to the wartime commission: "A colored man ran away with a white girl, and a colored man, speaking of the affair, said 'I always looked upon him as a respectable man. I didn't think he would fall so low as to marry a white girl.'" Even approval on the part of black communities indicates black convictions of the depraved nature of white women. A black bishop from the British Methodist Episcopal Church, who had also left the South for Canada, told the commissioners that when a white woman and a black man got married, "If the man is an upright man, and the woman an upright woman, they treat them as if they were both colored." This man also mentioned two white women married to black men who were both accorded as much respect as "any black woman." . . .

In the end, the American Freedmen's Inquiry Commission kept the testimony they had heard about sex between white women and black men a secret from the Secretary of War and from Congress. Hinton's testimony had covered thirty-two pages, with the information on white women and black men occupying the last six of those pages. On the cover sheet, someone had penciled: "This paper can be printed as far as this mark x on page 27. The remaining portion should be suppressed." The "x" marked Hinton's disclosure about sex between white women and black men. Neither of the two major reports printed by the AFIC addressed the subject of sex between white women and black men. The commission clearly judged it too detrimental to let the Secretary of War and Congress, or any other readers, believe that emancipation would bring sex between white women and black men in its wake, especially if such liaisons could not be written off as the province of the poorer classes of white women.

Ultimately, it was the conflation of politics and sex in the minds of white southerners that would generate so much of the Reconstruction-era violence in the South. With the demise of slavery, the separation of black and white became essential to white southerners who wished to retain racial supremacy. Thus did sex across the color line become a much more severe taboo than it had ever been before. Because it was the men among the former slave population who gained political power, and therefore had the potential to destroy the racial caste system, southern whites focused on the taboo of sex between white women and black men with a new urgency. Sexual transgressions in the form of liaisons between white women and black men that had previously been the province of local communities and courts took on national political dimensions after the war. In testimony about the Ku Klux Klan taken before Congress in 1871, white southerners often charged black men with illicit sexual conduct toward or with white women alongside charges of Republican activism or successful crops, that is for political or economic independence.

. . . When a congressional investigating committee asked a North Carolina Klansman about the purpose of his organization, the man said: "It was to keep down the colored un's from mixing with the whites." And by what means would this be accomplished? "To keep them from marrying, and to keep them from voting," he answered. Another white North Carolina man said: "[T]he common white people of the country are at times very much enraged against the negro population. They think that this universal political and civil equality will finally bring about social equality." He added: "[T]here are already instances . . . in which poor white girls are having negro children." After the war, then, with the determination of white southerners to retain dominance through the construction of a rigid color line, whites conflated the new political power of black men with sexual transgressions against white women.

While white ideology about the hypersexuality of all black men developed swiftly from emancipation forward, the twin ideology about the purity of all white women never took on the same ironclad quality. Rather, class distinctions in white ideology about white female sexuality remained. The reputation and character of white women was constantly assessed by white southerners in the 1871 congressional testimony about the Klan, and the investigating committee participated in this discourse, with both sides identifying white female transgressors as "low-down," as "tramps," and as women of "bad character." The sexual coercion of black men by white women was in fact still understood to be a possibility. In the narrative of freedman Henry Lowther, who survived castration by Klansmen, one white witness said that the white woman with whom Lowther was accused of consorting had followed Lowther into the woods and "solicited him to have intercourse with her." Of this woman, a white judge remarked, "the inference I drew was that she was a very bad, abandoned character." White women judged by Klansmen to be lacking in virtue were, like black women, also subject to abuse ranging from insulting language to rape and sexual mutilation.

The wartime dialogues on sex between white women and black men got no farther than a government commission composed of three white, northern, abolitionist men. Yet the voices of black men recorded therein now serve to better illuminate both the nature of sexual liaisons between white women and black men in the slave South, and white ideologies of sexuality in the crucial transitional period of war and emancipation. At the same time, the wartime suppression of the testimony, along with southern whites' conflation of black male political power and black male sexuality, indicate how sex between white women and black men came to be a deeply political issue connected directly to the maintenance of racial hierarchy from emancipation forward.

❊ *F U R T H E R   R E A D I N G*

Ben Barker-Benfield, *The Horrors of the Half-Known Life: Male Attitudes Toward Women and Sexuality in Nineteenth Century America* (1976)

Janet Farrell Brodie, *Contraception and Abortion in Nineteenth-Century America* (1994)

Patricia Cline Cohen, "The Helen Jewett Murder: Violence, Gender, and Sexual Licentiousness in Antebellum America," *NWSA Journal* 2 (Summer 1990), 374–389

Blanche Wiesen Cook, "Female Support Networks and Political Activism: Lillian Wald, Crystal Eastman, Emma Goldman," *Chrysalis,* No. 3 (1977), 43–61

Nancy Cott, "Passionlessness: An Interpretation of Victorian Sexual Ideology, 1790–1850," *Signs* 4 (1978–1979), 219–236

John D'Emilio and Estelle Freedman, *Intimate Matters: A History of Sexuality in America* (1988)

Lawrence Foster, *Religion and Sexuality: Three American Communal Experiments of the Nineteenth Century* (1981)

John Haller, "From Maidenhood to Menopause: Sex Education for Women in Victorian America," *Journal of Popular Culture* VI (Summer 1972), 46–49

John and Robin Haller, *The Physician and Sexuality in Victorian America* (1974)

Darlene Clark Hine, "Rape and the Inner Lives of Black Women in the Middle West: Preliminary Thoughts on the Culture of Dissemblance," *Signs* 14 (Summer 1989), 912–920

Lucie Cheng Hirata, "Free, Indentured, Enslaved: Chinese Prostitutes in Nineteenth-Century America," *Signs* 5 (Autumn 1979), 3–29

David Pivar, *Purity Crusade: Sexual Morality and Social Control 1868–1900* (1973)

Ruth Rosen, *The Lost Sisterhood: Prostitution in America: 1900–1918* (1982)

Charles Rosenberg, "Sexuality, Class, and Role in Nineteenth-Century America," *American Quarterly* XXV (1973), 131–154

Nancy Sahli, "Smashing: Women's Relationships Before the Fall," *Chrysalis,* No. 8 (Summer 1979), 17–27

William Shade, " 'A Mental Passion': Female Sexuality in Victorian America," *International Journal of Women's Studies* I (1978), 13–29

Daniel Scott Smith, "Family Limitation, Sexual Control, and Domestic Feminism in Victorian America," *Feminist Studies* I (1973), 40–57

Carroll Smith-Rosenberg and Charles Rosenberg, "The Female Animal: Medical and Biological Views of Woman and Her Role in Nineteenth-Century America," *Journal of American History* LX (1973), 332–356

Ann Snitow et al., eds., *Powers of Desire: The Politics of Sexuality* (1983)

C H A P T E R
10

The "New Woman": Suffrage and Social Reform

In the decades surrounding the turn of the century American women joined a myriad of women's organizations, hoping both to expand opportunities for their sex and to "uplift" the nation's culture, government, and politics. Women's long campaign for suffrage was finally victorious when Congress ratified the Nineteenth Amendment to the Constitution in 1920. Other reform campaigns spearheaded by women produced a federal children's bureau, protective labor legislation, pure food and drug acts, juvenile courts, kindergartens, city beautification projects, and a wide array of public health and social welfare programs for mothers and children. Organized women did not always act in concert; indeed, they were often divided by strategy and social background. For example, black women's collective experience taught them that racial and sexual oppression must be challenged simultaneously; yet the majority of white women refused to participate in efforts to combat racist ideology, segregation, or lynching. Although they experienced disunity and disagreement, organized women also struggled with a common problem: how to balance their profound faith in the distinctive power of womanhood with a quest for social and political equality. In what various ways did organized women try to combine a belief in sexual difference with the pursuit of equality? What benefits and limitations did this approach to reform take?

✻ D O C U M E N T S

In 1901, Mary Church Terrell, the president of the National Association of Colored Women, praised the reform efforts of organizations composed entirely of black women; her essay is excerpted as the first document. In the second document, dated three years later, Terrell calls on white women, especially those from the South, to join in the fight against lynching. Harriet Wheeler Moyer, a member of the National Congress of Mothers, describes in the third document how she was able to organize a school for poor mothers "with no expense" in 1909. Speaking at a suffrage convention in 1906, Jane Addams, the founder of Hull House, explained (in the fourth document) why it was imperative that urban women gain the right to vote. The fifth document, taken from a 1911 article in *The Woman Voter,* reveals the views of a woman in domestic service who supported the ongoing campaign in California to secure women's right to vote; in October of that year California's male citizens approved women's suffrage by a slim electoral margin. Finally, the last document is an excerpt from a 1914 speech in which the historian and activist Mary Ritter Beard explained why the newly formed Congressional Union wanted no part in existing state-by state campaigns for suffrage, and why it planned instead to fight for a federal suffrage amendment. These documents reveal two widely held views of the time: that women were different from men and that women desired equal rights. They also present the numerous programs and strategies that women devised at the turn of the century to advance their rights and to promote social reforms beneficial to women.

Mary Church Terrell,
"Club Work of Colored Women," 1901

Should anyone ask me what special phase of the Negro's development makes me most hopeful of his ultimate triumph over present obstacles, I should answer unhesitatingly, it is the magnificent work the women are doing to regenerate and uplift the race. Though there are many things in the Negro's present condition to discourage him, he has some blessings for which to be thankful: not the least of these is the progress of our women in everything which makes for the culture of the individual and the elevation of the race.

For years, either banding themselves into small companies or struggling alone, colored women have worked with might and main to improve the condition of their people. The necessity of systematizing their efforts and working on a larger scale became apparent not many years ago, and they decided to unite their forces. Thus it happened that in the summer of 1896 the National Association of Colored Women was formed by the union of two large organizations, from which the advantage of concerted action had been learned. From its birth till the present time its growth has been steady. Interest in the purposes and plans of the National Association has spread so rapidly that it has already been represented in twenty-six states. Handicapped though its members have been, because they lacked both money and experience, their efforts have for the most part been crowned with success.

Kindergartens have been established by some of its organizations, from which encouraging reports have come. A sanitarium with a training school for nurses has been set on such a firm foundation by the Phyllis Wheatley Club of New Orleans, Louisiana, and has proved itself to be such a blessing to the entire community, that the municipal government of that Southern city has voted it an annual appropriation of several hundred dollars. By the members of the Tuskegee branch of the association the work of bringing the light of knowledge and the gospel of cleanliness to their poor benighted sisters on the plantations in Alabama has been conducted with signal success. Their efforts have thus far been confined to four estates, comprising thousands of acres of land, on which live hundreds of colored people yet in the darkness of ignorance and in the grip of sin, and living miles away from churches and schools.

Plans for aiding the indigent orphaned and aged have been projected, and in some instances have been carried into successful execution. One club in Memphis, Tenn., has purchased a large tract of land on which it intends to erect an Old Folks' Home, part of the money for which has already been raised. Splendid service has been rendered by the Illinois Federation of Colored Women's Clubs, through whose instrumentality schools have been visited, truant children looked after, parents and teachers urged to cooperate with each other, rescue and reform work engaged in, so as to reclaim unfortunate women and tempted girls, public institutions investigated, and garments cut, made and distributed to the needy poor.

Questions affecting our legal status as a race are sometimes agitated by our women. In Tennessee and Louisiana colored women have several times petitioned the legislature of their respective states to repeal the obnoxious Jim Crow car laws. . . .

Homes, more homes, better homes, purer homes, is the text upon which our sermons have been and will be preached. There has been a determined effort to have heart-to-heart talks with our women, that we may strike at the root of evils, many of which lie at the fireside. If the women of the dominant race, with all the centuries of education, culture and refinement back of them, with all the wealth of opportunity ever present with them, feel the need of a Mothers' Congress, that they may be enlightened upon the best methods of rearing their children and conducting their homes, how much more do our women, from whom shackles were stricken but yesterday, need information on the same vital subjects! And so the Association is working vigorously to establish mothers' congresses on a small scale, wherever our women can be reached.

From this brief and meagre account of the work which has been and is still being accomplished by colored women through the medium of clubs, it is easy to observe how earnest and effective have been our efforts to elevate the race. No people need ever despair whose women are fully aroused to the duties which rest upon them, and are willing to shoulder responsibilities which they alone can successfully assume. The scope of our endeavors is constantly widening. Into the various channels of generosity and beneficence the National Association is entering more and more every day.

Some of our women are urging their clubs to establish day nurseries, a charity of which there is an imperative need. The infants of wage-earning mothers are frequently locked alone in a room from the time the mother leaves in the morning until she returns at night. Not long ago I read in a Southern newspaper that an infant thus locked alone in the room all day had cried itself to death. When one reflects on the slaughter of the innocents which is occurring with pitiless persistency every day, and thinks of the multitudes who are maimed for life or are rendered imbecile, because of the treatment received during their helpless infancy, it is evident that by establishing day nurseries colored women will render one of the greatest services possible to humanity and to the race. . . .

Nothing lies nearer the heart of colored women than the cause of the children. We feel keenly the need of kindergartens, and are putting forth earnest efforts to honeycomb this country with them from one extreme to the other. The more unfavorable the environments of children the more necessary is it that steps be taken to counteract baleful influences upon innocent victims. How imperative is it then, that, as colored women, we inculcate correct principles and set good examples for our own youth, whose little feet will have so many thorny paths of prejudice, temptation and injustice to tread. . . .

And so, lifting as we climb, onward and upward we go, struggling, striving and hoping that the buds and blossoms of our desires will burst into glorious fruition ere long. With courage born of success achieved in the past, we look forward to a future large with promise and hope. Seeking no favors because of our color, nor patronage because of our needs, we knock at the bar of Justice and ask for an equal chance.

Mary Church Terrell,
"Lynching from a Negro's Point of View," 1904

Before 1904 was three months old, thirty-one negroes had been lynched. Of this number, fifteen were murdered within one week in Arkansas, and one was shot to death in Springfield, Ohio, by a mob composed of men who did not take the trouble to wear masks. Hanging, shooting and burning black men, women and children in the United States have become so common that such occurrences create but little sensation and evoke but slight comment now. . . . In the discussion of this subject, four mistakes are commonly made.

In the first place, it is a great mistake to suppose that rape is the real cause of lynching in the South. Beginning with the Ku Klux Klan the negro has been constantly subjected to some form of organized violence ever since he became free. It is easy to prove that rape is simply the pretext and not the cause of lynching. Statistics show that, out of every 100 negroes who are lynched, from 75–85 are not even accused of this crime, and many who are accused of it are innocent. . . .

In the second place, it is a mistake to suppose that the negro's desire for social equality sustains any relation whatsoever to the crime of rape. . . . It is safe to assert that, among the negroes who have been guilty of ravishing white women, not one had been taught that he was the equal of white people or had ever heard of social equality. . . .

The third error on the subject of lynching consists of the widely circulated statement that the moral sensibilities of the best negroes in the United States are so stunted and dull, and the standard of morality among even the leaders of the race is so low, that they do not appreciate the enormity and heinousness of rape. . . . Only those who are densely ignorant of the standards and sentiments of the best negroes, or who wish wilfully [*sic*] to misrepresent and maliciously slander a race already resting under burdens greater than it can bear, would accuse its thousands of reputable men and women of sympathizing with rapists, either black or white, or of condoning their crime. . . .

What, then, is the cause of lynching? At the last analysis, it will be discovered that there are just two causes of lynching. In the first place, it is due to race hatred, the hatred of a stronger people toward a weaker who were once held as slaves. In the second place, it is due to the lawlessness so prevalent in the section where nine-tenths of the lynchings occur. . . .

Lynching is the aftermath of slavery. The white men who shoot negroes to death and flay them alive, and the white women who apply flaming torches to their oil-soaked bodies today, are the sons and daughters of women who had but little, if any, compassion on the race when it was enslaved. The men who lynch negroes to-day are, as a rule, the children of women who sat by their firesides happy and proud in the possession and affection of their own children, while they looked with un-pitying eye and adamantine heart upon the anguish of slave mothers whose children had been sold away, when not overtaken by a sadder fate. . . . It is too much to ex-pect, perhaps, that the children of women who for generations looked upon the hardships and the degradation of their sisters of a darker hue with few if any protests, should have mercy and compassion upon the children of that oppressed race now. But what a tremendous influence for law and order, and what a mighty foe to mob violence Southern white women might be, if they would arise in the pu-rity and power of their womanhood to implore their fathers, husbands and sons no longer to stain their hands with the black man's blood! . . .

Harriet Wheeler Moyer on Organizing a School for Mothers, 1909

Editor THE DELINEATOR: Through THE DELINEATOR articles and Miss Howe's talk at the National Congress of Mothers at New Orleans, in February of this year, where she was sent by THE DELINEATOR, I became very much interested in the infant mortality question. Our Mothers' Club was already providing the salary of a probation officer for our part of the city, was carrying on a social center for poor children, and had as-sisted financially in the Public Playground movement. As president of our club, I felt diffident about presenting a new work and an additional expense. Then the thought came, why can not this work be done without money? I applied to the directors of our hospital for the use of a room once a week, where doctors and nurses could lecture and demonstrate to mothers how to care for their babies — how to *prevent* babies' ills as well as how to relieve them. The superintendent was much interested, and promised to help me in securing the necessary doctors and nurses.

This is a manufacturing section of our city. Many of the people do not read the papers, so I asked our probation officer and the secretary of the associated charities to tell all the mothers with whom they came in contact. Then I asked the principals of the public schools to allow the children for their writing lesson to make copies of an invitation prepared for them and take it home to their parents. This, with the aid of the local papers, spread the news. The doctors and nurses entered heartily into the plan and we held our first meeting this week. The doctor talked on the care of a young baby, bathing, bandaging, clothing and nourishment, after which the nurse gave a demonstration lesson, using only such material as the poorer mothers could provide. Through these meetings we will lessen the high mortality rate and prevent many children's diseases. THE DELINEATOR deserves great praise for first present-ing the infant-mortality question to the public.

Jane Addams on the Political Role
of Urban Women, 1906

It has been well said that the modern city is a stronghold of industrialism quite as the feudal city was a stronghold of militarism, but the modern cities fear no enemies and rivals from without and their problems of government are solely internal. Affairs for the most part are going badly in these great new centres, in which the quickly-congregated population has not yet learned to arrange its affairs satisfactorily. Unsanitary housing, poisonous sewage, contaminated water, infant mortality, the spread of contagion, adulterated food, impure milk, smoke-laden air, ill-ventilated factories, dangerous occupations, juvenile crime, unwholesome crowding, prostitution and drunkenness are the enemies which the modern cities must face and overcome, would they survive. Logically their electorate should be made up of those who can bear a valiant part in this arduous contest, those who in the past have at least attempted to care for children, to clean houses, to prepare foods, to isolate the family from moral dangers; those who have traditionally taken care of that side of life which inevitably becomes the subject of municipal consideration and control as soon as the population is congested. To test the elector's fitness to deal with this situation by his ability to bear arms is absurd. These problems must be solved, if they are solved at all, not from the military point of view, not even from the industrial point of view, but from a third, which is rapidly developing in all the great cities of the world — the human-welfare point of view. . . .

City housekeeping has failed partly because women, the traditional housekeepers, have not been consulted as to its multiform activities. The men have been carelessly indifferent to much of this civic housekeeping, as they have always been indifferent to the details of the household. . . . The very multifariousness and complexity of a city government demand the help of minds accustomed to detail and variety of work, to a sense of obligation for the health and welfare of young children and to a responsibility for the cleanliness and comfort of other people. Because all these things have traditionally been in the hands of women, if they take no part in them now they are not only missing the education which the natural participation in civic life would bring to them but they are losing what they have always had.

A Working Woman Explains Why She Wants the Vote, 1911

"We are the homeless ones. We spend our lives in other people's homes, cooking the food in other people's kitchens, sweeping and dusting in other people's parlors, and incidentally rocking the cradles of other people's children. Yet we, too, are human beings, and we, too, have our needs like other women.

"When they passed the eight-hour law they left us out. I don't suppose any Senator would think of including the so-called 'servant girl.' I wanted to write and ask for an amendment to put us in, but then I was afraid it might wreck the whole bill, and I wanted other working women to have that great happiness, even if we couldn't have it ourselves. So you see, we, too, have souls. But now, at last, we will have the power to help ourselves, for, thank God, we will be able to vote. The despised 'servant girl' will also be a citizen."

Mary Ritter Beard Defends the Place of the Congressional Union in the Suffrage Movement, 1916

The Congressional Union claims a distinct and vital place in the suffrage movement for two reasons: (1) because it works solely for the Federal amendment, and (2) because it works politically.

The Congressional Union works only for the Federal amendment because it considers that a quicker, more economical and more certain way of securing an extension of suffrage in the United States. It does not believe that state and national work go hand in hand necessarily. Each successive failure to win in a campaign state increases the obstacles in the way of a Federal amendment. State work does not, therefore, inevitably promote a Federal amendment. . . .

An organization that is working for the Federal and state amendments at the same time will find that one or the other holds its major interest and gets the bulk of its money. It is easily surmised where that major interest will lie. One phase of the work will lag behind, and if the referendum loses one time, its second trial must absorb still more of the attention and energy and money of its supporters.

The Congressional Union, therefore, refuses to attempt to work for the two things. It chooses the Federal way exclusively at this moment because it believes that there is an extraordinary political situation which justifies that course. It chooses the Federal way, too, because it wishes to save women's time, money and nervous strength. The Federal way has other advantages: a progressive education, for suffragists, in politics and government; a broadening of the mental horizon from local to National issues; a concerted and intelligent move on the part of women throughout the country; and an opponent who is a responsible representative voting in the open. . . .

The Congressional Union, moreover, works to secure favorable action in Congress by political pressure. That also represents to it excellent chances of victory coupled with economy and dignity of effort. President Cleveland was elected by 1,049 votes; President Wilson by a little over two million votes. There are some four million possible women's votes in this crisis we are facing. Disfranchised women do not have to argue, plead or cajole if enfranchised women will but vote under the slogan: "SUFFRAGE FIRST!" Some of them may not. It is not essential that they all do. It is essential that many do and enough will. . . .

The Congressional Union believes the Federal amendment can be ratified by enough states. It has taken that matter into consideration as a vital part of its emphasis upon the Federal way. It is not a band of dreamers or youthful fanatics.

All sorts of objections are raised against the policies of the Congressional Union, naturally. Enthusiasts of the state referendum place their hope of victory in education and its "ultimate" triumph over selfish economic and political interests. They may be content with a progressive vote. Education is their real aim, and not suffrage first. . . .

Enthusiasts of the Federal way place their hope of victory in immediate political necessities which strengthen all the older and more abstract appeals by women. They are willing to get the vote through representatives of the "people" and let the vote itself educate.

The tactics of the Congressional Union have been sometimes called an English importation, not applicable to American conditions and to American government. It is even disputed as to whether we have party government at all in this country. This seems almost incredible in face of the facts. . . .

The political tactics of the Congressional Union are abundantly justified by the analyses of the way Congress works made by United States Senators and Congressmen themselves. . . .

The Congressional Union is responsible for recognition now in Washington of the grave political significance of this situation. It has insisted on placing responsibility where it belongs. The Congressional Union has not become thereby a partisan organization. It has merely become an efficient organization. It is strictly nonpartisan, in fact, because it asks enfranchised women to put suffrage above party.

In the National political campaign that has already indeed begun, it will not be individuals who will be discussed, but the deeds of the Party as a whole. Why, then, should suffragists alone discuss individuals when they are not the point? The point is: SUFFRAGE FIRST.

❋ E S S A Y S

In the opening essay, Elinor Lerner explores the reasons for Jewish women's unflagging support for the suffrage cause in New York City, suggesting that Jewish women came from a cultural tradition that valued political activism and democratic ideals. In the second essay, Robyn Muncy of the University of Maryland at College Park examines the creation of the U.S. Children's Bureau in 1912 by women who had long been part of the settlement movement. Through the Children's Bureau, women succeeded in institutionalizing a distinctive set of female values within the federal government, even as they pursued an equal rights agenda by developing new professional opportunities for women. Over time, Muncy shows, the values of women who worked in government changed somewhat as they became integrated into the federal bureaucracy. Finally, in the last essay, Eileen Boris of Howard University argues that by embracing an identity of "true motherhood," organized black women challenged the racism of the dominant culture. Finding much to praise in this approach, Boris suggests that black women created a new "justice standard" by combining a quest for equality with pride in their racial and gender difference.

Suffrage parade held in New York City, May 6, 1912. Suffrage parades were a common occurrence in New York City in the 1910s, attracting women of different classes and occupations. The marchers often wore white dresses to signify their unity of purpose. Perhaps to convey the hope that women would use the vote to improve the lives of America's children, some mothers brought their youngsters with them to the parades.

Jewish Involvement in the New York City Woman Suffrage Movement

ELINOR LERNER

The American woman suffrage movement is usually characterized as predominantly white, Protestant, Anglo-Saxon, and upper- and middle-class in composition and support. Although this may be true as far as the formal organizations are concerned, the issue of woman suffrage was supported, often actively, by large segments of immigrants and the working class. This has been noted by some writers, but few detailed accounts of this support have appeared. This study will describe the crucial role played by the Jewish community in the suffrage victory in New York State.

New York occupied a strategic position in the struggle for woman's suffrage. Most early suffrage victories had taken place in western, rural states, and suffragists were convinced that farmers and native Americans were their main support rather than the urban, working classes. New York was the first eastern, industrial state to

"Jewish Involvement in the New York City Woman Suffrage Movement" by Elinor Lerner from *American Jewish History* 70 (June 1981), pp. 442–461. Reprinted courtesy the American Jewish Historical Society.

give women the vote prior to the Constitutional amendment of 1920, and a victory in New York was considered crucial for convincing Congress to act on the federal amendment. Suffragists also believed that New York City presented almost insurmountable problems. In 1910 approximately 37% of its population was Roman Catholic and 31% Jewish. Thirteen percent were either first or second generation Irish and a similar number first or second generation Italian. By 1920 at least 78% of Manhattan was either foreign-born or had foreign-born parents.

New York conducted two referenda on suffrage in 1915 and 1917. In the earlier vote the issue was defeated by a narrow margin in both New York City and the state. In 1917, however, the amendment passed both in the city and the state as a whole, although losing in the state outside of New York City. It was the city, with its large Catholic, Jewish, immigrant, and working-class population which carried the state for woman suffrage. . . .

In both elections the largest, strongest and most consistent support came from the Jewish community, from Jews of all economic levels living both in Harlem and on the Lower East Side. The strongest and most consistent opposition came from working- and middle-class Irish. Italians were not unified on suffrage: most voted against the amendment, but the largest concentration of Italians in Greenwich Village was consistently pro-suffrage. . . .

The question, of course, remains why New York Jewry was so supportive of the suffrage movement and what role the Jewish community played in its final success. During the . . . [late] nineteenth and early twentieth century, the suffrage movement in New York followed a fairly conservative approach. The years 1907–1911, however, saw a resurgence of activity in New York City with many new organizations appearing together with increased popular support. The impetus for much of this change came from working-class women, especially young Jewish workers on the Lower East Side. Suffrage leaders realized the need for new organizations and tactics when working with immigrant women on other issues. We can see this by analyzing the development of several such organizations. It would seem that the working-class and immigrant women thought more highly of the militant British suffrage movement and favored more aggressive tactics by the Americans.

The National Progressive Women's Suffrage Union, following the British movement and seeking a working-class constituency, was formed in New York City around 1907. Although many of its members appear to have been German-Americans, its main bases of support were Jewish garment workers on the Lower East Side and in Harlem around 111th to 125th streets. The Union shocked the established suffrage organizations and the public by going to "the people direct, in the streets, on the highways and byways." It was the first suffrage group in the city to hold open air meetings, attempt a foot parade and to approach the urban working class at such public places as ball games, beaches and amusement parks. Its members staged a series of demonstrations and street meetings which were reported in the press and attracted crowds of thousands. They also distributed leaflets and demonstrated outside of factories and formed alliances with workers on union and labor issues. In November, 1909 union members addressed a meeting of striking necktie workers on the Lower East Side, and were well received by the largely Jewish workers. They were then invited to address a mass meeting of the union and forty or more women left the meeting wearing suffragette buttons.

Another militant organization, the Equality League of Self-Supporting Women, was established in January, 1907 by Harriet Stanton Blatch, the daughter of Elizabeth Cady Stanton. Upon returning to the United States in 1902 after many years' involvement in British socialist and suffrage activities, Blatch was disappointed by the stagnation in the American suffrage movement. Channeling her energies elsewhere, she became involved in civic reforms and the Women's Trade Union League (WTUL), which consisted of a group of middle- and working-class women attempting to organize women into trade unions. In working with young Jewish women on the Lower East Side in 1906, she became aware of the interest in suffrage among working women and the possibility of establishing an organization in the working class. League membership was open to any self-supporting woman, working-class or professional, and organizations of working women could also affiliate with the League. By 1909 the League contained over 1,000 individual members and 22,000 from affiliated societies. . . .

In 1911, the Wage Earners' League was formed by the Woman Suffrage Party (WSP), the major suffrage organization in New York City, and the WTUL. According to Elizabeth Freeman, one of the organizers, the idea of forming the League began when WTUL and WSP workers attempted to enlist working women and immigrants on the Lower East Side to march in a suffrage parade. Impressed with the strong interest in suffrage and enthusiasm for the parade, Freeman and Lavinia Dock (a nurse at the Henry Street Settlement) thought of starting a suffrage organization for working women and addressed clubs at the Henry Street, College and Christadora settlements about such a possibility. As with Blatch's League of Self-Supporting Women, the initial interest in the formation of the Wage Earners' League came from working-class, immigrant women on the Lower East Side. . . .

Initially based on the Lower East Side, the League soon extended its activities throughout the city. A house-to-house canvass to contact working men and women of Manhattan was planned, open air meetings at factories employing women were held, a "distinctive" leaflet published and a press committee established. Several mass meetings and large rallies were held, at least one conducted with black women workers.

The last organization to be discussed is the Political Equality League (PEL) founded by Alva Belmont, a wealthy New York society woman who devoted her fortune and time to the suffrage movement. Founded in 1909, the PEL had at least twelve branches by April, 1911 which were used to contact New York immigrants, the working class and blacks. . . . The Wage Earners branch, located in the center of pro-suffrage sentiment on the Lower East Side, opened with a meeting in which a crowd of hundreds "literally packed the halls," which "many more would have entered if it had been possible." The officers of the branch were Jewish women who planned to hold alternate indoor and outdoor meetings nearly every evening at the Manhattan end of the Williamsburg bridge. . . .

The major involvement of Manhattan Jewry in the formal suffrage organizations occurred at the lower level of organization. Since the WSP was structured like a political party, it had leaders and organizational units in both assembly and election districts. Organizational work was thus carried out in the small election districts of immigrant communities. . . . Of the five assembly districts with the highest concentration of Jews, four had a continuous history of Jewish assembly district chairmen, often the same women for many years. It is also a testimony to the chairmen's hard work and effectiveness that these four assembly districts had the highest pro-suffrage votes in Manhattan in 1915.

Another indication of working-class and immigrant involvement in the suffrage movement can be obtained by analyzing the suffrage activity in certain neighborhoods. The WSP journal, the *Woman Voter,* published a monthly calendar of events and detailed reports of the previous month's work. The Jewish neighborhoods on the Lower East Side were among the most active in Manhattan. . . . Over the years there were thousands of street meetings, larger meetings in local parks, indoor meetings, and special events such as dances and parties, with speeches both in English and Yiddish.

The reports written by [Lillian] Wald and Lavinia Dock, as South Manhattan organizers, often commented on and praised the quality of local workers and leaders. Local Jewish women were noted for their political acumen, hard work and ability to relate to the community. One was commended for the "good practical speech in Yiddish" given to a large crowd at Seward Park. In 1911, Dock praised the "splendid captains and workers" who were "making woman suffrage known in shops and homes and even in the political life of the district.". . .

Although most of this effort was done by local workers, it was planned and directed to a great extent by central city headquarters. The Woman Suffrage Party had carefully worked out plans for contacting all of Manhattan's population. The Press and Publicity Committee . . . prepared articles on suffrage for New York newspapers on a regular basis, having established contact with 893 papers, including 683 trade journals, 21 religious papers and 126 foreign language papers. Some felt that if suffrage was covered in the Yiddish press it would be easier to receive coverage in other foreign-language papers, so special efforts were directed toward this end. By 1915, it was reported that all the Yiddish press were in favor of suffrage editorially and all gave space to suffrage news.

The Press and Publicity Committee also published millions of pamphlets, leaflets and flyers, many in Yiddish, German, Italian and Bohemian. Those designed to appeal to Jewish voters carried endorsements by Jewish community, political and labor leaders. The only surviving copies of Yiddish leaflets are those directed to tenement mothers, suggesting that the problems of poor housing and unhealthy food would only be solved if women had the vote.

One city-wide strategy, employed with great success on the Lower East Side, was the neighborhood canvass. Long range plans developed by the WSP called for several visits to each household in Manhattan, with special attention to those with registered voters. Carefully coordinated from central headquarters, women canvassers were to keep card files, recording on different colored cards the sentiments of each voter toward woman suffrage, how often each had been contacted, what type of literature had been distributed, and whether they signed "enrollment slips" indicating support for suffrage and the WSP. Copies of these files were kept both in central Manhattan headquarters, and in the assembly district headquarters. . . .

Another approach, originating from central headquarters and used in various parts of Manhattan including immigrant neighborhoods, was the use of a traveling team of suffrage workers who would go from area to area with a special demonstration designed to attract a sizeable crowd. One tactic employed by such groups was the "voiceless speech," consisting of twenty to thirty large cards printed in plain letters that could be seen at a distance. Placed on a big easel, they were used where suffrage workers were not allowed to make speeches or in addressing an audience that did not speak English. They were so successful on the Lower East Side that for a time they were held weekly in Seward Park with signs in Yiddish. Voiceless speeches were used a year later, during the summer of 1914, to appeal to working men on their way home in the evening, and again were well received.

Another very popular practice on the Lower East Side was the torchlight parade. Suffrage workers provided free yellow caps to those who wished to join in and, carrying yellow lanterns, the marchers went through the Lower East Side, leaving small groups to conduct street meetings at points along the way. According to one suffrage worker: "The East Side loved the night parades, with music, and great balls of yellow light bearing suffrage messages. Mothers . . . with babies on their hips, the green grocer, the delicatessen owner, all came out to watch. Children and dogs swarmed under foot, shrieking with joy at the lights and the bands, and it was all so lively and appealing that even tired housewives and young working girls fell in to help carry the banners."

Formal suffrage organizations, however, were not the only link with the Jewish community. . . . In 1909 the women members of the New York Socialist Party voted, with party support, to wage an aggressive suffrage campaign independently from the formal suffrage organizations. In 1914, New York Socialist Party women voted to work with the Woman Suffrage Party in a joint campaign for the 1915 referendum. . . .

Closely allied to the Socialist Party within the Jewish community were the garment trade unions. But the importance of these unions was less in the area of active campaign than in providing a structure by which the suffrage message could be sent. Needle trade unions provided a handy vehicle for Jewish feminists to reach voters and also for suffragists to contact large numbers of young, working Jewish women. Woman suffrage was formally endorsed by many labor organizations which contained a large segment of the working class Jewish community of Manhattan. . . . This endorsement was important since like that of the Socialist Party it lent credibility and legitimacy to the cause for those workers whose primary allegiance was to working class politics. . . .

Unions also facilitated the spread of suffrage propaganda and the involvement of Jewish working women in the suffrage movement. . . . Many female union organizers had several political affiliations and were active suffragists. For example, both Rose Schneiderman and Clara Lemlich were active members of the Socialist Party and the Women's Trade Union League and worked closely with the Woman Suffrage Party. . . . Clara Lemlich used her union contacts to organize a large contingent of women trade unionists to march in the 1912 suffrage parade.

Suffragists also became very involved with working women during strikes. During the 1909 shirtwaist strike and the 1916 kimono and housedress workers strike, suffragists aided the strikers with money, publicity and picketing. . . .

Many attempts to reach the Jewish working men and women were conducted under the auspices of or by the efforts of women connected with the settlement houses. Most notable were Lavinia Dock and Lillian Wald of the Henry Street Settlement and Mary Simkhovitch of Greenwich House. . . . Because of their physical facilities and contacts with the local community, settlements were ideal for local suffrage work. The Henry Street Settlement Suffrage Club, in existence from at least 1912 to 1915, was one of the most active. It sponsored dances, social gatherings, and indoor and outdoor meetings. . . . In the summer and fall of 1915 the club conducted a series of large outdoor meetings in various parks on the Lower East Side on Sunday evenings so that working people and religious Jews could attend. . . . A festive mood was created with suffrage banners and decorations, flower girls with baskets of flowers, and young boys with yellow lanterns. "To the delight of the music loving East Side" music was provided, ranging from opera to Jewish and Polish folk songs played by a Polish band. Meyer London, Socialist Party Congressman from the district, frequently spoke at these meetings. . . .

Of course, given the liberal and radical political sentiment in the pre-World War I Jewish community, it is not totally surprising that suffrage was supported so strongly. Many Jewish men and women who came to the United States had been active in labor and radical politics in Europe and continued these activities within the radical Jewish unions and the Socialist Party. Some American Jews justified their support for female suffrage on universalistic principles. Stephen S. Wise stated: "The women's movement is not a feminist movement at all, but a human movement. It is not a sectional movement but is international in scope."

But, generally, more specific reasons were given. At a suffrage rally on the Lower East Side, Meyer London said: "The last persons to oppose granting suffrage . . . should be the foreign-born men who had fled the political oppression of their own countries." Compared to other immigrants and working women in Manhattan, Jewish women seemed more politically aware, more concerned with education and intellectual matters, relatively easier to organize and more socially concerned. Some attributed this to uniquely Jewish characteristics, as did Rose Schneiderman when explaining why Jewish working women responded to unionization attempts: "We find the Jewish girl especially responsive to its call. Perhaps it is because of the centuries of persecution that the race has had to endure, that she is easier to reach than the American girl who believes there is freedom of opportunity for all. Then, too, the Jewish people are idealists and are ready to fight injustice whether it be industrial or political."

The cultural and economic position of Jewish women in Eastern Europe is also offered as an explanation for the political and economic activism of American Jewish women. In Eastern Europe Jewish women functioned as an integral part of the family economic unit, especially where the male head was primarily a religious scholar and the responsibility for family support rested on the wife and older daughters. The most common occupations of women were shop owners, peddlers and seamstresses. When the mass immigration from Eastern Europe began, many Jewish women were also working in industry, usually the garment trades, in the large cities. Many Jewish women had also been active in labor and radical political movements in Eastern Europe and many middle class Jewish women were highly educated. All these factors came together and enabled Jewish women to face an easier transition to industrial city life and participate more easily in politics than women of other ethnic groups.

The American Jewish community also contained no significant organization or institution that was outspokenly anti-suffrage. Unlike the Catholic Church, which was highly centralized, hierarchical and vocally anti-suffrage, Jewish religious institutions were decentralized and attitudes on suffrage were determined largely by the individual rabbi. As early as 1912, mass meetings for the woman's vote were being held in temples in Jewish Harlem. And by 1917 several religious organizations, including the Eastern Council of Reform Rabbis and the Central Conference of American Rabbis, had endorsed woman suffrage.

The American woman suffrage movement was faced with the task of convincing men to share their political power. Its success depended on the ability of women, who had no formal access to the vote, to persuade men to grant them that right. Its success in a community, therefore, depended on strong support from women, a channel through which women could effectively convey their demands to men and the belief, on the part of the men in the community, that woman suffrage was, in some way, to their own advantage. Due to both past European and present American circumstances noted above, the Jewish community in Manhattan lent itself most readily to provide support for woman suffrage. In addition, because of family and occupational structure, male and female members of the household frequently worked in the same occupation. This, together with the high rate of unionization, provided a structure in which men and women had many of the same political and occupational interests and where it was possible for women to press feminist demands upon males in their workplace and family. Suffrage was thus seen by many Jewish men in political, rather than personal, terms. Women's votes were seen as being beneficial to union and radical politics and as advancing the interests of the worker and also those of the Jewish community. . . .

Female Reformers Create the U.S. Children's Bureau

ROBYN MUNCY

In 1905, Florence Kelley claimed: "The noblest duty of the Republic is . . . so cherishing all its children that they . . . may become self-governing citizens. . . . The care and nurture of childhood," she continued, "is thus a vital concern of the nation." These assertions indicated the direction that Hull House women would take in the early twentieth century: they and their growing network of reforming women would begin seeking national influence, and child welfare policy would provide the field for their broader authority.

Representing the success of this new, national focus was the creation of the Children's Bureau in 1912. Situated in the Department of Commerce and Labor, the new agency became the first female stronghold in the federal government, and it provided the widening circle of female reformers an official leadership. In fact, by the time America entered World War I, the Children's Bureau presided over an

Robyn Muncy, *Creating a Female Dominion in American Reform: 1890–1935* (New York: Oxford University Press, 1991), 38–65.

interconnected set of organizations that joined the Bureau in attempting to control child welfare policy in the United States. Thus materialized a female dominion in policymaking, the evolution of which illuminates the continued interrelationship between the professional interests of white, middle-class women and their participation in progressive reform.

Settlement culture was partly responsible for the idea of a federal bureau devoted exclusively to children. Legend holds that, in 1903, Lillian Wald and Florence Kelley were enjoying breakfast as usual at the Henry Street Settlement, and in the habit of settlement breakfasts, residents were reading their mail and exchanging the morning papers. . . . To Kelley fell the task of opening a letter that asked why nothing was done about the high summertime death rate among children. Tossing the letter to her colleague, Kelley suggested that Wald answer the inquiry. As Wald mused that she knew no source of information on variable death rates among children, Kelley read aloud an article from the morning paper, which announced that the federal government was sending the Secretary of Agriculture to investigate damage inflicted by the boll weevil in southern cotton fields. Wald is purported to have retorted: "If the Government can have a department to take such an interest in what is happening to the cotton crop, why can't it have a bureau to look after the nation's child crop?"

Given the times, there seemed no reason at all. . . . Already by 1903, the robust [President Theodore] Roosevelt was urging the federal government to exert itself in new ways. . . . In the year of Wald's brainstorm, for instance, Roosevelt won congressional approval for a new cabinet-level Department of Commerce and Labor and appointed a public lands commission to study the consequences of public land laws. . . . Roosevelt's new executive agencies . . . represented the arrival of progressive reform at the federal doorway.

Wald's proposal for a federal bureau to harvest data on "the child crop" fit perfectly into this new scheme of federal activity. . . . Industrialism, the source of so many Progressive-era maladies, exploited children in numerous ways, according to Wald: sometimes through their own employment at early ages, other times through poverty resulting from their families' low wages. In order to know exactly what ills afflicted the nation's youngest citizens, to learn the causes of those ills, and to know whether any existing programs had yet remedied the sicknesses, reformers needed information gathered from all over the country. They needed comprehensive and continuous studies that only a federal agency could conduct. . . .

From 1903 forward, Kelley and Wald made the creation of a children's bureau one of their top priorities. They opened this crusade as they had opened many others — with a search for public support. . . . They began by tapping into their organizational network. Jane Addams, of course, allied immediately with her friends and hooked them into Chicago's reform circles. As general secretary of the National Consumers' League, Kelley represented a national group dedicated to the reform of working conditions for women and children. Its support for Wald's idea was never in doubt. Edward Devine's backing won the cause editorial support in *Charities,* a powerful generator of favor among the nation's reformers, and eventually Wald and Kelley garnered endorsements from the settlements, the National Conference of Charities and Corrections, the General Federation of Women's Clubs, the Mothers' Congress, and local child welfare societies such as Chicago's Juvenile Protective Association.

To draft legislation for the creation of a children's bureau and to steer the bill through the maze of congressional procedure, the women approached the National Child Labor Committee. Both women belonged to this temporary union of northern and southern opponents of child labor. . . .

But it was not a women's organization. Indeed, in October 1904, the general committee of the NCLC comprised 35 men and only five women. . . . When, in the spring of 1905, Wald and Kelley convinced the NCLC to sponsor the fight for a federal children's bureau, they entrusted their idea to a sex-integrated organization concerned primarily with child labor. Female dependence on male help in this particular endeavor revealed the special stage of women's public involvement at the turn of the century. . . . Women as yet had little experience with the national government. Female campaigns for reform had previously succeeded at the local and state levels, where reformers used the influence especially of their wealthy sisters to pass legislation. At the national level, women had not yet established reputations compelling enough to assure a hearing without help from prominent men. . . . The pattern continued when Wald and Kelley chose a sex-integrated organization to carry their program for a federal children's bureau into the all-male national Congress. . . . The NCLC saw that a new bill appeared before Congress every year until its passage in 1912.

While the NCLC intensified its lobbying through these years, the broader Wald/Kelley network strove for recognition as a national policymaking body. Only since the 1890s had reformers wrenched child welfare out of parental hands and subjected it to public authority. They had made juvenile delinquency, recreation, education, and child labor the subject of municipal and even state legislation. . . . So far, children had not been scooped into the basket of federal concerns, an omission that left experts in child welfare outside the assembly of national policymakers. Through their campaign for a federal children's bureau, Wald and Kelley were thus edging child welfare onto the federal stage for the first time, and of course *female* reformers were inching onto the national platform simultaneously.

The first big break for these relative unknowns came in January 1909, when President Roosevelt allowed them a national audition. . . . Roosevelt invited over two hundred delegates representing the country's child welfare agencies to the first White House Conference on the Care of Dependent Children. . . . Roosevelt's invitation to the conference . . . asked . . . that attendees offer a recommendation on the creation of a federal children's bureau. . . . The stakes for female reformers were especially high. If the conference could persuade Congress that children should become a subject of federal legislation, then women would have their main chance for joining the national policymaking establishment. Jane Addams herself insisted that the convening of this conference alone gave child welfare work "a dignity and a place in the national life which it had never had before." And by association, it gave child welfare workers — women included — a wholly new authority in national life.

At the conference, . . . not a single voice objected to the proposal for the bureau, a tribute to the success of Wald's and Kelley's outreach to the prime movers in child welfare work. Disagreements did erupt, however, over the job description for a federal bureau. . . . Wald imagined the children's bureau as a national consensus builder, actively publicizing its findings, drafting recommendations, and working directly with local organizations to pass legislation that embodied its proposals. . . .

Several of Wald's male colleagues at the conference argued passionately that the United States Constitution would not allow a government agency to do what one participant called "promotion work.". . . At the turn of the century, men who were in the process of creating the social sciences wrestled with the relationship between their emerging disciplines and politics. . . . As the new professions matured, their most powerful practitioners decided that they must avoid the appearance of passionate attachment to any particular political ideals. . . . In other words, by the time of the Conference on [the Care of] Dependent Children, male social scientists had agreed that if they openly combined research and advocacy, they cast doubt on the objectivity of their research and thus lost credibility for themselves and their professions. . . .

To Wald and her settlement colleagues, this bifurcation of research and advocacy seemed false. . . . The history of female professions easily explained this special refusal of women to divorce social investigation from political engagement. Because women in the newer female professions had defined their mission as self-sacrificing service, because they had won support for their public lives by offering themselves as funnels of aid from one class to another, they did not have the freedom to withdraw their research from some immediately useful end. . . . Women coming through the settlement network of the 1890s had a gender-specific need to reconcile their professional goals with Victorian ideals of womanhood, and this need produced a version of professionalism and a justification for public participation peculiar to women. Wald's insistence on the bureaucratic union of research and advocacy was one of the implications of that justification for female professionals and reformers in the early twentieth century. . . .

Despite differences of opinion, the Conference on the Care of Dependent Children proved a great success and inspired congressional hearings on the children's bureau bill. During January and February 1909, both the House and the Senate heard testimony on the proposal, and women increased their visibility in Washington by counting among the witnesses called. . . . During subsequent hearings, too, the women bolstered their reputations as experts in a field struggling to enter the federal government's domain. . . .

Congress finally created the Children's Bureau during the reforming fervor of 1912. The new agency received a broad mandate, which was to "investigate and report upon all matters pertaining to the welfare of children and child life among all classes of our people." Among the issues suggested for study were "infant mortality, the birth rate, orphanage, juvenile courts, desertion, dangerous occupations, accidents and diseases of children in the several States and Territories."

With this wide range of issues from which to choose, the Bureau's chief had extraordinary discretion in determining the character of the new agency. The Bureau might become the leading opponent of child labor and harass employers the country over. Concentrating on orphans, it might advocate more efficient and humane institutions for dependent children. It might focus on the birth rate, become the chief herald of race suicide, and condemn educated women for not bearing enough children. Or, serving as an adjunct to the Census Bureau, it might simply compile vital statistics on the child population and advocate nothing in particular. The predilections of the Bureau's first chief, therefore, took on great significance.

As it turned out, that appointment held other importance as well. When President [William Howard] Taft signed the children's bureau bill, no one could have predicted that the new agency would establish the primacy of women in its area of public policy. After all, the Bureau enjoyed the support of a good mix of male and female reformers. Moreover, many congressmen expected that the Bureau's chief would be male. . . . Only three days after the children's bureau bill became law, however, female reformers made their move: Jane Addams wired both Lillian Wald and President Taft to say that "the Chicago group" supported Julia Lathrop's appointment to the new office. . . . "Let's try hard for a woman first." . . . On April 17, 1912, Taft sent Lathrop's appointment to the Senate, where it received confirmation that same day. Thus, Lathrop became the first woman to head a federal bureau.

Female settlement workers were following their pattern. Rather than competing with men for positions of authority in established areas of policy, they led in the creation of a brand-new field. When the logic of separate spheres encouraged men to cede this particular territory — child welfare — to women, female reformers were able to win their first bid for a position of official authority in the national government. Female reformers did not, of course, lobby for a children's bureau in hopes of gaining professional and political power for themselves, but in this case as in others, professional advancement for women was intimately connected to progressive reform.

In her own words, Lathrop was "dazed to find myself appointed" as chief of the United States Children's Bureau, and dazed was an appropriate response. Although the new bureau chief had pioneered in the juvenile court movement and the creation of psychiatric facilities for children, her most spectacular achievements had occurred at the state level in her work on behalf of the insane. Only because of support from the likes of Jane Addams could she have found herself in the country's most prominent child welfare position. . . .

Just as Addams had initiated Lathrop's elevation to head the Children's Bureau, Lathrop determined to lift other women. . . . The Civil Service rules — ostensibly written to assure that merit alone qualified an applicant for government jobs — explicitly allowed the heads of agencies to specify the sex of candidates for all positions. Once in power, Lathrop took full advantage of that permission to promote female hiring. In 1914, for instance, she wrote to the Civil Service Commission: "Most of our field agents must be women." She argued that, to investigate many issues, the Bureau (emulating the door-to-door technique introduced by Hull House residents) intended to conduct frank interviews with mothers, which would include questions about childbirth, breast-feeding, and child care. Lathrop insisted that it was inappropriate for men to ask women such questions.

This argument illuminates the complexities of Lathrop's motives for hiring women. Certainly she preferred women in part because she wanted to increase female participation in America's public life, and this commitment amounted to a rejection of nineteenth-century prescriptions for female behavior. But equally as supportive of her exclusively female hiring was Lathrop's acceptance of those aspects of the Victorian gender system that deemed it improper for men to talk to women about such personal experiences as breast-feeding. In the context of hiring at the Children's Bureau, then, even a sort of prudishness inadvertently advanced the cause of middle-class women. . . .

By March 1919, the Bureau listed only 14 men among its 169 staff members, and women outnumbered men in every occupational category except that of messenger. . . . Most of the women . . . were white, middle-class, well-educated, and unmarried. Many were also midwesterners and formed by the same reform traditions and institutions that Lathrop herself had helped to fashion. Emma O. Lundberg, for instance, who joined the Children's Bureau staff as head of the Social Service Division in 1914, had graduated from the University of Wisconsin before doing graduate work at both the New York School of Philanthropy and the Chicago School of Civics and Philanthropy, where Lathrop was an officer. She had already proven her research abilities in her work for the Wisconsin Industrial Commission. . . . Thus the ardent opponent of patronage systems based on affiliation with political parties actually began to build her own sort of patronage system based on gender and culture. . . .

Lathrop's Bureau re-created life in the settlements. . . . Most workers lived in boarding houses or apartment hotels . . . [and] thus enjoyed many of the advantages offered by settlements: private rooms, freedom from cooking, and a communal dining arrangement. . . . Close friends showed special concern for each other on the job. One employee, for instance, intervened to protect the health of an overworked friend: in a private note to Lathrop, she recommended that her friend be granted a long vacation and forbidden during that time to conduct any of the Bureau's work. The chief complied. . . .

Bureau workers also showed warm concern for the countless women who wrote letters to them. Having read about the Bureau in a local newspaper or received one of its pamphlets, women often turned to the Bureau for personal advice and material aid. The Bureau's files became repositories for innumerable supplications that revealed the most intimate details of women's lives, a testimony to the Bureau's popularity among women and to the lonely, fragmented lives of many American wives and mothers. Women wrote to the Bureau to confide beatings, ignorance about birth control, menstrual problems, and pregnancies outside marriage. . . . Every plea for help elicited a personal reply from the Bureau's staff and often involved long hours attempting to ensure adequate care. Usually that care came from an appropriate local agency to which the Bureau referred the supplicant.

In this way, the Children's Bureau carried the settlement ethos into the federal government and with it the culture of female professionalism created in the settlements. . . . Here, the Bureau contradicted latter-day preconceptions about bureaucracies: it was not simply an impersonal machine cranking out studies and forms according to standard operating procedures but also a flexible institution, responding to problems outside its official ken. . . .

In the context of a government agency, even Julia Lathrop could not precisely duplicate settlement life. While the hierarchy at Hull House had operated informally, lines of authority at the Bureau were formally delineated: every employee had a title that proclaimed her place in the structure and controlled her salary. Status descended from the chief to the assistant chief; from there to the five division heads;

next to the special agents and research assistants; and so on. Women who filled these slots were ambitious. To reach the Bureau, they had beaten out a good many applicants and, once there, competed against equally capable women for the best assignments, promotions, and admission to Lathrop's inner circle of favorite daughters. Imperatives dictated by the job market and governmental structure modified female professional culture as they set limits on the possibilities for simply shifting to this federal agency the values and strategies of the settlements.

Also pulling at the seam of intraoffice intimacies were bureaucratic procedures. Memoranda and travel vouchers hardly promoted close, personal relationships. Moreover, the staff had an enormous amount of work to do and little space in which to do it. . . . Office ambience militated against the gentility expected of the workers and may have made some feel torn between two, sometimes conflicting, sets of expectations. Though these tensions between competition and community, between personal relationships and impersonal procedures, were central to professional experience and had certainly existed before the founding of the Children's Bureau, they intensified for women with the increasing bureaucratization of professional life and the opening of greater professional opportunities for women. The point needs to be clear, however, that bureaucratic structure did not utterly control the working lives of women in the Children's Bureau. . . . Within the limits set by bureaucratic rationality, women in the Bureau created a work space that valued responsiveness, individual initiative, and personal relationships.

Indeed, while bureaucratization eroded some settlement traditions, it increased the effectiveness of others. Once women had taken control of the Children's Bureau, they used the agency to promote their reform agenda on a national scale, just as Lillian Wald had hoped. During her first months in office, Lathrop settled her strategy. Because child labor attracted controversy, she had her staff quietly compile child labor laws and concentrated the balance of her precious resources on infant mortality studies and a drive to improve birth registration in the states. In addition, she determined to begin publishing a series of popular pamphlets on prenatal and infant care.

In her implementation of this strategy, Lathrop employed such tactics of female professional culture as popularizing technical information. . . . Though Lathrop involved doctors in the preparation of the series, she chose Mary Mills West to write the pamphlets. West, a widow with five children to put through college, proved worthy of Lathrop's confidence.

West's publications became the best-selling pamphlets of the Government Printing Office in the 1910s. The first edition of West's pamphlet, *Prenatal Care,* sold out in two months. . . . Nearly a million and a half copies of West's second pamphlet, *Infant Care,* were disseminated between 1914 and 1921. When the Bureau added *Child Care* and *Milk: The Indispensable Food for Children* to its list of popular dodgers, it was distributing hundreds of thousands of pamphlets each year and was never able to meet the demand. To help satisfy some of the need, local women's groups began to print up excerpts for local distribution. . . . The confidence that Lathrop and her colleagues had in publicity inspired them not to settle for the use of print media alone to disseminate their advice but to pioneer in the use of public exhibits, demonstrations, eventually radio spots, and motion pictures.

Women in the Children's Bureau used each method of publicity in several ways. First — and most obviously — they distributed information from the

Bureau's research. Sometimes that information aimed toward the reform of child-rearing; sometimes toward the reform of public policy. But in either case, that publicity served a second purpose: it drew attention to the Children's Bureau itself. And as it spotlighted the Bureau, it began to establish the agency as the national authority on matters of child welfare. Strategies at Lathrop's agency thus continued the trend developed at Hull House. In the process of responding to demonstrable material problems, for example, maternal and infant death, middle-class women created new professional opportunities for themselves and increased their own authority in national life. . . .

To extend the Bureau's influence into America's policymaking bodies, Lathrop needed even more help than the media could offer. . . . Lathrop used the national network of female voluntary organizations which she knew through her work in the settlements. Thus, the interdependence of professional and lay women, a salient feature of settlement life, continued. . . .

Lathrop drew the voluntary organizations under her leadership, testing them first in her campaign for better birth registration. . . . Lathrop believed that all other efforts to improve the lives of children depended on adequate birth registration. Without it, the country could not collect reliable statistics on infant mortality or discover its causes; officials could not document a child's age and thereby enforce school attendance or child labor laws. . . .

With an original staff of only fifteen people, Lathrop could not hope to conduct a national campaign, so she called in the female voluntary associations. Florence Kelley committed the Consumers' League and the National Child Labor Committee to the cause in 1913, and the two groups carried the crusade into the South, where they were working against child labor. In 1914, the General Federation of Women's Clubs took up the standard. In 1915, the Association of Collegiate Alumnae joined, and in 1916, so did the Women's Christian Temperance Union. By 1918, women's organizations were vying for the honor of helping the Bureau. The chair of Child Hygiene for the Congress of Mothers and Parent-Teacher Associations, for instance, reminded Lathrop that her organization comprised 8000 groups devoted "to the interests of childhood" and was very well-organized. According to the chair, the large membership and effective organization of the Congress better qualified it than the General Federation of Women's Clubs to aid the Bureau. . . .

From the state of Washington to Florida, club women marched door-to-door to do the Bureau's bidding. . . . After each door-to-door canvass had provided volunteers with a list of babies recently born to a neighborhood, the women checked their records against official documentation in local registrars' offices. Most found the public registry deficient, sent the Bureau their results, and lobbied state legislatures for better laws, local officials for better enforcement, and both doctors and midwives for compliance with the laws. Pressure from women and the publicity they gave to the issue of birth registration prompted state health officials to back the movement and to plead for help from the Bureau in achieving the 90 percent registration rate. Mothers and fathers anxiously wrote the Bureau to ask how they could obtain birth certificates for their children. . . .

Lathrop's bureau was proving itself true to Wald's vision of an activist agency, and was, in the process, creating a female dominion within the larger empire of policymaking. . . . With the Children's Bureau at its head and female voluntary organizations serving as second in command, this group of associations was establishing a monopoly over child welfare policy and childrearing advice. Moreover, in the process of reforming America's treatment of children, white, middle-class, female progressives were increasing their own professional opportunities and public authority.

Into the governmental arena, these women carried the female professional culture that had emerged from experiences in female communities such as Hull House. They maintained commitments to the combination of research and advocacy; to public service; to popularizing expert knowledge; to the interdependence of professionals and laity; and to the integration of their private and public lives. But all of these values were modified by integration into an increasingly bureaucratic order and an ever-more competitive job market. In turn, bureaucratic operations took on a peculiarly female cast at the Children's Bureau, where personal relationships both within the Bureau and with volunteers outside the agency carried great weight, and where standard operating procedure included door-to-door visits with mothers of new babies. . . .

Black and White Women Bring the Power of Motherhood to Politics

EILEEN BORIS

Yes, it is the great mother-heart reaching out to save her children from war, famine and pestilence; from death, degradation and destruction, that induces her to demand 'Votes for Women,' knowing well that fundamentally it is really a campaign for 'Votes for Children.'

> — [Mrs.] Carrie W. Clifford, Honorary President of the
> Federation of Colored Women's Clubs of Ohio, 1915.

Good women try always to do good housekeeping. Building inspectors, sanitary inspectors and food inspectors owe their positions to politics. Who then is so well informed as to how these inspectors perform their duties as the women who live in inspected districts and in inspected houses, and who buy food from inspected markets?

> — Adella Hunt Logan of the Tuskegee Women's Club, 1912.

In the early twentieth century United States, women of African descent constructed a political voice that refused to be bounded by the separation of public from private, of work from home. Just as African-American women lived lives that knew no such false divisions, so those active in national and local women's organizations drew upon their strength as mothers to argue for a legal equality that recognized their difference as black and female from the dominant white society. They offered an interpretation of political life that emphasized the role of women as saviors of the race, justifying their activity because they were mothers. Indeed, they connected women's rights, unlike men's, to the experience of motherhood.

"The Power of Motherhood: Black and White Activist Women Redefine the 'Political,'" by Eileen Boris, *Yale Journal of Law and Feminism*, Vol. 2 No. 1 (Fall 1989), pp. 25–49. Reprinted by permission of the author and the publisher.

This language of social housekeeping extended women's realm from the home into the community, city, and nation. By claiming expertise and responsibility for non-familial social spaces, black suffragists were redefining the political and demanding votes for women on the basis of their *work* as — rather than their mere being — mothers. Black suffragists' discourse of female difference provided them with a unifying vocabulary, one that co-existed with, indeed complemented, another set of metaphors based on equal rights and universal claims.

In their own context, white women activists in the early twentieth century employed a similar vocabulary. But while analysis of the speeches, writing, and programs of women reformers reveal African-American and Euro-American women sharing language, metaphor, and position in relation to lower class women of their groups, the power of "motherhood" led to different outcomes for black and white women when it came to status and rights.

. . . What does it mean that black and white activist women both created texts that relied on motherhood as image, experience, and rhetoric to forge a new, more inclusive definition of the "political"? How similar were the social programs that complemented, followed, or explained such linguistic constructs of womanhood as motherhood? What were the political consequences of a discourse that relied on the same central image — the altruistic, protective, and nurturing mother — that was embodied in the dominant male supremacist and racist culture and the judge-made law of the period, but concurrently harnessed to a reform agenda?. . .

At the turn of the century, infant mortality and mothers working outside the home were both more common in the black community than in the white. In Washington, D.C., from 1888 to 1892, the death rate among black children stood at 15 per thousand, nearly three times greater than among whites. As early as the 1870 census, at least three times as many black, compared to white, Southern urban women listed an occupation, while by the early twentieth century, up to 70% of black women were earning wages at some point during the year, which meant that five times the number of married black, compared to white, women were in the labor force. Reporting on Atlanta, Nashville, and Cambridge, Massachusetts, the United States Department of Labor found that females supported "wholly or in part" nearly 60% of black families. Most worked as domestics which led them, according to Lucy Laney at the first Atlanta University Conference in 1896, to "be away from the home all day" so that children received inadequate care from an absent and/or exhausted mother. Nearly all of the 80% of Southern blacks who were rural lived the poverty-stricken and hard life of the tenant or sharecropper. These women engaged in family labor (reproduction, dependent care, housework, and sex/affective labor), joined in the farm labor, and sometimes worked for wages for white farmers and housewives. Fertility for both rural and urban women was declining at the turn of the century, but still, among African-Americans, wives of nonagricultural men had, on average, four to six children, with rural women having about eight, actually less than white Southern women. Yet the amount of household work under non-mechanized conditions remained staggering.

At the same time, the cultural construction of womanhood took middle-class white women as the norm, even though privileged black women appeared to live by its tenets. A 1908 study by Atlanta University defended the virtue of black women but still gave credence to the stereotype of the "bad," "loose" black woman by arguing that "sexual immorality is probably the greatest single plague spot . . . ," although the study did go on to argue that, "[the plague spot's] greatest cause is slavery and the present utter disregard of a black woman's virtue and self-respect, both in law court and custom in the South." Defined by the dominant white culture as breeder and slut, though subjected to sexual harassment, rape, and intimidation, black women existed outside the boundaries of an ideal of womanhood that the very absence of black women shaped. . . .

Because black women stood outside the boundaries of "true womanhood," as defined by the dominant culture, by being black and descended from slaves (even if their actual ancestors were free), black activists' references to "highest womanhood," to "true motherhood," appeared to subvert a social script written for them by the larger culture that sought to deny them the possibility of nurturing, motherhood, and family maintenance. That is, words that seemed to reflect the hegemonic culture, that seemed to suggest a consciousness steeped in a limited domesticity, in fact challenged that dominant culture.

Thus, through organized self-help, African-American women — the most unequal and the most different in a culture where white men were and are the norm — simultaneously sought equal rights and celebrated their femaleness and their blackness. They sought to advance their race, to uplift black womanhood from the slurs of racism and the legacy of slavery, and they redefined the political and motherhood in the process. They demonstrated that difference need not stand in binary opposition to equality, that, as one feminist has put it, "equality is not the elimination of difference, and difference does not preclude equality." They understood their womanhood as a qualification for citizenship, as a characteristic that enabled them to serve the community rather than as a distinction that hampered participation in the larger social life.

Moreover, they showed that equal rights and cultural differences or diversity can co-exist. After all, they were, for the most part, strong *race* women, asserting their bonds with black men and children while claiming the same rights for which white women struggled. This maintenance of difference as distinction within the search for equal rights before the law and in social practice predominated, although activist black women shared both Victorian values (such as the work ethic and gentility) and the religiosity associated with white America. Still an equilibrium, not an opposition, between equality and difference existed in the midst of persistent sexual and class divisions within the race, along with racial divisions among women.

Formed in 1896 from the merger of the National Federation of Afro-American Women with the Colored Women's League of Washington, D.C., the National Association of Colored Women (NACW) unified the philanthropic, self-improvement, and racial uplift efforts of "bourgeois" black women until the mid-1930's when Mary McLeod Bethune, a former president, founded the National Council of Negro Women. By then, the NACW had limited its efforts to two major departments, "Mother, Home, Child" and "Negro Women in Industry," with its focus on the first of these. Yet from the start, the association had concentrated on the status of black womanhood, the activities of mothers, and the quality of home life.

. . . As "an army of organized women standing for purity and mental worth," black activists would represent womanhood, a womanhood that was "self-sacrificing," "noble," "fine cultured," "good." They would claim a motherhood previously associated with white women but which black women would redefine in universal terms. But they also stood for "colored women," with special interest in applying universal precepts of home life and womanhood to "the peculiar conditions" of a people only a quarter century removed from slavery and ever caught in the noose of racism through actual lynchings, job discrimination, poverty, and lack of educational opportunity.

Mary Church Terrell best articulated this combination of racial uplift and social motherhood, identity with the race and upholding of genteel values, in her speeches and writings as first President of the NACW between 1896 and 1901. This daughter of the South's first black millionaire, graduate of Oberlin College, speaker of numerous European languages, and first black member of the District of Columbia Board of Education combined a philosophy of activism grounded in the idea of female difference with promotion of racial and sexual equality based on rights discourse. . . . She was a feminist, a member of the National Women's Party, and a maternalist, a woman who lost three children within days of their births, who had her daughter Phyllis in 1898 in the midst of her NACW presidency, and who would adopt her brother's daughter seven years later.

For Terrell, motherhood was felt experience as well as an ideal. . . . Images of mothers, children, and homes dominated [her] NACW speeches and writings. . . . At the first Biennial Convention of the organization in 1897, she proclaimed in words repeated in her widely distributed pamphlet, "The Progress of Colored Women":

> Believing that it is only through the home that a people can become really good and truly great, the NACW shall enter that sacred domain to inculcate right principles of living and correct false views of life. . . . [M]ore homes, purer homes, better homes is the text upon which our sermons to the masses must be preached.

. . . Relying on knowledge gleaned from education and on example, Terrell urged rescue work for the race. The clubwomen would lighten the darkness of the masses. The secular became sacred; the impure, transformed by the "lightness" of the reformers' touch. Terrell's metaphor reflected both the chasm of class within the black community and the effort to lessen that gap.

But unlike their white counterparts, black women activists shared a common heritage with the poor. Like other women with class privilege, they practiced a politics of maternalism, a superiority of knowledge that led them to dictate standards for those judged below them. Yet their fate interlocked with the objects of their uplift. . . . Racism bound together the "lesser" with the "better," and may have contributed to the creation of those very categories; certainly class privilege intensified such divisions. Not surprisingly, "Lifting As We Climb" became the motto of the NACW, a motto which embodied the ties of gender and race and reflected a wish to bridge the gulf of class — but on terms set by the clubwomen themselves. . . .

Black activists took their work directly into the home. While organizations like the white National Mothers' Congress were intellectually organized by the era's thrust towards scientism, black women's own Mothers' Conferences were grounded in the black church. . . . The Conferences relied on religion to provide the text for education. Respectability became this text's major lesson.

. . . Baptist and African Methodist Episcopal women throughout Arkansas, Tennessee, Alabama, Georgia, and North Carolina established in the early 1890's fire-side schools, bible bands, and mother's clubs out of the belief that "we *must have good mothers* before we can develop a good race of people." Assuming that mothers are responsible for the moral, religious, and social development of their children, the movement under Sister Moore counseled women to train their children for God, teach them values rather than good dress, and make a happy, clean, comfortable but not luxurious home. The group's *Resolutions on Improving the House in Which We Live,* for example, called for having, if possible, more than the common one room house of the rural South, separate bedroom areas for boys and girls, and a dining room arranged so the family could sit down and eat together — goals that would be taken up by the NACW. In the various guidelines of the clubs — including the "Mother's pledge" — Victorian values of work and deportment joined with celebrations of the mother-child bond and exhortations to labor for God and the race. . . .

Mothers' clubs . . . not only improved home life but also turned into a popular vehicle for cross-class association and for social betterment among African-American women. The Ladies Auxiliary of the District of Columbia reported on their mothers' meetings, held weekly in a chapel, with coffee and rolls after short talks: "The mothers are composed of working women, taught to make their own clothing. They are permitted to pay so much per week for the material until paid for and are entitled to the garments they make. They are also instructed how to keep their own houses neat and clean." The Woman's Civic League of the State of Illinois also claimed success: "Mothers have gone out encouraged, homes have been made better and happier; good resolutions have been made and kept by those who had felt almost alone.". . .

Recognizing that the mothers of their race often had to leave their children to work, the clubwomen accepted the working mother as a worthy mother. They understood how racism and discrimination insured the inadequacy of most black men's wages, making wage-earning a necessity for thousands of black mothers. Labor issues, then, became an area for club work. . . .

Local clubs practiced a larger social motherhood that provided necessary services to the community. They established kindergartens, old age homes, working girls' lodgings, social purity projects, female protective leagues, orphanages, and settlements. Such actions were political. As educator Lucy C. Laney noted, "[w]omen are by nature fitted for teaching very young children. . . . In the kindergarten and primary school is the salvation of the race." Between 1892 and 1898, the Woman's League of Washington, D.C., for example, organized seven kindergartens serving more than a hundred children. It opened a "mending bureau" to provide sewing for the poor and conducted classes in tailoring. Like white women's clubs, it sought to establish a "diet kitchen" to provide pure milk for infants and thus curb the alarming black infant mortality rate in the nation's capitol. Clubwomen in Providence, Rhode Island organized a day nursery for mothers "who must go out to work — to leave their little ones to be cared for, instead of having them roam the streets uncared for." Other locals, such as the Progress Study Club of Kansas City, combined philanthropy with self-improvement, setting up free kindergartens and devoting one afternoon a month to their own efforts at art needlework and lace making. . . .

Applying their education to the home, especially to lower mortality rates, the women of A + M College, Normal, Alabama formed the Women's Mutual

Improvement Circle. Like the Tuskegee Women's Club, these college women (teachers, students, and faculty wives) attempted to induce women from the community to hear talks on sanitation, general health, the mother-child relationship, child development, and related matters. Cooking and sewing classes, along with friendly visiting, brought the ideal of educated motherhood to the black belt for the purpose of individual but also race improvement. "A Mother's Reception" of the Colorado state federation summarized the major themes of all the NACW affiliates, ranging from "Ventilation and Sanitation" to "The Mother's Influence in the Home." It advocated patience instead of whipping and called for "pure mothers for pure children.". . .

The centrality of motherhood to the arguments and programs of white women reformers at the turn of the century is better known. Since the 1840's, the women's movement "believed in both sexual equality and gender-defined society." Prominent reformers of the Progressive era "did not see feminism as a rejection of domesticity, but rather as an extension of woman's role and power within the home into the larger society." . . . White women activists offered an alternative vision of a nurturing society, a vision projected from the social experience of women — as defined by such women — onto the entire society. The NWTUL [National Women's Trade Union League] adopted an even more powerful image: "$acred Motherhood," a portrait of a mother running a foot-powered sewing machine in a tenement while nursing her baby. The League made a postcard of this picture which it used to fundraise milk money for the children of strikers and to publicize the plight of women workers during the great Chicago garment strike of 1910–1911.

Such visual texts emphasize how the social welfare measures which historians link to Progressivism were sold through appeals to maternalism on the part of women who represented the mothers of "the race," that is, the human — which, in general dialogue, was often equated with white — race. As Frances Perkins, later Secretary of Labor under Franklin Roosevelt, recalled, success in gaining legislation came from behaving so as to remind politicians "subconsciously of their mothers." Such images also suggest how the larger culture substituted paeans to motherhood and childlife for any adequate resolution of the conflict between capitalist development and the real needs of mothers and children. . . .

Yet actual implementation of programs produced a more complex understanding of motherhood, one shaped by recipients and not merely by reformers. To take one example, those fighting tenement homework and sweated labor believed that waged labor had no place in real homes; it degraded motherhood, childhood, and family life. Immigrant women, in contrast, regarded making artificial flowers, sewing garments, and the hundred other activities they performed for wages at home as enabling them to fulfill their duty as mothers and sought to convince judges and investigators to allow them to continue such labor at home. . . . Motherhood became contested terrain, the ground upon which reformers battled both capitalists and the immigrant working class. . . .

Perhaps the power of motherhood reached its rhetorical heights in the women's peace movement, also of the World War I era. Founders of the Women's Peace Party (WPP) in 1915 (of which Mary Church Terrell was a member), believed that women's qualities as women — their actual or potential motherhood, their ability to talk things out rather than resolve disagreements through violence — generated a desire to preserve life. Women pacifists criticized American foreign policy on the basis of their experience with nurturing and their expectation of what it took to perform that act. Motherhood, then, provided a moral basis for action, a direction for politics.

If the discourse of white women reformers promised a new vision of the industrial city, indeed, a new world, it failed to escape its ties to the dominant culture's conception of womanhood as embodied in the law. . . . The famous Brandeis brief in *Muller v. Oregon* . . . reflected pre-existing understandings of women's place and female difference. The arguments of Josephine Goldmark of the National Consumers' League (NCL), who researched much of the brief, reinforced the idea that women were different from men. But her arguments that women were weaker than men sprang from the reality that women working in factories were injuring themselves and, because they were unorganized, had no recourse outside of the law. For Goldmark, using women's alleged "weakness" was a practical tactic in seeking to ensure that the law would improve the lives of these otherwise unprotected, suffering workers.

Significantly, the decision in *Muller* justified maximum hours for women on the basis of protecting motherhood; women carried with them responsibility for "the well-being of the race." *Muller* represents the sanctification of motherhood which had existed for nearly a century alongside women's attempts to increase their power through their position as mothers. However, the hours laws upheld in *Muller,* as well as attempts at minimum wage bills and exclusionary legislation like night work laws, applied only to limited groups of women because the legislation exempted from coverage agricultural, non-profit, and usually domestic workers (though not necessarily the black-dominated occupation of laundresses in laundries). That these were the very jobs held by women of color further suggests how the term "mother" in the judge-made discourse referred to white women. Laws which protected immigrant working women who labored outside the home, then, did not apply to the women on the plantation who were the subjects of efforts by the NACW to uplift the race.

Nearly a century ago, black activist women understood the complex relation between gaining civil rights and maintaining one's heritage, culture, and self-determination. . . . African-American women did not discredit motherhood as a female experience shaped by male demands; rather, they based their political programs as well as their epistemology on their own understanding of it. . . .

White women reformers did not have to defend their reputations as mothers, as black women activists often did, because the dominant culture found in them the prototype for "woman" and "mother." White women could use dominant cultural conceptions as a political tool for exposing the gaps between sentimentality and reality, as embodied in the image of $acred Motherhood. But, working to improve the actual conditions of mothers and children, as did the black women's clubs, white women still ran up against a difference standard defined by men, including white male judges.

In the case of white activist women, the male dominance of the time shaped both their understandings of difference and equality, which helps to explain the disappointing impact of their efforts. Women's culture, an alternative set of values based on women's perceptions and experiences as mothers, failed to transform the relations between the sexes or usher in an era of gender justice. Its understanding of motherhood — equated with peace and social nurturance — never overturned the hegemonic culture's equation of motherhood with biology and female dependence on men. Instead, the concept of women as mothers or potential mothers justified limiting women's labor market options without elevating the value of motherhood or nurturing. Social programs would protect working women, but not mothers in the home. Home and workplace remained separate spheres, with the male values of the workplace conflated with the whole of social life.

The work of bourgeois black women also must be evaluated in the context of unequal power relations. To deny the reality of patriarchy, or male power over women, would be to romanticize black male-female relations and to ignore the power of ruling-class white men over all other groups in the society. Yet black women's reliance on motherhood, a status and experience disrupted and denied to their mothers and grandmothers, challenged the subordination of African-Americans. Like their white counterparts, they addressed the actual needs of mothers and children. Even though their own classism, along with the racism and sexism of others, sometimes stymied their efforts, the history of black activist women at the turn of the century suggests that justice and difference can co-exist under the banner of self-determination, if not liberation. This history may encourage us to replace an equality standard that fails to incorporate the historic position of African-Americans and of women with a justice standard that incorporates the ethics of care.

※ *F U R T H E R   R E A D I N G*

Joyce Antler, "After College, What? New Graduates and the Family Claim," *American Quarterly* XXXII (1980), 409–434

Paula Baker, "The Domestication of Politics: Women and American Political Society, 1780–1920," *American Historical Review* 89 (June 1984), 620–647

G. J. Barker-Benfield, "Mother Emancipator: The Meaning of Jane Addams' Sickness and Cure," *Journal of Family History* IV (1979), 395–420

Karen Blair, *The Clubwoman as Feminist: True Womanhood Redefined* (1980)

———, *The Torchbearers: Women and Their Amateur Arts Associations in America, 1890–1930* (1994)

Jill K. Conway, "Women Reformers and American Culture, 1870–1930," *Journal of Social History* V (1971–1972), 164–177

Allen Davis, *Spearheads for Reform: The Social Settlements and the Progressive Movement, 1890–1914* (1967)

———, *American Heroine: The Life and Legend of Jane Addams* (1973)

Noralee Frankel and Nancy S. Dye, eds., *Gender, Class, Race, and Reform in the Progressive Era* (1992)

Robert Frankfort, *Collegiate Women: Domesticity and Career in Turn-of-the Century America* (1977)

Estelle Freedman, "Separatism as Strategy: Female Institution Building and American Feminism, 1870–1930," *Feminist Studies* V (1979), 512–529

Paula Giddings, *When and Where I Enter: The Impact of Black Women on Race and Sex in America* (1984)

Linda Gordon, "Black and White Visions of Welfare: Women's Welfare Activism, 1890–1945," *Journal of American History* 78 (September 1991), 559–590

Dolores Hayden, *The Grand Domestic Revolution: A History of Feminist Design for American Homes, Neighborhoods, and Cities* (1981)

Evelyn Brooks Higginbotham, *Righteous Discontent: The Women's Movement in the Black Baptist Church* (1993)

Aileen Kraditor, *Ideas of the Women Suffrage Movement* (1978)

Ellen Lageman, *A Generation of Women: Education in the Lives of Progressive Reformers* (1979)

Elizabeth Lasch-Quinn, *Black Neighbors: Race and the Limits of Reform in the American Settlement House Movement, 1890–1945* (1993)

Gerda Lerner, "Early Community Work of Black Club Women," *Journal of Negro History* LIX (1974), 158–167

Rivka Shpak Lissak, *Pluralism and Progressives: Hull House and the New Immigrants, 1890–1919* (1989)

David Morgan, *Suffragists and Democrats* (1972)

Rosalind Rosenberg, *Beyond Separate Spheres: The Intellectual Roots of Modern Feminism* (1982)

Sheila Rothman, *Woman's Proper Place* (1978)

John Rousmaniere, "Cultural Hybrid in the Slums: The College Woman and the Settlement House, 1889–1914," *American Quarterly* XXII (1970), 45–66

Dorothy Salem, *To Better Our World: Black Women in Organized Reform, 1890–1920* (1990)

Anne Firor Scott, *Natural Allies: Women's Associations in American History* (1992)

Margaret Gibbons Wilson, *The American Woman in Transition: The Urban Influence, 1870–1920* (1979)

Allis R. Wolfe, "Women, Consumerism, and the National Consumer's League in the Progressive Era, 1900–1923," *Labor History* XVI (1975), 378–392

Marlene Stein Wortman, "Domesticating the Nineteenth-Century American City," *Prospects* III (1977), 531–572

CHAPTER
11

Work Culture in the Early Twentieth Century

During the early twentieth century women became a significant presence in the American labor force, accounting for nearly 22 percent of all wage earners by 1930. Though they were not yet welcome in the majority of occupations and professions, millions of women found employment as factory operatives, retail clerks, and clerical workers.

Women workers had not always been so conspicuous. For most of the nineteenth century the labor force was overwhelmingly male; women were limited to a handful of occupations, the most common being domestic service. But in the decades after the Civil War the rise of industrialization created millions of new jobs in manufacturing and commerce. Many of these positions required only modest skills or strength and were highly repetitive. Employers quickly hired single women to fill them, reasoning that "working girls" would accept low wages and monotony with fewer complaints than would men. To some extent, these assumptions proved correct. Since women were usually ignored by unions, most could ill afford to complain about their wages or the conditions of their work. Moreover, because the majority of working women planned to work only until they married, they felt they had no vested interest in pursuing formal improvements in the workplace. With great advantage accruing to employers, then, the industrial workforce became highly sex segregated. In addition, women were segregated among themselves by ethnicity, class, and race. Working-class and European immigrant women flocked to factory positions, while middle-class women with some high-school education sought white-collar employment. Prevented by racial prejudice from taking jobs in either of these fields, black women (married and single) filled the domestic-service jobs abandoned by their more fortunate sisters.

Although historians have recognized the disadvantages under which women labored in the early twentieth century, recently they have begun evaluating what the experience of wage earning actually meant to women workers and the society around them. Did contemporary observers consider women's growing presence in the labor force a sign of meaningful change in gender roles or social relations? Did wage work alter women's sense of self and their relations with family members and the wider community? Were women able to challenge or subvert disagreeable features of their work despite lacking the formal authority to do so? Finally, despite the intentions of their employers, did women discover in patterns of segregation a basis for gender or workplace solidarity?

※ D O C U M E N T S

By 1891 the number of young women working in clerical positions had risen so dramatically that *Cosmopolitan* magazine noted the trend in a lengthy article by Clara Lanza, reprinted here as the first document. Harriet Brunkhurst, writing for the *Ladies Home Journal* in 1910, wrote sympathetically (in what is the second document) of the new difficulties that young women were encountering at home as they joined the workforce. In the third document, Fannie Barrier Williams comments on the employment difficulties that black women faced in 1903; she urges them to make the best of segregation and to treat domestic service as a field open to "unlimited improvement." The fourth document, from 1914, is a report from *The Survey* magazine on New York City's first organized protest of unemployed women, in which participants, refusing to submit passively to their plight, demanded that they be given jobs. In a 1929 article from *The Nation* that serves as the fifth document, Marion Bonner reports on the women who joined the textile strikes that were taking place in a number of southern states. Observing a group of protesters who had traveled to the Southern Summer School for Women Workers in North Carolina to speak about their strike experience with other women wage earners, Bonner emphasizes the terrible working and living conditions of the strikers as well as their indomitable spirit.

Clara Lanza, "Women Clerks in New York," 1891

The close of the nineteenth century brings us face to face with many noteworthy progressive movements that point triumphantly to the promotion of free thought; but perhaps none is more vital and significant than the progress that is based upon a high standard of womanly independence and is the direct outcome of a purely feminine inspiration. With the increase of educational advantages has come a corresponding evolution in habits and manners. Old-time prejudices lie buried. Work has become fashionable. By work, I do not mean dilettante dalliance with the implements of labor, but actual exercise of brain and muscle as a means of livelihood. Feminine dignity is nowadays in nowise imperiled by legitimate employment used as a means of existence. It is an accepted fact, and one that is wholly in accordance with a proper American spirit of democracy, that girls should be educated with a view to earning their own living. . . .

Among the woman workers in New York there are none who afford a more interesting study than the vast army of clerks; the work of a clerk being admirably adapted to the sex. You may count almost on the fingers of one hand the number of years that have elapsed since the women clerks appeared. Yet so prevalent have they become in all our large cities, that one might say they have entirely superseded the men in this particular department. Nine employers out of ten prefer women as clerks. If this statement appears to be a sweeping one, it can be verified by the fact that the demand for women as clerical workers is steadily on the increase, while men stand a comparatively poor chance of securing positions. The circumstance is amply justified by many reasons, not the least of these being the superior quality of the work performed by women.

Speaking not long ago, to the head of a large publishing house where women were employed as cashiers and book-keepers, I ventured to ask whether the women compared favorably with men in the fulfilment of their respective duties.

"Women," was the answer, "are much to be preferred for a number of reasons. They are capable and industrious, and, so far as my personal experience goes, absolutely reliable. Besides, a woman is more conscientious about her work. . . .

"Men are troublesome. They complain about trifles that a woman wouldn't notice. The office boys don't suit, or the temperature of the building is too hot or too cold, or the light is not properly adjusted. Then, if they have a slight headache, they stay at home. Most of them are married, and their wives fall ill, or their mother-in-law comes on a visit, and all these things are made an excuse for absence. The women come whether they have headaches or not. They never want a day off to attend a baseball match. They undertake the work with a full understanding of what is required of them, and they are steadfast in the performance of their duties. We treat them well and never refuse to grant them any trifling favor. There is only one thing we exact over and above their business qualifications. We do not employ a woman unless she lives at home with her family.

"This has the appearance of injustice, but if you reflect a moment you will recollect that the temptations to which a woman living by herself is exposed in a great city are manifold and dangerous, and for our own sake we find it necessary that our clerks, like Caesar's wife, should be above suspicion as to character and antecedents. We must know all about them and their families." . . .

The above proved conclusively that capability and a readiness to work did not in every instance insure a desirable occupation to the woman who sought it. A girl who had no "family," and who was obliged to depend upon her individual exertions for the food she ate and the clothes she wore, could not hope to get any position of trust. A woman who handles large sums of money that do not belong to her must be surrounded on all sides by a definite respectability; and while it sounds a bit quixotic to insist that she must have family connections over and above all her other virtues, it is perfectly just in the abstract. Unfortunately, respectable relations cannot be manufactured to order; therefore she who has them not would better become a typewriter, a stenographer, or a telegraph operator.

The large schools of stenography and typewriting turn out annually hundreds of women who rank easily with the most accomplished men clerks. Typewriting, being in great demand, is perhaps the most lucrative of the minor employments open to women. It is claimed that the market is decidedly overstocked with typewriters, and that there are not half enough positions for the largely increasing number of candidates. But this is a mistake. The market may be overcrowded with women who claim to be typewriters and stenographers, but in reality there is not a sufficient number of well-trained and capable clerks to supply the demand.

"By far the greatest difficulty I have to contend with," says Miss Seymour, who presides over the Union School of stenography and typewriting, "is to keep my best operators with me. Although I pay them liberal salaries and do everything I can to secure their services permanently, they are in constant receipt of offers that men would be glad to receive. Many pupils of the school receive offers of positions at salaries varying from eight to twelve dollars a week before they have finished the six months' course of instruction. I mention this for the purpose of showing how popular the employment of women clerks has become, that is, if they are properly trained for the work. It is positive that an intelligent woman is especially fitted for clerical work. If she does not succeed her failure is due to faulty training. Business men tell me they prefer women as shorthand amanuenses for one particular reason. It is because, contrary to accepted tradition, women are less likely than men to disclose the business secrets of their employers. Then, too, they are more faithful and more apt to remain for a long period in the service of one employer.

"Of course, a number of employers engage women under the prevailing impression that they will work for lower wages; but while this is true in the majority of cases, it is equally true that efficient women can command as high salaries as men, particularly if they refuse to work for less, which is usually the case."

Typewriting and stenography are not of themselves very difficult of comprehension or execution, and it does not take long in order to familiarize one's self with either; but a clerk who wishes to succeed must know many more things. She must possess a ready knowledge of English composition and orthography. She must be able to punctuate properly, and above all, be quick to grasp an idea. Large numbers of girls spend their last penny in an attempt to fit themselves for clerical work, only to discover that, owing to their rudimentary education and total inaptitude, it is impossible for them to fill any responsible position. A few study and persevere, contenting themselves with a meagre salary, five or six dollars a week perhaps, and thus gradually work themselves up to a higher rung of the ladder. But there are scores of discouraged plodders who have not the spirit of hopeful aspiration to guide them, and these fall by the wayside and sink into obscurity, while their braver sisters pass on to victory. . . .

Most clerks have comfortable homes with their parents, and numbers of them enjoy not only the ordinary necessaries of life, but a considerable portion of its luxuries. As a rule, the clerk's entire salary is at her disposal for her personal requirements. She must dress neatly, and then there are petty vanities that every woman likes to indulge, no matter what her station may be. The woman clerk is rarely frivolous in her demeanor. She cannot afford frivolity; the mere fact of her self-dependence invests her with a certain outward dignity that one sees seldom displaced even when brought into collision with the powerful exuberance of youthful animal spirits. Not that she is prim and puritanical. She does not eschew legitimate pleasure nor regard amusement as superfluous. But she seems impressed by the consciousness that being forced to trust her mental resources for whatever she now has and is destined to enjoy in the future constitutes an inspiring duty that is not the less evident or sacred because it happens to devolve entirely upon herself. Temptations descend and threaten her, temptations whose very existence is ignored by those who, in the peaceful serenity of home and protected from the world, are dimly aware of the actual meaning of life, and faintly appreciate the devastating force that lurks about, seeking so-called "independence" for its prey.

If individual fidelity marks an interesting step on the road to progress, a great deal also depends upon judicious coöperation. There are several clubs and societies in New York that are maintained by clerical workers for the purpose of mutual advancement. One or two of these admit men as well as women to membership. These associations offer much that is both attractive and useful. A clerk, typewriter or stenographer who is out of employment can practice at the club rooms. At a stated evening of each week literary exercises are conducted for the benefit of those who desire to attend, and once a month some distinguished lecturer is invited to address the society. The initiation fee is one dollar, and additional monthly dues of fifty cents are demanded. . . .

The matrimonial achievements of women clerks have become a species of national pleasantry. So many women employed in offices and mercantile houses have married men with whom they would hardly have come in contact in another sphere, that the subject has long ceased to be a matter of speculation, and has gradually drifted from witty comment to the more sober attention that bespeaks a recognized fact. . . .

From all I am able to gather the girls make good wives. There is nothing in clerical training that detracts from the finest womanly qualities, and men have outgrown their admiration for feminine helplessness and have come to look upon independence as something worth having. Clerical training educates the mind to accuracy in details, punctuality in the daily affairs of life, economy in the adjustment of time and quickness of perception. Perhaps this is the reason why so many men choose a wife amid the deft-fingered clerks in preference to the society misses. The woman clerk has studied the value of concentration, learned the lesson that incites to work when a burden bears heavily upon her strength. She knows the worth of self-reliance, and the fine courage that springs from the consciousness that a good result has been accomplished by a well-directed effort.

Harriet Brunkhurst on the Home Problems of "Business Girls," 1910

That the girl who goes to business frequently faces home problems more difficult than those she meets in an office is a fact that comparatively few people recognize. The status of the girl in the home changes when she becomes a breadwinner, yet there are many homes where the new order not only is not accepted, but is also stoutly combated. Perhaps the main difficulty arises from the fact that although the girl is out in the world and may develop capabilities and breadth unattainable to the one whose life lies in a narrower groove, yet she is still but a girl, shrinking, sensitive, possessed of all the whims, fancies and weaknesses that have marked her sex from the beginning of things.

The mother whose daughter goes to business, as do the husband and sons, finds it difficult to realize that anything is changed beyond the mere fact that the girl is away all day. When she returns she slips into her old place; not "all in a minute" can the mother bring herself to acknowledge that the daughter's position in the home is, in fact, precisely like that of her brother. If the mother is long in recognizing this so is the rest of the world. Meanwhile the daughter may be having a hard time.

A certain little woman whose daughter is the household provider has a grievance that seems to her almost insupportable. The daughter, Rose, is advertising manager in a big store; she has a private office, a stenographer, errand-boys and clerical workers to assist her; she employs no heavier implement than pen or scissors; her hours are from nine to five, six, seven — possibly ten at night, as the occasion may demand. She earns a comfortable salary, and she pays into the family exchequer whatever sum is necessary, with never a question as to where the money goes.

The mother is careful in her expenditure and an excellent housekeeper; she refuses to keep a maid because they have no room for her, but the rough work is done by outside hands. Her ideas of housekeeping demand rising at five-thirty A.M. She sleeps lightly, having a midday siesta, and she prefers to do her work in the early morning. She is ready for breakfast at six-thirty. There is no necessity for Rose to breakfast before eight, but the mother begins each day with a complaint at the late breakfast hour. This point of difference, trivial in itself, causes continual irritation.

Rose, capable executive head of a big department though she is, simply cannot fight the matter to a finish. The same girl who calmly gives orders right and left, once the office is reached, chokes with tears and has not a word to say when the little mother, who does not know even the rudiments of business, tells her that she is indolent and selfish. Rose knows that she herself is right — that she must have recreation and rest; deprivation of her morning sleep might be serious to the point of a breakdown — and she must not be ill, for she is the breadwinner. It is the principle of the thing, the mother avers, and she means just the best in the world, of course. But there is only one right way, and that is her way.

This mother is overlooking some very pertinent facts, even excluding the unhappiness she causes her daughter. Rose is actually, by right of her earnings, the head of the house; yet the mother, who would yield without question to husband or son occupying the same position, debates Rose's every movement simply because she is a girl. Were Rose to take her courage in her own hands and face her mother it would avail nothing. So she accepts an unnecessary unhappiness simply because she can see no solution. If the mother could see things in their true light she would be appalled.

There is another mother whose daughter, Cecil, carries a similar burden in the home. The latter finds that many little economies are necessary in order to conduct the home liberally. With fingers as nimble as her brain she finds a woman's innumerable tasks about her wardrobe — lace to be mended, fresh ribbons needed, a stitch here and there that she may be immaculate and insure the longest possible service from her clothing. When Cecil returns from her work, however, she is too weary to attempt any sewing. If she is to remain bright and alert, hold her position and not become ill, she must have relaxation in the evening. She goes to the theater, opera, concerts, has friends to see her, or spends a quiet evening with a book. At nine in the morning she is at her desk, bright-eyed and with a clear brain.

That their support is absolutely dependent upon Cecil's remaining "fit" the mother knows; but that recreation is necessary to maintain the condition she cannot grasp. Consequently, when Cecil takes Sunday morning for the little fussy tasks about her wardrobe the mother sees only sheer perversity, to say nothing of incipient depravity, about it. And there is the incontrovertible fact that Cecil "has all her evenings free." Moreover the mother wails: "She never has time to do anything for me!" It does not occur to her that she is asking of Cecil, whose strength already is fully taxed, more than she would ask from a man. She is the type of woman who would say of her husband: "John is so tired when he returns from work!" That Cecil may be tired she never considers. . . .

One of the most difficult phases of the situation appears with the subject of housework. While going to business absolves the daughter, even as it does the husband and sons, it is a fact not so fully recognized as it might be. To the mother seven or eight hours of work followed by complete release appear so easy in comparison with her own lot that a few additional duties seem no more than fair. Moreover there is the family, its relations and friends, to make the contention should the mother take a different view of the matter.

Maud's mother, for instance, is criticised severely by her relatives for her careful fostering of her daughter's strength.

"It is perfectly ridiculous for you to iron Maud's shirtwaists," declared an elderly aunt. "She doesn't work half as hard as you do, and it wouldn't hurt her a bit to do her ironing in the evening. We used to do ours, and we were none the worse for it."

Maud's mother made no reply as she hung the sixth white blouse in a row with its mates. The years had gifted her with a sweet wisdom the other had not attained, and she knew well the futility of argument.

"I did my own fine ironing at home," she said afterward, "but there was never an afternoon or a morning when I could not go out if I chose. A task in the evening, unless it was for our pleasure, we never knew. Maud goes to the office in sun and in storm; she has never a day or an afternoon, except holidays, when she is free to do as she pleases. Days of headache or other slight indisposition, when I would have been on the sofa or comfortably in bed, she trudges bravely away. Often she is too tired even for recreation, to say nothing of work, when she returns in the evening."

"But six white shirtwaists!" exclaimed the listener.

"She works in an office where the furnishings are of mahogany, with rich rugs, polished brass and other things in harmony. How long could she hold her position were she to appear in a soiled blouse?"

Now that was only plain, practical good sense, clear-eyed recognition of pertinent facts; but astonishingly few people can boast it.

Mabel's mother, for example, takes a different and a more usual view of a similar situation. True, her work is far heavier than is that of Maud's mother, but Mabel works eight hours a day while Maud works seven. She is home in time to assist in preparing dinner, she helps with the dishes afterward, and there are innumerable little "odd jobs" that frequently keep her busy until nine o'clock. If she goes out there is a mad rush to finish the dinner work and be dressed sufficiently early. She does not go out very much, however, for she must rise at six-thirty, assist with the preparation of breakfast, and be at the office by eight-thirty o'clock.

That Mabel is fagged continually is inevitable. "I am so tired, Mother," she said once, when an additional bit of work was suggested.

"Aren't you ashamed to say that when you see how your mother works?" demanded the father.

Mabel did the required work with no further comment, although the tears smarted in her eyes, her heart ached with the injustice of the taunt, and her weary little body seemed ready to fail her. She could earn her own living, but she could not fight her own battles. . . .

The problems these girls face are delicate, whichever way they are viewed. Perhaps part of the trouble arises from non-recognition of arrival at "years of discretion." We are all of us individuals first, and members of a family afterward. The family fosters and develops, but it may hamper freedom as well. There must be dependence upon one another, there must be community of interests; but in the successful home there must also be a clearly-defined recognition of individual existence. The girl attains her "majority" when she goes to business, and the home must learn when to "let go." It is not a question of independence — a word often misapplied and misunderstood — but simply one of self-reliance, and acknowledgment of the girl's right to it.

Fannie Barrier Williams, "The Problem of Employment for Negro Women," 1903

It can be broadly said that colored women know how to work, and have done their full share of the paid and unpaid service rendered to the American people by the Negro race. This is a busy world; the world's work is large, complicated, and increasing. The demand for the competent in all kinds of work is never fully supplied. Woman is constantly receiving a larger share of the work to be done. The field for her skill, her endurance, her finer instincts and faithfulness is ever enlarging; and she has become impatient of limitations, except those imposed by her own physical condition. In this generalization, colored women, of course, are largely excepted. For reasons too well understood here to be repeated, ours is a narrow sphere. While the kinds and grades of occupation open to all women of white complexion are almost beyond enumeration, those open to our women are few in number and mostly menial in quality. The girl who is white and capable is in demand in a thousand places. The capable Negro girl is usually not in demand. This is one of the stubborn facts of to-day. . . .

In the city of Chicago domestic service is the one occupation in which the demand for colored women exceeds the supply. In one employment office during the past year there were 1,500 applications for colored women and only 1,000 of this number were supplied. Girls of other nationalities do not seem to compete with colored women as domestics. It is probably safe to say that every colored woman who is in any way competent can find good employment. Her wages for general housework range from four to seven dollars per week, while a good cook receives from seven to ten dollars. Now what is the condition of this service? The two most important things are that the wages paid are higher than those given for the same grade of intelligence in any other calling; and that colored women can command almost a monopoly of this employment.

It might be safe to presume that as our women are so much in demand for this service they give perfect satisfaction. In considering that it is important to bear in mind that there are two kinds of colored women who perform domestic service: — First, there are those who take to the work naturally and whose training and habits make them perfectly satisfied with it; and second, those who have had more or less education and who are ambitious to do something in the line of "polite occupations." The women of the latter class do not take to domestic service very kindly. They do not enter the service with any pride. They feel compelled to do this work because they can find nothing else to do. They are always sensitive as to how they may be regarded by their associates and friends, and shrink from the term servant as something degrading "per se." . . .

It is of course an easy thing to condemn our young women who have been fairly educated and have had good home training, because they prefer idleness to domestic service, but I am rather inclined to think we must share in that condemnation. If our girls work for wages in a nice home, rather than in a factory or over a counter, they are ruthlessly scorned by their friends and acquaintances. Our young men, whose own occupations, by the way, will not always bear scrutiny, will also give them the cut direct, so that between the scorn of their associates and the petty tyranny of the housewife, the colored girls who enter domestic service are compelled to have more than ordinary strength of character.

But after all is said, I believe that it is largely in the power of the young woman herself to change and elevate the character of domestic service. She certainly cannot improve it by taking into it ignorance, contempt, and inefficiency. There is no reason why a woman of character, graciousness, and skill should not make her work as a domestic as respectable and as highly regarded as the work of the girl behind a department-store counter. For example, if by special training in domestic service, a girl can cook so well and do everything about a house so deftly and thoroughly that she will be called a real home helper and an invaluable assistant, it is in her power, with her intelligent grasp upon the possibilities of her position, to change the whole current of public opinion in its estimate of domestic service. . . .

When domestic service becomes a profession, as it surely will, by the proper training of those who follow it, what will be the condition of colored girls who would participate in its benefits? It is now time to prepare ourselves to answer this question. In my opinion, the training for this new profession should be elevated to the dignity and importance of the training in mathematics and grammar and other academic studies. Our girls must be made to feel that there is no stepping down when they become professional housekeepers. The relative dignity, respectability, and honor of this profession should first be taught in our schools. As it is now, the young woman in school or college knows that if she enters domestic service, she loses the relationships that she has formed. But schools of domestic science cannot do it all. The everyday man and woman who make society must change their foolish notions as to what is the polite thing for a young woman to do. The kind of stupidity that calls industrial education drudgery is the same kind of stupidity that looks upon the kitchen as a place for drudges. We must learn that the girl who cooks our meals and keeps our houses sweet and beautiful deserves just as high a place in our social economy as the girl who makes our gowns and hats, or the one who teaches our children. In what I have said on this particular phase of our industrial life, I do not wish to be understood as advocating the restriction of colored girls to house service, even when that service is elevated to the rank of a profession. My only plea is that we shall protect and respect our girls who honestly and intelligently enter this service, either from preference or necessity. . . .

There is still another consideration which suggests the importance to the colored people of taking the lead in helping to improve and elevate this service. Race prejudice is kept up and increased in thousands of instances by the incompetent and characterless women who are engaged in this work. While there are thousands of worthy and really noble women in domestic service who enjoy the confidence and affection of their employers, there is a large percentage of colored women who, by their general unworthiness, help to give the Negro race a bad name, for white people North and South are very apt to estimate the entire race from the standpoint of their own servant girls. When intelligence takes the place of ignorance, and good manners, efficiency, and self-respect take the place of shiftlessness and irresponsibility in American homes, one of the chief causes of race prejudice will be removed.

It should also be borne in mind that the colored girl who is trained in the arts of housekeeping is also better qualified for the high duties of wifehood and motherhood.

Let me say by the way of summary that I have dwelt mostly upon the opportunities of domestic service for the following reasons: —

1. It is the one field in which colored women meet with almost no opposition. It is ours almost by birthright.
2. The compensation for this service, in Northern communities at least, is higher than that paid for average clerkships in stores and offices.
3. The service is susceptible of almost unlimited improvement and elevation.
4. The nature of the work is largely what we make it.
5. White women of courage and large intelligence are lifting domestic service to a point where it will have the dignity of a profession, and colored women are in danger, through lack of foresight, of being relegated to the position of scrub women and dishwashers.
6. The colored girl who has no taste or talent for school teaching, dressmaking, or manicuring is in danger of being wasted in idleness, unless we can make domestic service worthy of her ambition and pride.
7. There can be no feature of our race problem more important than the saving of our young women; we can perhaps excuse their vanities, but idleness is the mildew on the garment of character.
8. Education has no value to human society unless it can add importance and respectability to the things we find to do.
9. Though all the factories and offices close their doors at our approach, this will be no calamity if we are strong enough to so transform the work we must do that it shall become an object of envy and emulation to those who now deny us their industrial fellowship.

The Survey Reports on a Protest of Unemployed Women in New York City, 1914

The meeting in Cooper Union on January 28, under the auspices of the Woman's Trade Union League was the first organized protest of unemployed women and girls ever held in New York city, perhaps in America.

The speakers on the platform railed against capitalism and the present system of industry. In turn they laid unemployment at the door of child labor, excessive hours of work, and capitalist ownership. They could do nothing toward the alleviation of the "problem," and they declared as much.

The audience listened grimly. The simple stolid demand was for work — "We want work, not charity," was displayed on a placard over the platform where Lincoln spoke.

These unemployed women had drifted into the hall with the half-hearted hope that in a mysterious way the mayor or the governor or some other vague potentate would dole out jobs to each in turn. Whatever the causes, whatever the cure, the solid, immediate fact was this roomful of workless women.

Department store help, stenographers, garment workers, scrub women, widows with children, young, middle-aged and old women of all races, nationalities and creeds followed each other in describing heart-rending experiences of looking for work. They told stories of sordid misery, of hungry children, of cold and suffering, of ragged clothing and broken shoes, of ceaseless, agonizing search for the work that was not forthcoming, of the alternatives of suicide or prostitution.

A German woman, thin and stoop shouldered, but dressed in tidy black, told how she and her fifteen-year-old daughter had been living since Christmas on three dollars a week. At one time she made fifteen and eighteen dollars a week as a dressmaker, but since her husband's death she had barely been able to support her daughter.

"My girl," she cried brokenly, "she is as pure as gold and I must keep her so. Everywhere I go they say I am too old to work, and my daughter they say she is too young. If I am too old do I have to die? Does my daughter have to die? No work anywhere. What can I do? That's what I say."

A young girl who said she had been out of work since October told of her experiences in trying to get a job as a saleswoman. She repeated the insults heaped upon her by some employers who told her that so young and pretty a girl should not be looking for work.

Another woman, who speaks several languages, said that she was told in one place that if she did not want a $6-a-week job offered to her she could join the bread line as there were many girls anxious to get work at $4 and $5 a week.

"It is suicidal," declared a frail young girl. "In my shop, braid-making, they get a girl fifteen years old to tend ten machines. She don't last long. She soon breaks down and then they throw her out and get a fresh one."

And so they told their stories, one after another: a laundry worker who had not been able to get work since she was blacklisted in the laundry strike two years ago; a sickly girl who spoke for two or three minutes and then sat down, explaining in a weak voice that she was no longer able to stand on her feet; a machine operator who had made complete shirt waists for fifty cents a dozen until she could stand the place no longer; a stenographer who had been turned aside for a younger girl.

Two or three things reiterated by woman after woman emphasized certain discouragements in the search for work which were common to many present. One was the way in which newspaper "want ads" and the employment agencies, without any discrimination, send hundreds of applicants to one open position. Another was the time wasted by superintendents and managers in "taking a girl's pedigree" when there was absolutely no idea of hiring her.

A noticeable feature of the meeting was the fact that Christmas was the starting point of unemployment for most of the girls and that a large number of speakers were department store employes.

The number of women present was not so large as some had expected, but the meeting was in deadly earnest. It closed with a resolution, adopted by a rising vote, reciting that "Whereas thousands of working women and young girls who are dependent upon themselves for support," are idle; "we, the unemployed women and girls in mass meeting assembled, do hereby call upon the city and state authorities to provide us with work. . . . We emphatically protest against our enforced idleness."

One outcome of the Cooper Union meeting was a permanent conference on unemployment, which has established a free employment bureau for women and girls.

Marion Bonner on the Women of the Southern Textile Strikes, 1929

"We're fightin' for our rights. We didn't want no strike. We went to the president and asked him to give us a ten-hour day without cuttin' our wages and to take back the fifteen men and women he fired for joinin' the union." . . .

A thin, wiry woman with a pinched face that looked at least ten years older than it was, was talking to a group of faculty and students of the Southern Summer School for Women Workers in Industry. On July 11 when the school began its session of six weeks at Burnsville, North Carolina, about six hundred and fifty men and women joined the United Textile Workers Union and went on strike against conditions in the Marion Manufacturing Company. Some of the strike leaders, knowing that the Southern Summer School was teaching economics, public speaking, and health, brought seven girls over the forty miles of beautiful mountain road to the school.

. . . Five girls from Elizabethton, Tennessee, who had been in the strikes in the Glanzstoff and Bemberg silk mills, mountain born, too, understood her and nodded approvingly. Girls from cities, in some cases making no more than ten dollars a week, but dressed in silk and speaking the language of cities, looked at her half in amusement, half in admiration. Some of the girls from Marion, seeing the amused glances, became self-conscious and whispered that they wished "J——— wasn't so talky." . . .

Gradually her intelligence, earnestness, intensity won the respect of most of the students. Other girls from Marion emerged from their protective shells and grew communicative. Sensitive, proud, feeling a chasm between themselves and some of the girls who had lived in the cities, they would often anticipate superiority and at first were on their guard. Girls who felt superior because they had toilets and bathrooms in their houses and did not have to draw their water from a street pump, and who had gone through several years of high school and had heard of grammar became interested in the struggle of these women of Marion to get better conditions and began to listen attentively to their speeches. . . .

One of the Marion girls described her work on the farm. "We raised corn, potatoes, cane, and tobacco. We also had lots of hay to take care of. My two older sisters married, and my two older brothers got jobs and left home to make wages. That left just my sister and me out of a family of eight large enough to work. My mother's health failed her and so my sister and I had most of the house-work to do and to help father on the outside. We got up at four o'clock every morning to get the house-work done, the cows milked, the chickens fed to get to the fields early. We would hoe corn all day long; come home at night and help mother get supper. Very often she would have beans picked or apples gathered so we could string beans after supper or peel apples to be dried. I have helped father saw wood time after time and I have driven a team of horses day after day hauling rock, hay, corn. After we got our crop planted father would get a job somewhere and tell us what he wanted done on the farm."

Those who have known life back in the mountains, on poor hillside farms that furnished inadequate nourishment to the large families living on them, know too the inadequacy of the mental food. Interference of work at home, short terms, teachers not too well trained — it is amazing that they learned to read, write, and figure. The following experience related by one of the girls from Marion is representative.

"I started to school at the age of seven. The first three or four years I attended regularly but after I got large enough to work and after my sisters married and my older brothers left home, I was in school a day or two and out a day or two. I was kept out of school to help take fodder, gather corn, hand tobacco, and take care of all the crops. We had only six months school the first five years of my school days. Our school building had only one room. There were two teachers and about eighty pupils. The room was very noisy. We had straight back benches with two or three students on each bench, and the students talked more than they studied. I went to school until I finished the eighth grade. I couldn't go any farther in school at home in the country. I told my parents I had a desire to go to high school, that if they would buy my clothes I would work my way through school, but they would not consent. They told me they needed me to help at home. I went off badly discouraged.

"Two years ago I told father and mother I would get a job in a factory and work and get enough money to go to school. I went to work in the cotton mill. I made $9.35 a week. I paid $5 a week for board and I also had my laundry bill and insurance, so after all I didn't get the money to go on to school."

Of course, some girls are glad enough to stop school and go to work as soon as possible with the hope of getting clothes and beaus, but the girls who are sent to the Southern Summer School for the most part are almost pathetic in their desire for an education.

In the hope of bettering their conditions the girls left the farm and went to live in the mill village of East Marion. Here is a description given by one of the students. "There are families of eight and ten living in three-room houses. Roofs on many of the houses leak. Most of the houses need repairing and painting. There are dry-pit toilets strung up at the back door of all these houses. The water the people use is drawn from pumps. There are but two or three pumps on each street and on part of the mill village there are sixteen families that use water from two pumps. The company recently built a Y. M. C. A. It has a swimming pool, a ten-pin alley, library, sewing and cooking department, shower baths, and a basket-ball court. The people of the village pay ten cents for a shower bath, ten cents for bathing in the pool, and ten cents for a game of ten pins. The only store that most of the working class ever trade in is the company store, for most of them eat up today what they work out tomorrow."

Conditions that would make many of us shudder were related by the thirty-five students; the girls from Marion could tell a story of the longest working day and of the most unsanitary conditions. . . .

One of the girls gave this account:

"I work twelve hours and twenty minutes a day and I am completely worn out at stopping time. Men and women who work in the mill are weak and sallow looking, some of them just dragging along half dead and overworked until they don't know what it is to take a rest and feel good. The average workingman or woman makes from $1.60 to $2.70 a day, and some have families of from three to seven and some-times more depending on them for a living. The employees of the mill walked out on a strike on July 11 for shorter hours and for the same pay they were getting for longer hours. Do you blame us for striking?"

. . . To some of the young strikers the strike meant excitement, a chance for the spectacular; to some of the older ones it meant a chance to rest; to most of them it was a reaching out for more tolerable conditions of life and work not only for them-selves but for their families and neighbors. . . .

※ *E S S A Y S*

In the first essay, Howard University's Elizabeth Clark-Lewis examines the experiences of black women who moved from the rural South to become domestic workers in Washington, D.C., in the early twentieth century. Clark-Lewis finds that, despite the constraints imposed by race, gender, and class, domestic workers discovered novel ways to enhance their auton-omy. In the second essay, Susan Porter Benson of the University of Connecticut asserts that young white women working in department stores created a subculture that "bent the rules" of store managers while generally avoiding direct confrontation. By way of contrast, Jacquelyn Dowd Hall, of the University of North Carolina at Chapel Hill, explores in the last essay how community alliances and cultural values drawn from the new consumer culture made it possible for women workers in Tennessee to become central players in the textile strikes of 1929.

Community Life and Work Culture Among African-American Domestic Workers in Washington, D.C., 1910–1940

ELIZABETH CLARK-LEWIS

When African-American women migrated from the rural South to the urban centers of the North to work as live-in servants, few imagined they were beginning an escape from restraints imposed by race, gender, and class. But escape they did, and this essay examines the transition of twenty-three such women as they moved beyond live-in household servitude to self-employment during the first three decades of this century. It also demonstrates that as their roles changed, they experienced a new freedom to exercise control over their own lives, and their perceptions about themselves and their relationships to others underwent a significant change. It is important to recognize, however, that these changes occurred within a restrictive cultural environment.

. . . When foreign immigration slowed to a trickle after World War I, an impor-tant source of new white servants was eliminated. Within the first two decades of the twentieth century, household work lost its importance as an occupation for

Adapted from Elizabeth Clark-Lewis, "'This Work Had a End': African-American Domestic Workers in Washington, D.C., 1910–1940" in *"To Toil the Livelong Day": America's Women at Work, 1780–1980,* edited by Carol Groneman and Mary Beth Norton, pp. 196–212. Copyright © 1987, by Cornell Univer-sity. Used by permission of the publisher, Cornell University Press.

white women. By contrast, the number of African-American female household workers *increased* by 43 percent. Nationally, during the 1900–1930 period, the southern exploitive system triumphed: African-American women were forced into a "servant caste."

Surveys of specific northern urban centers found that the sharp rise in the number of African-American household workers had three sources: the new, large-scale migration of African-Americans to urban centers outside the South; the fact that African-American women were twice as likely as white women to be employed; and discriminatory policies that barred African-American women from 86 percent of employment categories. By 1926 the predominance of African-American migrant women in household service in Washington, D.C., was well established. . . . In 1900, 54 percent of the employed African-American women in the District were working in domestic service; by 1930, that figure had risen to 78 percent.

Expanded employment opportunities lured a stream of migrants to the urban North, where they moved into segregated communities that coalesced around churches, schools, philanthropic institutions, and businesses. But because of antimigrant biases in the established African-American communities, only rarely could the newcomers find work in businesses owned by African-Americans or in the segregated schools of the communities where they settled. Disproportionately young, female, and poorly educated, they found themselves in urban centers where the pattern of racial segregation combined with class and gender restrictions to limit the jobs available to them. In overwhelming numbers the female migrants became household workers. . . .

Fourteen of the twenty-three women I interviewed grew up on farms owned by their parents; nine lived on share-tenant farms. Nearly all were reared in extended family households consisting of mothers, fathers, grandparents, siblings, and other relatives. They were all born between 1884 and 1911. Each household included at least one former slave; thus every woman in the study vividly recalled hearing firsthand descriptions of the degrading conditions of slavery. Further, the women were able to cite beliefs held by those former slaves regarding patterns and practices that enabled slave families to survive under the harshest of circumstances.

Family support, according to all of the women interviewed, was a focal point of rural churches. In addition to religious instruction, churches provided the only mutual aid, educational, and recreational activities available to African-American families in the rural South. After the family, the church was the most important means of individual and community expression.

The education of all of the women in the study had been severely limited by the need to help support the family, which they recognized as their primary responsibility by the age of seven. They worked first on the family farm, caring for the youngest children and serving as apprentices to older girls and women. Each of the twenty-three women recalled her mother's leaving home for residential (live-in) employment in white households in the surrounding area and recognized that independently employed children were an important part of the family's survival strategy. "Like everybody, by eight years old I went in to work with Mama," said Bernice Reeder in discussing the short period of outside tutelage which preceded a girl's first employment as live-in servant to a white family. She was alone on her first job, "at just nine years old! I was so scared," she continued. "Nobody cared you were a child. . . . You was a worker to them." The economic constraints faced by African-Americans in the rural South in the late nineteenth and early twentieth centuries made such early labor an unavoidable and accepted part of family and community life.

. . . By the age of ten, the women in this study told me, they also had to show clearly that they had the maturity to take another step: to travel to Washington, D.C., where sisters and aunts who worked as live-in servants (and sent money home) needed support in the form of child care and housekeeping by younger family members. These girls made the journey north by train. None had ever been out of her home state before. Twenty were taken to the train station by a male relative; all left their places of birth in the early morning, traveled alone, and were met by other relatives upon arrival in Washington.

When sharing reminiscences of their northbound journey, the women always described the feeling of freedom they experienced. "When you got on the train," Velma Davis exclaimed, "you felt different! Seem like you'd been bound up, but now this train untied you. It's funny . . . like being untied and tickled at the same time!" The girls understood that their first obligation was to carry on the rural-based family survival strategy in the homes of kin who served Washington's white households as live-in workers. The only significant change in their lives, initially, was the move to the North. . . .

Urban kin gave support to the migrant in several ways, if we may judge from information provided by the women interviewed. They paid all of her travel expenses to Washington, helped her adjust to urban life, and found employment for her within twelve months. In all the cases studied, the women were hired where their kin had contacts; in twenty-one of twenty-three cases, the coresident kin acquired employment for the migrants in households where they themselves were currently living. The girls migrated originally to provide support only to their urban kin; once they themselves became employed, however (after an average of one year), they were expected to assume responsibility for meeting the needs of both the urban and rural segments of the family.

As newly hired live-in servants, these female migrants learned that their primary role was to serve the mistress of the house, not just to complete the assigned tasks — a departure from the way they had worked in southern households. In the South, these African-American household workers had received daily task assignments from the white male head of the household. Migrants stressed that in Washington they slowly learned a new employment reality. Through trial and error, and with the advice of the more experienced earlier migrants, they learned to act in response to the needs of the wife rather than the husband.

Each of the twenty-three women was dismayed to learn that uniforms were mandatory in the District of Columbia. The wearing of uniforms was perceived by all as the major difference between their servant *work* in the South and their servant *role* in Washington. For these women, the uniform objectified the live-in servant and determined her fate in the workplace. The home was the white mistress's stage and major realm of influence, and the uniform legitimized her power. Ophilia Simpson recalled that "them uniforms just seemed to make them know you was theirs. Some say you wore them to show different jobs you was doing. Time in grey. Other times serving in black. But mostly them things just showed you was always at their beck and call. Really that's all them things means!" . . .

Despite the fact that each woman (and her family in the rural South) desperately needed the income her labor generated, within seven years these women were actively trying to leave the "servant life." There were several aspects of live-in employment that they all disliked. The uniform formalized the serving of the family for long hours, which they could not control. The wife as the authority figure had little respect for their needs. Worse still, they were forced to live in small quarters completely isolated from the African-American community.

But it was the question of church participation that first stimulated more than half of those interviewed to seek a change. Not being able to attend regular services on Sundays and generally feeling left out of the continuing life of their churches became for these women a potent symbol of the restrictions of live-in labor. "Even working-out down home, you'd go to church," Costella Harris explained, bedridden at eighty-six after a lifetime of household employment in Georgetown. "Everybody did," she continued slowly. "Now, most came just to hear the Word. But some came to keep from being in a kitchen somewhere. . . . Church gave you six, not seven days of work. But up here you never saw inside any church on Sunday, living-in."

Painful as all these restrictions were, however, they were probably not sufficient by themselves to lead the women to reject live-in servant work. The *ability* to make the change emanated from the phenomenon known as "penny savers clubs." Twenty-one of the twenty-three women actively associated themselves with such mutual benefit associations, which sponsored social gatherings and provided sickness and death benefits to members. . . . Although rarely mentioned in the literature, the penny savers clubs served as a vital economic base for the female migrant. After an average of six years of saving, the women were able to develop the important economic leverage they needed to leave servant life.

The role of the church and of the penny savers clubs in first awakening the desire for change and then facilitating the process of that change cannot be overestimated. The clubs permitted the women, during the transition from live-in service to household day work, to maintain financial security for themselves and their kin in the rural South. No woman left live-in work until she had saved enough money to maintain herself and send money monthly to rural kin. . . . They sought to find a less circumscribed economic and employment environment without abandoning one of the original motivations for leaving their rural families — relief of the family's economic distress.

The women soon identified laundresses as critical figures in their search for autonomy. Laundresses served as role models: unlike the other staff members, they did not belittle the migrant woman's desire to gain household work on a nonresidential basis, and they alone knew the categories and rules related to operating within several households simultaneously. The laundress also brought information about households that were seeking the services of women on a live-out basis for one or two days a week. . . .

The women saw six major benefits to the shift from live-in servant to household day worker. First, as indicated by the language they used to describe their experiences, their work seemed more their own. They spoke of their earlier jobs in depersonalized language because they sought detachment from their employers and a buffer against the employers' insensitivity to them as workers and African-Americans. . . . Velma Davis recalled, "When I say 'my job,' I mean a job I got and

I'd keep if they acted decent. 'They job' is for them; a job that you did and did, more and more — from one thing to another, early to late, and you worked!" . . .

Second, the previously isolated African-American women began to make contact with one another amid their newly flexible working conditions, encountering many others like themselves. The structure that had created social marginality among African-Americans in Washington was slowly being dismantled; the women's isolated and restrictive living circumstances were relegated to an oppressive past. . . .

Third, as the women changed jobs, they moved to rooms in boardinghouses and began to adopt a sharply different lifestyle. The other girls in the house where Velma Davis became a boarder "was all doing day-work, too," and "soon I was doing just about everything with them. I just liked being with these girls [who] was single, nice." After the move from live-in servant work, Velma Davis said that she did not see her family for long periods of time. She said that it was when she moved to the boardinghouse that she began to feel she had finally left home. . . .

Fourth, their places of work changed. Employers usually hired someone other than their former live-in servants to work as daily household employees. The women acknowledged this policy; thus, in communicating their new plans to their employers, they understood that future employment in that household would not be considered. . . .

Fifth, each woman indicated that turning to day work produced a subtle change in her relationship to the white women for whom she worked. Virginia Lacey described the new experience with an employer this way: "She'd meet you at the door, tell you how she wanted her house done, and she'd be gone. You did the work without her in the way, slowing you up. On a day job we all knew how to get everything done — but, in your own way. Having anybody around will make you work slower.". . .

Finally, all of the women stressed that as they moved out of live-in work, they shed their uniforms and other symbols of their identities as live-in servants. Each had felt locked into a narrow and constricted role by the need to wear uniforms of "black for this" and "gray for that." Discarding that badge of their station in life clearly disaffiliated them from their previous work. . . .

Virginia Lacey agreed: "I'd go to whatever house I'd have to be to work at. I change to my work clothes and then clean the house. . . . I never liked to be in the uniform. I guess serving in a uniform made you be back on staff. And you wasn't, so you'd just not want to wear that uniform." She paused for a moment, reflecting. "Wearing your own clothes — that's like you being your own boss! You was on your own job for a day and pay, then go home."

Some scholars and artists who are sensitive to the problems of domestic service have tended to view negatively the bags in which day workers carried their clothes. But these women took pride in the fact that they "carried work clothes" to their jobs; they felt that the bags were symbols of personal freedom and in that sense were positive. In fact, Marie Davis reported that workers often called them "freedom bags"; she observed, "When I got to carry clothes, I was finally working in what I wanted to. No black or gray uniforms or castoffs from the whites down home. I was proud to put my stuff in a bag at home. I guess I wanted to finally show I didn't wear a uniform. I wasn't a servant.". . .

A new identity was gained. Gone was the identity to which they were born or which had been ascribed to them; this new one they had *achieved* on their own, and their newly acquired friends and associates validated their achieved status. As Bernice Reeder explained, "Once you got some work by the day and got around people who did it, you'd see how you could get ahead, get better things. You'd see how to get more and more days, some party work, extra sewing, stuff like that." Velma Davis agreed: "When I started working days, other people [other household day workers] would show you how to get a few extra dollars. In this town you could make more money, and they'd sure show you how."

The women's transformed identities and modified employment modes led to several other changes in the African-American community. For one, the women's interest in the penny savers clubs waned. . . . Although the associations continued to exist . . . household day workers perceived them as institutions serving the needs of live-in servants. The day workers transferred their money to banks, in part because their new jobs gave them the opportunity to do so. As Eula Montgomery remarked, "I'd have used them [banks] earlier, but with that woman you never got time to go to a place like that. I know I didn't." Minnie Barnes verified this point: "I used a bank as a day worker because it was on my streetcar line home." . . .

The waning of the mutual benefit associations did not, however, mean the decline of support for rural kin. On the contrary, economic assistance typically increased after the transition to household day work. In speaking of the support she provided her relatives still living in the South, Velma Davis said, "I didn't miss a month. . . . That's why I got myself set before I left live-in. I never missed sending my share home." If anything, the women adhered even more strongly to their premigration beliefs concerning kinship obligations. . . .

The level of these women's participation in the African-American churches of Washington also changed significantly. Live-in servant work had greatly restricted their attendance and involvement in church activities. Velma Davis recalled, "Living in? You never dreamed of going to day service. Sundays, you'd be out of there [the live-in household], if you was good, by four or five." Regular participation in daytime church services was also an indication of status. "Big people, like government messengers, or people working in a colored business office, that's who'd be regular at Sunday day services," Eula Montgomery said. Individuals who worked in those types of jobs, she pointed out, had their Sundays free; they could also, therefore, "be on the church's special committees."

Live-in service had limited all aspects of interactions with other church members. Eula Montgomery went on: "If you lived in a room in the attic, how could you be in any of them clubs? You couldn't bring nobody over there. . . . You never got to be in a fellowship. That was for people who got off on Saturday and Sunday. They had a nice place to have people over to — not no kitchen." . . .

Regular church attendance, achieved through less confining employment, was accompanied by more leisure-time activity. A married couple could go to morning church services, and in summer they could go out for picnics, Dolethia Otis pointed out.

Participation in church and leisure activities was viewed, not surprisingly, as representative of the attainment of *better* work; according to Nellie Willoughby, a migrant from Virginia, "it showed you had work you didn't live at." It did not mean that these women did *easier* work. The point was that the work they did — even if more strenuous — permitted some previously unavailable free time. . . .

All of the women interviewed asserted that household day work was directly responsible for their ability to participate in the churches. The result of this change was wider church membership. Previously, working-class women had not been well represented in the African-American churches. "Most women down at Mason Street Baptist who were real active," said Helen Venable, "were educated good and had jobs like teaching. As people got more away from live-in you saw a lotta different people in all the things that church has. Then more and more people got in the church's clubs or work."

The growth of African-American churches in Washington, then, was a direct consequence of the steady influx of these working-class (former live-in) women. They strongly supported church expansion because their participation in the church activities further separated them from the stigma of servitude. . . .

Live-in servant work imposed countless burdens upon African-American female migrants to the District of Columbia before the Depression, yet "service-class" women developed and controlled philanthropic organizations that allowed them eventually to escape the boundaries of live-in servant employment. Although the African-American women quoted here remained in household service work all their lives, they restructured its salient features and created more freedom for themselves.

Reformers who rely only on archival records may view household service work as "a dead end." Scholars all too often see household workers as merely products of change, never as its causes; as objects of events, not as their subjects; as passive reactors, not as active forces in history. The words and lives of these women refute such views. Orra Fisher's response sums up best what the women expressed when asked about the progress and the success they have seen in their lives:

> I worked hard to serve God and to see that my three girls didn't have to serve nobody else like I did except God. I satisfied to know I came a long way. From a kitchen down home to a kitchen up here, and then able to earn money, but live with my children and grands. Now Jesus took me every step — that's real.
>
> But look at me, with more than I ever dreamed I'd have. And my three, with houses, and jobs. My girls in an office, and the baby — my son — over twenty years in the Army. I get full thinking about it. I had it bad, but look at them.

The Work Culture of Sales Clerks in American Department Stores, 1890–1940

SUSAN PORTER BENSON

When a woman chose — for whatever reason — to become a department-store saleswoman, she moved into the orbit of a powerful work culture which helped to shape and define daily working life. The world of women's work intersected with the world of the department-store industry on the selling floor, and the culture which emerged from that conjunction built upon both elements. The heart of saleswomen's lives from every perspective was skill in social interaction. As women,

Susan Porter Benson, "The Clerking Sisterhood," from *Counter Cultures: Saleswomen, Managers, and Customers in American Department Stores, 1890–1940,* 227–231, 253–258, 268–271. Copyright © 1986 by University of Illinois Press. Reprinted by permission.

Female clerks and their customers in a busy dry-goods and leather-goods store, 1915. The women clerks pictured in the photograph are assisting both male and female customers. The man standing behind the rear counter appears to be their supervisor.

they had been socialized to become adept at interpersonal relations and — lacking formal authority — to use influence. As clerks they were trained to be masters of the complex social situation involved in persuading someone of another class background to make a purchase. As members of occupational and departmental groups, they used their social skills to forge a resilient and cohesive work culture.

Saleswomen, no less than managers and customers, had their own ideas about how they should do their work. Observers of workers' conduct on the shop floor have long recognized that custom and informal rules compete with employer's prescriptions to govern day-to-day life on the job. Building on the insights of observers such as Stanley Mathewson and Frances Donovan, labor historians are now writing the history of these shop-floor practices and of the ideology and social organization which support them. Frequently focusing on a single industry or workplace, detailed studies recapture the complex history of the social relations of production as they developed through daily contact among and between workers and managers. When a third element — the patient in a hospital, for example, or the customer in a department store — enters into the equation, the possibilities for workers to manipulate the situation become that much greater. Labor history written from this point of view focuses on daily interaction within the workplace rather than upon formal union organization and dramatic events such as strikes.

The concept of work culture — the ideology and practice with which workers stake out a relatively autonomous sphere of action on the job — is a useful tool for analyzing these interactions. A realm of informal, customary values and rules mediates the formal authority structure of the workplace and distances workers from its impact. Work culture is created as workers confront the limitations and exploit the possibilities of their jobs; it is transmitted and enforced by oral tradition and social sanctions within the work group. Generated partly in response to specific working conditions, work culture includes both adaptation and resistance to these structural constraints. More than simply reactive, work culture embodies workers' own defini- tion of a good day's work, their own sense of satisfying and useful labor. While condemning oppressive aspects of the job, it also celebrates the skill it demands and the rewards it brings. Work culture is very much an in-between ground: it is neither a rubber-stamp version of management policy nor is it a direct outcome of the per- sonal — class, sex, ethnic, race, age — characteristics of the workers. It is the prod- uct of these forces as they interact in the workplace and result in collectively formed assumptions and behaviors.

The study of work culture opens the way to a fuller understanding of the forma- tion of workers' consciousness and of the strategies through which they resist and accommodate to employers' demands. Both processes are currently the subject of much discussion among students of the labor process; the writings of Harry Braver- man, Michael Burawoy, and Leslie Tentler show the range of the debate. Braver- man and Burawoy, devoting their closest attention to male workers, maintain that forces inside the workplace are the prime shapers of consciousness; Braverman ig- nores and Burawoy discounts the influence of life beyond the factory gates. Tentler, focusing on women factory workers, argues that consciousness is formed most powerfully by gender, particularly by women's experience in the family and the home, and that women's labor-force experience only reinforced their progress to- ward "conventional maturity." For Braverman and Burawoy changes in the labor process are controlling; for Tentler, they are incidental to the central fact of women's workplace subordination. All three agree that, ultimately, workers' sub- mission to the conditions of their jobs surpasses their resistance: Braverman as- sumes that the process of rationalization crushes workers; Burawoy affirms the transformation of resistance into consent; Tentler argues that women abandoned their grueling and demeaning jobs for the higher status and greater satisfactions of marriage and the family. In the end, of course, it is difficult to fault their shared judgment that workers' accommodation in whatever form has outweighed workers' resistance, but for students of work culture the process is as interesting as the result, the study of the small struggles, victories, and losses of daily life equal in signifi- cance to the exploration of the larger political context.

My discussion of the work culture of department-store saleswomen departs from two common assumptions, often all the more powerful because implicit, made by writers on labor and the labor process. First, I view skill not as an objective cate- gory but rather as a judgment based on social and economic imperatives which may be far removed from the nature of the work itself. In studies of the working class, the notion of skill has been biased in favor of men's work and artful manual work, with jobs performed by men labeled as more skilled than those performed by women, and the highest skill attributed to those engaged in custom production. All workers, in fact, whatever the level of skill attributed to their jobs, shape their work- place experience in ways that revise and expand managers' notions of the job, using the special "working knowledge" they develop. In the case of women workers, this working knowledge is often grounded in social interaction — as it is in retailing — and is thus doubly devalued. Second, I find that the family consciousness/work consciousness dichotomy distorts and oversimplifies the process by which forces both within and outside the workplace shape the outlook of male and female workers alike. Department-store saleswomen's work culture reflected a consciousness of themselves as workers, as women, and as consumers, reflecting the complexities and contradictions of their lives. . . .

Managers' efforts to rationalize the selling floor created the ideal conditions for the flourishing of saleswomen's work culture. Typically, department stores had conflicting lines of authority: members of the buying, operations, advertising, personnel, accounting, and sales promotions staffs all had some degree of leverage over the salespeople. In theory, this meant more thorough supervision, but in practice it meant that authority was hopelessly fragmented and frequently inconsistent. Saleswomen's work culture both exploited this weakness and mediated the contradictions in the situation. Management's decision to increase productivity by encouraging more and larger sales through "personal" or "skilled" or "suggestive" selling rather than resorting to self-service further enhanced the power of salespeople; managers relied increasingly on their initiative, originality, and skills at social interaction. This policy had a powerful double potential, since the skilled saleswoman could manipulate not just her customers but also her relationship with her bosses and her coworkers. The most valued employee could also be the most subversive.

Class and gender also played an important role in work culture. When managers tried through training and discipline to erase signs of working–class origins and to apply a veneer of middle-class or elite culture to the saleswomen, they raised the issue of class in a persistent and emphatic way. It would have been difficult for a saleswoman to avoid learning the lesson: that she was different from bosses and customers, that she and her peers formed a group apart. On the other hand, by encouraging clerks to form a womanly rapport with women on the other side of the counter, store managers set the stage for saleswomen to ally with customers and other saleswomen in ways that hurt the store's profits. Managers tried to harness class and gender to further their own ideas of selling efficiency, but in fact they unwittingly encouraged connections that could as easily do the opposite. . . .

Departmental work culture helped to manage the ties of interdependence between saleswomen and their buyers. Although the formal structure of the store defined clerks as simply subordinate to buyers, in fact the two were linked by almost feudal ties of dependence, loyalty, and obligation. The buyer bought the merchandise — but depended upon saleswomen to sell it. The buyer could provide the merchandise information for which saleswomen were eager — but saleswomen controlled the shop-floor knowledge about customers' wishes and demands which was vital to buyers' success. As a rule, saleswomen disliked classroom-type training and preferred to receive information from their buyers, whom they regarded as more expert than staff executives such as training directors. A good buyer was one who helped them learn about the stock; a bad buyer was one who did not. They disliked written materials and classroom lectures because their work culture and their entire work lives depended upon oral tradition and persuasion and they preferred to sharpen their skills through similar means. Older saleswomen whose stock-in-trade was experience rather than formal education especially resisted the classroom setting. Saleswomen perceived merchandise training as useful information; they scorned salesmanship training as an insult to their shop-floor skills. When training was given in a dictatorial or condescending fashion, they simply ignored it.

Buyers, for their part, came to saleswomen to learn what was selling, what customers were saying about the merchandise, what the department needed, what trends they observed in customer demand. This information was enormously important to buyers in planning for the future, in solving problems before they crippled the department, and in petitioning upper management for more merchandise, space, or personnel. Saleswomen, predictably, gave buyers this information in a way that reflected well on themselves and worked in their best interests. Merchandise managers and general managers eager to break the power of buyers and salespeople alike tried to switch the source of shop-floor knowledge from salespeople to accounting figures so that "[s]alespeople can't hornswoggle [buyers] any more with threats and cajoleries." But simple figures lacked the subtleties and the qualitative information saleswomen could provide. This exchange of knowledge about merchandise and customers formed a powerful link between buyers and saleswomen. Buyers could reward faithful and effective saleswomen with good recommendations and performance reports, juicy store gossip, and perquisites such as out-of-town buying trips and special bargains on merchandise.

Buyers and saleswomen were also involved in a tacit alliance against other managers. The buyers acted as a buffer between saleswomen and floorwalkers or upper-level management. She could shield her clerks from harassment by other executives and enforce rules in a lax manner. When salespeople clashed with upper management, buyers often pleaded their cases. Saleswomen in one department at Filene's appealed the store's decision to deny them supper money on a technicality. The general manager argued to the Board of Arbitration that the sales force was uncooperative about giving overtime: "the people should be willing to do a little of the giving and not demand the last drop of blood every time anything special comes up." The department head objected angrily to the "drop of blood" phrase, asserting that "[t]his is a question of justice." Such advocacy earned the loyalty of department members; they could, moreover, reciprocate by protecting the buyer from her superiors. Managers understood that a good way to get saleswomen's compliance with a storewide procedure or rule was to make it a test of cooperation with and loyalty to the buyers. Filene's top management learned the hard way that salespeople would resist anything that smacked of betrayal of the buyers; in 1922, the store announced a "Complete Stocks" contest offering workers a 50¢ prize for each report of an article or size that was out of stock. In the first two weeks of the contest, they received only nine reports because salespeople were well aware that incomplete selections reflected badly on a buyer. Only after A. Lincoln Filene himself met with the buyers and convinced them that the information would not be used against them did the reports come rushing in — eight hundred in a single week. . . .

Other managers — floorwalkers, staff executives, and those above buyers in the merchandising hierarchy — were equally aware of saleswomen's work culture but tended to see it as evidence of stupidity, stubbornness, or indifference to self-interest rather than as a sign of workers' informal self-government. Not unlike the slave owners of the antebellum South, they interpreted the actions of their subordinates in a self-serving fashion, refusing to acknowledge explicitly what most dimly perceived: the existence of an oppositional set of rules which simultaneously challenged and sustained the functioning of the store. On one hand, work culture helped the store to run smoothly by arbitrating interdepartmental conflicts, socializing new members, and fostering selling skill; on the other, it sanctioned the stint and various kinds of insubordination, its influence countering management's authority. To crush saleswomen's work culture would have damaged selling service by angering and alienating the saleswomen; to ignore it would have damaged selling service by giving free rein to the stint and departmental sociability. Most managers chose a middle ground which focused limited efforts on specific offenses.

Saleswomen bent rules at every turn, showing that they sensed their employers' hesitancy. Bosses and floorwalkers constantly complained of high spirits and boisterous sociability in the departments and did their unsuccessful best to stamp out loud laughing, talking, singing, and horseplay. Saleswomen openly ridiculed petty regulations and simply refused to comply with managers' demands that they complete "want slips" for every customer request they were unable to fill. They intentionally omitted their numbers from sales checks so that returned goods could not be subtracted from their sales totals. Rule-breaking was a way of life at Filene's; the *Echo** contained many exhortations to employees to be more conscientious. Saleswomen so frequently violated the dress rules with improprieties such as sleeveless dresses and sheer blouses that management began in the mid-1920s to send them home to change clothes and to dock their pay for time lost. They exploited the seasonal rhythms of retailing; twice as many arrived late for work during the summer doldrums as during the busier spring season. When an antitardiness campaign pushed too hard on the rank and file, a wit in the *Echo* suggested that the Tardiness Committee would have to hire Mechanic's Hall, a large auditorium, to hear all the cases of executive tardiness.

Saleswomen most dramatically defied managers when they felt that their dignity had been attacked or their prerogatives undermined. Such was the case in a drapery department in a Pittsburgh store. When the display department assumed the task of decorating the department, saleswomen viewed it as an insult to their abilities; they criticized the display department's work and ostentatiously refused to straighten out displays which became disarranged during the day. A saleswoman whom an executive offended spread the word among her co-workers, and "in a few minutes all the salespeople [were] aroused and doing all they [could] to ignore or annoy him." In dealing with staff personnel, floorwalkers, and upper management, saleswomen maintained a stern unity.

Management's major offensive against saleswomen's work culture was an effort to break the hold of the stint through incentive systems of payment. Saleswomen, like skilled craftsmen and less skilled factory operatives, resisted these tactics. Managers found to their sorrow that these plans might raise sales levels only to cause other problems. Saleswomen became more ruthless about weeding out those whom they supposed to be lookers and concentrated on the most likely prospects,

---

*The *Echo,* the newspaper of the Filene Co-operative Association, contained news of store policy but also published views critical of management.

particularly those who appeared to be more prosperous. They became fixated on their books; as one rueful manager put it, they "look at the records their sales are going to show this month, and they do not look at *the customer*." They shunned stock work as if to point out to management that they would play the game of higher sales with a vengeance, to the exclusion of other aspects of their work. They kept a wary eye out for any among them who might take the incentives too seriously and become a grabber. They ignored less popular merchandise and sold along the lines of least resistance, leaving large portions of the stock untouched until it had to be marked down. And, perhaps most alarming of all, they administered collectively what was designed to be an individualistic system. One manager reported that "[t]here was a tendency for some salespeople who had no prospects of making their quota to turn their sales over to someone who had made their quota and split the commission." Despairing of material incentives, one harried buyer simply resorted to pitting one saleswoman against another with vicious gossip in order to foster a competitive selling spirit. She succeeded in the short run, but in the long run she was left with a foul-tempered and backbiting department that was unable to deliver good selling service.

As universally as managers complained about the power of saleswomen's work culture, no boss testified to the successful and total elimination of its practices. Dire threats and draconian discipline might break its grip on an individual: the manager of an Ohio store told of his year-long battle to get one saleswoman to sell occasionally in other departments. She stood firm in her refusal, affirming "I'm a coat girl," invoking work culture's pride in and identification with her merchandise. Only his threat to fire her forced her to sell other merchandise, and even then he hedged his bets by demanding that she sign a letter promising to sell anywhere in the store. But more impressive are tales of saleswomen's small, quiet, collective victories against management. In 1915, for example, a desperate floorwalker mounted a major offensive against an obstreperous and temperamental department. He succeeded in subduing the saleswomen temporarily and in whipping them on to higher sales levels, but his success was short-lived. The store manager, faced with imminent insurrection among the saleswomen, finally had to transfer him to another floor. Even in the depth of the Depression, managers lost their battles with work culture. A retailing student reported on an extremely cohesive women's shoe department where the saleswomen enforced the stint rigorously, flaunted the dress code by wearing large hoop earrings, unilaterally extended their lunch hour from forty-five minutes to an hour, and resolutely ignored all storewide activities. Not even the specter of Depression-era unemployment deterred them. . . .

The nature of saleswomen's work culture shows their notable ability to exploit a flexible and ambiguous situation. Because there was no rigid formula for successful selling, clerks could liberally interpret employers' rules and instructions with relative impunity. For example, managers urged saleswomen to help one another, and they went overboard in forming close-knit work groups which subverted management goals. Managers emphasized selling skill, and saleswomen made those skills the basis of a resourceful work culture. Management encouraged saleswomen to use their domestic knowledge and women's culture in the store, and they went a step further in forming the "clerking sisterhood." Management encouraged clerks to become adept at social interaction, and they huddled on the selling floor, using their social skills with their peers as well as with their customers. Management emphasized the importance of fashion, and saleswomen used their arguments to justify insurrections against dress rules.

Saleswomen's techniques for disciplining unruly customers were similar to their ways of dealing with their bosses. They withheld their knowledge about merchandise from customers, and often sullenly withheld the merchandise itself. Clerks had enormous discretion in dealing with customers as well as in dealing with their employers: they could calculatingly fawn over or condescend to them; they could terrorize them or kill them with kindness; they could ignore them or overwhelm them with attention.

The study of saleswomen's work culture not only illuminates the lives of those legions of women who were part of it, but also suggests ways of revising the history of women workers in particular and life on the shop floor in general. At least one group of women workers, and doubtless others, developed a shop-floor culture that combined a keen sense of themselves as workers and as women. Both elements contained contradictions. As workers, saleswomen developed an appreciation of the skill of selling but an unwillingness to use that skill as their employers wished. As women, they integrated both a traditional home-and-family outlook and a more critical feminist stance into their work culture. The long-standing assumption that women's consciousness is overwhelmingly the product of domestic imperatives oversimplifies the complicated dynamic of women workers' daily lives.

The tactics of saleswomen's work culture were those long familiar to male skilled workers, but now mobilized to protect interpersonal and consumer skills rather than artisanal or mechanical ones. It is time to ask if these tactics are less specific to skilled workers than generalized among workers under conditions of capitalist production. All workers have a knowledge of the work they do that surpasses the prescriptions of their employers; to understand the modes by which workers protect and expand their knowledge can help to fix the boundary between the struggle and the acquiescence that are part of every worker's life.

One of male skilled workers' major weapons was conspicuously absent from saleswomen's work culture: the labor union. Until the CIO-sparked drives of the middle and later 1930s, barely a handful of the nation's saleswomen carried union cards. The Retail Clerks' International Protective Association (RCIPA), the principal pre-CIO retail union, claimed only two thousand female members in the mid-1920s — an insignificant .4 percent of the nation's women sales workers, many of them in small-town shops rather than in urban department stores. The organizing efforts of the late 1930s brought the unionized proportion nearer 5 percent. For most of the half-century between 1890 and 1940, then, labor unions had very little impact on the day-to-day life of the selling floor.

Far from surprising, this fact is doubly predictable because of the tendency of both women and white-collar workers to organize less often than men and blue-collar workers. Virtually all of the factors which conspire against women's unionization converged in department-store selling: high labor turnover; possibilities for upward mobility for the longer-term worker; a union (the RCIPA) which was at best paternalistic and often outright hostile to the organizing of saleswomen; and managers who were especially ruthless in firing union sympathizers uncovered by their pervasive and effective spy networks. Given the array of circumstances undermining unionization, it is remarkable not how little but how often saleswomen tried to organize. First during the pre–World War I burst of women's militancy, then after World War I, and again during the late 1930s, some department-store saleswomen saw unionization as desirable and possible. As historians begin to ask not why women fail to organize but why they sometimes try and succeed, the motivations, victories, and failures of this minority will be recaptured for the historical record.

One of the questions a study of department-store saleswomen's union efforts will have to consider is that of the relation of saleswomen's work culture to labor unions. Recent writers have argued both that work culture fed into union strength and that it thwarted it; an understanding of saleswomen's work culture suggests that the two possibilities coexisted and that work culture was indeed a flexible resource. Work culture fostered persuasive skills and ease at dealing with the public which served saleswomen well in their union struggles; news reports frequently note the energy and verve that saleswomen brought to the picket line and support meetings. Even as they displayed workers' militancy, however, saleswomen could still act out their pride in their white-collar status and their vision of themselves as the arbiters of fashion and consumption: during the 1937 San Francisco strike saleswomen from the carriage-trade stores showed up for picket duty dressed to the nines, making the strike action look "like a fashion show."

Seen from another point of view, of course, work culture was a hindrance to and an inferior substitute for unionization. Reinforcing the fragmentation of the store into departments, work culture's base in the departmental work group could undercut the storewide solidarity required to build a union. The aspects of work culture which provided channels for expressing hostility toward managers and customers could legitimate that anger, but could also defuse it by allowing saleswomen to act out their workers' consciousness in the sheltered context of the department rather than taking the enormous risks of union activity. Moreover, sales work did not involve the dyadic worker-manager relationship of the factory; the complex saleswoman/customer/manager triangle obscured and transformed the content of class conflict on the selling floor. It was not always clear who the enemy was. Finally, and perhaps most important of all, work culture functioned in an informal, customary fashion while unions adopted formalized legalistic agreements; shop-floor action was not always readily transferable to the bargaining table or the grievance procedure. Labor unions might regularize management practice, but work culture protected the "perks," and the two could clash as well as reinforce each other. It would be equally inappropriate to romanticize saleswomen's work culture and to blame it for their failure to unionize. Work culture in itself cannot insure dignity and justice for workers, but it did shape the daily lives of thousands of saleswomen, providing organizing principles and a sense of right even as it lacked the authority to enforce them. Placed alongside the cultural factors inhibiting the organization of white-collar women, the impotence of the RCIPA, and the grimly anti-union policies of their employers, saleswomen's work culture pales into insignificance as a block to unionization. . . .

"Disorderly Women" and Labor Militancy in the Appalachian South, 1920s

JACQUELYN DOWD HALL

The rising sun "made a sort of halo around the crown of Cross Mountain" as Flossie Cole climbed into a neighbor's Model T and headed west down the gravel road to Elizabethton, bound for work in a rayon plant. Emerging from Stony Creek hollow, the car joined a caravan of buses and self-styled "taxis" brimming with young people from dozens of tiny communities strung along the creek branches and nestled in the coves of the Blue Ridge Mountains of East Tennessee. The caravan picked up speed as it hit paved roads and crossed the Watauga River bridge, passing beneath a sign advertising Elizabethton's new-found identity as a "City of Power." By the time Cole reached the factory gate, it was 7:00 A.M., time to begin another ten-hour day as a reeler at the American Glanzstoff plant.

The machines whirred, and work began as usual. But the reeling room stirred with anticipation. The day before, March 12, 1929, all but seventeen of the 360 women in the inspection room next door had walked out in protest against low wages, petty rules, and high-handed attitudes. Now they were gathered at the factory gate, refusing to work but ready to negotiate. When 9:00 A.M. approached and the plant manager failed to appear, they broke past the guards and rushed through the plant, urging their co-workers out on strike. By 1:40 P.M. the machines were idle and the plant was closed.

The Elizabethton conflict rocked Carter County and made national headlines. Before March ended, the spirit of protest had jumbled the Blue Ridge and spread through the Piedmont. Gastonia, Marion, and Danville saw the most bitter conflicts, but dozens of towns were shocked by an unexpected workers' revolt.

The textile industry has always been a stronghold of women's labor, and women were central to these events. The most well-known protagonist in the 1929 strikes was, and remains, Gastonia's Ella May Wiggins, who migrated from the mountains, composed ballads for the union, and became a martyr to the workers' cause. But even Ella May Wiggins has been more revered than explained. . . .

Until recently, historians of trade unionism, like trade unionists themselves, neglected women, while historians of women concentrated on the Northeast and the middle class. There were few scholarly challenges to the assumption that women workers in general and southern women in particular were "hard to organize" and that women as family members exercised a conservative pull against class cohesion. Instances of female militancy were seen and not seen. Because they contradicted conventional wisdom, they were easily dismissed.

. . . Our task is not only to describe and celebrate but also to contextualize, and thus to understand. In Elizabethton the preindustrial background, the structure of the work force and the industry, the global forces that impinged on local events — these particularities of time and place conditioned women's choices and shaped their identities. Equally important was a private world traditionally pushed to the margins of labor history. Female friendships and sexuality, cross-generational and

"Disorderly Women: Gender and Labor Militancy in the Appalachian South," by Jacquelyn Dowd Hall, *Journal of American History* 73 (September 1986): 354–382. Reprinted by permission of the Organization of American Historians.

cross-class alliances, the incorporation of new consumer desires into a dynamic regional culture — these, too, energized women's participation. Women in turn were historical subjects, helping to create the circumstances from which the strike arose and guiding by their actions the course the conflict took. . . .

In 1925 the J. P. Bemberg Company of Barmen, Germany, manufacturer of high-quality rayon yarn by an exclusive stretch spinning process, began pouring the thick concrete floors of its first United States subsidiary. Three years later Germany's leading producer of viscose yarn, the Vereinigte Glanzstoff Fabriken, A.G., of Elberfeld opened a jointly managed branch nearby. A post–World War I fashion revolution, combined with protective tariffs, had spurred the American rayon industry's spectacular growth. As one industry publicist put it, "With long skirts, cotton stockings were quite in order; but with short skirts, nothing would do except sheer, smooth stockings. . . . It was on the trim legs of post-war flappers, it has been said, that rayon first stepped out into big business." Dominated by a handful of European giants, the rayon industry clustered along the Appalachian mountain chain. By World War II over 70 percent of American rayon production took place in the southern states, with 50 percent of the national total in Virginia and Tennessee alone. . . .

Frontier families had settled the fertile Watauga River Valley around Elizabethton before the Revolution. Later arrivals pushed farther up the mountains into the hollows carved by fast-falling creeks. Stony Creek is the oldest and largest of those creek-bed communities. . . . Descendants of the original settlers cultivated their own small plots, grazed livestock in woods that custom held open to all, hunted and fished in an ancient hardwood forest, mined iron ore, made whiskey, spun cloth, and bartered with local merchants for what they could not produce at home.

In the 1880s East Tennessee's timber and mineral resources attracted the attention of capitalists in the United States and abroad, and an era of land speculation and railroad building began. The railroads opened the way to timber barons, who stripped away the forests, leaving hillsides stark and vulnerable to erosion. Farmers abandoned their fields to follow the march of the logging camps. Left behind, women and children did their best to pick up the slack. But by the time Carter County was "timbered out" in the 1920s, farm families had crept upward to the barren ridge lands or grown dependent on "steady work and cash wages." Meanwhile, in Elizabethton, the county seat, an aggressive new class of bankers, lawyers, and businessmen served as brokers for outside developers, speculated in land, invested in homegrown factories, and looked beyond the hills for their standards of "push, progress and prosperity." . . .

The coming of the rayon plants represented a coup for Elizabethton's aspiring businessmen, who wooed investors with promises of free land, tax exemptions, and cheap labor. But at first the whole county seemed to share the boomtown spirit. Men from Stony Creek, Gap Creek, and other mountain hamlets built the cavernous mills, then stayed on to learn the chemical processes that transformed the cellulose from wood pulp and cotton linters (the short fibers that remain on cotton seeds after longer, spinnable fibers are removed) into "artificial silk." Women vied for jobs in the textile division where they wound, reeled, twisted, and inspected the rayon yarn. Real-estate prices soared as the city embarked on a frenzied improvement campaign and private developers threw up houses in subdivisions of outlying fields. Yet for all the excitement it engendered, industrialization in Carter County retained a distinctly rural cast. Although Elizabethton's population tripled (from 2,749 in 1920 to 8,093 in 1930), the rayon workers confounded predictions of spectacular urban growth, for most remained in the countryside, riding to work on chartered buses and trains or in taxis driven by neighbors and friends.

Women made up a large proportion of the 3,213 workers in the mills. According to company sources, they held 30 percent of the jobs at the Bemberg plant and a full 44 percent at the larger Glanzstoff mill — where the strike started and the union gained its firmest hold. Between 75 and 80 percent of those female employees were single and aged sixteen to twenty-one. . . . Adult married men, together with a smaller number of teenage boys, dominated the chemical division, while young women, the vast majority of whom commuted from farm homes, processed the finished yarn. . . .

The women who beat a path to the rayon plants came from families that had already been drawn into an economy where money was a key to survival. . . . The timber industry, which attracted Carter County's men, undermined its agricultural base, and destroyed its natural resources, created few opportunities for rural women. No wonder that farm daughters in the mills counted their blessings and looked on themselves as pioneers. . . . Whether they sought employment out of family need, adventurousness, or thwarted aspiration — or a combination of the three — most saw factory labor as a hopeful gamble rather than a desperate last resort. . . .

Pay scales were low even for the southern textile industry, and workers quickly found their income eaten away by the cost of commuting or of boarding in town. When the strike came it focused on the issue of Glanzstoff women's wages, which lagged behind those at the older Bemberg plant. But workers had other grievances as well. . . . In the chemical division men waded through water and acid, exposed all day to a lethal spray. Women labored under less dangerous conditions, but for longer hours and less pay. Paid by the piece, they complained of rising production quotas and what everyone referred to as "hard rules."

Women in particular were singled out for petty regulations, aimed not just at extracting labor but at shaping deportment as well. They were forbidden to wear makeup; in some departments they were required to purchase uniforms. Most galling of all was company surveillance of the washroom. According to Bessie Edens, who was promoted to "forelady" in the twisting room, "men could do what they wanted to in their own department," but women had to get a pass to leave the shop floor. "If we went to the bathroom, they'd follow us," Flossie Cole confirmed, "'fraid we'd stay a minute too long." If they did, their pay was docked; one too many trips and they lost their jobs. . . .

Efforts to organize the plants by local American Federation of Labor (AFL) craft unionists had begun at least as early as 1927. But the strike was initiated on March 12, 1929, by women in the Glanzstoff inspection department, by what one observer called "girls in their teens [who] decided not to put up with the present conditions any longer." . . . Christine Galliher remembered the moment well: "We all decided in that department if they didn't give us a raise we wasn't going to work." One by one the other sections sent word: "We are more important than any other department of the plant. . . . Why don't you walk out and we will walk out with you?" At 12:30 the inspectors left their jobs.

On March 13 the women returned to the plant and led the rest of the work force out on strike. Five days later Bemberg workers came out as well. By then the Carter County Chancery Court had handed down two draconian injunctions forbidding all demonstrations against the company. When strikers ignored the injunctions, plant managers joined town officials in convincing the governor to send in the National Guard. The strikers secured a charter from the AFL's United Textile Workers (UTW). Meeting in a place called the Tabernacle, built for religious revivals, they listened to a Baptist preacher from Stony Creek warn: "The hand of oppression is growing on our people. . . . You women work for practically nothing. You must come together and say that such things must cease to be." Each night more workers "came forward" to take the union oath.

Meanwhile, UTW and Federal Conciliation Service officials arrived on the scene. On March 22 they reached a "gentlemen's agreement" by which the company promised a new wage scale for "good girl help" and agreed not to discriminate against union members. The strikers returned to work, but the conflict was far from over. Higher paychecks never materialized; union members began losing their jobs. On April 4 local businessmen kidnapped two union organizers and ran them out of town. Eleven days later a second strike began, this time among the women in the Glanzstoff reeling room. "When they blew that whistle everybody knew to quit work," Flossie Cole recalled. "We all just quit our work and rushed out. Some of 'em went to Bemberg and climbed the fence. [They] went into Bemberg and got 'em out of there." . . .

This time the conflict quickly escalated. More troops arrived, and the plants became fortresses, with machine guns on the rooftops and armed guardsmen on the ground. The company sent buses manned by soldiers farther up the hollows to recruit new workers and to escort them back to town. Pickets blocked narrow mountain roads. Houses were blown up; the town water main was dynamited. An estimated 1,250 individuals were arrested in confrontations with the National Guard.

As far as can be determined, no women were involved in barn burnings and dynamitings. . . . Men "went places that we didn't go," explained Christine Galliher. "They had big dark secrets . . . the men did." But when it came to public demonstrations, women held center stage. At the outset "hundreds of girls" had ridden down main street "in buses and taxis, shouting and laughing at people who watched them from windows and doorsteps." Now they blocked the road at Gap Creek and refused soldiers' orders that they walk twelve miles to jail in town. . . . At Valley Forge women teased the guardsmen and shamed the strikebreakers. In Elizabethton after picket duty, women marched down the "Bemberg Highway . . . draped in the American flag and carrying the colors" — thereby forcing the guardsmen to present arms each time they passed. Inventive, playful, and shrewd, the women's tactics encouraged a holiday spirit. They may also have deflected violence and garnered community support.

Laughter was among the women's most effective weapons. But they also made more prosaic contributions, chief among which was taking responsibility for the everyday tasks of the union. . . . And beneath high spirits the terms of battle had begun to change. The militancy of Alfred Hoffmann, the UTW's chief organizer at Elizabethton, matched the strikers' own. But he was hobbled by a national union that lacked the resources and commitment to sustain the strike. Instead of translating workers' grievances into a compelling challenge, the UTW pared their demands down to the bone. On May 26, six weeks after the strike began, the union agreed to a settlement that made no mention of wages, hours, working conditions, or union recognition. The company's only concession was a promise not to discriminate against union members. The workers were less than enthusiastic. According to the strike's most thorough chronicler, "It took nine speeches and a lot of question answering lasting two and a half hours to get the strikers to accept the terms." . . .

Observers at the time and historians since saw the Elizabethton strike as a straightforward case of labor-management strife. But the conflict appeared quite different from within. Everyone interviewed put the blame for low wages on an alliance between the German managers and the "leading citizens" of the town. Preserved in the oral tradition is the story of how the "town fathers" promised the company a supply of cheap and unorganized labor. Bessie Edens put it this way: They told the company that "women wasn't used to working, and they'd work for almost nothing, and the men would work for low wages. That's the way they got the plant here." In this version of events the strike was part of an ongoing tug-of-war. On one side stood workers, farmers, and small merchants linked by traditional networks of trade and kin. On the other, development-minded townspeople cast their lot with a "latter day industrialism" embodied by the rayon plants. . . .

Stony Creek farmers were solidly behind the sons and daughters they sent to the factories. . . . Solidarity flowed not only from the farm families of striking workers but also from small merchants who relied on those families for their trade. . . . In this context of family- and community-based resistance, women had important roles to play. Farm mothers nurtured the strikers' independence simply by cleaving to the land, passing on to their children a heritage at odds with the values of the new order and maintaining family production as a hedge against the uncertainties of a market economy. But the situation of farm mothers had other effects as well, and it would be a mistake to push the argument for continuity too far. As their husbands ranged widely in search of wage labor, women's work intensified while their status — now tied to earning power — declined. The female strikers of Elizabethton saw their mothers as resourceful and strong but also as increasingly isolated and hard pressed. Most important, they no longer looked to their mothers' lives as patterns for their own. . . .

Women . . . , it seems, sensed the devaluation of women's handicraft labor in the face of cheap consumer goods. They feared the long arm of their mother's fate, resented their father's distant authority, and envied their brother's exploits away from home. By opting for work in the rayon plants, they struck out for their own place in a changing world. When low wages, high costs, and autocratic managers affronted their dignity and dashed their hopes, they were the first to revolt. . . .

The fact of women's initiative and participation in collective action is instructive. Even more intriguing is the gender-based symbolism of their protest style. Through dress, language, and gesture, female strikers expressed a complex cultural identity and turned it to their own rebellious purposes.

Consider, for instance, Trixie Perry and a woman who called herself "Texas

Bill." Twenty-eight-year-old Trixie Perry was a reeler in the Glanzstoff plant. She had apparently become pregnant ten years before, had married briefly and then divorced, giving her son her maiden name. Her father was a butcher and a farmer, and she lived near her family on the edge of town. Perry later moved into Elizabethton. She never remarried but went on to have several more children by other men. Texas Bill's background is more elusive. All we know is that she came from out of state, lived in a boardinghouse, and claimed to have been married twice before she arrived in town. These two friends were ringleaders on the picket line. Both were charged with violating the injunction, and both were brought to trial.

Trixie Perry took the stand in a dress sewn from red, white, and blue bunting and a cap made of a small American flag. . . .

The main charge was that Perry and her friend had drawn a line across the road at Gap Creek and dared the soldiers to cross it. Above all they were accused of taunting the National Guard. The defense attorney, a fiery local lawyer playing to a sympathetic crowd, did not deny the charges. Instead, he used the women to mock the government's case. Had Trixie Perry threatened a lieutenant? "He rammed a gun in my face and I told him to take it out or I would knock it out." Had she blocked the road? "A little thing like me block a big road?" What had she said to the threat of a tear gas bomb? "That little old fire cracker of a thing, it won't go off."

Texas Bill was an even bigger hit with the crowd. The defense attorney called her the "Wild Man from Borneo." . . . Texas Bill both affirmed and subverted her reputation. Her nickname came from her habit of wearing "cowboy" clothes. But when it was her turn to testify, she "strutted on the stand" in a fashionable black picture hat and a black coat. Besides her other transgressions, she was accused of grabbing a soldier's gun and aiming it at him. What was she doing on the road so early in the morning? "I take a walk every morning before breakfast for my health," Texas Bill replied with what a reporter described as "an assumed ladylike dignity." . . .

Mock gentility, transgressive laughter, male egos on the line — the mix made for wonderful theater and proved effective in court as well. The judge reserved maximum sentences for three especially aggressive men; all the women and most of the men were found not guilty or were lightly fined. In the end even those convictions were overturned by the state court of appeals. . . .

But Trixie Perry and Texas Bill were not just out of line in their public acts; they also led unconventional private lives. It was that erotic subtext that most horrified officialdom and amused the courtroom crowd. . . . In the heat of the trial, the question of whether or not women — as workers — had violated the injunction took second place to questions about their status *as women,* as members of their sex. Had they cursed? Had they been on the road at odd hours of the day or night? Was Texas Bill a lady or a "wild man from Borneo"? Fearing that "lewd women" might discredit the organizing drive, the organizers tried to send them home. To protect the community's "moral tone," the city council threatened to lock them up.

There is nothing extraordinary about this association between sexual misbehavior and women's labor militancy. . . . Since female aggressiveness stirs up fears of women's sexual power, opponents have often undercut union organizing drives by insinuations of prostitution or promiscuity. Fearing guilt by association, "respectable" women stay away.

What is impressive here is how Trixie Perry and Texas Bill handled the dichotomy between ladyhood and lewdness, good girls and bad. Using words that, for women in particular, were ordinarily taboo, they refused deference and signaled disrespect. Making no secret of their sexual experience, they combined flirtation with fierceness on the picket line and adopted a provocative courtroom style. And yet, with the language of dress — a cap made of an American flag, an elegant wide-brimmed hat — they claimed their rights as citizens and their place in the female community.

Moreover, that community upheld their claims. The defense attorney chose "disorderly women" as his star witnesses, and the courtroom spectators enthusiastically cheered them on. . . . The other female defendants may have been less flamboyant, but they were no less sharp-tongued. Was Vivian King a member of the UTW? "Yes, and proud of it." . . . Did Lena May Jones "holler out 'scab'"? "No, I think the statement made was 'I wouldn't be a scab' and 'Why don't you come and join our organization.'" Did she laugh at a soldier and tell him his gun wouldn't shoot? "I didn't tell him it wouldn't shoot, but I laughed at him . . . and told him he was too much of a man to shoot a lady."

Interviewed over fifty years later, strike participants still refused to make invidious distinctions between themselves and women like Trixie Perry and Texas Bill. Bessie Edens was a settled, self-educated, married woman. But she was also a self-described "daredevil on the picket line," secure in the knowledge that she had a knife hidden in her drawstring underwear. To Edens, who came from a mountain hamlet called Hampton, the chief distinction did not lie between herself and rougher women. It lay between herself and merchants' wives who blamed the trouble on "those hussies from Hampton." When asked what she thought of Trixie Perry and Texas Bill, she answered simply, "There were some girls like that involved. But I didn't care. They did their part." . . .

Family and community solidarity were obvious in the courtroom, implicit in press reports, and confirmed by interviews. By inference, they can also be seen in the living situations of female strikers. Of the 122 activists whose residences could be determined, only six lived or boarded alone. Residing at home, they could hardly have joined in the fray without family toleration or support. . . .

This is not to say that the women of Elizabethton were simply acting on tradition. On the contrary, the strikers dressed the persona of the disorderly woman in unmistakably modern garb. Women's behavior on the witness stand presupposed a certain sophistication: A passing familiarity allowed them to parody ladyhood and to thumb a nose at the genteel standards of the town. Combining garments from the local past with fragments of an expansive consumer culture, the women of Elizabethton assembled their own version of a brash, irreverent Jazz Age style.

By the early 1920s radios and "Ford touring cars" had joined railroads and mail-order catalogs as conduits to the larger world. Record companies had discovered hill-country music, and East Tennessee's first country-music stars were recording hits that transformed ballad singing, fiddle playing, and banjo picking into one of America's great popular-music sounds. . . . Arriving for work in the rayon plants, young people brought with them the useable past of the countryside, but they quickly assimilated the speeded-up rhythms, the fashions, the popular culture of their generation's changing times.

Work-related peer groups formed a bridge between traditional loyalties and a novel youth culture. Whether married or single, living with parents or on their own, women participated in the strike in same-sex groups. Sisters boarded, worked, and demonstrated together. Girlfriends teamed up in groups or pairs. . . . Most of the Elizabethton women were in their teens or early twenties, the usual age of marriage in the region, and the strike provided unaccustomed opportunities for courtship. Rather than choosing a neighbor they had known all their lives, under watchful parental eyes, women flirted on the picket lines or the shop floor. Romance and politics commingled in the excitement of the moment, flowering in a spectrum of behavior — from the outrageousness of Trixie Perry to a spate of marriages among other girls.

What needs emphasis here is the dynamic quality of working-class women's culture — a quality that is sometimes lost in static oppositions between modernism and traditionalism, individualism and family values, consumer and producer mentalities. This is especially important where regional history has been so thoroughly mythologized. Appalachian culture, like all living cultures, embraced continuity and discontinuity, indigenous and borrowed elements. . . . The Elizabethton strikers were "new women," making their way in a world their mothers could not have known but carrying with them values handed down through the female line. . . .

※ *F U R T H E R   R E A D I N G*

Lizabeth Cohen, *Making a New Deal: Industrial Workers in Chicago, 1919–1939* (1990)

Ileen A. DeVault, *Sons and Daughters of Labor: Class and Clerical Work in Turn-of-the-Century Pittsburgh* (1990)

Faye Dudden, *Serving Women: Household Service in Nineteenth-Century America* (1983)

Nancy Schrom Dye, *As Equals and As Sisters: Feminism, the Labor Movement, and the Women's Trade Union League of New York* (1981)

Sarah Einsenstein, *Give Us Bread But Give Us Roses* (1983)

Elizabeth Faue, *Community of Suffering and Struggle: Women, Men, and the Labor Movement in Minneapolis, 1915–1945* (1991)

Lisa Fine, *The Souls of the Skyscraper: Female Clerical Workers in Chicago, 1870–1930* (1990)

Martha Fraundorf, "The Labor Force Participation of Turn-of-the-Century Married Women," *Journal of Economic History* XXXIX (1979), 401–418

Dee Garrison, *Apostles of Culture: The Public Librarian and American Society, 1876–1920* (1979)

Evelyn Nakanno Glenn, *Issei, Nisei, War Bride: Three Generations of Japanese American Women in Domestic Service* (1986)

Susan A. Glenn, *Daughters of the Shtetl: Life and Labor in the Immigrant Generation* (1990)

Claudia Goldin, "The Work and Wages of Single Women, 1870–1920," *Journal of Economic History* XL (1980), 81–88

Tamara Hareven, *Family Time and Industrial Time* (1982)

Barbara Harris, *Beyond Her Sphere: Women and the Professions in American History* (1978)

Darlene Clark Hine, *Black Women in White: Racial Conflict and Cooperation in the Nursing Profession, 1890–1950* (1989)

Joan Jensen and Sue Davidson, eds., *A Needle, A Bobbin, A Strike* (1984)

Jacqueline Jones, *Labor of Love, Labor of Sorrow: Black Women, Work, and the Family from Slavery to the Present* (1985)

David Katzman, *Seven Days a Week: Women and Domestic Service in Industrializing America* (1978)

Alice Kessler-Harris, *Out of Work: A History of Wage-Earning Women in the United States* (1982)

Joanne Meyerowitz, *Women Adrift: Independent Wage Earners in Chicago, 1880–1930* (1988)

Stephen Norwood, *Labor's Flaming Youth: Telephone Operators and Worker Militancy, 1878–1923* (1990)

Kathy Peiss, *Cheap Amusements: Working Women and Leisure in Turn-of-the-Century New York* (1986)

Joanne Reitano, "Working Girls Unite," *American Quarterly* XXXVI (1984), 112–134

Elyce Rotella, *From Home to Office: United States Women at Work, 1870–1930* (1981)

Barbara Miller Soloman, *In the Company of Educated Women* (1985)

Meredith Tax, *The Rising of the Women: Feminist Solidarity and Class Conflict, 1880–1917* (1981)

Mary Roth Walsh, *Doctors Wanted: No Women Need Apply* (1977)

Winifred Wandersee, *Women's Work and Family Values, 1920–1940* (1981)

Women and Politics

in the 1920s

In 1920 women finally achieved the goal they had been striving for since 1848: The Nineteenth Amendment, granting women the right to vote, was added to the United States Constitution. Though suffragists often had been divided by race, class, and political ideology, in the two decades prior to ratification they had forged a successful coalition, working on the assumption that access to the ballot would benefit all women as well as society at large. Listening to suffragists speak of the day when the ballot would be theirs, hostile journalists and politicians concluded that women would likely vote as a bloc, damaging democracy and individualism in the process. This conclusion was drawn hastily; nonetheless, the issue of a "woman's bloc" has long influenced historical scholarship on women in the twenties.

As it turned out, American women in the 1920s did not vote as a unified group. Moreover, the suffragist coalition collapsed, and feminists divided over a number of issues. For example, Florence Kelley and other advocates of women's protective labor legislation became entangled in a bitter debate with the National Woman's Party over the party's fight for an Equal Rights Amendment. Does the absence of a "woman's bloc" suggest that American women had grown indifferent to politics? Should we interpret the controversy over the ERA as proof of the failure of organized feminism or, rather, as evidence of meaningful differences of opinion among activist women? How should we characterize feminism and describe women's relationship to politics in the 1920s?

❋ D O C U M E N T S

In October 1920, in an effort at interracial cooperation, the Women's Council of the Methodist Episcopal Church, South, whose members were white, issued a statement supporting a number of reforms desired by African-American women. Conspicuously absent from the council's list was suffrage — a right long denied to black men in the South and one now likely to be withheld from black women as well. The omission was not lost on the Southeastern Federation of Colored Women's Clubs, which pointedly responded to the white women's statement in June 1921; these two statements appear here as the first document. In the second document, published the following year in *The Nation*, Elsie Hill of the National Woman's Party calls for the elimination of all legal distinctions between men and women. In the third document, Florence Kelley, in the same issue of *The Nation*, sharply criticizes Hill's position, arguing that the National Woman's Party misunderstands women's legal interests and seems intent on undermining the protective labor laws that benefit female wage earners. In a 1925 speech (the fourth document), Alice Drysdale Vickery explains why feminists should support a woman's right to obtain and use contraception. Three years later, Carrie Chapman Catt, the former president of the National American Woman Suffrage Association, made a speech at a Washington, D.C., peace convention exploring the means by which women and men might substitute world peace for war; an excerpt from this speech is the fifth document. In 1931, a decade after the vote had been won, Emily Newell Blair — a vice chairman of the National Democratic Committee from 1922–1928 — expressed discouragement at women's lack of progress in politics, as is revealed in the final document.

Two Statements on Race Relations

Women's Council of the Methodist Episcopal Church, South, 1920

We, a company of Southern white women, in conference assembled on the invitation of the Commission on Inter-Racial Cooperation, find ourselves with a deep sense of responsibility to the womanhood and childhood of the Negro race, and also with a great desire for a Christian settlement of the problems that overshadow the homes of both races. . . .

We recognize and deplore the fact that there is friction between the races, but we believe that this can be largely removed by the exercise of justice, consideration, and sympathetic cooperation.

In order that the results of this conference may be perpetuated and enlarged, we recommend:

That a Continuation Committee be appointed to devise ways and means for carrying out the work considered by this conference; that this committee be composed of one woman from each denomination and Christian agency here represented, and that it be empowered to add to its membership as may seem necessary; that each local community form a Woman's Inter-Racial Committee, which may include representatives from all religious, civil and social service bodies working in the community, and that this Continuation Committee recommend plans by which this may be accomplished.

Desiring that everything that hinders the establishment of confidence peace justice and righteousness in our land shall be removed in order that there shall be better understanding and good will in our midst, we call attention to the following points as possible causes of friction, which if corrected, may go far toward creating a better day.

Domestic Service. We acknowledge our responsibility for the protection of the Negro women and girls in our homes and on the streets. We therefore recommend: That the domestic service be classed as an occupation and coordinated with other world service in order that better relations may be established by both employer and employee.

Child Welfare. We are persuaded that the conservation of the life and health of Negro children is of the utmost importance to the community. We therefore urge:

That day nurseries and kindergartens be established in local communities for the protection, care and training of children of Negro mothers who go out to work; that free baby clinics be established and that government leaflets on child welfare be distributed to expectant mothers, thus teaching the proper care of themselves and their children; that adequate playgrounds and recreational facilities be established for Negro children and young people.

Sanitation and Housing. Since good housing and proper sanitation are necessary for both physical and moral life, we recommend: That a survey of housing and sanitary conditions be made in the Negro section in each local community, followed by an appeal to the proper authorities for improvements when needed.

Education. Since sacredness of personality is the basis for all civilization, we urge: That every agency touching the child life of the nation shall strive to create mutual respect in the hearts of the children of different races. We are convinced that the establishment of a single standard of morals for men and women, both black and white, is necessary for the life and safety of a nation. We therefore pledge ourselves to strive to secure respect and protection for womanhood everywhere, regardless of race or color. Since provision for the education of Negro children is still inadequate, we recommend: More equitable division of the school fund, suitable school buildings and equipment, longer school terms, higher standards and increased pay for teachers.

Travel. Since colored people frequently do not receive fair treatment on street cars, on railroads and in railway stations and recognizing this as one of the chief causes of friction between the races, we urge: That immediate steps be taken to provide for them adequate accommodations and courteous treatment at the hands of street car and railway officials.

Lynching. As women, we urge those who are charged with the administration of the law to prevent lynching at any cost. We are persuaded that the proper determination on the part of the constituted officials, upheld by public sentiment, would result in the detection and prosecution of those guilty of this crime. Therefore we pledge ourselves to endeavor to create a public sentiment which will uphold these officials in the execution of justice.

Justice in the Courts. We recommend: That our women everywhere raise their voices against all acts of violence to property and person, wherever and for whatever cause occurring. We further recommend: That competent legal assistance be made available for colored people in the local communities in order to insure to them the protection of their rights in the courts.

Public Press. Since the public press often gives undue prominence to the criminal element among Negroes, and neglects the worthy and constructive efforts of law-abiding citizens, we pledge ourselves to cooperate with the men's committees in endeavoring to correct this injustice, and to create a fair attitude to Negroes and Negro news. . . .

Southeastern Federation of Colored Women's Clubs, 1921

We desire to state our position on some matters relating to the welfare of colored people, and to enlist the sympathy and cooperation of Southern white women in the interest of better understandings and better conditions, as these affect the relations between white and colored people.

We take this opportunity to call to your attention certain conditions which affect colored women in their relations with white people and which if corrected will go far toward decreasing friction, removing distrust and suspicion and creating a better atmosphere in which to adjust the difficulties which always accompany human contacts.

Conditions in Domestic Service. The most frequent and intimate contact of white and colored women is in domestic service. Every improvement made in the physical, moral and spiritual life of those so employed must react to increase the efficiency of their service to their employers.

We, therefore, direct your attention to: Long and Irregular Working Hours; (1) lack of provision for wholesome recreation; (2) undesirable housing conditions. We recommend, therefore, (1) definite regulation for hours and conditions of work; (2) sanitary, attractive and wholesome rooming facilities; (3) closer attention to personal appearance and deportment; (4) provision for and investigation of character of recreation.

Child Welfare. The large burden of economic responsibility which falls upon many colored women results in their prolonged absence from home and the consequent neglect of the children of the homes. We direct your attention to: Child Welfare — (1) neglected homes (irregularity in food, clothing, conduct, training); (2) truancy; (3) juvenile delinquency. We therefore recommend — Welfare Activities — (1) day nurseries, play grounds, recreation centers; (2) home and school visitation; (3) probation officers and reform schools.

Conditions of Travel. Race friction is perhaps more frequent in street cars and railroad trains than in any other public places. To reduce this friction and remove causes for just complaint from colored passengers we call your attention to: (1) seating accommodations on street cars; (2) unsanitary surroundings, at stations and on trains; (3) toilet facilities, at stations and on trains; (4) difficulty in securing tickets, Pullman accommodations and meals; (5) abuse of rights of colored passengers by train crew and white passengers occupying seats while colored passengers stand, smoking, profane language, overcrowding; (6) as corrective measures we suggest provision of equal accommodations in all public carriers and courteous treatment at the hands of street car and railway officials, for all passengers.

Education. Without education for all the children of all the people we cannot sustain a democracy. Ignorance and crime are the twin children of neglect and poverty. We urge your increasing effort for better educational facilities so that there may be provided: adequate accommodations for all Negro children of school age, vocational training in all secondary schools, improved rural schools — longer terms, suitable buildings, training schools for teachers, adequate salaries for teachers.

Lynching. We deplore and condemn any act on the part of any men which would tend to excite the mob spirit. We believe that any man who makes an assault upon any woman should have prompt punishment meted out to the limit of the law, but not without thorough investigation of the facts and trial by the courts. The continuance of lynching is the greatest menace to good will between the races, and a constant factor in undermining respect for all law and order. It is our opinion that mob violence incites to crime rather than deters it; and certainly it is less effective in discouraging crime than the watchful, thorough and deliberate processes of a fair and just trial.

Toward the suppression of this evil, we appeal to white women to: (1) raise their voices in immediate protest when lynchings or mob violence is threatened; (2) encourage every effort to detect and punish the leaders and participants in mobs and riots; (3) encourage the white pulpit and press in creating a sentiment among law-abiding citizens and urge outspoken condemnation of these forms of lawlessness.

The Public Press. In the great majority of cases the white press of the South gives undue prominence to crime and the criminal element among Negroes to the neglect of the worthy and constructive efforts of law-abiding Negro citizens. We feel that a large part of friction and misunderstanding between the races is due to unjust, inflammatory and misleading headlines, and articles appearing in the daily papers. We suggest that white women include in their local community program a united effort to correct this evil and to secure greater attention to worthy efforts of Negro citizens.

Suffrage. We regard the ballot as the democratic and orderly method of correcting abuses and protecting the rights of citizens; as the substitute of civilization for violence. As peace loving, law-abiding citizens we believe the ultimate and only guarantee of fair dealing and justice for the Negro, as well as the wholesome development of the whole community, lies in the peaceful, orderly exercise of the franchise by every qualified Negro citizen. We ask therefore, that white women, for the protection of their homes as well as ours indicate their sanction of the ballot for all citizens as representing government by the sober, reasoned and deliberate judgment of all the people.

In these articles offered at your request we are stating frankly and soberly what in our judgement, you as white women may do to correct the ills from which our race has so long suffered, and of which we as a race are perhaps more conscious now than ever. We recall how in the recent days of our nation's peril so many of us worked side by side for the safety of this land and defense of this flag which is ours as it is yours. In that same spirit of unselfishness and sacrifice we offer ourselves to serve again with you in any and every way that a courageous facing of duty may require as you undertake heroically this self-appointed yet God-given task. We deeply appreciate the difficulties that lie before you, but as you undertake these things which are destined to bless us all, we pledge you our faith and loyalty in consecration to God, home and country.

Elsie Hill on Why Women Should Have Full Legal Equality, 1922

The removal of all forms of the subjection of women is the purpose to which the National Woman's Party is dedicated. Its present campaign to remove the discriminations against women in the laws of the United States is but the beginning of its determined effort to secure the freedom of women, an integral part of the struggle for human liberty for which women are first of all responsible. Its interest lies in the final release of woman from the class of a dependent, subservient being to which early civilization committed her.

The laws of various States at present hold her in that class. They deny her a control of her children equal to the father's; they deny her, if married, the right to her own earnings; they punish her for offences for which men go unpunished; they exclude her from public office and from public institutions to the support of which her taxes contribute. These laws are not the creation of this age, but the fact that they are still tolerated on our statute books and that in some States their removal is vigorously resisted shows the hold of old traditions upon us. Since the passage of the Suffrage Amendment the incongruity of these laws, dating back many centuries, has become more than ever marked. . . .

The National Woman's Party believes that it is a vital social need to do away with these discriminations against women and is devoting its energies to that end. The removal of the discriminations and not the method by which they are removed is the thing upon which the Woman's Party insists. It has under consideration an amendment to the Federal Constitution which, if adopted, would remove them at one stroke, but it is at present endeavoring to secure their removal in the individual States by a blanket bill, which is the most direct State method. For eighty-two years the piecemeal method has been tried, beginning with the married women's property act of 1839 in Mississippi, and no State, excepting Wisconsin, where the Woman's Party blanket bill was passed in June, 1921, has yet finished. . . .

The present program of the National Woman's Party is to introduce its Woman's Equal Rights Bill, or bills attaining the same purpose, in all State legislatures as they convene. It is building up in Washington a great headquarters from which this campaign can be conducted, and it is acting in the faith that the removal of these discriminations from our laws will benefit every group of women in the country, and through them all society.

Florence Kelley Explains Her Opposition to Full Legal Equality, 1922

"The removal of all forms of subjection of women is the purpose to which the National Woman's Party is dedicated."

A few years ago the Woman's Party counted disfranchisement the form of subjection which must first be removed. Today millions of American women, educated and uneducated, are kept from the polls in bold defiance of the Suffrage Amendment. Every form of subjection suffered by their white sisters they also suffer. Deprivation of the vote is theirs alone among native women. Because of this discrimination all other forms of subjection weigh a hundred fold more heavily upon them. In the family, in the effort to rent or to buy homes, as wage-earners, before the courts, in getting education for their children, in every relation of life, their burden is greater because they are victims of political inequality. How literally are colored readers to understand the words quoted above?

Sex is a biological fact. The political rights of citizens are not properly dependent upon sex, but social and domestic relations and industrial activities are. All modern-minded people desire that women should have full political equality and like opportunity in business and the professions. No enlightened person desires that they should be excluded from jury duty or denied the equal guardianship of children, or that unjust inheritance laws or discriminations against wives should be perpetuated.

The inescapable facts are, however, that men do not bear children, are freed from the burdens of maternity, and are not susceptible, in the same measures as women, to poisons now increasingly characteristic of certain industries, and to the universal poison of fatigue. These are differences so far reaching, so fundamental, that it is grotesque to ignore them. Women cannot be made men by act of the legislature or by amendment of the Federal Constitution. This is no matter of today or tomorrow. The inherent differences are permanent. Women will always need many laws different from those needed by men.

The effort to enact the blanket bill in defiance of all biological differences recklessly imperils the special laws for women as such, for wives, for mothers, and for wage-earners. . . .

Why should wage-earning women be thus forbidden to get laws for their own health and welfare and that of their unborn children? Why should they be made subject to the preferences of wage-earning men? Is not this of great and growing importance when the number of women wage-earners, already counted by millions, increases by leaps and bounds from one census to the next? And when the industries involving exposure to poisons are increasing faster than ever? And when the overwork of mothers is one recognized cause of the high infant death rate? And when the rise in the mortality of mothers in childbirth continues?

If there were no other way of promoting more perfect equality for women, an argument could perhaps be sustained for taking these risks. But why take them when every desirable measure attainable through the blanket bill can be enacted in the ordinary way? . . .

Is the National Woman's Party for or against protective measures for wage-earning women? Will it publicly state whether it is for or against the eight-hour day and minimum-wage commissions for women? Yes or No?

Alice Drysdale Vickery, "The Place of Birth Control in the Woman's Movement," 1925

This seems to me a very critical period in the world's history. Either the world's inhabitants must face the problem of controlling the numbers of succeeding generations in proportion to the supply of necessaries, or the struggle between the various races and nations will become intensified and lead to world-wide disaster.

This is a time in which it is of the utmost importance that women shall learn to realize their responsibility, in view of the fact that the peopling of the world belongs to them. It is essential then that women shall come to the front and insist that they will no longer consent to be deprived of the knowledge which will allow them to fulfill their function in the way which will reflect credit upon themselves individually and collectively, and benefit the world at large. Sir Arbuthnot Lane has written of "the crass stupidity of man," and when we recall the obstacles which have been placed in the way of women's education generally, and education in physiology, biology, and all that concerns the reproduction of the human species in particular, we cannot think the phrase misplaced. The church has always looked with disfavor on the education of young people, more particularly women, in sex matters. Men also have very largely desired ignorance in their mates. The legal profession have placed obstacles in the way of woman's power of acting on her own judgment, by making her in the past so largely dependent on the husband as to feel it impossible to form or take any action of which he might not approve.

The subject which above all others craves the woman's outlook is that of maternity and reproduction.

As woman did not know how to control reproduction and as she naturally, as did man, desired a mate in the early days of maturity, she fell, almost of necessity, into a state of dependence, and that dependence has been fruitful of evil results. But with the knowledge of contraception, of Birth Control, there is no longer the same reason why she should accept a position of dependence. The young girl like the young man should find the same opportunities for employment and self-dependence open to her. She can postpone marriage until she meets with a suitable partner. And when she does meet with an apparently suitable partner (say at 21 years of age) she will not be faced with the necessity of forfeiting her independent position for fear of the premature arrival of offspring. She will by means of birth control methods be able to maintain a position of self-dependence for some years. There is much to be said for a temporary postponement of parentage after marriage.

First as the age of physiological maturity is 25, it will doubtless be granted that parentage should be delayed to that age in order that maturity and not immaturity should produce the next generation. Again, is it not well that the young couple should be able to enjoy to the full (say from 21 to 25 years) the delight of intimate companionship, until they can feel assured that they are well suited to one another, that their characters and ideals are likely to develop along mutually sympathetic lines; also that their career (industrial or otherwise) may not be hampered by the premature arrival of another mouth to feed and care for, obliging the young mother to cease her independent employment.

The young couple owe to each other fidelity and companionship, mutual solace and assistance. They will learn in this period of experience to understand each other more fully, not merely trusting to the more or less superficial attraction which brought them together. They will besides be more able to assure their future, to build up the home and create and develop the little capital which will enable them to face the responsibility of parentage without alarm. The prospective mother, with health assured, will be willing to cease her contribution to the family budget at a suitable period, having laid by what she deems sufficient for the time being. She will be prepared to give to the new-comer her time, her strength, her thoughts, so that together the young parents will mutually enjoy the delights of parentage, and by the careful use of contraceptive methods will feel assured that no second birth will come to cut short prematurely the mother-care due to the first comer.

Think what all this power of direction means to the young couple in their early married life. The power to go slow, to adjust their expenses to their means to avoid all the overstrain of being always a little behind. Poverty is held at bay. Slums are not being created. The child will enjoy its childhood. He will have time for play, for education. If accidents happen, if ill-health supervene, the strain is materially lessened. Woman with efficient knowledge of birth control can practically abolish poverty in the home. Collectively she will learn how to abolish poverty in the town, the city, the village, the nation.

There need be no sex-promiscuity either for men or women. Rational early marriage laws will allow for needful changes.

Carrie Chapman Catt Explores the Cause and Cure of War, 1928

Ten years after the Great War we may solemnly inquire of events whether the civilized nations are drifting toward that much advertised "next war" or toward the certainties of perpetual peace.

To the most casual observer it is evident that the advocates of peace are growing in number, that the various groups are more tolerant toward each other, that there is more friendliness between them, and that slowly but certainly they are being convinced of the need of a common program, a unanimous aim, and the advantage of a common directing agency. Yet these highly desirable ends are as yet remote and their probability uncertain.

On the other hand, it is also clear that the advocates of war are increasing in number, and that there is a greater solidarity among them than among peace forces. Using as a symbol the game called "The Tug of War," the war forces are pulling hard at one rope, the peace forces are pulling at many ropes and thus distributing their energy in many directions. . . .

War is an institution as old as human records and is almost inextricably entwined with the law, the precedents and the thought of nations. It is bound up with social stability, education, and even religion. War is picturesque, heroic, dramatic, romantic, vivid. . . . This combination grips human sensibilities with well-nigh unshakable power.

War is also a mighty vested interest and millions live by it. Not only is war the daily support of soldiers and sailors and their officers, but the profit from the supplies of war itself and from the supplies of hundreds of the ramifications of the war machine is the chief support of many an industry. The combination of traditional opinion plus the widespread bread-and-butter interest in war furnishes a colossal support of the institution of war and a well-nigh insurmountable resistance to peace.

More, the war forces have a slogan that appears to be so logical that millions believe it to be unanswerable. . . . The slogan is, "The way to maintain peace is to prepare for war." . . .

An examination of the utterances of the Presidents would probably reveal that each, in turn, has repeated that same belief — certainly many did. . . . The precedents of most foreign policies of the nations are based upon it. . . . It leads in press editorials and colors the news. . . . No fallacy ever held the minds of men in its grasp more tenaciously than this one, yet fallacy it is. Whenever Nation A has adopted a new armament, Nation B has followed its example and improved upon it. Then Nation A adopted the improvement and added another, and so the competition proceeded, each laying the full blame for the rivalry upon the wicked ambition of the other. Meanwhile each prepared for war, but for *defense* only. . . . So a nation, all prepared for defense, is a safe neighbor when the public mind is undisturbed, but at any moment an incident, whose meaning is undetermined, may stir that nation into an hysterical emotion. The mental excitement of that nation arouses another and without knowing quite how it happened, war is on. . . .

. . . It is always with agony that new trails are blazed. It is not the business of departments of the army and navy to create a new policy of peace. There can be no compromise with the old war slogan and, therefore, the way out of the present maze of tradition, precedent, and unclear thinking is the substitution of a wholly new slogan for the old one. "The way to maintain peace is to prepare for peace." . . .

As the result of 10 years of hard reading about war and peace, I have arrived at six very definite conclusions. . . . I have long believed that when the rubbish surrounding war discussions could be cleared away, the problem of transition from war policies to peace policies would be very simple. Naturally the process must include a change of the public mind all along the line. That may be a slow and tedious process, but it is never impossible, since all men and women have some sense of logic. My conclusions are:

1. War, as an institution, a policy, can be abolished by civilized nations as between themselves; and that can be done when they so will.

2. The only way to treat the problem of war is to isolate it absolutely from all other questions. Treat it as a sin, a crime, an iniquity, an unethical institution, an unpractical policy, or what you will. It is, in truth, a barbarism with no rightful place in an enlightened age. Whatever you may call it, set it apart from all other problems and deal with it in that sense.

I well remember the time when woman suffrage was as much surrounded with rubbish as is the whole problem of war. Looking backward, how simple that question looks now when the rubbish has been torn away. And looking a little farther back, reading about it in history, there was the same kind of rubbish surrounding the question of human slavery. How simple it looks now when it is isolated from everything else. Yet it took a hundred years of campaigning and a civil war to clear the rubbish away. I ask you to try to get this question away from the rubbish and to treat it as an isolated problem itself.

3. Wars now have no causes; they have excuses, and wars go on because nations have the habit and move by precedent. I came to this conclusion when I had listed 257 causes, alleged to have been the actual causes of wars of history.

4. Wars cannot settle anything. The strong nation, not the right nation, wins. I note that Napoleon, who knew a great deal more than I about war, said the same thing in several ways.

5. The problems that now confront nations, and their number is legion, are far too momentous, too crucial, to be tried by the arbitrament of guns and bombs; how irrational to attempt to settle them that way. They call for statesmen with brains, not soldiers with guns; for reason, not submarines; for round tables, not battlefields; for conciliation, not poison gas, and let me add, they call for prayer, not because God is necessarily on our side, but because He supposedly is on the right side.

6. The only possible substitute for war, and, therefore, the foundation of world peace, are compacts between and among all civilized nations to proscribe war ab-

solutely as between themselves and in agreements to find the means of settling all disputes arising by peaceful means. The unit of this foundation of world peace is the compact between two nations. . . .

Emily Newell Blair, "Why I Am Discouraged About Women in Politics," 1931

Five years ago I wrote an article on women in politics in which I said that women were already participating in politics to some extent, and that the promise was good that they would participate more and more. My conclusions were based upon the situation as it appeared then. After the first five years of woman suffrage I was encouraged. The beginning was good. The future looked bright. Since then the going has been bad. Having expressed my optimism, I must now in fairness to myself report my pessimism and its causes.

Let me note at the outset two things. I am not disappointed in those women who have succeeded in politics. I am disappointed with what politics has done for women. I am not discouraged because I feel that I have been ineffective as a politician, for I do not. I am discouraged because I have been ineffective in politics as a feminist.

To me the aim of woman suffrage was to make women co-partners with men in government. I thought it would make it possible for women with ambition and political ability to enter politics as a career without disqualification because they were women. I never had any illusions that women would "clean up" politics, for I never believed that women were better than men. Also, I knew enough about politics to understand that its ethics and practices were caused by other conditions than the dominance of men. But I did think woman suffrage would widen the opportunities of women.

I hoped to see women candidates exemplifying women's right to participate with men in politics and to have enough of them elected to accustom men and women to women in office, and thus serve to overcome the prejudice against women in positions of importance. . . .

Now at the end of ten years of suffrage, I find politics still a male monopoly. It is hardly any easier for women to get themselves elected to office than it was before the Equal Suffrage Amendment was passed. Women still have little part in framing political policies and determining party tactics.

Far from participating equally with men in politics, they participate in leadership hardly at all — less, as a matter of fact, than they did in 1920. To realize this, I have only to recall the national political conventions of 1920, when candidates for the presidential nominations selected as women-managers leaders of women, when they emphasized in their campaign literature their sympathy with the recognition of women, when women spoke from the convention rostrums on debatable planks, when women delegates cast their votes without advice from men associates, when men on the Resolutions Committees conferred with and kept in touch with leaders of women, and women in the delegations kept in touch with the same leaders and forced their members of the Resolutions Committee to vote for the measures they favored. Since then I have attended two national conventions of my own party and one of the other party, and at no one of them have I seen women, as feminists, of so much importance.

If this is not convincing that there has been a decline in the participation of women in politics, let us turn to the political party organization and see what has happened there. When it appeared that women might be given the right to vote before the next national election, politicians of both parties rushed to place women on their party committees. In their choice, the men paid women a high compliment. They believed, it was evident, that women would want the highest type of women to represent them. And in their eagerness to capture the women's votes for their party they put this type on their committees. They also believed that women would want women on these committees who could lead women. They therefore named women whose leadership had been tried and tested. And then these men listened to these women whom they had chosen: even when they did not have a vote on the committees, their opinions had weight. And why? Because the men saw them as powerful leaders of women.

Since then, women have come officially to have a place on party committees. They are elected to them as are the men. But in too many cases these first women have been succeeded by a different type, who give their proxies at committee meetings to the men by whose influence they have been elected, who do what they are told by these men to do, and who are without achievement or previous leadership of women. . . .

Such women never bother with so-called women's measures or movements. They have no use for feminism. The League of Women Voters, for instance, is anathema to them. And so they do nothing to forward the participation of women in politics. Small wonder that politicians think woman suffrage a success. The bogie of the feminine influence, of the woman-vote, has been laid.

But there are also women on these committees who went into politics desirous of representing women and strengthening their position in politics. I was one of them once myself. I owed my election to the National Committee and my subsequent position with the committee in Washington to the fact that I had been associated with women in pre-suffrage activities. For I was elected to this committee and position in the days when men still feared women's votes and it was thought that I would have influence with women and so win them to the support of the party. But once in politics I found myself entirely surrounded by men. . . .

Unfortunately for feminism, it was agreed to drop the sex line in politics. And it was dropped by the women. Even those who ran for office forgot that they were women. "I am not running as a woman, but as a Democrat (or as a Republican)!" How many times have I heard it! No appeal to women to put a woman into office, no argument as to her right to hold office, but a minimizing always of her sex. And yet thousands of votes were cast against her, for no other reason than that she was a woman. For let us not think, because we cease to talk of it, that the prejudice against women in public office has been overcome. . . .

Of all the women the country over who have been elected to office, I know of only one who went into politics as a feminist; that is, who made an appeal to women to support a woman, organized women to back her because she was a woman, stressed the right of women to hold office, thus making that an issue in her campaign, and owed her election to a following of women instead of a political following dominated by men. I refer to Florence Allen, Judge of the Supreme Court of Ohio. There are probably others scattered about the country in state legislatures and county offices, but their number is without doubt small. . . .

❈ *E S S A Y S*

In the first essay, Nancy F. Cott of Yale University pointedly rejects the familiar assertion that organized feminism was in decline in the twenties. Women abandoned neither politics nor feminism; rather, Cott asserts, historians have defined politics too narrowly, and have been looking for evidence of women's involvement in it in the wrong places. A careful reevaluation shows that women's political behavior in the twenties was similar in many ways to their behavior in the years before they won the vote, with much of their activism occurring through voluntarist organizations rather than political parties. Stressing change rather than continuity, Joan G. Zimmerman in the second essay examines the legal contest between women who supported protective labor legislation and women who supported the Equal Rights Amendment. She argues that feminists on both sides were forced by contemporary legal doctrines into a sharply polarized debate that undermined the goals of both factions and constrained the debate over equality. Like Zimmerman, Rosalyn Terborg-Penn of Morgan State University highlights differences between women. Although African-American women continued to be involved in politics in the 1920s, they rarely worked on feminist projects because of the racism of white women, Terborg-Penn says.

Across the Great Divide: Women in Politics Before and After 1920

NANCY F. COTT

The 1920 marker has been crucial to historians' treatment of women in politics and has undergirded claims that organized feminism declined in the 1920s. Despite cautions from observers at the time that "all feminists are suffragists, but not all suffragists are feminists," the suffrage victory in 1920 is seen as the height from which feminism broke down; the earlier suffrage movement is assumed to be the matrix of women's politics and also a proxy for feminism. . . .

The composite portrayal of women's politics in the 1920s supplied by historians emphasizes the following points: After the achievement of the vote, the large coalition movement among women disintegrated; now insiders rather than outsiders, women (ironically) lost influence within the political process. Suffragists' predictions of transformation in politics through women's contributions were not realized. No longer operating from strong women-only voluntary organizations nor avidly showing their strength as unified voices, women were not as aggressive as men in pursuing political advantage in a still highly male-dominated system. Historians have often evaluated women's progress in politics after 1920 with reference to the realization of a "woman bloc," in tacit parallel to the woman suffrage

Nancy F. Cott, "Across the Great Divide: Women in Politics Before and After 1920," reprinted from *Women, Politics, and Change,* edited by Louise A. Tilly and Patricia Gurin, © 1990 by Russell Sage Foundation. Used with the permission of Russell Sage Foundation.

coalition (although the woman suffrage movement was not a voting entity but a great voluntarist effort formed around a single issue). This portrayal generally holds out the possibility of a woman bloc and links its failure to the destructive controversy over the Equal Rights Amendment, which was first proposed in 1923 by the minority National Woman's Party and then vigorously opposed by most other women's organizations.

. . . I intend to complicate this portrayal . . . by showing that some of its elements are false and that it all looks different when the marker of 1920 is suppressed to some extent and the history is seen as continuous and related to the larger political milieu. Neglecting the political watershed of 1920 would be obtuse, and cavalier, since not only was the sex barrier to the ballot eliminated but also the movement for the vote ended. Too great a focus on the achievement of the Nineteenth Amendment, however, obscures the similarities in women's political behavior before and after it and the relation of that behavior to broaden political and social context. . . .

Although the campaign for suffrage is usually presented as a unity in contrast to the disunity of the 1920s, there is reason to see disunity among politically active women as typical of both the 1910s and 1920s. For instance, suffragists were opposed by female antisuffragists; white suffragists raised racial bars to blacks. In other matters great and small, from the conflicts between clubwomen and entertainers over the status and standards of dance halls to stand-offs between pacifists and preparedness advocates during the Great War, there were strategic, ideological, class-based, and race-based differences among groups of women that were acted out in the public arena before as well as after 1920. . . . Intense internal conflicts over leadership, finances, and tactics so racked the National American Woman Suffrage Association (NAWSA) in 1911 that long-time suffragist Reverend Olympia Brown called her colleagues' "shallow false talk of love excellence harmony &c &c . . . so false that it makes me vomit." The bitter split between NAWSA and the Congressional Union–National Woman's Party leaderships beginning in 1913 was the latest but not the only such cleavage.

The way that suffragists built coalitions during the 1910s acknowledged that women had variant and perhaps clashing loyalties. Suffrage leaders purposely addressed defined groups (mothers, wage earners, black women, white women, professionals) with specifically designed instrumental appeals, tacitly acknowledging that not all women shared the same definition of self-interest. . . .

Even when maintaining that women would exercise civic duties differently from men, suffragists rarely if ever portrayed a future voting "bloc" of women. . . . It is striking that the one time that a small minority of suffragists *did* attempt to marshal women's votes into a voting bloc, they were condemned by the majority of their colleagues. In 1914 and 1916 the suffragist group the Congressional Union (CU), predecessor of the National Woman's Party, campaigned among enfranchised women of the western states to defeat all Democrats. They intended to "punish the party in power" in Washington for failure to adopt a constitutional amendment for woman suffrage. Their effort to make women's power at the polls count on a single issue inspired horrified rejection from mainstream suffragist leaders and little agreement from women voters. . . .

Suffragists spoke of issues — safeguarding children's health, eliminating political corruption, ending the liquor traffic, improving the economic leverage of women wage-earners — but rarely addressed exactly how or for whom women's votes would be collected, whether electing women to office was a high priority, or whether women's votes were adjuncts or substitutes for the established practice of lobbying and educational work by women's voluntary associations. As much as suffragists talked about women's inclinations, duties, and contributions, they rarely specified by what means, exactly, the injection of women's votes into the polity was to bring about change. . . . During the 1915 New York campaign, Carrie Chapman Catt even warned suffragist speakers against promising "what women will do with the vote."

The idea that women's votes would line up in one direction certainly existed in an implicit imprecise form, in the views of both suffragists *and* their opponents. As prospective voters, women were often expected to punish candidates who did not show deference to women's organizations' aims and to embrace those who supported Prohibition and social legislation. There was some evidence in the 1910s (mainly from Scandinavia) that women were "conservative" voters and some claims (from New York City) that women swelled the "radical" vote. . . . However, most big-city machine politicians had dropped objections to woman suffrage by the late 1910s after observing and reasoning that enfranchised women had *not* shown a habit of voting together to oppose existing political organizations. Claims about the impact of women's votes were so speculative and contradictory by 1919, in fact, that social scientists William Ogburn and Inez Goltra, after studying "how women vote," could conclude only that there might be some significant sex differences *or* that "the enfranchisement of women will have no other effect than approximately to double the number of votes previously cast." . . .

The unspoken notion that adding women to the electorate should transform politics did prompt some suffragists' disappointment in the 1920s, but they were not the only ones looking dourly at the scene. . . . Social scientists stressed the irrational motivations driving individual political behavior, the inability of the mass public to make objective judgments in popular government, and the likelihood that politicians would manipulate these failings. Observers' discouragement about democratic participation found corroboration in the deepening decline in voter participation, a trend continuous from 1896 and intensifying from the 1910s to the 1920s. . . .

In light of such reforms as direct election of senators, direct primaries, the initiative, referendum, and recall, it seems ironic, even tragic, that the Progressive era should have ushered in the decade of the lowest voter participation ever. But if Progressive reforms intended to keep the reins of the state in the hands of the expert or the economically powerful few — as some "reforms" more than others indicate — then the decline in voter turnout fulfilled rather than undid that aim. Voting reforms included the continuing disfranchisement of blacks and Populist or Republican whites in the South by means of poll taxes, literacy tests, and other bars to registration and balloting; more complicated and rigorous residency and registration requirements in northern states which limited immigrant voting; and, at the municipal level, replacement of district voting with at-large elections, which predestined minority interest-group candidates to fail.

While Progressive reformers embraced the salutary aim to eliminate corrupt influence-peddling and substitute neutral and informed standards, their emphasis on expert presence and management in the state also diverted control away from the populace to an elite of professional and business-managerial experts. The results could be seen institutionalized in the 1920s in various forms, from city-manager rule in municipalities, to federal and state commissions, to such quasi-governmental institutions as the National Bureau of Economic Research. . . . The most persuasive explanations of downsliding voter turnout from 1896 to the 1920s also have to do with the entrenchment of the Democratic party's hold on the South and the Republican party's domination of the North and West (and thus of the national government) to the extent that the interest of voters in partisan contest, and voter sense of efficacy, collapsed. . . . The context in which to look at women's voting behavior in the 1920s is that of declining voter participation overall.

A few vigorous female voices, such as that of former National Woman's Party leader Anne Martin of Nevada, urged women to enter the electoral arena in force and move directly to claim "woman's share, woman's *half* in man-controlled government." The much more general trend — and one deplored by Martin as merely "indirect influence" — was women's reliance on voluntary associations rather than the electoral arena for political efficacy. Since the early nineteenth century, women had influenced what took place in electoral and legislative halls from outside, not only by seeking suffrage but by inquiring about a range of health, safety, moral, and welfare issues. . . . Women's organizations' lobbying route should be seen as pioneering in the modern mode of exerting political force — that is, interest-group politics. This voluntarist mode, with its use of lobbying to effect political influence, and the kinds of interests pursued (that is, health, safety, moral, and welfare issues), prevailed in women's political participation both before and after 1920.

. . . Although historians often cite as evidence of decimation in activism the contrast between the 2 million women in the NAWSA in the 1910s and the tiny proportion of that membership — probably 5 percent — who joined in the NAWSA's successor group, the National League of Women Voters (LWV), the two figures are not really comparable. The two organizations differed widely in form and intent: The first was a federation which pursued one specific goal, made few demands on its local members, imposed no homogeneity upon affiliates, and used all volunteer labor; the subsequent organization stated many aims (including civic reform, citizenship education, international peace, and women's rights), made strenuous demands on its local members, attempted standardized national procedure, and employed professional staff.

Quickly evolving into a "good government" rather than a feminist organization, its premise being to ready women for political life, the LWV found itself, ironically, competing with women's partisan activity as much as preparing women for it. When all women became fair game for party organizations, Republican and Democratic women's divisions vied with the nonpartisan league for the time and loyalty of women interested in politics. Some leading NAWSA suffragists went directly into party organizations instead of into the LWV. . . . Women's divisions in state and national party committees should be seen, as logically as the LVW, as successor organizations to the NAWSA.

More generally, where one large or vital pre-1920 women's organization declined or ended, more than one other arose to take its space, if not its exact task. While the General Federation of Women's Clubs seemed to decline in vigor (although not clearly in membership), the National Congress of Parents and Teachers Associations (PTA) rose into a mass membership whose local units took up efforts similar to those of many unnamed women's clubs of the earlier generation, working to establish playgrounds, libraries, and health clinics, as well as lobbying at the national level on issues from film standards to international peace. More than quintupling during the 1920s, the membership of the PTA reached over 1.5 million by 1931. Its color bar (in effect) led to the founding in 1926 of a National Colored Parent-Teacher Association, which had at least the cooperation of the older group. . . .

The WTUL's [Women's Trade Union League] intention to raise the trade-union consciousness of industrially employed women as well as sweeten their lives through association was seized by industrial clubs formed by the Young Women's Christian Association (YWCA). In 1926 the YWCA stopped requiring that members be Protestant Christians, and membership grew; by 1930 the organization boasted over 600,000 members, 55,000 volunteer advisers, and a dispersed professional staff of almost 3,500. The YWCA industrial clubs educated and helped to organize both black and white women workers in southern textile mills and brought them to testify before legislatures about industrial conditions. These clubs also served as recruitment grounds for summer schools for women workers. The summer schools themselves, founded during the 1920s by labor reformers and academics, formed a sequel to the WTUL cross-class efforts earlier in the century. . . .

The alliance with professionals — social workers, social researchers, college and university professors — so noticeably important in efforts on behalf of women workers and in the YWCA in the 1920s was also apparent in the birth control movement. In 1919 Margaret Sanger, leader in the American Birth Control League, left behind her former socialist politics, along with her purposeful law-breaking and agitation in working-class communities and her emphasis on women's control of their own bodies. Sanger thenceforward emphasized eugenic reasoning about better babies. The American Birth Control League organized and educated the public and lobbied for the legalization of birth control on the premise of allowing "doctors only" to provide information and methods. Women who saw the virtues of that approach and volunteered their time for birth control in the 1920s were mainly middle-class matrons, more socially and politically conservative than the birth control advocates of the 1910s, and also more numerous. The American Birth Control League claimed over 37,000 members in 1926, almost 90 percent female. Fewer women followed the approach of civil libertarian Mary Ware Dennett, founder of the Voluntary Parenthood League, which stood on First Amendment rights and aimed to decriminalize birth control by removing it from federal obscenity statutes. . . .

Group consciousness among minority-group women was a major source of new organizations. Both Jewish women and Catholic women founded numerous voluntary associations during the 1920s and 1930s. Black women continued the National Association of Colored Women (NACW), the organizational hub which had been central to black suffragist efforts and had linked black clubwomen in communities across the nation. Its umbrella covered between 150,000 and 200,000 members in forty-one states in the mid 1920s. Many of its leaders also pursued their aims of racial uplift through male-dominated black organizations, especially the National Association for the Advancement of Colored People (NAACP), the Urban League, and the Commission on Interracial Cooperation. All through the decade, black women campaigned vigorously against lynching and for the federal antilynching bill languishing in the southern-dominated U.S. Senate — their numbers far beyond Ida B. Wells Barnett's lone crusade in an earlier generation. . . .

In an unprecedented tide of public concern, a range of peace groups from the conservative and nationalistic American Peace Society, through Protestant church agencies, to the left-wing pacifist War Resisters League formed during and after the war. In the 1920s they proposed competing alternatives, including the League of Nations, the World Court, international arbitration conferences, disarmament, and noncooperation with the military. Women could follow a number of avenues instigated and dominated by men; they appeared in all the peace societies, but clustered in their own organizations. Two groups were founded in 1919; the Women's International League for Peace and Freedom (WILPF), whose U.S. section included such luminaries of social reform as Jane Addams, Lillian Wald, and Alice Hamilton, and the much smaller, more extremely nonresistant Women's Peace Society. The founding of the Women's Peace Union of the Western Hemisphere and the Women's Committee for World Disarmament followed in 1921. In addition, the major women's organizations — the LWV, the AAUW, the WCTU [Women's Christian Temperance Union], the NFBPW [National Federation of Business and Professional Women's Clubs], and the PTA — all put international peace prominently on their agendas. In 1925 Carrie Chapman Catt, the former general of NAWSA, assembled from the memberships of the major women's organizations with peace departments the National Committee on the Cause and Cure of War (NCCCW). That collectivity met annually for many years and formed a basis for peace lobbying; it claimed a cumulative membership of over 5 million at the start and 8 million — or one out of five adult women in the United States — by the 1930s.

The level of organization among American women after 1920 thus appears to compare very favorably with that before. . . . Repeated foundings and aggregate memberships make it clear that women were still joining women's organizations, as they had for generations. By their very constitution of specialized memberships (professional women, religious women, mothers, women of a particular political bent) and purposes (birth control, education, antilynching, peace, and so on), such organizations were as likely to sustain or even to rigidify the differentiations and diversities among women according to racial, ethnic, class, and political grounds, however, as to make women feel a common cause. . . . While these were women's organizations, they were not purporting to emanate from or to operate in a separate sphere, as had many of their forebears in the nineteenth century. Consequently, there was an omnipresent potential for the groups working on issues not peculiar to women — peace, for example — to self-destruct by routing their members toward male-dominated organizations that had more funds and thus seemed more effective (as happened with the NACW). . . .

Not all women's organizations entered politics, but most of the national organizations did. They adopted the mode of pressure politics — forwarding public education and lobbying for specific bills as they had during the suffrage campaign, rather than running their own candidates. . . . The considerable unity of method among women's organizations contrasted with the diversity — often acrimony — among their specific goals. . . . Differences among women's groups were at least as characteristic as their techniques of pressure politics. The controversy over the Equal Rights Amendment in the 1920s is well known: When the National Woman's Party had introduced into Congress in December 1923 an amendment to the U.S. Constitution reading "Men and women shall have equal rights throughout the United States and every place subject to its jurisdiction," it was immediately — and for decades after — opposed by the LWV and most other major women's organizations. What is not so well recognized are the other equally important divisions among politically active women and the fact that these divisions were multiple and could cross-cut. Partisan loyalty has been wrongly slighted in historians' assessments of women's political behavior in the 1920s; partisan women not only conflicted across parties but also, importantly, with women who wanted to organize nonpartisan alliances.

On the peace issue — where at first glance women seemed most wholeheartedly united — women's groups that urged disarmament were opposed by patriotic women's organizations that boosted military preparedness. To counter the antimilitarist impact that WILPF was making, the DAR [Daughters of the American Revolution] and allied groups in 1924 formed a National Patriotic Council. When WILPF speakers testified in Congress in 1928 against the naval building program, for instance, members of the DAR and the Dames of the Loyal Legion were also present, and Mrs. Noble Newport Potts, president of the National Patriotic Council, outspokenly warned the House Naval Affairs Committee chairman about Dorothy Detzer, executive secretary of the WILPF, "That's a dangerous woman you've been talking to!" In that particular instance WILPF and other antimilitarists had the desired effect, and the 1928 cruiser bill did not pass. The House Committee, deluged by adverse mail, cut the authorization from seventy-one to sixteen vessels. Nonetheless, confidence that antimilitarism was "women's" stance was shattered. The impact that women activists made on one side or another of the pacifism/militarism question proved, ironically, the absence rather than the substance of gender solidarity. . . .

On Prohibition — generally presumed in the 1910s to command women's support — the late 1920s revealed another crevasse. Pauline Morton Sabin recalled being motivated to found the Women's Organization for National Prohibition Reform (WONPR) when she heard Ella Boole, president of the WCTU, announce to the Congress, "I represent the women of America!" Sabin felt, "Well, lady, here's one woman you don't represent." . . . The WONPR actively challenged the stereotype that women supported Prohibition. For instance, it disputed the WCTU's public assurance that the 3 million women under the aegis of the General Federation of Women's Clubs (GFWC) endorsed the Eighteenth Amendment. After WONPR leaders dared the GFWC to poll its membership on Prohibition — emphasizing that WONPR members also belonged to GFWC clubs — the WCTU no longer made that assertion.

. . . The quantity of evidence that women arrayed themselves on opposing political sides (even if they used gender-dependent justifications to do so) calls into question the very possibility of a woman bloc. Given the divisions among women and given the nature of the political system, a woman's voting bloc — or even the possibility of a lobbying bloc representing *all* women — must be considered an interpretive fiction rather than a realistic expectation, useful perhaps to some minds, but requiring a willing suspension of disbelief. . . .

As much as suffragist rhetoric had stressed women's need to represent themselves and women's duty to become voters because their interests and expertise differed from men's, it had also stressed that women and men were equally citizens and individuals in relation to the state. A *New York Times* editorialist heard the suffragists' clarion to be that "women are people — human beings sharing certain fundamental human interests, aspirations, and duties with men." That very important strand of suffragist rationale was renewed in the 1910s along with rationales stressing women's differences from men; it justified and anticipated women's integration into men's political associations rather than the formation of a woman bloc.

There were also strategically defensive reasons why most women active in politics did not pursue nor speak of their goals in terms of mobilizing a woman bloc. The notion of a woman bloc was portrayed as the deployment of destructive sex antagonism and was condemned in the harshest terms by mainstream male politicians as well as by right-wing ideologues. Once when the fledgling LWV did try to marshal a woman's voting bloc — in New York in 1920, trying to unseat Republican Senator James Wadsworth, an intransigent opponent of woman suffrage whose wife headed the National Association Opposed to Woman Suffrage — the organization was violently condemned by New York's Republican governor as *"a menace to our free institutions and to representative government."* . . .

Although the woman bloc could only have been an interpretive fiction, it was, curiously, a large enough looming specter for male politicians to slay it again and again. Those who have imagined that women entering politics in the 1920s should have or could have constituted a bloc of woman voters similar to the coalition formed on behalf of woman suffrage have underestimated how profoundly at crosspurposes to the existing party system such a proposition really was. Yet how else could women lobbyists, without economic resources to speak of (as Mary Anderson admitted), swing any weight? Women leaders in the political arena faced a classic double bind: damned outright for attempting to form a woman bloc, damned (in effect) by male politicians' indifference or scorn for failing to form one. There was the dilemma for women who intended to make it clear that politics was no longer a man's world. . . .

Women's Rights, Feminist Conflict, and the Jurisprudence of Equality

JOAN G. ZIMMERMAN

Talk of rights has always been an undercurrent in American constitutional history, but there were few times between the Reconstruction amendments and *Brown v. Board of Education* in 1954 when the rights of a previously excluded group were so quickly and intensely debated and adjudicated as in the three years after the Nineteenth Amendment was ratified. Alice Paul's effort to draft the first Equal Rights

Joan G. Zimmerman, "The Jurisprudence of Equality: The Women's Minimum Wage, the First Equal Rights Amendment, and *Adkins v. Children's Hospital,* 1905–1923," *Journal of American History,* vol. 78, no. 1 (June 1991): 188–225. The author is grateful for a Fellowship for University Teachers provided by the National Endowment for the Humanities in 1988–1989. Reprinted by permission of the Organization of American Historians.

Amendment (ERA) between 1920 and 1923 initiated a wide-ranging debate among lawyers and among women about women's "proper position in society" and about legal barriers to reform. The participation of legal scholars such as Felix Frankfurter and Roscoe Pound drew this argument over women's legal equality with men into a larger debate. That debate pitted proponents of a new sociological jurisprudence or instrumentalism, which held that the law should respond more directly to social needs, against defenders of legal formalism, which held that the law was separate from politics and internally rational. . . .

The debate over the language of the first ERA, which went through over thirty-five drafts, intersected with proposals for statutory reforms designed to improve working conditions for women in the labor force. Advocates of such hours and wage legislation for women had developed strategies to evade the barriers created by legal formalism — particularly the courts' interpretation of the Fourteenth Amendment's due process clause — and to establish a new basis for talk of rights. As an outspoken and effective proponent of protective labor legislation for women, Florence Kelley sought to redefine rights and the meaning of equality for women in an industrial economy. Her arguments raised questions about how useful an emphasis on individualism and equality with men was for women seeking to articulate their political and social goals. After 1920, conflicts among women themselves over the meaning of their new republican citizenship were drawn into and became part of the jurisprudential debate over formalism and instrumentalism. Whether talk of rights among women would challenge legal barriers or be co-opted by those with power would be decided in the first women's minimum wage case after the Nineteenth Amendment. The directors of the Children's Hospital in Washington, D.C., challenged the power of the District of Columbia minimum wage board (chaired by Jesse Adkins) to set wages for the hospital's women employees. Drawing on conceptions of liberty in the legal formalist tradition, the hospital's lawyers argued that the 1918 law establishing the board conflicted with the Fourteenth Amendment's guarantees because it deprived both the hospital and its employees of liberty of contract without due process of law. That case, *Adkins v. Children's Hospital*, not only reconstructed rights talk but also showed that at least for the leaders of the National Woman's Party (NWP), legal formalism was not a barrier, but an avenue to desired reforms.

Many historians have discussed the split in the women's movement in the 1920s between the National Woman's Party and the promoters of protection. Some have framed the controversy as an argument over the meaning of feminism or as evidence of class differences. Other historians have emphasized the results of protective legislation: Such laws stereotyped women as weak and institutionalized a sex-segregated labor force. In analyzing the intentions of proponents of protection, historians have generally pointed to assumptions about women's maternal role. For example, Nancy Cott has recently argued that Kelley's "approach stressed maternal nature and inclination as well as conditioning and implied that the sexual division of labor was eternal." In all of these historiographical frameworks, the ERA has been juxtaposed to protection to show that an innovative alternative was available to women opposed to protective legislation in the early 1920s.

. . . A more complete understanding of the split in the women's movement requires a closer analysis of the peculiar legal context in which protective legislation was structured and pre-1923 drafts of the ERA were discussed. . . . Kelley and Paul wrote drafts of laws and a constitutional amendment; they faced attacks on those drafts; they heard judges and lawyers give opinions; and they started again with new proposals. Kelley and Paul thus discovered that in order to convince judges that the laws they proposed were constitutional, they had to fit their proposals into structures of legal thought. . . . As Kelley observed how the courts interpreted regulatory statutes, she came to realize that the broad reforms of working conditions that she desired had a better chance of success if she focused on women. As she learned how the courts used the principle of liberty of contract and applied a means-ends test to laws, Kelley recognized that she had to develop a special defense. That defense not only relied on common law views of women as dependents but also stressed, in new ways, women's differences from men. . . . Paul, in contrast, discovered that her interest in expanding married women's contractual capacity beyond common law restrictions conformed neatly with a formalist emphasis on liberty of contract. . . .

The litigation that culminated in the *Adkins* decision altered the course of social reform, recast women's claims to constitutional rights, and propelled Kelley and Paul toward different, incompatible kinds of arguments. The close relationship between the *Adkins* decision and the emergence of the ERA — a relationship clearly understood by participants in the debate over equality — illustrates how specific reforms can intersect with legal doctrines and principles. In broader terms, the jurisprudential divisions that helped polarize the women's movement may also illuminate other struggles for reform in the Progressive Era.

As the argument over the first ERA sharpened in 1921, the disagreement between formalists and instrumentalists became more pronounced and more specific. . . . For legal formalists, law was internally coherent both logically and morally. The morality of the law was not contingent upon some external standard or ideal. Legal formalism can be characterized by several assumptions that Robert Summers has called "meanings of formalism." First, "pre-existing law" was "virtually comprehensive and complete." The law was "like a static and closed logical system." Second, judges were objective discoverers of the law rather than creators of law. Third, statutes were presumptively invalid if they seemed to "conflict with [the] literal wording of [a] constitutional text." Fourth, existing law was coherent, harmonious, logical, and conceptually unitary. Finally, conclusions could be arrived at through deductive reasoning from general rules. In short, legal formalism in the words of one critic was "mechanical jurisprudence."

By the beginning of the twentieth century, those assumptions were under attack from legal scholars who were creating an alternative approach known as sociological jurisprudence or instrumentalism. For Roscoe Pound, whose name is most closely associated with sociological jurisprudence, the law was not static and complete, but subject to growth and change. According to Pound, legal analysis could not be limited to abstract concepts but should consider the real results of legal decision making. Pound assumed that judges were not necessarily objective discoverers of law, but creators of law — overtly or covertly. Pound believed that statute making was a useful expression of the will of the people. Judges should not treat it as a hostile invasion into common law adjudication. Instead of exalting conceptual coherence, Pound argued that the law could be stated only in more narrow and limited generalities. Overgeneralization could lead to distortion in particular situations or to legal fictions designed to shore up the illusion of conceptual coherence.

In the late nineteenth century, legal formalism reinforced a view of economic relationships that assumed a free market unencumbered by state intrusion, individuals motivated by self-interest, and the right of individuals to make their own contracts. Those with power found it convenient to assume that the law was conceptually complete; there was no room for creativity. Conservative judges often used the due process clause of the Fourteenth Amendment as the legal basis for the protection of individual economic rights. . . . The due process clause of the Fourteenth Amendment provided that no state could "deprive any person of life, liberty, or property, without due process of law." Out of this language, conservative judges had created a legal fiction, "liberty of contract.". . . Frequently, judges decided that statutes were unconstitutional because they denied both parties their liberty to contract and therefore due process of law. The liberty-of-contract fiction not only enhanced judges' authority at the expense of lawmakers' authority but also ignored the real inequality in bargaining power between individual employees and their employers. . . . By the end of the nineteenth century, the realities of industrial life for many workers made the liberty to contract the basis of an empty freedom. The liberty-of-contract fiction became a major target both for sociological legal scholars and for Progressive reformers.

As a lawyer and as one of the most articulate reformers of the Progressive Era, Florence Kelley, the executive secretary of the National Consumers' League (NCL), not only fashioned a series of statutes designed to remedy the worst aspects of industrial labor but also wrote one of the first books to outline a sociological approach to the law. Kelley believed that the meaning of rights had to be broadened to include the new social relations and responsibilities of industrial life. . . . The clearest statement of Kelley's theory of reform was *Some Ethical Gains through Legislation*, published in 1905. In *Ethical Gains* Kelley argued that industrialization had disrupted working-class family life by forcing children and women into the labor force to work for low wages and long hours in poor conditions. . . . The due process clause as interpreted by the courts was a formidable barrier to Kelley's plan to use the police power — the inherent power of a state to pass laws that protect the health, safety, and welfare of its citizens — to enact laws that served the interests of working people, and women and children in particular. In its assumption that the law was changeable and its emphasis on statute making, *Ethical Gains* tacitly challenged two basic tenets of formalism. . . .

In *Ethical Gains* Kelley framed her remedies for the social ills caused by industrialization in terms of rights. Each chapter showed how protecting the rights of one group guaranteed the rights of all and contributed to the welfare of the whole society. In the chapter on "The Right to Childhood," Kelley wrote: "It is no aim of this chapter to prove that the right to childhood exists. That right follows from the existence of the Republic. . . . The noblest duty of the Republic is that of self-preservation by so cherishing all its children that they, in turn, may become enlightened self-governing citizens." Kelley pointed out the dangers of child labor and explained that children's education and nurture should not be sacrificed to the needs of employers. . . . By referring to her program as "ethical gains," Kelley emphasized the moral necessity of using legislation to preserve the commonwealth tradition and the notion of mutual obligation. By combining the individual rights tradition with the commonwealth tradition, Kelley was theoretically restoring a balance that had been lost during the period of industrial growth. . . .

The plan she had outlined in *Ethical Gains* entailed efforts to construct statutes that would protect all workers, and women and children in particular, from the worst forms of exploitation: child labor and the employment of women for low wages and long hours. Kelley's first attempt to solve the problem of overwork came in Illinois in 1893 when, as the state's first factory inspector, she drafted a law requiring an eight-hour day for women in factories. . . . In *Ritchie v. People* the Illinois Supreme Court declared the law unconstitutional on the grounds that it denied liberty of contract and therefore due process of law under the Fourteenth Amendment. . . .

The court pointed out that the Married Woman's Act of 1874 in Illinois had authorized a married woman to sue and be sued, and it provided "that contracts may be made and liabilities incurred by her and enforced against her to the same extent and in the same manner as if she were unmarried." . . . Since the court viewed liberty of contract as the rule, it demanded strong reasons for making an exception. Sex alone was no longer enough.

The court had made a logical connection based on the rule of liberty of contract and on an assumption that all women could be classified as one group. Kelley, however, viewed the problem in social or class terms. . . . She knew that poorer women would not benefit from the liberty to contract that the court was so eager to extend to them because there was no bargaining over the hours they were expected to work. Rather than making an explicit class argument, Kelley invoked the image of women's physical dependence to prevent the liberty-of-contract principle from extending to overworked women workers. . . . The *Ritchie* opinion shaped Kelley's strategy for promoting ethical gains by forcing her to emphasize women's physical weaknesses and differences from men to achieve legal precedents that would, she hoped, eventually benefit both men and women.

The famous *Lochner* [*v. New York*] case decided by the United States Supreme Court in 1905 . . . concluded that the state did not have the power to pass an hours law for bakers since there was no relation . . . between the public good and the hours worked. Once again, judges ruled that the means used (limiting hours) bore no relation to the ends of the statute (preserving health and safety). When she read *Lochner*, Kelley asked, "How can the gradual, cumulative effect of working conditions, and of living conditions, upon the public health, be made obvious to the minds of the judges composing the courts of last resort?" Kelley soon recognized that the answer to her question lay in creating her own fiction — the dependent woman. By emphasizing women's role as mothers, Kelley sought not only to exclude them from the liberty-of-contract rule but also to balance means and ends in her statutes.

By inviting reformers to demonstrate a connection between the public good and the hours worked, the *Lochner* opinion provided an opening that Kelley and her ally, Louis Brandeis, used to promote ethical gains for women. In 1908, thirteen years after *Ritchie* and three years after *Lochner*, the Supreme Court upheld a ten-hour law for women in Oregon. Brandeis argued the case for the state of Oregon, using a novel legal approach. In the "Brandeis brief" prepared for *Muller v. Oregon*, Kelley and Josephine Goldmark, Brandeis's sister-in-law, showed that overwork and fatigue were dangerous for the health of women. The brief, characterized by sociological evidence rather than deductive reasoning, exemplified an instrumental approach to the law. Taking up the argument that women's health was endangered by long hours, Justice David J. Brewer's majority opinion emphasized the importance of women as mothers of the race. In so doing, Brewer acknowledged the link between the means used, the ten-hour law, and the ends of the statute, preservation of public health and welfare. By relying on the common law view of women as dependents, which accommodated the cultural conservatism of judges, Kelley had been able to build a series of legal precedents that could enhance the state police power and secure more ethical gains. . . . *Muller v. Oregon* marked the most effective challenge to formalism and the liberty-of-contract doctrine of the Progressive Era.

This victory in 1908 paved the way not only for the overturning of the *Ritchie* decision in Illinois in 1910 but also for Kelley's next project: legislating the minimum wage for women. Having found a way around the liberty-of-contract barrier, Kelley and a new ally, Professor Felix Frankfurter of the Harvard Law School, sought to extend the police power still further. . . . Kelley and Frankfurter stressed women's dependence, their inequality in bargaining, and the impact of low wages paid women on public health and morals. Kelley first introduced the idea of a women's minimum wage in the United States in 1910. Within two years, Massachusetts had enacted the first minimum wage law for women. By 1917, twelve states had passed women's minimum wage laws. . . .

Based on these successes, Kelley and Frankfurter lobbied for and achieved passage of a model women's minimum wage law for the District of Columbia in the fall of 1918. This law was especially significant since Congress legislated for the district; Kelley and Frankfurter hoped the district's minimum wage law would become a model for all the states. The law provided for a minimum wage board composed of members of the public, employers' groups, and employees. On the basis of hearings and investigations in various industries, the board would issue orders mandating minimum living wages for different occupations. The legislation assumed that the law should respond to social needs. In testimony on behalf of the law, Frankfurter had specifically addressed the problem of due process since the Fifth Amendment, like the Fourteenth Amendment, provided that "no person . . . shall be deprived of life, liberty or property, without due process of law." Frankfurter implied that the "liberty of contract" construction of that phrase was obsolete. . . . Just as *Muller* had been a test case for women's hours laws, the district's law, Kelley and Frankfurter expected, would provide a constitutional test for women's minimum wage laws. . . .

Within a few months, Kelley's plan for ethical gains became hopelessly entangled in the debate over the drafting of the first Equal Rights Amendment. While Florence Kelley had seen suffrage as only one of several possible advances for women, Alice Paul, head of the newly reorganized National Woman's Party, viewed the ratification of the Nineteenth Amendment as the end of one era in the struggle for women's rights and the beginning of a drive to enact full equality between men and women. The timing of her efforts to construct an equal rights amendment between 1921 and 1923 forced her to confront the program for ethical gains Kelley was pursuing. In particular, the women's minimum wage became the battleground between Kelley and her protectionist allies on one hand and Paul and the National Woman's Party on the other. The litigation over the District of Columbia minimum wage act, which began in 1920, would not only determine the victor in the first round of a continuing struggle over the meaning of rights and equality for women but would also test the limits of the dependent woman theory.

Paul was much less familiar than Kelley with legal thinking and the jurisprudential context. Paul's initial efforts to free married women from common law constraints made her increasingly wary of legislation that relied on a theory of women's dependence. Throughout 1921, the dramatic shifts in the language of Paul's drafts of the ERA reflected her reliance on and confrontation with several lawyers and legal scholars, many of whom were hostile to the new sociological jurisprudence. During the struggle to draft the first ERA, Paul consistently embraced the nineteenth-century heritage of women's rights as it had been developed by Susan B. Anthony and Elizabeth Cady Stanton. Her understanding of that heritage led Paul to insist on women's individualism and equality with men. How these apparently timeless demands were interpreted and refashioned in the legal environment of the early 1920s was one of the ironies of Paul's seemingly radical insistence on an ERA for women.

Paul's attempt to enact her view of women's equality first through legislation and then through an amendment to the Constitution went through roughly five stages from 1920 through 1923. Paul's initial attempts to draft legislation for the District of Columbia and for the states gave way to efforts to draft an equal rights amendment by May of 1921. In the summer and fall of 1921, Paul approached protective legislation for women first by incorporating it into her amendment, then by attempting to avoid it, and finally by attacking it. By 1923, Paul had decided to allow the courts to determine whether the dependent woman theory or her view of the equal rights of women and men would prevail. . . .

To understand how the women's minimum wage issue shaped the emergence of the first ERA, it is necessary to look at the activities of the minimum wage board and the motives of the attorney who launched the most effective campaign against the idea of a women's wage in the 1920s and 1930s. That attorney, Challen Ellis, helped forge the critical link between equal rights for women and the liberty-of-contract principle. It was precisely this link that Kelley sought to avoid.

Once the minimum wage board was set up in 1919, its members . . . began to issue orders mandating minimum wages for women in specified occupations. As they did so, Ellis initiated four suits in the Supreme Court of the District of Columbia (a trial court) between May and December 1920, all aimed at having the minimum wage act declared unconstitutional. . . . Ellis's clients were the directors of the Children's Hospital in Washington, D.C., and Willie Lyons, a hotel elevator operator. In the two cases that were appealed to the District of Columbia Court of Appeals, *Children's Hospital v. Adkins* and *Willie Lyons v. Adkins*, Ellis argued that the minimum wage act prevented his clients from forming their own contracts without state interference. Since the act had been passed by Congress, Ellis claimed that it must conform to the Fifth Amendment's due process clause. The clause, he argued, protected independently formed contracts.

In February 1921, the District of Columbia Court of Appeals heard arguments in the Children's Hospital and Willie Lyons cases. Frankfurter appeared on behalf of the minimum wage board, and his brief, like the Brandeis brief, included an extensive statistical analysis showing the need for a living wage for women in the district. Four months later, Frankfurter was pleased when the Court of Appeals decided that the minimum wage act was constitutional.

Rather than appealing immediately to the United States Supreme Court, Ellis decided to press his suit again in the Court of Appeals. Ellis's determination and persistence were not simply the characteristics of an eager lawyer. A graduate of the Harvard Law School in 1900, Ellis harbored a personal animosity toward Frankfurter. Together with his brother, Wade, with whom he shared a law practice, Challen vigorously pursued the defeat of the women's minimum wage. Ellis realized that the dependent woman theory, which formed the basis of a growing body of laws undermining the liberty-of-contract principle, could be attacked most effectively by women themselves. Paul's claim that men and women should have equal rights would be the most useful counter to Kelley's and Frankfurter's argument that women employees could not bargain effectively for wages. . . .

The Court of Appeals decision in the *Adkins* case . . . was issued on November 6, 1922. Justice Van Orsdel's opinion was a fitting complement for Paul's nationwide assault on Kelley's dependent woman theory. In declaring the District of Columbia minimum wage act unconstitutional, Van Orsdel pointed out that women no longer deserved special treatment since they now had the right to vote. "No reason is apparent why the operation of the law should be extended to women to the exclusion of men, since women have been accorded full equality with men in the commercial and political world. Indeed, this equality in law has been sanctioned by constitutional amendment." Van Orsdel's interpretation of the Nineteenth Amendment vindicated Paul's goals. . . . Predictably, Kelley quickly sensed the dangers in the decision of the Court of Appeals. "If the United States Supreme Court should decide adversely," she warned, "the state laws would be seriously undermined, if not destroyed outright." . . .

In April 1923 in the case of *Adkins v. Children's Hospital*, the United States Supreme Court struck down the District of Columbia law authorizing the establishment of minimum wages for women. The five-to-three majority opinion in the *Adkins* case not only joined women's legal equality with formalism but also undermined Kelley's vision of ethical gains in a revived Republic. In the opinion, [Supreme Court Justice George] Sutherland used the Nineteenth Amendment to show that women were no longer dependents and that they could now be treated as equals to men. There was no longer any reason to exempt them from the rule of liberty of contract.

> We cannot accept the doctrine that women of mature age, *sui juris*, require or may be subjected to restrictions upon their liberty of contract which could not lawfully be imposed in the case of men under similar circumstances. To do so would be to ignore all the implications to be drawn from the usage, by which woman is accorded emancipation from the old doctrine that she must be given special protection or be subjected to special restraint in her contractual and civil relationships.

Sutherland pointed out that the minimum wage law had not balanced means and ends. He saw no connection between morals and health on one hand and a minimum wage on the other. Sutherland had effectively closed the opening Kelley and

Brandeis had spotted in Peckham's *Lochner* opinion in 1905. Sutherland's opinion demonstrated that the idea of liberty of contract made famous in *Lochner* not only survived but applied with full force to women who worked for wages. Kelley's dependent woman theory as it applied to minimum wage laws had been undone. . . .

In later years, [Burnita] Matthews [a National Woman's Party lawyer] hailed Sutherland's words in the *Adkins* opinion as "the *Magna Charta* of women's rights." The National Woman's Party adopted women's right to make their own contracts as the cornerstone of liberty for women. Paul's ambitious vision of women's complete equality with men in all social and legal relations had been reduced to a legal fiction. By formalizing Paul's talk of rights, Sutherland had co-opted Paul's view and narrowed it to serve the most conservative economic and legal interests. Her attempt to seek public power for women had shown that individualism and equality, rather than being timeless values, could be turned against women by conservative judges. . . . The NWP got what those with power wanted it to have. . . .

To women seeking access to power and control of legal definitions of women's rights after achieving the right to vote, the *Adkins* decision demonstrated the hazards a conservative legal environment posed. Legal requirements had forced both Kelley and Paul to frame their arguments about women's equality to conform to judicial expectations. As both compromised themselves, they drew further apart. The narrow judicial definition of women's rights that emerged from their struggle exacted heavy costs. By establishing a male standard that was itself based on a legal fiction, the *Adkins* opinion polarized the women's movement and limited the debate over equality. Kelley's imaginative vision of social reform and civic responsibility for women and for all groups in the Republic was lost not only to the women of the 1920s but also to the historians who have studied their debate. Long after the liberty-of-contract fiction dropped out of judicial discourse, the legacy of formalism persisted both in women's definition of equality as legal identity with men and in exaggerated defenses of protective legislation based on women's weaknesses. What had begun as an attempt to capture constitutional definitions of rights on behalf of women's interests and the interests of the Republic ended as a war of fictions.

Discontented Black Feminists

ROSALYN TERBORG-PENN

On the eve of the passage of the Nineteenth Amendment, black women leaders could be counted among other groups of women who had worked diligently for woman suffrage. At least ninety black women leaders endorsed woman suffrage, with two-thirds of these women giving support during the decade immediately before passage of the amendment. Afro-American women organized suffrage clubs, participated in rallies and demonstrations, spoke on behalf of the amendment, and

Rosalyn Terborg-Penn, "Discontented Black Feminists: Prelude and Postscript to the Passage of the Nineteenth Amendment," originally published in *Decades of Discontent: The Women's Movement, 1920–1940*, Lois Scharf and Joan M. Jensen, eds. (Contributions in Women's Studies, No. 28, Greenwood Press, Westport, CT, 1983), pp. 261–268. Copyright © 1983 by Lois Scharf and Joan M. Jensen. Abridgement and reprinting with permission.

wrote essays in support of the cause. These things they had done since the inception of the nineteenth-century woman's rights movement. However, the largest woman suffrage effort among black women's groups occurred during the second decade of the twentieth century. Organizations such as the National Federation of Afro-American Women, the National Association of Colored Women (NACW), the Northeastern Federation of Colored Women's Clubs, the Alpha Kappa Alpha Sorority, and the Delta Sigma Theta Sorority actively supported woman suffrage. These organizations were national or regional in scope and represented thousands of Afro-American women. Some of the women were from the working class, but most of them were of middle-class status. Across the nation, at least twenty black woman suffrage organizations or groups that strongly endorsed woman suffrage existed during the period.

Three examples provide an indication of the diversity in types of woman suffrage activities among black women's organizations. In 1915 the Poughkeepsie, New York, chapter of the Household of Ruth, a working-class, black women's group, endorsed woman suffrage by sending a resolution to the New York branch of the National Woman's Party (NWP) in support of the pending state referendum on woman suffrage. With the need for an intelligent female electorate in mind, black women of Texas organized voter leagues in 1917, the year Texas women won the right to vote. Among these was the Negro Women Voters' League of Galveston. Furthermore, in 1919, the Northeastern Federation of Colored Women's Clubs, representing thousands of women from Montreal to Baltimore, petitioned the National American Woman Suffrage Association (NAWSA) for membership.

The enthusiastic responses of black women to woman suffrage may seem astonishing when one realizes that woman suffrage was a predominantly middle-class movement among native born white women and that the black middle class was very small during the early twentieth century. Furthermore, the heyday of the woman suffrage movement embraced an era that historian Rayford Logan called "the nadir" in Afro-American history, characterized by racial segregation, defamation of the character of black women, and lynching of black Americans, both men and women. It is a wonder that Afro-American women dared to dream a white man's dream — the right to enfranchisement — especially at a time when white women attempted to exclude them from that dream.

The existence of a double standard for black and white women among white woman suffragists was apparent to black women on the eve of Nineteenth Amendment passage. Apprehensions from discontented black leaders about the inclusion of black women as voters, especially in the South, were evident throughout the second decade of the twentieth century. During the early years of the decade, black suffragists such as Adella Hunt Logan, a club leader and suffragist from Tuskegee, Alabama; Mary B. Talbert, president of the National Association of Colored Women; and Josephine St. Pierre Ruffin, a suffragist since the 1880s from Boston and the editor of the *Woman's Era*, a black women's newspaper, complained about the double standard in the woman suffrage movement and insisted that white suffragists set aside their prejudices to allow black women, burdened by both sexism and racism, to gain political equality. . . .

By 1919, the year before the Nineteenth Amendment was adopted by Congress, antiblack woman suffrage sentiments continued to plague the movement. Shortly before the amendment was adopted, several incidents occurred to further disillusion black feminists. Mary Church Terrell, a Washington, D.C., educator and national leader among black club women, reported that white suffragists in Florida discriminated against black women in their attempts to recruit support for the campaign. In addition, the NAACP [National Association for the Advancement of Colored People], whose policy officially endorsed woman suffrage, clashed with Alice Paul, president of the NWP, because she allegedly said "that all this talk of Negro women voting in South Carolina was nonsense." Later, Walter White, the NAACP's assistant to the executive secretary, complained to Mary Church Terrell about Alice Paul and agreed with Terrell that white suffrage leaders would be willing to accept the suffrage amendment even if it did not enfranchise black women.

Within a week after receiving Walter White's letter, Mary Church Terrell received a letter from Ida Husted Harper, a leader in the suffrage movement and the editor of the last two volumes of the *History of Woman Suffrage*, asking Terrell to use her influence to persuade the Northeastern Federation of Colored Women's Clubs to withdraw their application seeking cooperative membership in the NAWSA. Echoing sentiments expressed earlier by NAWSA president Carrie Catt, Harper explained that accepting the membership of a black organization was inexpedient for NAWSA at a time when white suffragists sought the cooperation of white southern women. Harper noted that the major obstacle to the amendment in the South was fear among whites of the black woman's vote. She therefore asked federation president Elizabeth Carter to resubmit the membership application after the passage of the Nineteenth Amendment.

At its Jubilee Convention in Saint Louis in March 1919, the NAWSA officially catered to the fears of their southern white members. In response to a proposal by Kentucky suffragist Laura Clay that sections of the so-called Susan B. Anthony amendment that would permit the enfranchisement of black women be changed, the convention delegates agreed that the amendment should be worded so as to allow the South to determine its own position on the black female vote.

During the last months before the passage of the Susan B. Anthony amendment, black suffragists had been rebuffed by both the conservative wing of the suffrage movement, the NAWSA, and by the more radical wing, the NWP. Why then did Afro-American women continue to push for woman suffrage? Since the 1880s, most black women who supported woman suffrage did so because they believed that political equality among the races would raise the status of blacks, both male and female. Increasing the black electorate, they felt, would not only uplift the women of the race, but help the children and the men as well. The majority of the black suffragists were not radical feminists. They were reformers, or what William H. Chafe calls social feminists, who believed that the system could be amended to work for them. Like their white counterparts, these black suffragists assumed that the enfranchised held the key to ameliorating social ills. But unlike white social feminists, many black suffragists called for social and political measures that were specifically tied to race issues. Among these issues were antimiscegenation legislation, jim crow legislation, and "lynch law." Prominent black feminists combined the fight against sexism with the fight against racism by continuously calling the public's attention to these issues. Ida B. Wells-Barnett, Angelina Weld Grimke, and

Mary Church Terrell spoke out against lynching. Josephine St. Pierre Ruffin and Lottie Wilson Jackson, as well as Terrell and Wells-Barnett took steps to challenge jim crow facilities in public accommodations, and antimiscegenation legislation was impugned by Terrell, Grimke, and Wells-Barnett. . . .

The inability of the NAACP to protect the rights of black women voters led the women to seek help from national woman suffrage leaders. However, these attempts failed also. The NWP leadership felt that since black women were discriminated against in the same ways as black men, their problems were not woman's rights issues, but race issues. Therefore, the woman's party felt no obligation to defend the rights of black women.

That they would be abandoned by white female suffragists in 1920 came as no surprise to most black women leaders. The preceding decade of woman suffrage politics had reminded them of the assertions of black woman suffrage supporters of the past. Frederick Douglass declared in 1868 that black women were victimized mainly because they were blacks, not because they were women. Frances Ellen Watkins Harper answered in 1869 that for white women the priorities in the struggle for human rights were sex, not race. By 1920 the situation had changed very little, and many black suffragists had been thoroughly disillusioned by the machinations of the white feminists they had encountered.

Afro-American women continued to be involved in local and national politics during the post–World War I years. However, few organized feminist activities were apparent among the disillusioned black feminists of the period. Afro-American women leaders and their organizations began to focus on issues that continued to plague both the men and the women of the race, rather than upon issues that concerned white feminists. The economic plight of black women kept most of them in poverty and among the lowest of the working classes. Middle-class black women were still relatively few in number. They were more concerned about uplifting the downtrodden of the race or in representing people of color throughout the world than in issues that were limited to middle-class feminists. Hence, during the 1920s there was little concern among black women over the Equal Rights Amendment debate between the more conservative League of Women Voters (LWV) and the more radical NWP. Although the economic roles of many white American women were expanding, the status of black women remained basically static between the wars. As a result, black feminists identified more with the plight of Third World people who found themselves in similar oppressed situations. Former black suffragists were more likely to participate in the Women's International League for Peace and Freedom (WILPF) or the International Council of Women of the Darker Races than in the LWV or the NWP. . . .

A look at the 1920s reveals that most of the black women's organizations that were prominent during the woman suffrage era remained so. Nonetheless, new groups were organized as well. Elizabeth Carter remained president of the Northeastern Federation of Colored Women's Clubs, which celebrated its twenty-fifth anniversary in 1921. The leadership of the NACW was in transition during the 1920s. Mary B. Talbert retired as president and was succeeded by a former suffragist, Hallie Q. Brown, in 1922. In the middle of the decade Mary McLeod Bethune assumed the presidency. In 1922 several NACW leaders organized the International Council of Women of the Darker Races. Margaret Murray Washington, the wife of the late Booker T. Washington and the first president of the National Federation of Afro-American Women, was elected president.

In addition to these established black women's organizations, there was the women's arm of Marcus Garvey's United Negro Improvement Association (UNIA). At its peak, in 1925, the UNIA had an estimated membership of 2 million and can be considered the first mass movement among working-class black people in the nation. Amy Jacques Garvey, Marcus Garvey's wife, was the articulate leader of the women's division and the editor of the women's department of the UNIA official newspaper, *Negro World.* A feminist in the international sense, Amy Jacques Garvey's feminist views embraced the class struggle as well as the problems of Third World women. A black nationalist, Garvey encouraged women of color throughout the world to organize for the benefit of themselves as well as their own people. Although she gave credit to the old-line black women's clubs, Garvey felt their approach to the problems of Third World women was limited. A Jamaican by birth, she called for revolutionary strategies that did not merely reflect the reform ideas of white middle-class women. Instead Garvey called upon the masses of black women in the United States to acknowledge that they were the "burden bearers of their race" and to take the lead in fighting for black independence from white oppression. Amy Jacques Garvey combined the UNIA belief in the power of the black urban working class with the feminist belief that women could think and do for themselves. The revolutionary implications of her ideas are reflected in the theme of the women's pages of *Negro World* — "Our Women and What They Think." Garvey called for black women's dedication to social justice and to national liberation, abroad as well as at home.

Garvey was a radical who happened to be a feminist as well. Her views were ahead of her time; thus, she would have fit in well with the mid-twentieth century radical feminists. However, the demise of the UNIA and the deportation of Marcus Garvey in 1927 shattered much of Amy Jacques Garvey's influence in the United States and she returned to Jamaica. In the meantime, the majority of black feminists of the 1920s either joined the white social feminists, such as Jane Addams and the WILPF, or bypassed the feminists altogether to deal with race issues within black organizations.

The leadership of the WILPF was old-line and can be characterized as former progressives, woman suffragists, and social feminists. Jane Addams presided over the organization before U.S. entry into World War I and brought black women such as Mary Church Terrell, Mary B. Talbert, Charlotte Atwood, Mary F. Waring, and Addie W. Hunton into the fold. Terrell had been a member of the executive committee since 1915. As a league representative, she was elected a delegate to the International Congress of Women held in Paris in 1919. Upon her arrival, Terrell was impressed with the conference delegates but noticed that there were none from non-western countries and that she was the only delegate of color in the group. As a result, she felt obliged to represent the women of all the nonwhite countries in the world, and this she attempted to do. At the conference meeting in Zurich, Switzerland, Terrell agreed to represent the American delegation and did so by speaking in German before the largely German-speaking audience. In addition, she submitted her own personal resolution to the conference, despite attempts by American committee members to change her wording. "We believe no human being should be deprived of an education, prevented from earning a living, debarred from any legitimate pursuit in which he wishes to engage or be subjected to humiliations of various kinds on account of race, color or creed." Terrell's position and thinking were in keeping with the growing awareness among black women leaders in the United States that Third World people needed to fight oppression together.

Although Mary Church Terrell remained an active social feminist, her public as well as her private views reflected the disillusionment of black feminists of the woman suffrage era. In 1921 she was asked by members of the WILPF executive committee to sign a petition requesting the removal of black troops from occupied German territory, where they were alleged to be violating German women. Terrell refused to sign the petition because she felt the motives behind it were racist. In a long letter to Jane Addams, the executive committee chairman, Terrell explained why she would not sign the petition. She noted that Carrie Catt had investigated the charges against the black troops and found them to be unfounded. The troops, from French colonies in Africa, were victims, Terrell contended, of American propaganda against black people. Making a dramatic choice between the feminist organization position and her own loyalty to her race, Terrell offered to resign from the executive committee. Addams wrote her back, agreeing with Terrell's position and asking her not to resign. In this case, when given the choice between the politics of feminism and race pride, Terrell felt that her energies were needed most to combat racism, and she chose to take a nationalist position in the controversy.

Several other attempts were made at interracial cooperation among women's groups during the early 1920s, but most of these efforts were white-dominated and short-lived. An exception was the Cooperative Women's League of Baltimore, founded in 1913 by Sarah C. Fernandis. This group maintained relations with white women's civic leagues in connection with local health and sanitation, home economics, art, and education projects. In 1925 the league initiated its twelfth annual program. This organization was quite conventional, a far cry from feminist — black or white. However, the activities were, like most black women's group activities of the times, geared to strengthen local black communities.

Other black-white cooperative ventures on a grander scale included the Commission on Inter-Racial Cooperation of the Women's Council of the Methodist Episcopal Church South. In October 1920 the commission held a conference on race relations. Only four black women were invited and they were selected because of their husbands' prominence, rather than for their feminist views. The conference pledged a responsibility to uplift the status of black women in the South, calling for a reform of the conditions under which black domestics worked in white homes. The delegates passed resolutions supporting improved sanitation and housing for blacks, fair treatment of blacks in public accommodations, the prevention of lynching, and justice in the courts. Significantly, no mention of protecting black women's suffrage was made. Several months later, the National Federation of Colored Women's Clubs met at Tuskegee, Alabama, and issued a statement that seemed to remind the Methodist Episcopal women of their pledge and called for increased cooperation and understanding from southern white women. Interestingly, the black women included suffrage in their resolution.

Nothing came of this attempt at interracial cooperation, for neither the social nor the economic status of black women improved in the South during the 1920s. The trend toward interracial cooperation continued nevertheless, and in 1922 the YWCA appointed a joint committee of black and white women to study race problems. Once again, only four black women were invited to participate. Principles were declared, but little came of the gathering.

In the meantime, most black women's organizations had turned from attempts to establish coalitions with white women's groups to concentrate upon pressing race problems. Lynching was one of the major American problems, and black women organized to fight it. On the national front, black women's groups used political strategies and concentrated their efforts toward passage of the Dyer Anti-Lynching Bill. In 1922 the Northeastern Federation of Colored Women's Clubs appointed a delegation to call on Senator Lodge of Massachusetts to urge passage of the Dyer bill. In addition, the Alpha Kappa Alpha Sorority held its national convention in Indianapolis and sent a telegram to President Warren Harding urging the support of his administration in the passage of the bill. Also that year, the NACW met in Richmond and appointed an antilynching delegation to make contact with key states needed for the passage of the Dyer bill in Congress. In addition, the delegation was authorized to meet with President Harding. Among the black women in the delegation were veteran antilynching crusader Ida B. Wells-Barnett, NACW president Hallie Q. Brown, and Rhode Island suffragist Mary B. Jackson.

Perhaps the most renowned antilynching crusader of the 1920s was Spingarn Medal winner Mary B. Talbert. In 1922 she organized an executive committee of 15 black women, who supervised over 700 state workers across the nation in what Talbert called the Anti-Lynching Crusade. Her aim was to "unite a million women to stop lynching," by arousing the consciences of both black and white women. One of Talbert's strategies was to provide statistics that showed that victims of lynching were not what propagandists called sex-hungry black men who preyed upon innocent white women. The crusaders revealed that eighty-three women had been lynched in the United States since Ida B. Wells-Barnett had compiled the first comprehensive annual report in 1892. The Anti-Lynching Crusade was truly an example of woman power, for the crusaders believed that they could not wait for the men of America to stop the problem. It was perhaps the most influential link in the drive for interracial cooperation among women's groups. As a result of its efforts, the 1922 National Council of Women, representing 13 million American women, resolved to "endorse the Anti-Lynching Crusade recently launched by colored women of this country."

Although the Dyer bill was defeated, it was revised by the NAACP and introduced again in the House of Representatives by Congressman Leonidas C. Dyer of Missouri and in the Senate by William B. McKinley of Illinois in 1926. That year the bill failed again, as did similar bills in 1935, 1940, and 1942. However, it was the effort of blacks and white women organized against lynching that pressed for legislation throughout the period. Without a doubt, it was the leadership of black women, many of whom had been active in the late nineteenth-century women's club movement and in the woman suffrage movement, who motivated white women in 1930 to organize the Association of Southern Women for the Prevention of Lynching. Although a federal antilynching bill never passed the Congress, by the end of the 1940s public opinion had been sufficiently convinced by the efforts of various women's groups that lynching was barbarous and criminal. Recorded incidents of lynching ceased by 1950.

Even though interracial cooperation in the antilynching campaign was a positive factor among black and white women, discrimination against black women by white women continued to plague feminists. In 1925, for example, the Quinquennial of the International Council of Women met at the Washington Auditorium in the District of Columbia. The council sought the cooperation of NACW president Mary McLeod Bethune and arrangements were made to have a mass choir of black women perform. The night of the concert, black guests were placed in a segregated section of the auditorium. Mary Church Terrell reported that when the singers learned of what was happening, they refused to perform. Foreign women delegates were in the audience, as well as white women from throughout the nation. Many of them were angry because the concert had to be canceled. Terrell felt that this was one of the most unfortunate incidents of discrimination against black women in the club movement. However, she agreed with the decision of her black sisters not to sing.

National recognition of black women did not really come until 1936, when Mary McLeod Bethune was appointed director of the Division of Negro Affairs, National Youth Administration, under the Franklin D. Roosevelt administration. The founder of Bethune-Cookman Institute in Daytona, Florida, Bethune had been a leader in the black women's club movement since the early 1920s. NACW president from 1924 to 1928, she founded the National Council of Negro Women (NCNW) in 1935. What feminist consciousness Bethune acquired was thrust upon her in the mid-1930s because for the first time, a black woman had the ear of the president of the United States and the cooperation of the first lady, who was concerned not only about women's issues, but about black issues. In 1936 Bethune took advantage of her new status and presented the concerns of the NCNW to Eleanor Roosevelt. As a result, sixty-five black women leaders attended a meeting with Eleanor Roosevelt to argue the case for their greater representation and appointments to federal bureaus. They called for appointments of professional black women to the Children's Bureau, the Women's Bureau, and each department of the Bureau of Education that dealt with the welfare of women and children. The NCNW also wanted the appointment of black women to administrative positions in the Federal Housing Administration and Social Security Board. In addition, they called for enlarging the black staff of the Bureau of Public Health and for President Roosevelt to suggest to the American Red Cross that they hire a black administrator.

The NCNW requests reflect two trends among middle-class women in the mid-1930s. First, they were calling for positions that black women had never held, nor would achieve until a generation later; consequently, their ideas were revolutionary ones in terms of federal policies. Second, they were calling for policies to benefit not only their sex, but their race; hence, the NCNW reflected the position established by black feminists a generation before. . . .

Although President Roosevelt made good his promise to Mary McLeod Bethune, so that by 1945 four black women had received outstanding federal appointments, the political viability of black women in the early 1940s was bleak. The list of black elected officials from 1940 to 1946 included no women. Agents of white supremacy continued to subvert what vestiges of political influence blacks held. For example, in 1942 Congressman Martin Dies, chairman of the congressional committee investigating un-American activities, attempted to link several national black leaders to the Communist party. Among the group was Mary McLeod Bethune, who remained the only black woman prominent in national politics.

Hence, over twenty years after the passage of the Nineteenth Amendment racial discrimination festered in most areas of American life, even among feminists and women in political life. Prejudice did not distinguish between middle-class and working-class black women, nor between feminists and nonfeminists who were black. Although black women continued to use what political rights they maintained, the small number of those politically viable made little impact upon public policies.

※ *F U R T H E R   R E A D I N G*

Susan D. Becker, *The Origins of the Equal Rights Amendment* (1981)

Kathleen M. Blee, *Women of the Klan: Racism and Gender in the 1920s* (1991)

William Chafe, *The Paradox of Change: American Women in the 20th Century* (1991)

Ellen Chesler, *Woman of Valor: Margaret Sanger and the Birth Control Movement* (1992)

Nancy F. Cott, *The Grounding Modern Feminism* (1987)

Richard J. Evans, *The Feminists: Women's Emancipation Movements in Europe, America and Australasia 1840–1920* (1977)

Paula Fass, *The Damned and the Beautiful: American Youth in the 1920s* (1977)

Estelle Freedman, "The New Woman: Changing Views of Women in the 1920s," *Journal of American History* LXI (1974), 372–393

Peter Geidel, "The National Woman's Party and the Origins of the Equal Rights Amendment, 1920–1923," *The Historian* XLII (1980), 557–582

Paula Giddings, *When and Where I Enter: The Impact of Black Women on Race and Sex in America* (1984)

Linda Gordon, *Woman's Body, Woman's Right: A Social History of Birth Control in America* (1976)

Jacquelyn Dowd Hall, *Revolt Against Chivalry: Jessie Daniel Ames and the Women's Campaign Against Lynching* (1979)

Patrice M. Hummer, *The Decade of the Elusive Promise: Professional Women in the United States 1920–1930* (1981)

J. Stanley Lemons, *The Woman Citizen: Social Feminism in the 1920s* (1973)

Christine Lunardini, *From Equal Suffrage to Equal Rights: Alice Paul and the National Woman's Party, 1913–1928* (1986)

Rosalind Rosenberg, *Beyond Separate Spheres: Intellectual Roots of Modern Feminism (1982)*

Lois Scharf and Joan Jensen, eds., *Decades of Discontent: The Women's Movement 1910–1940* (1983)

Frank Stricker, "Cookbooks and Lawbooks: The Hidden History of Career Women in Twentieth-Century America," *Journal of Social History* X (1976–1977), 1–19

Decades of Crisis: The Great

Depression and World War II

In 1929 the United States descended into the worst economic crisis of its history, a crisis that ruined thousands of businesses and left nearly one-quarter of the workforce unemployed by 1933. In the 1930s, President Franklin Delano Roosevelt's New Deal created federal job programs, boosted unionization, established social security and unemployment funds, and mandated a federal minimum wage; however, it did not end the Great Depression. Instead, it took another crisis — World War II — to finally reinvigorate the economy, but this one also created new sources of hardship and anxiety for Americans.

Historians have long debated the significance of these two decades of crisis for women, questioning whether the Depression and World War II caused Americans to affirm or forsake traditional gender roles and expectations. Two facts are well known and oft-repeated. First, during the Depression, federal agencies, state governments, school districts, and various businesses fired married women, or refused to hire them, hoping to create more work opportunities for married men with dependents. Second, the nation's involvement in World War II produced a temporary surge in new job opportunities for women in munitions work and related war industries; these jobs disappeared when the war ended. But the basic facts raise more questions than they answer. Did women, married or single, believe that the members of their sex were being discriminated against during the 1930s? Did they profit from New Deal job programs, social welfare policies, or unionization efforts? What did women think of their wartime jobs? Did they work out of a sense of patriotism, because they wanted the money, or for other reasons? Did the expansion of job opportunities during the war benefit women of color as much as it did white women? Japanese-American women who were interned in relocation centers would have had no opportunity to work at high-paying jobs in the war industry; how did internment alter their lives and their sense of self?

※ D O C U M E N T S

Ann Marie Low, a single, college-educated white woman, kept a diary during the 1930s, while she and her North Dakota family were struggling to withstand the hardships of the Depression and life in the Dust Bowl. Excerpted as the first document, Low's diary is a record of her feelings about lost job opportunities, family obligations, and marriage. Writing for *The Daily Worker* in 1940, Louise Mitchell, in the second document, discloses the harsh conditions under which African-American women sought work in New York City during the Depression years, given that, as domestic servants, they lacked job security and were ineligible for New Deal work benefits or entitlements. In the third document, from 1939, Mary Sweet, a black garment presser who was interviewed by the Federal Writer's Project, speaks with measured optimism about unionizing black women garment workers. In October 1942, in a *Ladies Home Journal* article, a female psychiatrist explored the problems that employed mothers faced during World War II. Dr. Leslie Hohman's emphatic "yes" to the question, "Can Women in War Industry Be Good Mothers?" (the fourth selection) broke sharply with the traditional prewar wisdom on the subject. The fifth selection, a prize-winning essay by an African-American munitions worker, Hortense Johnson, appeared in *Opportunity* magazine in 1943. In the last selection, Jeanne Wakatsuki Houston, in an excerpt from her memoir, describes her experiences as a ten-year-old schoolgirl interned in the Manzanar, California, relocation camp for Japanese-Americans during World War II. Taken together, these documents show how women and the larger culture adjusted to the demands and trials of economic depression and war.

Ann Marie Low on Life in the Dust Bowl, 1934

April 25, 1934, Wednesday

Last weekend was the worst dust storm we ever had. We've been having quite a bit of blowing dirt every year since the drouth started, not only here, but all over the Great Plains. Many days this spring the air is just full of dirt coming, literally, for hundreds of miles. It sifts into everything. After we wash the dishes and put them away, so much dust sifts into the cupboards we must wash them again before the next meal. Clothes in the closets are covered with dust.

Last weekend no one was taking an automobile out for fear of ruining the motor. I rode Roany to Frank's place to return a gear. To find my way I had to ride right beside the fence, scarcely able to see from one fence post to the next.

Newspapers say the deaths of many babies and old people are attributed to breathing in so much dirt.

May 7, 1934, Monday

The dirt is still blowing. Last weekend Bud and I helped with the cattle and had fun gathering weeds. Weeds give us greens for salad long before anything in the garden is ready. We use dandelions, lamb's quarter, and sheep sorrel. I like sheep sorrel best. Also, the leaves of sheep sorrel, pounded and boiled down to a paste, make a good salve.

Still no job. I'm trying to persuade Dad I should apply for rural school #3 out here where we went to school. I don't see a chance of getting a job in a high school when so many experienced teachers are out of work.

He argues that the pay is only $60.00 a month out here, while even in a grade school in town I might get $75.00. Extra expenses in town would probably eat up that extra $15.00. Miss Eston, the practice teaching supervisor, told me her salary has been cut to $75.00 after all the years she has been teaching in Jamestown. She wants to get married. School boards will not hire married women teachers in these hard times because they have husbands to support them. Her fiancé is the sole support of his widowed mother and can't support a wife, too. So she is just stuck in her job, hoping she won't get another salary cut because she can scarcely live on what she makes and dress the way she is expected to.

Dad argues the patrons always stir up so much trouble for a teacher at #3 some teachers have quit in mid-term. The teacher is also the janitor, so the hours are long.

I figure I can handle the work, kids, and patrons. My argument is that by teaching here I can work for my room and board at home, would not need new clothes, and so could send most of my pay to Ethel and Bud. . . .

May 21, 1934, Monday

Ethel has been having stomach trouble. Dad has been taking her to doctors though suspecting her trouble is the fact that she often goes on a diet that may affect her health. The local doctor said he thought it might be chronic appendicitis, so Mama took Ethel by train to Valley City last week to have a surgeon there remove her appendix.

Saturday Dad, Bud, and I planted an acre of potatoes. There was so much dirt in the air I couldn't see Bud only a few feet in front of me. Even the air in the house was just a haze. In the evening the wind died down, and Cap came to take me to the movie. We joked about how hard it is to get cleaned up enough to go anywhere. . . .

Sunday the dust wasn't so bad. Dad and I drove cattle to the Big Pasture. Then I churned butter and baked a ham, bread, and cookies for the men, as no telling when Mama will be back.

July 6, 1934, Friday

I am still herding cows, and it is awfully hot. Where they have eaten every weed and blade of grain, Bud is plowing so the ground will be softened to absorb rain (if it comes). He is very fed up and anxious to get away to school and fit himself for a job.

Poor Bud. He has worked so hard and saved so hard. He has done without nice clothes and never went to a dance or movie oftener than about once a year because he was saving every penny for college. He hoped his livestock would pay his way for four years. The price was so low he didn't sell any last year. This year they are worth less, and he absolutely must sell them because there is not enough feed for them and no money to buy feed. All the stock he has won't pay his way through one year of college. . . .

July 9, 1934, Monday

Saturday night Cap and I went to the movie, Claudette Colbert in *The Torch Singer*. Afterward he bought ice cream cones and we sat in the car in front of the store eating them. He brought up the subject of marriage. I reminded him that he promised, if I would go out with him occasionally, he would not mention marriage. I also pointed out the impossibility. He has to run the farm until Sonny is old enough and then will have nothing to start out on his own. I have to work until Ethel gets through college and can help Bud, at least two years. If she doesn't help Bud, we are looking at four years. Though I didn't mention it, in four years Cap will be thirty-six years old. Forget it.

He insisted he wants to get married now. Then I turned shrewish and said I'd seen him leave a dance last year with Joan. If he wants a wife, she would doubtless marry him.

He said he did take her home from a dance once, but there is absolutely nothing between him and Joan and I know it — I am all he wants and I know it.

"Let's not quarrel," I murmured. "Things will work out somehow."

He leaned back against the car seat, saying somberly, "Oh, how I wish it would rain."

The light from the store window was on his face. He is really a handsome man, with a John Barrymore profile and thick wavy auburn hair. Suddenly I seemed to see what his face will be someday — a tombstone on which is written the epitaph of dead dreams. I shivered.

"Oh, Sweetheart, you are cold and have no wrap. I'll take you home."

I didn't tell him I wasn't shivering from cold.

Louise Mitchell on the "Slave Markets" Where Domestics Are Hired, New York City, 1940

Every morning, rain or shine, groups of women with brown paper bags or cheap suitcases stand on street corners in the Bronx and Brooklyn waiting for a chance to get some work. Sometimes there are 15, sometimes 30, some are old, many are young and most of them are Negro women waiting for employers to come to the street corner auction blocks to bargain for their labor.

They come as early as 7 in the morning, wait as late as four in the afternoon with the hope that they will make enough to buy supper when they go home. Some have spent their last nickel to get to the corner and are in desperate need. When the hour grows late, they sit on boxes if any are around. In the afternoon their labor is worth only half as much as in the morning. If they are lucky, they get about 30 cents an hour scrubbing, cleaning, laundering, washing windows, waxing floors and woodwork all day long; in the afternoon, when most have already been employed, they are only worth the degrading sum of 20 cents an hour.

Once hired on the "slave market," the women often find after a day's back-breaking toil, that they worked longer than was arranged, got less than was promised, were forced to accept clothing instead of cash and were exploited beyond human endurance. Only the urgent need for money makes them submit to this routine daily.

Throughout the country, more than two million women are engaged in domestic work, the largest occupational group for women. About half are Negro women. . . .

Though many Negro women work for as little as two dollars a week and as long as 80 hours a week . . . they have no social security, no workmen's compensation, no old age security. . . .

The Women's Bureau in Washington points out that women take domestic work only as a last resort. Largely unprotected by law they find themselves at the mercy of an individual employer. Only two states, Wisconsin and Washington, have wage or hour legislation. But enforcement is very slack. . . .

The tradition of street corner markets is no new institution in this city. As far back as 1834, the statute books show, a place was set aside on city streets where those seeking work could meet with those who wanted workers. This exchange also functions for male workers. . . . At present markets flourish in the Bronx and Brooklyn where middle-class families live. However, this method of employment is also instituted in Greenwich Village, Richmond and Queens. . . .

The prosperity of the nation can only be judged by the living standards of its most oppressed group. State legislatures must pass laws to protect the health and work of the domestic. A world of education is still needed both for employees and employers.

Many civic and social organizations are now working toward improving conditions of domestics. Outstanding among these is the Bronx Citizens Committee for Improvement of Domestic Employees. The YWCA and many women's clubs are interested in the problem. Mayor LaGuardia . . . must be forced to end these horrible conditions of auction block hiring with the most equitable solution for the most oppressed section of the working class — Negro women.

Mary Sweet on the Difficulties of Organizing Black Garment Workers, 1939

All workers, white or colored, are hard to organize. They're afraid for their jobs. With the Negro the fear is much greater; it's much harder for them to find jobs. And the union has been dumb in its attitude towards the Negro garment workers in Boston. You see, the important workers in the shops are the cutters and pressers. If you're going to organize a shop you got to get those two. Now, many of the colored girls are pressers and the union simply wouldn't take them in. They weren't prejudiced against our race. It was just that the men in the ILGWU [International Ladies' Garment Workers' Union] here wanted to keep the pressing jobs for the men, and they kept the union from taking in women pressers. They'd take in the other colored workers, but they couldn't get them. You see, you couldn't tell the colored girls that it wasn't prejudice. I didn't believe that, but almost all of them did. Besides, it wouldn't do 'em much good to get the other girls if they wouldn't organize the pressers.

I lost my job because of the union. In 1933 we had a general strike in Boston. The ILGWU called out everybody, the union and non-union shops. My shop had about

From *First Person America,* Ann Banks, ed., 1980, pp. 133–135. Reprinted by permission of the editor.

half union members. . . . They expected I'd go out, but I didn't. My foreman, who was a pretty good union member, said, "Mary, I'm surprised at you." And I said, "Well you wouldn't take me in the union so I'm independent and I'll do what I want. You gotta take me in before I'll strike." The boss asked if I was afraid and I said no. We had to sneak in and out through the back way. Near the end of the strike he hired thugs to protect us. They finally settled the strike. Our shop signed a union agreement and the women pressers had to get out. They gave us four months to find other jobs.

I loafed for a while and things were tough, real tough. Meanwhile the ILGWU got around to looking at the women pressers the same way that they did in New York and other places; besides, they felt that it was important to organize the colored garment workers of Boston. One day my old foreman came down to see me. He said, "I want you to come with me to talk to some officials of the ILGWU." We went to an Italian restaurant for dinner and they asked me to go to work for the ILGWU as an organizer. They wanted to organize the colored workers, and experience had shown them that it wouldn't be done by white organizers. They had put one white woman on the job as an organizer and then another, and they couldn't get to first place. We talked about it for a while and I said okay. The union sent me to New York and got me a job in a shop and I learned about the union setup and how it worked. I lived while I was there in the home of Mark Starr, the educational director of the ILGWU. He's a fine man and a fine unionist. Then they sent me to Brookwood Labor College for a six-week course, and when that was over I went to Boston and began to work.

It was very discouraging. I sent out a hundred letters for the first meeting I called of colored girls. Six turned out. They told me that wasn't so bad. I kept calling meetings and only a few turned out for each meeting and never the same few. I also went house to house to talk with the girls. Some refused to let me in; some threatened me with knives or said they'd beat me up. One woman in Somerville said, "I'll let you in only because it's freezing out but I'm telling you now that you can talk from now till next week an' it won't do no good, my mind is made up." Some said the boss'd told them they didn't need no union.

I worked a little over a year and then the union gave me one week's pay and laid me off. I told them they were making a big mistake, that the only way to organize the colored girls was to stick to it even if it takes years and I knew it would, though they thought it was something that could be done in a few months.

We've got about a hundred in the union today but we're not organizing anymore. I'm an active union member. I work a union shop, but it's really a sweat shop. I guess I average about twenty-five dollars a week. I've got hopes that we may be able to do a lot to make our people union-minded through a Negro Labor Committee such as they have in New York. We've set up such a committee here and I'm the secretary.

The most inspiring thing I ever knew was in New York. A manufacturer, a Jew, ran away from the union and opened up a shop in Harlem. He hired experienced colored girls, and paid them the lowest sweat-shop wages, next to nothing. On the front of the building he put up a sign, "Jesus Saves." He needed an experienced man to cut, so he hired a little Jewish cutter. Before very long the ILGWU organized the girls, about thirty of them, and a strike was called. The Jewish cutter joined the union, too. The strike went on for several weeks and the workers were having a real tough time. They were new to the union and flat broke after a few days. But they stuck it out and the boss cracked first. The union and the boss sat down to negotiate and the boss gave in to almost every demand, but one thing he wouldn't do. He wouldn't take the Jewish cutter back to work. He felt that the cutter should have stuck by him because they both were Jewish. Well, they called a meeting of the crew, the thirty girls and the Jewish cutter, and the strikers were told what the boss offered and they were to vote on it. Mind you, they were all dead broke, but they voted unanimously to stay on strike until every one of them was taken back. And they won.

Dr. Leslie Hohman Asks, "Can Women in War Industry Be Good Mothers?" 1942

The task of working women who are mothers, too, involves unquestionable difficulties which we must face squarely. Yet it gives women and their husbands a chance to prove dramatically and quickly where their deepest interests are.

If I had had any doubts on the question, my trip to the Hartford home of Fred and Mary Berckman would have converted me. Their whole household teems with evidence that their children are to them the most important consideration in the world. Their unflagging interest is the solid foundation for the first of the specific rules to be drawn from their highly successful experience.

The first rule is that mothers who are working must deliberately and determinedly plan to spend ample time with their children. To Mary this is not in the least burdensome. She delights in helping with the lessons of all her merry brood — second-grader son Junie, and the daughters Eileen, Fredrica and the eldest, Catherine, in the fifth grade. Mary sings with them, laughs with them, tells them stories in her fine Irish brogue of County Mayo, where she was born and lived until she came to America nineteen years ago.

"We make things interesting in this house," Mary said — an excellent boost for girls and boys along the road to happiness and security.

With all her fondness for her children, Mary could not accomplish so much time with them if both she and Fred had not organized their days carefully with that very purpose in mind. Her early shift at the Colt arms plant brings her home in the afternoons about the time the children arrive from school. She mixes them a malted milk, does preliminary work on dinner, then lies down for an hour until the children call out that their father is home from work. Fred is there at noon, too, from the Royal Typewriter plant just across the street, to help the youngsters prepare the lunch that has been arranged by Mary before she left for work.

Not much is to be gained by a detailed study of the exact schedule Fred and Mary use. Each working mother will have to arrange a schedule according to her individual working hours and her individual problems. We can be sure in advance that those who haven't the will to succeed will seek excuses for not doing so well as Fred and Mary — such as, "Neither my husband nor I can come home at noon." We can be equally sure that those who sincerely try will find some way to make certain that their children are well cared for while they are at work.

One mother I know who has an important executive position and commutes every working day to her desk rises much earlier every morning than she otherwise would have to, so that she can have breakfast and a long chat with her daughter. In the evenings, also, she always manages to spend some time with the child. They talk gaily of topics which interest the little girl. Their companionship is far closer than that of most daughters with mothers who haven't any outside work to do.

A writing assistant on a daily radio program who has few unfilled hours at home during the week still arranges to find brief and happy intervals for her young son every day. The main feature of her admirable plan comes every Sunday. The entire day is her son's. Any reasonable suggestion he makes on how they shall spend his day, she follows merrily. They have grand fun. The scheme often means that she and her husband decline weekend invitations, but they hold to their plan and enjoy themselves more than they would on the missed parties. The result is that the son is held to his parents by the strongest possible bonds of wholesome affection.

The general attitude of mothers — and fathers too — is a more powerful influence than the actual number of hours they spend with their children. Couples who want to act childless and who find association with their children irksome and dull, do not fool their children by staying home and snapping at them. Fewer hours and more companionship would be much better.

A child's sense of security is fostered psychologically by stability in his environment. Despite all protestations of love at odd moments, young children in a harum-scarum household are likely to develop unstable emotional habits and a feeling of insecurity.

I am convinced that jobs for mothers outside the home generally help to create the stability of environment that is so essential. The gain usually more than offsets the loss of the hours in which the mother has to be away. Besides the scheduling of household routine imposed by regular employment, there is the added advantage for children that the inefficient mothers whose home management is hit-or-miss and disturbingly unreliable will learn to be more efficient by working where efficiency is required.

The skill and willingness in housework which Fred acquired when he took it over completely while his heart would not permit more strenuous exertion, makes him an ideal partner for a working wife. This suggests still another flat rule:

If children are to be reared successfully in families with employed mothers who haven't enough money for nursemaids and servants, it is absolutely necessary for husbands to help their wives with home duties and with the children's training.

Many unemployed wives would say offhand that their husbands could never learn. They probably would be pleasantly surprised. An outside job for a wife usually seems to cause a striking improvement in the husband's domesticity. Every husband of a working wife to whom I have mentioned the problem assured me that he felt obligated to help. "I never did before my wife got a job," several said. "After all, why should I when I had done my part and she had nothing else to do?" Not taking the husbands' statements of their own virtues as final, I made extensive inquiries among employed wives I knew. With hardly any exceptions, they cited their husbands for extraordinary household accomplishments.

Even when father knuckles down to do his share, there will be plenty of chores left for children in homes where both parents have outside jobs and abundant assistance cannot be hired. That is a great good fortune for the children. If we had enough working mothers, there would be a reinstatement of work training and early feeling for useful accomplishment. Too many young boys and girls are missing this valuable training.

Watching the Berckman children, I thought how much more fortunate they were than the ten-year-old son of an idle, prosperous mother who recently sought my advice because she saw, at last, that something was going wrong with him. Something had been going wrong since infancy. His mother and nursemaid and later his whole family waited on him hand and foot. An important part of my prescription was that useful chores be found for him. The family is having a hard time following the prescription after its long habit of spoiling the boy.

The troubles of mothers who have jobs will be greatly lessened if they and their husbands enforce good training while they are at home. Mary and Fred established a cornerstone by affectionate discipline from infancy, not shying from occasional punishment when it was necessary to stop the development of traits that would handicap their children.

Merely the presence of a mother in the house will not make children behave — as harried neighbors can testify. Mothers cannot incessantly watch children old enough to go out and play, and it would be harmful to the children's self-reliance if they could. The best guaranty is the trained-in reliability and independence that enable Mary to say confidently: "My children never have done anything I told them not to do. I can trust them completely."

War or no war, outside work should never be undertaken by mothers until adequate care and training of their young children are assured. The arrangements frequently are hard to make, but rarely impossible. Where there is money enough, a qualified woman can be paid to come in and take charge. In most neighborhoods where money is not too plentiful, some woman who has proved her skill with her own children will be glad to augment the family income a little by taking care of one or two more for eight or nine hours a day.

No story of the problems and difficulties that working mothers meet could give a complete picture without prominent mention of the intangible gain that is nearly always overlooked. With few exceptions, women are made more interesting to their girls and boys by an outside job. Mary Berckman is a shining example. She is in brisk step with the world of today. She has sorted out her values under the test of stern realities. She has no time to be bored, no time for gossip. She always has time for companionship. It is not surprising that she, with Fred's excellent help, fills her children's lives with happiness.

Hortense Johnson on Black Women and the War Effort, 1943

Of course I'm vital to victory, just as millions of men and women who are fighting to save America's chances for Democracy, even if they never shoulder a gun nor bind a wound. It's true that my job isn't so exciting or complicated. Perhaps there

Hortense Johnson, "First Essay," *Opportunity* 21 (April 1943): 50–51.

are millions of girls who could do my job as well as I — certainly there are thousands. I am an inspector in a war plant. For eight hours a day, six days a week, I stand in line with five other girls, performing a routine operation that is part of our production schedule. We inspect wooden boxes that are to hold various kinds of munitions, and that range in size from eight inches to six feet. When we approve them they are ready to be packed with shells, bombs, fuses, parachutes — and other headaches for Hitler and Hirohito.

Not much to that, you say. Well, that all depends on the way you look at it. A missing or projecting nail, a loose board or hinge — these are some of the imperfections that we watch for. If we miss them, they may be checked later on, or they may not. If they are not, they may mean injury for a fellow worker on a later operation or an explosion in another part of the plant with dozens of lives lost — or they might even spell disaster for American soldiers in a tight spot in North Africa.

Did I say my job isn't exciting or complicated? I take that back. It may be a simple matter to inspect one box or a dozen, but it's different when you are handling them by the hundreds. The six of us in my crew sometimes inspect as many as fourteen or fifteen hundred boxes during one shift. That means two hundred and fifty apiece — an average of one every two minutes, regardless of size and not counting any rest periods. Try that sometime and see if it's a simple job! You stand at your bench all day long, with rest periods sometimes seeming years apart. You fight against the eye fatigue that might mean oversight. You probe with your fingers and tap here and there. Your back aches, your legs get weary, your muscles scream at you sometimes — groan at you all the time. But the dozen and one little operations must be carried on smoothly and efficiently if your work output is to keep up. It's exciting all right, and it's plenty complicated — in the same way that jungle warfare must be, hard and painstaking and monotonous — until something goes off with a bang!

And then when your shift is finished, you stalk off stiffly to the washroom and hurry to get ready for the bus that brings you forty-five miles back from the plant to your home in the city. You slip on an extra sweater and heavy woolen socks, because the unheated bus is apt to be cold and damp. Even when you get into the bus your day's job isn't over, for you work almost as hard as the driver. You strain with him to see through the heavy winter fog that blankets the highway. You watch with him for the tricky ice that waits at curves to throw you into dangerous skids. When sleet has covered the road and made all travel seem suicidal, you sit ready to get out at the worst spots and walk with the rest of your crowd until the bus pulls across to safety.

So when you get back home, you're glad to jump into bed and die until morning — or until your alarm-clock tells you it's morning, no matter how black it is. Then your two-hour experience of traveling back to the job begins all over again, because in spite of rain, snow, cold or illness, the job is there to be done, and you're expected to do your share. It never occurs to you to figure out how much money you're making, because it isn't much anyhow — after you've had your victory tax deducted, paid for your war bond, set aside money for your bus commutation ticket. By the time you've given grandmother the food and rent money, and paid the doctor for helping you to fight off your frequent colds, and bought the extra-heavy clothes the job calls for, you're just about where the boys in New Guinea are. Don't let Senator Wheeler fool you with his talk about "high wages for war workers!"

So if it's as tough as all that — and it is! — why do you stick on the job? Why did you leave the comfortable job you held with a city business house? Why don't you go back to it and make as much money as you're making now? Why? Because it's not that easy to leave, and it's not that tough to stay! Of course the work is hard and sometimes dangerous, but victory in this war isn't going to come the easy way, without danger. And we brown women of America need victory so much, so desperately. America is a long way from perfect. We resent the racial injustices that we meet every day of our lives. But it's one thing to resent and fight against racial injustices; it's another thing to let them break your spirit, so that you quit this struggle and turn the country over to Hitler and the Talmadges and Dies' who will run this country if Hitler wins. America can't win this war without all of us, and we know it. We must prove it to white Americans as well — that our country can't get along without the labor and sacrifice of her brown daughters, can't win unless we *all* fight and work and save.

So the hardships of war work become willing sacrifices to victory, not to victory for Democracy, but to victory by a country that some day, please God, will win Democracy. In such a spirit, even some of the hardships are forgotten in the daily rewards of the job. After all, we *are* working today and drawing regular pay checks. . . . Frayed nerves and short tempers show themselves sometimes, and that's understandable, but a real quarrel seldom develops. Ill-tempered remarks are usually understood, and passed over without comeback.

I imagine that our boys at the front develop the same kind of tolerance, the same kind of partnership, for the same reason. Wouldn't it be great if the white workers who are fellow-fighters with us in war production, would develop more of the same spirit of partnership? What can we do to make them realize that colored people must be given equal opportunity in every walk of life to make that partnership real — to build an impregnable, free, and democratic America. . . .

I'm not fooling myself about this war. Victory won't mean victory for Democracy — yet. But that will come later, because most of us who are fighting for victory today will keep on fighting to win the peace — maybe a long time after the war is over, maybe a hundred years after. By doing my share today, I'm keeping a place for some brown woman tomorrow, and for the brown son of that woman the day after tomorrow. Sterling Brown once wrote, "The strong men keep a-comin' on," and millions of those men have dark skins. There will be dark women marching by their side, and I like to think that I'm one of them.

Jeanne Wakatsuki Houston, A Schoolgirl at Manzanar, 1940s

Once we settled into Block 28 that ache I'd felt since soon after we arrived at Manzanar subsided. It didn't entirely disappear, but it gradually submerged, as semblances of order returned and our pattern of life assumed its new design.

For one thing, [my older brother] Kiyo and I and all the other children finally had *a school*. During the first year, teachers had been volunteers; equipment had been makeshift; classes were scattered all over camp, in mess halls, recreation rooms, wherever we could be squeezed in. Now a teaching staff had been hired. Two blocks were turned into Manzanar High, and a third block of fifteen barracks was set up to house the elementary grades. We had blackboards, new desks, reference books, lab supplies. . . .

My days spent in classrooms are largely a blur now, as one merges into another. What I see clearly is the face of my fourth-grade teacher — a pleasant face, but completely invulnerable, it seemed to me at the time, with sharp, commanding eyes. She came from Kentucky. . . . A tall, heavyset spinster, about forty years old, she always wore a scarf on her head, tied beneath the chin, even during class, and she spoke with a slow, careful Appalachian accent. She was probably the best teacher I've ever had — strict, fair-minded, dedicated to her job. Because of her, when we finally returned to the outside world I was, academically at least, more than prepared to keep up with my peers. . . .

Outside of school we had a recreation program, with leaders hired by the War Relocation Authority. During the week they organized games and craft activities. On weekends we often took hikes beyond the fence. A series of picnic groups and camping sites had been built by internees — clearings, with tables, benches, and toilets. The first was about half a mile out, the farthest several miles into the Sierras. As restrictions gradually loosened, you could measure your liberty by how far they'd let you go — to Camp Three with a Caucasian, to Camp Three alone, to Camp Four with a Caucasian, to Camp Four alone. As fourth- and fifth-graders we usually hiked out to Camp One, on the edge of Bair's Creek, where we could wade, collect rocks, and sit on the bank eating lunches the mess hall crew packed for us. . . .

In addition to the regular school sessions and the recreation program, classes of every kind were being offered all over camp: singing, acting, trumpet playing, tap-dancing, plus traditional Japanese arts like needlework, judo, and kendo. The first class I attended was in baton twirling, taught by a chubby girl about fourteen named Nancy. In the beginning I used a sawed-off broomstick with an old tennis ball stuck on one end. When it looked like I was going to keep at this, Mama ordered me one like Nancy's from the Sears, Roebuck catalogue. Nancy was a very good twirler and taught us younger kids all her tricks. For months I practiced, joined the baton club at school, and even entered contests. Since then I have often wondered what drew me to it at that age. I wonder, because of all the activities I tried out in camp, this was the one I stayed with, in fact returned to almost obsessively when I entered high school in southern California a few years later. By that time I was desperate to be "accepted," and baton twirling was one trick I could perform that was thoroughly, unmistakably American—putting on the boots and a dress crisscrossed with braid, spinning the silver stick and tossing it high to the tune of a John Philip Sousa march.

Even at ten, before I really knew what waited outside, the Japanese in me could not compete with that. It tried — in camp, and many times later, in one form or another. My visit to the old geisha who lived across the firebreak was a typical example of how those attempts turned out. She was offering lessons in the traditional dancing called *odori*. A lot of young girls studied this in order to take part in the big *obon* festival held every August, a festival honoring dead ancestors, asking them to bring good crops in the fall.

She was about seventy, a tiny, aristocratic-looking woman. She took students in her barracks cubicle, which was fitted out like a little Buddhist shrine, with tatami mats on the floor. She would kneel in her kimono and speak very softly in Japanese, while her young assistant would gracefully swing closed knees or bend her swan-like neck to the old geisha's instructions.

I sat across the room from her for an hour trying to follow what was going on. It was all a mystery. I had never learned the language. And this woman was so old, even her dialect was foreign to me. She seemed an occult figure, more spirit than human. When she bowed to me from her knees at the end of the hour, I rushed out of there, back to more familiar surroundings. . . .

Among my explorations during these months, there was one more, final venture into Catholicism. The Maryknoll chapel was just up the street now and easy to get to. I resumed my catechism. Once again I was listening with rapt terror to the lives of the saints and the martyrs, although that wasn't really what attracted me this time. I had found another kind of inspiration, had seen another way the church might make me into something quite extraordinary.

I had watched a girl my own age shining at the center of one of their elaborate ceremonies. It appealed to me tremendously. She happened to be an orphan, and I figured that if this much could befall an orphan, imagine how impressive *I* would look in such a role. . . .

This girl had already been baptized. What I witnessed was her confirmation. She was dressed like a bride, in a white gown, white lace hood, and sheer veil, walking toward the altar, down the aisle of that converted barracks. Watching her from the pew I was pierced with envy for the position she had gained. At the same time I was filled with awe and with a startled wonder at the notion that this girl, this orphan, could become such a queen.

A few days later I let it be known that I was going to be baptized into the church and confirmed as soon as the nuns thought I was ready. I announced this to the Sisters and they rejoiced. I announced it at home, and Papa exploded.

"No," he roared. "Absolutely not!"

I just stood there, stunned, too scared to speak.

"You're too young!"

I started to cry.

"How are you going to get married?" he shouted. "If you get baptized a Catholic, you have to marry a Catholic. No Japanese boys are in the Catholic church. You get baptized now, how are you going to find a good Japanese boy to marry?"

I ran to Mama, but she knew better than to argue with him about this. I ran to the chapel and told Sister Bernadette, and she came hurrying to the barracks. She and Papa had become pretty good friends over the months. Once every week or so she would visit, and while he sipped his apricot brandy they would talk about religion. But this time, when she came to the door and called "*Wakatsuki-san?*" he met her there shouting, "No! No baptism!"

She raised her eyebrows, trying to stare him down.

He rose to his full height, as if she, about the size of Mama, were the general of some invading army, and said, "Too young!"

"Old enough to know God!"

"Who knows anything of God at ten?"

This made her angry. At any other time they would have taken an hour hearing each other out. But now, when she opened her mouth to reply, his upheld flat palm stopped her. He was not going to argue. He wouldn't even let her past the door.

In exasperation she glared at him, then turned and walked away. I ran to my bunk, devastated, and wept, hating him. I was too ashamed to go back to catechism after that. I just hated Papa, for weeks, and dreamed of the white-gowned princess I might have become. Late afternoons, practicing my baton in the firebreak, angrily I would throw him into the air and watch him twirl, and catch him, and throw him high, again and again and again.

※ *E S S A Y S*

In the first essay, Alice Kessler-Harris of Rutgers University examines letters written by ordinary men and women to Eleanor and Franklin Roosevelt about women wage earners and the prudence of Depression-era policies that excluded married women from the workforce. Kessler-Harris argues that American men and women defended such exclusionary policies in the hope that they would serve to undermine selfish individualism and reinforce an ethic of cooperation among family members and neighbors. In the second essay, Karen Tucker Anderson of the University of Arizona examines the discrimination faced by African-American women during World War II. Although black women were able to move out of the rural South into urban industrial centers, they were denied access to many well-paying jobs despite a chronic labor shortage. Valerie Matsumoto of the University of California at Los Angeles examines in the last essay the lives of Japanese-American women during World War II. Although the relocation camps deprived Japanese-Americans of citizenship rights and undermined family harmony, internment also presented young women with new opportunities for work, travel, and education.

Gender Ideology and Family Survival During the Depression

ALICE KESSLER-HARRIS

On 10 May 1933, Earl Leiby of Akron, Ohio, wrote to Franklin Delano Roosevelt, President of the United States:

> You are probably aware of the fact that homes are being wrecked daily due to the fact that married women are permitted to work in factories and offices in this land of ours. You and we all know that the place for a wife and mother is at home, her palace. The excuse is often brought up that the husband cannot find employment. It is the writers' belief that if the women were expelled from places of business, . . . these very men would find employment. These same womens' husbands would naturally be paid a higher salary, inasmuch as male employees demand a higher salary than females.

Like other people who chose the early months of a new administration to pass on suggestions for relief to the president, Mr Leiby was convinced that the solution to

---

Alice Kessler-Harris, "Gender Ideology in Historical Reconstruction: A Case Study from the 1930s," *Gender and History* 1 (Spring 1989): 31–44.

three long years of economic depression lay in a return to old values. For him, as for others, a restoration of women and men to their appropriate spheres would return peace and prosperity to the land. But if Mr Leiby's belief in a particular form of domesticity was widespread, it was not universal.

Consider the following letter from Mrs Blanche Crumbly, a weaver of McDonough, Georgia, who wrote to FDR on 26 October 1933. The letter, written in pencil, on lined foolscap paper, protested the failure of her textile mill employers to pay her an expected $12 a week. 'I am sending you my checks to show you what I made', she wrote.

> I want to let you see that they didn't pay me enough. I worked eight hours a day and you will see they have me marked up forty hours a week and didn't pay twelve dollars and by law they were supposed to pay twelve dollars whether you operated one machine or not but I worked in the weave shop and run five looms so I want you to see that I get my money that is due me for I am just a poor woman and was working trying to make some money but they didn't pay enough to keep me working so I want you to write right back to me and let me know what you can do.

Nothing in this letter speaks to the values of domesticity. . . . Mrs Crumbly wants action, not on the basis of her place in the household, but as a matter of workplace justice. She had worked in the weave shop running five looms; she had earned her pay; she was a poor woman who needed the money.

These letters seem to reflect opposing positions on the issue of domesticity: the first assumes its inevitability and explicitly validates it; the second fails even to acknowledge its existence, much less its role in shaping the labour force. From the perspective of the first letter writer, the world appears to be structured around the household whose effective regulation would have a salutary effect on the economy. In that of the second, work and wages are central — their just resolution by state agencies is demanded independently of the writer's household role. Taken together, these letters raise questions about the persistence of the ideology of separate spheres — a concept that has dominated American women's history for the past two decades.

Traditionally 'separate spheres' connotes a middle class world of privatized households in which women, excluded from the public arena, protect the values associated with piety, purity and domesticity against a competitive, aggressive, and individualistic world. Historians, who first perceived separate spheres as an ideology adopted by women to justify their exclusion from public life and to rationalize the effects of an economy that increasingly removed production from the household, have, more recently, found in the idea the capacity of women to create networks of female power and access routes to political influence. In that appealing form, the values engendered by domesticity, which constitute the core of the ideology of separate spheres, have moved far beyond their original boundaries. Stretched across class lines, and now widely applied to analyses of poor, black and immigrant women, the idea of separate spheres underlines female participation in and control of, neighbourhood activity. It is used, for example, to illuminate the emergence of spontaneous protests against rising prices for bread, meat and rents, as well as to explain how cross-class alliances are sustained. Thus, the notion of separate spheres, which once suggested the limits of family life, is now offered by many historians as the most important source of female power.

If the major contribution of separate spheres as a historical construct has been to allow us to evaluate women on their own terms what are we to make of those women — wage earning women — who demonstrably functioned in the male work-world on a daily basis? The idea of separate spheres requires us as historians to attribute to women a conception of identity that is primarily gender based (rooted that is in the things that women primarily do). This might accurately reflect the self-images of those whose lives were undivided between family and paid work, but it is problematic for the vast majority whose daily existence straddled both arenas. And it raises questions we have not yet learned how to pose. To what extent do historically specific circumstances define a gendered identity? As the nineteenth century gave way to the twentieth, can we still argue that, whatever its validity among privileged women who lived in a predominately commercial setting in the 1820s, domestic values continue to reflect the daily lives of most women? And what of men? Are we willing to argue that their identity, too, is gender based? If so, then the social construction of gender must become a major historical issue, replacing class formation as the central problematic of social history. For the moment, however, I pose a simpler question: does gender constitute the single most important level at which men and women self-identify in a given historical period or at a particular phase in their lives? . . .

The depression of the 1930s provides an ideal place to examine this question because its a-typicality opens working people's world views to public examination. The previous decade had witnessed a dramatic rise in the proportion of married workers among wage-earning women, heightening public concern about the breakdown of the traditional family among some sectors while encouraging others to claim that female wage work helped hold families together. Increased concern preceded and was sharply exacerbated by a fearsome and rising tide of unemployment that engulfed the country beginning in the winter of 1929. In the period between the election of Franklin D. Roosevelt in November 1932, and his inauguration four months later, nearly a quarter of the labour force was unemployed, and emergency conditions prevailed everywhere. The result was an unprecedented discussion of who was and was not entitled to work.

One of the nation's first and most immediate responses was to exclude the spouses of wage earners from the labour force. Pressure was brought on employers to fire married women; states passed laws discriminating against married women teachers, and the Federal government responded by passing section 213 of the National Economy Act which allowed only one partner in a marriage to draw a federal salary. But though public pressure continued, neither the numbers nor the proportion of married women working declined in response. So great was sentiment against married women holding jobs that it provoked hundreds of letters to President Roosevelt, the National Recovery Act (NRA) code authorities, Eleanor Roosevelt, Frances Perkins and the Women's Bureau of the Department of Labour. Beginning in 1932, and reaching a crescendo in the spring of 1933, writers suggested that married women with employed husbands had no right to work and ought to be forcibly ejected from jobs. The letters came from single and married women, from widows and from men of all kinds. Many were nearly illiterate. Most were handwritten, sometimes in pencil. Some were written on the letterheads of apparently prosperous businesses; others on foolscap. They complained of injustices done, asked for help, and offered solutions to the depression crisis.

My reading of these letters is not scientific in any sense. It could not be for the letters themselves represent no known sample of the population, and the context that motivated them is often obscure. . . . Nonetheless, they offer a unique opportunity to explore the meanings of work as they appear in a spontaneous outburst. The letters tell us about much more than gendered responses under emergency conditions. They speak to a sense of social order that is much more consistent than the contradictions implied by a superficial reading. Read carefully and together, they illuminate a moral code that transcends gender lines.

In the lexicon of separate spheres, these letters appear at first to reflect the importance of that concept, though they offer no immediately apparent distinctions between those written by men and women. Many of both sexes insist, like Earl Leiby, on 'a woman's place.' . . . The panic will be over, suggested an insurance agent from Kansas City, Missouri, 'when and only when women no longer have to work . . . or . . . when men again become *men* and provide for their mothers, sisters, wives and daughters, and womanhood is again restored to its pedestal motherhood of the yesterday and man to the manhood of the yesterday.' Such perceptions are not gender specific. Miss B. Wohlmaker of Brooklyn wrote to Roosevelt: 'I have heard so much about prosperity. I don't think it will ever return as long as married women are taking the Bread and Butter out of the men who have familys to support.'

The common wisdom, then is that women have a primary domestic role while men are responsible for earning their families' livings. . . . But a closer examination reveals that the domestic role is far from a separate sphere. Concerns over both work and family life converged in a widely shared conception of justice. Though it did not contradict a felt perception of role difference, this vision of justice was not rooted in it. Rather, it seems to have been shaped by the impact of the material world around them. These letters reveal an integration of wage work and family life that belies the dualistic paradigms of work and domesticity normally utilized by historians. They present instead a perception of social reality far more unified than that embodied within a notion of separate spheres.

The first thing revealed by these letters is the sharp distinction made by those who believed work to be an individual right and the vast majority who did not. A pre-depression world of job opportunity, where ambition might be rewarded, could afford to make room for personal goals for both men and women. In the depression world, the concept that a job was a right of citizenship appeared to be selfish, and continued to be expressed by relatively few. One person who held to that position was the female assistant postmaster of Deerfield, Michigan, who wrote to Frances Perkins: 'I can't see why if we women are American Citizens why we haven't just as much right to work as anybody. I would have written to the Post Master General but woman to Woman I thought you would understand better.' But this letter was as unusual as the June 1932 petition from the Texas Federation of Business and Professional Women which declared, 'We do not believe this country has reached the point where it is willing to be sovietized, and to have employment granted or denied as a dole. . . . '

Such sentiments, while surely deeply felt among the better off, were not characteristic of either the working or the non-working poor before or after the depression. Most of those who put pen or pencil to paper believed that work was the prerogative of those who must support themselves and their families. In the code of honour of working people, jobs belonged to providers. Though this typically meant married men, the scales of justice encompassed widows, single women and married women with unemployed or disabled husbands as well. And they just as clearly excluded men with other means of support. As one writer explained the priorities, 'The idea is to first place to work all men who have dependents, then girls who have dependents. The remaining jobs to be given to those not having dependents.'

. . . Such comments affirm ideas of justice among the working poor that certainly antedate economic crisis. They can be found for example, among communities of textile workers in the South, and among immigrant women in the North. They enable us to make sense of the general hostility that surrounded married women's work while they simultaneously explain how a Blanche Crumbly functioned outside the orbit of apparently traditional roles. Since at least part of the issue around married women's work was unfair competition, single women, widows and the wives of unemployed workers constituted a large proportion of the cacophonous complainants. Indeed, they were often the most virulent advocates of removing married women from jobs. Identifying not with their sex, but with their work/family positions, they complained on behalf of others like them. 'How can the youth of our land eliminate married women from working and taking from us every means of support, every hope, every chance for morality and high standards?' asked a young single woman from Bellingham, Washington. 'If there were not so many women working who have husbands working and no family, we single women might stand a better show in getting a job,' wrote another. . . . And Loreua Ankron of Pawhusku, Oklahoma, wanted to oust married women with 'husbands who have good jobs' because 'widow women with children should have this kind of work.'

If women self identified not only as women but as young people, family supporters, parents and dependents, they were vulnerable to any who threatened to undermine their family roles, whether such people were male or female. Men and women translated their sense of grievance to any who seemed to undermine the provider role, including most especially farmers, country people, foreigners and nameless racketeers. The free-flowing relationships of these categories appear in the following letter to Frances Perkins. After first insisting that married women ought to 'be compelled by law to give up their positions to single girls and married men', the writer went on to complain about foreigners along with married women holding 'most of our city and country positions and consuming 90% of the welfare money.' In other words, males who had other means of support faced the same criticism as married women. This was especially true in communities (like the textile mills of the Piedmont) where family wage work was the norm rather than the exception. Mr L. A. Cook, a fixer at the Cannon Mills in Concord, North Carolina, complained to General Hugh Johnson, chief of the National Recovery Administration,

> about so many farmers working in the mill a farmer will come by they will hire them before they will an experienced hand they make their crops raise most of what they eat lights water, rent not costing anything when people here in town can't get jobs . . . the way it is the farmer is holding a job down here and farming too. . . .

At issue here is a question broader than gender but in which gender participates, and to some extent becomes the scapegoat. A careful reading of these letters suggests that while the perspective of domesticity was certainly an available angle of vision, it was not the only perspective that guided the attack on married women workers. Where, then, is the outrage rooted? The privileges of relative affluence, whether they resided in a gendered role or in farm ownership, sparked outrage when they prevented those with greater need from earning a living. . . . For the men and women who complained that jobs were going to the undeserving, conceptions of dignity did not lie in equal opportunity, or in equality, but rather in the intertwined reality of their own complex images of themselves and in their expectations about the meaning of jobs. At one level, what was at issue was whether the free market (which gave employers the prerogative of hiring most cheaply) would prevail over indigenous standards of justice. This is apparent in the various levels of exasperation with which writers asked why the government couldn't take control of the situation. . . . Behind the frequent complaints of writers that they, or someone they knew, had been fired and replaced by someone who would work for less, lay a refusal to acquiesce to a system that seemed patently unfair. A self described 'business girl' who had lost her job asked for the removal of women with external support such as 'married women and home girls.' They were, she argued 'inefficiently taking the place of some man or efficient business girl as they are working for a lower salary.' The meaning of efficiency to her is clear. The complaint here is against a system in which values other than those of social conscience regulate job holding.

In expressing their scepticism about the capacity of the market to sustain what seemed to be elementary notions of justice, writers conflated public and private spheres. Indeed one of the most striking things about these letters is their consistent inability or unwillingness to separate the two. The family may have been the private domain of individuals but male and female workers interpreted its survival and protection as a public duty. In a situation such as the depression the most intimate details of one's life became a public issue — the idea of a distinct domestic sphere scarcely existed. Most letter writers translated work into wages — wages that held the capacity to sustain or undermine the moral precepts thought to reside in the family. Thus, the income produced by work constituted the glue that melded the family, that joined public and private together. Like some modern epoxies, it had to be mixed just right.

While few doubted that only an adequate income could preserve family values, most correspondents feared that an income that was either too low or too high would yield moral disaster for the individual, the family and the community as a whole. They spoke of 'necessity' wages as opposed to 'luxury' wages. Depriving families of the first — the result of allowing the wrong people to hold jobs — would yield moral degeneration. It encouraged the 'less strong in character' to spend their time 'loafing and resorting to crime for a living' and reduced them to 'standing on the street corners planning to rob someone. . . . ' It could result in 'deplorable conditions, moral issues with which we are constantly confronted' like ' . . . forcing many young girls on the streets because they have to get along the best they can.'

But the relatively high income — the luxury wage — of the dual income family was perceived as no less threatening, destroying character and contributing to private and public moral degeneration. 'All over the country,' wrote a self described 'unemployed young woman,' 'women marry and immediately return to their jobs, instead of endeavoring to live within their husband's income and living a domesticated life, building a home, etc.' Even worse, 'The women consistently dodge motherhood and go home after their work is done with a paper carton in one hand and a can opener in the other.'

. . . While the maldistribution of jobs could cause degeneration of the moral fibre of the family and therefore of the nation, so, too, could it distort the economic priorities of the nation's families. In the public mind, women's wages did not buy the same things as men's wages did, a factor that raised public concern about the nation's future. A male who worked would, in the popular parlance,

> spend his income to the support of this family while the woman spends for permanent waves, lip sticks. But those things do not pay the grocer and all the other bills that father is expected to pay walking up and down the street looking and praying for something to do. The woman comes home says she works for her money and she will do as she pleases with it which is a fact. . . .

Such maldistribution violated notions of fairness because it allowed some to fritter money away on luxuries while it prevented others from sustaining the provider role. . . . Encoded in these comments is the sense that married women are acting unfairly. They are taking jobs from men and from single women; they are destroying the moral fibre of men, and reducing men's respect for women. They are responsible for the delinquency of children and for the disintegration of the family. The continuing depression is laid at their feet — the future of the nation placed in their hands. These messages, as the letters convey, are deeply held, and virulently argued. They mitigate against a continuing demand for equality and go some distance towards explaining why the assertion of individual rights, which brought the nation to such a pass, is seen as unfair.

Many of the married women who earned wages would not have disagreed with these sentiments. Those who continued to work, like Blanche Crumbly, clearly thought of themselves as providers. Their work was part of a long tradition in which wages were seen as part of their contribution to family well-being. As the Women's Bureau of the Department of Labour put it in 1924, married women worked 'for one purpose and generally speaking, for one purpose only — to provide necessities for their families or to raise their standard of living.' During the depression, they resisted removal from the work force not out of ideological commitment, but because they clearly did not feel themselves to be the selfish neglectful women described in many of the letters.

Understanding their self-image should give us some insight into workplace behaviour as well — into the sense of justice on which women will act. If the provider role was central, then the failure of employers to live by it would yield tension. Mrs Crumbly protested the insufficient $12 a week, but she quit because 'they didn't pay enough to keep me working.' A year or two later, under other circumstances, she might have joined the CIO organizing drive. While the felt injustice of married women working cannot be read as other than hostility, it takes on a different cast when seen from the perspective of work, rather than that of separate spheres. From the point of view of domesticity, it is a conservative plea for a return to traditional roles. From the perspective of workplace concerns, it becomes a demand for justice — for cooperation and sharing, and, arguably, for a different kind of market system. Articulated by both men and women, the injustice of wage work for those with alternate sources of income or for those without dependents was an idea that might have been conceived in, and sustained by, domesticity, but it took on a larger resonance in the prevailing climate of industrial distress. In practice it was not gender neutral, and yet it reflects a conception of work-related roles that transcends a simple division into separate spheres.

What appears at first reading to be a defense of separate spheres and an affirmation of female domesticity contains a more complex statement about social reality. The letters articulate a vision of social order in which the provider role is related to both family and individual life cycle, and in which men and women provide in different ways. They suggest a perception of jobs as a public resource to be disposed of fairly, and though there are clearly job hierarchies that are gender specific, the letters assume a pool of work that is available to be divided among the deserving. The definition of deserving rested not on sex, but on the need to support oneself and others. The letters reveal an inability or unwillingness to separate public and private values, and an acknowledgement that dignity for both men and women lay in the preservation of both work possibilities and household order. . . .

Persistent Discrimination Against Black Women During World War II

KAREN TUCKER ANDERSON

As a result of the increasing demand for workers in all categories of employment, and especially in the high-paying manufacturing sector, the full employment economy of World War II posed the most serious challenge in American history to the traditional management preference for white male labor in primary-sector jobs. The war years were especially important for blacks, who benefited from an expanding labor force, changing racial values, a revitalized migration out of the rural South, and the attempted enforcement of equal employment opportunity under a presidential executive order. Although scholars have given some attention to the labor-force fortunes of blacks in the war economy, few have considered the impact of the wartime expansion on black women, who constituted 600,000 of the 1,000,000 blacks who entered paid employment during the war years. Those who have focused on black women have stressed the degree to which the war opened new job categories and fostered mobility. William Chafe, for example, contends that the opportunities generated by the wartime economy and the long-term changes they fostered constituted a "second emancipation" for black women. According to Dale L. Hiestand, occupational shifts by black women workers during the 1940s promoted substantial income improvement.

A careful examination of the labor-force status of black women during the 1940s brings into question such sanguine pronouncements. Focusing on the

Karen Tucker Anderson, "Last Hired, First Fired: Black Women Workers During World War II," *Journal of American History* 69 (June 1982): 82–97. Reprinted by permission of the Organization of American Historians.

African-American women training to become auto mechanics in 1943 at the Bethune-Cookman College in Daytona Beach, Florida. The College, a vocational school for blacks, was founded by Mary McLeod Bethune, an educator, leader in the black women's club movement, and outspoken member of Franklin Delano Roosevelt's "black cabinet." Bethune was a tireless advocate of federal programs to train blacks in the skilled trades; the auto mechanics program at Bethune-Cookman was sponsored by the National Youth Administration, a New Deal agency in which Bethune served as the director of the Negro Division. During the 1940s black women were drawn into auto mechanics, a traditionally masculine field, by the exigencies of war.

wartime experiences of black women provides insight into the nature of prejudice as manifested and experienced by women and into the sources and mechanisms of labor-force discrimination in a particular historical context. It also facilitates an examination of the relative importance of managerial intransigence and coworker prejudice in perpetuating discriminatory employment practices. In addition, it gives an indication of the importance of tight labor markets in fostering economic mobility for minority group women.

Labor force statistics support the contention that the war marked an important break with the historic allocation of work by race and sex. Between 1940 and 1944 the proportion of employed black women engaged in domestic service declined from 59.9 percent to 44.6 percent, although their share of jobs in this field increased because white women exited from private household work in even greater proportions. In addition, the percentage of the black female labor force in farm work was cut in half, as many from the rural South migrated to urban areas in response to the demand for war workers. The shift of large numbers of black women from work in farms and homes to work in factories resulted in the proportion of black females employed in industrial occupations rising from 6.5 percent to 18 percent during the war. A comparable expansion also occurred in personal service work outside of the private household, which claimed 17.9 percent of black women workers in 1944.

To stress only the improvement wrought during the war, however, is to under-state the extent to which discrimination persisted and to ignore the fact that the as-sumptions of a historically balkanized labor force continued to determine the distri-bution of the benefits of a full employment economy. When faced with a shortage of white male workers, employers had various options. They could seek workers from other areas of the country, hoping that this would enable them to minimize the changes produced by the wartime expansion, or they could rely on underutilized el-ements of the local labor supply — workers in nonessential employment, women, blacks, and older and younger workers. If unable to secure large numbers of white male in-migrants and unwilling to modify hiring patterns too dramatically, they could limit production, sacrificing output to prejudice.

Those who decided to employ substantially increased numbers of women and/or minorities established a complex hierarchy of hiring preferences based on the composition of the local labor force and the nature of the work to be done. In light industries, women workers became the first recourse of employers unable to recruit large numbers of white males. In the airframe industry, for example, women constituted 40.6 percent of the employees by November 1943, while blacks claimed only 3.5 percent of airframe jobs. Employers in heavy industries, by contrast, sought minority males as a preferred source of labor, with the result that the level of utilization of women depended on the minority population of an area. In Baltimore, for example, blacks comprised up to 20 percent of the shipbuilding workers while women represented only 4 percent. Seattle, which had only a small black popula-tion, relied on women for 16 percent of its shipyard employees.

Whatever the hierarchy of preference, however, black women could always be found at the bottom. The dramatic expansion of jobs for women did not necessarily mean the opening up of new categories of employment for minority group women. A survey conducted by the United Auto Workers (UAW) in April 1943 found that only 74 out of 280 establishments that employed women in production work were willing to hire black women. Similarly, a 1943 study by the National Metal Trades Association revealed that only twenty-nine out of sixty-two plants that used women workers had black women in their employ. Moreover, most of them used black women only in janitorial positions. Even some employers willing to hire white women and black men in large numbers balked at including black women in their work forces. At the Wagner Electric Corporation in Saint Louis, for example, 64 percent of the employees were white women, 24 percent were black males, and 12 percent were white males. The company refused to hire black women throughout the war, even in the face of a January 1945 order from the President's Committee on Fair Employment Practice (FEPC) to cease all discrimination.

Because of the mobilization of large numbers of young men by the military, the availability of white women for aircraft and munitions work, the nature of the jobs being created during the war, and the depth of the prejudice against black women, the male labor force proved to be more racially flexible than the female labor force. While the number of all blacks employed in manufacturing increased 135 percent between April 1940 and January 1946, the number of black women in such work rose only 59 percent. Blacks made their greatest wartime gains in heavily male-employing industrial fields; by January 1945 they constituted 25 percent of the labor force in foundries, 11.7 percent in shipbuilding, and 11.8 percent in blast furnaces and steel mills. By contrast, nonwhites accounted for only 5.8 percent of employees in aircraft and 2.7 percent of those in electrical equipment production. In the traditional female fields of clerical and sales, the gains of black women were negligible — their share of female clerical jobs rose from 0.7 percent to 1.6 percent while their proportion in the female sales force declined from 1.2 percent to 1.1 percent.

One of the most important and obdurate of the industries that fought the employment of black women during the war was the auto industry. Led by the negative example of the Ford Motor Company, which refused to hire nonwhite women in any but token numbers, the auto companies persisted in rejecting trained black female applicants or in limiting their employment to a few work categories until very late in the war. When referred to the automakers by the United States Employment Service (USES) in response to calls for women workers, black women found that the white women accompanying them would be hired immediately while they would be told to await a later call, a call that would never come. When Samella Banks, along with five white women, applied to Cadillac Motor Company in November 1942, she was told that there might be a janitress opening in a day or two while they were hired as welder trainees. As a result, much of the expansion of the female labor force in industrial work occurred before economic or political pressures necessitated the hiring of black women. By February 1943 nonwhite women had claimed only 1,000 of the 96,000 jobs held by women in major war industries in Detroit. Consequently, most nonwhite females were confined to work in low-paying service and other unskilled categories, and those who landed industrial jobs had so little seniority that their postwar fate was guaranteed.

As was generally the case with wartime racial discrimination in employment, the most frequent employer rationale for excluding nonwhite women was the fear that white opposition to the change might cause work slowdowns or strikes. An examination of the nature and goals of coworker prejudice during the war years provides some possible answers to the question of whether such prejudice is rooted in an aversion to social contact in a context of equality or is primarily a calculated attempt on the part of whites to maintain an exploitative economic advantage. When the former issue is the basic concern, it is manifested in a desire to exclude blacks altogether or to segregate them on the job. When the latter is the wellspring of white workplace prejudice, it is evidenced, not in a wish to segregate black workers, but in an attempt to prevent the hiring of blacks or to limit them to particular low-paying job categories.

During the war years, white male hostility to expanded job opportunities for black men focused primarily on the issue of promotion rather than on hiring or segregation. Although some strikes occurred when black men were admitted to entry-level jobs or over the issue of integrating the workplace, most white-male hate strikes took place when black male workers were promoted into jobs at higher skill and pay levels. This was a product of the fact that black men had been employed as janitors and unskilled laborers in many defense industries prior to the war and sought promotions as opportunities expanded. White males thus seemed to be concerned primarily with maintaining their advantaged economic position. Moreover, their resistance to the elimination of discrimination was more tenacious and more effective than was the opposition of white women to the opening of opportunities for black women. Control over labor unions, whose opposition to black entry into previously white jobs proved an effective barrier to change in many cases, gave white males more power to translate prejudice into employer discrimination.

For women workers, on the other hand, the desire to maintain social distance, rather than a wish to safeguard economic prerogatives, seemed to be the dominant motivation in many cases. White female workers frequently objected to working closely with black women or sharing facilities with them because they feared that blacks were dirty or diseased. Work stoppages occurred in several places after the introduction of black women into the female work force. More than 2,000 white women employed at the U.S. Rubber plant in Detroit walked off the job in March 1943, demanding separate bathroom facilities. A similar walkout occurred at the Western Electric plant in Baltimore in summer 1943. In both cases management refused to segregate the facilities and appealed to patriotic and egalitarian values to persuade the striking workers to return to their jobs. Significantly, the one hate strike by white women workers that focused on upgrading as well as integration, the Dan River strike in 1944, was in a traditional female-employing industry. . . .

As a result of the idiosyncratic nature of employer practices during the war, some areas and some employers offered greater employment opportunities for black women than others. Aircraft plants in the Los Angeles area, for example, began hiring black women for production work relatively early by comparison with similar operations in other areas of the country. As a result, by 1945 black women could be found doing industrial work in all Los Angeles aircraft plants; 2,000 were employed by North American Aviation alone. Among the automakers, the Briggs plant in Detroit deviated from industry patterns and hired substantial numbers of black women. In Saint Louis, where defense industry discrimination against black women was the general rule, the Curtiss-Wright Company and the U.S. Cartridge Company eased the situation somewhat by providing industrial jobs for hundreds of nonwhite women. These examples, however, were not typical of employer response; restrictive hiring and segregation remained the rule, even in industries faced with severe labor shortages. Nowhere was this truer than in the South, where traditional practices remained virtually unchanged.

Even when defense employers broke with tradition and hired nonwhite women, they generally segregated them from other women workers and employed them only for certain kinds of work, usually that which was arduous, dirty, hot, or otherwise disagreeable. A cursory study of black women workers done by the Women's Bureau of the United States Department of Labor in 1945 revealed that in many cases nonwhite women were disproportionately represented among women employed in outside labor gangs, in foundries, and in industrial service work. On the ore docks of the Great Lakes, for example, the survey found women, predominantly black, shoveling the leavings of ore from the bottoms of ships onto hoists. According to the USES, the meat-packing industry in Detroit resorted to black women in large numbers during the war years to take jobs others had spurned. On the railroads minority group women found employment in substantial numbers as laborers, loaders, car cleaners, and waitresses. The city of Baltimore first broke with its policy of hiring only whites for street-cleaning work in the immediate prewar period when it began hiring black males; by 1943, when the black male labor force was completely exhausted, the city turned to the only labor reserve left — the large numbers of unemployed and underemployed black females.

The insistence by some employers on segregated work arrangements and facilities served as a rationale for excluding black women altogether or limiting their numbers to conform to physical plant requirements. The Glenn Martin Aircraft Company, for example, hired the same proportion of nonwhite women for its integrated plant in Omaha, where the black population was quite small, as it did for its Baltimore operations, where black women constituted a substantial proportion of the local labor supply. In Baltimore, however, their numbers were limited because they had to be assigned only to a small separate subassembly plant. A small aircraft parts firm in Los Angeles asserted that it could not hire black women because it separated workers by sex as well as by race and could not further complicate its managerial and supervisory difficulties. At the Norfolk Navy Yard, management excluded black women from most production jobs on the grounds that women workers had to be segregated by race, although the racial integration of male workers was an accomplished fact. As a result, black men worked in a wide variety of jobs at all skill levels in the yard while the jobs assigned to women were virtually monopolized by whites. . . .

The major agency charged with enforcing equal opportunity in employment regardless of race, religion, or national origin was the FEPC, an agency created in 1941 by executive order of President Franklin D. Roosevelt in response to a threatened march on Washington by civil rights groups protesting discriminatory policies by war contractors. Although the FEPC could theoretically recommend the removal of war contracts from those who continued to discriminate and the WMC [War Manpower Commission] could restrict work permits to enforce federal hiring policies, the federal government was not inclined to hamper the production of essential war materials in order to foster racial equity. As a result, the agency had to rely on behind-the-scenes negotiations and the possibility of adverse publicity generated by public hearings. Although effective in some cases, such tools proved ineffectual against recalcitrant violators, whose ranks included some major war industries. The large volume of complaints and the bureaucratic delays inherent in the situation facilitated evasion, even on the part of blatant violators officially ordered to cease restrictive hiring practices. Moreover, the reliance on individual, documented complaints rather than on employer hiring patterns as the basis for action hampered effective enforcement.

The decision by Roosevelt to place the FEPC under the jurisdiction of the WMC in July 1942 also handicapped the agency in its efforts to end employment discrimination. WMC head Paul McNutt, never enthusiastic regarding the FEPC's goals and afraid that they were incompatible with his agency's responsibility for allocating scarce manpower within war industries, canceled scheduled FEPC hearings on discrimination by the railroads and generally made racial equity a low priority within WMC. Even after the FEPC was removed from the WMC in May 1943, it was hampered in its efforts to enforce the law by the unwillingness of southern representatives of the WMC and the USES to cooperate in reporting and seeking to change discriminatory practices. Although the USES had agreed in September 1943 to refuse to fill employer requests for workers when they included racial restrictions, its agents in the South frequently disregarded this directive. Thus, when blacks with defense training applied for appropriate work, they were often referred to jobs outside the area. The persistence of discrimination, despite a federal commitment to eliminate it, hampered the ability of all blacks, male and female, to find industrial employment in the region that still claimed a majority of the black population.

In its official policies the FEPC treated discrimination against black women as seriously as discrimination against black males, although its rate of success in enforcing compliance in women's cases lagged somewhat behind the rate for men. After its 1944 hearings in Saint Louis, the FEPC ruled that a company that hired black males while discriminating against black women was still in violation of the executive order, noting that "partial compliance is partial violation." Despite pressure from civil rights groups on behalf of black women workers and occasional threats of strikes by black male workers, the equal opportunity machinery of the government proved unable to aid minority women in any substantial way. By the time the agency had investigated, negotiated, or held hearings, much valuable time had been lost. For women, this could be especially damaging because it meant that anything beyond token conformity could be jeopardized by employer unwillingness to expand the female work force late in the war.

The Carter Carburetor Company in Saint Louis, for example, managed a minimal compliance with an FEPC order to cease discriminating when it came to black men, but refused in April 1944 to hire any black women on the grounds that it had no intention of hiring any more women. Although the government continued to pressure the company, it stood by its policies. The Allied Tent Manufacturing Company in New Orleans claimed to have instituted a nondiscriminatory policy regarding women workers when it announced its intention in June 1945 to replace all its women machine operators with men (white and black), having decided that women workers had proved themselves "unsatisfactory." Federal enforcement officials thus found that labor-market forces late in the war provided a rationale and a means for continued resistance by those employers intent on circumventing federal hiring policies regarding black women.

The organization that was most cognizant of persisting discrimination against black women and most active in fighting against it was the National Association for the Advancement of Colored People (NAACP). As early as August 1942, Detroit NAACP officer Gloster Current wrote to McNutt of the WMC, complaining that the Ford Motor Company was discriminating against black females as it hired thousands of whites for work at the Willow Run Bomber Plant. In March 1943 the Detroit NAACP cooperated with the United Auto Workers Inter-Racial Committee in staging a large rally to protest continued discrimination against black women in hiring and black men in promotion on the part of Detroit's war industries. Thereafter both groups continued to pressure employers and government officials at all levels on the issue. In a statement prepared for presentation to the House manpower committee, the NAACP evinced its awareness that the situation was not unique to Detroit but was a national problem resulting in the serious underutilization of black womanpower. . . .

Job retention was a serious issue for those women who landed industrial work during the war. The persistence of discrimination and the late entry of black women into production work, rather than their on-the-job conduct, meant that nonwhite females were more likely than others to experience layoffs resulting from contract completions or seasonal cutbacks. Once fired, they faced great difficulties in finding comparable work. According to an official of the Baltimore Urban League, white women there with industrial experience were easily reabsorbed by war industries while black women were being referred by the USES to work as maids, counter girls, and laundry pressers. As would be the case for all unemployed women after the war, those who turned down such jobs faced the possibility of losing their unemployment benefits for refusing suitable work. Black women thus experienced a much greater degree of job discontinuity than others during the war, hampering their ability to accumulate seniority.

Once the war was over and American industry began its postwar contraction, those black women who had held industrial jobs during the war found that their concentration in contracting industries, their low seniority, and their sex contributed to employment difficulties in the postwar period. American women, black and white, were overrepresented among those experiencing layoffs in durable good industries. When management began rehiring workers in the reconversion period, it reinstituted most prewar discriminatory policies regarding working women, even to the point of disregarding their seniority rights, a practice facilitated by union acquiescence. USES officials reinforced employer policies by denying unemployment benefits to those women who refused referrals to jobs in traditional female-employing fields. To a greater extent than white women, black women were victimized by the postwar eviction of women from jobs in durable goods industries. . . .

In other work categories black women fared somewhat better in the postwar years. Although some apparently lost employment in service, sales, and clerical work as a result of competition from displaced white women, most managed to maintain their hold on lower-level jobs in the female work force. Despite attempts by USES officials in some local offices to force black women to return to domestic service work by threatening to withhold unemployment compensation benefits, enough job opportunities in other categories remained available to prevent a massive return to household work. Even so, domestic service remained the primary occupation of black women, providing employment to 782,520 in 1950, 40 percent of the black female work force.

As a result of the wartime experience, black women made substantial progress in the operatives occupational category, although their position in this area deteriorated somewhat in the late 1940s. One of the most important areas of expansion for nonwhite women was the apparel industry, which witnessed a 350 percent increase in black female employment during the 1940s. By 1950, it offered employment to 56,910 black women and ranked second in the operatives category behind laundry and dry cleaning establishments, where 105,000 black females were employed. Other major sources of industrial work for women, including textiles, remained virtually closed to blacks during the 1940s. In the durable goods industries, which had experienced the greatest wartime expansion, black women were a rarity in the postwar period. In 1950, only 60 black women held jobs as operatives in aircraft plants, while 2,730 claimed similar positions in the auto industry.

In the long run, the greatest benefit of the wartime experience for black women workers derived from their movement in large numbers out of the poverty of the rural South to the possibilities provided by an urban, industrialized economy. The extent to which those possibilities were realized in the decade of the 1940s can be overstated, however. Both during and after the war, black women entered the urban female labor force in large numbers only to occupy its lowest rungs. Largely excluded from clerical and sales work, the growth sectors of the female work force, black women found work primarily in service jobs outside the household and in unskilled blue-collar categories. Although many experienced some upward mobility during the war, their relative position within the American economy remained the same.

Wartime circumstances illustrate the extent to which an economic system that had historically allocated work according to race and sex could tolerate a high level of unemployment and underemployment even in a time of labor shortage in order to minimize the amount of change generated by temporary and aberrant conditions. By stressing the modification of traditional patterns fostered by rapid economic growth, scholars ignore the degree to which prejudices inhibited change and constrained the rate of economic expansion even in the face of strong patriotic, political, and economic incentives favoring expanded output at all cost. For black women, especially, what is significant about the war experience is the extent to which barriers remained intact.

Japanese American Women During World War II

VALERIE MATSUMOTO

The life here cannot be expressed. Sometimes, we are resigned to it, but when we see the barbed wire fences and the sentry tower with floodlights, it gives us a feeling of being prisoners in a "concentration camp." We try to be happy and yet oftentimes a gloominess does creep in. When I see the "I'm an American" editorial and write-ups, the "equality of race etc." — it seems to be mocking us in our faces. I just wonder if all the sacrifices and hard labor on [the] part of our parents has gone up to leave nothing to show for it?

— Letter from Shizuko Horiuchi,
Pomona Assembly Center, May 24, 1942

Thirty years after her relocation camp internment, another Nisei woman, the artist Miné Okubo, observed, "The impact of the evacuation is not on the material and the physical. It is something far deeper. It is the effect on the spirit." Describing the lives of Japanese American women during World War II and assessing the effects of the camp experience on the spirit are complex tasks: factors such as age, generation, personality, and family background interweave and preclude simple

---

"Japanese American Women During World War II" from *Frontiers*, 8 (1984), pp. 6–14—with abridgements as approved by Valerie Matsumoto.

generalizations. In these relocation camps Japanese American women faced severe racism and traumatic family strain, but the experience also fostered changes in their lives: more leisure for older women, equal pay with men for working women, disintegration of traditional patterns of arranged marriages, and, ultimately, new opportunities for travel, work, and education for the younger women.

I will examine the lives of Japanese American women during the trying war years, focusing on the second generation — the Nisei — whose work and education were most affected. The Nisei women entered college and ventured into new areas of work in unfamiliar regions of the country, sustained by fortitude, family ties, discipline, and humor. My understanding of their history derives from several collections of internees' letters, assembly center and relocation camp newspapers, census records, and taped oral history interviews that I conducted with eighty-four Nisei (second generation) and eleven Issei (first generation). Two-thirds of these interviews were with women. . . .

A century ago, male Japanese workers began to arrive on American shores, dreaming of making fortunes that would enable them to return to their homeland in triumph. For many, the fortune did not materialize and the shape of the dream changed: they developed stakes in small farms and businesses and, together with wives brought from Japan, established families and communities.

The majority of Japanese women — over 33,000 immigrants — entered the United States between 1908 and 1924. The "Gentlemen's Agreement" of 1908 restricted the entry of male Japanese laborers into the country but sanctioned the immigration of parents, wives, and children of laborers already residing in the United States. The Immigration Act of 1924 excluded Japanese immigration altogether.

Some Japanese women traveled to reunite with husbands; others journeyed to America as newlyweds with men who had returned to Japan to find wives. Still others came alone as picture brides to join Issei men who sought to avoid army conscription or excessive travel expenses; their family-arranged marriages deviated from social convention only by the absence of the groom from the *miai* (preliminary meeting of prospective spouses) and wedding ceremony. Once settled, these women confronted unfamiliar clothing, food, language, and customs as well as life with husbands who were, in many cases, strangers and often ten to fifteen years their seniors.

Most Issei women migrated to rural areas of the West. Some lived with their husbands in labor camps, which provided workers for the railroad industry, the lumber mills of the Pacific Northwest, and the Alaskan salmon canneries. They also farmed with their husbands as cash or share tenants, particularly in California where Japanese immigrant agriculture began to flourish. In urban areas, women worked as domestics or helped their husbands run small businesses such as laundries, bath houses, restaurants, pool halls, boarding houses, grocery stores, curio shops, bakeries, and plant nurseries. Except for the few who married well-to-do professionals or merchants, the majority of Issei women unceasingly toiled both inside and outside the home. They were always the first to rise in the morning and the last to go to bed at night.

The majority of the Issei's children, the Nisei, were born between 1910 and 1940. Both girls and boys were incorporated into the family economy early, especially those living on farms. They took care of their younger siblings, fed the farm animals, heated water for the *furo* (Japanese bath), and worked in the fields before and after school — hoeing weeds, irrigating, and driving tractors. Daughters helped with cooking and cleaning. In addition, all were expected to devote time to their studies: the Issei instilled in their children a deep respect for education and authority. They repeatedly admonished the Nisei not to bring disgrace upon the family or community and exhorted them to do their best in everything.

The Nisei grew up integrating both the Japanese ways of their parents and the mainstream customs of their non-Japanese friends and classmates — not always an easy process given the deeply rooted prejudice and discrimination they faced as a tiny, easily identified minority. Because of the wide age range among them and the diversity of their early experiences in various urban and rural areas, it is difficult to generalize about the Nisei. Most grew up speaking Japanese with their parents and English with their siblings, friends, and teachers. Regardless of whether they were Buddhist or Christian, they celebrated the New Year with traditional foods and visiting, as well as Christmas and Thanksgiving. Girls learned to knit, sew, and embroider, and some took lessons in *odori* (folk dancing). The Nisei, many of whom were adolescents during the 1940's, also listened to the *Hit Parade,* Jack Benny, and *Gangbusters* on the radio, learned to jitterbug, played kick-the-can and baseball, and read the same popular books and magazines as their non-Japanese peers.

The Issei were strict and not inclined to open displays of affection towards their children, but the Nisei were conscious of their parents' concern for them and for the family. This sense of family strength and responsibility helped to sustain the Issei and Nisei through years of economic hardship and discrimination: the West Coast anti-Japanese movement of the early 1920's, the Depression of the 1930's, and the most drastic ordeal — the chaotic uprooting of the World War II evacuation, internment, and resettlement. . . .

The bombing of Pearl Harbor on December 7, 1941, unleashed war between the United States and Japan and triggered a wave of hostility against Japanese Americans. On December 8, the financial resources of the Issei were frozen, and the Federal Bureau of Investigation began to seize Issei community leaders thought to be strongly pro-Japanese. Rumors spread that the Japanese in Hawaii had aided the attack on Pearl Harbor, fueling fears of "fifth column" activity on the West Coast. Politicians and the press clamored for restrictions against the Japanese Americans, and their economic competitors saw the chance to gain control of Japanese American farms and businesses.

Despite some official doubts and some differences of opinion among military heads regarding the necessity of removing Japanese Americans from the West Coast, in the end the opinions of civilian leaders and Lieutenant General John L. DeWitt — head of the Western Defense Command — of Assistant Secretary of War John McCloy and Secretary of War Henry Stimson prevailed. On February 19, 1942, President Franklin Delano Roosevelt signed Executive Order 9066, arbitrarily suspending the civil rights of American citizens by authorizing the removal of 110,000 Japanese and their American-born children from the western half of the Pacific Coastal States and the southern third of Arizona.

During the bewildering months before evacuation, the Japanese Americans were subject to curfews and to unannounced searches at all hours for "contraband" weapons, radios, and cameras; in desperation and fear, many people destroyed their belongings from Japan, including treasured heirlooms, books, and photographs. Some families moved voluntarily from the Western Defense zone, but many stayed, believing that all areas would eventually be restricted or fearing hostility in neighboring states.

Involuntary evacuation began in the spring of 1942. Families received a scant week's notice in which to "wind up their affairs, store or sell their possessions, close up their businesses and homes, and show up at an assembly point for transportation to an assembly center." Each person was allowed to bring only as many clothes and personal items as he or she could carry to the temporary assembly centers that had been hastily constructed at fairgrounds, race tracks, and Civilian Conservation Corps camps: twelve in California, one in Oregon, and one in Washington.

The rapidity of evacuation left many Japanese Americans numb; one Nisei noted that "a queer lump came to my throat. Nothing else came to my mind, it was just blank. Everything happened too soon, I guess." As the realization of leaving home, friends, and neighborhood sank in, the numbness gave way to bewilderment. A teenager at the Santa Anita Assembly Center wrote, "I felt lost after I left Mountain View [California]. I thought that we could go back but instead look where we are." . . .

Overlying the mixed feelings of anxiety, anger, shame, and confusion was resignation. As a relatively small minority caught in a storm of turbulent events that destroyed their individual and community security, there was little the Japanese Americans could do but shrug and say, *"Shikata ga nai,"* or, "It can't be helped," the implication being that the situation must be endured. The phrase lingered on many lips when the Issei, Nisei, and the young Sansei (third generation) children prepared for the move — which was completed by November 1942 — to the ten permanent relocation camps organized by the War Relocation Authority: Topaz, Utah; Poston and Gila River, Arizona; Amache, Colorado; Manzanar and Tule Lake, California; Heart Mountain, Wyoming; Minidoka, Idaho; Denson and Rohwer, Arkansas. Denson and Rohwer were located in the swampy lowlands of Arkansas; the other camps were in desolate desert or semi-desert areas subject to dust storms and extreme temperatures reflected in the nicknames given to the three sections of the Poston Camp: Toaston, Roaston, and Duston.

The conditions of camp life profoundly altered family relations and affected women of all ages and backgrounds. Family unity deteriorated in the crude communal facilities and cramped barracks. The unceasing battle with the elements, the poor food, the shortages of toilet tissue and milk, coupled with wartime profiteering and mismanagement, and the sense of injustice and frustration took their toll on a people uprooted, far from home.

The standard housing in the camps was a spartan barracks, about twenty feet by one hundred feet, divided into four to six rooms furnished with steel army cots. Initially each single room or "apartment" housed an average of eight persons; individuals without kin nearby were often moved in with smaller families. Because the partitions between apartments did not reach the ceiling, even the smallest noises traveled freely from one end of the building to the other. There were usually fourteen barracks in each block, and each block had its own mess hall, laundry, latrine, shower facilities, and recreation room.

Because of the discomfort, noise, and lack of privacy, which "made a single symphony of yours and your neighbors' loves, hates, and joys," the barracks often became merely a place to "hang your hat" and sleep. As Jeanne Wakatsuki Houston records in her autobiography, *Farewell to Manzanar,* many family members began to spend less time together in the crowded barracks. The even greater lack of privacy in the latrine and shower facilities necessitated adjustments in former notions of modesty. There were no partitions in the shower room, and the latrine consisted of two rows of partitioned toilets "with nothing in front of you, just on the sides. Lots of people were not used to those kind of facilities, so [they'd] either go early in the morning when people were not around, or go real late at night. . . . It was really something until you got used to it."

The large communal mess halls also encouraged family disunity as family members gradually began to eat separately: mothers with small children, fathers with other men, and older children with their peers. "Table manners were forgotten," observed Miné Okubo. "Guzzle, guzzle, guzzle; hurry, hurry, hurry. Family life was lacking. Everyone ate wherever he or she pleased." Some strategies were developed for preserving family unity. The Amache Camp responded in part by assigning each family a particular table in the mess hall. Some families took the food back to their barracks so that they might eat together. But these measures were not always feasible in the face of varying work schedules; the odd hours of those assigned to shifts in the mess halls and infirmaries often made it impossible for the family to sit down together for meals.

Newspaper reports that Japanese Americans were living in luxurious conditions angered evacuees struggling to adjust to cramped quarters and crude communal facilities. A married woman with a family wrote from Heart Mountain:

> Last weekend, we had an awful cold wave and it was about 20° to 30° below zero. In such a weather, it's terrible to try going even to the bath and latrine house. . . . It really aggravates me to hear some politicians say we Japanese are being coddled, for *it isn't so*!! We're on ration as much as outsiders are. I'd say welcome to anyone to try living behind barbed wire and be cooped in a 20 ft. by 20 ft. room. . . . We do our sleeping, dressing, ironing, hanging up our clothes in this one room.

After the first numbness of disorientation, the evacuees set about making their situation bearable, creating as much order in their lives as possible. With blankets they partitioned their apartments into tiny rooms and created benches, tables, and shelves as piles of scrap lumber left over from barracks construction vanished; victory gardens and flower patches appeared. Evacuees also took advantage of the opportunity to taste freedom when they received temporary permits to go shopping in nearby towns. These were memorable occasions. A Heart Mountain Nisei described what such a trip meant to her in 1944:

> for the first time since being behind the fences, I managed to go out shopping to Billings, Montana — a trip about 4 hours ride on train and bus. . . . It was quite a mental relief to breathe the air on the outside. . . . And was it an undescribable sensation to be able to be dressed up and walk the pavements with my high heel shoes!! You just can't imagine how full we are of pent-up emotions until we leave the camp behind us and see the highway ahead of us. A trip like that will keep us from becoming mentally narrow. And without much privacy, you can imagine how much people will become dull.

Despite the best efforts of the evacuees to restore order to their disrupted world, camp conditions prevented replication of their prewar lives. Women's work experiences, for example, changed in complex ways during the years of internment. Each camp offered a wide range of jobs, resulting from the organization of the camps as model cities administered through a series of departments headed by Caucasian administrators. The departments handled everything from accounting, agriculture, education, and medical care to mess hall service and the weekly newspaper. The scramble for jobs began early in the assembly centers and camps, and all able-bodied persons were expected to work.

Even before the war many family members had worked, but now children and parents, men and women all received the same low wages. In the relocation camps, doctors, teachers, and other professionals were at the top of the pay scale, earning $19 per month. The majority of workers received $16, and apprentices earned $12. The new equity in pay and the variety of available jobs gave many women unprecedented opportunities for experimentation, as illustrated by one woman's account of her family's work in Poston:

> First I wanted to find art work, but I didn't last too long because it wasn't very interesting . . . so I worked in the mess hall, but that wasn't for me, so I went to the accounting department — time-keeping — and I enjoyed that, so I stayed there. . . . My dad . . . went to a shoe shop . . . and then he was block gardener. . . . He got $16. . . . [My sister] was secretary for the block manager; then she went to the optometry department. She was assistant optometrist; she fixed all the glasses and fitted them. . . . That was $16.

As early as 1942, the War Relocation Authority began to release evacuees temporarily from the centers and camps to do voluntary seasonal farm work in neighboring areas hard hit by the wartime labor shortage. The work was arduous, as one young woman discovered when she left Topaz to take a job plucking turkeys:

> The smell is terrific until you get used to it. . . . We all wore gunny sacks around our waist, had a small knife and plucked off the fine feathers.
>
> This is about the hardest work that many of us have done — but without a murmur of complaint we worked 8 hours through the first day without a pause.
>
> We were all so tired that we didn't even feel like eating. . . . Our fingers and wrists were just aching, and I just dreamt of turkeys and more turkeys.

Work conditions varied from situation to situation, and some exploitative farmers refused to pay the Japanese Americans after they had finished beet topping or fruit picking. One worker noted that the degree of friendliness on the employer's part decreased as the harvest neared completion. Nonetheless, many workers, like the turkey plucker, concluded that "even if the work is hard, it is worth the freedom we are allowed."

Camp life increased the leisure of many evacuees. A good number of Issei women, accustomed to long days of work inside and outside the home, found that the communally prepared meals and limited living quarters provided them with spare time. Many availed themselves of the opportunity to attend adult classes taught by both evacuees and non-Japanese. Courses involving handcrafts and traditional Japanese arts such as flower arrangement, sewing, painting, calligraphy, and wood carving became immensely popular as an overwhelming number of people turned to art for recreation and self-expression. Some of these subjects were viewed as hobbies and leisure activities by those who taught them, but to the Issei women they represented access to new skills and a means to contribute to the material comfort of the family.

The evacuees also filled their time with Buddhist and Christian church meetings, theatrical productions, cultural programs, athletic events, and visits with friends. All family members spent more time than ever before in the company of their peers. Nisei from isolated rural areas were exposed to the ideas, styles, and pastimes of the more sophisticated urban youth; in camp they had the time and opportunity to socialize — at work, school, dances, sports events, and parties — in an almost entirely Japanese American environment. Gone were the restrictions of distance, lack of transportation, interracial uneasiness, and the dawn-to-dusk exigencies of field work.

Like their noninterned contemporaries, most young Nisei women envisioned a future of marriage and children. They — and their parents — anticipated that they would marry other Japanese Americans, but these young women also expected to choose their own husbands and to marry "for love." This mainstream American ideal of marriage differed greatly from the Issei's view of love as a bond that might evolve over the course of an arranged marriage that was firmly rooted in less romantic notions of compatibility and responsibility. The discrepancy between Issei and Nisei conceptions of love and marriage had sturdy prewar roots; internment fostered further divergence from the old customs of arranged marriage.

In the artificial hothouse of camp, Nisei romances often bloomed quickly. As Nisei men left to prove their loyalty to the United States in the 442nd Combat Team and the 100th Battalion, young Japanese Americans strove to grasp what happiness and security they could, given the uncertainties of the future. Lily Shoji, in her "Fem-a-lites" newspaper column, commented upon the "changing world" and advised Nisei women:

> This is the day of sudden dates, of blind dates on the up-and-up, so let the flash of a uniform be a signal to you to be ready for any emergency. . . . Romance is blossoming with the emotion and urgency of war.

In keeping with this atmosphere, camp newspaper columns like Shoji's in *The Mercedian, The Daily Tulean Dispatch*'s "Strictly Feminine," and the *Poston Chronicle*'s "Fashionotes" gave their Nisei readers countless suggestions on how to impress boys, care for their complexions, and choose the latest fashions. These evacuee-authored columns thus mirrored the mainstream girls' periodicals of the time. Such fashion news may seem incongruous in the context of an internment camp whose inmates had little choice in clothing beyond what they could find in the Montgomery Ward or Sears and Roebuck mail-order catalogues. These columns, however, reflect women's efforts to remain in touch with the world outside the barbed wire fence; they reflect as well women's attempt to maintain morale in a drab, depressing environment. . . .

Relocation began slowly in 1942. Among the first to venture out of the camps were college students, assisted by the National Japanese American Student Relocation Council, a nongovernmental agency that provided invaluable placement aid to 4,084 Nisei in the years 1942–46. Founded in 1942 by concerned educators, this organization persuaded institutions outside the restricted Western Defense zone to accept Nisei students and facilitated their admissions and leave clearances. A study of the first 400 students to leave camp showed that a third of them were women. Because of the cumbersome screening process, few other evacuees departed on indefinite leave before 1943. In that year, the War Relocation Authority tried to expedite the clearance procedure by broadening an army registration program aimed at Nisei males to include all adults. With this policy change, the migration from the camps steadily increased.

Many Nisei, among them a large number of women, were anxious to leave the limbo of camp and return "to normal life again." With all its work, social events, and cultural activities, camp was still an artificial, limited environment. It was stifling "to see nothing but the same barracks, mess halls, and other houses, row after row, day in and day out, it gives us the feeling that we're missing all the freedom and liberty." An aspiring teacher wrote: "Mother and father do not want me to go out. However, I want to go so very much that sometimes I feel that I'd go even if they disowned me. What shall I do? I realize the hard living conditions outside but I think I can take it." Women's developing sense of independence in the camp environment and their growing awareness of their abilities as workers contributed to their self-confidence and hence their desire to leave. Significantly, Issei parents, despite initial reluctance, were gradually beginning to sanction their daughters' departures for education and employment in the Midwest and East. One Nisei noted:

> [Father] became more broad-minded in the relocation center. He was more mellow in his ways. . . . At first he didn't want me to relocate, but he gave in. . . . I said I wanted to go [to Chicago] with my friend, so he helped me pack. He didn't say I could go . . . but he helped me pack, so I thought, "Well, he didn't say no."

The decision to relocate was a difficult one. It was compounded for some women because they felt obligated to stay and care for elderly or infirm parents, like the Heart Mountain Nisei who observed wistfully, "It's getting so more and more of the girls and boys are leaving camp, and I sure wish I could but mother's getting on and I just can't leave her." Many internees worried about their acceptance in the outside world. The Nisei considered themselves American citizens, and they had an allegiance to the land of their birth: "The teaching and love of one's own birth place, one's own country was . . . strongly impressed upon my mind as a child. So even though California may deny our rights of birth, I shall ever love her soil." But evacuation had taught the Japanese Americans that in the eyes of many of their fellow Americans, theirs was the face of the enemy. Many Nisei were torn by mixed feelings of shame, frustration, and bitterness at the denial of their civil rights. These factors created an atmosphere of anxiety that surrounded those who contemplated resettlement: "A feeling of uncertainty hung over the camp; we were worried about the future. Plans were made and remade, as we tried to decide what to do. Some were ready to risk anything to get away. Others feared to leave the protection of the camp."

Thus, those first college students were the scouts whose letters back to camp marked pathways for others to follow. May Yoshino sent a favorable report to her family in Topaz from the nearby University of Utah, indicating that there were "plenty of schoolgirl jobs for those who want to study at the University." Correspondence from other Nisei students shows that although they succeeded at making the dual transition from high school to college and from camp to the outside world, they were not without anxieties as to whether they could handle the study load and the reactions of the Caucasians around them. . . .

Several incidents of hostility did occur, but the reception of the Nisei students at colleges and universities was generally warm. Topaz readers of *Trek* magazine could draw encouragement from Lillian Ota's "Campus Report." Ota, a Wellesley student, reassured them: "During the first few days you'll be invited by the college to teas and receptions. Before long you'll lose the awkwardness you might feel at such doings after the months of abnormal life at evacuation centers." Although Ota had not noticed "that my being a 'Jap' has made much difference on the campus itself," she offered cautionary and pragmatic advice to the Nisei, suggesting the burden of responsibility these relocated students felt, as well as the problem of communicating their experiences and emotions to Caucasians.

> It is scarcely necessary to point out that those who have probably never seen a nisei before will get their impression of the nisei as a whole from the relocated students. It won't do you or your family and friends much good to dwell on what you consider injustices when you are questioned about evacuation. Rather, stress the contributions of [our] people to the nation's war effort.

Given the tenor of the times and the situation of their families, the pioneers in resettlement had little choice but to repress their anger and minimize the amount of racist hostility they encountered.

In her article "a la mode," Marii Kyogoku also offered survival tips to the departing Nisei, ever conscious that they were on trial not only as individuals but as representatives of their families and their generation. She suggested criteria for choosing clothes and provided hints on adjustment to food rationing. Kyogoku especially urged the evacuees to improve their table manners, which had been adversely affected by the "unnatural food and atmosphere" of mess hall dining:

> You should start rehearsing for the great outside by bringing your own utensils to the dining hall. Its an aid to normality to be able to eat your jello with a spoon and well worth the dishwashing which it involves. All of us eat much too fast. Eat more slowly. All this practicing should be done so that proper manners will seem natural to you. If you do this, you won't get stagefright and spill your water glass, or make bread pills and hardly dare to eat when you have your first meal away from the centers and in the midst of scrutinizing caucasian eyes.

Armed with advice and drawn by encouraging reports, increasing numbers of women students left camp. A postwar study of a group of 1,000 relocated students showed that 40 percent were women. The field of nursing was particularly attractive to Nisei women; after the first few students disproved the hospital administration's fears of their patients' hostility, acceptance of Nisei into nursing schools grew. By July 1944, there were more than 300 Nisei women in over 100 nursing programs in twenty-four states. One such student wrote from the Asbury Hospital in Minneapolis: "Work here isn't too hard and I enjoy it very much. The patients are very nice people and I haven't had any trouble as yet. They do give us a funny stare at the beginning but after a day or so we receive the best compliments."

The trickle of migration from the camps grew into a steady stream by 1943, as the War Relocation Authority developed its resettlement program to aid evacuees in finding housing and employment in the East and Midwest. A resettlement bulletin published by the Advisory Committee for Evacuees described "who is relocating":

> Mostly younger men and women, in their 20s or 30s; mostly single persons or couples with one or two children, or men with larger families who come out alone first to scout opportunities and to secure a foothold, planning to call wife and children later. Most relocated evacuees have parents or relatives whom they hope and plan to bring out "when we get re-established."

In early 1945, the War Department ended the exclusion of the Japanese Americans from the West Coast, and the War Relocation Authority announced that the camps would be closed within the year. By this time, 37 percent of the evacuees of sixteen years or older had already relocated, including 63 percent of the Nisei women in that age group.

For Nisei women, like their non-Japanese sisters, the wartime labor shortage opened the door into industrial, clerical, and managerial occupations. Prior to the war, racism had excluded the Japanese Americans from most white-collar clerical and sales positions, and, according to sociologist Evelyn Nakano Glenn, "the most common form of nonagricultural employment for the immigrant women (issei) and their American-born daughters (nisei) was domestic service." The highest percentage of job offers for both men and women continued to be requests for domestic workers. . . . However, Nisei women also found jobs as secretaries, typists, file clerks, beauticians, and factory workers. By 1950, 47 percent of employed Japanese American women were clerical and sales workers and operatives; only 10 percent were in domestic service. The World War II decade, then, marked a turning point for Japanese American women in the labor force.

Whether they were students or workers, and regardless of where they went or how prepared they were to meet the outside world, Nisei women found that leaving camp meant enormous change in their lives. Even someone as confident as Marii Kyogoku, the author of much relocation advice, found that reentry into the Caucasian-dominated world beyond the barbed wire fence was not a simple matter of stepping back into old shoes. Leaving the camps — like entering them — meant major changes in psychological perspective and self-image.

> I had thought that because before evacuation I had adjusted myself rather well in a Caucasian society, I would go right back into my former frame of mind. I have found, however, that though the center became unreal and was as if it had never existed as soon as I got on the train at Delta, I was never so self-conscious in all my life.

Kyogoku was amazed to see so many men and women in uniform and, despite her "proper" dining preparation, felt strange sitting at a table set with clean linen and a full set of silverware.

> I felt a diffidence at facing all these people and things, which was most unusual. Slowly things have come to seem natural, though I am still excited by the sounds of the busy city and thrilled every time I see a street lined with trees. I no longer feel that I am the cynosure of all eyes.

Like Kyogoku, many Nisei women discovered that relocation meant adjustment to "a life different from our former as well as present way of living" and, as such, posed a challenge. Their experiences in meeting this challenge were as diverse as their jobs and living situations.

"I live at the Eleanor Club No. 5 which is located on the west side," wrote Mary Sonoda, working with the American Friends Service Committee in Chicago:

> I pay $1 per day for room and two meals a day. I also have maid service. I do not think that one can manage all this for $1 unless one lives in a place like this which houses thousands of working girls in the city. . . . I am the only Japanese here at present. . . . The residents and the staff are wonderful to me. . . . I am constantly being entertained by one person or another.
>
> The people in Chicago are extremely friendly. Even with the Tribune screaming awful headlines concerning the recent execution of American soldiers in Japan, people kept their heads. On street cars, at stores, everywhere, one finds innumerable evidence of good will.

Chicago, the location of the first War Relocation Authority field office for supervision of resettlement in the Midwest, attracted the largest number of evacuees. Not all found their working environment as congenial as Mary Sonoda did. Smoot Katow, a Nisei man in Chicago, painted "another side of the picture":

> I met one of the Edgewater Beach girls. . . . From what she said it was my impression that the girls are not very happy. The hotel work is too hard, according to this girl. In fact, they are losing weight and one girl became sick with overwork. They have to clean about fifteen suites a day, scrubbing the floors on their hands and knees. . . . It seems the management is out to use labor as labor only. . . . The outside world is just as tough as it ever was.

These variations in living and work conditions and wages encouraged and sometimes necessitated a certain amount of job experimentation among the Nisei.

Many relocating Japanese Americans received moral and material assistance from a number of service organizations and religious groups, particularly the Presbyterians, the Methodists, the Society of Friends, and the Young Women's Christian Association. . . .

The Nisei also derived support and strength from networks — formed before and during internment — of friends and relatives. The homes of those who relocated first became way stations for others as they made the transition into new communities and jobs. In 1944, soon after she obtained a place to stay in New York City, Miné Okubo found that "many of the other evacuees relocating in New York came ringing my doorbell. They were sleeping all over the floor!" Single women often accompanied or joined sisters, brothers, and friends as many interconnecting grapevines carried news of likely jobs, housing, and friendly communities. Ayako Kanemura, for instance, found a job painting Hummel figurines in Chicago; a letter of recommendation from a friend enabled her "to get my foot into the door and then all my friends followed and joined me." Although they were farther from their families than ever before, Nisei women maintained warm ties of affection and concern, and those who had the means to do so continued to play a role in the family economy, remitting a portion of their earnings to their families in or out of camp, and to siblings in school.

Elizabeth Ogata's family exemplifies several patterns of resettlement and the maintenance of family ties within them. In October 1944, her parents were living with her brother Harry who had begun to farm in Springville, Utah; another brother and sister were attending Union College in Lincoln, Nebraska. Elizabeth herself had moved to Minneapolis to join a brother in the army, and she was working as an operative making pajamas. "Minn. is a beautiful place," she wrote, "and the people are so nice. . . . I thought I'd never find anywhere I would feel at home as I did in Mt. View [California], but I have changed my mind." Like Elizabeth, a good number of the 35,000 relocated Japanese Americans were favorably impressed by their new homes and decided to stay.

The war years had complex and profound effects upon Japanese Americans, uprooting their communities and causing severe psychological and emotional damage. The vast majority returned to the West Coast at the end of the war in 1945—a move that, like the initial evacuation, was a grueling test of flexibility and fortitude. Even with the assistance of old friends and service organizations, the transition was taxing and painful, the end of the war meant not only long-awaited freedom but more battles to be fought in social, academic, and economic arenas. The Japanese Americans faced hostility, crude living conditions, and a struggle for jobs. Few evacuees received any compensation for their financial losses, estimated conservatively at $400 million, because Congress decided to appropriate only $38 million for the settlement of claims. It is even harder to place a figure on the toll taken in emotional shock, self-blame, broken dreams, and insecurity. One Japanese American woman still sees in her nightmares the watchtower searchlights that troubled her sleep forty years ago.

The war altered Japanese American women's lives in complicated ways. In general, evacuation and relocation accelerated earlier trends that differentiated the Nisei from their parents. Although most young women, like their mothers and non-Japanese peers, anticipated a future centered around a husband and children, they had already felt the influence of mainstream middle-class values of love and marriage and quickly moved away from the pattern of arranged marriage in the camps. There, increased peer group activities and the relaxation of parental authority gave them more independence. The Nisei women's expectations of marriage became more akin to the companionate ideals of their peers than to those of the Issei.

As before the war, many Nisei women worked in camp, but the new parity in wages they received altered family dynamics. And though they expected to contribute to the family economy, a large number did so in settings far from the family, availing themselves of opportunities provided by the student and worker relocation programs. In meeting the challenges facing them, Nisei women drew not only upon the disciplined strength inculcated by their Issei parents but also upon firmly rooted support networks and the greater measure of self-reliance and independence that they developed during the crucible of the war years.

❈ *F U R T H E R   R E A D I N G*

Karen Tucker Anderson, *Wartime Women: Sex Roles, Family Relations, and the Status of Women During World War II* (1981)

M. Joyce Baker, *Images of Women in Film: The War Years, 1941–1945* (1981)

Julia Kirk Blackwelder, *Women of the Depression: Caste and Culture in San Antonio, 1929–1939* (1984)

D'Ann Campbell, *Women at War with America* (1984)

William Chafe, *The American Woman: Her Changing Social, Economic, and Political Roles, 1920–1970* (1972)

Blanche Weisen Cook, *Eleanor Roosevelt: Volume One, 1884–1933* (1992)

Sherna Berger Gluck, ed., *Rosie the Riveter Revisited: Women, the War and Social Change* (1987)

Susan Hartmann, *The Home Front and Beyond* (1982)

Joan Hoff-Wilson and Marjorie Lightman, eds., *Without Precedent: The Life and Career of Eleanor Roosevelt* (1984)

Maureen Honey, *Creating Rosie the Riveter: Class, Gender, and Propaganda During World War II* (1984)

Amy Kesselman, *Fleeting Opportunities: Women Shipyard Workers in Portland and Vancouver During World War II and Reconversion* (1990)

Valerie J. Matsumoto, *Farming the Home Place: A Japanese American Community in California, 1919–1982* (1993)

Ruth Milkman, *Gender at Work: The Dynamics of Job Segregation by Sex During World War II* (1988)

Paddy Quick, "Rosie the Riveter: Myths and Realities," *Radical America* IX (1975), 115–132

B. Joyce Ross, "Mary McLeod Bethune and the National Youth Administration: A Case Study of Power Relationships," *Journal of Negro History* 60 (January 1975), 1–28

Leila Rupp, *Mobilizing Women for War* (1978)

Lois Scharf, *To Work or to Wed: Female Employment, Feminism, and the Great Depression* (1980)

Mary Schweitzer, "World War II and Female Labor Force Participation Rates," *Journal of Economic History* XL (1980), 89–95

Theda Skocpol, *Protecting Mothers and Soldiers: The Political Origins of Social Policy in the United States* (1992)

Karen Beck Skold, "The Job He Left Behind: American Women in the Shipyards During World War II," in *Women, War, and Revolution,* Carol Berkin and Clara Lovett, eds. (1980), 55–75

Sheila Tobias and Lisa Anderson, *What Really Happened to Rosie the Riveter?* MSS Modular Publication no. 9 (1973)

Winifred Wandersee, *Women's Work and Family Values, 1920–1940* (1981)

Susan Ware, *Beyond Suffrage: Women in the New Deal* (1981)

——, *Partner and I: Molly Dewson, Feminism, and New Deal Politics* (1987)

CHAPTER
14

Women and the Feminine Ideal
in Postwar America

Throughout the 1940s and 1950s, American men and women married at an earlier age and had larger families than their own parents, thus reversing the long-standing downward trend in the nation's birthrate. These adults, the parents of the baby boom generation, moved by the thousands to suburban neighborhoods, where childrearing became the focal point of private and public life. Meanwhile, movies and popular magazines gave generous coverage to family matters, and seemed to revive, though with a modern twist, a feminine ideal based in domesticity. Writing for the lay public, many educators and mental health professionals also stressed women's identification with marriage and motherhood.

Historians have vigorously debated the meaning of womanhood in the postwar era. What are we to make of the nation's popular celebration of a domestic feminine ideal? Was this ideal in some way shaped by its political context — that is, the nation's Cold War policies and concerns? Did the popular media offer any alternative images of womanhood? How did women respond to the media's representations of themselves? And, just as important, did definitions of womanhood differ for women by social and racial group? Finally, how and under what circumstances did women ignore, subvert, or manipulate normative standards of postwar womanhood? With what gains, and at what cost?

※ DOCUMENTS

In 1946, Louisa Randall Church wrote an article for *American Home* magazine (excerpted as the first selection) that explored the vital duties of parents who lived in a nation worrying over Soviet expansionism and atomic warfare. Church urged men and women to regard parenting as a noble duty; in an interesting twist, she also urged them to embrace gender equity. Psychiatrist Marynia F. Farnham and her colleague, sociologist Ferdinand Lundberg, coauthors of *Modern Woman: The Lost Sex* (1947), an excerpt of which appears as the second document, had no use for gender equity; instead, as staunch antifeminists, they offered strong praise for women who devoted themselves to domesticity, and called women who tried to compete with men "neurotic" and "unfeminine." Also writing in 1947 but from a decidedly feminist perspective, Pauli Murray, an African-American deputy attorney general for California, described the rebellion of educated and professional black women against racial and sexual subordination; in an article published in *Negro Digest* — the third selection — Pauli particularly lamented the tendency of black men to vent frustrations borne of racism against black women. The fourth selection is an anonymous letter from an African-American reader to *The Ladder,* America's first lesbian magazine, which began publication in 1956. The author of the letter sees nothing wrong with her sexual identity; this same self-assurance is evident in the fifth document, which consists of the statements of four women whose answers to the question, "Why am I a lesbian?" appeared in *The Ladder* in 1960. Finally, in the last document, Joyce Johnson, a young woman who was part of the nonconformist "Beat Generation," describes what it was like to obtain an illegal abortion in New York City in 1955. Together, these documents point both to the varied social identities that women endorsed in the postwar decades and to the obstacles that they encountered.

Louisa Randall Church, "Parents, Architects of Peace," 1946

On that day in August 1945, when the first atomic bomb fell on Hiroshima, new concepts of civilized living, based on the obligations of world citizenship and un-selfish service to mankind, were born. Out of the smoke and smoldering ruins arose a great cry for leadership equipped to guide the stricken people of the world along the hazardous course toward peace. On that day parenthood took on added responsibilities of deep and profound significance.

Today, months later, lacking sufficient and adequate leadership the nations of the earth flounder in a perilous state of distrust, suspicion, confusion and impotency. As one historian has said, "We stand at the very door of a golden age fumbling at the lock." How right he is.

Frightened scientists warn us of dire disaster — unspeakable catastrophe — the possible atomic murder of millions of peace-loving human beings. They tell us that bombs never again will come in ones and twos; they will come in hundreds, even thousands. More frightening still, they say there is no defense. Surely, in all history, the parents of the world were never so challenged.

However, there is a defense — an impregnable bulwark — which lies in meeting the world's desperate cry for leadership. Upon the shoulders of parents, everywhere, rests the tremendous responsibility of sending forth into the next generation men and women imbued with a high resolve to work together for everlasting peace.

There is no time to lose. We must gear our thoughts and actions for this new task as we did for winning the war. The noble instincts — sacrifice, heroism, generosity, unselfishness — which stirred us to action then must stir us now.

In every American home parents ought to be thinking and talking about these questions. What has caused the scarcity of qualified leaders? What are the requirements of worthy citizenship from which leaders can be expected to emerge? What changes must be made in our concepts of family living and parenthood if our children are to become wise, co-operative, courageous world citizens? How can parents help to eradicate the underlying causes of war: poverty and despair, inequality of opportunity, hatred and greed? . . .

Louisa Randall Church, "Parents, Architects of Peace," *American Home* XXXVI (November 1946).

In order to develop the qualities of leadership necessary to insure peace — vision to see the needs of all humanity, willingness to work, sacrifice and co-operate for a common goal — parents must give their children not social security but personal security.

Personal security is attained only when the individual has achieved an inner harmony of spirit, self-confidence and a sense of mastery — in short — when he has achieved complete triumph over himself and his environment. Only then can he meet the exigencies of worthy citizenship in the world of tomorrow. Personal security cannot be bought for or taught to a child. It is a by-product of harmonious family living which is based on: **(1) Love and Affection.** Psychologists tell us our first duty is to surround a child, from the moment of birth, with a never-failing love, affection and the assurance of being wanted. . . . When we push a child aside as a nuisance, ignore his needs, allow ourselves to become bored with his care, or fail to accept him as a real person, is it strange that he becomes confused and troublesome? . . .

(2) Equal Rights. Parenthood is a partnership for the mutual welfare of the father and the mother, the children and the whole society and should be governed by the rules which apply to all professional partnerships. In the discipline of their children, in policies of home management or control of family finances neither father nor mother should reign supreme. There can be no harmony in a home where favoritism is shown, where the spirit of rivalry and competitive striving is encouraged or where equality of opportunity is denied. Since, more and more, women will be taking their rightful places in world affairs, girls should be provided with the same opportunities, intellectually, professionally, socially and economically as boys.

(3) Discipline. It is in the home that a child should develop his first sense of responsibility to himself and to others. From intelligent guidance in habit formation he gains self-reliance, self-control and self-direction. Such self-discipline cannot be achieved by parental tyranny which molds a child according to selfish ambitions and foolish pride. It cannot be achieved by pampering. . . .

(4) Freedom. Unless a child senses a growing inner freedom to think, act, and achieve according to his interests, his talents, his abilities and his ambitions, he cannot gain the sense of security which is his right. Parents who go through life, pruning shears in hand — clipping here, clipping there every spontaneous outburst of enthusiasm which fails to conform to their plans and desires for their children are building future robots.

(5) Enrichment. . . . A child's desire for self-expression and recognition is a basic personality need. Parents have no greater responsibility than to provide him with opportunities to develop hobbies which will open to him the world of arts, crafts and mechanical skills. Essential to his personal security, his ability to co-operate with others and to a high standard of social behavior are friendships and contacts with people from all walks of life. . . .

(6) Co-operation. Good behavior of the individual is basic to harmony in the group. Obedient, thoughtful, helpful, unselfish children are a reflection of the parent's ability to co-operate with them, and to win co-operation from them. . . . Nothing in parenthood is more important than . . . willingness to share in the dreams, ambitions and problems of their children — to share those rare, golden moments when a child bares his mind, heart and soul. At such moments parental guidance can go into action and do its best work in wise, constructive counselling. At such moments, listening with honest sincerity and understanding breeds in a child confidence, a sense of inner security and power. When he feels security in the home he will feel at home in his community, his nation and the world. . . . There is no place in today's world for the "getters" — those who seem, always, to be in trouble, who create tensions, who cause most of the problems of society. Leaders of a new stamp — the "givers" will be needed, not alone at the peace table, but in community activities, church life, education, public welfare services and youth groups.

(7) **Education.** . . . The time has come when potential parents should be trained for the serious business of marriage, family living, and parenthood. . . . One thing is certain: parents cannot create harmony in the home and personal security in their children if they, themselves, lack the assurance and confidence which comes from knowledge gained in advance of need. School officials, everywhere, and citizens, too, should give active support to the idea of training for parenthood. . . .

Success as a parent involves the expenditure not of money and material advantages, but of one's self; one's time, imagination, skill and effort; one's companionship and counsel; one's faith, patience and love. It involves a knowledge and an acceptance of the obligations of marriage; an understanding of the needs of children, and a willingness to co-operate with schools, churches and civic agencies for their welfare. When we build personal security not alone for our own child but for all children, everywhere, then we shall, indeed, be architects of peace!

Marynia F. Farnham and Ferdinand Lundberg on Modern Woman, the "Lost Sex," 1947

. . . The woman arriving at maturity today does so with certain fixed attitudes derived from her background and training. Her home life, very often, has been distorted. She has enjoyed an education identical with that of her brother. She expects to be allowed to select any kind of work for which she has inclination and training. She also, generally, expects to marry. At any rate, she usually intends to have "a go" at it. Some women expect to stop working when they marry; many others do not. She expects to find sexual gratification and believes in her inalienable right so to do. She is legally free to live and move as she chooses. She may seek divorce if her marriage fails to gratify her. She has access to contraceptive information so that, theoretically, she may control the size and spacing of her family. In very many instances, she owns and disposes of her own property. She has, it appears, her destiny entirely in her own hands.

All of this serves less to clarify and simplify her life than to complicate it with conflict piled on conflict. These conflicts are between her basic needs as a woman and the destiny she has carved out for herself — conflicts between the head and the heart, if you will. . . .

Thus she finds herself squarely in the middle of the most serious kind of divided purpose. If she is to undertake occupation outside her home with any kind of success, it is almost certain in the present day to be time-consuming and energy-demanding. So it is also with the problems she faces in her home. Certainly the tasks of a woman in bearing and educating children as well as maintaining, as best she may, the inner integrity of her home are capable of demanding all her time and best attention. However, she cannot obtain from them, so attenuated are these tasks now, the same sort of community approval and ego-satisfaction that she can from seemingly more challenging occupations which take her outside the home. Inevitably the dilemma has led to one compromise after another which we see exemplified on every hand in the modern woman's adaptation — an uneasy patchwork. . . .

It is becoming unquestionably more and more common for the woman to attempt to combine both home and child care and an outside activity, which is either work or career. Increasing numbers train for professional careers. When these two spheres are combined it is inevitable that one or the other will become of secondary concern and, this being the case, it is certain that the home will take that position. This is true, if only for the practical reason that no one can find and hold remunerative employment where the job itself doesn't take precedence over all other concerns. All sorts of agencies and instrumentalities have therefore been established to make possible the playing of this dual role. These are all in the direction of substitutes for the attention of the mother in the home and they vary from ordinary, untrained domestic service through the more highly trained grades of such service, to the public and private agencies now designed for the care, supervision and emotional untanglement of the children. The day nursery and its more elegant counterpart, the nursery school, are outstanding as the major agencies which make it possible for women to relinquish the care of children still in their infancy.

All these services and facilities produce what appears on the surface to be a smoothly functioning arrangement and one that provides children with obviously highly trained, expert and efficient care as well as with superior training in early skills and techniques and in adaptation to social relations. This surface, however, covers a situation that is by no means so smoothly functioning nor so satisfying either to the child or the woman. She must of necessity be deeply in conflict and only partially satisfied in either direction. Her work develops aggressiveness, which is essentially a denial of her femininity. . . .

Work that entices women out of their homes and provides them with prestige only at the price of feminine relinquishment, involves a response to masculine strivings. The more importance outside work assumes, the more are the masculine components of the woman's nature enhanced and encouraged. In her home and in her relationship to her children, it is imperative that these strivings be at a minimum and that her femininity be available both for her own satisfaction and for the satisfaction of her children and husband. She is, therefore, in the dangerous position of having to live one part of her life on the masculine level, another on the feminine. It is hardly astonishing that few can do so with success. One of these tendencies must of necessity achieve dominance over the other. The plain fact is that increasingly we are observing the masculinization of women and with it enormously dangerous consequences to the home, the children (if any) dependent on it, and to the ability of the woman, as well as her husband, to obtain sexual gratification. . . .

The dominant direction of feminine training and development today . . . discourages just those traits necessary to the attainment of sexual pleasure: receptivity and passiveness, a willingness to accept dependence without fear or resentment, with a deep inwardness and readiness for the final goal of sexual life — impregnation. It doesn't admit of wishes to control or master, to rival or dominate. The woman who is to find true gratification must love and accept her own womanhood as she loves and accepts her husband's manhood. Women's rivalry with men today, and the need to "equal" their accomplishments, engenders all too often anger and resentfulness toward men. Men, challenged, frequently respond in kind. So it is that women envy and feel hostile to men for just the attributes which women themselves require for "success" in the world. The woman's unconscious wish herself to possess the organ upon which she must thus depend militates greatly against her ability to accept its vast power to satisfy her when proffered to her in love.

Many women can find no solution to their dilemma and are defeated in attempts at adaptation. These constitute the array of the sick, unhappy, neurotic, wholly or partly incapable of dealing with life. . . .

It is not only the masculine woman who has met with an unhappy fate in the present situation. There are still many women who succeed in achieving adult life with largely unimpaired feminine strivings, for which home, a husband's love and children are to them the entirely adequate answers. It is their misfortune that they must enter a society in which such attitudes are little appreciated and are attended by many concrete, external penalties. Such women cannot fail to be affected by finding that their traditional activities are held in low esteem and that the woman who voluntarily undertakes them is often deprecated by her more aggressive contemporaries. She may come to believe that her situation is difficult, entailing serious deprivations, as against the more glamorous and exciting life other women seemingly enjoy. She may be set away from the main stream of life, very much in a backwater and fearful lest she lose her ability and talents through disuse and lack of stimulation. She may become sorry for herself and somewhat angered by her situation, gradually developing feelings of discontent and pressure. As her children grow older and require less of her immediate attention, the feelings of loss increase.

. . . In this way she may easily and quickly develop attitudes of discontent and anger injurious to her life adjustment. She may begin to malfunction sexually, her libidinal depths shaken by her ego frustrations.

So it is that society today makes it difficult for a woman to avoid the path leading to discontent and frustration and resultant hostility and destructiveness. Such destructiveness is, unfortunately, not confined in its effects to the woman alone. It reaches into all her relationships and all her functions. As a wife she is not only often ungratified but ungratifying and has, as we have noted, a profoundly disturbing effect upon her husband. Not only does he find himself without the satisfactions of a home directed and cared for by a woman happy in providing affection and devotion, but he is often confronted by circumstances of even more serious import for his own emotional integrity. His wife may be his covert rival, striving to match him in every aspect of their joint undertaking. Instead of supporting and encouraging his manliness and wishes for domination and power, she may thus impose upon him feelings of insufficiency and weakness. Still worse is the effect upon his sexual satisfactions. Where the woman is unable to admit and accept dependence upon her husband as the source of gratification and must carry her rivalry even into the act of love, she will seriously damage his sexual capacity. To be unable to gratify in the sexual act is for a man an intensely humiliating experience; here it is that mastery and domination, the central capacity of the man's sexual nature, must meet acceptance or fail. So it is that by their own character disturbances these women succeed ultimately in depriving themselves of the devotion and power of their husbands and become the instruments of bringing about their own psychic catastrophe.

But no matter how great a woman's masculine strivings, her basic needs make themselves felt and she finds herself facing her fundamental role as wife and mother with a divided mind. Deprived of a rich and creative home in which to find self-expression, she tries desperately to find a compromise. On the one hand she must retain her sources of real instinctual gratification and on the other, find ways of satisfying her need for prestige and esteem. Thus she stands, Janus-faced, drawn in two directions at once, often incapable of ultimate choice and inevitably penalized whatever direction she chooses.

Pauli Murray on Why Negro Girls Stay Single, in *Negro Digest,* 1947

There exists in the United States a system of discrimination based upon sex which I call "Jane Crow" because it is so strikingly similar to "Jim Crow," or prejudice based upon race.

Women still occupy a subordinate position as citizens of the American community, even though they may represent a majority of the potential voting population. The rationalizations upon which this sex prejudice rests are often different from those supporting racial discrimination in label only.

I should like to cite two examples of this prejudice. Harvard University, for three centuries the "prestige" school of presidents, supreme court justices, ambassadors and financiers, still does not permit a woman student to darken the doors of its law school, although I am unaware of any special relation between legal acumen and sex identity. Recently, however, Harvard Law School did weaken to the degree that a Hunter College graduate, Soia Memchikoff, was appointed as a member of the law school faculty.

Secondly, I winced considerably the other day when, upon picking up a copy of Ebony Magazine, a Negro pictorial publication, and seeing a current "spread" on Negro lawyers, I saw the pictures of many personal friends and associates of mine but observed that Negro women lawyers were conspicuous by their absence. . . . I wondered what quirk of the editor's attitude had permitted him or her to ignore the contributions of women attorneys like Edith Alexander and Judge Jane Bolin, just to mention two of our outstanding lawyers who have won their spots unquestionably in the legal profession.

These two "case studies" suggest that despite their numerical size, women in

Excerpted from Pauli Murray, "Why Negro Girls Stay Single," *Negro Digest,* July 1947, pp. 4–8.

the United States and perhaps throughout the world, with rare exceptions, are a minority group and suffer minority status. This minority status operates independently of race, religion or politics.

Every time I begin to bemoan the submerged status of the Negro woman among my white women friends, they hastily assure me that my problems are not unique and that they suffer just as much from "Jane Crow" as I do, particularly when it comes to advancement in their professional endeavors.

Within this framework of "male supremacy" as well as "white supremacy" the Negro woman finds herself at the bottom of the economic and social scale.

She is obviously in a state of revolt. This revolt proceeds in part from the consciousness on the part of the Negro woman that she has been compelled to act as breadwinner and cementer of family relationships in the Negro community since its inception. Historically, few Negro women have belonged to the leisure class, and what few social privileges they now enjoy have very often come "the hard way."

The rebellion against racial and sexual status is felt most keenly among Negro college-trained and professional women. With reference to my own generation, people now in their thirties, it is a matter of history that more Negro women proportionately have availed themselves of higher education than Negro men.

The complete hopelessness and dejection which led Negro boys of my age group to abandon their studies in droves before they completed a high school education or a trade, and to flounder about for years without vocational direction, is one of the tragic sources of frustration to the Negro woman of marriageable age. If professionally trained, she finds a shortage of her educational peers among men in Negro circles. She very often cannot find a mate with whom she can share all the richness of her life in addition to its functional aspects.

Having stayed in school far beyond the period of the average Negro boy, she now emerges with certain educational skills and often has a potential earning power far beyond the range of the majority of available single males — a social handicap if she wants marriage. Men usually shy away from women more highly trained than they are when the question of marriage is involved. It is too great a threat to their security.

Since the chances of the Negro trained woman for economic security are necessarily precarious because of the general underprivileged economic status of the Negro minority, in her relationship to the Negro male she can hope for little beyond emotional security.

But here again she is defeated. Emotional security arises from mature relationships among free and uninhibited individuals. The American Negro male is not prepared to offer emotional security because he has rarely, if ever, known it himself. His own emotional balance is that of a blindfolded tightrope walker before a jeering crowd. His submerged status in American life places unnatural stresses and strains upon his already inadequate equipment inherited from an immature democracy.

Our general mis-education of the sexes and our outmoded social tabus have helped to form rigid moulds into which the sexes are poured and which determine in advance the role men and women are to play in community life. Men are expected to act as if they are the lords of creation, the breadwinners and the warriors of our time and of all time. They play the role with varying degrees of ham-acting and success. . . .

The discerning eye soon discovers that many Negro men are well marked products of this sex mis-education. Charming individual exceptions appear here and there, but they are few. The Negro man who attempts to play the role of the dominant sex in a setting where the Negro woman has partially emancipated herself by dint of hard labor is face to face with emotional disaster. Particularly is this true in the case of the trained Negro woman who has become perhaps the most aggressive of the human species.

This impending emotional disaster is born of the contradictions in the life of the Negro male. He is the victim of constant frustration in his role as a male because socially he is subordinate to the white woman although he is trained to act as a member of the dominant sex. He is required to fit his human emotions into a racially determined pattern which may have nothing to do with his desires.

There is no earthly reason why a Negro man should not admire in a clean and healthy sort of way physical beauty, whether the bearer of the beauty be a Nordic Blonde or a West Indian Bronze. There is no reason why the Negro man today should find the white woman less attractive than did his white slave-owning ancestor find the African slavewoman desirable. Yet what sister of a Negro boy or man today does not know the family terror at the thought that some unguarded and unconscious look or gesture, though completely spontaneous and meaningless, may lead straight to ostracism, the faggot or the lynchman's noose!

The frustrations implicit in being a Negro are not only catastrophic to the Negro male's emotions, but lead him often to vent his resentments upon the Negro woman who may become his sex partner. The situation may be described in the homely saying, "Pa beats Ma, Ma beats me, and I beat hell out of the cat." Here, the Negro woman is without doubt "the cat."

On top of these difficulties, census figures suggest an unbalance between the sexes within racial groupings. Negro females far outnumber Negro males.

If the emotional security of the Negro woman depends upon proper mating and marriage, she is confronted with the inexorable logic of numbers which demands that she find a mate elsewhere than among Negro males, unless the American society which enforces bi-racialism also permits legal racial polygamy. From a biological and functional point of view, the logical solution to a shortage of available Negro males would be that Negro women find their mates in other ethnic groups.

This alternative faces the practical difficulty that there is a shortage of available males of marriageable age today in all groups. Secondly, to consciously seek interracial marriage would be denounced as sheer "treason" in the eyes of the "no social equality" advocates throughout the country. Yet, what other alternatives are open?

On the other hand, our racial stockades being what they are, Negro men who are in the market for Negro wives are not required to face honest and above-board competition from white members of their sex. Few white men are either mature or courageous enough to lift their emotional attractions for Negro women outside of the red light districts within the ghetto or the sub-rosa arrangements outside the ghetto into the clean light of healthy sex relationships looking toward legal marriage.

The Negro male, therefore, not only has no outside stimulus which operates to force him to improve his relationships with the Negro woman, but more damning, he stores up huge resentments against his rival, the white male who "slinks across the line" after dark, and very often turns this resentment upon himself and the Negro woman.

All of this contributes to a Jungle of human relationships, aggravates among Negroes the alienation of the sexes, intensifies homosexuality and often results in a rising incidence of crimes of passion, broken homes and divorces.

The problem of the Negro male cannot be solved within the Negro group unless it is being resolved simultaneously in the larger society. Readers of Negro periodicals will recall that Miss Almena Davis, editor of the Los Angeles Tribune, attempted more than a year ago to articulate the resentment of the Negro woman against the exposed position in which she finds herself by directing a critical editorial toward the sex habits of the Negro male. She won the Willkie Award in Journalism for her pains but incurred the wrath of almost every Negro male journalist in the country. Ann Petry added another fragment to the growing literature of revolt "from way down under," with her recent article, "What's Wrong With Negro Men," in NEGRO DIGEST. I have now jumped into the arena with both feet. What I think Almena Davis, Ann Petry and Pauli Murray are trying to say from their varied approaches is this:

We desire that the Negro male accept the Negro female as his equal and treat her accordingly and that he cease his ruthless aggression upon her and his emotional exploitation of her made possible by her admittedly inferior position as a social human being in the United States. That he strive for emotional maturity himself and see the Negro woman as a personality, an individual with infinite potentialities, and that in turn he require from the Negro woman an equal maturity and acceptance of responsibility in human relationships. That he maintain the dignity and respect for human personality with relation to the Negro woman in the sanctity of the marital chamber which he is expected to show in the law office or other professional set-up.

Despite the numerous limitations forced upon Negro men and women by our society, nevertheless certain improvements between the sexes are desirable and can be achieved.

A Letter to the Editor of *The Ladder* from an African-American Lesbian, 1957

"Please find enclosed a money order for $2.00. I should like to receive as many of your back issues as that amount will cover. In the event $2.00 is in excess of the cost of six issues — well, fine. Those few cents may stand as a mere downpayment toward sizeable (for me, that is) donations I know already that I shall be sending to you.

"I hope you are somewhat interested in off-the-top-of-the-head reactions from across the country because I would like to offer a few by way of the following:

"(1) I'm glad as heck that you exist. You are obviously serious people and I feel that women, without wishing to foster any strict *separatist* notions, homo or

L.H.N., *The Ladder*, vol. 1, no. 8 (May 1957): 26.

A couple at a New Orleans lesbian bar in the early 1950s. Lesbians were shunned and misunderstood by heterosexuals in the postwar era. Nonetheless, they constructed a number of viable subcultures. Working-class and younger lesbians like the ones pictured here developed a subculture that centered around gay bars and the adoption of butch/femme roles. In contrast, middle-class and older lesbians socialized in their homes, wore conservative feminine attire, and blamed women who adopted butch/femme roles for helping to create stereotypes that hurt lesbians. Middle-class lesbians also founded the Daughters of Bilitis, an organization whose official magazine, *The Ladder,* tried to prove that lesbians were "normal" women who deserved acceptance by mainstream America.

hetero, indeed have a need for their own publications and organizations. Our problems, our experiences as women are profoundly unique as compared to the other half of the human race. Women, like other oppressed groups of one kind or another, have particularly had to pay a price for the intellectual impoverishment that the second class status imposed on us for centuries created and sustained. Thus, I feel that THE LADDER is a fine, elementary step in a rewarding direction.

"(2) Rightly or wrongly (in view of some of the thought provoking discussions I have seen elsewhere in a homosexual publication) I could not help but be encouraged and relieved by one of the almost subsidiary points under Point I of your declaration of purpose, '(to advocate) a mode of behaviour and dress acceptable to society.' As one raised in a cultural experience (I am a Negro) where those within were and are forever lecturing to their fellows about how to appear acceptable to the dominant social group, I know something about the shallowness of such a view as an end in itself.

"The most splendid argument is simple and to the point, Ralph Bunche, with all his clean fingernails, degrees, and, of course, undeniable service to the human race, could still be insulted, denied a hotel room or meal in many parts of our country. (Not to mention the possibility of being lynched on a lonely Georgia road for perhaps having demanded a glass of water in the wrong place.)

"What ought to be clear is that one is oppressed or discriminated against because one is different, not 'wrong' or 'bad' somehow. This is perhaps the bitterest of the entire pill. HOWEVER, as a matter of facility, of expediency, one has to take a critical view of revolutionary attitudes which in spite of the BASIC truth I have mentioned above, may tend to aggravate the problems of a group.

"I have long since passed that period when I felt personal discomfort at the sight of an ill-dressed or illiterate Negro. Social awareness has taught me where to lay the blame. Someday, I expect, the 'discreet' Lesbian will not turn her head on the streets at the sight of the 'butch' strolling hand in hand with her friend in their trousers and definitive haircuts. But for the moment, it still disturbs. It creates an impossible area for discussion with one's most enlightened (to use a hopeful term) heterosexual friends. Thus, I agree with the inclusion of that point in your declaration to the degree of wanting to comment on it.

"(3) I am impressed by the general tone of your articles. The most serious fault being at this juncture that there simply is too little.

"(4) Would it be presumptuous or far-fetched to suggest that you try for some overseas communications? One hears so much of publications and organizations devoted to homosexuality and homosexuals in Europe; but as far as I can gather these seem to lean heavily toward male questions and interests.

"Just a little afterthought: considering Mattachine; Bilitis, ONE; all seem to be cropping up on the West Coast rather than here where a vigorous and active gay set almost bump one another off the streets — what is it in the air out there? Pioneers still? Or a tougher circumstance which inspires battle? Would like to hear speculation, light-hearted or otherwise."

L.H.N., New York, N.Y.

Extracts from *The Ladder* Survey, "Why Am I a Lesbian?", 1960

Statement #1

Personally, I do not believe there is any "cause" of Lesbian or homosexual personalities or character traits . . . any more than one can say there is a "cause" for the behaviour and personality of people elsewhere on the emotional scale — any single cause or identifiable group of causes, that is. I'm inclined to agree with a wise, travelled and psychologically subtle man I know who once said in a lecture: "There is no such thing, basically, as homosexuality . . . only sexuality. How it will be expressed is a complex matter of mores, accident, social pressures and attitudes, convenience, habit, glandular activity, and much more, determinable and not determinable."

"Why Am I a Lesbian?" *The Ladder,* vol. 4, no. 9 (June 1960): 20–24.

He might have added that much of it is also semantic. A young man or woman who for one reason or another, or no particular reason, happens to become aware of affection or sexual desire in relation to his or her own sex is immediately labeled — or self-labeled — homo. We are all so hypnotised by labels these days that if you pin one on a person he starts acting and feeling the stereotypes of the label. Gets stuck. Actually, any one form of sexual expression may constitute repression. In a society that was less sexually puritanical than ours I feel sure we should find the sane persons spontaneously indulging in a far wider range of sexual play all along the possible scale. If this were possible, and the guilt removed, we'd probably have fewer neurotic personalities; also fewer rigidly heterosexual — or homosexual — personalities.

Statement #2

I'm not sure of the causes — who is? I'm much more sure that some things often given as causes of homosexuality are *not true* for my case.

1. Was I rejected by my parents or given inadequate love? *No.* Neither parent rejected me; and mother, who raised me (along with grandparents), almost smothered me with excessive love and care.
2. Did my family want a boy, or try to raise me as one? No! They wanted a girl, and did everything within their power to try to make me "feminine." It never worked — I disliked frilly clothes, dolls, and the rest. I wanted to play with electric trains (which I never got), and climb trees (which I wasn't allowed to). The more they tried to enforce their pattern on me the more I rebelled against it.
3. Was I sheltered from contact with boys during adolescence, or made by parents to feel that sex and marriage were undesirable? No. Mother tried her best to interest me in these things (despite her own unhappy marriage). It didn't take.
4. Was I seduced into homosexuality by another lesbian? No! I wish I had been — it might have spared me many lonely years. My love objects were for years heterosexual women, and for too many years no overt action took place. When overt action did take place at last with one of them — in my late twenties — I did the initiating myself, completely "uninitiated" as I was.

Then, do I think my lesbianism is innate? No, not directly. My guess is as follows:

First, there was an indirect genetic influence through my having been born with a temperament that was different from the other women of my family and culture-group, and more like that of the men. This didn't make me lesbian, but did have a lot to do with my self-conceptions. The attempt to thwart my interests, likes and dislikes only intensified my dissatisfaction at my sex role.

Second, as an infant and young child, I never learned to love men. The closest man in the family (my father) was not himself an object of love by either my mother, myself (as far as I can remember), or anyone else in the family in which I grew up — which was mother's family. After the first four years, he was not present at all. There was probably a strong early attachment to mother, as the "books" suggest.

Both these factors probably reinforced each other, and stamped me so early in life and so indelibly that it might just as well have been "innate."

Statement #3

I do not subscribe to the myth of "the well of loneliness" that a lesbian is born that way.

I do subscribe to the theory of the Kinsey group, found on page 447 of "Sexual Behavior in the Human Female":

> The inherent physiologic capacity of an animal to respond to any sufficient stimulus, seems, then, the basic explanation of the fact that some individuals respond to stimuli originating in other individuals of their own sex — and it appears to indicate that every individual could so respond if the opportunity offered and one were not conditioned against making such responses. . . .

I am a woman — physically and emotionally. I have the capacity to respond sexually either to a member of my own sex or of the opposite sex. I have been a wife and mother. But I am a lesbian by choice. The basic reason for this choice I believe is the freedom of expression of the personality with its many-faceted manifestations. Oddly enough, as a lesbian I have lifted the veil of repression imposed by society. As a lesbian I may be myself.

In discussions of homosexuality stress is always placed on the sexual act. Seldom is there any mention of the fulfillment of a lasting lesbian liaison based on love, understanding and companionship. Any consideration of lesbianism must necessarily recognize the fact that it is a way of life — the emotional, physical and spiritual expression of the love of one woman for another.

Statement #4

Reasons for lesbianism as stated by many authorities include:

Fear of pregnancy or venereal disease

Heterosexual trauma or disappointment

Society's heterosexual taboos

Seeing parents in the sex act

Seduction by older females

Masturbation

Endocrine imbalance

Penis envy and castration complex

Father fixation or hatred toward mother

Mother fixation

Defense against or flight from incestuous desires

These are cited as conditioning factors, and we have been "conditioned" to believe that any or all of these factors in the background of a young woman may lead her into lesbianism. If this is true, then I must ask why heterosexual women (whose backgrounds also have included many of the above factors) did not develop into lesbians? Or is there perhaps a predisposition to homosexuality which, when one or more of these conditioning factors is added, results in lesbianism?

I would suspect that a more likely factor leading to lesbianism would be the protest against domination by the male and the inability of the lesbian to emulate the female role as set forth by society. There would seem to be a withdrawal from the heterosexual market-place of glamour and emphasis placed rather upon the independence of the individual and the development of the full personality.

Joyce Johnson On Obtaining an Illegal Abortion, New York City, 1955

In June I didn't get my period. First it was a little late, and then a lot, but I still thought it would come anyway, and I waited, thinking I felt it sometimes. But finally it didn't come. A tangible, unbelievable fact, like sealed doom.

I was going to have a baby. But it was impossible for me to have a baby. . . .

The father was a child of my own age — a wrecked boy I'd known from Columbia who already had a drinking problem and lived, doing nothing, with his parents in Connecticut. I didn't love this boy. Sometimes you went to bed with people almost by mistake, at the end of late, shapeless nights when you'd stayed up so long it almost didn't matter — the thing was, not to go home. Such nights lacked premeditation, so you couldn't be very careful; you counted on a stranger's carefulness. The boy promised to pull out before the danger — but he didn't. And although I could have reminded him of his promise in time, I didn't do that either, remembering too late it was the middle of the month in a bedroom on East Ninety-sixth Street that smelled of smoke and soiled clothing, with leftover voices from that night's party outside the closed door.

I'd gotten a therapist by then — a $7.50 man, a rejected boyfriend of the woman whose apartment I was living in. I told him my problem. "I see," he said, rubbing his large chin, staring out over Central Park West.

There was a box of Kleenex on the small Danish-modern table near my head. He had pointedly placed boxes of tissues in several locations in his office. But I never cried.

I explained to this therapist why I didn't see how I could become a mother. Aside from being twenty years old, I lived on fifty dollars a week and had cut myself off from my family. I said I would rather die. And then I asked him what Elise had told me to: "Could you get me a therapeutic abortion?" (I'd never heard the term before she explained what it meant.)

"Oh, I wouldn't even try," he said.

I hadn't thought he wouldn't try.

Life was considered sacred. But independence could be punishable by death. The punishment for sex was, appropriately, sexual.

There were women in those days who kept slips of paper, like talismans to ward off disaster, on which were written the names of doctors who would perform illegal abortions. Neither Elise nor I knew any of these women. You had to ask around. You asked friends and they asked friends, and the ripples of asking people widened until some person whose face you might never see gave over the secret information that could save you. This could take time, and you only had two months, they said, and you'd lost one month anyway, through not being sure.

The therapist called my roommate, got from her the name of the boy who had made me pregnant. He called the boy and threatened to disclose the whole matter to his parents unless the boy came up with the money for an illegal abortion. The boy called me, drunk and wild with fear. I hadn't expected anything of this boy except one thing — that when I had an abortion he'd go there with me; there had to be someone with you, I felt, that you knew. But as for blaming this boy — I didn't. I knew I had somehow let this happen to me. There had been a moment in that bedroom on Ninety-sixth Street, a moment of blank suspension, of not caring whether I lived or died. It seemed important to continue to see this moment very clearly. I knew the boy wouldn't come with me now.

I went to see the therapist one last time to tell him he had done something terribly wrong.

"Yes," he admitted, looking sheepish. "I've probably made a mistake."

I said, "I'm never coming back. I owe you thirty-seven fifty. Try and get it."

Someone finally came up with a person who knew a certain doctor in Canarsie. If you called this person at the advertising agency where he worked, he wouldn't give you the doctor's name — he'd ask you if you wanted to have a drink with him in the Rainbow Room, and over martinis he might agree to escort you out to see the doctor. This person wasn't a great humanitarian; he was a young man who had a weird hobby — taking girls to get abortions. He'd ask you if you wanted to recuperate afterward at his house on Fire Island. You were advised to say no.

Blind dates were a popular social form of the fifties. As I sat in the cocktail lounge of the Rainbow Room, staring through the glass doors at crew-cutted young men in seersucker suits who came off the elevator lacking the red bow tie I'd been told to watch out for, I realized that despite the moment in the bedroom, I probably didn't want to die, since I seemed to be going to an enormous amount of effort to remain living. If it happened that I died after all, it would be an accident.

He turned up a half-hour late in his blue and white stripes. "Why, you're pretty," he said, pleased. He told me he liked blondes. He made a phone call after we had our drinks, and came back to the table to say the doctor would see us that night. "I hope you don't have anything lined up," he said.

He offered me sticks of Wrigley spearmint chewing gum on the BMT to Canarsie. People in jokes sometimes came from there, but I'd never been to that part of Brooklyn in my life.

Canarsie was rows of small brick houses with cement stoops and yards filled with wash and plaster saints. Boys were playing stickball in the dusk. You could disappear into Canarsie.

The doctor seemed angry that we had come, but he led us into his house after we rang the bell, and switched on a light in his waiting room. He was fat, with a lot of wiry grey hair on his forearms; a white shirt wet and rumpled with perspiration stretched over his belly. The room looked like a room in which only the very poor would ever wait. There were diplomas on the walls, framed behind dusty glass; I tried to read the Latin. He glared at me and said he wanted me to know he did tonsillectomies. To do "the other" — he didn't say *abortions* — disgusted him. I made efforts to nod politely.

My escort spoke up and said, "How about next week?"

"All right. Wednesday."

I felt panic at the thought of Wednesday. What if my mother called the office and found out I was sick, and came running over to the apartment? "No," I said, "Friday. It has to be Friday."

"Friday will cost you extra," the doctor said. . . .

I'd managed to borrow the five hundred dollars from a friend in her late twenties, who'd borrowed it from a wealthy married man who was her lover. With the cash in a sealed envelope in my purse, I stood for an hour that Friday morning in front of a cigar store on Fourteenth Street, waiting for the young advertising executive. I got awfully scared that he wouldn't come. Could I find the doctor's house myself in those rows of nearly identical houses?

There was a haze over Fourteenth Street that made even the heat seem grey. I stared across the street at Klein's Department Store, where my mother had taken me shopping for bargains, and imagined myself dying a few hours later with the sign KLEIN'S the last thing that flashed through my consciousness.

But finally the young man did materialize out of a cab. "Sorry to have kept you waiting." He'd brought some back issues of *The New Yorker,* and planned to catch up on his reading during the operation.

Upstairs in Canarsie, the doctor who did tonsillectomies had a room where he only did abortions. A freshly painted room where every surface was covered with white towels. He himself put on a mask and a white surgeon's gown. It was as if all that white was the color of his fear.

"Leave on the shoes!" he barked as I climbed up on his table almost fully clothed. Was I expected to make a run for it if the police rang his doorbell in the middle of the operation? He yelled at me to do this and do that, and it sent him into a rage that my legs were shaking, so how could he do what he had to do? But if I didn't want him to do it, that was all right with him. I said I wanted him to do it. I was crying. But he wouldn't take the money until after he'd given me the local anesthetic. He gave me one minute to change my mind before he handed me my purse.

The whole thing took two hours, but it seemed much longer through the pain. I had the impression that this doctor in all his fear was being extremely careful, that I was even lucky to have found him. He gave me pills when it was over, and told me I could call him only if anything went wrong. "But don't ever let me catch you back here again, young lady!"

I staggered down the cement steps of his house with my life. It was noon in Canarsie, an ordinary day in July. My escort was saying he thought it would be hard to find a cab, we should walk in the direction of the subway. On a street full of shops, I leaned against the window of a supermarket until he flagged one down. Color seemed to have come back into the world. Housewives passed in floral nylon dresses; diamonds of sunlight glinted off the windshields of cars.

On the cab ride across the Manhattan Bridge, the young man from the ad agency placed his hand on my shoulder. "I have this house out on Fire Island," he began. "I thought that this weekend — "

"No thanks," I said. "I'll be okay in the city."

He removed his hand, and asked if I'd drop him off at his office — "unless you mind going home alone."

I said I'd get there by myself.

❋ *E S S A Y S*

In the first essay, Elaine Tyler May of the University of Minnesota examines the causes and implications of the postwar baby boom. She suggests that the anxieties of the Cold War, amplified and embellished in the popular media, produced a true "reproductive consensus"; women embraced a domestic feminine ideal because the culture's values precluded other options. In sharp disagreement with May, Joanne Meyerowitz of the University of Cincinnati contends that America's postwar popular media delivered "multiple messages" to women by simultaneously glorifying and subverting domesticity. The last essay, by Donna Penn, examines the meanings of lesbianism in postwar America. While Penn acknowledges the predominance of a psychiatric and social discourse that condemned lesbians because of their putative rejection of femininity, she finds evidence of a lesbian subculture in which "butch" women played an important role. Taken together, these essays offer a number of ways of looking at the construction of female identity in the postwar era.

The Reproductive Consensus in the Postwar Era

ELAINE TYLER MAY

Procreation in the cold war era took on almost mythic proportions. . . . Children were a "defense — an impregnable bulwark" against the terrors of the age. For the nation, the next generation symbolized hope for the future. But for individuals, parenthood was much more than a duty to posterity; the joys of raising children would compensate for the thwarted expectations in other areas of their lives. For men who were frustrated at work, for women who were bored at home, and for both who were dissatisfied with the unfulfilled promise of sexual excitement, children might fill the void. Through children, men and women could set aside the difficulties of their sexual relationships and celebrate the procreative results. In so doing, they also demonstrated their loyalty to national goals by having as many children as they could "raise right and educate and be a benefit to the world," in the words of one postwar father. Rather than representing a retreat into private life, procreation was one way to express civic values. . . .

The baby boom was not the result of the return to peace, or of births to older parents postponed because of the war. Rather, the baby boom began *during* the war and continued afterward because younger couples were having babies earlier. Part of the boom can be explained by the drop in the marriage age, which was encouraged by sexual pressures. But a lower marriage age would not necessarily result in a higher birthrate. . . . Demographers have shown that the baby boom did not result from women suddenly having a huge number of children; the number of children per family went up modestly. Women coming of age in the thirties had an average of 2.4 children; those who reached adulthood in the fifties gave birth to an average of 3.2 children. What made the baby boom happen was that *everyone* was doing it — and at the same time. . . .

Along with the baby boom came an intense and widespread endorsement of pronatalism — the belief in the positive value of having several children. A major study conducted in 1957 found that most Americans believed that parenthood was the route to happiness. Childlessness was considered deviant, selfish, and pitiable. Twenty years later, these pronatal norms began to break up. But in the 1940s and 1950s, nearly everyone believed that family togetherness, focused on children, was the mark of a successful and wholesome personal life. One study of 900 wives in the 1950s found that the desire for children was second only to companionship in stated marriage goals.

In spite of these widespread beliefs, and the fact that the baby boom was well under way, numerous postwar observers expressed fears that women might be inclined to shirk their maternal role — to the nation's detriment, as well as to their own. J. Edgar Hoover, director of the Federal Bureau of Investigation, spoke to "homemakers and mothers" about their unique role in fighting "the twin enemies of freedom — crime and communism." Hoover was careful to address these housewives as "'career' women. . . . I say 'career' women because I feel there are no careers so important as those of homemaker and mother." Many agreed with Hoover that women should focus their talents and expertise on the home, and argued that the new opportunities for education and employment would reduce a woman's reproductive potential. . . .

As late as 1956 — the peak of the baby boom — *U.S. News and World Report* echoed this concern: "America's college women are marrying earlier than they did, having more children." Nevertheless, the article continued with the misperception that college-educated women "are failing to keep up with the baby boom. It is the relatively uneducated women who keep the U.S. population on the rise." The report was inaccurate. Although women with less education continued to have a higher overall birthrate, as had been the case for decades, the increase in the birthrate among these women during the baby-boom years was relatively modest. Actually, the sharpest increase in the birthrate was among the most highly educated women. Nevertheless, distorted observations like these reports suggested that "inferior" groups were overpopulating the nation. . . .

Of course, idealized motherhood was nothing new in the United States. It had its heyday in the nineteenth century when Victorian values were at their zenith. During that era, the declining birthrate contributed to the idealization of motherhood, for women could then spend more time and energy nurturing each child. In the twentieth century, the Victorian notions of motherhood were recast in the form of powerful sentiments encouraging women to have more, rather than fewer, babies.

This new glorification of motherhood reflected the twentieth-century idea of the sexualized home.

The notion that motherhood was the ultimate fulfillment of female sexuality surfaced suddenly and visibly in the media at the beginning of World War II. Female film celebrities began to offer a new maternal model for identification and emulation. In mass circulation magazines such as *Photoplay,* the shift in the portrayal of female stars was dramatic. Celebrities who were noted for their erotic appeal were suddenly pictured as contented mothers, nestled comfortably in their ranch-style suburban homes with their husbands and children. The most striking thing about the new image of women was the sudden introduction of babies. While children almost never appeared in stories or photographs of female stars in the 1930s, they became featured along with their famous moms in the war years.

One issue of *Photoplay* in 1940 ran a story headlined, "Hollywood Birth Rate — Going Up! A Bumper Crop of Babies Brings a Message of Renewed Faith and Courage." By 1943, babies had taken center stage. Significantly, it was the sex symbols who were now featured as mothers. "Hollywood's Newest Pin-up Girl" was none other than the infant of Lana Turner, noted World War II "pin-up" herself. The article accompanying the picture stated approvingly that Lana Turner was giving up her film career to raise her daughter, suggesting that her sexual energy and her ambition now found fulfillment through motherhood. Joan Crawford, featured in the 1930s for her independence and ambition, became "another incredibly devoted and capable mother . . . Every time she talked of her children I knew a sense of unreality. . . . It is a wonderful thing that these glamor girls insist upon being mothers." . . . The message in the popular culture was clear: motherhood was the ultimate fulfillment of female sexuality and the primary source of a woman's identity. . . .

In 1941, as the depression gave way to wartime and the declining marriage rate and birthrate began to turn around, *Penny Serenade* captivated film audiences around the country. Virtually every anxiety of the early 1940s appears in this film, with one solution offered to all the problems of the age: children. The film begins with Roger (Cary Grant), the restless newspaperman, wooing Julie (Irene Dunne), a young working woman. The night before the hero is transferred overseas (not to war but to become a foreign correspondent in Japan), the couple wed. Three months later, Julie joins Roger in Tokyo, where he has leased a luxurious house with Japanese servants (who have three cherubic children). Julie tells Roger she is pregnant, obviously since their wedding night. For Julie, it is a dream come true, but she worries about Roger's reckless extravagance. With the depression fresh in the mind of the audience, Julie chastises Roger for giving up a steady job to chase a dream of owning his own newspaper, and for buying her fancy clothes and planning an international vacation when they should be saving for the child. But all the plans are thwarted when an earthquake strikes, causing Julie to miscarry and rendering her permanently infertile. When Roger promises to give up his foolish ways and to settle down in a nice home of their own, Julie tells him that nothing matters to her anymore, since "the only thing that would have made me happy I can't have."

. . . Happiness comes their way when they adopt a baby daughter. Long scenes focus on the mundane routines of feeding, diapering, and bathing the baby, with endless close-up shots of the face of the angelic girl. . . . But the joy does not last. Just after the child enters school, she becomes ill and dies. We never see the dying child, only the miserable parents whose meaning in life, and in their relationship, have been destroyed. Roger withdraws into silence, and Julie prepares to leave. Just as Julie heads out the door, the phone rings. It is the adoption agency, with another child for them. Instantly the two burst into smiles and embrace. They will have another chance to renew their purpose in life and to find meaning in their marriage.

Penny Serenade won an oscar nomination for Cary Grant and for the writers of the screenplay, Garson Kanin and Ruth Gordon. It was an ideal film to inaugurate the 1940s. Like the hero, men would need to accept positions of subordination in large organizations rather than risk insecurity by going into business for themselves. Compensation for the loss of independence and creativity would be provided in the family, where fatherhood gave life meaning. The arrival of the child tamed the husband's extravagance and recklessness, making him a responsible provider. For the woman, the child meant everything. Without the child, even the marriage was worthless. . . .

Fatherhood became a new badge of masculinity and meaning for the postwar man, and Father's Day a holiday of major significance. Men began attending classes on marriage and family in unprecedented numbers. In 1954, *Life* announced "the domestication of the American male." Fatherhood was important not just to give meaning to men's lives, but to counteract the overabundance of maternal care. Although mothers were, of course, expected to devote themselves full-time to their children, excessive mothering posed dangers that children would become too accustomed to and dependent on female attention. The unhappy result would be "sissies," who were allegedly likely to become homosexuals, "perverts," and dupes of the communists. Fathers had to make sure this would not happen to their sons. "Being a real father is not 'sissy' business," a male psychiatrist wrote in *Parents Magazine* in 1947. "It is an occupation . . . the most important occupation in the world."

The outpouring of attention to fatherhood in the popular media belies an undercurrent of uncertainty: were fathers really involved in childrearing? A writer in *Better Homes and Gardens* asked, "Are we staking our future on a crop of sissies? . . . You have a horror of seeing your son a pantywaist, but he won't get red blood and self reliance if you leave the whole job of making a he-man of him to his mother." The author recounted an incident in which a well-meaning mother tried to stop her small son from a harmless frolic. Her husband restrained her gently, saying, "Let him go, he'll be all right." The author explained that the mother "was exercising a mother's perfectly normal and necessary instinct to protect her children from harm," but the father "knew that a boy has to have chances to try things on his own, to go off on new adventures. He understood that it is a father's job to encourage his son to adventure." Even in parenting, strict gender roles applied: it was as inappropriate for the man to protect the child as for the wife to encourage the adventure. . . .

Given the strong connections among female sexuality, marriage, and motherhood, one might expect the birth control movement to have withered during these years. On the contrary, the movement gained momentum. Under the leadership of Margaret Sanger, birth control had gained a significant amount of liberal support during the twenties and thirties, with roots in feminism and socialism. The number of birth control clinics in the nation grew from 55 in 1930 to over 800 in 1942. In 1942, the Birth Control Federation of America changed its name to the Planned Parenthood Federation of America (PPFA), signaling a major shift in the movement's direction. New goals included the strengthening of the family through the liberation of female sexuality in marriage. . . . By eliminating the fear of pregnancy, birth control would contribute to women's sexual satisfaction and would tame and channel the power of female sexuality into rationally planned families.

The effect of the new direction was to bring contraception under professional control, making birth control devices more widely available and ultimately more effective. Most of all, PPFA gave the birth control movement "a clean image," emphasizing not women's rights, individual freedom, or sexuality, but, as *Scientific American* noted, "the need for individual couples to plan their families and for nations to plan their populations." . . .

Historian James Reed showed how the major funding for research that ultimately led to the development of intrauterine devices and oral contraceptives resulted directly from cold war concerns: "Nations newly liberated from colonial status wanted to share the prosperity of the West. Failure to develop their economies would lead to more bitter internal divisions and rejection of Western alliances in favor of communist models of development. Thus, political stability depended on rapid economic development and that development in turn could only succeed if the rate of population growth did not eat up the capital needed to finance development." The anticommunist thrust of the funding for contraceptive research was obvious at the time. The Hugh More Fund distributed a pamphlet, frequently reprinted through the fifties and early sixties, entitled *The Population Bomb.* It claimed, "There will be 300 million more mouths to feed in the world four years from now — most of them hungry. Hunger brings turmoil — and turmoil, as we have learned, creates the atmosphere in which the communists seek to conquer the earth."

Scientific, rational procreation at home and abroad fit the needs of the cold war and justified the acceptance of contraception by many liberal institutions. Throughout the 1950s, religious groups, with the notable exception of the Catholic Church, began to sanction birth control for family planning. . . .

By 1961, the National Council of Churches of Christ had approved the use of birth control devices. Nonorthodox Protestant and Jewish organizations, according to one study, moved "from uncompromising hostility to birth control to fervid endorsement of its use, even making it a moral obligation to control family size." The medical establishment concurred. At the same time, legislatures were loosening their restrictions on birth control. Before the war, most states banned the dissemination of contraceptive information and materials, even for doctors. But by the late 1950s, only two states, Connecticut and Massachusetts, still had these statutes on the books. Within the space of a few decades, major institutions shifted their perceptions of birth control from a threat to the social order to a positive tool for the nation's benefit. Throughout the 1950s, proponents of contraception continued to promote it as a means of controlling fertility abroad and spacing children at home.

Increased availability and legitimation led to the widespread use of birth control devices among married couples. American society was certainly ready to accept birth control as a means of improving marital sex and family planning. But it was not ready to accept its potential for liberating sex outside marriage or for liberating women from childbearing to enable them to pursue careers outside the home. As a result, contraception in the postwar years encouraged scientific family planning, rather than premarital sexual experimentation or alternatives to motherhood for women. American public opinion, legislative bodies, and the medical establishment all did their part to make sure that the birth control technology would encourage marriage and family life. . . .

Unlike contraceptives, which were promoted as a means of strengthening the family, abortion was considered a threat to sexual morality and family life. While contraception was the reward for the virtuous, abortion was the punishment for the immoral. . . . Legal abortions had been available for several decades at the discretion of physicians, but they became more difficult to obtain in the 1940s and 1950s. "Therapeutic" abortions could be performed legally in hospitals only if the physicians decided that continuing the pregnancy would present a danger to the life or health of the woman, and criteria were haphazard and arbitrary. In most states, physicians were able to interpret the danger as they saw fit, and some women were able to have safe operations. Legal abortions, however, accounted for only part of the terminated pregnancies. A thriving underground business provided illegal and often dangerous abortions to an estimated 250,000 to 1 million women each year during the postwar years. These illegal abortions were also responsible for an estimated 40 percent of all maternal deaths. . . . A few voices called for legalized abortion, but they were faint compared to the roar that condemned the practice. The weight of public opinion was on the side of reproduction: women who have sex should be married, and married women should have babies. Medical advances in contraception might assist that effort, but abortion represented a threat to the family planning ideal. . . .

The rising birthrate, then, was not just a demographic phenomenon. It was the result of a fully articulated baby-boom ideology that found expression in Hollywood, in the political culture, in the prescriptive literature, and in the thoughts and aspirations of women and men at the time. Postwar Americans wholeheartedly endorsed this reproductive consensus. It fit their belief in abundance, progress, and productivity. As one man declared in 1955, "I'd like six kids . . . it just seems like a minimum production goal." Although many people experienced confusion and discord over sexuality, most had the same procreative ideals and followed the same procreative behavior. They used contraception, spaced their children, and created large families. . . .

Competing Images of Women in Postwar Mass Culture

JOANNE MEYEROWITZ

In 1963 Betty Friedan published *The Feminine Mystique,* an instant best seller. Friedan argued, often brilliantly, that American women, especially suburban women, suffered from deep discontent. In the postwar era, she wrote, journalists, educators, advertisers, and social scientists had pulled women into the home with an ideological stranglehold, the "feminine mystique." This repressive "image" held that women

Joanne Meyerowitz, "Beyond the Feminine Mystique: A Reassessment of Postwar Mass Culture, 1946–1958," *Journal of American History,* vol. 79, no. 4 (March 1993). Reprinted by permission of the Organization of American Historians.

could "find fulfillment only in sexual passivity, male domination, and nurturing maternal love." It denied "women careers or any commitment outside the home" and "narrowed woman's world down to the home, cut her role back to housewife." In Friedan's formulation, the writers and editors of mass-circulation magazines, especially women's magazines, were the "Frankensteins" who had created this "feminine monster." In her defense of women, Friedan did not choose a typical liberal feminist language of rights, equality, or even justice. Influenced by the new human potential psychology, she argued instead that full-time domesticity stunted women and denied their "basic human need to grow." For Friedan, women and men found personal identity and fulfillment through individual achievement, most notably through careers. Without such growth, she claimed, women would remain unfulfilled and unhappy, and children would suffer at the hands of neurotic mothers.

The Feminine Mystique had an indisputable impact. Hundreds of women have testified that the book changed their lives, and historical accounts often credit it with launching the recent feminist movement. But the book has also had other kinds of historical impact. For a journalistic exposé, Friedan's work has had a surprisingly strong influence on historiography. In fact, since Friedan published *The Feminine Mystique,* historians of American women have adopted wholesale her version of the postwar ideology. While many historians question Friedan's homogenized account of women's actual experience, virtually all accept her version of the dominant ideology, the conservative promotion of domesticity.

According to this now-standard historical account, postwar authors urged women to return to the home while only a handful of social scientists, trade unionists, and feminists protested. As one recent rendition states: "In the wake of World War II . . . the short-lived affirmation of women's independence gave way to a pervasive endorsement of female subordination and domesticity." Much of this secondary literature relies on a handful of conservative postwar writings, the same writings cited liberally by Friedan. In particular, the work of Dr. Marynia F. Farnham, a viciously antifeminist psychiatrist, and her sidekick, sociologist Ferdinand Lundberg, is invoked repeatedly as typical of the postwar era. In this standard account, the domestic ideology prevailed until such feminists as Friedan triumphed in the 1960s.

When I first began research on the postwar era, I accepted this version of history. But as I investigated the public culture, I encountered what I then considered exceptional evidence — books, articles, and films that contradicted the domestic ideology. I decided to conduct a more systematic investigation. This essay reexamines the middle-class popular discourse on women by surveying mass-circulation monthly magazines of the postwar era (1946–1958). The systematic sample includes nonfiction articles on women in "middlebrow" magazines (*Reader's Digest* and *Coronet*), "highbrow" magazines (*Harper's* and *Atlantic Monthly*), magazines aimed at African Americans (*Ebony* and *Negro Digest*), and those aimed at women (*Ladies' Home Journal* and *Woman's Home Companion*). The sample includes 489 nonfiction articles, ranging from Hollywood gossip to serious considerations of gender. In 1955 these magazines had a combined circulation of over 22 million. Taken together, the magazines reached readers from all classes, races, and genders, but the articles seem to represent the work of middle-class journalists, and articles written by women seem to outnumber ones by men.

My goal in constructing this sample was not to replicate Friedan's magazine research, which focused primarily on short story fiction in four women's magazines. Rather my goal was to test generalizations about postwar mass culture (that is, commodified forms of popular culture) by surveying another side of it. To this end, I chose nonfiction articles in a larger sample of popular magazines. Some of the magazines of smaller circulation, such as *Harper's* and *Negro Digest,* were perhaps outside the "mainstream." But including them in the sample enabled me to incorporate more of the diversity in American society, to investigate the contours of a broader bourgeois culture and some variations within it. Since my conclusions rest on a sample of nonfiction articles in eight popular magazines, they can provide only a tentative portrait of postwar culture. Future studies based on different magazines or on fiction, advertisements, films, television, or radio will no doubt suggest additional layers of complexity in mass culture and different readings of it.

. . . For Betty Friedan and for some historians, popular magazines represented a repressive force, imposing damaging images on vulnerable American women. Many historians today adopt a different approach in which mass culture is neither monolithic nor unrelentingly repressive. In this view, mass culture is rife with contradictions, ambivalence, and competing voices. We no longer assume that any text has a single, fixed meaning for all readers, and we sometimes find within the mass media subversive, as well as repressive, potential.

With a somewhat different sample and a somewhat different interpretive approach, I come to different conclusions about postwar mass culture than did Friedan and her followers. Friedan's widely accepted version of the "feminine mystique," I suggest, is only one piece of the postwar cultural puzzle. The popular literature I sampled did not simply glorify domesticity or demand that women return to or stay at home. All of the magazines sampled advocated both the domestic and the nondomestic, sometimes in the same sentence. In this literature, domestic ideals coexisted in ongoing tension with an ethos of individual achievement that celebrated nondomestic activity, individual striving, public service, and public success. . . .

In popular magazines, the theme of individual achievement rang most clearly in the numerous articles on individual women. These articles appeared with frequency throughout the postwar era: they comprised over 60 percent, or 300, of the 489 nonfiction articles sampled. These articles usually recounted a story of a woman's life or a particularly telling episode in her life. In formulaic accounts, they often constructed what one such article labeled "this Horatio Alger success story — feminine version." Of these articles, 33 percent spotlighted women with unusual talents, jobs, or careers, and another 29 percent focused on prominent entertainers. Typically they related a rise to public success punctuated by a lucky break, a dramatic comeback, a selfless sacrifice, or a persistent struggle to overcome adversity. Such stories appeared in all of the magazines sampled, but they appeared most frequently in the African-American magazines, *Ebony* and *Negro Digest,* and the white "middlebrow" magazines, *Coronet* and *Reader's Digest.* Journalists reworked the formula for different readers: In *Negro Digest,* for example, articles returned repeatedly to black performers who defied racism; in *Reader's Digest* they more often addressed white leaders in community service. In general, though, the articles suggested that the noteworthy woman rose above and beyond ordinary domesticity. Or, as one story stated, "This is the real-life fairy tale of a girl who hurtled from drab obscurity to sudden, startling fame."

At the heart of many such articles lay a bifocal vision of women both as feminine and domestic and as public achievers. In one article, "The Lady Who Licked Crime in Portland," the author, Richard L. Neuberger, juxtaposed domestic stereotypes and newsworthy nondomestic achievement. The woman in question, Dorothy McCullough Lee, was, the article stated, an "ethereally pale housewife" who tipped "the scales at 110 pounds." But more to the point, she was also the mayor of Portland, Oregon, who had defeated, single-handedly it seems, the heavyweights of organized crime. Before winning the mayoral election in 1948, this housewife had opened a law firm and served in the state legislature, both House and Senate, and as Portland's commissioner of public utilities. Despite her "frail, willowy" appearance, the fearless mayor had withstood ridicule, recall petitions, and threatening mail in her "relentless drive" against gambling and prostitution. She was, the article related without further critique, a "violent feminist" who had "intense concern with the status of women." And, according to all, she was "headed for national distinction." The article concluded with an admiring quotation describing Mayor Lee's fancy hats as the plumes of a crusading knight in armor. Here the feminine imagery blended with a metaphor of masculine public service. . . .

While feminine stereotypes sometimes provided convenient foils that enhanced by contrast a woman's atypical public accomplishment, they also served as conservative reminders that all women, even publicly successful women, were to maintain traditional gender distinctions. In their opening paragraphs, numerous authors described their successful subjects as pretty, motherly, shapely, happily married, petite, charming, or soft voiced. This emphasis on femininity and domesticity (and the two were often conflated) seems to have cloaked a submerged fear of lesbian, mannish, or man-hating women. This fear surfaced in an unusual article on athlete Babe Didrikson Zaharias. In her early years, the article stated, the Babe's "boyish bob and freakish clothes . . . [her] dislike of femininity" had led observers to dismiss her as an "Amazon." But after her marriage, she "became a woman," a transformation signaled, according to the approving author, by lipstick, polished nails, and "loose, flowing" hair as well as by an interest in the domestic arts of cooking, sewing, and entertaining. In this article, as in others, allusions to femininity and domesticity probably helped legitimate women's public achievements. Authors attempted to reassure readers that conventional gender distinctions and heterosexuality remained intact even as women competed successfully in work, politics, or sports. . . .

Nonetheless, the emphasis on the domestic and feminine should not be overstated; these articles on women's achievement did not serve solely or even primarily as lessons in traditional gender roles. The theme of nondomestic success was no hidden subtext in these stories. In most articles, the rise to public achievement was the first, and sometimes the only, narrative concern. When addressing both the domestic and the nondomestic, these articles placed public success at center stage: they tended to glorify frenetic activity, with domesticity at best a sideshow in a woman's three-ring circus. . . .

Marriage and domesticity were not prerequisites for star status in magazine stories. Over one-third of the articles on individual women featured unmarried women, divorced women, or women of unmentioned marital status. The African-American magazines seemed least concerned with marital status, but all of the magazines included articles that did not conjoin public success with connubial harmony. While a few such articles advocated marriage, others discounted it directly. Still other articles related the public achievements of divorced women, with consistent sympathy for the women involved. . . .

Magazines articles, of course, do not reveal the responses of readers. Formulaic stories of success do not seem to have provoked controversy: those magazines that published readers' responses rarely included letters regarding these stories. Some supplementary evidence, however, suggests that the language used in success stories also appeared in the language of at least some readers. The *Woman's Home Companion* conducted opinion polls in 1947 and 1949 in which readers named the women they most admired. In both years the top four women were Eleanor Roosevelt, Helen Keller, Sister Elizabeth Kenny (who worked with polio victims), and Clare Boothe Luce (author and congresswoman), all distinctly nondomestic women. Why did readers select these particular women? They seemed to offer the same answers as the success stories: "courage, spirit, and conviction," "devotion to the public good," and "success in overcoming obstacles." While a feminine version of selfless sacrifice seems to have won kudos, individual striving and public service superseded devotion to home and family.

On the one hand, one might see these success stories as pernicious. They applied to women a traditionally male, middle-class discourse of individual achievement that glorified a version of success, honor, and fulfillment that was difficult enough for middle-class white men, highly unlikely for able-bodied women of any class and race, and nearly impossible for the ill, disabled, and disfigured. As fantasies of unlikely success, they offered false promises that hard work brought women public reward. They probably gave women readers vicarious pleasure or compensatory esteem, but they provided no real alternatives to most women's workaday lives. They usually downplayed the obstacles that women faced in the public arena, and they implicitly dismissed the need for collective protest. Further, they did not overtly challenge traditional gender roles. With frequent references to domesticity and femininity, narrowly defined, they reinforced rigid definitions of appropriate female behavior and sexual expression, and they neglected the conflicts between domestic and nondomestic demands that many women undoubtedly encountered.

On the other hand, these articles subverted the notion that women belonged at home. They presented a wide variety of options open to women and praised the women who had chosen to assert themselves as public figures. They helped readers, male and female, envision women in positions of public achievement. They tried openly to inspire women to pursue unusual goals, domestic or not, and they sometimes suggested that public service brought more obvious rewards than devotion to family. By applauding the public possibilities open to women, including married women, they may have validated some readers' nondomestic behavior and sharpened some readers' discontent with the constraints they experienced in their domestic lives. At least one contemporary observer noticed this subversive side to stories of individual success. Dr. Marynia Farnham, the antifeminist, railed not only against the "propaganda of the feminists" but also against "stories about famous career women," which, she claimed, undermined the prestige of motherhood. . . .

The postwar popular discourse on women, then, did not simply exhort women to stay at home. Its complexity is also seen in . . . articles that addressed questions of gender directly. The topics of those articles ranged from women in India to premenstrual tension, but most fell into four broad categories: women's paid work, women's political activism, marriage and domesticity, and glamour and sexuality. . . .

On the issue of paid employment, there was rough consensus. Despite concerns for the postwar economy, journalists in this sample consistently defended wage work for women. Articles insisted that women, including married women, worked for wages because they needed money. . . . Articles praised women workers in specific occupations, from secretaries to doctors. These articles related exciting, stimulating, or rewarding job possibilities or the "practically unlimited" opportunities allegedly available to women. Like the success stories, these articles sometimes encouraged individual striving. "Advancement," one such article claimed, "will be limited only by [a woman's] intelligence, application, and education." The African-American magazines, *Ebony* and *Negro Digest,* alert to racism, showed more explicit awareness of institutional barriers to individual effort and sometimes noted discrimination based not only on race but also on gender. One article, for example, not only praised black women doctors but also denounced the "stubborn male prejudice" faced by "petticoat medics." In general, though, the articles on specific occupations did not attack sexism or the sexual division of labor directly; they simply encouraged women to pursue white-collar jobs in business and the professions.

Beneath the consensus, though, a quiet debate exposed the tensions between the ideals of nondomestic achievement and of domestic duty. Echoing earlier debates of the 1920s, some authors advised women to subordinate careers to home and motherhood while others invited women to pursue public success. The question of careers was rarely discussed at any length, and the relative silence itself underscores how postwar popular magazines often avoided contended issues. But throwaway lines in various articles sometimes landed on one side of the debate or the other. In a single article in *Ebony,* for example, one unmarried career woman warned readers, "Don't sacrifice marriage for career," while another stated, "I like my life just as it is." . . .

The postwar popular magazines were more unequivocally positive on increased participation of women in politics. The *Ladies' Home Journal,* not known for its feminist sympathies, led the way with numerous articles that supported women as political and community leaders. In 1947, lawyer and longtime activist Margaret Hickey, former president of the National Federation of Business and Professional Women's Clubs, launched the *Journal*'s monthly "Public Affairs Department," which encouraged women's participation in mainstream politics and reform. In one article, Hickey stated bluntly, "Make politics your business. Voting, office holding, raising your voice for new and better laws are just as important to your home and your family as the evening meal or spring house cleaning." Like earlier Progressive reformers, Hickey sometimes justified nondomestic political action by its benefits to home and family, but her overall message was clear: women should participate outside the home, and not just by voting. . . .

Reports on women politicians stressed the series' recurring motif, "They Do It . . . You Can Too." This article presented women politicians as exemplars. With direct appeals to housewives, it praised women who ran for office, even mothers of "babies or small children" who could "find time and ways to campaign and to win elections." It presented political activism not only as a public service but also as a source of personal fulfillment. For women who held political office, it claimed, "there is great pride of accomplishment and the satisfaction of 'doing a job.'" . . .

Historians sometimes contend that the Cold War mentality encouraged domesticity, that it envisioned family life and especially mothers as buffers against the alleged Communist threat. But Cold War rhetoric had other possible meanings for women. In the *Ladies' Home Journal,* authors often used the Cold War to promote women's political participation. One such approach contrasted "free society" of the United States with Soviet oppression, including oppression of women. . . . Other articles stressed that Soviet citizens, male and female, did not participate in a democratic process. American women could prove the strength of democracy by avoiding "citizen apathy," by "giving the world a lively demonstration of how a free society can serve its citizens," by making "free government work well as an example for the undecided and unsatisfied millions elsewhere in the world." . . .

The role of the housewife and mother was problematic in the postwar popular discourse. On the one hand, all of the magazines assumed that women wanted to marry, that women found being wives and mothers rewarding, and that women would and should be the primary parents and housekeepers. In the midst of the baby boom, some articles glorified the housewife, sometimes in conscious attempts to bolster her self-esteem. On the other hand, throughout the postwar era, numerous articles portrayed domesticity itself as exhausting and isolating, and frustrated mothers as overdoting and smothering. Such articles hardly glorified domesticity. They provided their postwar readers with ample references to housewife's discontent. . . .

In the postwar magazines, marriage also presented problems. . . . An article in *Ebony* stated, "Most women would rather be married than single but there are many who would rather remain single than be tied to the wrong man." The magazines gave readers contrasting advice on how to find a good husband. One article told women, "Don't fear being aggressive!," while another considered "aggressive traits" as "handicaps . . . in attracting a husband." Within marriage as well, journalists seemed to anticipate constant problems, including immaturity, incompatibility, and infidelity. They saw divorce as a difficult last resort and often advised both husbands and wives to communicate and adjust.

. . . Postwar authors did not, as Friedan's *Feminine Mystique* would have it, side automatically with "sexual passivity, male domination, and nurturing maternal love." They portrayed the ideal marriage as an equal partnership, with each partner intermingling traditional masculine and feminine roles. One article insisted: "The healthy, emotionally well-balanced male . . . isn't alarmed by the fact that women are human, too, and have an aggressive as well as a passive side. . . . He takes women seriously as individuals." This article and others condemned men who assumed an attitude of superiority. . . . Yet, to many it seemed that "individualism" could go too far and upset modern marriage. While husbands might do more housework and wives might pursue nondomestic activities, men remained the primary breadwinners and women the keepers of the home. . . .

The postwar magazines seemed least willing to entertain alternatives in the area of sexuality. As Friedan argued, popular magazines emphasized glamour and allure, at least for young women, and as Elaine Tyler May has elaborated, they tried to domesticate sexual intercourse by containing it within marriage. Magazines presented carefully framed articles with explicit directives about appropriate behavior. Young women were to make themselves attractive to men, and married women were to engage in mutually pleasing sexual intercourse with their mates. Articles presented "normal" sex through voyeuristic discussion of sexual problems, such as pregnancy before marriage and frigidity after. Other forms of sexual expression were rarely broached, although one article in *Ebony* did condemn "lesbians and nymphomaniacs" in the Women's Army Corps.

While all of the magazines endorsed a manicured version of heterosexual appeal, the African-American magazines displayed it most heartily. This may have reflected African-American vernacular traditions, such as the blues, that rejected white middle-class injunctions against public sexual expression. But it also reflected an editorial decision to construct glamour and beauty as political issues in the fight against racism. Articles admired black women's sex appeal in a self-conscious defiance of racist white standards of beauty. In this context what some feminists today might read as sexual "objectification" presented itself as racial advancement, according black womanhood equal treatment with white. Thus, *Ebony,* which in most respects resembled a white family magazine like *Life,* also included some of the mildly risqué cheesecake seen in white men's magazines like *Esquire.* One editorial explained: "Because we live in a society in which standards of physical beauty are most often circumscribed by a static concept of whiteness of skin and blondeness of hair, there is an aching need for someone to shout from the housetops that black women are beautiful." . . .

Still, despite the magazines' endorsement of feminine beauty and heterosexual allure, Friedan's polemical claim that "American women have been successfully reduced to sex creatures" seems unabashedly hyperbolic. Try as they might, popular magazines could not entirely dictate the responses of readers. In most cases, we have little way of knowing how readers responded to magazine articles, but in the case of sex appeal we have explicit letters of dissent. In the African-American magazines, some readers, women and men both, objected to the photos of semiclad women. One woman complained that the "so-called beauties" were "really a disgrace to all women." And another protested "those girl covers and the . . . so-called realism (just a cover up name for cheapness, coarseness, lewdness, profanity and irreverence)." . . .

In his ground-breaking 1972 book, *The American Woman,* William Henry Chafe offers what still stands as the best summary of the debates on womanhood in the postwar era. In Chafe's reconstruction, a popular "antifeminist" position, promoted by such authors as Farnham and Lundberg, stood opposed to a more feminist "sociological" perspective, promoted primarily by social scientists such as Mirra Komarovsky and Margaret Mead. While the antifeminists insisted on marriage and domesticity, the social scientists called for new gender roles to match modern conditions. In the popular magazines sampled for this essay, this debate rarely surfaced. Articles sometimes drew on one position or even both, but the vast majority did not fall clearly into either camp. Still, the antifeminist position did appear occasionally as did an opposing "women's rights" stance. These positions emerged in various magazines, but they both appeared most unequivocally in the highbrow magazines, the *Atlantic Monthly* and *Harper's,* which did not avoid controversy as assiduously as did others.

The antifeminist authors promoted domesticity as a woman's only road to fulfillment. Women should not compete with men, they argued; instead, they should defer to, depend on, and even wait on men, especially their husbands. According to these conservatives, women and men differed fundamentally, and attempts to diminish sexual difference would lead only to unhappiness. Often invoking a version of Freudian thought, these authors sometimes engaged in psychological name-calling in which they labeled modern woman neurotic, narcissistic, unfeminine, domineering, nagging, lazy, materialistic, and spoiled. These conservative arguments and the attendant name-calling were by no means typical of popular discourse. Of the 489 articles sampled, only 9, or less than 2 percent, even approached such starkly conservative claims.

This is where the oft-cited Dr. Marynia Farnham stood in the postwar discourse, at the conservative margin rather than at the center. For Farnham, modern women who attempted to compete with men or expressed discontent with their natural career as mothers suffered from mental instability, bitterness, and worse. Industrialization, Farnham claimed, had undermined women's productive functions in the home. Women, "frustrated at the inmost core of their beings," attempted tragically to emulate men in the world of work, led "aimlessly idle," "parasitic" lives as frigid housewives, or indulged in "overdoting, overstrict or rejecting" mothering, with a cumulative outcome of neurotic children, including future Adolph Hitlers. Farnham called for a renewed commitment to motherhood, dependence on men, and "natural" sexual passivity. She spelled out these arguments in ceaseless detail in her 1947 book, *Modern Woman: The Lost Sex,* coauthored with Ferdinand Lundberg.

Although Farnham's position had some influence, especially among psychologists, it did not represent the mainstream in the mass culture; rather, it generated "a storm of controversy." Book reviews, some of them scathing, called *Modern Woman* "neither socially nor medically credible," "dogmatic and sensational," "intensely disturbing," "unfair," and "fundamentally untrue." And Farnham's articles in *Coronet* provoked enough letters that the editors promised to include opposing viewpoints in future issues, this in a magazine that generally avoided any inkling of debate. While bits and pieces of Farnham's arguments appeared in other popular magazines, the antifeminist position was rejected more often than embraced. In the era of positive thinking, magazines tended toward more upbeat and celebratory representations of women.

Also at the boundaries of the discourse, a few "women's rights" articles counterbalanced the conservative extreme. . . . While conservatives insisted on domestic ideals, women's rights advocates insisted on women's right to nondomestic pursuits. Like the antifeminists, the authors of these articles often argued that women's functions in the home had declined, and they, too, often found the modern housewife restless and discontented. These authors, however, condemned isolation in the home and subordination to men. They admired women who pursued positions of public responsibility and leadership, and they identified and opposed discrimination in the workplace and in politics. They insisted that women were individuals of infinite variety. In *Harper's,* Agnes Rogers wrote, "there would be a healthier distribution of civic energy if more attention were paid to individuals as such and if it were not assumed that men hold the executive jobs and women do what they are told." In contrast with antifeminist writings, these articles either downplayed sex differences or derogated men for their militaristic aggression or "masculine self-inflation." The women's rights articles were only slightly less common than the antifeminist attacks. (With a conservative count, there were five, about 1 percent of the sample.) Like the antifeminist articles, they sometimes generated controversy, especially when readers read them as frontal attacks on the full-time housewife.

The antifeminists and the women's rights advocates competed for mainstream attention. Both tempered their arguments in seeming attempts to broaden appeal: antifeminists sometimes disavowed reactionary intention and denied that married women had to stay in the home, and women's rights advocates sometimes disavowed feminist militance and denied that married women had to have careers. Through the 1950s, though, neither position in any way controlled or dominated the public discourse, at least as seen in nonfiction articles in popular magazines. Both antifeminists and women's rights advocates clearly represented controversial minority positions. . . .

Why does my version of history differ from Betty Friedan's? The most obvious, and the most gracious, explanation is that we used different, though overlapping, sources. The nonfiction articles I read may well have included more contradictions and more ambivalence than the fiction on which Friedan focused. But there are, I think, additional differences in approach. Friedan did not read the popular magazines incorrectly, but she did, it seems, cite them reductively. . . . For the postwar era, she cited both fiction and nonfiction stories on domesticity. But she downplayed the articles on domestic problems (belittling one by saying "the bored editors . . . ran a little article"), ignored the articles on individual achievement, and dismissed the articles on political participation with a one-sentence caricature. Her forceful protest against a restrictive domestic ideal neglected the extent to which that ideal was already undermined.

My reassessment of the "feminine mystique" is part of a larger revisionist project. For the past few years, historians have questioned the stereotype of postwar women as quiescent, docile, and domestic. Despite the baby boom and despite discrimination in employment, education, and public office, married women, black and white, joined the labor force in increasing numbers, and both married and unmarried women participated actively in politics and reform. Just as women's activities were more varied and more complex than is often acknowledged, so, I argue, was the postwar popular ideology. Postwar magazines, like their prewar and wartime predecessors, rarely presented direct challenges to the conventions of marriage or motherhood, but they only rarely told women to return to or stay at home. They included stories that glorified domesticity, but they also expressed ambivalence about domesticity, endorsed women's nondomestic activity, and celebrated women's public success. They delivered multiple messages, which women could read as sometimes supporting and sometimes subverting the "feminine mystique." . . .

The Meanings of Lesbianism in Postwar America

DONNA PENN

> I had been a closet gay before I got married, about 1948, which means I had a relation-ship with a woman, and I'd been in love with her but I thought I was the only person in the world. There was no others in the world. I had never read a gay book. I didn't even know the word 'gay' . . . I didn't know the word 'lesbian' . . . And I really believe that women used to dress mannish simply to get you to know who they were . . . In those days it was very important.

In recounting her experience as a young lesbian in the 1950s, Joan reminds us of the very different cultural landscape that existed for gays and lesbians in the days be-fore the emergence of the gay liberation movement. With the relative absence of strictly defined gay political institutions and social organizations, women who 'used to dress mannish' played a vital role in introducing others to gay life and its social centers. They were the vehicle by which those who thought they were the 'only ones' found others. Further, by dressing mannish during a period when strict gender boundaries were being revitalized and reinforced, these women announced lesbian-ism to the general public as well. Now publicly identifiable, the masculine woman became the object of study among experts on sexual deviance, while popular dis-seminators of expert opinion embarked on something resembling a crusade to make meaning of the masculine woman. This essay explores the various meanings as-signed to the masculine woman by social scientists and their popularizers and by lesbians themselves, in an effort to unravel the competing and conflicting dis-courses over lesbianism during the post-war years. . . .

By the 1950s, some consensus had been reached concerning the etiology of ho-mosexuality. Theories of glandular and hormonal imbalance as well as those of con-genital or hereditary defect gave way to the opinion that homosexuality was psy-chological in origin. Although opinion differed as to the exact nature of the psychogenesis of this defective condition, most experts and popularizers agreed that at its heart, lesbianism was a flight from adult responsibility. They argued that it was a flight, as well, from heterosexuality, but sexual object choice was not the key here. Rather, heterosexuality was taken to mean all the concomitant social responsi-bilities associated with a heterosexual way of life, most importantly marriage and family. Frank Caprio stated this position clearly in his 1954 study of what he called the psychodynamics of lesbianism. He asserted:

> The lesbian who deliberately renounces marriage and motherhood is blind to the realiza-tion that her attitude represents a defensive rationalization for her inadequacy and flight from life's responsibilities.

W. Beran Wolfe, former Director of the Community Church Mental Hygiene Clinic of New York, concurred, claiming that 'lesbian love . . . represents an evasion of the responsibilities of marriage and motherhood. . . . '

Donna Penn, "The Meanings of Lesbianism in Post-War America," *Gender and History* 3 (Summer 1991): 190–203.

According to the experts, this failure to assume life's responsibilities relegated the lesbian to a life of frustration and loneliness unless she could find a substitute outlet for her unconscious maternal desires. In some cases, this might be accomplished, in Caprio's view, by 'lavish[ing] their affections on a pet cat, dog, or bird, or they become attached to some childlike male invert and practically "mother him."' For others, the adjustment to maternal desires was thought to be satisfied by a woman developing a mother/child relationship with her sexual partner. In both cases, she sublimated her 'natural' instincts in socially, culturally, and psychologically deficient ways.

The blame for what was perceived to be the rising rate of lesbianism was placed at the doorsteps of so-called emancipated women and of parents who did not offer culturally appropriate gender role models for their children. In the wake of wartime changes, cultural anxiety concerning the future of the American family led experts and popularizers to view 'psychic masculinity,' of the so-called defeminization of American women, as both the cause and symptom of lesbianism.

This sentiment was echoed time and again by purveyors of the dominant discourse. The degree to which sexual maladjustment was a consequence of an improper balance between masculine and feminine attributes in both the parent(s) and the lesbian herself was most explicitly argued by George Henry who went so far as to describe homosexuals as 'those who suffer from masculine-feminine conflicts.' While director of the Committee on Sex Variants, he conducted studies of hundreds of sexually deviant types. His cases and findings are reported in his over 1000 page tome entitled *Sex Variants* which was then rewritten for a lay audience under the title *All the Sexes* in 1955.

In this volume, notably subtitled 'A Study of Masculinity and Femininity,' Henry was explicit about his belief that meddling in the balance between prescribed gender roles was both the source of and description for homosexuality. Domineering or masculine mothers and weak or feminine fathers produced children who failed to identify with and socialize to their appropriate sex role. The consequence was sexually deviant children who themselves suffered from false gender identification. Nonetheless, he was hopeful that if girls and women were encouraged to pursue feminine ideals they would be capable of attaining the 'preferred goal in life; [that is] establishing and maintaining a home which involves the rearing of children.' . . .

Caprio credits noted German sexologist Magnus Hirschfeld for providing him with a picture of a typical lesbian's childhood which included a preference for boys' games and a distaste for 'feminine occupations.' Henry's study concurred. Masculinizing influences and tendencies were reported in over forty percent of the 'female variants' in his sample 'who wished they had been boys . . . which agrees with the general impression that female sex variants are inclined to be masculine.' His evidence, like Hirschfeld's, harkened back to the subjects' childhoods during which a dislike of dolls was offered as an indication of masculine tendencies. Other masculine propensities included an interest in sports, fishing, and male clothing. . . .

The obsession with the so-called masculine lesbian reached a feverish pitch in Henry's book. With meticulous detail, he measured every inch of the variant's body in an effort to describe with exact precision the adaptation to gender characteristics of the opposite sex. Despite widespread belief in the psychosexual origins of homosexuality and lesbianism, and despite the contentions of historians who have argued that by this era homosexuality was understood as same-sex sexual object choice, Henry's tabulations suggested that lesbianism still had everything to do with gender inversion and a 'flight from femininity.' What Henry called 'Sex Variant Characteristics' were reduced to a two-page table including the following images of lesbians:

> athletic with broad shoulders and narrow hips . . . ; hair kept short, coarse, straight, brushed straight back with an excess on face, body and extremities; eyes are subtle with a scrutinizing appraisal of women; mouth is small with thin lips and demonstrate a limited, conservative movement of lips and tongue; voice is deep, . . . sharp, . . . and petulant with cold, harsh, cautious, and biting speech, though sometimes soft, seductive, appealing or babyish with own sex. . . .

The table continues, in the same vein, to chart clothing, presence or absence of jewelry and cosmetics, build and body type, carriage and gait — all decidedly unfeminine.

The near hysteria reflected in such writings was the culmination of at least a half century of anxiety with regard to the transformation of prescribed gender roles particularly as they pertained to women. Although experts have offered examples of lesbian activity in all ages and cultures, there was an apocalyptic quality to its appearance at this particular juncture in human history. By reading properly the disturbance in the masculine-feminine balance, those focused on female sexual deviance believed one could foretell the destruction of the human race, albeit a white middle-class race.

This disturbance in gender identity was, according to the prevailing wisdom, due in no small part to the so-called emancipation of women which had been accelerated by war and women's labor force participation. Failure to restore equilibrium between the sexes would result in future generations of sexual variants whose failure to reproduce would bring an end to civilization. Henry asserted:

> The rebellion of women . . . in the form of feminism . . . has resulted in equal suffrage and virtual elimination of the double standard of morals. Women now own more property than do men, they outlive men, and if they united they could control the government. . . . The present Occidental trend is in the direction of a matriarchal system, with increasing masculinity on the part of women. The ascendancy of women has been fostered by political and industrial competition between the sexes, the increasing tendency on the part of both sexes to avoid parental and homemaking responsibilities, and the destruction of masculine males and preservation of feminine males by modern warfare. This gradual change may foreshadow for Western civilization a decline and fall such as that of the Roman Empire.

Note that these are not the voices of a lunatic fringe, but in fact represent the opinion of respected mainstream 'experts.'

This conflation of gender and sexuality was presented again by Richard Robertiello in a tedious 1959 account of his psychoanalytic sessions with a woman named Connie called *Voyage From Lesbos.* The author cites as an indication of the success of treatment Connie's awakening interest in things female. He notes, 'during the next session she told me that she was getting very interested in sewing and that she was busy fixing up her apartment. She said she was thinking how nice it would be to get into a domestic life again. She spoke of getting a rotisserie. The role of the housewife was beginning to look a little more appealing to Connie.' He further encouraged her to believe that the level of responsibility she brought to her analytic work indicated that she was certainly responsible enough to handle the role of wife and mother. The assumption operating here was that if Connie's interests could be made consistent with her gender, a reassignment in her choice of sexual object would necessarily follow. . . .

This preoccupation with the masculine lesbian, the butch, was in no small part a consequence of her obvious violation of prescribed gender roles as reflected in her appearance. The concern with feminine lesbians, or femmes, on the part of the experts, centered around their being unfortunate victims of the aggressive masculine type. The femme was a suitable candidate for successful psychotherapy since it was believed she could readjust her sexual desires towards men, and thereby achieve heterosexuality and its attendant virtues of home and family. She was not a 'true homosexual' in that she did not suffer from gender inversion, thus what barred her form achieving normal sexuality could be eliminated by some hours on the couch. For the butch, however, her choice of an inappropriate sexual object was desperately compounded by a gender misidentification. Whereas, according to Ward and Kasselbaum, 'the butch changes the love object *and* her own appearance and behavior, thereby substituting a role; the femme changes only the love object.' (emphasis mine)

Frequently, experts on homosexuality like to make note of the perception that public sanctions against lesbianism are not as severe as those pertaining to male homosexuality. They argue that, unlike male homosexuality, lesbianism has gone largely unnoticed by the culture or by professionals, owing to a variety of factors. First, they suggest that lesbians are not considered responsible for the spread of syphilis which was the venereal disease of primary concern during the period under consideration. Therefore, they did not pose a public health threat. In addition, lesbians, they argued, practiced discretion in their sexual activity which kept them relatively free of the legal authorities. Reported instances of solicitation or sexual activity in public places, the two crimes along with child molestation that formed the basis of much public fear of homosexuality and that landed many a gay man in prison, are statistically insignificant with respect to lesbians. Finally, experts and popularizers repeatedly stressed, almost with a taint of regret, that in this culture women are permitted significant latitude in their affectionate expressions which, at best, masks female homosexuality behind acceptable standards of interaction, and at worst, arouses no suspicion. Thus, according to these experts, female homosexuality is generally overlooked. Further, they admit with disdain that many identified lesbians have no wish to change and staunchly assert that they are happy with their lives.

If then, these women do not break the taboos of sexual expression and are not often tormented by their condition, what's the fuss? What is the basis upon which they are labelled 'deviant'? I would argue that lesbians were labelled deviant to the degree that they symbolized, represented and actualized lives that defied strict gender distinctions during a period of profound anxiety regarding gender roles and the post-war restoration and maintenance of 'normal' family life. Thus, increasingly, masculine appearance became the yardstick against which lesbianism was measured. . . .

And yet, despite my emphasis on the trespassing of gender boundaries as the defining characteristic for lesbianism during this period, we must be careful as scholars to not falsely dichotomize between gender and sex. Perhaps butch style was as much about sex as it was about gender, for acting and dressing like a man — assuming male privilege — included having sexual access to other women. Clearly lesbians of the time, like Joan whose words open this essay, understood that butch women would lead them to other women who chose women for sex. The 'others' were not merely other women who dressed like men but, rather, other lesbians — women whose sexual object choices were other women. Among social scientists, as well, the concern about gender identity may have been a code for sexual desire. Therefore, in our efforts to reintroduce gender as a variable, we must be careful not to lose sight of the role of sex. The work of Liz Kennedy and Madeleine Davis, Joan Nestle, and Esther Newton all point to the sexual meanings of butch attire and remind us that butch style signalled, at least in part, someone who sought female sexual partners. Consequently, although this essay focuses on the ways in which lesbianism was signified by butch women who defied gender role characteristics, at the very least in their appearance, we must not understate the extent to which traits of gender inversion also marked the presence of an 'inverted' or 'deviant' sexual identity.

The concern with masculine women did not escape the attention of lesbians themselves. Some attempted to dispel the notion of lesbians as masculine women by defending what they perceived as the very real femininity they experienced in lesbian circles. One mid-1950s witness, in discussing her distaste for the butchy portrayal of Stephen in the *Well of Loneliness,* asserted:

> I think it was bad science to suggest that an interest in sports, the habit of wearing tailored clothes, a desire to have a career are symptoms of sexual inversion in women. These things are not signs of sexual inversion and anyone who has any real knowledge of the subject knows that they are not. Most [female] homosexuals are usually very feminine in appearance, behavior, mannerisms, [and] tastes. . . .

In this context, DOB (Daughters of Bilitis) represented quite an interesting position. To the extent that they, too, understood that deviation from prescribed gender roles was the root of social discomfort and worse against lesbians, they sought to remedy the situation, in part, by helping lesbians rediscover their femininity. DOB asserted that by adhering to the rules of the subculture, particularly with respect to butch/femme appearance, an alternative conformity emerged that directed women away from their true nature as women. A primary mission of DOB was to reaffirm and reassert womanly qualities among lesbians. They viewed the bar as a site of false gender consciousness in which conformity to perverse notions of gender were encouraged. Whereas, according to DOB, the bars fostered a complete depreciation of femininity, DOB sought to help lesbians be proud of their womanliness and femininity and to refuse to transform themselves into a 'mockery' of men of 'perversion' of themselves.

This tension within the subculture between those who participated in the lesbian bar culture with its attendant commitment to a butch and femme way of life and those who held the DOB position was articulated in the pages of the DOB journal, *The Ladder.* A message from the president of the organization that appeared in the November 1956 issue speaks directly to the organization's interest in clarifying the gender identity of lesbians by reminding them that they are women first, regardless of the object of their sexual desires. She stated: 'Our organization has already . . . converted a few to remembering that they are women first and a butch or femme secondly, so their attire should be that which society will accept.'

Such notable literary figures as Marion Zimmer Bradley and Lorraine Hansberry addressed this point directly in letters to the editor. They each reaffirmed and supported DOB's position that the lesbian should adopt a mode of dress and behavior acceptable to society. Zimmer expressed her feelings in the following way:

> I think Lesbians themselves could lessen the public attitudes by confining their differences to their friends and not force themselves deliberately upon public notice by deliberate idiosyncracies of dress and speech . . . I believe that homosexuals and Lesbians might well . . . realize that their private life is of little interest to the public and to keep it to themselves.

The efforts of the DOB to encourage lesbians to reassert and recommit themselves to an appropriate gender identity was in part intended as a challenge to a flourishing and largely working-class bar culture that was rooted in a butch/femme sensibility.

Given this context how do we make meaning of the stories lesbians tell about their lives? Although there is a great range of opinion on the butch/femme dichotomy in the subculture itself, there remains a singular acknowledgement of its importance in the lesbian world, particularly the post-war lesbian world. Even those who were appalled by it, comment on it with vigor — their distaste frequently rooted in the often expressed sentiment, 'we didn't really like the idea that they [butches and femmes] were representing' us to the outside world.

And yet, to the lesbian who sought access to a gay world beyond herself, who sought a remedy to her isolation, who sought to interrupt the often held belief that she was the only one, the butch played an absolutely key role that cannot be overemphasized. 'Masculine' women made lesbianism public; they made an otherwise privatized sexuality visible. For the very reasons the purveyors of the dominant discourse, as well as members of DOB, were disturbed by these women, women who sought access to others found them crucial. Through butch women, they found their way to a lesbian subculture in which they could be among others like themselves. As one woman explains her own introduction to the gay world:

> When I was 22, I brought my car to the car wash . . . and I see these butches, these women all in men's clothes working in this car wash and they fascinated me . . . So I had my car washed almost every day . . . I feel that in the '50s the only way we brought the ones that came out into our community was by usually looking gay to let them know 'here we are, come join us.' And it was the butch that did that . . . I look at it as, if I had never found them, what would my life have been like? If you stop and think of it, how [else] would I have met them?

This woman went on to explain her own experience of serving as the so-called masculine woman through whom others found access to the lesbian world. She and her friend, dressing in full butch attire, entered a straight bar in downtown Worcester for a quick drink:

... there were two women in there ... and through the waitress they sent us a note, they said, 'we would like to meet you but not in here. Outside' ... what happened was they were gay and they lived down in the other section of town and they didn't know anybody who was gay and they spotted us. We introduced them to the other people and they came to our house parties and before you knew it, they were part of the community. So you see where that worked? Being butch brought other people into the community ... That's what the butch role was as far as I was concerned because that's how we made friends, that's how people came into our community, became our family ... The butch role had a reason, a purpose of identification ... A real important purpose. ...

In a field as new as lesbian history, there remain numerous areas yet untouched as well as important conceptual issues still unsolved. In my own work I have encountered a critical problem represented in this essay, the problem of whether the 'experts' constructed lesbianism or merely discovered and described it. Recent scholarship in this field has tended to focus on the subculture and its institutions as the context from which cultural meaning was derived, developed, and imparted to new members. Yet, this community did not exist in a subcultural vacuum. However alternative or oppositional the subculture was, it and its members did not exist completely detached or distanced from the messages of the dominant culture. How then do we evaluate the relationship between hegemonic and oppositional discourses? How do we explore the language of the experts without offering them complete cultural authority over defining the meaning of lesbianism? At the same time, when examining the words of lesbians themselves, how do we make meaning of their experiences without, similarly, presenting a world untouched by dominant cultural messages? If, as Joan states at the beginning of this essay, she never even knew the word lesbian, in what ways and in what contexts did this world acquire meaning for her? Was her relationship to the meaning and experience of lesbianism completely shaped by her participation in the lesbian subculture or was it in part derived from popular and expert ideology concerning lesbianism?

Clearly at issue here is the question of who gains authority over the discourse and following from that, who holds cultural authority over defining the meaning of the experience. I have tried in this essay to convey a sense of competing discourses over the meanings of lesbianism during the post-war period even though the essay presents 'expert' ideology first and then asks how well lesbians themselves subverted, resisted, or absorbed the opinions of the authorities. In so doing, I have given these 'experts' at least partial control of *my* discourse. Only when we find a remedy to this problem will we be able to paint a more reliable portrait of the cultural history of lesbianism in America.

※ *F U R T H E R   R E A D I N G*

William Chafe, *The Paradox of Change: American Women in the 20th Century* (1991)

Stephanie Coontz, *The Way We Never Were: American Families and the Nostalgia Trap* (1992)

Lillian Faderman, *Odd Girls and Twilight Lovers: A History of Lesbian Life in Twentieth-Century America* (1991)

Herbert Gans, *The Levittowners: Ways of Life and Politics in a New Suburban Community* (1967)

Cynthia Harrison, *On Account of Sex: The Politics of Women's Issues, 1945–1968* (1988)

Kenneth T. Jackson, *Crabgrass Frontier: The Suburbanization of the United States* (1985)

Jacqueline Jones, *Labor of Love, Labor of Sorrow: Black Women, Work, and the Family from Slavery to the Present* (1985)

Eugenia Kaledin, *Mothers and More: American Women in the 1950s* (1984)

Elizabeth Lapovsky Kennedy and Madeline D. Davis, *Boots of Leather, Slippers of Gold: The History of a Lesbian Community* (1993)

Mirra Komarovsky, *Blue Collar Marriage* (1964)

Susan Lynn, *Progressive Women in Conservative Times: Racial Justice, Peace, and Feminism, 1945 to the 1960s* (1992)

Margaret Marsh, *Suburban Lives* (1990)

Joanne Meyerowitz, ed., *Not June Cleaver: Women and Gender in Postwar America, 1945–1960* (1994)

Jo Ann Gibson Robinson, *The Montgomery Bus Boycott and the Women Who Started It* (1987)

Leila J. Rupp and Verta Taylor, *Surviving the Doldrums: The American Women's Rights Movement, 1945 to the 1960s* (1987)

Rickie Solinger, *Wake Up Little Susie: Single Pregnancy and Race Before Roe v. Wade* (1992)

Nancy Pottishman Weiss, "The Invention of Necessity: Dr. Benjamin Spock's 'Baby and Child Care'," *American Quarterly* 29 (Winter 1977), 519–546

Political Activism and Feminism

in the 1960s and Early 1970s

The sixties and early seventies were years of extraordinary political and cultural unrest in the United States. Young adults, members of the baby boom generation, participated in a frontal attack on American society and its institutions, condemning the nation's misuse of military power abroad, especially in Vietnam, and its indifference to oppression and inequality at home. Women of various class, racial, and ethnic backgrounds devoted tremendous energy to the political movements of the era, including the civil rights and Black Power struggles and the anti-war, anti-poverty, and labor movements.

Eventually, some women — many of them former members of the Student Nonviolent Coordinating Committee (SNCC) and Students for a Democratic Society (SDS), and nearly all of them white and middle class — launched a new, radical feminist movement. Radical feminists organized small "consciousness-raising" groups that combined investigations of gender discrimination in employment, education, and politics with analyses of gender oppression in private, familial, and sexual contexts. Like Black Power activists, these feminists were often frankly separatist, doubting the dominant society's willingness to grant women (or African-Americans) true equality. Meanwhile, a group of older, more moderate women (also predominantly white and middle class) formed the National Organization for Women (NOW) in 1966, adopting integrationist goals that paralleled those of the National Association for the Advancement of Colored People (NAACP) and the Southern Christian Leadership Conference. (In many ways, NOW could be seen as heir to the National Woman's Party.) These two branches of feminism often disagreed over goals and tactics, but together they helped to bring about massive changes in attitudes toward the role of women in American society.

What were the circumstances that provoked feminist activism in the sixties? Why did the new feminist movement claim the sympathies of women who were primarily white and middle class? What roles did working-class women and women of color play in the movements that claimed their allegiance? And did these women embrace a "feminist" consciousness, even if they did not join the movement?

D O C U M E N T S

In 1963, Betty Friedan described "the problem that has no name" in her groundbreaking book *The Feminine Mystique;* an excerpt appears as the first selection. Two years later, Casey Hayden and Mary King, white activists with both SNCC and SDS, wrote "A Kind of Memo" (the second document) to others in the peace and freedom movements in an attempt to draw attention to the issue of gender oppression. In 1966, NOW's founding statement (extracted in the third document) laid out the organization's central premises. Note the striking differences between that statement and the fourth selection, the Redstockings Manifesto of 1969, a creation of the radical wing of the feminist movement. In 1970 Frances Beale published an essay (parts of which appear as the fifth document) condemning the sexism of the Black Power movement and the racism of the women's movement; she claimed that such attitudes created a "double jeopardy" for those who, like her, were both black and female. One year later, Mirta Vidal wrote an essay on the critical importance of feminism for Chicanas; portions of it make up the last document.

Betty Friedan on "The Problem That Has No Name," 1963

The problem lay buried, unspoken, for many years in the minds of American women. It was a strange stirring, a sense of dissatisfaction, a yearning that women suffered in the middle of the twentieth century in the United States. Each suburban wife struggled with it alone. As she made the beds, shopped for groceries, matched slipcover material, ate peanut butter sandwiches with her children, chauffeured Cub Scouts and Brownies, lay beside her husband at night — she was afraid to ask even of herself the silent question — "Is this all?"

For over fifteen years there was no word of this yearning in the millions of words written about women, for women, in all the columns, books and articles by experts telling women their role was to seek fulfillment as wives and mothers. Over and over women heard in voices of tradition and of Freudian sophistication that they could desire no greater destiny than to glory in their own femininity. Experts told them how to catch a man and keep him, how to breastfeed children and handle their toilet training, how to cope with sibling rivalry and adolescent rebellion; how to buy a dishwasher, bake bread, cook gourmet snails, and build a swimming pool with their own hands; how to dress, look, and act more feminine and make marriage more exciting; how to keep their husbands from dying young and their sons from growing into delinquents. They were taught to pity the neurotic, unfeminine, unhappy women who wanted to be poets or physicists or presidents. They learned that truly feminine women do not want careers, higher education, political rights — the independence and the opportunities that the old-fashioned feminists fought for. Some women, in their forties and fifties, still remembered painfully giving up those dreams, but most of the younger women no longer even thought about them. A thousand expert voices applauded their femininity, their adjustment, their new maturity. All they had to do was devote their lives from earliest girlhood to finding a husband and bearing children. . . .

The suburban housewife — she was the dream image of the young American women and the envy, it was said, of women all over the world. The American housewife — freed by science and labor-saving appliances from the drudgery, the dangers of childbirth and the illnesses of her grandmother. She was healthy, beautiful, educated, concerned only about her husband, her children, her home. She had found true feminine fulfillment. As a housewife and mother, she was respected as a full and equal partner to man in his world. She was free to choose automobiles, clothes, appliances, supermarkets; she had everything that women ever dreamed of.

In the fifteen years after World War II, this mystique of feminine fulfillment became the cherished and self-perpetuating core of contemporary American culture. Millions of women lived their lives in the image of those pretty pictures of the American suburban housewife, kissing their husbands goodbye in front of the picture window, depositing their stationwagonsful of children at school, and smiling as they ran the new electric waxer over the spotless kitchen floor. They baked their own bread, sewed their own and their children's clothes, kept their new washing machines and dryers running all day. They changed the sheets on the beds twice a week instead of once, took the rug-hooking class in adult education, and pitied their poor frustrated mothers, who had dreamed of having a career. Their only dream was to be perfect wives and mothers; their highest ambition to have five children and a beautiful house, their only fight to get and keep their husbands. They had no thought for the unfeminine problems of the world outside the home; they wanted the men to make the major decisions. They gloried in their role as women, and wrote proudly on the census blank: "Occupation: housewife."

For over fifteen years, the words written for women, and the words women used when they talked to each other, while their husbands sat on the other side of the room and talked shop or politics or septic tanks, were about problems with their children, or how to keep their husbands happy, or improve their children's school, or cook chicken or make slipcovers. Nobody argued whether women were inferior or superior to men; they were simply different. Words like "emancipation" and "career" sounded strange and embarrassing; no one had used them for years. When a Frenchwoman named Simone de Beauvoir wrote a book called *The Second Sex,* an American critic commented that she obviously "didn't know what life was all about," and besides, she was talking about French women. The "woman problem" in America no longer existed.

If a woman had a problem in the 1950's and 1960's, she knew that something must be wrong with her marriage, or with herself. Other women were satisfied with their lives, she thought. What kind of a woman was she if she did not feel this mysterious fulfillment waxing the kitchen floor? She was so ashamed to admit her dissatisfaction that she never knew how many other women shared it. If she tried to tell her husband, he didn't understand what she was talking about. She did not really understand it herself. For over fifteen years women in America found it harder to talk about this problem than about sex. Even the psychoanalysts had no name for it. When a woman went to a psychiatrist for help, as many women did, she would say, "I'm so ashamed," or "I must be hopelessly neurotic." "I don't know what's wrong with women today," a suburban psychiatrist said uneasily. "I only know something is wrong because most of my patients happen to be women. And their problem isn't sexual." Most women with this problem did not go to see a psychoanalyst, however. "There's nothing wrong really," they kept telling themselves. "There isn't any problem."

But on an April morning in 1959, I heard a mother of four, having coffee with four other mothers in a suburban development fifteen miles from New York, say in a tone of quiet desperation, "the problem." And the others knew, without words, that she was not talking about a problem with her husband, or her children, or her home. Suddenly they realized they all shared the same problem, the problem that has no name. They began, hesitantly, to talk about it. Later, after they had picked up their children at nursery school and taken them home to nap, two of the women cried, in sheer relief, just to know they were not alone.

Gradually I came to realize that the problem that has no name was shared by countless women in America. As a magazine writer I often interviewed women about problems with their children, or their marriages, or their houses, or their communities. But after a while I began to recognize the telltale signs of this other problem. I saw the same signs in suburban ranch houses and split-levels on Long Island and in New Jersey and Westchester County; in colonial houses in a small Massachusetts town; on patios in Memphis; in suburban and city apartments; in living rooms in the Midwest. Sometimes I sensed the problem, not as a reporter, but as a suburban housewife, for during this time I was also bringing up my own three children in Rockland County, New York. I heard echoes of the problem in college dormitories and semi-private maternity wards, at PTA meetings and luncheons of the League of Women Voters, at suburban cocktail parties, in station wagons waiting for trains, and in snatches of conversation overheard at Schrafft's. The groping words I heard from other women, on quiet afternoons when children were at school or on quiet evenings when husbands worked late, I think I understood first as a woman long before I understood their larger social and psychological implications.

Just what was this problem that has no name? What were the words women used when they tried to express it? Sometimes a woman would say "I feel empty somehow . . . incomplete." Or she would say, "I feel as if I don't exist." Sometimes she blotted out the feeling with a tranquilizer. Sometimes she thought the problem was with her husband, or her children, or that what she really needed was to redecorate her house, or move to a better neighborhood, or have an affair, or another baby. Sometimes, she went to a doctor with symptoms she could hardly describe: "A tired feeling . . . I get so angry with the children it scares me . . . I feel like crying without any reason." (A Cleveland doctor called it "the housewife's syndrome.") . . .

Most men, and some women, still did not know that this problem was real. But those who had faced it honestly knew that all the superficial remedies, the sympathetic advice, the scolding words and the cheering words were somehow drowning the problem in unreality. A bitter laugh was beginning to be heard from American women. They were admired, envied, pitied, theorized over until they were sick of it, offered drastic solutions or silly choices that no one could take seriously. They got all kinds of advice from the growing armies of marriage and child-guidance counselors, psychotherapists, and armchair psychologists, on how to adjust to their role as housewives. No other road to fulfillment was offered to American women in the middle of the twentieth century. Most adjusted to their role and suffered or ignored the problem that has no name. It can be less painful for a woman, not to hear the strange, dissatisfied voice stirring within her.

It is no longer possible to ignore that voice, to dismiss the desperation of so many American women. This is not what being a woman means, no matter what the experts say. For human suffering there is a reason; perhaps the reason has not been found because the right questions have not been asked, or pressed far enough. I do not accept the answer that there is no problem because American women have luxuries that women in other times and lands never dreamed of; part of the strange newness of the problem is that it cannot be understood in terms of the age-old material problems of man: poverty, sickness, hunger, cold. The women who suffer this problem have a hunger that food cannot fill. It persists in women whose husbands are struggling internes and law clerks, or prosperous doctors and lawyers; in wives of workers and executives who make $5,000 a year or $50,000. It is not caused by lack of material advantages; it may not even be felt by women preoccupied with desperate problems of hunger, poverty or illness. And women who think it will be solved by more money, a bigger house, a second car, moving to a better suburb, often discover it gets worse.

It is no longer possible today to blame the problem on loss of femininity: to say that education and independence and equality with men have made American women unfeminine. I have heard so many women try to deny this dissatisfied voice within themselves because it does not fit the pretty picture of femininity the experts have given them. I think, in fact, that this is the first clue to the mystery: the problem cannot be understood in the generally accepted terms by which scientists have studied women, doctors have treated them, counselors have advised them, and writers have written about them. Women who suffer this problem, in whom this voice is stirring, have lived their whole lives in the pursuit of feminine fulfillment. They are not career women (although career women may have other problems); they are women whose greatest ambition has been marriage and children. For the oldest of these women, these daughters of the American middle class, no other dream was possible. The ones in their forties and fifties who once had other dreams gave them up and threw themselves joyously into life as housewives. For the youngest, the new wives and mothers, this was the only dream. They are the ones who quit high school and college to marry, or marked time in some job in which they had no real interest until they married. These women are very "feminine" in the usual sense, and yet they still suffer the problem. . . .

If I am right, the problem that has no name stirring in the minds of so many American women today is not a matter of loss of femininity or too much education, or the demands of domesticity. It is far more important than anyone recognizes. It is the key to these other new and old problems which have been torturing women and their husbands and children, and puzzling their doctors and educators for years. It may well be the key to our future as a nation and a culture. We can no longer ignore that voice within women that says: "I want something more than my husband and my children and my home."

Casey Hayden and Mary King, "A Kind of Memo" to Women in the Peace and Freedom Movements, 1965

We've talked a lot, to each other and to some of you, about our own and other women's problems in trying to live in our personal lives and in our work as independent and creative people. In these conversations we've found what seem to be recurrent ideas or themes. Maybe we can look at these things many of us perceive, often as a result of insights learned from the movement:

• Sex and caste: There seem to be many parallels that can be drawn between treatment of Negroes and treatment of women in our society as a whole. But in particular, women we've talked to who work in the movement seem to be caught up in a common-law caste system that operates, sometimes subtly, forcing them to work around or outside hierarchical structures of power which may exclude them. . . . It is a . . . system which, at its worst, uses and exploits women.

This is complicated by several facts, among them: 1) The caste system is not institutionalized by law (women have the right to vote, to sue for divorce, etc.); 2) Women can't withdraw from the situation (a la nationalism) or overthrow it; 3) There are biological differences (even though those biological differences are usually discussed or accepted without taking present and future technology into account so we probably can't be sure what these differences mean). Many people who are very hip to the implications of the racial caste system, even people in the movement, don't seem to be able to see the sexual-caste system and if the question is raised they respond with: "That's the way it's supposed to be. There are biological differences." Or with other statements which recall a white segregationist confronted with integration.

• Women and problems of work: The caste-system perspective dictates the roles assigned to women in the movement, and certainly even more to women outside the movement. Within the movement, questions arise in situations ranging from relationships of women organizers to men in the community, to who cleans the freedom house, to who holds leadership positions, to who does secretarial work, and to who acts as spokesman for groups. Other problems arise between women with varying degrees of awareness of themselves as being as capable as men but held back from full participation, or between women who see themselves as needing more control of their work than other women demand. And there are problems with relationships between white women and black women.

• Women and personal relations with men: Having learned from the movement to think radically about the personal worth and abilities of people whose role in society had gone unchallenged before, a lot of women in the movement have begun trying to apply those lessons to their own relations with men. Each of us probably has her own story of the various results, and of the internal struggle occasioned by trying to break out of very deeply learned fears, needs, and self-perceptions, and of

---

Mary King and Casey Hayden, "A Kind of Memo from Casey Hayden and Mary King to a Number of Other Women in the Peace and Freedom Movements," in Mary Elizabeth King, *Freedom Song: A Personal Story of the 1960s Civil Rights Movement* (New York: William Morrow, 1987), appendix 3, 571–574.

what happens when we try to replace them with concepts of people and freedom learned from the movement and organizing.

• Institutions: Nearly everyone has real questions about those institutions which shape perspectives on men and women: marriage, childrearing patterns, women's (and men's) magazines, etc. People are beginning to think about and even to experiment with new forms in these areas.

• Men's reactions to the questions raised here: A very few men seem to feel, when they hear conversations involving these problems, that they have a right to be present and participate in them, since they are so deeply involved. At the same time, very few men can respond nondefensively, since the whole idea is either beyond their comprehension or threatens and exposes them. The usual response is laughter. That inability to see the whole issue as serious, as the straitjacketing of both sexes, and as societally determined often shapes our own response so that we learn to think in their terms about ourselves and to feel silly rather than trust our inner feelings. The problems we're listing here, and what others have said about them, are therefore largely drawn from conversations among women only — and that difficulty in establishing dialogue with men is a recurring theme among people we've talked to.

• Lack of community for discussion: Nobody is writing, or organizing or talking publicly about women in any way that reflects the problems that various women in the movement come across and which we've tried to touch above. . . .

The reason we want to try to open up dialogue is mostly subjective. Working in the movement often intensifies personal problems, especially if we start trying to apply things we're learning there to our personal lives. Perhaps we can start to talk with each other more openly than in the past and create a community of support for each other so we can deal with ourselves and others with integrity and can therefore keep working.

Objectively, the chances seem nil that we could start a movement based on anything as distant to general American thought as a sex-caste system. Therefore, most of us will probably want to work full time on problems such as war, poverty, race. The very fact that the country can't face, much less deal with, the questions we're raising means that the movement is one place to look for some relief. Real efforts at dialogue within the movement and with whatever liberal groups, community women, or students might listen are justified. That is, all the problems between men and women and all the problems of women functioning in society as equal human beings are among the most basic that people face. We've talked in the movement about trying to build a society which would see basic human problems (which are now seen as private troubles), as public problems and would try to shape institutions to meet human needs rather than shaping people to meet the needs of those with power. To raise questions like those above illustrates very directly that society hasn't dealt with some of its deepest problems and opens discussion of why that is so. (In one sense, it is a radicalizing question that can take people beyond legalistic solutions into areas of personal and institutional change.) The second objective reason we'd like to see discussion begin is that we've learned a great deal in the movement and perhaps this is one area where a determined attempt to apply ideas we've learned there can produce some new alternatives.

NOW's Statement of Purpose, 1966

We, men and women who hereby constitute ourselves as the National Organization for Women, believe that the time has come for a new movement toward true equality for all women in America, and toward a fully equal partnership of the sexes, as part of the world-wide revolution of human rights now taking place within and beyond our national borders.

The purpose of NOW is to take action to bring women into full participation in the mainstream of American society now, exercising all the privileges and responsibilities thereof in truly equal partnership with men.

We believe the time has come to move beyond the abstract argument, discussion and symposia over the status and special nature of women which has raged in America in recent years; the time has come to confront, with concrete action, the conditions that now prevent women from enjoying the equality of opportunity and freedom of choice which is their right as individual Americans, and as human beings.

NOW is dedicated to the proposition that women first and foremost are human beings, who, like all other people in our society, must have the chance to develop their fullest human potential. We believe that women can achieve such equality only by accepting to the full the challenges and responsibilities they share with all other people in our society, as part of the decision-making mainstream of American political, economic and social life.

We organize to initiate or support action, nationally or in any part of this nation, by individuals or organizations, to break through the silken curtain of prejudice and discrimination against women in government, industry, the professions, the churches, the political parties, the judiciary, the labor unions, in education, science, medicine, law, religion and every other field of importance in American society. . . .

There is no civil rights movement to speak for women, as there has been for Negroes and other victims of discrimination. The National Organization for Women must therefore begin to speak.

WE BELIEVE that the power of American law, and the protection guaranteed by the U.S. Constitution to the civil rights of all individuals, must be effectively applied and enforced to isolate and remove patterns of sex discrimination, to ensure equality of opportunity in employment and education, and equality of civil and political rights and responsibilities on behalf of women, as well as for Negroes and other deprived groups.

We realize that women's problems are linked to many broader questions of social justice; their solution will require concerted action by many groups. Therefore, convinced that human rights for all are indivisible, we expect to give active support to the common cause of equal rights for all those who suffer discrimination and deprivation, and we call upon other organizations committed to such goals to support our efforts toward equality for women.

WE DO NOT ACCEPT the token appointment of a few women to high-level positions in government and industry as a substitute for a serious continuing effort to recruit and advance women according to their individual abilities. To this end, we urge American government and industry to mobilize the same resources of ingenuity and command with which they have solved problems of far greater difficulty than those now impeding the progress of women.

WE BELIEVE that this nation has a capacity at least as great as other nations, to innovate new social institutions which will enable women to enjoy true equality of opportunity and responsibility in society, without conflict with their responsibilities as mothers and homemakers. In such innovations, America does not lead the Western world, but lags by decades behind many European countries. We do not accept the traditional assumption that a woman has to choose between marriage and motherhood, on the one hand, and serious participation in industry or the professions on the other. We question the present expectation that all normal women will retire from job or profession for ten or fifteen years, to devote their full time to raising children, only to reenter the job market at a relatively minor level. This in itself is a deterrent to the aspirations of women, to their acceptance into management or professional training courses, and to the very possibility of equality of opportunity or real choice, for all but a few women. Above all, we reject the assumption that these problems are the unique responsibility of each individual woman, rather than a basic social dilemma which society must solve. True equality of opportunity and freedom of choice for women requires such practical and possible innovations as a nationwide network of child-care centers, which will make it unnecessary for women to retire completely from society until their children are grown, and national programs to provide retraining for women who have chosen to care for their own children full time.

WE BELIEVE that it is as essential for every girl to be educated to her full potential of human ability as it is for every boy — with the knowledge that such education is the key to effective participation in today's economy and that, for a girl as for a boy, education can only be serious where there is expectation that it will be used in society. We believe that American educators are capable of devising means of imparting such expectations to girl students. Moreover, we consider the decline in the proportion of women receiving higher and professional education to be evidence of discrimination. This discrimination may take the form of quotas against the admission of women to colleges and professional schools; lack of encouragement by parents, counselors and educators; denial of loans or fellowships; or the traditional or arbitrary procedures in graduate and professional training geared in terms of men, which inadvertently discriminate against women. We believe that the same serious attention must be given to high school dropouts who are girls as to boys.

WE REJECT the current assumptions that a man must carry the sole burden of supporting himself, his wife, and family, and that a woman is automatically entitled to lifelong support by a man upon her marriage, or that marriage, home and family are primarily woman's world and responsibility — hers, to dominate, his to support. We believe that a true partnership between the sexes demands a different concept of marriage, an equitable sharing of the responsibilities of home and children and of the economic burdens of their support. We believe that proper recognition should be given to the economic and social value of homemaking and child care. To these ends, we will seek to open a reexamination of laws and mores governing marriage and divorce, for we believe that the current state of "half-equality" between the sexes discriminates against both men and women, and is the cause of much unnecessary hostility between the sexes.

WE BELIEVE that women must now exercise their political rights and responsibilities as American citizens. They must refuse to be segregated on the basis of sex into separate-and-not-equal ladies' auxiliaries in the political parties, and they must demand representation according to their numbers in the regularly constituted party committees — at local, state, and national levels — and in the informal power structure, participating fully in the selection of candidates and political decision-making, and running for office themselves.

IN THE INTERESTS OF THE HUMAN DIGNITY OF WOMEN, we will protest and endeavor to change the false image of women now prevalent in the mass media, and in the texts, ceremonies, laws, and practices of our major social institutions. Such images perpetuate contempt for women by society and by women for themselves. We are similarly opposed to all policies and practices — in church, state, college, factory, or office — which, in the guise of protectiveness, not only deny opportunities but also foster in women self-denigration, dependence, and evasion of responsibility, undermine their confidence in their own abilities and foster contempt for women.

NOW WILL HOLD ITSELF INDEPENDENT OF ANY POLITICAL PARTY in order to mobilize the political power of all women and men intent on our goals. We will strive to ensure that no party, candidate, President, senator, governor, congressman, or any public official who betrays or ignores the principle of full equality between the sexes is elected or appointed to office. If it is necessary to mobilize the votes of men and women who believe in our cause, in order to win for women the final right to be fully free and equal human beings, we so commit ourselves.

WE BELIEVE THAT women will do most to create a new image of women by *acting* now, and by speaking out in behalf of their own equality, freedom, and human dignity — not in pleas for special privilege, nor in enmity toward men, who are also victims of the current half-equality between the sexes — but in an active, self-respecting partnership with men. By so doing, women will develop confidence in their own ability to determine actively, in partnership with men, the conditions of their life, their choices, their future and their society.

Redstockings Manifesto, 1969

I. After centuries of individual and preliminary political struggle, women are uniting to achieve their final liberation from male supremacy. Redstockings is dedicated to building this unity and winning our freedom.

II. Women are an oppressed class. Our oppression is total, affecting every facet of our lives. We are exploited as sex objects, breeders, domestic servants, and cheap labor. We are considered inferior beings, whose only purpose is to enhance men's lives. Our humanity is denied. Our prescribed behavior is enforced by the threat of physical violence.

Because we have lived so intimately with our oppressors, in isolation from each other, we have been kept from seeing our personal suffering as a political condition. This creates the illusion that a woman's relationship with her man is a matter of interplay between two unique personalities, and can be worked out individually. In reality, every such relationship is a *class* relationship, and the conflicts between individual men and women are *political* conflicts that can only be solved collectively.

III. We identify the agents of our oppression as men. Male supremacy is the oldest, most basic form of domination. All other forms of exploitation and oppression (racism, capitalism, imperialism, etc.) are extensions of male supremacy: men dominate women, a few men dominate the rest. All power structures throughout history have been male-dominated and male-oriented. Men have controlled all political, economic and cultural institutions and backed up this control with physical force. They have used their power to keep women in an inferior position. *All men* receive economic, sexual, and psychological benefits from male supremacy. *All men* have oppressed women.

IV. Attempts have been made to shift the burden of responsibility from men to institutions or to women themselves. We condemn these arguments as evasions. Institutions alone do not oppress; they are merely tools of the oppressor. To blame institutions implies that men and women are equally victimized, obscures the fact that men benefit from the subordination of women, and gives men the excuse that they are forced to be oppressors. On the contrary, any man is free to renounce his superior position provided that he is willing to be treated like a woman by other men.

We also reject the idea that women consent to or are to blame for their own oppression. Women's submission is not the result of brainwashing, stupidity, or mental illness but of continual, daily pressure from men. We do not need to change ourselves, but to change men.

The most slanderous evasion of all is that women can oppress men. The basis for this illusion is the isolation of individual relationships from their political context and the tendency of men to see any legitimate challenge to their privileges as persecution.

V. We regard our personal experience, and our feelings about that experience, as the basis for an analysis of our common situation. We cannot rely on existing ideologies as they are all products of male supremacist culture. We question every generalization and accept none that are not confirmed by our experience.

Our chief task at present is to develop female class consciousness through sharing experience and publicly exposing the sexist foundation of all our institutions. Consciousness-raising is not "therapy," which implies the existence of individual solutions and falsely assumes that the male-female relationship is purely personal, but the only method by which we can ensure that our program for liberation is based on the concrete realities of our lives.

The first requirement for raising class consciousness is honesty, in private and in public, with ourselves and other women.

VI. We identify with all women. We define our best interest as that of the poorest, most brutally exploited woman.

We repudiate all economic, racial, educational or status privileges that divide us from other women. We are determined to recognize and eliminate any prejudices we may hold against other women.

We are committed to achieving internal democracy. We will do whatever is necessary to ensure that every woman in our movement has an equal chance to participate, assume responsibility, and develop her political potential.

VII. We call on all our sisters to unite with us in struggle.

We call on all men to give up their male privileges and support women's liberation in the interest of our humanity and their own.

In fighting for our liberation we will always take the side of women against their oppressors. We will not ask what is "revolutionary" or "reformist," only what is good for women.

The time for individual skirmishes has passed. This time we are going all the way.

July 7, 1969

Frances Beale, "Double Jeopardy: To Be Black and Female," 1970

In attempting to analyze the situation of the Black woman in America, one crashes abruptly into a solid wall of grave misconceptions, outright distortions of fact, and defensive attitudes on the part of many. The system of capitalism (and its afterbirth — racism) under which we all live has attempted by many devious ways and means to destroy the humanity of all people, and particularly the humanity of Black people. This has meant an outrageous assault on every Black man, woman, and child who reside in the United States.

In keeping with its goal of destroying the Black race's will to resist its subjugation, capitalism found it necessary to create a situation where the Black man found it impossible to find meaningful or productive employment. More often than not, he couldn't find work of any kind. And the Black woman likewise was manipulated by the system, economically exploited and physically assaulted. She could often find work in the white man's kitchen, however, and sometimes became the sole breadwinner of the family. This predicament has led to many psychological problems on the part of both man and woman and has contributed to the turmoil that we find in the Black family structure.

Unfortunately, neither the Black man nor the Black woman understood the true nature of the forces working upon them. Many Black women tended to accept the capitalist evaluation of manhood and womanhood and believed, in fact, that Black men were shiftless and lazy, otherwise they would get a job and support their families as they ought to. Personal relationships between Black men and women were thus torn asunder and one result has been the separation of man from wife, mother from child, etc.

America has defined the roles to which each individual should subscribe. It has defined "manhood" in terms of its own interests and "femininity" likewise. Therefore, an individual who has a good job, makes a lot of money, and drives a Cadillac is a real "man," and conversely, an individual who is lacking in these "qualities" is less of a man. . . .

The ideal model that is projected for a woman is to be surrounded by

A demonstration sponsored by the Congress of Racial Equality (CORE) outside Harlem Hospital Center in New York City, May 1970. After the early 1960s, urgent demands for racial justice were made in America's northern ghettos, not just in southern communities. The demonstrators in this photograph, many of them women from the local community, were protesting excessive delays in emergency room treatment and a lack of common courtesy from staff members at the hospital. Knowing that blacks suffered a higher rate of disease than other Americans, Harlem residents were bitterly disappointed in the failure of the hospital, recently moved to a brand-new building, to provide African-Americans with adequate care.

hypocritical homage and estranged from all real work, spending idle hours primping and preening, obsessed with conspicuous consumption, and limiting life's functions to simply a sex role. We unqualitatively reject these respective models. A woman who stays at home caring for children and the house often leads an extremely sterile existence. She must lead her entire life as a satellite to her mate. He goes out into society and brings back a little piece of the world for her. His interests and his understanding of the world become her own and she cannot develop herself as an individual having been reduced to only a biological function. This kind of woman leads a parasitic existence that can aptly be described as legalized prostitution.

Furthermore it is idle dreaming to think of Black women simply caring for their homes and children like the middle-class white model. Most Black women have to work to help house, feed, and clothe their families. Black women make up a substantial percentage of the Black working force, and this is true for the poorest Black family as well as the so-called "middle-class" family. . . .

Unfortunately, there seems to be some confusion in the Movement today as to who has been oppressing whom. Since the advent of Black power, the Black male has exerted a more prominent leadership role in our struggle for justice in this country. He sees the system for what it really is for the most part, but where he rejects its values and mores on many issues, when it comes to women, he seems to take his guidelines from the pages of the *Ladies' Home Journal.* Certain Black men are maintaining that they have been castrated by society but that Black women somehow escaped this persecution and even contributed to this emasculation.

Let me state here and now that the Black woman in America can justly be described as a "slave of a slave." By reducing the Black man in America to such abject oppression, the Black woman had no protector and was used, and is still being used in some cases, as the scapegoat for the evils that this horrendous system has perpetrated on Black men. Her physical image has been maliciously maligned; she has been sexually molested and abused by the white colonizer; she has suffered the worse kind of economic exploitation, having been forced to serve as the white woman's maid and wet nurse for white offspring while her own children were more often than not starving and neglected. It is the depth of degradation to be socially manipulated, physically raped, used to undermine your own household, and to be powerless to reverse this syndrome.

It is true that our husbands, fathers, brothers, and sons have been emasculated, lynched, and brutalized. They have suffered from the cruelest assault on mankind that the world has ever known. However, it is a gross distortion of fact to state that Black women have oppressed Black men. The capitalist system found it expedient to enslave and oppress them and proceeded to do so without consultation or the signing of any agreements with Black women.

It must also be pointed out at this time that Black women are not resentful of the rise to power of Black men. We welcome it. We see in it the eventual liberation of all Black people from this corrupt system of capitalism. Nevertheless, this does not mean that you have to negate one for the other. This kind of thinking is a product of miseducation; that it's either X or it's Y. It is fallacious reasoning that in order for the Black man to be strong, the Black woman has to be weak.

Those who are exerting their "manhood" by telling Black women to step back into a domestic, submissive role are assuming a counter-revolutionary position. Black women likewise have been abused by the system and we must begin talking about the elimination of all kinds of oppression. If we are talking about building a strong nation, capable of throwing off the yoke of capitalist oppression, then we are talking about the total involvement of every man, woman, and child, each with a highly developed political consciousness. We need our whole army out there dealing with the enemy and not half an army.

There are also some Black women who feel that there is no more productive role in life than having and raising children. This attitude often reflects the conditioning of the society in which we live and is adopted from a bourgeois white model. Some young sisters who have never had to maintain a household and accept the confining role which this entails tend to romanticize (along with the help of a few brothers) this role of housewife and mother. Black women who have had to endure this kind of function are less apt to have these utopian visions.

Those who project in an intellectual manner how great and rewarding this role will be and who feel that the most important thing that they can contribute to the Black nation is children are doing themselves a great injustice. This line of reasoning completely negates the contributions that Black women have historically made to our struggle for liberation. These Black women include Sojourner Truth, Harriet Tubman, Mary McLeod Bethune, and Fannie Lou Hamer, to name but a few.

We live in a highly industrialized society and every member of the Black nation must be as academically and technologically developed as possible. To wage a revolution, we need competent teachers, doctors, nurses, electronics experts, chemists, biologists, physicists, political scientists, and so on and so forth. Black women sitting at home reading bedtime stories to their children are just not going to make it. . . .

Much has been written recently about the white women's liberation movement in the United States, and the question arises whether there are any parallels between this struggle and the movement on the part of Black women for total emancipation. While there are certain comparisons that one can make, simply because we both live under the same exploitative system, there are certain differences, some of which are quite basic.

The white women's movement is far from being monolithic. Any white group that does not have an anti-imperialist and anti-racist ideology has absolutely nothing in common with the Black woman's struggle. In fact, some groups come to the incorrect conclusion that their oppression is due simply to male chauvinism. They therefore have an extremely anti-male tone to their dissertations. Black people are engaged in a life-and-death struggle and the main emphasis of Black women must be to combat the capitalist, racist exploitation of Black people. While it is true that male chauvinism has become institutionalized in American society, one must always look for the main enemy — the fundamental cause of the female condition.

Another major differentiation is that the white women's liberation movement is basically middle-class. Very few of these women suffer the extreme economic exploitation that most Black women are subjected to day by day. This is the factor that is most crucial for us. It is not an intellectual persecution alone; it is not an intellectual outburst for us; it is quite real. We as Black women have got to deal with the problems that the Black masses deal with, for our problems in reality are one and the same.

If the white groups do not realize that they are in fact fighting capitalism and racism, we do not have common bonds. If they do not realize that the reasons for their condition lie in the system and not simply that men get a vicarious pleasure out of "consuming their bodies for exploitative reasons" (this kind of reasoning seems to be quite prevalent in certain white women's groups), then we cannot unite with them around common grievances or even discuss these groups in a serious manner because they're completely irrelevant to the Black struggle. . . .

Mirta Vidal on Chicanas and the Women's Liberation Movement, 1971

At the end of May 1971, more than 600 Chicanas met in Houston, Texas, to hold the first national conference of Raza women. For those of us who were there it was clear that this conference was not just another national gathering of the Chicano movement.

Chicanas came from all parts of the country inspired by the prospect of discussing issues that have long been on their minds and which they now see not as individual problems but as an important and integral part of a movement for liberation.

The resolutions coming out of the two largest workshops, "Sex and the Chicana" and "Marriage — Chicana Style," called for "free, legal abortions and birth control for the Chicano community, controlled by *Chicanas*." As Chicanas, the resolution stated, "we have a right to control our own bodies." The resolutions also called for "24-hour child-care centers in Chicano communities" and explained that there is a critical need for these since "Chicana motherhood should not preclude educational, political, social and economic advancement."

While these resolutions articulated the most pressing needs of Chicanas today, the conference as a whole reflected a rising consciousness of the Chicana about her special oppression in this society.

With their growing involvement in the struggle for Chicano liberation and the emergence of the feminist movement, Chicanas are beginning to challenge every social institution which contributes to and is responsible for their oppression, from inequality on the job to their role in the home. They are questioning "machismo," discrimination in education, the double standard, the role of the Catholic Church, and all the backward ideology designed to keep women subjugated. . . .

The oppression suffered by Chicanas is different from that suffered by most women in this country. Because Chicanas are part of an oppressed nationality, they are subjected to the racism practiced against La Raza. Since the overwhelming majority of Chicanos are workers, Chicanas are also victims of the exploitation of the working class. But in addition, Chicanas, along with the rest of women, are relegated to an inferior position because of their sex. Thus, Raza women suffer a triple form of oppression: as members of an oppressed nationality, as workers, *and* as women. Chicanas have no trouble understanding this. At the Houston conference 84 percent of the women surveyed felt that "there is a distinction between the problems of the Chicana and those of other women."

On the other hand, they also understand that the struggle now unfolding against the oppression of women is not only relevant to them, but *is* their struggle.

Because sexism and male chauvinism are so deeply rooted in this society, there is a strong tendency, even within the Chicano movement, to deny the basic right of Chicanas to organize around their own concrete issues. Instead they are told to stay away from the women's liberation movement because it is an "Anglo thing."

We need only analyze the origin of male supremacy to expose this false position. The inferior role of women in society does not date back to the beginning of time. In fact, before the Europeans came to this part of the world women enjoyed a position of equality with men. The submission of women, along with institutions such as the church and the patriarchy, was imported by the European colonizers, and remains to this day part of Anglo society. Machismo — in English, "male chauvinism" — is the one thing, if any, that should be labeled an "Anglo thing."

When Chicano men oppose the efforts of women to move against their oppression, they are actually opposing the struggle of every woman in this country aimed at changing a society in which Chicanos themselves are oppressed. They are saying to 51 percent of this country's population that they have no right to fight for their liberation.

Moreover, they are denying one half of La Raza this basic right. They are denying Raza women, who are triply oppressed, the right to struggle around their specific, real, and immediate needs.

In essence, they are doing just what the white male rulers of this country have done. The white male rulers want Chicanas to accept their oppression because they understand that when Chicanas begin a movement demanding legal abortions, child care, and equal pay for equal work, this movement will pose a real threat to their ability to rule.

Opposition to the struggles of women to break the chains of their oppression is not in the interest of the oppressed but only in the interest of the oppressor. And that is the logic of the arguments of those who say that Chicanas do not want to or need to be liberated. . . .

Stripped of all rationalizations, when Chicanos deny support to the independent organization of Chicanas, what they are saying is simply that Chicanas are not oppressed. And that is the central question we must ask: are Chicanas oppressed?

All other arguments aside, the fact is that Chicanas *are* oppressed and that the battles they are now waging and will wage in the future, are for things they need: the right to legal abortions, the right to adequate child care, the right to contraceptive information and devices, the right to decide how many children they do or do not want to have. In short, the right to control their own bodies. . . .

Coupled with this campaign to repeal all abortion laws, women are fighting to end all forced sterilizations, a campaign in which Chicanas will play a central role. This demand is of key importance to Chicanas who are the victims of forced sterilizations justified by the viciously racist ideology that the problems of La Raza are caused by Raza women having too many babies.

In line with other brutal abuses of women, Chicanas have been used as guinea pigs for experimentation with contraception. This was done recently in San Antonio by a doctor who wanted to test the reaction of women to birth control pills. Without informing them or asking their opinion, he gave some of the women dummy pills (placebos) that would not prevent conception, and as a result some of the women became pregnant. When questioned about his action, his reply was: "If you think you can explain a placebo test to women like these you never met Mrs. Gomez from the West Side."

The feminist movement today provides a vehicle for organizing against and putting an end to such racist, sexist practices. And that is what women are talking about when they talk about women's liberation.

Another essential fight that Chicanas have begun is around the need for adequate child care. While billions of dollars are spent yearly by this government on war, no money can be found to alleviate the plight of millions of women who, in addition to being forced to work, have families to care for. . . .

Demands such as twenty-four hour child-care centers financed by the government and controlled by the community, are the kinds of concrete issues that Chicanas are fighting for. As Chicanas explain in "A Proposal for Childcare," published in *Regeneración,* "Child care must be provided as a public service, like public schools, unemployment insurance, social security, and so forth. The potential for a mass movement around this initiative is clear."

An important aspect of the struggles of Chicanas is the demand that the gains made through their campaigns be *controlled by Chicanas.* The demand for community control is a central axis of the Chicano liberation struggle as a whole. Thus, when Chicanas, as Chicanas, raise demands for child-care facilities, abortion clinics, etc., controlled by Chicanas, their fight is an integral part of the Chicano liberation struggle.

When Chicanas choose to organize into their own separate organizations, they are not turning away from La Causa or waging a campaign against men. They are saying to Chicanos: "We are oppressed as Chicanas and we are moving against our oppression. Support our struggles." The sooner that Chicanos understand the need for women to struggle around their own special demands, through their own organizations, the further La Raza as a whole will be on the road toward liberation.

It is important to keep in mind that many of the misunderstandings that have arisen so far in the Chicano movement regarding Chicanas are due primarily to the newness of this development, and many will be resolved through the course of events. One thing, however, is clear — Chicanas are determined to fight. . . .

The struggle for women's liberation is the Chicana's struggle, and only a strong independent Chicana movement, as part of the general women's liberation movement and as part of the movement of La Raza, can ensure its success.

※ *E S S A Y S*

In the first essay, Anne Standley, an independent historian, examines the role and consciousness of African-American women in the civil rights movement. She argues that these women were reluctant to acknowledge or challenge sexism in the movement because they feared that doing so would undercut black men or divert attention from the issue of racism. In the second essay, Alice Echols of Occidental College examines the origins of radical feminism, and explores why the champions of "women's liberation" were mostly white and middle class. In the last essay, Margaret Rose recounts the history of women's involvement in the United Farm Workers of America (UFW) union, which César Chávez organized in 1962 to improve the lives of Mexican and Chicano farm laborers. Although Chicanas and Mexicanas were most often asked to perform the UFW's domestic tasks, the union inadvertently laid the foundation for a feminist consciousness among its female workers.

The Role of Black Women in the Civil Rights Movement

ANNE STANDLEY

The role of black women in the civil rights movement has received scant attention from historians. Most studies of the movement have examined such organizations as the Southern Christian Leadership Conference, the Student Nonviolent Coordinating Committee, the Congress of Racial Equality, and the National Association for the Advancement of Colored People, and accordingly have focused on the black ministers who served as officers in those organizations, all of whom were men. Harvard Sitkoff's list of the leaders of the movement, for example, consisted exclusively of men — Martin Luther King, Jr., of SCLC, James Forman and John Lewis of SNCC, James Farmer of CORE, Roy Wilkins of the NAACP, and Whitney Young of the National Urban League. The accounts of other historians, such as Aldon Morris, Clayborne Carson, and August Meier, also showed male preachers spearheading the various protests — boycotts of bus companies and white-owned businesses, voter registration drives, and marches — that constituted the movement. Likewise, the vast majority of students leading the sit-ins and freedom rides named by Sitkoff were men. He cited only two of the many women who held positions of leadership in the movement — Fannie Lou Hamer, who was elected delegate to the Democratic National Convention by the Mississippi Freedom Democratic Party in 1964, and Ella Baker, executive secretary of SCLC — and understated their influence. . . .

The argument that men were the principal leaders of the civil rights movement is not wholly inaccurate. According to women who achieved prominence within the movement, such as Septima Clark, who trained teachers of citizenship schools for SCLC, or Ella Baker, and historians Jacqueline Jones and Paula Giddings, the ministers' sexism and authoritarian views of leadership prevented women from assuming command of any of the movement organizations. Indeed, in light of the advantages men possessed in establishing themselves as leaders of the movement — the preachers' virtual monopoly on political power within the black community and the exclusion of women from the ministry in many black churches — it is remarkable that any women achieved positions of authority.

Yet, in fact, women exerted an enormous influence, both formally, as members of the upper echelon of SNCC, SCLC, and the Mississippi Freedom Democratic Party, and informally, as spontaneous leaders and dedicated participants. Many of

"The Role of Black Women in the Civil Rights Movement" by Anne Standley from *Black Women's History*, ed. Darlene Clark Hine, 10 (1990), pp. 183–201.

the protests that historians describe as led by ministers were initiated by women. For example, Martin Luther King, Jr., is usually cited as the leader of the Montgomery Bus Boycott, since it was King who was appointed director of the organization that coordinated the boycott, the Montgomery Improvement Association. Yet the boycott was started by a woman, Jo Ann Robinson, and by the women's group that she headed, the Women's Political Council. Black women directed voter registration drives, taught in freedom schools, and provided food and housing for movement volunteers. As members of the MFDP, women won positions as delegates to the national Democratic convention in 1964 and as representatives to Congress. They demonstrated a heroism no less than that of men. They suffered the same physical abuse, loss of employment, destruction of property, and risk to their lives.

Black women also deserve credit for the refusal within the movement to accept halfway measures towards eradicating Jim Crow practices. Fannie Lou Hamer's rejection of the compromise offered the MFDP delegation at the Democratic National Convention in 1964 typified the courage of black women, who formed the majority of the preachers' congregations and whose pressure forced the ministers in SCLC, CORE, and the other movement associations to persist in the face of white opposition to their demands. Paula Giddings reported that when the ministers of Montgomery met after the first day of the bus boycott to discuss whether to continue the boycott, they agreed on the condition that their names not be publicized as the boycott leaders. E. D. Nixon, former head of the Montgomery NAACP, shamed them into giving their public endorsement by reminding them of the women to whom they were accountable: "How you gonna have a mass meeting, gonna boycott a city bus line without the white folks knowing about it? You guys have went around here and lived off these poor washerwomen all your lives and ain't never done nothing for 'em. Now you got a chance to do something for 'em, you talking about you don't want the White folks to know about it."

As well, black women were responsible for the movement's success in generating popular support for the movement among rural blacks. Ella Baker convinced SCLC to jettison plans to take control of SNCC, allowing the student-run group to remain independent of the other movement organizations and to adopt, with Baker's encouragement, an egalitarian approach to decisionmaking. Because SNCC workers formulated the organization's objectives by soliciting the views of members of black communities in which the volunteers worked, they were able to build considerable grass-roots support for the movement.

Despite the exclusion of black women from top positions in movement organizations and the little recognition they received from either blacks or whites for their contributions, the published accounts of black women activists suggest that the movement gave women as well as men a sense of empowerment. . . . Yet these women differed in their analyses of the cause of the racial oppression that they combatted. Two of the older women leaders — Daisy Bates, who was president of the NAACP State Conference of Branches, and who led the integration of Central High School in Little Rock, Arkansas, and Jo Ann Robinson — and a younger leader, Diane Nash, who organized sit-ins and freedom rides for SNCC, viewed racism as politically motivated. They believed that if blacks could obtain the vote, white politicians would be forced to act against racial discrimination at the polls, segregated schools, and the varied forms of extralegal violence carried out against blacks. Blacks could use their political influence to improve their economic status, which in turn would enhance their image among whites.

Because they saw themselves as having to convince whites to support the movement, and because they identified so completely with the struggle for civil rights, Bates, Robinson, and Nash refrained from making critical judgments about the movement or their roles within it. . . . Consequently their behavior showed contradictions — on the one hand a boldness in initiating protests and applying pressure on whites in power, while at the same time a submissiveness in their acceptance of the authority of the black male clergy.

Jo Anne Robinson was born in 1916 in Colloden, Georgia, twenty-five miles from Macon. She was the youngest of twelve children. Her family subsequently moved to Macon, where she graduated first in her class from an all black high school. Robinson received a bachelor's degree from Georgia State College in Fort Valley, taught for five years at a public school in Macon, and earned a master's degree in English literature from Atlanta University. In 1949, after teaching for a year at Mary Allen College in Crockett, Texas, she moved to Montgomery to join the faculty at Alabama State University. Robinson chaired the Women's Political Council in Montgomery, an organization of professional women that sought to raise the status of blacks by working with juvenile and adult delinquents and organizing voter registration. She also served on the Executive Board of the Montgomery Improvement Association and edited the MIA newsletter.

Robinson declared that in publishing her memoir, she hoped to improve whites' image of blacks by demonstrating blacks' courage, dedication, and self-discipline in their fight for their rights. Robinson saw the movement as blacks' attempt to overcome the circumstances that degraded them — to secure the same living conditions and opportunities as whites — so as to live decently and thereby prove their equality with whites. . . .

Robinson's view of the movement as the first step towards blacks' redemption in the eyes of whites, and the role she assumed as the movement's publicist, left little room for a candid evaluation of the male leadership or for challenging its authority. She briefly criticized the ministers in Montgomery for their timidity, stating that only when they read a circular advertising the bus boycott and realized that "all the city's black congregations were quite intelligent on the matter and were planning to support the one-day boycott with or without the ministers' leadership" did they endorse it. She offset this reproach, however, with praise for the preachers' work, and attributed the boycott's success to the clergymen.

> Had it not been for the ministers and the support they received from their wonderful congregations, the outcome of the boycott might have been different. The ministers gave themselves, their time . . . and their leadership . . . which set examples for the laymen to follow. They gave us confidence, faith in ourselves, faith in them and their leadership, that helped the congregations to support the movement every foot of the way.

In her memoir, *The Long Shadow of Little Rock,* Daisy Bates displayed similar contradictions between her readiness to confront her white oppressors, which she demonstrated both as a child and as an adult, and her acceptance of what she regarded as a flawed black leadership. Bates grew up in southern Arkansas, in a town controlled by a sawmill company. She first experienced discrimination at the age of eight, when a white grocer refused to serve her until he had waited on all of the white customers. . . .

Bates not only challenged whites while growing up; she also defied the authority of her parents and members of the black community. . . . Bates's narrative showed that as an adult, she continued to challenge those in power. She met with the governor of Arkansas and the U.S. Attorney to urge them, unsuccessfully, to respond to the whites' violence. In contrast, however, she appears to have deferred to the male leadership in the black community. She made only a passing reference to her irritation at the black ministers' silence in the face of the whites' terrorism carried out against the black students, suggesting that she suppressed her frustration. In her conclusion, she assailed Congress and the Eisenhower administration for their lackluster support of desegregation, but like Robinson, refrained from placing any blame for the movement's slow progress on its leadership.

One can see similar inconsistencies in the actions of Diane Nash, a SNCC volunteer. Nash grew up in Chicago and came to Nashville to attend Fisk University. Nash's shock at the segregation of restaurants, water fountains, and other public facilities in the south prompted her to join SNCC. In 1965, Nash wrote an article for *Ebony* that implied that she accepted the prevailing view that the civil rights movement, and specifically SCLC, should be led primarily by men. Nash's article, "The Men Behind Martin Luther King" profiled the male staff members of SCLC. She depicted the women on the staff, who numbered three out of a total of twelve, as important but peripheral figures. . . . At no point did Nash question the women's secondary status within SCLC.

Nash's prominence in protest efforts, however, seemed to contradict the unspoken assumption of her article that men should lead the movement. Nash chaired the central committee of the sit-in movement in Nashville. She also assembled a second group of freedom riders to continue the journey when harassment forced the first group to disperse in Birmingham before they reached their destination of New Orleans. . . .

While Bates, Robinson, and Nash attributed racism to blacks' lack of representation in the political process, the majority of black women leaders who left accounts of their experiences regarded racial oppression as symptomatic of a structurally flawed society. Disheartened by the movement's fragmentation in the late sixties and by what they regarded as its limited success, they concluded that racial oppression formed part of a larger system of inequities that characterized American society and that could not be eradicated without addressing the other injustices to which it was connected. One activist who became disillusioned was Jean Smith, a student at Howard University who registered voters for SNCC in 1963 and who organized the MFDP meetings that elected an integrated delegation to the Democratic National Convention in 1964. Smith maintained that the right to vote, while unifying the black community and giving blacks the confidence to assert themselves and challenge racist laws or customs, had proved ineffectual in diminishing white hegemony and improving the living conditions of blacks.

The best way to understand is to look at what the Negro people who cast their lot with the Movement believed. They believed, I think, that their participation in the drive for voting rights would ultimately result in the relief of their poverty and hopelessness. They thought that with the right to vote they could end the exploitation of their labor by the plantation owners. They thought they could get better schools for their children; they could get sewers dug and sidewalks paved. They thought they could get adequate public-health facilities for their communities. And of course they got none of these. . . . They believed there was a link between representation in government and making that government work for you. What they — and I — discovered was that for some people, this link does not exist. . . .

This disenchantment with the civil rights movement led some activists to temporarily embrace separatism. Smith, for example, in 1968 argued for a self-sufficient black community as the solution to blacks' political impotence. . . . Two years earlier, in 1966, [Joyce] Ladner [a SNCC volunteer] had also abandoned integration as a goal, convinced by the unrelenting brutality of whites that black power offered the most effective means of improving the status of blacks.

> When Vernon Dahmier [Ladner's mentor] was killed, my faith in integration was shaken. I found myself trying to justify my belief that "Black and white together" was still the solution to the race problem . . . What Blacks needed to do, I thought, was to unite as a group and develop their own institutions and communities. What they needed was Black power! . . .

In addition to embracing separatism, Ladner turned to marxism for a diagnosis and a solution to racial oppression, along with Frances Beale, a former SNCC activist. Ladner asserted that in aspiring to middle-class goals of upward mobility and wealth, blacks condoned a structure of economic inequality. For Ladner, it was not blacks' lowly position in the hierarchy, but their acceptance of a capitalist economy which required a hierarchy, in which the fortunes of a few came from the exploitation of many, that oppressed them. Similarly, Frances Beale claimed that the feminists who sought only to improve their own position, demanding, for example, equal pay for equal work, failed to attack capitalism as the root of inequality and thus perpetuated an unjust system. . . .

Robinson, Bates and Nash sought to present a united front to white authorities. Consequently, they suppressed their differences with the male leadership. In contrast, the other activists aired their disagreements with the men managing the movement organizations, although most did so only in hindsight.

Only two of the women, Ella Baker and Septima Clark, confronted the male leaders of the movement while working with them to challenge their policies. Baker, like Robinson and Bates, belonged to the older generation of women civil rights leaders. She was 57 when SCLC appointed her as executive secretary in 1960. Baker was born in 1903 in Norfolk, Virginia. . . . Baker's father waited on tables for the Norfolk-Washington ferry; her mother tended to the sick in the community. After graduating from Shaw University in Raleigh, Baker began a long career of activism. She worked for a WPA [Works Progress Administration] consumer education project in New York City during the depression. The NAACP hired her in 1938 to recruit members and raise money in the south, and five years later named her national director of branches. Baker helped found SNCC in 1960. In 1964 she gave the keynote address at the MFDP convention in Jackson and established the MFDP Washington office.

Baker's readiness to confront the male officers in SCLC may have come in part from her commitment to participatory decisionmaking. . . . Baker's account of the debate within SCLC on a strategy to bring SNCC under SCLC's control showed her opposing SCLC's hierarchical style of management — her efforts to democratize the leadership of the movement by lobbying for an autonomous SNCC, and her refusal to defer to King.

> The Southern Christian Leadership Conference felt that they could influence how things went. They were interested in having the students become an arm of SCLC. They were most confident that this would be their baby, because I was their functionary and I had called the meeting. At a discussion called by the Reverend Dr. King, the SCLC leadership made decisions [about] who would speak to whom to influence the students to become part of SCLC. Well, I disagreed. There was no student at Dr. King's meeting. I was the nearest thing to a student, being the advocate, you see. I also knew from the beginning that having a woman be an executive of SCLC was not something that would go over with the male-dominated leadership. And then, of course, my personality wasn't right, in the sense I was not afraid to disagree with the higher authorities. I wasn't one to say, yes, because it came from the Reverend King. So when it was proposed that the leadership could influence the direction by speaking to, let's say, the man from Virginia, he could speak to the leadership of the Virginia student group, and the assumption was that having spoken to so-and-so, so-and-so would do what they wanted done, I was outraged. I walked out.

Septima Clark, the other activist who challenged the male staff of SCLC, was also a member of the older generation of women civil rights leaders. Clark was born in 1898 in Charleston, North Carolina. She taught in the Charleston public schools until she lost her job in 1956 when the legislature passed a law prohibiting state employees from belonging to the NAACP. The Highlander Folk School, which brought blacks and whites together to discuss social issues at a farm in Tennessee, hired Clark to lead workshops training members of rural communities to teach their neighbors to read and to register to vote. In 1961, when the Tennessee legislature moved to close Highlander, SCLC and the United Church of Christ provided the funds to enable Clark to continue organizing citizenship schools, which in 1964 numbered 195.

Clark talked freely about what she saw as the sexism of the SCLC staff.

> I was on the executive staff of the SCLC, but the men on it didn't listen to me too well. They like to send me into many places, because I could always make a path in to get people to listen to what I have to say. But those men didn't have any faith in women, none whatsoever. They just thought that women were sex symbols and had no contributions to make. That's why Reverend Abernathy would say continuously, "Why is Mrs. Clark on this staff?" Dr. King would say, "Well she has expanded our program. She has taken it into eleven deep south states." Rev. Abernathy'd [sic] come right back the next time and ask again.
>
> I had a great feeling that Dr. King didn't think much of women either . . . when I was in Europe with him, when he received the Nobel Peace Prize in 1964, the American Field Service Committee people wanted me to speak. In a sort of casual way he would say "Anything I can't answer, ask Mrs. Clark." But he didn't mean it, because I never did get the chance to do any speaking to the AFS committee in London or to any of the other groups.

Like Baker, Clark communicated to King her differences with his style of leadership, urging him in a letter to run SCLC more democratically by delegating authority. She also attacked other ministers for their dependence on King, in which they assumed that only King could lead the movement, and for their belief that to suggest expanding the leadership of the movement cast doubt on King's own capabilities. . . .

Kathleen Cleaver . . . reported in 1971 that she joined the women's movement because she observed while working for SNCC, beginning in 1966, that women did most of the work but that few women held positions of authority. Those women who obtained administrative posts, Cleaver noticed, carried the double burden of their jobs and their duties as wives and mothers, and also had to contend with the male staff members' refusal to accept them as their equals. Cleaver attributed the death of Ruby Doris Smith, Executive Secretary of SNCC, to sheer exhaustion from the many demands and from having to fight racism and sexism simultaneously. "What killed Ruby Doris was the constant outpouring of work, work, work, with being married, having a child, the constant conflicts, the constant struggles that she was subjected to because she was a woman."

A letter written in 1977 by Cynthia Washington, who directed a freedom project for SNCC in Mississippi in 1963, suggested that the position of black women in the movement was more ambiguous than the deference of Robinson, Bates, or Nash to the male leadership, or the anger of Baker, Clark, or Cleaver at women's subordinate status indicated. . . .

> During the fall of 1964, I had a conversation with Casey Hayden about the role of women in SNCC. She complained that all the women got to do was type, that their role was limited to office work no matter where they were. What she said didn't make any particular sense to me because, at the time, I had my own project in Bolivar County, Mississippi. A number of other black women also directed their own projects. What Casey and other white women seemed to want was an opportunity to prove they could do something other than office work. I assumed that if they could do something else, they'd probably be doing that.

Washington said that while some black men viewed the women as inferior — she quoted Stokely Carmichael's jeer that the only position for women in SNCC was prone — she believed that the authority she enjoyed as project director demonstrated that few shared his view. "Our relative autonomy as projects directors seemed to deny or override his statement. We were proof that what he said wasn't true — or so we thought." . . . Yet Washington . . . later concluded that sexism did exist, despite her lack of awareness of it at the time. "In fact, I'm certain that our single-minded focus on the issues of racial discrimination and the black struggle for equality blinded us to other issues."

The ambiguity in the status of women in the movement brought out by Washington's letter paralleled the activists' ambivalence towards the male leaders, in which even those women who criticized the male activists for their condescending attitudes towards women did not hold the men responsible for their sexism. Some, such as Clark, saw the men's treatment of women as reflecting their hostility towards a racially oppressive society that put down black men even more than black women. Clark thought that black men's sexism was a reaction against their overprotective mothers, who tried to shield their sons from the violence of whites to which black men were particularly susceptible. . . .

Other movement workers, such as Beale and Cleaver, blamed capitalism as well as racism for black men's discrimination against women. Sexism, like racism, they argued, was a device by which whites reinforced the exploitation of the masses. Just as racism perpetuated lower-class whites' poverty by preventing them from joining forces with blacks to overthrow their oppressors, so too, by internalizing the sexism of whites, black men contributed to the marginal economic status of blacks. Their complicity in the segregation of jobs by sex, which limited black women's access to all but the lowest paid jobs, and which treated women as a source of surplus labor and as strikebreakers, impoverished blacks as a group.

Cleaver agreed with Clark that black men developed sexist attitudes because they were oppressed, although Cleaver saw their oppression as economic. The black men, according to Cleaver, resented the "strong" role black women had had to assume as breadwinners as well as mothers. They vented their frustration by asserting their power over women — treating them as inferior, abusing them — or by abandoning their families to escape their guilt at their inability to find employment. . . .

All of the women leaders agreed that discrimination against women was of secondary importance to the subjection of all blacks and the inequitable distribution of power in society. Cleaver, for example, insisted that to focus on sexism diverted blacks from attacking the root of all injustice, "colonization," or economic exploitation of white women and minority men and women. . . .

Moreover, these activists held differing views of the relationship between the status of black women and that of blacks as a whole. Cleaver thought that women's equality was a necessary precondition to achieving the equality of all blacks—a means of ensuring the full utilization of blacks' resources. . . . Ladner, on the other hand, feared that the assertiveness of women made black men look relatively weak, . . . and hindered the men from proving their equality to whites. . . .

The inconsistencies in the behavior of these women leaders, in which they challenged white authorities but deferred to black ministers, or criticized the male activists, but only in hindsight, or directly challenged the male officers of movement organizations, yet nevertheless accepted their leadership, cannot entirely be explained by their various theories on the source of racism. Indeed, only in the case of three of the activists, Robinson, Bates, and Nash, do their ideologies seem consistent with their actions. A more plausible explanation for their contradictory behavior is that these women, for the reasons given by Washington, did not consider themselves oppressed by black men, either in or out of the movement, and in some respects believed that black men were worse off than black women. Consequently they did not seek to change their roles in the movement. In addition, the women had conflicting feelings about whom to hold responsible for sexism, if they thought that it did exist, and were uncertain as to how the assertion of their rights as women would affect the status of blacks as a group. These women leaders' reflections suggest that the role of black women in the civil rights movement, largely ignored by historians, was complicated by their ambivalence about what it ought to be and defies a definitive answer.

White Women and the Origins
of the Women's Liberation Movement

ALICE ECHOLS

. . . Before we explore the ways in which the civil rights movement and the new left helped to generate the second wave of feminism, we must first acquaint those readers who are strangers to the world of '60s radicalism with the Student Nonviolent Coordinating Committee (SNCC) and Students for a Democratic Society (SDS) — two groups that are virtually synonymous with what is commonly referred to as the "Movement."

SNCC was founded in 1960 by black students who had participated in the lunch-counter sit-ins that swept across the South in early 1960. SNCC established voter registration projects throughout the South and initiated Freedom Summer, the 1964 voter registration campaign that brought 800 northern white students to Mississippi to help with the registration effort. SNCC also organized the Mississippi Freedom Democratic Party, an alternative political party for disenfranchised blacks, whose delegates unsuccessfully challenged the all-white regular delegation from Mississippi at the 1964 Democratic Convention. Like the civil rights activists in the Congress of Racial Equality (CORE) and the Southern Christian Leadership Conference (SCLC), the college students who founded SNCC were committed to nonviolent direct action. However, in many other respects SNCC had more in common with the newly established SDS than with other civil rights organizations. Like SDS, its membership was young, valued action, and its politics were typically more expressive than strategic. SNCC deliberately provoked confrontations with the Southern power structure and ventured into areas of the deep South considered untouchable by other groups. Through their dedication to the cause and their willingness to "put their bodies on the line," SNCC workers quickly gained a reputation as the "shock troops" of the civil rights movement. In contrast to other civil rights groups, SNCC struggled to develop local leadership — an idea embodied in the slogan "let the people decide" — and, especially in its early years, was committed to participatory democracy. SNCC disintegrated by the end of the decade, but throughout much of the '60s it was the cutting edge of the black freedom movement, becoming the first civil rights group to oppose the Vietnam war and advocate black power.

SDS was founded in 1960 as the youth group of the League for Industrial Democracy (LID), an old left group whose politics were social-democratic and staunchly anti-Communist. Its manifesto, "The Port Huron Statement," drafted by Tom Hayden in 1962, lamented the evisceration of American democratic traditions and called for their revitalization through "participatory democracy." Stifling bureaucratic structures would be replaced by new institutions that would allow "the individual [to] share in those social decisions determining the quality and direction of his life." Despite (or perhaps because of) its affiliation with LID, SDS evolved in a manner that put it light years away from the old left, both philosophically and

Alice Echols, *Daring to Be Bad: Radical Feminism in America 1967–1975* (Minneapolis: University of Minnesota Press, 1989), pp. 23–49. Copyright © 1989 by the Regents of the University of Minnesota. Reprinted with permission of the publisher.

organizationally. While the old left focused on "class-based economic oppression," SDS stressed "how late capitalist society creates mechanisms of psychological and cultural domination over everyone." . . . Nothing confused political pundits more than SDS's indifference toward traditional political activity, especially electoral politics. SDS'ers were less interested in repairing society than in developing new forms that would prefigure the desired society. . . . And, most heretical of all, at least from the standpoint of the old left, was SDS's anti-anti-communism.

From 1964 to 1965 SDS tried to ignite an "interracial movement of the poor" by organizing community unions in northern ghettoes. Its architects hoped that the Economic Research and Action Project (ERAP) would "bring poor whites into an alliance with the Negro freedom movement on economic issues," thereby averting a backlash against the civil rights movement. ERAP organizers failed to organize a poor people's movement, but they did gain valuable organizing experience and their work did lay the basis for a revitalized welfare rights movement. In 1965 SDS began to turn its attention to the war, and in April of that year it organized the first national demonstration against the Vietnam war. Frustrated by liberals' unwillingness to move decisively to end civil-rights abuses in the South and their apparent eagerness to expand the war in Vietnam, many SDS'ers were coming to feel by 1965 that liberalism was the problem. But, . . . it proved easier to identify the deficiencies of liberalism than to build a genuinely American radicalism. SDS grew tremendously during the decade, from 2,500 in 1964 to between 80,000 and 100,000 in 1968. Until its dissolution in 1969 SDS was "a wedge into American society," as it struggled to "build a democratic and humane society in which Vietnams are unthinkable, in which human life and initiative are precious."

. . . Both the new left and the civil rights movement were dominated by men who were, at best, uninterested in challenging sexual inequality. Unlike the old left which acknowledged the existence of male chauvinism and gave token support to women's issues, the new left initially lacked any critical consciousness of gender relations. . . . Barbara Epstein, who was at one point active in both old and new left groups, recalled:

> SDS members criticized certain aspects of American culture, but the sexism of American culture was for the most part adopted uncritically. . . . "Male chauvinism" was a phrase that one did not utter unless one was ready to be laughed at. . . .

Despite the sexism of the new left and the civil rights movement, women's experiences in these movements were not of unrelieved and unmitigated oppression. . . . These movements also gave white women the opportunity to develop skills and to break out of confining, traditional roles. Both in the civil rights movement and in northern community organizing projects, like SDS's Economic Research and Action Project (ERAP), women began to acquire political skills. The danger of civil rights work and the persistent tradition of chivalry generally confined white women to the office or the freedom school. But even though women in the new left and the civil rights movement were often engaged in "women's work," they nonetheless felt themselves to be involved in socially meaningful work. . . .

Furthermore, white female activists began to question culturally received notions of femininity as they met powerful, young black women in SNCC and older women in the black community who were every bit as effective as male organizers and community leaders. Civil rights activist Dorothy Dawson Burlage explained that "[f]or the first time I had role models I could really respect." And, later in the decade, radical women found role models in those Vietnamese and Cuban women who were playing critical roles in their respective national liberation struggles.

In ERAP projects white women not only encountered positive female role models, but became seasoned community organizers. Although the male architects of ERAP had imagined themselves organizing unemployed white and black men in Northern ghettoes, this was not how the projects evolved. . . .

Before long, ERAP projects abandoned all hope of mobilizing unemployed men and began to focus on "nitty-gritty" issues such as improved schools, housing, lighting, and garbage removal. With this shift women assumed greater importance both as organizers and as the organized. . . . Neighborhood women were more organizable than men because they were generally more affected by community issues and more accessible to organizers. But while ERAP women developed skills and self-confidence, their accomplishments were not readily acknowledged by their male co-workers. . . .

The new left contributed to the development of feminist consciousness in another important way. While the new left lacked the old left's awareness of the "woman question," its rejection of the old left's narrow understanding of politics encouraged female activists to define apparently personal concerns as political issues. . . . By expanding political discourse to include the subject of personal relations, new leftists paved the way for feminists to criticize marriage, the family, and sexuality. Moreover, in contrast to the old left, which demanded the subordination of personal needs to "the struggle," the new left encouraged people to seek personal fulfillment through the Movement. Thus, when women felt their needs trivialized, they were somewhat less inclined to push their needs aside for the sake of the Movement.

But at the same time that the Movement was building women's self-confidence and giving them the opportunity to break out of stultifying roles, it was, paradoxically, becoming a less congenial place for white women. . . . Within SNCC, white women, even "powerful insiders" like Mary King and Casey Hayden, saw their influence wane in the aftermath of the 1964 Freedom Summer. . . . Many black civil rights workers resented the white volunteers whose behavior they often found patronizing and imperious. Moreover, the frequency with which black men and white women became sexually involved with each other infuriated many black women staffers. . . . If a white woman accepted a black man's sexual advance, she risked being ridiculed as loose; if she spurned him, she left herself vulnerable to the charge of racism. Of course, the interracial relationships that developed in these projects often grew out of genuine caring and affection. But some black men used white women in an effort to reclaim their manhood and some white women used black men to prove their liberalism or to "expiate their guilt."

Given the heightened sexual and racial tensions, it was hardly surprising that the first serious discussions of sexual inequality within the Movement occurred during Freedom Summer. Having resolved to write a position paper on women for the upcoming SNCC staff meeting, King spent a good deal of time that summer raising the issue of sex roles with Casey Hayden and her other women friends in SNCC. . . . King drafted the paper with help from Casey Hayden, and it was among the thirty-seven papers discussed at the November 1964 SNCC meeting in Waveland, Mississippi. Hayden and King decided against assuming authorship of the paper because they feared they would be ridiculed. However, other staffers quickly pegged them as the authors. The paper cited instances of sexual discrimination, likened male supremacy to racial supremacy, and took SNCC to task for denying women an equal role in the decision-making process. The authors worried that their paper would meet with "crushing criticism." And, indeed, some staffers did mock their concerns.

It was at this November meeting that Stokely Carmichael uttered his legendary one-liner about women's position in SNCC. After the meeting had ended, . . . according to King, . . .

> [Carmichael] made fun of everything that crossed his agile mind. Finally, . . . he came to the no-longer-anonymous paper on women. Looking straight at me, he grinned broadly and shouted, "What is the position of women in SNCC?" Answering himself, he responded, "The position of women in SNCC is prone!" . . . We all collapsed with hilarity. His ribald comment . . . drew us all closer together, because, even in that moment, he was poking fun at his own attitudes. . . .

Several years later Cynthia Washington, a black woman who directed one of SNCC's projects, recalled that neither she nor Muriel Tillinghast, another project director, was amused by Carmichael's comment. However, neither did they understand or sympathize with those women who raised the issue of sex discrimination. . . . Certainly black women's tendency to dismiss women's liberation as "white women's business" was related to the fact that middle-class, white women were struggling for those things — independence and self-sufficiency — which racial and class oppression had thrust upon black women. For example, Washington explained that "[i]t seemed to many of us . . . that white women were demanding a chance to be independent while we needed help and assistance which was not always forthcoming." Moreover, while white women often found themselves sexually objectified and exploited within the Movement, black women were often treated as though they were somehow sexless. Washington complained that . . .

> Our skills and abilities were recognized and respected, but that seemed to place us in some category other than female. . . .

Another factor made white women like Hayden and King feel as though they were losing ground in SNCC. . . . By the time of the Waveland meeting, two factions were emerging within SNCC. Bob Moses (Parris), Mary King, and Casey Hayden were among those identified with the "freedom high" faction, which wanted SNCC to remain committed to decentralization and democratization. James Forman and Ruby Doris Smith Robinson were among the growing number of staffers who favored a more strategic, centralized, and hierarchical SNCC. . . . With the decline of expressive politics, first in SNCC and later in SDS, the Movement became a less hospitable place for women whose concerns were dismissed as "personal" or "apolitical."

. . . SDS was also changing in ways that made it less responsive to women's needs. After SDS's hugely successful antiwar march on Washington in April 1965, the organization's ranks swelled. SDS's hypertrophied growth made it markedly more competitive and its leadership more impenetrable for women. The sense of community which SDS veterans so valued dissipated as new members tried to assert themselves and the old guard struggled to defend itself. . . .

In fact, some men did respond favorably when the question of sex roles was first raised within SDS at the December 1965 National Council meeting. . . . The December "rethinking conference," as it was optimistically dubbed, was supposed to rekindle the spirit of the 1962 SDS Convention at Port Huron. . . . Casey Hayden and Mary King's "Sex and Caste" — a "kind of memo" they had circulated among women in the Movement — . . . finally prompted the National Council to hold a workshop on women's role in SDS. Their paper, an elaboration of the position paper they had written for SNCC a year earlier, . . . located the struggle for sexual equality within the new left tradition of dissolving the barrier between the personal and the political:

> . . . We've talked in the movement about trying to build a society which would see basic human problems (which are now seen as private troubles), as public problems and would try to shape institutions to meet human needs rather than shaping people to meet the needs of those with power. . . .

> . . . Marilyn Webb recalls that the issue

> galvanized enormous numbers of meetings of women endlessly. I don't even remember anything else happening at that convention. We always used to talk about other people's problems. The reason it was so incredibly interesting was that it was the first time we applied politics to ourselves. . . .

[Yet] the issue of "sex roles" remained dormant for the next year and one-half as other issues took precedence. . . . Between December 1965 and June 1967 the American political landscape changed irrevocably. Faced with the inexorability of white racism, a federal government apparently indifferent to Southern white terrorism, and the dissolution of the "beloved community" within SNCC itself, many young black activists were, by 1966, advocating that the civil rights movement abandon its original goal of integration and work instead toward black power. . . . To proponents of black power, integration, by presuming that blacks needed to become assimilated into white society, fostered the myth of white superiority. . . . Black power, by contrast, was a way to build racial consciousness, pride, and solidarity. And, to its original proponents, it seemed the way to build an independent, oppositional power base in the black community. . . .

Black power had enormous consequences for the Movement because it effectively barred whites from organizing in the black community. White organizers were told that they impeded the development of black consciousness and pride, and that their involvement in the civil rights movement smacked of liberal paternalism. . . . From mid-1966 until late 1967 the new left responded to the challenge of black power by concentrating its efforts upon draft resistance and student organizing. The draft resistance movement was launched by white veterans of the civil rights movement who, in Staughton Lynd's words, "wanted to retain a politics of daring, but wanted to get away from the role of . . . auxiliary to a radicalism [whose] center of gravity was in other people's lives." They were searching for "something white radicals could do which would have the same spirit, ask as much of us, and challenge the system as fundamentally as had our work in Mississippi."

Unfortunately, the draft resistance movement contributed to women's growing peripheralization within the Movement. Whereas men could engage in heroic action by resisting the draft, women were reduced to helpmates. Mimi Feingold, who had been active in both CORE and the Cleveland ERAP project, became alienated from the Resistance when she realized that:

> here was a movement where women were playing the most unbelievably subservient role, because that was the only role the women could play, because women couldn't burn draft cards and couldn't go to jail so all they could do was to relate through their men and that seemed to me the most really demeaning kind of thing.

In fact, one of the draft resistance movement's most popular slogans was "Girls Say Yes to Guys Who Say No!" Moreover, to counter the public's image of draft resisters as cowardly "draftdodgers," the movement often portrayed resistance as the quintessential act of courage and manliness. . . .

In late 1966 and early 1967, some women, like Heather Tobis Booth and Francine Silbar, tried to challenge the anti-draft movement's stance toward women. Booth organized a women's workshop at the December 1966 "We Won't Go" conference. However, most of the women who attended the conference avoided the workshop, and many of those who did show up agreed with Alice Lynd that "our duty [is] to support our men." In the March 1967 issue of *New Left Notes,* Francine Silbar pointed out that the resistance movement had placed women in a position similar to that experienced by whites in the civil rights movement as a result of black nationalism. Eventually white women, feeling themselves pushed out of the Movement, would follow the example of others and organize on their own behalf. . . .

By late 1967 SDS was, like SNCC before it, beginning to disassociate itself from the expressive politics which had so distinguished it from the old left. Much of its leadership claimed that SDS would have to become a more strategic organization if it was serious about fighting racism and imperialism and joining forces with the working class. This was not the first time SDS debated the merits of strategic versus expressive politics. Almost from the beginning there were SDS'ers who favored an economistic analysis and a more strategic orientation for the group. Former SDS president Paul Potter recalled that as early as 1965 some people began to dismiss "The Port Huron Statement" as a "kind of simpy, rhetorical exercise that had covered up or masked the hard, crisp, basic economic analysis that was now emerging." But by late 1967 discussion of personal issues, political process, and counter-institutions seemed a middle-class luxury which SDS could hardly afford to indulge. . . .

These debates may seem arcane and unrelated to women, but one cannot understand the emergence of the women's liberation movement without reference to them. First of all, it is hardly surprising that the issue of women's inequality resurfaced in the summer of 1967. The idea that a revolutionary must look first to her or his own oppression gave women the ideological ammunition they needed to examine their own situation. However, the idea was losing credibility at the very moment women were invoking it. Women who were demanding that their oppression be acknowledged ran up against a left concerned only with supporting the struggles of blacks, the working class, or the Vietnamese. Women who were declaring that the "personal is political" encountered a Movement reverting to the old left's definition of political.

There were other factors contributing to the women's revolt within SDS. . . . Women's position in the Movement deteriorated even further as countercultural ideas about free love penetrated the new left. . . . Men's desire for sexual relationships with emotional commitment . . . created a groundswell of resentment. And, in opening up new sexual vistas, the sexual revolution made it possible for women to demand genuine sexual self-determination.

In the spring of 1966 there were . . . signs of incipient feminism. Naomi Weisstein taught a course on women at the University of Chicago and Heather Booth organized the women's workshop at the anti-draft conference. . . . In the winter and spring of 1967, *New Left Notes* published articles by Jane Addams, Heather Booth, and Francine Silbar attacking the Movement's uncritical acceptance of sex roles. But these were isolated and individual protests. This all changed when radical women raised the issue of sexual inequality at SDS's June 1967 National Convention in Ann Arbor. This time the rhetoric and analysis were markedly different, reflecting the enormous changes that had occurred since 1965. And this time the women met with a far chillier reception.

The "Women's Liberation Workshop" thrashed out an analysis and a series of demands to present to the entire convention. The statement . . . declared:

> As we analyze the position of women in capitalist society and especially in the United States we find that women are in a colonial relationship to men and we recognize ourselves as part of the Third World.

They argued for communal child-care centers, accessible abortion, the dissemination of birth-control information, and the sharing of housework to free women from the confines of domesticity. They maintained that women's continued subordination within SDS would retard the revolutionary struggle, and they recommend that SDS pursue an aggressive educational campaign concerning women's liberation. However, after demanding that the men in SDS confront their "male chauvinism," the authors ended on a conciliatory if not an apologetic note:

> . . . We recognize the difficulty our brothers will have in dealing with male chauvinism and we will assume our full responsibility in helping to resolve the contradiction, freedom now! we love you!

> But the men's fears were not assuaged. . . .

> The meeting hall erupted. Men were yelling, arguing, cursing, objecting all over the floor. . . .

Although most of the men who spoke reportedly "agreed that women were the victims of a sexual caste system," they found the third-world analogy completely untenable. . . . The men probably also resented the women's analysis because it seemed to challenge their legitimacy as revolutionary actors. Attacked first by blacks as racist and then by women as male chauvinist, white men must have wondered what role, if any, they could comfortably play in the struggle.

. . . But it took yet another encounter with Movement chauvinism before some women decided to organize on their own behalf. During Labor Day weekend of 1967

2,000 activists from 200 organizations descended upon Chicago's elite Palmer House for the National Conference for New Politics (NCNP). Organizers of the NCNP had hoped that the convention would unite the disparate factions of the Movement — "the electoral reformers, radical organizers and Black militants." . . . However, the convention not only failed to unite the Movement, but it also shattered the assumption that there was *one* Movement. . . . By the time of the August convention, black power had been embraced by virtually everyone within the black liberation movement. While the white delegates hoped for an interracial coalition, many black delegates were extremely skeptical about any such undertaking. Some blacks favored a separatist stance, while others proposed working with whites, but on *their* terms, not on whites' terms. . . . The black caucus demanded that blacks, who comprised roughly one-sixth of all delegates, be given fifty percent representation on all committees. They further demanded that the convention condemn the "imperialist Zionist war" in the Middle East and encourage whites to humanize the "savage and beastlike character" of white communities. In his speech to the black caucus, James Forman of SNCC declared that black people, as the "most dispossessed," must lead the Movement and proclaimed that those who disagreed could "go to hell." . . . In the end, the convention voted three to one to accept the caucus'. . . points. The following day the black caucus demanded fifty percent of the convention vote, and again the white delegates capitulated. . . . But capitulation did not bring about the desired coalition, and at the convention's conclusion NCNP was in shambles. . . .

Although most press accounts focused exclusively upon the racial tension, the convention was also marked by conflicts over women's liberation. Of course, the NCNP convention occurred a mere two months after the SDS Convention where the issue of women's liberation had caused such a fracas. . . . Roughly fifty to seventy women, including NOW's Ti-Grace Atkinson, attended the women's workshop at the NCNP and drafted a resolution.

But whereas radical white men seemed eager to do penance for their racism, they actively resisted women's attempts to raise the issue of sexual inequality. When representatives from the women's workshop spoke with the resolution chairperson about getting their resolution on the agenda, they were rebuffed. The chairperson explained that Women Strike for Peace (WSP) had already submitted a women's resolution, the gist of which was simply that women should work for peace. He suggested that they meet with women from WSP to draft a compromise resolution. [Madlyn Murray] O'Hair [the women's workshop facilitator] met with two representatives from WSP and, according to Freeman, "sold out" the radical women's workshop. Only two of the points of the women's workshop were included in the new resolution. Freeman was outraged by the compromise resolution and stormed out of the meeting with O'Hair. The compromise resolution might well have gone unchallenged had Freeman not encountered Shulamith Firestone on her way out of the hall. Firestone was equally furious about the betrayal, and the two spent the rest of the night writing a new resolution. Freeman doubts that they would have acted separately, "but together we fed on each other's rage."

Following the example of the black caucus, Firestone and Freeman's resolution demanded that women receive fifty-one percent of the convention votes and committee representation because, they argued, women comprise fifty-one per cent of the population. They demanded that the convention condemn the mass media "for perpetuating the stereotype of women as always in an auxiliary position to men [and as] sex objects." They also called upon the convention to endorse "the revamping of marriage, divorce, and property laws." Finally, they demanded "complete control by women of their own bodies, the dissemination of birth control information to all women regardless of their age and marital status, and the removal of all prohibitions against abortion." After typing up the resolution — which differed from the original resolution — they paid a return visit to the resolutions chairperson. When he claimed that the convention lacked the time to debate their resolution, Freeman countered, "You know, there's an awful lot of women in that audience. We can tie up this conference on procedural motions for far longer than it will take you to debate our little resolution." With that, he agreed to make the women's resolution number eleven on the agenda. Freeman and Firestone made about 2,000 copies of the resolution and succeeded in recruiting three or four other women to their cause. However, when the time came to debate resolution number eleven, the chair introduced Madlyn Murray O'Hair's resolution, not theirs. According to Freeman:

> . . . Shulie Firestone and about three or four other people, who we didn't know, were ready to pull the place apart. Then [the chair] William Pepper patted Shulie on the head and said, "Move on little girl; we have more important issues to talk about here than women's liberation." That was the genesis. We had a meeting the next week with women in Chicago.

That fall the Chicago group issued a manifesto, "To the Women of the Left," which was subsequently published in *New Left Notes*. In it, they counseled new left women to avoid making "the same mistake the blacks did at first of allowing others (whites in their case, men in ours) to define our issues, methods, goals. Only we can and must define the terms of our struggle." Thus, they contended, "it is incumbent on us, as women, to organize a movement for women's liberation." . . .

Gender Awareness Among Chicanas and Mexicanas in the United Farm Workers of America

MARGARET ROSE

One of the labor movement's most inspiring struggles during the post–World War II era was the unionization of farm workers in the National Farm Workers Association (NFWA), precursor to the United Farm Workers of America (UFW). NFWA, founded in 1962 by César Chávez and Dolores Huerta, was an independent agricultural organization, composed primarily of Mexican and Chicano farm laborers. It gained national headlines in 1965 when it joined Filipino workers in the AFL-CIO sponsored Agricultural Workers Organizing Committee (AWOC) in the now famous Delano grape strike. Defeated by the combined economic and political power of corporate agriculture and its allies, the union survived through a national appeal

Margaret Rose, "From the Fields to the Picket Line: Huelga Women and the Boycott, 1965–1975," *Labor History* (Summer 1990): 271–293. Reprinted by permission of the author and the publisher.

for consumer boycotts of agricultural producers. Since its inception, the UFW has targeted over 200 different items in its campaigns against agribusiness. The public, however, is most familiar with its well-publicized boycotts of grapes, lettuce, and Gallo wines.

As part of its economic strategy, the union recruited male and female strikers from rural agricultural communities to live and organize boycotts in cities and towns across the U.S. Union leaders quickly recognized the key ingredient for a successful boycott formula. "Families are the most important part of the UFW," declared Dolores Huerta, "because a family can stick it out in a strange place, on $5 a week per person, the wages everyone in the union is paid (plus expenses)." . . .

This work examines the protest of a selected group of Chicanas and Mexicanas in the UFW — married women with children, particularly in the Washington, DC, boycott — who made the difficult transformation "from the fields to the picket lines" during the struggle for union recognition and collective bargaining rights.

In the early years, Anglo volunteers dominated the boycott operations across the nation. Farm worker participation was minimal. Anglo boycott staff in the urban centers were isolated from the turmoil and pressing realities of the California struggle. Originally, few Mexican or Mexican-American women and even fewer entire families went to boycott; the family pattern evolved gradually as the UFW experimented, through trial and error, with the most effective response to grower tactics and as union attitudes towards women began to change. Over the years, as the boycott strategy was refined, women were increasingly recognized as important players in the decision to relocate their families in urban locations.

When the union initially adopted the boycott strategy in 1965, it directed its first campaigns against highly visible major corporations, such as Schenley, DiGiorgio, and Perelli-Minetti, which depended on wine grapes for their products. In contrast to the later and much larger boycotts against the growers of table grapes and lettuce in the late 1960s and 1970s, the first boycotts were narrower in scope, concentrated primarily on the West Coast, and short in duration. Reliance on Anglo boycott supporters in the cities with only the temporary assistance from farm workers, primarily young single men or husbands usually dispatched without their families, proved unsatisfactory in creating the sustained economic pressure campaign necessary in the later more protracted struggles. . . .

Changes in farm worker organization began during the intensified boycott in 1968 against Giumarra, the largest producer of table grapes (and later extended against the entire industry). This long term effort which lasted two years required a greater financial commitment and a much larger staff in major cities all over North America. The union maintained operations in 40–50 large urban centers. Usually one or two farm worker families, in addition to single men, were assigned to large cities to work with a UFW director and an Anglo support staff often recruited from the local community.

In 1968 under pressure from her husband, Hijinio, and with urgent pleas from the union, María Luisa Rangel, a farm worker wife from Dinuba, a small agricultural town outside of Fresno, California, reluctantly agreed to transplant her family of eight children to Detroit to work on the Giumarra campaign. A writer who later interviewed her wrote:

She had a hard time in Detroit; she didn't know much English, the climate was completely strange and she had two operations in the city.

Nevertheless, María Luisa provided essential stability for family life and the boycott as she worked alongside her husband and children until the historic grape contracts were secured in 1970. Soon after the announcement of the agreements the
Rangels returned to California. From her Detroit experience, María Luisa emerged a
strong advocate of the union's cause. . . .

With the strike and boycott against lettuce growers in 1970, new personnel
were needed. This time recruitment of farm worker families was facilitated by
changing attitudes towards and more recognition of Chicanas and Mexicanas in the
UFW. In part a response to urgent staffing requirements and in part an outgrowth of
the emergence of the women's movement, these new views regarding the importance of women in the union effort were expressed in an increase of articles about
women in union publications. For example, news stories like "A Woman's Place
Is . . . On the Picket Line!" which featured the contributions of four women field
workers to *la causa* appeared in *El Malcriado*. . . .

During this period, the Juanita and Merced Valdez family and their seven children left the lettuce and strawberry fields in the Salinas Valley in northern California and moved to Cincinnati to help with the lettuce campaign. The parents tended
to the day-to-day chores of the boycott. Their children — Sergio (18), Mary (17),
Rego (15), Olga (14), Milly (10), Lucy (9), and Enedelia (8) — devoted their summers, weekends, and after-school hours to picket lines. . . . During the week the parents and older children appeared before community meetings to talk about their
work in the fields, their strike experiences, and to appeal for help for their union.
Their activities generated publicity for the boycott in the local press and on television news and public affairs programs. In this effort, the family worked with an
Anglo staff, volunteers, and a local community support group.

By 1973, when the UFW had intensified its lettuce campaign, renewed its boycott against table grapes, and initiated its drive against Gallo wines, the family pattern of boycott participation was firmly entrenched. . . . The Washington, DC, union
operation provides a good example of the family pattern of boycott participation. In
the family, in the fields, and in the boycott, responsibilities for men and women
were divided along gender lines. A patriarchal order characterized the organizational structure and personal relations from the leadership down to the rank-and-file
level.

Gilbert Padilla coordinated the union's effort in the nation's capital from 1973
to 1975. California-born Padilla, one of nine children, migrated with his family
throughout the agricultural valleys in the state, quitting school after the seventh
grade to work full time in the fields. . . . Meeting César Chávez in 1957, Gilbert was
impressed with his determination to stop abuses by labor contractors and to obtain
minimum wage and unemployment legislation for farm workers. He joined the local
chapter of the Community Service Organization (CSO) being established by
Chávez and later helped Chávez and Dolores Huerta found the Farm Workers Association in 1962. Subsequently, he led union membership drives in California and
South Texas; headed the union's Selma field office near Fresno; participated in

boycotts in Philadelphia and Wisconsin, and served as secretary-treasurer of the UFW. . . .

As director of the Washington, DC, boycott, Gilbert was the chief spokesman and strategist for the union in the federal district and the surrounding area. He coordinated picketing and sought the support of labor groups and politicians as well as clergy, students, and the general public. He concentrated on the male-dominated labor community. . . . Gilbert cultivated ties with national labor officials, such as Tom Donahue, executive assistant to George Meany, at the Washington, DC, office of the AFL-CIO. He also sought to develop regional labor support. . . . Different segments of the labor movement responded more favorably than others. The steel workers' union, for example, contributed important moral and financial support.

Gilbert was joined by his second wife, Esther, whom he married in 1971, and their baby daughter, Adelita. The 29-year-old Esther Negrete de Padilla, a California-born Chicana, brought sensitivity, educational training, and administrative experience to the Washington, DC, enterprise. The youngest of 14 children born to an immigrant farm worker family, Esther labored briefly in the fall cotton harvests in the Fresno area after school. Heeding the advice of her parents to "get a good education and do something positive," she finished high school and earned a bachelor's degree from the local college in 1966. Her academic training offered the opportunity for white-collar employment; she became a social worker in the Fresno Department of Social Services and later was a supervisor with the Head Start program. After several years of volunteer activity with the union, she officially joined the UFW in 1971.

While Gilbert oversaw the entire boycott operation, he received valuable help from Esther in gender-specific areas. This service, while critically important, did not attract wide notice because of its traditional nature and because it often occurred behind the scenes. A conventional female concern in the home was the care and management of the family. Esther not only met these responsibilities, but also managed the domestic side of the boycott. The two-story frame house in Takoma Park, a suburb of Washington, DC, that served as headquarters for the boycott, sheltered up to 14 people. Its four bedrooms, with a makeshift dormitory in the basement, was home to the Padillas and to the families and individual organizers who came and went in the course of the two-year campaign.

Esther dealt with the problems that inevitably arose from the interaction of many people. Using her knowledge of the welfare system, she obtained food stamps and medical benefits for the transplanted farm workers. When one farm worker woman required emergency care upon arrival in the city, Esther arranged for her hospitalization. Children required visits to the doctor and glasses. . . . For the new boycott recruits from the fields, Esther sought medical attention and acted as a counselor and morale booster. As such she served as a liaison between the boycott leadership and the farm worker families scattered around the metropolitan area.

Esther's contribution was not limited to personal and domestic details. Because of her educational and work experience, she was a valuable asset in the formal administration of the boycott. Her public duties ranged from dealing with produce managers and political representatives to office work. Esther's day began with early morning visits to the central produce market. Along with staff members Mike

Angelo and David Urioste, she harangued uncooperative fruit and vegetable dealers who continued to purchase boycotted grapes and lettuce. . . .

After these 5:30–7:30 am daily encounters, she devoted the bulk of her time to political lobbying on Capitol Hill. . . . Public officials who were not sufficiently supportive of the union became the target of UFW campaigns. Esther organized a sit-in at the Washington, DC, office of California Senator John Tunney in response to his failure to support UFW boycotts and his advocacy of labor legislation opposed by the union.

In addition to personal contacts with legislators and their staffs, Esther testified before congressional committees. One appearance arose out of the UFW recall campaign against Arizona Republican governor Jack Williams, who had signed into law a restrictive bill intended to thwart agricultural unionizing in the state. . . .

When she was not on Capitol Hill, Esther helped in the day-to-day operations of the enterprise. Working out of the boycott house in Takoma Park, she handled correspondence, issued press releases, supervised Anglo supporters who volunteered to help in the office, attended staff meetings, and kept minutes for important regional boycott conferences. With her expertise on congressional matters, her knowledge of the Washington, DC, office, and her dealings with farm worker personnel, she also served as a confidante and advisor to her husband. Thus besides being a family unit, the Padillas were a political team — Gilbert the official head of the boycott and Esther his trusted assistant. But within this formal patriarchal arrangement, there was a great degree of mutuality, cooperation, and female autonomy.

This family model of union activism also characterized the Washington, DC, boycott venture at the rank-and-file level. . . . By 1974 there was a staff of 23, supplemented from time to time by temporary non-Hispanic and non-paid volunteers. This figure did not take into account the younger children who often participated in the boycott. The majority of the staff consisted of five farm worker families — the Castillos, the Herreras, the Baldwins, the Salinases, and the Rodríguezes and three single males, José Salzar, Daniel Terrones, and David Urioste.

The family of Herminia and Conrado Rodríguez resided in the Arvin-Lamont area, south of Bakersfield, before their move to Washington, DC. . . . Conrado (also called Lalo) supported his family as a farm laborer, supplementing his income with carpentry jobs during the winter months. Herminia, following a traditional female pattern of part-time, seasonal work, contributed to the household economy as a field worker during harvest time. The young family migrated annually between Texas and California. In the Arvin-Lamont area, where they eventually settled, the Rodríguezes worked primarily in table and wine grape production and occasionally in the harvest of other local crops, such as carrots and cotton.

Like many other families, the Rodríguezes' politicization became a family affair. During the summer of 1973, the family participated in the widespread protests against local grape growers who balked at renewing the UFW contracts negotiated three years before. As a local leader at his company, Conrado hosted strategy meetings in his home attended by his co-workers and his family. As talks between grape producers and the union stalled, demonstrations intensified. When local grape industry representatives hastily concluded contracts with the Teamsters Union, protests heightened. While picketing against local growers, Conrado and his eldest teenage daughter, Lupe, were arrested along with other union supporters and transported to the county jail in Bakersfield. Herminia and the remaining children, together with other detainees' families, went into the city and denounced the incarcerations. Lupe Rodríguez stayed in jail for three or four days; her father was held a few days longer and then released.

The calamitous confrontations between agribusiness and the union in the summer of 1973 that resulted in the mass arrests of farm workers (men, women, and children) and their supporters politicized many families. When the UFW suspended picketing after the deaths of two union supporters in August, the activism of the Rodríguez family did not diminish. Packing up their personal belongings, they joined the caravans of farm worker families who left in the late summer and early fall 1973 to launch a renewed boycott campaign against corporate agriculture on a distant urban front, far away from the recent turmoil in the fields.

As with the Padillas, the Rodríguezes followed the family model of boycott participation with activities divided along gender lines. Herminia Rodríguez oversaw the domestic needs of her family and participated in traditionally female-defined boycott work. Like Esther Padilla, Herminia received much less attention than her husband and refrained from public speaking with the result that her actions, like those of most other Chicanas and Mexicanas, seemed "invisible." Since they appeared infrequently in news accounts and official union records, it is difficult to quote directly their personal reactions and experiences.

The traditional responsibility of making her family comfortable was not an easy task for Herminia Rodríguez given the disruptions in family life caused by the boycott. The Rodríguez family, like others, had to adjust to a strange environment, new people, different climate, an unfamiliar culture, and difficult living conditions. An entirely new system of survival and domestic decisions had to be adopted. For food, clothing, and housing, the family relied on the local community and fundraising drives. . . . When organizing needs shifted, the family relocated. Herminia moved her family four times during their two-year stay in Washington, DC. First, they lived in the Takoma Park boycott house with the Padillas and other boycotters. Later, they shared another house, a block away, with the Salinas family. Another move took them to an apartment downtown near the White House. Finally, the family stayed in the basement of a house in the same area. Frequent residential changes necessitated different arrangements for the entire family. Herminia's patient acceptance of this instability contributed to the smooth functioning of the boycott. . . . Personal discomforts and domestic duties translated into a strong female political statement.

In addition to managing difficult living conditions and family affairs, Chicanas and Mexicanas also participated in public boycott activities, short of public speaking which was left to the men. . . . The most tedious, but most essential, task was picketing. Chicanas and Mexicanas spent hours on picket duty, particularly during the summers when the objective was to maintain daily picket lines. At grocery stores, like Giant and Safeway, and at local liquor stores, such as Woodley Discount Liquor, Esther Padilla carried her two-year-old daughter, Adelita, and Herminia Rodríguez took her five children — Lupe, Oralia, Eduardo, Daniel, and Dalia. At times picket lines were composed of women and children. . . . Philippine-born

Luming Imutan related the typical difficulties picketers encountered from unsympathetic members of the public:

> One of the hardest parts about being on strike and being on picket lines is taking the insults that people give you. When I was in Los Angeles for the factory gate collections and the boycott lines for S & W [DiGiorgio product brand], people would ask, "Why should you tell us what to buy?" "Why do you have to beg?" "Why don't you to work?" There were many people who called us a disgrace to the public. . . .

Farm worker women engaged in supportive jobs in the office, depending on their skill level, but did not participate in the formal decision-making process which was reserved for men. Because of her education (and her position as wife of the director), Esther Padilla assumed a more visible role than did Herminia Rodríguez, who had received no formal education while growing up in Mexico. Herminia and other Mexicanas answered phones, stuffed envelopes, or ran office equipment. María Castillo, Herminia's friend, assumed the task of selling union bumper stickers, buttons, key chains, and other items at union-sponsored events. . . . Possessing a fine singing voice, María also provided entertainment performing Mexican folk songs and *corridos* (ballads), such as "De Colores," a union favorite, accompanied by guitar-playing Conrado Rodríguez. . . .

In contrast to Chicanas and Mexicanas at the rank-and-file level, their husbands exerted a more public and readily recognized presence in the boycott. The family model of social activism gave the male head of household more prominence, authority, and responsibility. Media coverage reinforced this division. . . . While both men and women walked picket lines, the men were photographed more frequently for union publications and were often jailed — a very public event — for their activities. Whereas in rural California mass arrests of both men and women occurred, especially during the summer of 1973, in the cities men were more frequently arrested than women. If both husband and wife underwent arrest there was no extended family to care for the children; thus the less public responsibility to stay out of jail usually fell to the wife.

By virtue of gender and patriarchal standing in the family, male farm workers, in the boycott assumed more administrative duties. For his special project, Conrado Rodríguez teamed with an Anglo staff member, Kay Pollock, to develop support for the boycott among religious groups. . . . Along with Pollock, he attended church-sponsored gatherings, spoke briefly about his experience in California agriculture, showed farm worker slides or films, and appealed for help to walk picket lines, write letters, donate food and clothing, and provide financial assistance. . . . The backing of the religious community proved an essential mainstay of the boycott effort. The overall effectiveness of Rodríguez' appeal relied on domestic cooperation and support from his wife, Herminia, and the able assistance of his Anglo female co-worker. . . .

The progress of the Washington, DC, boycott accelerated after the arrival of farm worker families in the city. The immediate attention of the boycott focused on pressuring supermarkets to remove non-union products and to create strong grass-roots support for UFW collective bargaining demands. Farm worker families, like the Rodríguezes, the Castillos, the Herreras, the Baldwins, and the

Salinases, were essential in the picketing strategy. Within the first three months of their arrival in the nation's capital, they had succeeded in gaining the cooperation of 137 independent and "Mom and Pop" stores. Local co-ops, such as the Beltsville Consumes, a group of 10 stores, joined the boycott. After the arrests of three farm workers, another small independent, Snider's market, agreed to remove grapes from its shelves. The California boycotters also achieved success in their campaign to pressure 275 liquor stores to stop selling Gallo wine products. Cooperation from black groups was notable in this effort; 110 stores in the black community quickly responded to the boycott. But as the local boycott leadership and farm worker families soon realized, the most difficult targets were the large supermarkets. After their initial accomplishments with small stores, farm workers and their supporters began picketing Giant Foods, a chain of 100 stores in the Washington area. The largest, and most intransigent chain was Safeway with 234 stores in the vicinity. Despite almost constant picketing at their stores and warehouses, and despite financial losses, both chains resisted demands of farm worker families to honor the boycott.

To create the necessary pressure to make the UFW campaign effective, the boycott leadership turned to the development of long-term community and regional support. Through the sustained cooperation of farm worker families, local organizers, and with the backing of labor, religious, political, consumer, and student groups, the Washington, DC, UFW office mounted a viable boycott effort. After organizing the nation's capital, the boycott spread to other areas. Using the experience they had gained in Washington, DC, farm worker families moved to other cities. Juanita and Alfredo Herrera and their five children went to Baltimore to build a campaign against the A & P grocery chain. Still other families accepted assignments in Norfolk and Alexandria, Virginia.

In this region, the most successful campaign was directed against Gallo wine because of its highly recognizable labels and the availability of other easily substituted brands. Although significant, the boycotts against grapes and lettuce yielded less impressive results. Overall, the nationally-coordinated campaign finally convinced agribusiness in California to endorse legislation, the Agricultural Labor Relations Act (ALRA), which guaranteed secret-ballot elections — an historic step in the state. . . .

The ultimate success of the two-year struggle, from 1973 to 1975, against the agricultural industry depended on a remarkable cooperation between Mexican and Chicano activists and field workers, Anglo organizers, and middle-class supporters in cities across the U.S. and Canada. Farm worker commitment to the boycott was intricately tied to the family approach to organization that preserved gender designated forms of labor activism.

The variety of Chicanas' and Mexicanas' participation in the Washington, DC, boycott reflected the diversity of experience of women of Mexican heritage in the U.S. during the second half of the 20th century. Class and generational distance from Mexico, in particular, shaped female activism. More acculturated and educated, U.S.-born Chicanas, like Esther Padilla, often exerted a prominent and visible position in the boycott and experienced more flexibility regarding their social activism. Recently immigrated, poorer, farm worker women from Mexico, such as

Herminia Rodríguez, influenced by a more conservative definition of female activism and limited by inadequate educational and language skills, received little recognition of their quiet, but vital, contributions to the boycott.

Regardless of ethnicity or class, gender remained the preeminent force shaping women's activism on the boycott. The family model of boycott organization reinforced the general expectation that Chicanas and Mexicanas would exert a crucial, but less visible, role in the boycott. Female cooperation and community prevailed over individual ambition. A familiar domestic culture eased the transition from the fields to the cities.

But because of its unconventional nature and its unorthodox and radical challenge to the established economic order, the boycott had perhaps the unintended consequence of undermining traditional social and gender relationships for this generation of women. New Mexican-born Carolina Vásquez, a grape striker from the Schenley company who worked in the boycott as a single woman in Philadelphia and later as a wife, after her marriage in 1969 to a farm worker boycotter in Connecticut, hinted at the potential of the boycott for relaxing conventional relationships between spouses.

> Now my husband and I work together, and sometimes we have different points of view, but we help each other as much as we can. We are up to our nerves in this strike most of the time from responsibilities we've confronted on the boycott. . . .

A few women, like Esther Padilla, developed feminist leanings. When she first participated in the boycott she became defensive when middle-class female supporters challenged the UFW's traditional attitudes towards women. As she observed that other unions in Washington, DC had established bureaus and committees to address the concerns of women, she became more sensitive to the issue. By the late 1970s her raised consciousness moved her to write to César Chávez to advocate the formation of a women's department in the UFW. The unusual circumstances of the boycott created a climate for altering traditional male-female relationships within marriage and in the union and for providing Mexicanas and Chicanas with new opportunities for personal growth. But the feminism of Esther Padilla remained an exception.

While the UFW provided an outlet for class solidarity and a means for expressing ethnic pride for an exploited minority, it reinforced traditional gender relations by confining women to traditionally female-defined work and social activism. However, by raising the ethnic and class consciousness of its female membership and by exposing them to novel situations, new ideas, and different cultural expectations, the UFW may have inadvertently laid the foundation for the emergence of a greater awareness of gender issues among Mexicanas and Chicanas.

✳ *F U R T H E R   R E A D I N G*

Lois W. Banner, *Women in Modern America* (1984)
Maren Lockwood Carden, *The New Feminist Movement* (1974)
William Chafe, *Women and Equality* (1977)
Vicki Crawford, Jacqueline Ann Rouse, and Barbara Woods, eds., *Women in the Civil Rights Movement: Trailblazers and Torchbearers, 1941–1965* (1990)

Robert Daniel, *American Women in the Twentieth Century* (1987)

Flora Davis, *Moving the Mountain: The Women's Movement in America Since 1960* (1991)

Barbara Deckard, *The Women's Movement* (1983)

John D'Emilio, *Sexual Politics, Sexual Communities: The Making of a Homosexual Minority in the United States, 1940–1970* (1983)

Bonnie Thornton Dill, "The Dialectics of Black Womanhood," *Signs* 4 (Spring 1979), 543–555

Sarah Evans, *Personal Politics: The Roots of Women's Liberation in the Civil Rights Movement and the New Left* (1979)

Cynthia Harrison, "A 'New Frontier' for Women: The Public Policy of the Kennedy Administration," *Journal of American History* LXVII (1981), 630–646

——, *On Account of Sex: The Politics of Women's Issues, 1945–1968* (1988)

Susan M. Hartmann, *From Margin to Mainstream: American Women and Politics Since 1960* (1989)

Judith Hole and Ellen Levine, *Rebirth of Feminism* (1971)

Gloria Joseph and Jill Lewis, *Common Differences: Conflicts in Black and White Feminist Perspectives* (1981)

Blanche Linden-Ward and Carol Hurd Green, *Changing the Future: American Women in the 1960s* (1993)

Nancy McGlen and Karen O'Connor, *Women's Rights* (1983)

Mary Rothschild, "White Women Volunteers in the Freedom Summers: Their Life and Work in a Movement for Social Change," *Feminist Studies* V (1979), 466–495

Leila J. Rupp and Verta Taylor, *Survival in the Doldrums: The American Women's Rights Movement, 1945 to the 1960s* (1987)

Winifred D. Wandersee, *On the Move: American Women in the 1970s* (1988)

Gayle Graham Yates, *What Women Want: The Ideas of the Movement* (1975)

An Elusive Sisterhood: Women and Politics Since 1972

In the early 1970s American feminists imagined a bright future for their movement. They had reason to be optimistic: In 1972, Congress passed an Equal Rights Amendment and sent it to the states for ratification. The following year the Supreme Court, in the landmark decision Roe v. Wade, *restricted states from prohibiting a woman's access to abortion during the first trimester of pregnancy. In the years that followed, however, the feminist movement appeared to founder. Anti-feminists with ties to the Catholic church, the Republican party, and fundamentalist Protestant churches, mounted a political campaign that obstructed the ratification of the ERA. The women and men of this so-called New Right pressured presidents Ronald Reagan and George Bush to appoint conservative justices to the Supreme Court in hopes of overturning* Roe v. Wade.*

Meanwhile, feminists divided sharply over the issue of pornography, and staked out positions that oddly paralleled older debates over separatism and integration. White, middle-class feminists struggled, without great success, to reach out to working-class women and women of color. Thus, in the controversy surrounding Clarence Thomas's 1991 nomination to the Supreme Court, white feminists, rallying to support Anita Hill in her allegations of sexual harassment, failed to realize that Hill needed support not only as a woman but as a black woman.

Why were thousands of women and men alienated by feminism during the last decades of the twentieth century, and how did the New Right give voice to their anxieties about widespread patterns of change in women's lives? What impact did the New Right have on the laws and policies that affect women's lives? Why did the issue of pornography become a source of intense controversy among feminists in the 1980s, provoking some feminist opponents of pornography to seek an uneasy alliance with the New Right? Finally, how and why were feminists in this era never fully able to acknowledge the needs and interests of women outside the white middle class?

The first document, the Equal Rights Amendment approved by Congress in 1972 and sent to the states for ratification, uses simple wording that was first proposed by Susan B. Anthony in the nineteenth century. In 1973 the U.S. Supreme Court, in *Roe* v. *Wade* (excerpted as the second document), issued a highly controversial opinion that restricted states' authority to pass laws prohibiting abortion. Nineteen years later, a divided Supreme Court reaffirmed the central holding of *Roe* in *Planned Parenthood* v. *Casey* (excerpts of which constitute the third selection) but gave states permission to enact rules and regulations that, short of imposing an "undue burden," encouraged women to seek alternatives to abortion. Anti-abortion and anti-feminist activists publicized their views widely during the seventies and eighties. In the fourth document, which appeared in 1980, Reverend Jerry Falwell gives his views on the potential destructiveness of the ERA. In 1988, Connaught C. Marshner, chair of the National Pro-Family Coalition, explored and defended the values of social conservatives; her opinions are excerpted here as the fifth document. The sixth document excerpts *American Booksellers Ass'n, Inc.* v. *Hudnut,* a 1985 decision by the Seventh Circuit Court: it declared unconstitutional a statute, favored by some feminists, banning pornography in Indianapolis. The last document consists of excerpts from Anita Hill's 1991 testimony before the Senate Judiciary Committee on the nomination of Clarence Thomas to the Supreme Court.

The Equal Rights Amendment, 1972

[Sent to the states, 1972]

Section 1   Equality of rights under the law shall not be denied or abridged by the United States or by any State on account of sex.

Section 2   The Congress shall have the power to enforce, by appropriate legislation, the provisions of this article.

Section 3   This amendment shall take effect two years after the date of ratification.

Roe v. *Wade,* 1973

Mr. Justice Blackmun delivered the opinion of the Court.

This Texas federal appeal and its Georgia companion, *Doe* v. *Bolton,* present constitutional challenges to state criminal abortion legislation. The Texas statutes under attack here are typical of those that have been in effect in many States for approximately a century. The Georgia statutes, in contrast, have a modern cast and are a legislative product that, to an extent at least, obviously reflects the influences of recent attitudinal change, of advancing medical knowledge and techniques, and of new thinking about an old issue.

We forthwith acknowledge our awareness of the sensitive and emotional nature of the abortion controversy, of the vigorous opposing views, even among physicians, and of the deep and seemingly absolute convictions that the subject inspires. One's philosophy, one's experiences, one's exposure to the raw edges of human existence, one's religious training, one's attitudes toward life and family and their values, and the moral standards one establishes and seeks to observe, are all likely to influence and to color one's thinking and conclusions about abortion.

In addition, population growth, pollution, poverty, and racial overtones tend to complicate and not to simplify the problem.

Our task, of course, is to resolve the issue by constitutional measurement, free of emotion and of predilection. We seek earnestly to do this, and, because we do, we have inquired into, and in this opinion place some emphasis upon, medical and medical-legal history and what that history reveals about man's attitudes toward the abortion procedure over the centuries. . . .

It perhaps is not generally appreciated that the restrictive criminal abortion laws in effect in a majority of States today are of relatively recent vintage. Those laws, generally proscribing abortion or its attempt at any time during pregnancy except when necessary to preserve the pregnant woman's life, are not of ancient or even of common-law origin. Instead, they derive from statutory changes effected, for the most part, in the latter half of the 19th century. . . .

Three reasons have been advanced to explain historically the enactment of criminal abortion laws in the 19th century and to justify their continued existence.

It has been argued occasionally that these laws were the product of a Victorian social concern to discourage illicit sexual conduct. Texas, however, does not advance this justification in the present case, and it appears that no court or commentator has taken the argument seriously. . . .

A second reason is concerned with abortion as a medical procedure. When most criminal abortion laws were first enacted, the procedure was a hazardous one for the woman. . . . Thus, it has been argued that a State's real concern in enacting a criminal abortion law was to protect the pregnant woman, that is, to restrain her from submitting to a procedure that placed her life in serious jeopardy.

Modern medical techniques have altered this situation. Appellants and various amici refer to medical data indicating that abortion in early pregnancy, this is, prior to the end of the first trimester, although not without its risk, is now relatively safe. Mortality rates for women undergoing early abortions, where the procedure is legal, appear to be as low as or lower than the rates for normal childbirth. Consequently, any interest of the State in protecting the woman from an inherently hazardous procedure, except when it would be equally dangerous for her to forgo it, has largely disappeared. Of course, important state interests in the area of health and medical standards do remain. . . .

The third reason is the State's interest — some phrase it in terms of duty — in protecting prenatal life. Some of the argument for this justification rests on the theory that a new human life is present from the moment of conception. The State's interest and general obligation to protect life then extends, it is argued, to prenatal life. Only when the life of the pregnant mother herself is at stake, balanced against the life she carries within her, should the interest of the embryo or fetus not prevail. Logically, of course, a legitimate state interest in this area need not stand or fall on acceptance of the belief that life begins at conception or at some other point prior to live birth. In assessing the State's interest, recognition may be given to the less rigid claim that as long as at least *potential* life is involved, the State may assert interests beyond the protection of the pregnant woman alone. . . .

The Constitution does not explicitly mention any right of privacy. In a line of decisions, however, the Court has recognized that a right of personal privacy, or a guarantee of certain areas or zones of privacy, does exist under the Constitution. . . .

This right of privacy, whether it be founded in the Fourteenth Amendment's concept of personal liberty and restrictions upon state action, as we feel it is, or, as the District Court determined, in the Ninth Amendment's reservation of rights to the people, is broad enough to encompass a woman's decision whether or not to terminate her pregnancy. The detriment that the State would impose upon the pregnant woman by denying this choice altogether is apparent. Specific and direct harm medically diagnosable even in early pregnancy may be involved. Maternity, or additional offspring, may force upon the woman a distressful life and future. Psychological harm may be imminent. Mental and physical health may be taxed by child care. There is also the distress, for all concerned, associated with the unwanted child, and there is the problem of bringing a child into a family already unable, psychologically and otherwise, to care for it. In other cases, as in this one, the additional difficulties and continuing stigma of unwed motherhood may be involved. All these are factors the woman and her responsible physician necessarily will consider in consultation.

On the basis of elements such as these, appellant and some amici argue that the woman's right is absolute and that she is entitled to terminate her pregnancy at whatever time, in whatever way, and for whatever reason she alone chooses. With this we do not agree. Appellant's arguments that Texas either has no valid interest at all in regulating the abortion decision, or no interest strong enough to support any limitation upon the woman's sole determination, is unpersuasive. The Court's decisions recognizing a right of privacy also acknowledge that some state regulation in areas protected by that right is appropriate. As noted above, a State may properly assert important interests in safeguarding health, in maintaining medical standards, and in protecting potential life. At some point in pregnancy, these respective interests become sufficiently compelling to sustain regulation of the factors that govern the abortion decision. The privacy right involved, therefore, cannot be said to be absolute. . . .

We, therefore, conclude that the right of personal privacy includes the abortion decision, but that this right is not unqualified and must be considered against important state interests in regulation. . . .

The appellee and certain amici argue that the fetus is a "person" within the language and meaning of the Fourteenth Amendment. In support of this, they outline at length and in detail the well-known facts of fetal development. If this suggestion of personhood is established, the appellant's case, of course, collapses, for the fetus' right to life is then guaranteed specifically by the Amendment. The appellant conceded as much on reargument. On the other hand, the appellee conceded on reargument that no case could be cited that holds that a fetus is a person within the meaning of the Fourteenth Amendment.

The Constitution does not define "person" in so many words. Section 1 of the Fourteenth Amendment contains three references to "person." The first, in defining "citizens," speaks of "persons born or naturalized in the United States." The word also appears both in the Due Process Clause and in the Equal Protection Clause.

"Person" is used in other places in the Constitution. . . . But in nearly all these instances, the use of the word is such that it has application only postnatally. None indicates, with any assurance, that is has any possible prenatal application.

All this, together with our observation, supra, that throughout the major portion of the 19th century prevailing legal abortion practices were far freer than they are today, persuades us that the word "person" as used in the Fourteenth Amendment, does not include the unborn. . . .

Texas urges that, apart from the Fourteenth Amendment, life begins at conception and is present throughout pregnancy, and that, therefore, the State has a compelling interest in protecting that life from and after conception. We need not resolve the difficult question of when life begins. When those trained in the respective disciplines of medicine, philosophy, and theology are unable to arrive at any consensus, the judiciary, at this point in the development of man's knowledge, is not in a position to speculate as to the answer. . . .

With respect to the State's important and legitimate interest in the health of the mother, the "compelling" point, in the light of present medical knowledge, is at approximately the end of the first trimester. This is so because of the now-established medical fact that until the end of the first trimester mortality in abortion may be less than mortality in normal childbirth. It follows that, from and after this point, a State may regulate the abortion procedure to the extent that the regulation reasonably relates to the preservation and protection of maternal health. . . .

With respect to the State's important and legitimate interest in potential life, the "compelling" point is at viability. This is so because the fetus then presumably has the capability of meaningful life outside the mother's womb. State regulation protective of fetal life after viability thus has both logical and biological justifications. If the State is interested in protecting fetal life after viability, it may go so far as to proscribe abortion during that period, except when it is necessary to preserve the life or health of the mother. . . .

To summarize and to repeat:

1. A state criminal abortion statute of the current Texas type, that excepts from criminality only a *life-saving* procedure on behalf of the mother, without regard to pregnancy stage and without recognition of the other interests involved, is violative of the Due Process Clause of the Fourteenth Amendment.
   a. For the stage prior to approximately the end of the first trimester, the abortion decision and its effectuation must be left to the medical judgment of the pregnant woman's attending physician.
   b. For the stage subsequent to approximately the end of the first trimester, the State, in promoting its interest in the health of the mother, may, if it chooses, regulate the abortion procedure in ways that are reasonably related to maternal health.
   c. For the stage subsequent to viability, the State in promoting its interest in the potentiality of human life may, if it chooses, regulate, and even proscribe, abortion except where it is necessary, in appropriate medical judgment, for the preservation of the life or health of the mother. . . .

Mr. Justice White, with whom Mr. Justice Rehnquist joins, dissenting.

At the heart of the controversy in these cases are those recurring pregnancies that pose no danger whatsoever to the life or health of the mother but are, nevertheless, unwanted for any one or more of a variety of reasons — convenience, family planning, economics, dislike of children, the embarrassment of illegitimacy, etc. The common claim before us is that for any one of such reasons, or for no reason at all, and without asserting or claiming any threat to life or health, any woman is entitled to an abortion at her request if she is able to find a medical advisor willing to undertake the procedure.

The Court for the most part sustains this position: During the period prior to the time the fetus becomes viable, the Constitution of the United States values the convenience, whim, or caprice of the putative mother more than the life or potential life of the fetus; the Constitution, therefore, guarantees the right to an abortion as against any state law or policy seeking to protect the fetus from an abortion not prompted by more compelling reasons of the mother.

With all due respect, I dissent. I find nothing in the language or history of the Constitution to support the Court's judgment. The Court simply fashions and announces a new constitutional right for pregnant mothers and, with scarcely any reason or authority for its action, invests that right with sufficient substance to override most existing state abortion statutes. The upshot is that the people and the legislatures of the 50 States are constitutionally disentitled to weigh the relative importance of the continued existence and development of the fetus, on the one hand, against a spectrum of possible impacts on the mother, on the other hand. As an exercise of raw judicial power, the Court perhaps has authority to do what it does today; but in my view its judgment is an improvident and extravagant exercise of the power of judicial review that the Constitution extends to this Court. . . .

Planned Parenthood v. *Casey,* 1992

Justice O'Connor, Justice Kennedy, and Justice Souter announced the judgment of the Court. . . .

Liberty finds no refuge in a jurisprudence of doubt. Yet 19 years after our holding that the Constitution protects a woman's right to terminate her pregnancy in its early stages, *Row v. Wade,* that definition of liberty is still questioned. Joining the respondents as *amicus curiae,* the United States, as it has done in five other cases in the last decade, again asks us to overrule *Roe.*

At issue in these cases are five provisions of the Pennsylvania Abortion Control Act of 1982 as amended in 1988 and 1989. . . .

After considering the fundamental constitutional questions resolved by *Roe,* principles of institutional integrity, and the rule of *stare decisis,* we are led to conclude this: the essential holding of *Roe v. Wade* should be retained and once again reaffirmed.

It is . . . tempting . . . to suppose that the Due Process Clause protects only

"Planned Parenthood v. *Casey,"* 112 S. Ct. 2791 (1992) from Leslie Friedman Goldstein, *Contemporary Cases in Women's Rights.* Copyright © 1994. Reprinted by permission of The University of Wisconsin Press.

those practices, defined at the most specific level, that were protected against government interference by other rules of law when the Fourteenth Amendment was ratified. . . . But such a view would be inconsistent with our law. It is a promise of the Constitution that there is a realm of personal liberty which the government may not enter. . . . Our law affords constitutional protection to personal decisions relating to marriage, procreation, contraception, family relationships, child rearing, and education. . . . Beliefs about these matters could not define the attributes of personhood were they formed under compulsion of the State.

These considerations begin our analysis of the woman's interest in terminating her pregnancy but cannot end it, for this reason: though the abortion decision may originate within the zone of conscience and belief, it is more than a philosophic exercise. Abortion is a unique act. It is an act fraught with consequences for others: for the woman who must live with the implications of her decision; for the persons who perform and assist in the procedure; for the spouse, family, and society which must confront the knowledge that these procedures exist, procedures some deem nothing short of an act of violence against innocent human life; and, depending on one's beliefs, for the life or potential life that is aborted. Though abortion is conduct, it does not follow that the State is entitled to proscribe it in all instances. That is because the liberty of the woman is at stake in a sense unique to the human condition and so unique to the law. The mother who carries a child to full term is subject to anxieties, to physical constraints, to pain that only she must bear. That these sacrifices have from the beginning of the human race been endured by woman with a pride that ennobles her in the eyes of others and gives to the infant a bond of love cannot alone be grounds for the State to insist she make the sacrifice. Her suffering is too intimate and personal for the State to insist, without more, upon its own vision of the woman's role, however dominant that vision has been in the course of our history and our culture. The destiny of the woman must be shaped to a large extent on her own conception of her spiritual imperatives and her place in society. . . .

The woman's right to terminate her pregnancy before viability is the most central principle of *Roe v. Wade*. It is a rule of law and a component of liberty we cannot renounce.

On the other side of the equation is the interest of the State in the protection of potential life. . . .

Though the woman has a right to choose to terminate or continue her pregnancy before viability, it does not at all follow that the State is prohibited from taking steps to ensure that this choice is thoughtful and informed. Even in the earliest stages of pregnancy, the State may enact rules and regulations designed to encourage her to know that there are philosophic and social arguments of great weight that can be brought to bear in favor of continuing the pregnancy to full term and that there are procedures and institutions to allow adoption of unwanted children as well as a certain degree of state assistance if the mother chooses to raise the child herself. . . . It follows that States are free to enact laws to provide a reasonable framework for a woman to make a decision that has such profound and lasting meaning. This, too, we find consistent with *Roe's* central premises, and indeed the inevitable consequence of our holding that the State has an interest in protecting the life of the unborn.

We reject the trimester framework, which we do not consider to be part of the essential holding of *Roe*. . . . The trimester framework suffers from these basic flaws: in its formulation it misconceives the nature of the pregnant woman's interest; and in practice it undervalues the State's interest in potential life, as recognized in *Roe*. . . .

Numerous forms of state regulation might have the incidental effect of increasing the cost or decreasing the availability of medical care, whether for abortion or any other medical procedure. The fact that a law which serves a valid purpose, one not designed to strike at the right itself, has the incidental effect of making it more difficult or more expensive to procure an abortion cannot be enough to invalidate it. Only where state regulation imposes an undue burden on a woman's ability to make this decision does the power of the State reach into the heart of the liberty protected by the Due Process Clause. . . . In our view, the undue burden standard is the appropriate means of reconciling the State's interest with the woman's constitutionally protected liberty. . . .

We permit a State to further its legitimate goal of protecting the life of the unborn by enacting legislation aimed at ensuring a decision that is mature and informed, even when in so doing the State expresses a preference for childbirth over abortion. . . . Requiring that the woman be informed of the availability of information relating to fetal development and the assistance available should she decide to carry the pregnancy to full term is a reasonable measure to insure an informed choice, one which might cause the woman to choose childbirth over abortion. This requirement cannot be considered a substantial obstacle to obtaining an abortion, and, it follows, there is no undue burden. . . .

The Pennsylvania statute also requires us to reconsider the holding in *Akron I* that the State may not require that a physician, as opposed to a qualified assistant, provide information relevant to a woman's informed consent. Since there is no evidence on this record that requiring a doctor to give the information as provided by the statute would amount in practical terms to a substantial obstacle to a woman seeking an abortion, we conclude that it is not an undue burden. . . .

Whether the mandatory 24-hour waiting period is . . . invalid because in practice it is a substantial obstacle to a woman's choice to terminate her pregnancy is a closer question. The findings of fact by the District Court indicate that because of the distances many women must travel to reach an abortion provider, the practical effect will often be a delay of much more than a day because the waiting period requires that a woman seeking an abortion make at least two visits to the doctor. The District Court also found that in many instances this will increase the exposure of women seeking abortions to "the harassment and hostility of antiabortion protestors demonstrating outside a clinic." . . .

These findings are troubling in some respects, but they do not demonstrate that the waiting period constitutes an undue burden. . . .

Section 3209 of Pennsylvania's abortion law provides, except in cases of medical emergency, that no physician shall perform an abortion on a married woman without receiving a signed statement from the woman that she has notified her spouse that she is about to undergo an abortion [or that she fits into one of the statute's exceptions.] . . .

In well-functioning marriages, spouses discuss important intimate decisions such as whether to bear a child. But there are millions of women in this country who are the victims of regular physical and psychological abuse at the hands of their husbands. Should these women become pregnant, they may have very good reasons for not wishing to inform their husbands of their decision to obtain an abortion. . . .

The spousal notification requirement is thus likely to prevent a significant number of women from obtaining an abortion. It does not merely make abortions a little more difficult or expensive to obtain; for many women, it will impose a substantial obstacle. . . . It is an undue burden, and therefore invalid. . . .

[As to parental consent w]e have been over most of this ground before. Our cases establish, and we reaffirm today, that a State may require a minor seeking an abortion to obtain the consent of a parent or guardian, provided that there is an adequate judicial bypass procedure. . . .

The judgment [of the Circuit Court] is affirmed. . . .

Justice Blackmun, concurring in part, concurring in the judgment in part, and dissenting in part. . . .

Three years ago, in *Webster v. Reproductive Health Serv.,* four Members of this Court appeared poised to "cas[t] into darkness the hopes and visions of every woman in this country" who had come to believe that the Constitution guaranteed her the right to reproductive choice. . . . All that remained between the promise of *Roe* and the darkness of the plurality was a single, flickering flame. Decisions since *Webster* gave little reason to hope that this flame would cast much light. . . . But now, just when so many expected the darkness to fall, the flame has grown bright.

I do not underestimate the significance of today's joint opinion. Yet I remain steadfast in my belief that the right to reproductive choice is entitled to the full protection afforded by this Court before *Webster.* And I fear for the darkness as four Justices anxiously await the single vote necessary to extinguish the light. . . .

Roe's requirement of strict scrutiny as implemented through a trimester framework should not be disturbed. No other approach has gained a majority, and no other is more protective of the woman's fundamental right. Lastly, no other approach properly accommodates the woman's constitutional right with the State's legitimate interests. . . .

Chief Justice Rehnquist, with whom Justice White, Justice Scalia, and Justice Thomas join, concurring in the judgment in part and dissenting in part.

The joint opinion, following its newly-minted variation on *stare decisis,* retains the outer shell of *Roe v. Wade,* but beats a wholesale retreat from the substance of that case. We believe that *Roe* was wrongly decided, and that it can and should be overruled consistently with our traditional approach to *stare decisis* in constitutional cases. We would adopt the approach of the plurality in *Webster v. Reproductive Health Services* and uphold the challenged provisions of the Pennsylvania statute in their entirety. . . .

In *Roe v. Wade,* the Court recognized a "guarantee of personal privacy" which "is broad enough to encompass a woman's decision whether or not to terminate her pregnancy." We are now of the view that, in terming this right fundamental, the Court in *Roe* read the earlier opinions upon which it based its decision much too broadly. Unlike marriage, procreation and contraception, abortion "involves the purposeful termination of potential life." *Harris v. McRae* (1980). . . . One cannot ignore the fact that a woman is not isolated in her pregnancy, and that the decision to abort necessarily involves the destruction of a fetus. . . .

We think, therefore, both in view of this history and of our decided cases dealing with substantive liberty under the Due Process Clause, that the Court was mistaken in *Roe* when it classified a woman's decision to terminate her pregnancy as a "fundamental right" that could be abridged only in a manner which withstood "strict scrutiny." . . . The Court in *Roe* reached too far when it . . . deemed the right to abortion fundamental. . . .

Jerry Falwell Condemns the ERA, 1980

I believe that at the foundation of the women's liberation movement there is a minority core of women who were once bored with life, whose real problems are spiritual problems. Many women have never accepted their God-given roles. They live in disobedience to God's laws and have promoted their godless philosophy throughout our society. God Almighty created men and women biologically different and with differing needs and roles. He made men and women to complement each other and to love each other. Not all the women involved in the feminist movement are radicals. Some are misinformed, and some are lonely women who like being housewives and helpmeets and mothers, but whose husbands spend little time at home and who take no interest in their wives and children. Sometimes the full load of rearing a family becomes a great burden to a woman who is not supported by a man. Women who work should be respected and accorded dignity and equal rewards for equal work. But this is not what the present feminist movement and equal rights movement are all about.

The Equal Rights Amendment is a delusion. I believe that women deserve more than equal rights. And, in families and in nations where the Bible is believed, Christian women are honored above men. Only in places where the Bible is believed and practiced do women receive more than equal rights. Men and women have differing strengths. The Equal Rights Amendment can never do for women what needs to be done for them. Women need to know Jesus Christ as their Lord and Savior and be under His Lordship. They need a man who knows Jesus Christ as his Lord and Savior, and they need to be part of a home where their husband is a godly leader and where there is a Christian family.

The Equal Rights Amendment strikes at the foundation of our entire social structure. If passed, this amendment would accomplish exactly the opposite of its outward claims. By mandating an absolute equality under the law, it will actually take away many of the special rights women now enjoy. ERA is not merely a political issue, but a moral issue as well. A definite violation of holy Scripture, ERA defies the mandate that "the husband is the head of the wife, even as Christ is the head of the church" (Ep. 5:23). In 1 Peter 3:7 we read that husbands are to give their wives honor as unto the weaker vessel, that they are both heirs together of the grace of life. Because a woman is weaker does not mean that she is less important.

Connaught C. Marshner Explains What Social Conservatives Really Want, 1988

By now everyone knows that pro-family conservatives are a powerful political force. . . . What follows are the presumptions of the moral traditionalists.

The family is the fundamental institution of society; in the traditional society, it was your main source of comfort and strength. When you were a child, your father geared his life to providing shelter for your mother and you. As you grew, your family imparted the skills of survival, and gave you your religion and your politics. In your old age, someone with a blood connection would offer you a bed and a seat by the fire.

Today, these functions have atrophied. Your existence needn't cause your father to change his lifestyle, and in many circles it changes your mother's as little as she can possibly arrange. It is no reason for your father to stay with your mother; in the modern myth, she may even be more "fulfilled" without him around. If they do stay together, they play an increasingly small role in your upbringing: the public-education system, backed by the courts, positively puts obstacles in the path of parents wishing to exercise control over what their children read and study, while government-sponsored clinics are permitted to dispense contraceptives and perform abortions on teenagers without their parents' even being told. In your old age, Medicare will pay the costs of your medical treatment if you are put into an institution, but not if your relatives care for you at home. It's likely that your children and their spouses will all have careers anyhow, which means they can hire someone to look after you but can't spend time with you themselves.

In one area after another, functions once performed by the family are now provided by the government or government-style agencies and institutions. The goal of the pro-family movement is not to destroy these institutions but to restore to the family its proper functions, and to restore to the institutions an understanding of the proper proportion of their role.

The family fulfills many functions — social, psychological, and even economic — but these are *not* the reason for its existence. The family has one overriding task: raising children. It is each individual's entry point into society and the staging area of his personality.

Children are thus a gift and a responsibility, a long-term duty that arises from the nature of marriage. Marriage is not a contract, balancing conflicting interests, measuring competing obligations, forcing compliance with fear of consequences; it is a covenant, a permanent and exclusive union that sets no limits on what is to be given or forgiven by either party. The purposes of this covenant are the mutual support of the partners and the procreation, education, and rearing of children. Human nature being what it is, in practice many marriages are more reminiscent of contract than of covenant. But public policy should not seek the lowest common denominator and proclaim it as the model.

Modern society has, admittedly, lost sight of marriage in convenant terms. Fifty per cent of marriages in the U.S. today are second marriages for at least one of the partners. In 1984, over one million children were involved in the divorce of their parents; we can expect that over 11 million children — about one-fifth of the nation's total — will experience the misery of divorce over the next decade.

That trauma is rarely studied. In the famous California Children of Divorce Project, Dr. Judith Wallerstein of UC Berkeley followed children over a period of years after their parents divorced. Ten years after a divorce, 42 per cent of children were functioning poorly (exhibiting consistent depression, drug or alcohol abuse, sexual promiscuity, and/or poor performance in school); 15 per cent were functioning unevenly; and only 43 per cent were doing well most of the time. And the decline in upward mobility is just beginning to be noted: Dr. Wallerstein found in one study that, although 41 per cent of their divorced fathers were professionals, only 27 per cent of the children had professional aspirations.

A further result of the contract approach is no-fault divorce, which regards children as options that can be adjudicated like cars and stereos, with no long-term consequence to anyone. Some women may feel their "sense of self-worth" enhanced by bearing the costs of child-rearing alone, but their babies have no such illusions of self-reliance. Thanks to divorce and illegitimacy, children are the poorest class in America today: 20.5 per cent of all children were below the poverty line in 1986.

Nor are children the only victims. Stanford professor Lenore Weitzman, in her landmark study, *The Divorce Revolution,* found that in the year after a divorce, women experience a 73 per cent decline in their standard of living, while their former husbands experience a 42 per cent increase. The typical liberal response to this is to lament the feminization of poverty and wonder what the Federal Government is going to do to force fathers to pay child support. But even if every father met every child-support payment, 97 per cent of divorced women with children would still be in poverty. The real problem, again, is state laws and judges that adhere to no-fault divorce, expecting divorced mothers to function like young professional men. Despite what many would like to believe, traits of gender and the condition of motherhood make a tremendous difference in the way people can and will act. Any world view that pretends otherwise is either dishonestly or maliciously inviting human misery.

Another distortion in the public consciousness is population-bomb rhetoric: the idea that there are too many of us. Couples contemplating parenthood frequently decide against it out of deference to a vague sense of "society's" need. But decisions about fertility are properly the responsibility of husband and wife — those who will bear the responsibility of *raising* the children. Outside pressure — whether public or private — is inappropriate.

Actually, if the long-term good of the nation were the controlling factor, *large* families ought to be the goal. We have come to expect in retirement a standard of living that formerly was the reward of those who had raised a large family of successful and generous children. But maintaining Social Security and the rest of the welfare state requires constant population growth to keep the pyramid game going. The unfunded liability of our entitlement programs for the elderly alone is staggering. By the year 2010, two-thirds of the federal budget will be needed just to meet current entitlement promises.

The current tax cost of the welfare state is in fact making the future revenue base smaller, because it penalizes those who bear and raise children. Not only is there the loss of the second income and the expense of child-rearing, but mortgage rates for decent homes are geared to two incomes. At best, a young couple must choose prosperity or children — and many don't even have that choice.

A perverse dynamic is in place in our society: youthful lust is indulged, so long as fertility is controlled. Later, when fertility is desired, many find that it has been destroyed. One in four American couples is infertile, report the Centers for Disease Control, the most common cause being damage from venereal disease. And so begins the shrill demand to have a baby. Just as it was a "right" to be infertile when 18, it now is declared a "right" to be fertile at 28 or 35, as if nature could be turned on and off to suit one's preferences.

The lengths gone to and the amounts of money spent in pursuit of pregnancy can be astonishing. There is a growing demand for high-tech obstetrics — *in vitro* fertilization, embryo transfer, and even more alarming techniques — to say nothing of surrogate parenting. Let there be no confusion about this demand for babies, however: far too often, it is not a manifestation of pro-life sentiment, but of an ego in pursuit of an alter.

If couples yearning for children but unable to conceive were satisfied by adoption, theirs would be a noble impulse. But adoption remains unfashionable, and government policy does not encourage it. Federal funds are available to keep children in foster care, but not to place them in permanent homes, and some social workers establish standards for adoption so high that if nature held to such standards, few of us would have been born.

It should be an achievable goal that every baby born have an adult male responsible for it, that the norm be children nurtured by their own, married parents. But support for the traditional family flies in the face of the reigning orthodoxy by hinting that there is something inherently superior in children's being raised by their own parents in an intact family. Many professional women, single parents, and human-services personnel seem to take this praise of the ideal as an insult to the good they do. Many single parents *are* doing an excellent job of raising their children. But should we pretend that divorce and unwed motherhood are symptoms of social *strength*?

Liberalism since the Sixties has repudiated the validity of the ideal, anxious to placate feminism and the demand for instant pleasure without negative consequences. The facts of human nature do not change, however: to develop into stable, virtuous men and women, children need the constant, loving, particular attention of one or two consistent adults.

If we are to reassert the ideal, we must re-examine employment policies that lure mothers into the workforce, change tax policies that favor working mothers over full-time homemakers, and create tax oases for families of young children. Technology can come to our aid here, if it is not trammeled by politics as it has been in previous opportunities. Thirteen million new jobs could be created at home (presumably mostly for women) if government resists pressure from organized labor to outlaw home employment. Local laws restricting businesses operated out of the home — including computer work — must be corrected.

For those unmoved by social and moral arguments, there are hard dollars-and-cents considerations. If children are given the right formation they become a net plus to the public treasury; if not, they end up as a drain on it. According to University of North Carolina sociologist Peter Uhlenberg, there were in 1976 more than 260 programs administered by twenty different agencies of the Federal Government whose primary mission was to benefit children and adolescents, from recreation programs to drug and alcohol rehabilitation, job training, delinquency prevention, juvenile justice services, nutrition guidance, and so on. Real per-capita social-welfare expenditures in the country increased about five-fold between 1960 and 1980, with youth programs keeping pace. The government was doing more and more, and families were doing less and less. But did the well-being of the "beneficiaries" increase?

Among white adolescents aged 15 to 19, Uhlenberg found that, between 1960 and 1980, the death rate from suicide increased 140 per cent; from homicide, 232 per cent. The gonorrhea morbidity rate increased 199 per cent. Just between 1972 and 1979, the proportion of children aged 12 to 17 using alcohol increased 56 per cent; using drugs, 139 per cent. From 1970 to 1980, the arrest rate in that age group for violent crimes increased 60 per cent. This is the future we buy with our "investments."

It all comes down to values. Traditional values work because they are the guidelines most consistent with human nature for producing happiness and achievement. Children who are not trained to traditional values are deprived of the best opportunity to understand their own nature and achieve that happiness. Children who *are* trained to these values are nonetheless free, upon maturity, to reject them: that is why, contrary to what the relativists insist, instilling them is not oppressive. But if these values are at least transmitted to all members of society, the possibility for a fundamental consensus on behavior exists.

Ronald Reagan got elected and reelected in large part because enough people agreed that the policies of the welfare state had failed, and enough wanted to hear more about traditional values. The public wanted government to shrink its role in their lives. That basic impulse has been developed for eight years now. In the meantime, we still have a welfare state that shows no signs of curing a single social ill, let alone withering away — it is, of course, intrinsically incapable of doing either. . . . This system perpetuates itself and the problems it pretends to solve; and yet we cannot follow the vision on which Ronald Reagan was elected until the way society organizes its approach to problems is changed — until people are again in charge of their own affairs, and those of their local community.

What can we do? An example comes from Texas. Jimmy Starkes runs the Dallas Life Foundation, a shelter for the homeless. It houses one thousand people, with over two hundred volunteers and fewer than fifty employees, many of both groups themselves former street people. Starkes estimates that out of every ten homeless people who come through his system, eight are employed and productive when he stops following them, whereas only one out of ten who go through a public shelter would have such a future. In 1987, Starkes raised $2 million in cash and in kind from the Dallas community to do this work — from people who are also paying taxes so government can do its ineffective work on the same mission.

Here is the answer: transfer, one by one, the functions of the welfare state from bureaucrats, whose vested interest is perpetuation of the problem, to service-oriented people whose only interest is solution of the problem in its current victims, and prevention of it in its future victims.

Sure, Jimmy Starkes gets the people he helps to commit their lives to Christ. Liberals would say that's unconstitutional; some conservatives would feel it's not fair. But Starkes would tell you that unless they do that first, he can't help them, because they're not willing to *let* him help them change their lives. Welfare agencies don't demand that change of heart, nor do they have Jimmy Starkes's low recidivism rate.

Liberal solutions don't work because institutions cannot change hearts or minds. *People* do that. That's why the family must hold onto as many functions as it can, and reclaim those that have been taken from it: because the consolidation of tasks in the family intensifies the interaction among members, and heightens awareness of and commitment to one another's welfare. That gives the long-range focus to our lives that connects us to society and enables us to extend our concern to our fellow citizens.

"Private-sector initiatives" is a fine watchword, but if it just means business voluntarily giving money to government-style programs, it is no solution to social problems. If it means empowering ancient institutions to do that which they do best, namely catalyze change in human hearts and actions, then it can invite a solution.

American Booksellers Ass'n, Inc. v. *Hudnut,* 1985

Frank H. Easterbrook, Circuit Judge:

. . . Under the First Amendment the government must leave to the people the evaluation of ideas. Bald or subtle, an idea is as powerful as the audience allows it to be. A belief may be pernicious — the beliefs of Nazis led to the death of millions, those of the Klan to the repression of millions. A pernicious belief may prevail. Totalitarian governments today rule much of the planet, practicing suppression of billions and spreading dogma that may enslave others. One of the things that separates our society from theirs is our absolute right to propagate opinions that the government finds wrong or even hateful.

Under the ordinance graphic sexually explicit speech is "pornography" or not depending on the perspective the author adopts. Speech that "subordinates" women and also, for example, presents women as enjoying pain, humiliation, or rape, or even simply presents women in "positions of servility or submission or display" is forbidden, no matter how great the literary or political value of the work taken as a whole. Speech that portrays women in positions of equality is lawful, no matter how graphic the sexual content. This is thought control. It establishes an "approved" view of women, of how they may react to sexual encounters, of how the sexes may relate to each other. Those who espouse the approved view may use sexual images; those who do not, may not.

Indianapolis justifies the ordinance on the ground that pornography affects thoughts. Men who see women depicted as subordinate are more likely to treat them so. Pornography is an aspect of dominance. It does not persuade people so much as change them. It works by socializing, by establishing the expected and the permissible. In this view pornography is not an idea; pornography is the injury.

There is much to this perspective. Beliefs are also facts. People often act in accordance with the images and patterns they find around them. People raised in a religion tend to accept the tenets of that religion, often without independent examination. People taught from birth that black people are fit only for slavery rarely rebelled against that creed; beliefs coupled with the self-interest of the masters established a social structure that inflicted great harm while enduring for centuries. . . .

Therefore we accept the premises of this legislation. Depictions of subordination tend to perpetuate subordination. The subordinate status of women in turn leads to affront and lower pay at work, insult and injury at home, battery and rape on the streets. In the language of the legislature, "[p]ornography is central in creating and maintaining sex as a basis of discrimination. Pornography is a systematic practice of exploitation and subordination based on sex which differentially harms women. The bigotry and contempt it produces, with the acts of aggression it fosters, harm women's opportunities for equality and rights [of all kinds]."

Yet this simply demonstrates the power of pornography as speech. All of these unhappy effects depend on mental intermediation. Pornography affects how people see the world, their fellows, and social relations. If pornography is what pornography does, so is other speech. Hitler's orations affected how some Germans saw Jews. Communism is a world view, not simply a *Manifesto* by Marx and Engels or a set of speeches. . . . Religions affect socialization in the most pervasive way. . . . Many people believe that the existence of television, apart from the content of specific programs, leads to intellectual laziness, to a penchant for violence, to many other ills. . . .

Racial bigotry, anti-semitism, violence on television, reporters' biases — these and many more influence the culture and shape our socialization. None is directly answerable by more speech, unless that speech too finds its place in the popular culture. Yet all is protected as speech, however insidious. Any other answer leaves the government in control of all of the institutions of culture, the great censor and director of which thoughts are good for us.

Sexual responses often are unthinking responses, and the association of sexual arousal with the subordination of women therefore may have a substantial effect. But almost all cultural stimuli provoke unconscious responses. Religious ceremonies condition their participants. . . . Television scripts contain unarticulated assumptions. People may be conditioned in subtle ways. If the fact that speech plays a role in a process of conditioning were enough to permit governmental regulation, that would be the end of freedom of speech.

It is possible to interpret the claim that the pornography is the harm in a different way. Indianapolis emphasizes the injury that models in pornographic films and pictures may suffer. The record contains materials depicting sexual torture, penetration of women by red-hot irons and the like. . . .

However . . . the image of pain is not necessarily pain. In *Body Double,* a suspense film directed by Brian DePalma, a woman who has disrobed and presented a sexually explicit display is murdered by an intruder with a drill. The drill runs through the woman's body. The film is sexually explicit and a murder occurs — yet no one believes that the actress suffered pain or died. . . . Depictions may affect slavery, war, or sexual roles, but a book about slavery is not itself slavery, or a book about death by poison a murder. . . .

A power to limit speech on the ground that truth has not yet prevailed and is not likely to prevail implies the power to declare truth. At some point the government must be able to say (as Indianapolis has said): "We know what the truth is, yet a free exchange of speech has not driven out falsity, so that we must now prohibit falsity." If the government may declare the truth, why wait for the failure of speech? Under the First Amendment, however, there is no such thing as a false idea. . . .

We come, finally, to the argument that pornography is "low value" speech, that it is enough like obscenity that Indianapolis may prohibit it. . . .

Indianapolis seeks to prohibit certain speech because it believes this speech influences social relations and politics on a grand scale, that it controls attitudes at home and in the legislature. This precludes a characterization of the speech as low value. True, pornography and obscenity have sex in common. But Indianapolis left out of its definition any reference to literary, artistic, political, or scientific value. The ordinance applies to graphic sexually explicit subordination in works great and small. The Court sometimes balances the value of speech against the costs of its restriction, but it does this by category of speech and not by the content of particular works. . . . Indianapolis has created an approved point of view and so loses the support of these cases. . . .

The definition of "pornography" is unconstitutional. No construction or excision of particular terms could save it. The offense of trafficking in pornography necessarily falls with the definition. . . .

The offense of coercion to engage in a pornographic performance . . . has elements that might be constitutional. Without question a state may prohibit fraud, trickery, or the use of force to induce people to perform — in pornographic films or in any other films. Such a statute may be written without regard to the viewpoint depicted in the work. . . .

But the Indianapolis ordinance, unlike our hypothetical statute, is not neutral with respect to viewpoint. The ban on distribution of works containing coerced performances is limited to pornography; coercion is irrelevant if the work is not "pornography," and we have held the definition of "pornography" to be defective root and branch. A legislature might replace "pornography" . . . with "any film containing explicit sex" or some similar expression, but even the broadest severability clause does not permit a federal court to rewrite as opposed to excise. Rewriting is work for the legislature of Indianapolis. . . .

No amount of struggle with particular words and phrases in this ordinance can leave anything in effect. The district court came to the same conclusion. Its judgment is therefore

Affirmed.

Anita Hill's Testimony Before the Senate
Judiciary Committee, 1991

. . . Mr. Chairman, Senator Thurmond, members of the committee, my name is Anita F. Hill, and I am a professor of law at the University of Oklahoma.

I was born on a farm in Okmulgee County, OK, in 1956. I am the youngest of 13 children. I had my early education in Okmulgee County. My father, Albert Hill, is a farmer in that area. My mother's name is Erma Hill. She is also a farmer and a housewife.

My childhood was one of a lot of hard work and not much money, but it was one of solid family affection as represented by my parents. I was reared in a religious atmosphere in the Baptist faith, and I have been a member of the Antioch Baptist Church, in Tulsa, OK, since 1983. It is a very warm part of my life at the present time.

For my undergraduate work, I went to Oklahoma State University, and graduated from there in 1977. . . .

I graduated from the university with academic honors and proceeded to the Yale Law School, where I received my J.D. degree in 1980.

Upon graduation from law school, I became a practicing lawyer with the Washington, DC, firm of Wald, Harkrader & Ross. In 1981, I was introduced to now Judge Thomas by a mutual friend. Judge Thomas told me that he was anticipating a political appointment and asked if I would be interested in working with him. He was, in fact, appointed as Assistant Secretary of Education for Civil Rights. After he had taken that post, he asked if I would become his assistant, and I accepted that position. . . .

During this period at the Department of Education, my working relationship with Judge Thomas was positive. I had a good deal of responsibility and independence. I thought he respected my work and that he trusted my judgment.

After approximately 3 months of working there, he asked me to go out socially with him. What happened next and telling the world about it are the two most difficult things, experiences of my life. It is only after a great deal of agonizing consideration and a number of sleepless nights that I am able to talk of these unpleasant matters to anyone but my close friends.

I declined the invitation to go out socially with him, and explained to him that I thought it would jeopardize what at the time I considered to be a very good working relationship. I had a normal social life with other men outside of the office. I believed then, as now, that having a social relationship with a person who was supervising my work would be ill advised. I was very uncomfortable with the idea and told him so.

I thought that by saying "no" and explaining my reasons, my employer would abandon his social suggestions. However, to my regret, in the following few weeks he continued to ask me out on several occasions. He pressed me to justify my reasons for saying "no" to him. These incidents took place in his office or mine. They were in the form of private conversations which would not have been overheard by anyone else.

My working relationship became even more strained when Judge Thomas began to use work situations to discuss sex. On these occasions, he would call me into his office for reports on education issues and projects or he might suggest that because of the time pressures of his schedule, we go to lunch to a government cafeteria. After a brief discussion of work, he would turn the conversation to a discussion of sexual matters. His conversations were very vivid.

He spoke about acts that he had seen in pornographic films involving such matters as women having sex with animals, and films showing group sex or rape scenes. He talked about pornographic materials depicting individuals with large penises, or large breasts involved in various sex acts.

On several occasions Thomas told me graphically of his own sexual prowess. Because I was extremely uncomfortable talking about sex with him at all, and particularly in such a graphic way, I told him that I did not want to talk about these subjects. I would also try to change the subject to education matters or to nonsexual personal matters, such as his background or his beliefs. My efforts to change the subject were rarely successful.

Throughout the period of these conversations, he also from time to time asked me for social engagements. My reactions to these conversations was to avoid them by limiting opportunities for us to engage in extended conversations. This was difficult because at the time, I was his only assistant at the Office of Education or Office for Civil Rights.

During the latter part of my time at the Department of Education, the social pressures and any conversation of his offensive behavior ended. I began both to believe and hope that our working relationship could be a proper, cordial, and professional one.

When Judge Thomas was made chair of the EEOC, I needed to face the question of whether to go with him. I was asked to do so and I did. The work, itself, was interesting, and at that time, it appeared that the sexual overtures, which had so troubled me, had ended.

I also faced the realistic fact that I had no alternative job. While I might have gone back to private practice, perhaps in my old firm, or at another, I was dedicated to civil rights work and my first choice was to be in that field. Moreover, at that time the Department of Education, itself, was a dubious venture. President Reagan was seeking to abolish the entire department.

For my first months at the EEOC, where I continued to be an assistant to Judge Thomas, there were no sexual conversations or overtures. However, during the fall and winter of 1982, these began again. The comments were random, and ranged from pressing me about why I didn't go out with him, to remarks about my personal appearance. I remember him saying that "some day I would have to tell him the real reason that I wouldn't go out with him."

He began to show displeasure in his tone and voice and his demeanor in his continued pressure for an explanation. He commented on what I was wearing in terms of whether it made me more or less sexually attractive. The incidents occurred in his inner office at the EEOC.

One of the oddest episodes I remember was an occasion in which Thomas was drinking a Coke in his office, he got up from the table, at which we were working, went over to his desk to get the Coke, looked at the can and asked, "Who has put pubic hair on my Coke?"

On other occasions he referred to the size of his own penis as being larger than normal and he also spoke on some occasions of the pleasures he had given to women with oral sex. At this point, late 1982, I began to feel severe stress on the job. I began to be concerned that Clarence Thomas might take out his anger with me by degrading me or not giving me important assignments. I also thought that he might find an excuse for dismissing me.

In January 1983, I began looking for another job. I was handicapped because I feared that if he found out he might make it difficult for me to find other employment, and I might be dismissed from the job I had.

Another factor that made my search more difficult was that this was during a period of a hiring freeze in the Government. In February 1983, I was hospitalized for 5 days on an emergency basis for acute stomach pain which I attributed to stress on the job. Once out of the hospital, I became more committed to find other employment and sought further to minimize my contact with Thomas.

This became easier when Allyson Duncan became office director because most of my work was then funneled through her and I had contact with Clarence Thomas mostly in staff meetings.

In the spring of 1983, an opportunity to teach at Oral Roberts University opened up. I participated in a seminar, taught an afternoon session in a seminar at Oral Roberts University. The dean of the university saw me teaching and inquired as to whether I would be interested in pursuing a career in teaching, beginning at Oral Roberts University. I agreed to take the job, in large part, because of my desire to escape the pressures I felt at the EEOC due to Judge Thomas.

When I informed him that I was leaving in July, I recall that his response was that now, I would no longer have an excuse for not going out with him. I told him that I still preferred not to do so. At some time after that meeting, he asked if he could take me to dinner at the end of the term. When I declined, he assured me that the dinner was a professional courtesy only and not a social invitation. I reluctantly agreed to accept that invitation but only if it was at the very end of a working day.

On, as I recall, the last day of my employment at the EEOC in the summer of 1983, I did have dinner with Clarence Thomas. We went directly from work to a restaurant near the office. We talked about the work that I had done both at Education and at the EEOC. He told me that he was pleased with all of it except for an article and speech that I had done for him while we were at the Office for Civil Rights. Finally he made a comment that I will vividly remember. He said, that if I ever told anyone of his behavior that it would ruin his career. This was not an apology, nor was it an explanation. That was his last remark about the possibility of our going out, or reference to his behavior.

In July 1983, I left the Washington, DC, area and have had minimal contacts with Judge Clarence Thomas since. I am, of course, aware from the press that some questions have been raised about conversations I had with Judge Clarence Thomas after I left the EEOC.

From 1983 until today I have seen Judge Thomas only twice. On one occasion I needed to get a reference from him and on another, he made a public appearance at Tulsa. On one occasion he called me at home and we had an inconsequential conversation. On one occasion he called me without reaching me and I returned the call without reaching him and nothing came of it. I have, at least on three occasions been asked to act as a conduit to him for others. . . .

It is only after a great deal of agonizing consideration that I am able to talk of these unpleasant matters to anyone, except my closest friends as I have said before. . . . Telling the world is the most difficult experience of my life, but it is very close to have to live through the experience that occasioned this meeting. I may have used poor judgment early on in my relationship with this issue. I was aware, however, that telling at any point in my career could adversely affect my future career. . . .

Perhaps I should have taken angry or even militant steps, both when I was in the agency or after I had left it, but I must confess to the world that the course that I took seemed the better, as well as the easier approach.

I declined any comment to newspapers, but later when Senate staff asked me about these matters, I felt that I had a duty to report. I have no personal vendetta against Clarence Thomas. I seek only to provide the committee with information which it may regard as relevant.

It would have been more comfortable to remain silent. . . . I took no initiative to inform anyone. But when I was asked by a representative of this committee to report my experience I felt that I had to tell the truth. I could not keep silent.

❋ E S S A Y S

In 1981, Rosalind Pollack Petchesky, currently of Hunter College, analyzed the rise of the New Right and its connections to the anti-abortion movement and to anti-feminism; her views appear in the first essay. In the second essay, Alida Brill, an independent researcher, analyzes the ideological issues dividing feminists who support laws banning pornography from those who view such laws as a dangerous form of censorship. Kim A. Taylor, a professor of law at Stanford Law School, argues in the third essay that Anita Hill was rendered "invisible" when she testified before the Senate Judiciary Committee in 1991. The members of the committee could not comprehend the dual impact of racism and sexism on Anita Hill in the workplace. Sadly, Taylor contends, feminists and members of the African-American community also ignored the intersection of race and gender in Hill's experience. Together these essays help to identify the nature of the obstacles, internal and external, to the advance of the feminist cause in the 1990s.

Antiabortion and Antifeminism

ROSALIND POLLACK PETCHESKY

Soon after the 1980 elections, it became all too clear that American society and the state were plunging day by day more deeply into conservative reactionism. Throughout its regime, the Reagan administration presented a power structure and political culture that were openly racist, antifeminist, and also antiliberal. To characterize such a basic political shift in terms of the conspiratorial maneuvering of a tightly organized New Right seems tempting but simplistic, given the pervasiveness of the conservative pull. For the 1980s threatened not only a well-orchestrated

"Antiabortion, Antifeminism, and the Rise of the New Right," reprinted from *Feminist Studies,* Volume 7, number 2 (Summer 1981): pp. 206–46, by permission of the publisher, Feminist Studies, Inc., c/o Women's Studies Program, University of Maryland, College Park, MD 20742.

A demonstration by antiabortion activists outside an abortion clinic in Robbinsdale, Minnesota, a suburb of Minneapolis, April 1993. The woman in the foreground is trying to engage in "sidewalk counseling" with the occupants of the car, women who have just left the clinic. Historically, American mothers have often brought their children with them to political parades and demonstrations (see the suffrage parade photo in Chapter 10); here, a boy carries a sign meant to convey youths' special interest in opposing abortion.

right-wing offensive, but also the demise of the liberal state and, along with it, some of its more progressive ideas — ideas such as individual freedom, "equality," and the responsibility of the state to provide for social welfare needs — in short, the tenets of bourgeois democracy. In practice, these ideas have historically stood in marked contrast to a capitalist, racist, and male-supremacist society. Although they were never either carried to their logical conclusions or made real for large groups of people, they nevertheless, until now, had a widespread ideological legitimacy, and as such were taken up and transformed by progressive movements, sometimes effectively, in the fight for radical social change. The antiliberal reaction obviously poses serious contradictions for socialists, feminists, gay rights activists, and others who have fought to transform the liberal state; at the same time, the attack on liberal reforms pushes those groups to organize on a much broader basis than they have done in the recent past.

Clearly, the New Right is not alone in abandoning liberalism. The dogma that social programs for the poor and working people represent "intrusiveness" and "overregulation" by the state, and that feminism and the sixties' counterculture represent "permissiveness" and "hedonism" (or "narcissism") in the society, emanates not only from the Moral Majority, but also from the dominant media and intellectual organs, the centers of corporate and state power, and even from some self-defined leftists. It is important to recognize the generality of these trends and also that Reagan's election and reelection cannot be read as a popular "mandate" for conservatism. And yet it is still the case that the New Right *is* an identifiable political reality, which had visible success in mobilizing conservative voters and in creating an effective organizational machine in the 1980s. Above all, I shall argue that what has given the New Right both ideological legitimacy and organizational coherence in this period has been its focus on reproductive and sexual issues. If there is anything genuinely "new" about the current right wing in the United States, it is its tendency to locate sexual, reproductive, and family issues at the center of its political program — not as manipulative rhetoric only, but as the substantive core of a politics geared, on a level that outdistances any previous right-wing movements in this country, to mobilizing a nationwide mass following. The politics of the family, sexuality, and reproduction — and most directly, of abortion — became a primary vehicle through which right-wing politicians achieved their ascent to state power in the late 1970s and the 1980s. My purpose here is to analyze the role of antiabortion and antifeminist politics in that rise to power. . . .

If the embodiment of absolute evil for an earlier generation of the Right was international communism, the Left, and labor movements in the United States, in the recent period, it is feminism and homosexuality — both representing movements for transcendance of a patriarchal form of family and for sexual liberation. This shift is not surprising given the weakness of the Left and labor movements at the present time; whereas the women's liberation movement in the 1970s has become the most dynamic force for social change in the country, the one most directly threatening not only to conservative values and interests, but also to significant groups whose way of life is challenged by ideas of sexual liberation. And of all feminist demands, the *right to abortion* is that which somehow appears most threatening to traditional sexual and social values.

The antiabortion movement, which began in the Catholic church and, despite disclaimers, has remained an essentially *religious* movement, has been the main vehicle through which the New Right has crystallized and developed both its mass base and its mass ideology. This particular crusade — which existed before the New Right and, I would argue, in many ways laid the groundwork for it — has provided the existing right wing with the perfect issue to "freeze" the political process into an absolute struggle between good and evil; an intensely palpable symbol of martyrdom, something "positive to fight for." But, while the religious, moralistic, and often mystical terms in which this crusade is couched resonate for many of its followers, religion should not be mistaken for the *content* of right-wing politics. Religion provides an "apocalyptic framework which validates [moral] absolutism," but the content of this framework is political in the most conventional sense: it has to do with how and by whom power is exercised — in the economy, the state, the family, and the churches.

From this perspective, it becomes clear that the major role of organized religion for the Right during elections has been to serve as a major organizational infrastructure, a nationally and locally established institutional network, one that exists outside the framework of the Democratic and Republican party structures, but which would give the Right access to an organized mass constituency. The two main institutions comprising this infrastructure, and around which New Right organizing strategy has revolved, are, first, the conservative wing and hierarchy of the Catholic church; and, second, the fundamentalist Protestant churches, particularly those affiliated with the Moral Majority. Both of these groups are already organized through the "right-to-life" movement, as well as through their own internal congregations and networks — a reality on which the New Right has sought to capitalize. Through a vigorous use of these conservative religious organizations, the New Right — and indirectly the Reagan forces — sought to achieve certain key ingredients of political power: votes and funds; active recruits and foot soldiers; and legitimacy (through association with a morally righteous cause). Already by 1978, its spokesmen were claiming that this base would give them potential access to one hundred million voters, and they were confident of commanding sufficient votes in the elections to give them control over the Senate, the Republican party, and, indeed, the presidency. Regardless of how one analyzes the deeper causes of the right-wing electoral victories in 1980, it is undeniable that a key element in the Right's strategy was to use the churches and particularly the "right-to-life" movement as an organizational model and base.

The "right-to-life" movement was originally a creation of the Family Life division of the National Conference of Catholic Bishops (NCCB), the directing body of the Catholic church in America. Immediately following the Supreme Court decision in *Roe* v. *Wade*, the NCCB Pro-Life Affairs Committee declared that they would not "accept the Court's judgment," and called for a major legal and educational battle against abortion. Since then, in numerous documents the bishops have summoned Catholics, both lay and clergy, to enter the antiabortion struggle: to defeat liberal abortion laws and proabortion candidates, and to work for a constitutional amendment that would, in accordance with Roman Catholic doctrine, declare the fetus a full human person from the moment of fertilization, and abortion thus a homicide. In 1975, the NCCB presented a detailed strategy for the church's antiabortion crusade, its "Pastoral Plan for Pro-Life Activity." It called for the establishment of a network of "prolife committees" based in the parishes, that would (1) effect the passage of a "prolife" amendment; (2) elect "prolife" sympathizers to local party organizations; (3) monitor officials on their abortion stands; and (4) "work for qualified candidates who will vote for a constitutional amendment and other prolife issues." In other words, from the outset, the "right-to-life" movement was set up to be a political action machine to influence national and local elections, but working primarily through the churches and the financial and organizational leadership of the hierarchy. . . .

The New Right could not help but be drawn to these winning ingredients: a tightly controlled organization geared to recruiting and influencing voters across party lines; an alleged eleven million members and three thousand chapters throughout the United States; and a sense of moral righteousness on behalf of conservative values and "a cause." It would seem that the "right-to-life" movement became for the New Right a *model* for building a mass base. In addition, the New Right has been the direct beneficiary of mass antiabortion organizing, which has helped to create a constituency and a consciousness that is both responsive to the New Right's "profamily" ideology (see below) and committed to participating in the electoral process. In a political climate in which the majority of liberals and radicals are disaffected nonvoters, such political socialization undoubtedly contributed to the Right's margin of victory.

In 1978, the New Right began to take the "prolife" message outside of the "right-to-life" committees, setting up its own network of "prolife" Political Action Committees (PACs), "leadership conferences," and "conservative Christian" organizations, all under the rubric of the "profamily" movement. The strategy adopted in 1977 was to absorb "groups devoted to preservation of the traditional social roles of the family, the churches, and the schools" (that is, groups that were antiabortion, antibusing, anti-ERA, and anti–gay rights) into a single coalition organized around four main planks: "prolife," "profamily," "promoral," and "pro-American," with "family" as the keystone. New Right organizers launched direct-mail campaigns aimed at politicizing the country's fundamentalist preachers and organized a series of "leadership conferences" and religious coalitions. In addition to the highly publicized Moral Majority, conferences and groups with names like Religious Roundtable, Christian Voice, and American Family Forum proliferated, with the same speakers and leaders appearing continually on their rosters. . . .

The main constituency "profamily" leaders sought to organize was the estimated fifty million "born-again" Christians in this country, reached through both the evangelical church pulpits and, even more directly, the vast broadcasting network (thirteen thousand radio stations, thirty-six television shows) to which the evangelical churches have access. As in the "right-to-life" movement, the key to this strategy was the *preachers,* but particularly the nationally known Bible-preaching broadcasters. For millions of evangelical Protestants, who are the most frequent listeners to religious broadcasts, radio and television have taken the place of the local church, reaching people in their cars and homes, not only on Sunday, but on every other day all across America. Religious broadcasting for right-wing political purposes has long been a tool of right-wing preachers. But today the use of high-wave frequencies and satellite technology magnifies the potential impact of such broadcasting, and its costs, tremendously. What is of interest here, of course, is not the high-powered technology of the fundamentalist broadcasters, but the large financial backing which allows the application of that technology on a massive scale; and the political and ideological purposes for which the "electronic church" was created. An important example is Rev. Jerry Falwell, founder of the "profamily" Moral Majority, which has a mailing list of seventy thousand pastors. Falwell broadcasts *daily* over 300 television stations and 280 radio stations in thirty-one states. The message he communicates through the electronic church is the essence of "profamily" ideology: antihomosexuality ("the bisexual and homosexual movements in America are antifamily, . . . the number one offender . . . in traditional man-woman relationships"); antifeminism ("we believe in *superior* rights for women"); antiabortion and antidivorce. . . .

The fundamentalists thus developed a formidable base of financial and corporate support. The main purpose of "profamily" organizing prior to 1980 was to mobilize the growing social force of Christian fundamentalism into conservative political activity, and to weld it to the already politicized and Catholic-dominated "right-to-life" movement. An alliance between conservative Catholics and Protestants would be historically unprecedented in the United States; and New Right leaders believe that the politics of "morality" — that is, conservative family and sexual politics — is the key to forging such an alliance, and thus to uniting a potential "100 million Americans" into right-wing political identity and votes. Their method is to tap — as the "right-to-life" movement has done so successfully — both religious guilt and emotional vulnerability to all the symbolic meanings of "family" and "morality." The "profamily" movement promises not only to save fetuses, but to save "the family" itself and the moral foundations of "Christian civilization." Through citation of scripture and an urgent appeal to Christian conscience ("out of the pew, into the precinct"), Christians are urged to get involved in politics for the sake of the family and morality. But the vision implied in Moral Majority rhetoric transcends the family. It is one of a Christian theocracy, a transformed political system in which the (conservative) clergy is at the center of state power, and the state is avowedly "Christian" — and patriarchal.

Yet, the relationship between the group of conservative politicians and political promoters who call themselves the New Right and the right-to-life movement is a complicated one, involving both close ties and potentially deep divisions. From its origins in the early 1970s, the right-to-life movement has been courted by and wedded to a whole series of right-wing political veterans, whose affiliations include the John Birch Society, the Young Americans for Freedom, the World Anti-Communist League, and the Conservative Caucus. These relations have developed into a symbiosis in which New Right organizers lend to prolife groups their expertise in direct mailings, targeting candidates, and managing PACs, in return for securing a mass base of voters and local organizers. . . . Although less successful in 1984, in the 1980 elections, the New Right succeeded in combining its direct-mail fundraising techniques with the church-based electoral machinery of the "prolife" movement to elect an impressive number of conservatives to national office, and to defeat liberals.

At the same time, the New Right's political aims go well beyond the abortion issue. The goal of their electoral strategy is to get rid of legislators considered liberal on *any* of the Right's favorite issues, including environmental regulation, welfare, defense spending, and civil rights. It is this connection of abortion to a much larger and more traditional set of rightist political ends that has sown the seeds of difference between hardcore "right-to-lifers" and their New Right and fundamentalist patrons. Even prior to 1980, some antiabortion leaders expressed suspicion of the New Right's motives and were reluctant to let their "single-issue" focus become absorbed in the larger "profamily"/"pro-America" agenda. Indeed, much of the rhetoric and organizing of the NRLC has attempted to appeal to liberal and "humanist" religious people who identify with the poor and the oppressed, to connect the "rights of the unborn" to other human rights issues. (There is even a "Prolife Feminists" caucus which meets at the NRLC national convention, as well as a small, "left" wing of the movement which opposes population control and nuclear power and favors welfare benefits.)

While the actual ideas and priorities of the antiabortion movement contradict the appearance of liberalism and grass-roots populism (to say nothing of feminism), the desire to maintain that appearance, in order to win on the abortion issue, is very real. A too-close association with the New Right could be damaging to the "right-to-life" movement's support among liberal Catholics and others who identify with humanist and pacifist traditions, who strongly favor many of the services and institutions (daycare, labor unions, environmental protection laws) that the New Right loudly condemns. In an editorial in early 1976, the liberal Catholic journal *Commonweal* gave prophetic warning to the Church hierarchy about the fellows it was bedding down with in the antiabortion campaign:

> The anti-abortion amendment is a right-wing issue, and the bishops will quickly become the tools of conservative so-called "pro-life" (and perhaps anti-busing, anti-'welfare chiselers,' pro-arms race, pro-CIA) candidates in the 1976 elections. The effort will fizzle and the church will have been had. . . .

Yet if we are to understand the specificity of New Right politics, we need to analyze the complex relationships between "economic," "political," and "moral" issues in their thinking. What I want to argue is, first, that the politics of the New Right seek legitimation from a common ideological core, the idea of *privatization;* and second, that the "privatization" impulse itself cuts in two interrelated directions: against social welfare and the poor, and against feminism and women. What is particularly important here is the ideology of the "private sphere" and its relation to both the family and states' rights. The New Right in its "profamily" program invokes deep fears of loss of control over what is considered most "private," most "personal." Historically, the concept of "privacy" for American conservatives has included not only "free enterprise" and "property rights," but also the right of the white male property owner to control his wife and his wife's body, his children and their bodies, his slaves and their bodies. It is an ideology that is patriarchal and racist, as well as capitalist. Part of the content of the formal appeal to "states' rights" is the idea of the family as a private, and above all male-dominated, domain. Control over families (one's wife and children) and control over local and state power structures are closely related conservative values, insofar as the latter is the means whereby the former is sought as an end. Thus what appear to be attacks on federalism are simultaneously attacks on movements by women, blacks, and young people to assert their right to resources, services, and a viable existence outside the family and the ghetto. . . .

The New Right must be understood as a response to feminist ideas and to their strong impact, in the 1970s, on popular consciousness. Joined by major segments of the corporate capitalist and state power structures, the New Right is trying to designate the private as "private" once again, but in a particular sense. The aim is surely to *reprivatize* every domain of social, public intervention that has been created through the struggles of working people, blacks, the poor, and women for the last twenty years. Not only abortion, sex education, and domestic violence services, but health care, education, the right to equal education, legal services, health and safety at work, access to the broadcasting media are all being pushed back into the unregulated anarchy of the private sector. The legitimation for this massive attempt to destroy the meager reforms that were won from the liberal state in the 1960s and 70s is the myth of "privatism" — the idea that what's wrong with busing or medicaid abortions or the Occupational Safety and Health Administration (OSHA) or the Environmental Protection Agency is that the federal government is "meddling in our 'private' business"; that, indeed, there even exists some private, safe, secure place — our neighborhoods, our churches, above all, the family — that would give us everything we needed if only the government would stay out.

But, although the language of New Right ideology evokes the sentiment of personal freedom from state interference, what distinguishes that ideology from classical conservatism is that it is spoken on behalf of *corporate* bodies rather than individuals. It is, in other words, corporate privatism — in the service of business, church, private school, and patriarchal family — that is intended, not individual privacy. In this regard, the New Right's appeal to privatism is much closer to fascism than to classical libertarian doctrine and is thus perfectly compatible, in theory as well as practice, with a program of massive state control over individuals' private lives. Of course, the fact that this ideology is being propagated widely in a period of severe economic crisis and recession is not particularly surprising. My argument here is that it is the context of a popular feminist movement and an antifeminist backlash that has, in this historical period, fueled that ideology and given it a certain popular momentum. In that context, by focusing on those realms which still have the greatest *appearance* as "private," or "personal," in our culture — sexuality, abortion, the relations between parents and children — the New Right has been able to achieve a much greater ideological legitimacy for its politics of racism and fiscal conservatism than it could have by calling things by their right names. . . .

Antiabortion ideology has been taken up by the right wing not only for its "profamily" and prochurch message, but also for its support of conservative sexual values. The "right-to-life" doctrine of the fetus's "personhood" and the aborting woman's "selfishness" is directly akin to the antihumanist philosophy of the "profamily" movement. Antihumanism, as professed by the "right-to-life" and "profamily" movements, pits itself squarely against every intellectual and philosophical tradition that grew out of the Enlightenment and secularism. Marxism and feminism both are clearly denounced by the "right-to-life"/"profamily" movement, but so are all philosophies, including radical Christian movements, whose central focus is social change on this earth or even human as opposed to divine, or scriptural, ends. When [Paul] Weyrich describes the Moral Majority as "a Christian democratic movement rooted in the authentic Gospel, not the social gospel," he is attacking, and distinguishing his politics from, those Christian and Catholic movements in the United States and Latin America who ally with the poor to change oppressive social conditions. All social movements — including labor movements, peasant uprisings, anticolonial struggles, civil rights, antinuclear protests — would thus be categorized by the New Right under "materialistic, atheistic humanism," charged with the sin of making human life and human pleasure on earth the measure of all value.

But a very particular condemnation is reserved for feminism and the movement for sexual liberation. . . . Over and over again in antiabortion and "profamily" literature, one is struck with a defiantly traditional middle-class morality regarding sexual behavior and an undisguised antipathy toward *all* forms of sexuality outside the marital, procreative sphere. Male homosexuality, lesbianism, extramarital sex, divorce — all are targets of the New Right's modern "purity crusade." But more than anything else, the subject that excites "prolifers" is premarital sex among teenagers. Increasingly it appears that antagonism to abortion stems less from concern for protecting the fetus than from a desire to prevent teenage sexuality. "Right-to-life" advocates assume as a matter of course that there is a causal relationship between legalized abortion and a rise in sexual promiscuity and illegitimacy, particularly among teenagers. Not only abortion but also birth control and sex education programs sponsored by clinics and schools are seen as giving official government sanction to "illicit" sex — and, therefore, as interfering with parents' control over the moral behavior and values of their children. Conversely, the way to eliminate premarital sexuality, it is thought, is to eliminate abortion, teenage contraceptive programs, and sex education. . . .

The theme of protecting children has also been applied in the movement's virulent, active campaign against homosexuals and lesbians. On the false pretext that male homosexuals and lesbians are child molesters, New Right legislative and political offensives have sought, with some success, to defeat local gay rights ordinances in cities around the country; to deny federally funded legal services to homosexuals; to bar homosexuals from teaching in the public schools (as in the defeated Briggs Amendment campaign in California); and to revive the ideology (abandoned even by the American Psychiatric Association) that homosexuality is "pathological" and "perverse." A longer-range goal is to prohibit the employment of homosexuals not only in education, but in *any* "public sector" or "high visibility public jobs"; as well as to prohibit federal funding of any organization that even "suggests" that homosexuality "can be an acceptable lifestyle." Conservatives both within and outside the Reagan administration have cruelly exploited the AIDS epidemic as "God's curse" on homosexuals, a pretext for discrimination and, in some quarters, proposals for quarantine.

The ideas behind the New Right's antihomosexual campaign are revealing of the political values that motivate the "profamily" movement, including the movement against abortion. They suggest that, while it may be true that "prolifers" are hostile to sexuality as such, it is really the social aspects of traditional gender identities — and particularly the position of male paternal and heterosexual authority — that they are determined to protect. Homosexuality is characterized by "profamily" representatives as "unnatural," "evil," and psychologically "perverse"; but male homosexuality is even more dangerous than female, in the "profamily" view, because it signals a breakdown of "masculinity" itself — or what one right-wing ideologue calls the "male spirit," or "the male principle." Thus, what is at stake in the New Right campaign against homosexuality is the very idea of what it means to be a "man" or a "woman," and the structure and meaning of the traditional family. These two concepts are clearly related, for the meaning of "masculinity" (as of "femininity") — that is, of gender itself — has been defined historically through the structure of the family and dominant position of the father within it. Paul Weyrich, a leader of the "profamily" movement, expresses an awareness of this reality when he says that

> there are people who want a different political order, who are not necessarily Marxists. Symbolized by the women's liberation movement, they believe that the future for their political power lies in the restructuring of the traditional family, and particularly in the *downgrading of the male or father role in the traditional family.*

The aim of the "profamily" movement is to restore heterosexual patriarchy, the control of men over their wives and children. Teenage sexuality; homosexuality; the freely determined sexuality of women as wives and daughters; abortion and contraception, insofar as they promote sexual freedom; even "test-tube babies," which hold out the prospect of totally removing procreation from heterosexual monogamy

— all are a direct threat to male authority and the identification of men as heads of families. Given this, it is not surprising that all these activities have become the central target of a movement that is led by middle-class conservative men. The men of the "profamily" movement, mainly upper-middle-class professionals, are not immune to the sense of personal loss and threat provoked by feminism and by recent changes in the family and women's work. Weyrich again captures the essence of this middle-class patriarchal *ressentiment* when he proclaims: "The father's word has to prevail." With this unambiguous call to arms, Weyrich speaks not only as a New Right general, but also as a husband and a father. And he speaks, too, as a leading patriarch in his church, aware of the Sonia Johnsons and the Sister Theresa Kanes and the other believing women who would perhaps turn traditional church governance upside down.

In the case of the Catholic Church, one could argue that it is feminism itself, within the church as outside it, that explains the singlemindedness and fury with which the church hierarchy has engaged in the current crusade against birth control and abortion. The hierarchy and the pope have evidenced strong concern about feminist and Marxist stirrings within the church's own ranks and the need to impose "discipline" and patriarchal authority in its own house. This was made clear in the pope's visit to the United States in 1979 and his outspoken endorsement there, and during the recent Synod of Bishops, of the most conservative views on women, birth control, sexuality and marriage — even in the face of widespread lay nonconformism and public appeals by nuns for a more modern approach. Feminism represents to the church a threat of insubordination, but also a threat of depopulation: not only have Catholic birth rates gone down as much as other groups', but Catholics today both approve of and *practice* abortion in nearly as large numbers as do other groups in the United States. Declining enrollments in parochial school may play no small part in motivating church attacks on birth control, abortion, and women's control over pregnancy.

Taking feminist ideas more seriously than do many liberals, the doctrinal leaders of the New Right relate women's sexuality to their place in society — only reversing the feminist vision. Connie Marshner, another prime mover behind the "profamily" movement and director of its "Library Court" legislative group, assures women that all they need is "to know 'that somebody will have the authority and make the decision, and that your job is to be happy with it.'" This is exactly what Schlafly and her anti-ERA forces have been vociferously promoting since 1973 — the idea that it is women's "right" to be dependent, cared for, subordinate to men, and defined by marriage and motherhood. At the center of anti-ERA ideology is the assumption that it is destructive of the family for married women to work outside the home. From this follows their opposition to federally funded childcare programs and their support for "protective" legislation that would exclude women from certain jobs, due to their "physical differences and family obligations," or would "give job preference . . . to a wage-earner supporting dependents" (meaning men). Most fundamentally of all, however, "prolife" and "profamily" ideology represent the urge to restore the values of motherhood as they have been propagated since the late eighteenth century: as woman's true destiny, her "calling," that which defines her above all else and so must take priority above all other tasks or commitments. Clearly, this is the underlying message of the antiabortion movement, that women who seek abortions are "selfish" because they attempt to deny the "life" of "their own child" and therefore their own "destiny" (both "natural" and God-given) to procreate, nurture, and suffer. One could speculate at length on the deeper cultural and psychological roots of the "promotherhood" backlash, yet it obviously touches something very profound — in men, a long-ingrained expectation of being taken care of, which feminism seems to threaten; in women, a long-ingrained vulnerability to guilt, which antifeminism evokes.

"Profamily"/"prolife" organizers understand all too well that the main threats to maintaining a traditional family structure in which men dominate women and children, and women seek their identity in motherhood, are women's economic independence from husbands and the existence of a strong feminist movement. The massive rise in women's labor force participation, particularly among married women; and, on a much smaller but still important scale, the existence of feminist alternatives outside the home (battered women's shelters, lesbian communities, "returning women's" programs in colleges, feminist health networks), create the possibility for women to imagine existing outside of traditional married life. For married women too, these possibilities have changed how they think about marital relations and motherhood, whether or not they remain married or remarry (which most of them do). Far more than an opportunistic appeal to the "irrational," the New Right represents a highly conscious conservative response to these broad and changing social conditions. It is a response that advocates a return to the values of privatism; that would throw the welfare and education of individuals back onto the resources of the family and the church; that would confine sexuality within the strict bounds of heterosexual marriage, and women within a patriarchal version of self-denying motherhood.

Describing the ideology and political program of a social movement is not at all the same as understanding the consciousness of the masses of people who make up that movement, much less the material and social conditions that bring a particular consciousness to light. We have to consider why that ideology is able to have a broad impact on people's consciousness; why, in this case, the resurgence of patriarchal authority, in its "prolife" and "profamily" incarnations, has come to play such a central role in American politics and its current bend to the right.

First, the simplest and most obvious explanation for the "prolife" movement's existence and its success in developing a mass-based organization is that the political values and social changes its members are fighting against are real and pervasive. Both the women's and gay liberation movements, on the one hand, and the structural changes in the family that have been both cause and effect of those movements, represent a genuine threat to the type of family system and the sexual morality that the New Right is seeking to preserve. While New Right language and symbolism often take a mystical and irrational form, their ends are nevertheless coherent and clear; the conflict between the values of the New Right and those they oppose, as they perceive better than many liberals, broaches no compromise. In this sense, the antiabortion/antigay/anti-ERA/"profamily" current is indeed a backlash movement, a movement to turn back the tide of the major social movements of the 1960s and 1970s. This backlash is aimed primarily at those organizations and ideas that have most directly confronted patriarchal traditions regarding the place of women in society and the dominant norms of heterosexual love and marriage. But it is also a reaction to the New Left and the counterculture generally, which many white middle-class parents experienced as having robbed them of their children, either literally or spiritually. The strength and determination of this backlash — particularly in regard to abortion, homosexuality, and the ERA — is in part a measure of the *effectiveness* of the women's and gay movements, the extent to which their ideas (and various commercial distortions of their ideas) have penetrated popular culture and consciousness, if not public policy. This ideological impact has, of course, been double-edged because it has brought with it a great deal of uncertainty about what will replace the old forms that are being challenged, and even about people's own identities. But it is also true, as Zillah Eisenstein has argued elsewhere, that there is no corner of the society where the basic liberal feminist idea of women's "equality" with men has not touched people in their daily relationships.

Second, the "profamily" movement is reacting to very real, dramatic changes in family life that have occurred most sharply during the past twenty years. The kind of family model the New Right would like to restore — in fact, to make morally and legally mandatory — has become practically extinct in America. By the early 1980s, fewer than 10 percent of all households were composed of husband-wife families with children where the husband was the sole "breadwinner." The majority of women with school-age children were working outside the home, increasing proportions of them (50 percent of Black families, 15 percent of white) as the primary supporters of their households.

These changes have been accompanied by much greater openness about homosexuality, nonmarital heterosexuality, living arrangements, and child-rearing arrangements that fall outside the traditional heterosexual-married-household pattern. Further, the whole pattern and social context of motherhood has changed as a result of these shifts. While most women will raise one or two children in their lives, they will do so in a context of nearly continuous work outside the home; and, for many, of decreasing economic dependence on husbands or other men.

The New Right's "prolife," "profamily" campaign thus cannot easily be written off as either religious fanaticism or mere opportunism. It has achieved a mass following and a measure of national political power because it is in fact a response to real material conditions and deep-lying fears, a response that is utterly *reactionary,* but nevertheless attune. It is not only those conditions and fears, however, that have given the New Right its leverage, but also the failure of the Left and feminist movements to develop an alternative vision, based on socialist and feminist values, that gives people a sense of orientation in dealing with the kinds of personal insecurity and disruption brought by recent changes in the family and sexual norms. The disjunctions in relations between parents and teenagers illustrate this lack of vision painfully. For the concerns of parents about their children getting pregnant, having abortions, being encouraged toward "sexual freedom," without any social context of sexual and reproductive responsibility, are rational and real and neither the Left nor the women's movement has offered a model for a better, more socially responsible way for teenagers to live. The "prolife" movement's critique of a certain kind of "hedonism," the cult of subjective experience and "doing whatever feels good," with no sense of values outside the self, is in part a response to the moral failure of contemporary capitalist culture.

In addressing these cultural dislocations, the New Right answers with the reassurance of moral absolutism: to deal with the problems of abortion, teenage sexuality, conflicts in female-male relations, simply abolish them. There are no decisions to make, no hard choices, no ambiguities. You have only to listen to "the word" — of the priest, of the husband, of the father. But this is a nonmorality, because it absolves human beings (especially those lacking patriarchal authority) of moral agency, and thus plays on people's weakness and insecurity. Moreover, it puts its own followers — for example, the activist women of the "right-to-life" movement — in a terrible dilemma, because the meaning of political activism, to which they are being called, is to think, to act, to be responsible. Indeed, the most stinging contradiction embodied in the "prolife" movement may be that confronting its apparently large numbers of female rank and file, most of them white, middle class and middle aged. On the one hand, we may speculate that these are the very women for whom the loss of a protective conjugal family structure and the idea of motherhood as the core of woman's fulfillment is a truly menacing specter. On the other hand, what can it mean to be active as a woman in a political movement, or a church, that stands for women's passivity and subordination? How will the women of the New Right begin to confront this dilemma?

Anita Bryant, for three years national symbol and leader of the anti–gay rights movement and a devout fundamentalist, may be a harbinger of a gathering storm. Finding herself divorced, jobless, and denounced by the male-dominated church that has made millions of dollars off her name, Bryant now claims to "better understand the gays' and the feminists' anger and frustration." She sees "a male chauvinist attitude" in "the kind of sermon [she] always heard" growing up in the Bible belt — "*wife submit to your husband even if he's wrong*"; and thinks "that her church has not addressed itself to women's problems":

> Fundamentalists have their head in the sand. The church is sick right now and I have to say I'm even part of that sickness. I often have had to stay in pastors' homes and their wives talk to me. Some pastors are so hard-nosed about submission and insensitive to their wives' needs that they don't recognize the frustration — even hatred — within their own households.

But there are also material contradictions that, I believe, will undo the "prolife" movement in the long run. The New Right's rejection of the now dominant ideology of the "working mother," their determination to bring women back into the home, represents a basic misunderstanding of current economic realities, including the long-range interests of the capitalist class as a whole, which continues to rely heavily on a (sex-segregated) female labor force. Emma Rothschild has cogently pointed out that the only real "growth" industries in the American economy in the current period — "eating and drinking places," "health services," and "business services" — are those whose labor force is predominantly women. Corporations are unlikely to fill these low paid, part-time, unprotected, high-turnover jobs with male workers; they are, in the existing division of labor, "women's work."

Finally, neither the practice of abortion and birth control nor the expression of sexual desire has ever been successfully stamped out by repressive religious or legal codes. As Jill Stephenson comments with regard to the failure of Nazi "promotherhood" ideology to raise the German birthrate:

The long history of birth control in Germany, with widespread resort to abortion if contraception had been unavailable, or had failed, could not be eliminated from popular consciousness by a few laws and even a mass of propaganda. . . . Repression could only drive these practices underground, where popular demand ensured that, somehow, they survived.

In the United States in the 1980s and 1990s, social needs and popular consciousness will also assure the survival of these practices. But whether survival will transform into political struggle will depend on the existence and strength of an organized popular movement.

Feminists and the Debate on Pornography

ALIDA BRILL

From the antiquated "filthy pictures" to the sophisticated horrors of modern pornographic films or the technological ease of sex videos for home use, pornography has long been with us as both notion and reality. The decision about what should, or can, be included in the free exchange of ideas is never a simple one, but in the case of pornography the definitional task itself becomes a venture into a fun-house hall of mirrors. Depending on the angle taken or the mirror used, the logic of control or freedom takes on a different image and shape. The attempt to control or eliminate pornography raises an eternally perplexing question in a democratic society: At what cost freedom? At what loss control? It is unlikely that any definition could successfully end the now centuries-old argument about the lewd versus the erotic, the sensual versus the offensive, the obscene and worthless versus the validly "socially redeeming." . . .

The current issues go beyond the challenge of finally, reliably identifying what is or is not obscene, pornographic, or otherwise repugnant. Instead, they confront another question: To what extent should (or can) a society tolerate a freedom which, by its exercise, many argue, humiliates, degrades, or harms half the population?

Not surprisingly, this battle about the control of pornography has captured a significant amount of feminist attention. The pornography debate has moved away from the consideration of constitutional protections and censorship to encompass major women's issues and to present a challenge to feminism. In this instance, the value of free expression collides with feminist goals and ideology, and feminist ideology, in turn, conflicts with presumed constitutional provisions and guarantees. In these developments, some women are participating in political strategies which, if successful, would force censorship. Most ironically, these strategies, and the beliefs from which they grow, locate feminists and members of the New Right on the same side for the first time. Censorship as a tool is not an unknown feature of conservative politics; it is, however, a seemingly less appropriate tactic for the advocates of women's rights. Other feminists, because of their suspicion and mistrust of any

Alida Brill, "Freedom, Fantasy, Foes, and Feminism: The Debate Around Pornography" reprinted from *Women, Politics, and Change,* edited by Louise A. Tilly and Patricia Gurin, © 1990 by Russell Sage Foundation. Used with the permission of Russell Sage Foundation.

legal remedy that would prescribe restriction, find themselves in the unhappy situation of being accused of championing the cause of pornographers.

Contemporary feminists opposed pornography early in the development of the women's movement. The well-publicized "Take Back the Night" demonstrations . . . predate the current drama by about ten years. Some feminist leaders have devoted large amounts of time and writing to the harmful effects of pornography. . . . Previously, however, feminist protests and other political strategies surrounding pornography did not threaten to split the movement or significantly alienate allies. Organizations such as Women Against Violence Against Women and Women Against Pornography (WAP) had their roots in the antirape and antibattery efforts of the 1970s.

In 1985, however, a significant departure in strategy occurred. Andrea Dworkin, a noted feminist writer and strong opponent of pornography, and Catharine MacKinnon, a law professor, proposed a novel ordinance that they hoped would sidestep the traditional obscenity versus freedom arguments by taking the issue out of the domain of the First Amendment. Defining pornography as an infringement on women's civil rights and basing cases on the proof of actual harm, the Dworkin-MacKinnon strategy attempted to have an ordinance enacted in a number of cities. They succeeded, temporarily, in Indianapolis. It is this ordinance and its approach that have so divided the feminist community.

An organization known as FACT (Feminists Against Censorship Taskforce) was formed and opposed the Indianapolis ordinance. "FACT feminists" question the presumed link between pornographic images and violent behavior against women, thus undercutting or challenging what has always been a main contention of "WAP feminists." FACT feminists challenge the uncomfortable alliance with the New Right and its fundamentalist colleagues, fearing that such dubious liaisons (whether admitted or not) will eventually thwart feminist goals and destroy any chance for true equality. . . .

Freedom is the primary concept that permeates all discussions about pornography; and while much of the debate is consumed by the loftier principles of the First Amendment and its possible infringement, there are other freedom issues beyond those involving speech and expression. That is, there are different kinds of freedoms at stake, such as those involving the privacy of sexual behaviors, as well as the notion of sexual freedom itself.

In reviewing the positions of the various actors — FACT, the American Civil Liberties Union (ACLU), WAP — what becomes clear is that they are arguing about vastly different kinds of freedoms. One could say that they are not in the same conversation. Essentially, the WAPs believe that to defend the indefensible, pornography, is to harm the already vulnerable and weak of society. If the views that must be protected by the guarantees of freedom of expression are the ones that preach a hatred of women and a justification for women's pain and inequality, the WAPs would argue that the First Amendment is no friend to women and as such does not deserve female reverence. While much the of WAP literature and the attempts to sidestep the traditional First Amendment considerations recognize constitutional reality, WAP feminists are in essence talking about the centrality of another kind of freedom — freedom from harm, pain, humiliation, and degradation.

An interesting question is why some feminists have fixated on pornography and its violent images of women as proof of the continuing exploitation of women and why others have fixated on the importance of safeguarding freedom as necessary ultimately for all women's safety, even at the expense and sensitivity of women in particular instances.

The diverging feminist positions might best be characterized by the difference between the concepts of *freedom from* and *freedom to*. For the WAPs, the desire to have *freedom from* a harmful world motivates the regulation of pornography; and in the ACLU/FACT view, the *freedom to* engage in pornographic modeling, distribution, and consumption is a highly regarded right. In the civil libertarian portion of the debate, pornography issues also involve the guarantees of privacy — the freedom to buy pornographic materials and to use them in the privacy of your home. Pornography is a part of the "new" privacy claims that are a far cry from the rather passive rights Brandeis described as the "right to be let alone." People now want to do something in their privacy, and one of the things they want to do is to partake of pornography.

Perhaps in their advocacy for an unrestricted First Amendment and an active use of the rights of privacy, the FACT and ACLU forces have closed their eyes to the most virulent forms of pornography. . . . When confronted with the question of repugnant violence as in the questionable "snuff" films in which women are apparently savagely murdered on screen, including one in which this was done to a pregnant woman, the civil libertarians argue that if the law was indeed broken in order to make the films, then criminal statutes cover criminal offenses such as kidnapping, battery, and murder. Feminists opposed to these violent depictions consider the constitutional protection of such films as ludicrous at best since if the acts had been committed, they would have been illegal and punishable by law. . . .

No matter how appalled individual FACT or civil libertarian feminists may be by the existence of pornography's worst examples, they must regard the First Amendment as sacred. Their arguments center exclusively around the protections of freedom offered by the Constitution. They see the liberties we enjoy as interdependent and fragile. Any legislated censorship of pornography passed for the benefit of women could one day harm blacks, homosexuals, and ultimately come back around to harm the very women who sought this shield. If liberties are fragile and interconnected, a compromise could lead to a collapse of the entire structure of freedom — like a constitutional house of cards. In the civil libertarian play, the chief actors must be freedom and access — for it is only in complete and unrestricted openness that truth can have its day. . . .

The main concern of the WAP feminists is the deprivation of full enfranchisement caused by pornography. It is the link between the political participation of women and pornography as well as the placing of these diminished citizenship rights of women into the sphere of sexuality that makes the MacKinnon approach particularly interesting.

> Pornography is a practice of discrimination on the basis of sex, on one level because of its role in creating and maintaining sex as a basis for discrimination. It harms many women one at a time and helps keep all women in an inferior status by defining our subordination as our sexuality and equating that with our gender.

What does the MacKinnon-Dworkin ordinance say? It defines pornography as one or more of the following:

Women are presented as sexual objects who enjoy pain or humiliation; or

women are presented as sexual objects who experience sexual pleasure in being raped; or

women are presented as sexual objects tied up or cut up or mutilated or bruised or physically hurt, or as dismembered or truncated or fragmented or severed into body parts; or

women are presented being penetrated by objects or animals; or

women are presented in scenarios of degradation, injury, abasement, torture, shown as filthy or inferior, bleeding, bruised, or hurt in a context that makes these conditions sexual; or

women are presented as sexual objects for domination, conquest, violation, exploitation, possession or use or through postures or positions of servility or submission or display.

Different from criminal proceedings under the existing obscenity laws . . . this ordinance provides for civil actions, based on the allegation of discrimination. Thus, the ordinance has at its foundations a complaint procedure involving the Office of Equal Opportunity, through hearings at the equal opportunity boards, and ultimately relief at the court level. . . .

By placing pornography within the domain of discrimination and under the larger consideration of equality, MacKinnon seeks to move away from the censorship considerations present in other attempts to control pornography. Although, if successful, her ordinance would clearly have to rely on censorship as the tool of enforcement, by casting the argument in this manner, she places the spotlight on something other than the First Amendment. . . . MacKinnon would have us believe that the decision to be made is not the more simplistic one about suppression of materials, but rather a more general one about civil rights, in which seeking legal remedy is appropriate. What is difficult to comprehend is the MacKinnon leap from pornography to the wholesale denial of women's civil rights and a full enjoyment of citizenship claims, a leap reminiscent of the sweeping statements made by the temperance feminists that harm is caused by alcohol and drunken men. . . . Whether it is the immoderate use of alcoholic beverage or the "ungentlemanly" sexual behaviors of both the pornographer and the consumer of pornography — it is the male appetite, seemingly wild and insatiable, that is the villain. . . .

Much scholarly attention has been given to civil libertarian concerns about the control of pornography, from both a legal and a feminist perspective. The one document that best exemplifies this side of the argument is the brief filed in the Seventh Circuit Court of Appeals by FACT and authored by Nan Hunter and Sylvia Law. . . .

The Hunter-Law brief confronts the MacKinnon-Dworkin ordinance on the freedom and the equality dimensions. Hunter and Law do not confine themselves to the rather straightforward considerations of the First Amendment and suppression of expression through censorship. Although the brief begins in much the way one might predict for a civil libertarian position, the authors quickly proceed to much more complex terrain in their discussion of the difficulties of achieving and maintaining sexual freedom for women.

> The violent and brutal images which Appellants use as examples cannot obscure the fact that the ordinance authorizes suppression of material that is sexually explicit, but in no way violent. . . . The material that could be suppressed . . . is virtually limitless.

The FACT brief is striking in how little it deals with the history of women's inequality or the origins of male dominance, which in turn is played out in pornography. Law and Hunter talk instead about how women have been injured by the erosion of freedom under the guise of the protection of women. . . . In their view all forms of control lead to unwanted suppression, and any attempt to remove the harm caused women by pornography diverts feminist goals and treats women as unequal, childlike, and vulnerable. Their brief traces previous laws which regulated sexual behaviors and contends that such laws imposed a double standard of legal codes and cultural norms. Hunter and Law, then, place the ordinance in the land of the double sexual standard. Throughout the brief an important point is that the ordinance denies women the freedom to be sexual and the right to choose what is enjoyable and reject what is not. Hunter and Law argue that the ordinance "resurrects the notion that sexually explicit materials are subordinating and degrading to women." They build a case against the ordinance on this foundation, relying on the history of such restrictions as those on birth control information (not remedied until the *Griswold* decision in 1965), the Mann Act, statutory rape laws, and the like. . . .

For these feminists the historical fragility of liberty, the recency of sexual freedom for women, and the still emerging case law on women's equality, coupled with the unavoidable reliance on the mechanism of control, outweigh other concerns about the possible effects of pornography on individual women's lives. Instead, they say, build the structure of freedom large enough and strong enough and everyone can live there. If women need protection, it is in freedom's house. . . .

Presumably pornography could not exist if there were no sexual fantasies in people's souls. Despite all the arguments about pornography, no one seems to dispute the existence of sexual fantasy. WAP feminists say that male fantasy, imbedded as it is in a hostile culture, inevitably involves desires that are harmful or degrading to women and that male sexual fantasy itself is a problem.

For those feminists the depictions of women in the pages of *Playboy* or other softer versions of pornography are unacceptable. These portrayals deliver the message that a woman, submissively posed, is inviting the sexual advances of a man. By their standards, this cannot be a freely given invitation but instead represents intrusion, or worse. Other feminists, however, feel that women can find sexual arousal through traditional forms of pornography and that to deny women that access not only curtails a kind of freedom, but in essence censors fantasy, which might otherwise lead to more profound sexual experiences for women: "By defining sexually explicit images of women as subordinating and degrading to them, the ordinance reinforces the stereotypical view that good women do not seek and enjoy sex." . . .

The FACT feminists fear that passage of a pornography ordinance or the enforcement of obscenity laws will destroy the fragile beginnings of open female sexual fantasy. While abhorrent pornography would disappear if the WAPs have their way, the FACT forces argue that so would the opportunities for women to begin to define for themselves a female sexual fantasy.

A number of FACT members and signers of the amicus brief are lesbian groups and coalitions; it is easy to see how lesbian images, fantasy, and identity could be adversely affected. The lesbians involved in the anticensorship campaign believe that such restrictions begin to set the stage for repression of all sexually explicit materials, including lesbian erotica. Even more important is their belief that such widespread control of materials could open the door to the repression of behavior defined by some as "deviant." . . .

At the heart of the struggle lies the question: Who is the foe? The real enemy? Many WAP feminists argue that the entire system is the culprit, which makes apparent the logic of the MacKinnon approach to system transformation through legal remedy. Beneath all WAP strategies or actions, however, is an assumption, or a conviction, that men are the enemy: dangerous and to be reckoned with. And, since institutions, indeed culture itself, are male creations, or at the least highly male identified and dominated, the belief that men *and* the system are the dual foes is not a contradictory vision. . . .

When Dworkin writes of men, she writes unmistakably of the enemy. One of WAP's most articulate and visible leaders, Dworkin denies any compromise or solution to the pornography question short of complete restraint. She cuts into the Law and Hunter argument, claiming that the individual behavior of men is not really the crucial question. For her, whether or not men "are attack dogs" is irrelevant. All men engaged in sexual intercourse, at any time or in any setting, are, by definition, behaving in a hostile and hurtful manner. Dworkin would not concede that if men controlled themselves and stopped producing and consuming pornography, they would become acceptable. The need to stop pornography goes much further, and the rationale cuts much deeper, for man is the enemy, a most vile creature whose only salvation might lie in teaching himself not to have erections. In Dworkin's terms, all sexual intercourse is the physical outcome of male hatred for women.

Although Dworkin represents the most radical end point of WAP ideology and rhetoric, it would not be wise to dismiss her message. Stripped of its more inflammatory words, Dworkin expresses the core of WAP belief: Men can never redeem themselves from their "other" or enemy status; the very reality of their gender precludes redemption. Since their natural sexual response to women is both painful and cruel, men, in the most literal WAP vision, can be neither trusted nor reasoned with. Whether expressed in conventional male-female sexual encounters, or in pornographic consumption or production, the only possible outcome of male sexuality is abuse of women. . . .

Another dilemma emerges in this immediate drama that addresses the very definition of a foe. What of the nonfeminists who have supported the MacKinnon ordinance as well — namely, New Right and fundamentalist groups? . . . Although the alliance with the New Right is largely unacknowledged by WAP, it is a very real phenomenon. The ordinance, which began as a feminist initiative in Minneapolis and Indianapolis, ended up in Suffolk County, New York, and in Maine as initiatives sponsored by the New Right and a reorganized or reconstituted version of the Decency League. Feminist presence was barely visible in later versions of the ordinance. New Right antipornography efforts make the image of a fun-house hall of mirrors especially vivid. Little is as ironic as the members of the ultra-right and representatives of WAP engaged in warm and friendly conversation following the filming of a television panel show in the spring of 1986, while FACT representatives were insulted or ignored by their feminist WAP sisters.

Empirical research seems to indicate that these nonfeminist groups are foes, not friends. New Right opponents of pornography also reject other aspects of freedom or equality for women, including the right to abortion, the passage of the ERA, and questions of sexual preference and other lifestyle options. For conservatives opposed to pornography, as demonstrated by the Meese Commission, conventional morality and a belief in the purity and sanctity of womanhood lead to an ideology valorizing a traditional lifestyle for women. Their desire to reform society, and turn back the clock to a time when a different code was honored, has special irony because they believe that they are responding to a higher order. This ideology, which proscribes universal values that must be enforced, could lead, of course, to the banning of all sorts of books and literature. . . .

For FACT feminists the foes are the ideological strangers. It is the crusade against repression and censorship that unites them, not the opposition to men, or to pornography, or even to the inequities of life in a sexist world. Here the WAP point about the disloyalty of defending those who bring harm to women is well taken. For there is no reason to believe that one's ACLU brothers care more about the rights of women than they care about the rights of Nazis to march; for various profound reasons they cannot. One might assume that the ACLU defends the rights of pornographers and the rights of Nazis (while in some sense "holding their noses"), but at heart, for civil libertarians, all groups must have equal standing. What unites a civil libertarian view and gives it cohesiveness is a commitment to an enduring ideology of individual rights. The civil libertarian agenda that the FACTs have subscribed to, then, is not differentiated for women; the FACTs see neither irony nor conflict in taking refuge in a shelter where the overall ideology of individual rights means that some roommates are incompatible with others. . . .

Perhaps the WAPs will win; this is less difficult to imagine than it once was, in light of the Bush presidency and the inevitable changes on the Supreme Court. What is more important to note here, however, is that the fight to eliminate pornography is being carried out on a traditional battleground, a symbolism that cannot be overlooked. The question of morality is replayed for women over and over again. Earlier women without protection in divorce, without the right to inherit from their own fathers, and with no adequate devices for the prevention of pregnancy saw sexual purity as a way to a better life and survival itself. Despite the modern players, this drama is an old one; the traditional battleground for reform has become a radical encampment. But the eternal question continues to plague women's political life: How to reconcile one's "womanness" with one's "citizenship," in the dual realm to which women are forever consigned.

Invisible Woman: Reflections
on the Clarence Thomas Confirmation Hearing

KIM A. TAYLOR

I am an invisible [wo]man. No I am not a spook like those who haunted Edgar Allan Poe; nor am I one of your Hollywood-movie ectoplasms. I am a [wo]man of substance, of flesh and bone, fiber and liquids — and I might even be said to possess a mind. I am invisible, understand, simply because people refuse to see me. Like the bodiless heads you see sometimes in circus sideshows, it is as though I have been surrounded by mirrors of hard, distorting glass. When they approach me they see only my surroundings, themselves, or figments of their imagination — indeed, everything and anything except me.*

As I sat behind Professor Anita Hill during the second round of hearings for the confirmation of Clarence Thomas to the Supreme Court, I felt as if I had stepped into a carnival fun house, where the world simultaneously becomes larger than life and fundamentally warped. Here were members of the United States Senate Judiciary Committee, despite promises to engage in a genuine factfinding hearing into the allegations of sexual harassment raised by Professor Hill, distorting the hearing process with the verbal equivalent of mirrors and lights. Even on the occasion of recommending a nominee for a lifetime appointment to this nation's highest court, United States senators appeared incapable of rising above their large egos and putting aside petty politics to take their investigatory task seriously. Because they could appreciate the complexity of neither the issue of sexual harassment nor the person who sat before them, they failed to establish a process that might have begun to unearth the truth about what had transpired between Clarence Thomas and Anita Hill. Instead, they allowed the hearing to degenerate into a circus sideshow.

I, like others, watched the conduct of the members of the Senate Judiciary Committee in utter disbelief. My disbelief did not spring from a naïve assumption that our governmental institutions function fairly or with much concern for the rights of the defenseless. From the vantage point of an African American growing up in Harlem and later through the professional lens of a public defender, I had seen and become accustomed to the inherent contradictions in a political system that pays lip service to cherishing diversity while using the dual weapons of power and privilege to subordinate those who happen to be a little too different.

Nor did my disbelief at the senators' behavior stem from political inexperience. For the preceding three years, I had served as the director of an independent government agency — the Public Defender Service for the District of Columbia. . . . Because of the District of Columbia's unique status, I engaged in seemingly endless battles over the agency's budget and various pieces of legislation, locking horns with local politicians in the Marion Barry administration and national politicians in the United States Congress. I became accustomed to the political maneuvering of often uninformed and, at times, malicious legislators as I lobbied on behalf of a constituency that could not vote and, consequently, wielded little traditional influence

---

*Ralph Ellison, *Invisible Man 7* (Signet Books, 1952) (1947).

Stanford Law Review, vol. 45, no. 2. (January 1993), 443–452.

over the political process. And, in episodes that I will not detail here, I had felt what it was like to have officials secretly investigate aspects of my personal life hoping to uncover information to use against me in our political battles. Still, I found unfathomable the depths to which the Senate sank in the October confirmation hearing.

Perhaps I was disturbed because the hearing was personal. It involved my friend, whom I knew to be a woman of enormous integrity. This woman should not have had to summon such strength in order to have her evidence considered. Of course, as a trial lawyer, I expected that she would be subjected to rugged cross-examination. She was leveling accusations that had never before been raised publicly against Clarence Thomas, and her allegations surfaced late in the confirmation process. Fairness to the nominee warranted a rigorous, probing inquiry. However, the unparalleled exhibition of demeaning questions and baseless accusations about her sanity and sexuality could neither substitute for a genuine inquiry nor be defended as a rigorous examination of her allegations.

The senators on the Judiciary Committee simply ignored their obligation to provide a process which could have explored the troubling issues which her allegations raised. These men, who appeared completely unconcerned about the impact of their demeaning treatment, could not begin to comprehend the dual impact of racism and sexism on African American women in the workplace. Yet, as factfinders in this process, they had an obligation to rise above their limited experiences. As investigators, they had an obligation to keep open minds about experiences which they obviously knew little about, at least from the perspective of a victim. As officials entrusted with the task of evaluating this evidence, they had an obligation to elevate the discussion above titillating images and to provide a regulated process for analyzing the substance of these allegations. And yet they never did.

I. How the Process Failed

> It is sometimes advantageous to be unseen, although it is most often wearing on the nerves. Then too, you're constantly being bumped against by those of poor vision. Or again, you often doubt if you really exist. You wonder whether you aren't simply a phantom in other people's minds. Say, a figure in a nightmare which the sleeper tries with all his strength to destroy.*

The Judiciary Committee did not have to adopt any particular design for the hearing on Professor Hill's allegations. Indeed, the Committee had an infinite variety of models from which to choose. It could have established a nonconfrontational setting, gathering facts through the presentation of statements and clarifying issues with open-ended questions. Or, the Committee could have borrowed roles and rules from litigation: It could have assigned advocates to Professor Hill and Clarence Thomas, and allowed them to conduct cross-examinations, raise objections, and present arguments about inferences to be drawn from the evidence. Using this model, the Committee members could have reserved for themselves the role of jurors. Instead, the Committee adopted a process which effectively ceded control of the hearing to the Republicans and made possible the one-sided inquisition of Professor Hill that would eventually unfold.

---

*Ellison, loc. cit.

The failure of the process was surprising, in part, because the Democrats controlled the Judiciary Committee. By virtue of that control, they could have shaped the proceeding in a way that would have promoted a clearer understanding of the issue the senators were expected to evaluate. However, the opening remarks of Senator Joseph Biden, the Chair of the Committee, revealed that he had made the conscious decision to suspend rules of evidence, to limit the scope of the hearing, and, apart from determining the order of the questioning, to place few, if any, restraints on the members of the Committee. Perhaps the Chair's decision to surrender control was motivated by personal concerns about the public criticisms leveled against him and the members of his committee for appearing intent on rushing Thomas' name through to a final vote while barely pausing to consider Professor Hill's allegations. Or perhaps this decision revealed his confusion about what steps were required to ensure a fair hearing on this complex issue. Whatever the ultimate excuse, the Democrats permitted the hearing to stray from its purported goal.

. . . Had the Democrats established some guidelines regarding the types of questions that could be properly posed, we might have been spared much of the misleading examination that characterized the hearing. In this unrestrained environment, examinations which recounted the graphic details of Professor Hill's testimony, not for the sake of scrutiny but for sensation, were to be expected. While such examinations may have provided the illusion of meaningful inquiry, they offered less insight into the nature and impact of the conduct Professor Hill alleged than into the senators' preoccupation with images of Coke cans and the anatomy of African American men.

Similarly, had the Democrats imposed basic rules of procedure, many of the *ad hominem* attacks against Professor Hill could have been eliminated. Certainly, as any trial lawyer will admit, the principal tactic for impeaching a victim is to suggest that her motive for testifying is suspect; however, any ethical lawyer will also concede that before she attributes an evil motive to the witness, she should have a good faith basis for doing so. In court, lawyers are routinely required to provide a factual basis for a line of questioning that will impute a negative motive. Had the Committee required such an offer of proof, any senator whose questions portrayed Professor Hill as a scorned woman would have been forced to provide credible evidence to support his accusations. It is difficult to imagine that the wild speculations of the likes of John Doggett would have satisfied any neutral arbiter.

Had the Democrats exercised any control over the conduct of the hearing, they might have restrained the chief examiner for the Republican members, Senator Arlen Specter. In the absence of rules governing the proceedings, Senator Specter's background as a prosecutor enabled him to slide into and out of the roles of prosecutor and judge whenever doing so served his purpose. For example, Senator Specter posed a series of questions that he believed demonstrated that Professor Hill had perjured herself. He then shed the role of examiner, assumed the position of arbiter of the facts, and expressed his judgment that her testimony amounted to "flat out perjury." By imposing some restriction on his conduct, the Democrats could have required that, while in the role of examiner, Senator Specter confine himself to posing questions without drawing conclusions until the examinations had been completed. In a courtroom, Specter would undoubtedly have been subject to at least this degree of restraint. Here, though, constrained by neither the rules of the proceeding nor by even a basic sense of fair play, Senator Specter was able to capitalize on these two roles with impunity.

The Democrats needed to embrace their roles as advocates in this process. Rather than sitting idly by as if dumbstruck, they should have begun to rebut the arguments raised by Senator Specter. For example, Senator Specter focused much of his examination on the suggestion that Professor Hill's testimony should be discounted because it would have been barred by the statute of limitations applicable to civil claims raised under Title VII had it been offered in court. At the very least, the Democrats should have reminded the viewing public that Professor Hill was not lodging a civil claim of sexual harassment, and that, consequently, statutes of limitation would not apply. Moreover, even conceding that statutes of limitation serve important functions in certain contexts, the Democrats never attempted to distinguish this situation. The Democrats could have argued that recent confirmation hearings should have placed Clarence Thomas on notice that not only his entire record but his character would be open to scrutiny. Furthermore, they could have stressed that the probative value of evidence suggesting that Thomas had abused a prior position of trust would outweigh any prejudicial impact, given the gravity of evaluating a nominee's fitness to receive a lifetime appointment to one of America's highest positions of trust. Yet the Committee Democrats never made these points.

As the Republicans raised questions concerning Professor Hill's "delay" in reporting Clarence Thomas' conduct, her choice to proceed with him to the Equal Employment Opportunity Commission, and her decision to maintain distant yet cordial relations with him, the Democrats should have responded. The Democrats had the opportunity and the responsibility to force the Committee to revisit its initial decision to preclude expert testimony on the issue of sexual harassment. Indeed, as Republican members gained mileage from their (and Thomas' witnesses') speculations about the meaning of her conduct, an examination of the context of Professor Hill's conduct and charges became not only relevant but critical. Even those who might have doubted the effectiveness of expert testimony, or feared that the hearing would become a battle of the experts, would have had to agree that expert testimony had long been permitted in court in precisely this situation: to explain matters considered "beyond the ken of the jury." Certainly, in the area of sexual harassment, which even today remains underreported and misunderstood, expert testimony could have served to inform the senators and the viewing public about inferences they were inclined to draw from Professor Hill's behavior, and could have dispelled popular misconceptions that her pattern of conduct was indicative of deceit.

With a clearer definition and understanding of their roles, the Democrats might have been better equipped to require that Clarence Thomas respond to Professor Hill's charges. While the Republicans on the Committee appeared fully capable of inquiring in depth into the personal aspects of Professor Hill's statements, using newspaper articles and quotes from witnesses, the Democrats failed to utilize anything approaching the same probing tactics with respect to Clarence Thomas or his witnesses. The *New York Times* reported that personal friends of Clarence Thomas could have corroborated his interest in pornographic material from 1974 on and could have verified that he discussed and joked about such matters. The Democrats were also aware of at least one witness who could have testified that as recently as the summer of 1991, Clarence Thomas continued to exhibit an active interest in pornography. These witnesses were important not because we as a nation possessed some prurient interest in Thomas' taste in movies. Rather, once the Republican members accused Professor Hill of fantasizing the events she described, it became relevant and appropriate to establish through corroborating testimony that both Thomas' interest in pornography and his habit of regaling his friends with pornographic plots were indeed real. The Democrats, however, failed to subpoena these witnesses, and the Chair declared the inquiry off limits.

The witnesses who appeared on behalf of Clarence Thomas presented the Democrats with yet another opportunity to advocate for Professor Hill. Even a basic understanding of cross-examination would require that the biases of witnesses be exposed, yet the Democrats were incapable of carrying out this elementary task. For example, Nancy Fitch, who testified on the first panel of witnesses called on behalf of Thomas, was never questioned about the fact that she was in the process of writing a biography of Clarence Thomas. Certainly, she had much to gain if she testified on his behalf, yet this basic point was never made.

While the Republican senators on the Committee used this free form hearing to further their short term political objective of discrediting Professor Hill in order to pave the way for confirmation of their nominee, the Democrats were hopelessly hamstrung by either their personal skeletons or their limited ability to assess the complexity of the issue before them. Had they been able to overcome these limitations and assume a role which would have protected Professor Hill, they might have enabled the Senate and the country to understand the issue that she raised. Without guidelines governing the scope of permissible inquiry or admissible evidence, and without better definition of the roles in the proceeding, we were left with a hearing mired in superficial analyses and incapable of unearthing the truth about what transpired between Clarence Thomas and Anita Hill.

II.   Why the Process Failed

> Nor is my invisibility exactly a matter of a bio-chemical accident to my epidermis. That invisibility to which I refer occurs because of a peculiar disposition of the eyes of those with whom I come in contact. A matter of the construction of their *inner* eyes, those eyes with which they look through their physical eyes upon reality.*

The stark image of a young African American woman seated alone at a table facing a panel of fourteen white male senators remains vivid one full year after the hearing. Even more striking than the visual image of Professor Anita Hill testifying before the Judiciary Committee is the realization that the men entrusted with the task of evaluating the evidence presented during the hearings were limited and, ultimately, blinded by their positions of privilege. Perhaps these men, who had rarely, if ever, been forced to see folks who resembled Professor Hill as their equals, had become all too accustomed to ignoring their concerns. Dismissing such voices had become so commonplace in our nation's capitol, that even when Professor Hill was brought center stage by the media, these men seemed unable, or at least unwilling, to see the woman of color who sat before them answering questions for seven

---

*Ellison, loc. cit.

hours. The senators failed to appreciate the significance of Professor Hill's experience as a woman in the workplace, and they were completely ignorant of her life struggles as an African American. The real Anita Faye Hill remained invisible to them.

It is now painfully apparent that the failure of the process was emblematic of society's inability to recognize and appreciate the double oppression of race and gender. Perhaps, as some have suggested, had this complaint been lodged by a *white* female law professor, the outcome would have been different. Southern Republican senators, such as Strom Thurmon and Jesse Helms, might not have embraced Clarence Thomas so readily because personal and cultural politics might have shifted their sympathies away from the "carousing" African American man to one of "their" women. Had she been white, the argument continues, the Judiciary Committee would have conducted a closed inquiry, away from the cameras, to determine the truth of the allegations. In my view, had she been a *different* woman of color, one who fit societal presumptions about politics and place, reactions by the Senate and the American public at the time of the hearing might have been dramatically different. Instead, in very complicated ways, Professor Hill challenged many of the myths and presumptions about people of color and, more specifically, about women of color. When the Senate and the public were asked to evaluate Professor Hill and her message, her differences made the task more difficult.

At the time of the hearing, not only the Senate, but the American public (at least those segments that were polled), failed to see and appreciate Professor Hill and the complexity of her situation. Even those groups that might have been expected to rally to her side seemed only to see those aspects of her which served their purposes. Perhaps this failure to understand Professor Hill was due in part to the fact that she did not fit into the tidy categories that we as a society use to define individuals. She appeared to be politically conservative, yet she was delivering testimony which could have derailed the nomination of a conservative judge to the Supreme Court. She poignantly discussed Clarence Thomas' conduct, but seemed reluctant either to characterize the conduct as sexual harassment or to use her testimony as a platform to raise the American consciousness about sexual harassment in the workplace. She appeared to be the product of a traditional African American family, yet she seemed to be breaking ranks with African Americans by openly attacking an African American man. In another setting, Professor Hill's complexities might have widened her appeal; during the hearing, those complexities only alienated her from much of the American public.

The Senate's failure to appreciate Professor Hill's complexity was highlighted by Senator Specter's cross-examination of her. Each time Senator Specter expressed his incredulity that a Yale Law School graduate could not simply have quit her job and accepted one of the supposed endless opportunities awaiting her, I found myself thinking, not for the first time, "he just doesn't get it." Perhaps Senator Specter based his conclusions about options available to a Yale Law School graduate on the experience of *white male* graduates. Or maybe his comments grew out of an exaggerated view of the "benefits" of affirmative action. Whatever the reason, Senator Specter's comments demonstrated precisely how little he knew about Professor Hill's reality: Doors that may have been open to her white male counterparts would not have been open to her. He simply refused to acknowledge that the double burden of race and gender might restrict the choices and opportunities facing a woman of color working in a profession dominated by white males.

Senator Specter seemed to forget that at the time Clarence Thomas began subjecting Anita Hill to the harassment that she described, she had not yet become the composed, tenured law professor who appeared before the senators. She was twenty-four years old and in only her second year of law practice. She had already resigned from a law firm and had assumed a position at the Department of Education. Anyone familiar with the legal profession would acknowledge that when seeking employment in the more conventional segments of the profession, two moves in as many years would not have been viewed favorably by most employers. Senator Specter once again displayed his ignorance when he contended that Professor Hill could have made a third move, after the harassment began, without consequence. As Professor Hill knew even from her limited experience in the workforce, she could not afford to leave her job no matter how much she longed to do so.

The interplay of race and gender that defined and delineated Professor Hill's dilemma was missed not just by the Senate, but by some white feminists as well. In their efforts to tout her as spokesperson for all women who had been victims of sexual harassment, some feminists attempted to distill her voice into simply that of a woman and, as a result, denied her complexity. Many who acknowledged the difficulty of finding the courage to speak as a victim of sexual harassment overlooked the additional measure of strength that Professor Hill needed to summon in order to speak those words against an African American man. Having been raised in a tradition that taught her not to "air our dirty laundry in public," Professor Hill did not violate that directive lightly. Yet many white feminists seemed, at best, unaware of or, worse, insensitive to the painful reality that speaking out could alienate Professor Hill from her African American community.

Indeed, at the time of the hearing, the loyalties of African American communities were divided. During those three days in October, the silence of my community was almost deafening. Although there were notable exceptions, which did not garner the type of media attention paid to those people of color who opposed Professor Hill, the second round of the confirmation process saw notably few African American activists raise their voices in support of Professor Hill. Voices from the NAACP and National Urban League, for example, were not even raised in condemnation of sexual harassment as it peculiarly affects African American women. Suddenly, those prominent African American leaders who had spoken so eloquently in opposition to Clarence Thomas in the first set of hearings seemed to have lost their voices. Instead of embracing Professor Hill's testimony as further evidence of Clarence Thomas' incompetence to serve, these "leaders" said nothing. And I wondered why.

Could these organizations have swallowed the Republican line that Professor Hill was acting on a personal vendetta? Or in the vernacular of my community, could they have believed that she was simply interested in "bringing a brother down"? Perhaps at a time when attacks on the African American man have increased in number and intensity, the airing of Professor Hill's complaint on prime time television was destined to be viewed as the latest in a wave of attacks. However, in their rush to define her testimony as an effort to malign an African American man, these designated spokespersons for the African American community inadvertently missed or, worse, consciously discounted *her* victimization. While the

African American community and our national organizations remained attuned to racial subordination and outraged over its impact, many within my community failed to recognize and acknowledge the devastating impact of gender subordination.

"Why didn't she quit if this *really* happened?" was a question that emerged not just from Senator Specter but from my community as well. Interestingly, African Americans who had been subjected to racist remarks in the workplace knew all too well that they had often tolerated such abuse and then swallowed their anger to maintain their jobs. Now these same individuals were suggesting that Professor Hill's experience was somehow different and less important; they were suggesting that she should be held to a different standard than the one they applied to their own behavior. The message behind these attitudes, which registered painfully in my head and heart, was that issues facing African American women should be sacrificed in our efforts to close ranks around an African American man. Our "leaders" and segments of my community quite simply chose to embrace a man (who had only recently discovered his own heritage in the first set of hearings) and elected to abandon this African American woman. Professor Hill stood alone, invisible to those entrusted with the task of seeing her and evaluating her words, and at best an enigma to the communities that should have understood and supported her most. . . .

FURTHER READING

Mary Frances Berry, *Why ERA Failed* (1986)

Janet Boles, *The Politics of the Equal Rights Amendment* (1979)

Patricia Collins, *Black Feminist Thought: Knowledge, Consciousness, and the Politics of Empowerment* (1990)

Jane DeHart-Matthews and Donald Matthews, *The Equal Rights Amendment and the Politics of Cultural Conflict* (1988)

Bonnie Thornton Dill, "Race, Class, and Gender: Prospects for an All-Inclusive Sisterhood," *Feminist Studies* IX (1983), 131–150

Barbara Ehrenreich, *Hearts of Men* (1983)

Zillah Eisenstein, *The Radical Future of Liberal Feminism* (1981)

Carol Felsenthal, *Sweetheart of the Silent Majority: The Biography of Phyllis Schlafly* (1981)

Janet Giele, *Woman and the Future* (1978)

Arlie Hochschild, *The Second Shift: Working Parents and the Revolution at Home* (1989)

Joan Hoff, *Law, Gender, and Injustice: A Legal History of U.S. Women* (1991)

Joan Hoff-Wilson, ed., *Rites of Passage: The Past and Future of the ERA* (1986)

bell hooks, *Ain't I a Woman? Black Women and Feminism* (1981)

———, *Talking Back: Thinking Feminist, Thinking Black* (1989)

Rebecca E. Klatch, *Women of the New Right* (1987)

Ethel Klein, *Gender Politics* (1984)

Lauren Lederer, ed., *Take Back the Night: Women on Pornography* (1980)

Dorchen Leidholdt and Janice G. Raymond, eds., *The Sexual Liberals and the Attack on Feminism* (1990)

Kristin Luker, *Abortion and the Politics of Motherhood* (1984)

Jane Mansbridge, *Why We Lost the ERA* (1986)

Susan Gluck Mezey, *In Pursuit of Equality: Women, Policy, and the Federal Courts* (1992)

James Mohr, *Abortion in America* (1980)

Susan Moller Okin, *Justice, Gender and the Family* (1989)

Rosalind Pollack Petchesky, *Abortion and Woman's Choice* (1990)

Rosalind Rosenberg, *Divided Lives: American Women in the 20th Century* (1992)

Ruth Sidel, *Women and Children Last: The Plight of Poor Women in Affluent America* (1986)

Ann Snitow et al., eds., *Powers of Desire: The Politics of Sexuality* (1983)

Carol Vance, ed., *Pleasure and Danger: Exploring Female Sexuality* (1984)

Lise Vogel, *Mothers on the Job* (1993)

Leonore J. Weitzman, *The Divorce Revolution: The Unexpected Social and Economic Consequences for Women and Children in America* (1985)